T0265532

UNCOMFORTABLY OFF

"Anyone interested in tackling the grotesque levels of inequality in our society needs to understand what the top 10% think, what motivates them and what will convince them that change is necessary. This book goes beyond a mapping of the economic status and attitudes of this influential top 10% and provides a fascinating insight into the choices that confront them and the potential there is to recruit them for progressive change."

John McDonnell MP

"The top 10% matter because of their loud political voice. This electrifying book warns us they don't feel rich on £60,000, ignorant that the great majority earn half as much. Everyone needs to know where they stand."

Polly Toynbee, *The Guardian*

"Fascinating and telling insights into the situations and views of the top 10%: an under-researched and in many ways invisible – yet politically significant – group."

Professor the Baroness (Ruth) Lister of Burtersett

"A brilliant study in how understanding the fears, feelings and hopes of the best-off tenth of our societies helps explain why we hold so tightly to inequality."

Danny Dorling, University of Oxford

"A must-read for anyone interested in how to build public support for progressive taxation and redistribution."

Daniel Edmiston, University of Leeds

"Both refreshingly honest and extremely pertinent, this book is well researched yet entertaining. Whether you are part of the top 10% or not, read it to better understand political polarisation, Brexit and the structural crisis that increasing inequality has become."

Alice Krozer, El Colegio de México

UNCOMFORTABLY OFF

Why the Top 10% of Earners Should Care about Inequality

Marcos González Hernando and Gerry Mitchell

With a foreword by
James Perry

First published in Great Britain in 2023 by

Policy Press, an imprint of
Bristol University Press
University of Bristol
1-9 Old Park Hill
Bristol
BS2 8BB
UK
t: +44 (0)117 374 6645
e: bup-info@bristol.ac.uk

Details of international sales and distribution partners are available at
policy.bristoluniversitypress.co.uk

© Bristol University Press, 2023

British Library Cataloguing in Publication Data
A catalogue record for this book is available from the British Library

ISBN 978-1-4473-6751-2 hardcover
ISBN 978-1-4473-6753-6 ePub
ISBN 978-1-4473-6754-3 ePdf

The right of Marcos González Hernando and Gerry Mitchell to be identified as
authors of this work has been asserted by them in accordance with the Copyright,
Designs and Patents Act 1988.

All rights reserved: no part of this publication may be reproduced, stored in a
retrieval system, or transmitted in any form or by any means, electronic, mechanical,
photocopying, recording, or otherwise without the prior permission of Bristol
University Press.

Every reasonable effort has been made to obtain permission to reproduce copyrighted
material. If, however, anyone knows of an oversight, please contact the publisher.

The statements and opinions contained within this publication are solely those of the
authors and not of the University of Bristol or Bristol University Press. The University
of Bristol and Bristol University Press disclaim responsibility for any injury to persons
or property resulting from any material published in this publication.

Bristol University Press and Policy Press work to counter discrimination on grounds of
gender, race, disability, age and sexuality.

Cover design: Mecob
Front cover image: Shutterstock/wk1003mike

Bristol University Press and Policy Press use
environmentally responsible print partners.

Printed and bound in Great Britain by TJ Books, Padstow

Contents

List of figures

About the authors

Marcos González Hernando is Honorary Research Fellow at UCL Social Research Institute, Postdoctoral Researcher at Universidad Diego Portales and Adjunct Researcher at the Centre for the Study of Conflict and Social Cohesion. He is also a Fellow of the Royal Society of Arts and has a PhD in sociology from the University of Cambridge. Marcos has experience working in universities and think tanks, both in Latin America and Europe. His research interests include think tanks and policy experts, intellectual change, attitudes towards inequality, and economic and political elites. He is also the author of *British Think Tanks after the 2008 Global Financial Crisis* (Palgrave, 2019). He recently moved to Santiago, Chile, where he lives with his wife, Irina, and his cat, Lily.

Gerry Mitchell is a freelance policy researcher and writer. Experienced in research, political campaigning, community engagement and teaching, she has degrees from Cambridge and the London School of Economics and Political Science where, based in the Centre for Social Exclusion, she completed a PhD in social policy. She has recently worked with Compass (London), the Edinburgh Voluntary Organisations' Council, the Foundation for European Progressive Studies (Brussels), Friedrich-Ebert-Stiftung (Stockholm and London) and the Think-tank for Action on Social Change (Dublin). She lives in Woking, Surrey, with her partner, Gareth, and their two children, Lilya and Noah, where she chaired Woking Labour Party and stood as its parliamentary candidate in the 2019 general election. She currently chairs local Compass and Make Votes Matter groups, is a secondary school governor and in 2022 opened Canalside Community Fridge.

Acknowledgements

We would like to begin by thanking our interviewees for sharing their time, personal experiences and thoughts with us. They were all extremely generous, interesting and thoughtful.

We also wish to thank our colleagues in the top 10% research report on which this book is based at Arena Idé, Compass, Foundation for European Progressive Studies, Fundación Alternativas and the Think-tank for Action on Social Change. They are Amy Barker, Belén Barreiro, Sylvia Byrne, Susana Cristo, Frances Foley, Jack Jeffrey, Johanna Lindell, Sidney Moss, Michelle O'Sullivan, Kishan Patel, Lisa Pelling, David Rinaldi, Jesús Ruiz-Huerta, Jorge San Vicente, Paul Sweeney, Rob Sweeney, Remco Van der Stoep, Gonzalo Velasco and Diana Volpe. Special thanks to Neal Lawson and Shana Cohen who have advised and supported us throughout the process.

We are also grateful to the team at Policy Press, particularly Kathryn King, Jessica Miles and Victoria Pittman.

We cannot forget our immediate families, for putting up with us (it can't have been easy). This book would not have been written without their love, support, generosity and patience: Irina, Marco, Marcela, Daniela, María Francisca, Gareth, Lilya, Noah, Margaret and Mary.

This book is also informed by the insightful comments of our readers: Valentina Ausserladscheider, Shana Cohen, Daniel Edmiston, Roxana Chiappa, Rodrigo Cordero, Nurjk Agloni, Danny Dorling, Naim Bro Khomasi, Ruth Lister, Victoria Redclift and Macarena Orchard. It also draws from the writings and conversations with Katharina Hecht, Martina Yopo, Katie Gaddini, Alfredo Joignant, Patrick Baert, Michaela Franceschelli, Jorge Atria, Michèle Lamont, Jordan Tchilingirian, Luis Garrido, Aris Komporozos-Athanasiou and Simon Susen.

James Perry, as readers will notice, wrote an extremely sharp and readable foreword. He was also gracious, patient and perceptive throughout the process and we cannot thank him enough.

We also cannot imagine having written this book without the influence and support of colleagues and friends: Rebecca Gibbs, Andy Berriman, Ognjen Bubalo, Carmen Campeanu, Franko Cancino, Fabien Cante, Manuela Cisternas, Zara Coombes, Eduardo Lobos, Nat O'Grady, Mark Perryman, Marcela Santana, Steve Sawh, Marita Unepiece, Thiago Vilas-Boas, Israel Yamaguchi, Compass colleagues, Woking Labour CLP and Make Votes Matter.

Finally, we wish to dedicate this book to the memory of Sir John Hills, Barbara Ehrenreich, Nigel Dodd and David Graeber.

Foreword

Something isn't working. Everyone can feel it. Why, when we live in an age of unparalleled prosperity does it seem so hard to make ends meet?

But surely the top 10% are okay, right? Everything is relative, and of course, their problems are largely 'first world problems'. But they're still problems.

A deep dive into the data shows that the distribution of income and wealth in the UK has experienced a hollowing out of the middle class over recent decades. And surprisingly, it shows that this hollowing out has also affected the top 10%. Where has all the wealth creation gone? Mostly to the top 1%. As the generation of new wealth has increasingly drifted into the hands of a very few, it has left behind most of us, even a largely professional 'top 10%'.

This top 10% aspire to a lifestyle that is increasingly beyond them. While from the outside they look like they are living the dream, in reality, they are beset by anxiety. Life to them is a hamster wheel, a constant struggle to keep the high-paying jobs that allow them to service their mortgages and keep up with expectations. They worry about their and their family's future, and so education becomes an arms race to ensure their children are fast enough to be able to get onto, and stay on, that same hamster wheel.

They believe in public services and, in theory, see that the burden for their cost should fall more on those doing well for themselves. But they don't count themselves among those people. Theirs is an uncomfortable existence, squeezed by the accelerating hamster wheel of expectations, both at home and at work. In short, a majority of this group has become uncomfortably off.

Meanwhile, in the higher reaches of the top 1%, there has been almost a total decoupling from everyone else. A super-class of extreme wealth has emerged – those at the top of the pyramid who have made great riches from finance, business, sport, showbiz.

This small group holds an astonishing amount of wealth and lives in a through-the-looking-glass world of privilege. The top 10% has become a microcosm of the entire wealth distribution in that those at the bottom of it are struggling to meet their expectations with an income of £55,000 to £60,000 while those at the top enjoy the compound annual growth of their wealth, accruing at a rate far faster than they could ever spend.

The implications for this modern phenomenon reach into everything. The state is no longer able to make enough tax revenue from the squeezed 99% to cover the social contract. Structural deficits lead the public debt markets to baulk, or at least to increase the interest cost on the national debt to a level greater than the budget of many government departments. Wealth continues to go untaxed, and discussion of any meaningful reform to the 13,000-page UK tax code has been made taboo by certain sections of the media – even in the face of high levels of political consensus on the necessity of some obvious simplifications and changes. Meanwhile, public services, on which the top 10% still rely, become ever more decrepit, unable to metabolise the needs of a population which gets more complex – whether in social care, health, education, social services or justice. And with all the local fires to put out, the government increasingly lacks the bandwidth or political will to meaningfully address the global fire that is about to engulf us all – climate breakdown. The intractability of these structural problems plays out in a political permacrisis. While the top 10% may have the most potential influence over our politicians, are they sufficiently aware of the underlying issues and long-term trends causing their own anxiety?

The discomfort of the top 10% is a logical conclusion to the system we have created. It is a symptom of prioritising individual advancement at all costs, as opposed to the wellbeing of the whole, so the only purpose (and duty) of business and finance is the maximisation of profits. People are reduced to individualised units of labour and consumption – whether consuming the products and services of business or of the state.

The core design idea that underpins our system is individualism. Yet, the truth is that if we are to move beyond our discomfort we have no choice but to look beyond ourselves. To replace the organising idea of individualism with the deeper truth of our interdependence. In recognising that we do not exist in a vacuum, we have no choice but to give prominence to the wellbeing of the whole if we are to create wellbeing for individuals.

The top 10%, the uncomfortably off, are the best-placed cohort in society to address this imperative for deeper change – to transition from individualism to interdependence. It is they who design, regulate and operate the current system. They are the people with both the knowledge and the access to design a better arrangement, based on the truth of our interdependence.

This important and timely book should be seen as a call to arms and a manual for this uniquely placed group, the uncomfortably off. If you are reading this, you may be one of them or perhaps closer than you thought. And if you want to feel comfortable, then the opportunity lies before you to mobilise and rethink the systems that you operate – for everyone in society, and so for yourself. And now, before it is too late.

James Perry
November 2022

James is co-Chair of COOK (www.cookfood.net), a certified B Corp since 2013. He co-founded the B Corp movement in the UK (www.bcorporation.uk), and serves on the global board of B Lab and the board of B Lab Europe. He is also a member of Patriotic Millionaires UK, a founding partner of Snowball (www.snowball.im) and a multi-asset impact investment manager.

Introduction:
Why bother with the well-off?

Three weeks before the UK's 2019 general election, a middle-aged man spoke up among the audience on BBC *Question Time* and briefly became a minor celebrity. Clearly angry, Rob Barber, an IT consultant from Lancashire, said that the Labour Party was lying to the public by claiming that people like him wouldn't be taxed more by a Labour government: "You are not going after the billionaires, you're going after the employees because it's easy money and I have no choice because it's PAYE [pay as you earn]. I have no choice."

The Labour Member of Parliament (MP) Richard Burgon, on the programme's panel, assured him that the proposal only targeted the top 5% of income earners, so most of the public wouldn't qualify and Labour would not be touching their taxes. Unconvinced, Barber retorted: "But you are! Because I've read your policy. It's above £80,000. And I am nowhere near the top 5%, let me tell you. I am not even in the top 50%."

At this point, a few other members of the audience muttered back "But you are!" and Burgon repeated that £80,000 would indeed make you part of the top 5%, but Barber remained undeterred: "Every doctor, every accountant, every solicitor in this country earns more than that. [...] The top 5%, they don't even work! They're not employees!"

For a few days, the exchange became the subject of much media attention. Most pieces on the topic mocked Barber for not realising he was a high earner. As inequality researchers, in the months before that programme we had been interviewing high-income earners just like him, and few if any of our respondents had guessed correctly where they sat in the income distribution.

But is there something to be learnt from this incident beyond Barber's lack of knowledge of income statistics? After all, that assurances had to be made repeatedly about the actual number is evidence itself of a much more generalised ignorance about the economic lives of others. This ignorance, we argue, is not politically anodyne. The fact that Barber and many of our respondents thought they are not even in the top 50% – that is, below the median income, a figure that rarely goes over £30,000 regardless of the statistical source – may paint a much rosier picture in their minds of the circumstances of their fellow citizens than is the case. This assured belief in where they sit is, we will argue, at least partly a result of a tendency to think of ourselves intuitively as 'normal', situated somewhere around the middle. They may have thought if most people are broadly like themselves, they probably earn roughly the same, and therefore their finances are also similar – that is, more likely to be negatively affected by a marginal income tax hike for earnings above £80,000 than benefited by the potential strengthening of welfare provision those funds may allow for.

These misunderstandings about incomes at the top, nevertheless, hide a kernel of truth. For many, the figure of the top 5% evokes images of Jeff Bezos, Elon Musk, yachts and private jets. These are the 'masters of the universe', the truly wealthy, whose economic reality is completely foreign to most. Although Barber may have underestimated the threshold for that kind of wealth, his insistence that he isn't part of it was not unjustified.

Torsten Bell, Head of the Resolution Foundation, wrote one of the best op-eds about the *Question Time* episode. He explained that the real hikes in the income distribution begin around the top 1% and even above.[1] It's no wonder, then, that a relatively well-earning employee or small business owner might resent being put in the same bracket as people whose incomes are exponentially larger. In absolute terms, those at the 5% mark sit much closer to the median income earner than to the super-rich and are arguably much more likely to fall below the former than to ever join the ranks of the latter.

It is also worth remembering that, when we refer to the top 5%, we are talking about 1.635 million people in employment (the total employed population in Britain, as of 2022, being 32.7 million).[2] This is not an insignificant number and one which can even decide elections on its own considering that, as studies have repeatedly shown, the higher your income, the more likely you are to vote.[3]

The fact we are generally unaware of the economic circumstances of those socially distant from us is only compounded by the taboos that exist around money. When we chat with friends and colleagues, we might talk about families, houses, our children, the intricacies of our health issues, our sex lives even, but it is beyond rude to ask about the details of someone else's finances. Money, even if it's everywhere and touches everything, is a subject too private to talk about. It is culturally both 'dirty' (linked to selfishness and philistinism) and 'valued' (associated with social esteem, effort and success). In other words, talking frankly about money makes the social and economic distance between us noticeable and leaves us feeling naked and objectified. If our incomes are higher than those around us, we fear being seen with resentment, or if they are lower, being considered inferior. However reasonable that taboo may be for interpersonal relationships, one important consequence of not broaching it is difficulty in understanding and connecting with the economic realities of others. The ignorance that derives from this may easily inform our politics.

Burgon later told the audience, trying to win them over, "the enemy of someone who is on 70 or 80 thousand pounds a year isn't someone on 20 or 25 thousand pounds a year [...] the people getting away with murder, in reality, are the billionaires, and it's the billionaires who are backing the Conservative Party". Regardless, three weeks later, a majority of the British electorate, Barber presumably included, gave the Tories their largest majority in decades.

At the time of writing (October 2022), the same misperceptions of the income distribution remain by those earning higher incomes. Kwasi Kwarteng, the Chancellor between 6 September and 14 October 2022, announced in a September mini-budget that the 45p tax rate for earnings above £150,000 was going to be abolished.[4] After much public backlash, he reversed the policy. Tony Parsons, a 68-year-old successful author, journalist and broadcaster living in London, tweeted in response to public outcry at the initial policy announcement: "If you think the men and women earning £150,000 a year are 'the super-rich,' you need to get out a bit more."[5]

3

This book is addressed to those who, like Rob Barber, are affluent in relative terms but do not necessarily feel so. For our purposes, this will include anyone who is part of the top 10% of income earners but is not near the very top – that is, what we believe to be an arbitrary but reasonable cut-off point for the upper-middle, professional-managerial class.[6] We aim to answer the following questions: what do members of the top 10% think about inequality, politics and their position in society? How will they react to the economic crisis, the cost of living, cuts to public services and the climate emergency? And how can a case be made for tackling inequality that appeals to this segment of the population?

But before we do any of that, we ought to have a clearer idea of who belongs to this group. After all, the boundaries of what constitutes being 'well-off' are fuzzy and depend on where we stand. Barber did not think he was, even though he is better off than 95% of the British public. Readers may wonder where they themselves sit. We asked ourselves the same thing.

Who exactly are we talking about? And who is doing the talking?

In current debates on economic inequality, most attention has been given either to the top 1% and their capacity to influence politics and shape society, or to those with the lowest incomes, and for good reason. However, the remainder of the top 10% of the income distribution, the top decile in statistical terminology, is just as significant for understanding how inequality works and is maintained. This group includes, for instance, engineers, head teachers, IT specialists, HR managers, senior academics and accountants, who are affluent but not excessively so.

Unless otherwise stated, the subject of this book is those in the top decile but below the top 1% or, if in the top 1%, only just – we were not recruiting for CEOs or tycoons. At this point, it is important to say that these are arbitrary cut-off points. It could be argued that the truly global elite only begins at the 0.1% mark,[7] or that the top quintile (20%) shares similar sociological characteristics with the top decile. We would agree; the economic distribution is not static, after all. Most of our examples will come from the UK, but given our previous research experience and the degree of international mobility and global outlook of this group, we also refer to other countries in Europe and the Americas.

Even though the overwhelming majority in the top 10% do not own yachts or have direct access to senior politicians, they still have disproportionate political influence. Indeed, almost by definition, this group includes all British MPs and most of the top echelons of government, as well as a sizeable proportion of decision makers in the media, the third sector, political parties, business and academia; not to mention senior doctors, lawyers, most judges, consultants and the like. In other words, they make up much of the higher ranks of the professions and institutions dominating the economy, politics and public conversation – with the possible exception of finance, which is firmly the remit of the 1%.

We, Gerry and Marcos, met in 2018, working on a research project focused on the top 10% of income earners in four European countries (Ireland, Spain, Sweden and the UK) led by TASC and FEPS, Irish and European Union (EU) think tanks, respectively. The evidence collected – which includes 110 interviews in those four countries – is the basis for this book.[8]

The report asked to what extent this group was sociologically distinct from the rest of society and whether its attitudes to welfare and redistribution were any different. We focused mostly on income (what people earn) rather than wealth (what they own). Some suggested it would perhaps be better to concentrate on the latter: it is even more unequally distributed than income and, as Thomas Piketty has shown, returns from owning (for instance, property or stocks) are increasing in importance relative to returns from working.[9] Nevertheless, also following Piketty, we thought looking at those at the top of the income distribution would be particularly interesting as they may see their work pay less and less and increasingly rely on what they own instead.

While we were carrying out those interviews, three well-established facts struck us about the literature on the top 10%. First, according to estimations from the HMRC survey of personal incomes, in the 2019–20 tax year, you only needed to earn over £58,300 to be part of it.[10] Many of those earning this amount are not necessarily part of the top 10% of households, especially if they have young children, but a couple where both partners earn around that are significantly above the top 10% mark.[11] Most people, be they interviewees, colleagues and friends, thought this figure was way too low. Perhaps for some readers, this doesn't sound like much either, especially if they are based in a large city such as London where well-paying jobs tend to concentrate and the cost of living is highest. But, and this is key if you are earning £58,300, it means that 90% of the population earns less. See Figure 0.1 for a dramatic representation of how incomes shoot up after the 90th percentile, and how far away the top 1% is from everybody else.

Second, if you are just about into the top 10%, or even the top 5% (£81,000, according to the same HMRC source quoted above for 2019/20), you are still further away from those in the top 1% (£180,000 and over) than from the UK's median income (around £26,000). The higher you go up the distribution, the steeper the climb. As many have noted, including Richard Burgon and Torsten Bell, the earnings of the truly rich are almost unimaginable for most. And as we climb closer to the very top of the distribution, those earnings are increasingly backed up by what people own (in other words, their capital) rather than only their wages. Furthermore, reporting actual income at both the top and the bottom of the distribution is difficult to ascertain, so the distances may be even bigger than we imagine.[12]

Third, while members of that top 10% tend to have relatively socially progressive attitudes to immigration, abortion, minority rights, same-sex marriage and foreign policy, their attitudes on all things economic are not so left of centre. Both surveys and interviews show they are more likely than the rest to oppose redistribution and to accept meritocratic explanations of social mobility.[13]

As bringing up the subject of income is often awkward, finding interviewees wasn't always easy.[14] We used our extended networks and LinkedIn, recruiting to reflect the composition of the top 10% in a few key respects. The most important of these was occupation, which we took as a proxy for income as we did not want to begin the interview with our respondents being immediately aware that they were in the top decile. In most cases that variable was enough to identify who should be

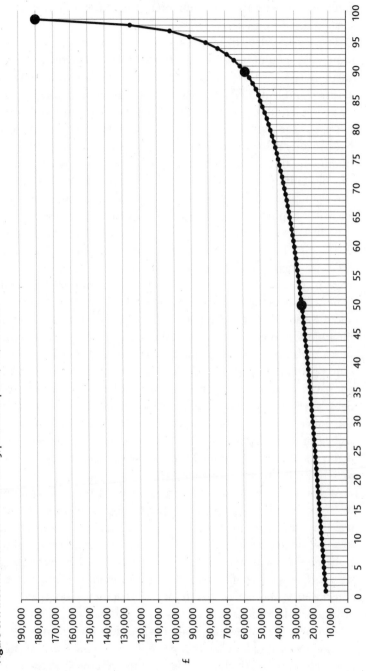

Figure 0.1: Income thresholds before tax by percentile point, UK, 2019/20

Source: HMRC, 2022

interviewed, with the exception of a young IT professional who earned significantly less.

To further reflect the top 10% in statistical terms, two thirds were men, ranging between 26 and 66 years of age, most being in their late forties and early fifties. A majority were White, married and had children.[15] Most lived in or close to the capitals or largest cities in each of the four countries; 16% of Londoners belong to the top 10%.[16] In the UK, that meant our respondents lived mainly in south-east England, perhaps a consequence of us both living there and the concentration of higher-paying jobs in this most affluent region of the country.[17] We acknowledge that this is a limitation and that the perceptions and attitudes of high earners living in other parts of the UK warrant further study.

Interviews were conducted between August 2018 and August 2019, plus a series of follow-ups between January and May 2022. A majority of these were carried out online, but some were in person. Most took just over an hour and all used the same semi-structured interview guide. We began with questions about respondents' biographies, followed by asking them about their work, careers and professional trajectory.[18] Later, we moved on to their attitudes on inequality, the rich and the poor; their views on taxation, the public and private sectors, and public services (including which ones they use); their social and political behaviour: whether they vote, participate in politics or volunteer. We ended with questions about their self-perception. Do they feel privileged? To what extent has hard work, good decision making and luck determined their status? Where do they think they fit in the income distribution?

At this stage, it's important to explain why we found this group worthy of attention and how it may affect how we see it. When we were carrying out this research, we were an early-career sociologist looking for a footing in a precarious, internationalised academic labour market and a freelance social policy researcher who had moved out of London to Woking, a solidly Conservative constituency, and ran as Labour's parliamentary candidate in the 2019 general election.

Marcos is the son of upwardly mobile doctors from Chile – themselves of middle-class background in the US sense of the term. He grew up during the decades that followed Pinochet's dictatorship, which saw his country become one of the wealthiest and most unequal in Latin America. In 2009, he came to the UK to study at some of the most prestigious universities in the world. For his Cambridge PhD and first book on think tanks after the 2008 financial crisis, he interviewed some elite figures of British policy making. After graduating, he spent a few years doing freelance research and taking occasional teaching and lecturing jobs across UK universities, because it was difficult to find permanent work. As anyone who knows academia will tell you, teaching means being paid only for the time spent in the classroom at a rate, when preparation and marking time are added, that often amounts to less than the minimum wage. The unspoken assumption is that this will only be temporary as junior academics work their way up the hierarchy. However, for many, this is not what happens, as evidenced by the increasing reliance of universities on underpaid fixed-term labour, without which they could not deliver their courses.[19] Marcos only found a more secure foothold when he was contracted by University College London to cover a permanent member of staff on maternity leave, after almost four years of applying for jobs. This is not uncommon.

Gerry is an only child and the first in her mother's family to go to university and private school. Though she moved around quite a bit during her childhood, she spent many years behind the scenes in luxury hotels in London, where her mother and stepfather worked as managers. Her classmates were children of some of the wealthiest families in the city. Living in such environments during the Thatcher years made her keenly aware of inequality. Following her undergraduate degree, Gerry spent ten years working in publishing, public sector and non-profit organisations, at which point she returned to university in the 2000s, completing a PhD at the London School of Economics and Political Science (LSE) on the impact of Tony Blair's New Labour welfare to work programmes on young people. At the same time, she also took contract teaching, lecturing and research positions at LSE and was a freelance Hansard reporter in parliament. She then took a career break to raise her own family, moving to Woking, just outside London. Before returning to research, Gerry worked in local schools and voluntary organisations and became heavily involved with the Labour Party. In those years, she saw the impact of austerity on her community, ostensibly one of the most affluent in the UK.

From that brief introduction to two people with fairly different backgrounds, it is apparent that there is much we share. We are both from families who became socially and geographically mobile, who provided privilege on the tacit expectation that our trajectories would be equally successful. Both of us have experienced the anxiety such expectations can often bring and owe our positions not only to scholarships but also to the early privilege provided by our parents being professionals or managers and finding the cash for private schools. Very few, even in the top 10%, ever get to write a book. Less than 2% of their children go to Oxbridge or the LSE. We share these privileges with many working in the social sciences, a relatively 'posh' academic subject. While as individuals we are not in the top 10%, we have been supported by our partners and wider network of relatives, friends and colleagues, many of whom are in this group themselves or have been for much of their working lives.

Having entered the privileged world of academia, we have both been broadly invested in the institution of the university, from which we expected to get the legitimacy to have something to say about society and the prerogative to belong to the middle class, however vaguely defined.[20] We have spent decades studying alongside, being taught by and working with individuals in academia and the policy research world who were – or could be expected to become – high-earning professionals and managers. However, neither of us expects to join the top 10% anytime soon, however close we are to some of its members in professional, educational or personal settings. The ground rules have changed and a PhD isn't able to guarantee the income it may have just a few decades ago.

Our own position, as authors of this book, is therefore instrumentally and ethically loaded. On the one hand, our professional biographies give us a keen understanding of how inequalities function and our relative proximity to our research subjects gives us a unique opportunity to identify their ways of thinking. On the other hand, there are ethical and methodological risks in that we find our own perspectives becoming entangled with worldviews that reflect and reinforce the status quo, and which are then given further legitimacy through our work. Our own relationship with the top 10% is, therefore, both potentially transformative (we have unique access) but also dangerous (it may reproduce current frames of thinking).

Conducting interviews with high-income earners, we were struck by the seeming familiarity of many of their views. Most were to the right of Jeremy Corbyn and to the left of Boris Johnson (or at least of his post-Brexit version). Those closer to the right (a majority, but not an overwhelming one), tended to have the kind of 'pro-austerity' views that are prevalent in the media and gave meritocratic explanations and values to justify their opposition to greater redistribution. Those closer to the political left often held similar ideas to those found in *The Guardian* and the kinds of institutions we are both familiar with (universities, NGOs, left-of-centre think tanks and political parties). Therefore, a crucial hurdle in deciphering this group was that – discounting their distorted sense of their own economic position – what they told us often simply sounded like the prevailing 'common sense' in media and politics.

We also soon discovered that the dominance and ubiquity of the top 10% in the public conversation perversely renders it almost invisible. We have become accustomed to its ways of thinking – including meritocratic explanations of its success – and its cultural trappings. It's the unspoken background of the dominant political culture in Britain, as represented, for example, by the BBC. Members of the top 10%, while not always identifying with that description of themselves, see the economic and social structures that support them simply as 'commonsensical' and 'reasonable'. Therefore, they are perplexed when confronted with anger against them. In their minds, a more irrational 'populism' seems to have taken over, especially in the fallout of the Brexit vote and after Trump became US president. We started wondering whether these ways of thinking, though seemingly unremarkable, are part of the explanation for our growing social divides.

The difficulty of making sense of the fact that their views are both apparently omnipresent and perceived to be under siege made us think. Academics frequently tend to 'other' their research subjects, ostensibly to give a voice to people we don't usually hear from or understand. In our case, the difficulty was exactly the opposite – we needed to interrogate the 'us' of the 'us and them'.

The research world is not immune to the naturalisation of such views, which makes writing this book particularly uncomfortable – reflecting on the growing distance between ourselves (the researchers), the people we study (most often those who are 'othered'), and those we report to (quite frequently, members of the top 10%). While nobody we know in the top decile would refer to themselves as 'us' or to the rest of the population as 'them', the structure of our work assumes a 'professional' distance between the researcher and a researched 'subject'. We study others through 'fieldwork' and return to elite environments to present 'findings' to our peers and employers to, in the best-case scenario, inform policy and the public conversation.

This privileged viewpoint comes with the tacit acceptance of a commonly held but rarely voiced view: if you are a high-income earner, you have proven yourself worthy of being in charge of your own life and politics and the state should leave you be. From that viewpoint, even researching the relatively well-off may seem indulgent. This book argues the opposite, that social structures affect the lives of 'us' as well as 'them'. For that reason, we look at high-income earners as a group to be studied sociologically and anthropologically, reflecting on how the failure to do so obscures so much of the dynamics of inequality. In that sense, thinking about the 'subjects' of our work requires what anthropologists call 'estranged intimacy': becoming intimately involved, while at the same time standing back.

That being said, we do not want to simply reproduce the kind of 'anti-metropolitan elites' arguments that have poisoned the well in Britain and elsewhere. As the last decade has made all of us painfully aware, denunciations of highly educated professionals and experts quite frequently mask reactionary politics under the guise of anti-elitism – and lead to trust being deposited into even more moneyed elites. We do not want to refuel nativist, anti-intellectual denunciations of the 'citizens of nowhere', which often end up benefiting the truly wealthy, the owners of capital. As we explore later in the book, taking that route – as countries like Hungary, Russia and increasingly the UK seem to have done – results in less free, less solidaristic and less sustainable societies.

Another issue we face with our chosen subject group is that while we don't want to antagonise the top 10%, we also don't want to seem excessively sympathetic to those who are, by definition, a privileged segment of society. They tend to be more mobile, healthy, educated, professionally fulfilled, economically secure and optimistic about the future than the 90%. Even though their incomes decrease at a larger rate after economic downturns, they recover faster and capture most subsequent growth.[21] More likely to hold a university degree, to access cheap credit and to feel financially secure, they have also been insulated from the worst effects of austerity and the post-COVID-19 economic crisis.

What we want instead is to prompt this group to question whether they are simply 'normal' and whether their own experiences and achievements can and should be the basis to judge the lives of everyone else. After all, soon after being granted a privilege, you get used to it, at which point it becomes normal, part of the background. However, this tendency becomes harmful when it forces on the majority standards that are increasingly beyond their reach. In other words, we want to elicit more 'sociological imagination' in a group in which those who have a voice in how society is run tend to concentrate.

Is all well with them?

As privileged as members of this subset of the population might be, we argue that cracks are beginning to show in their sense of security and self-worth. This has opened up a space to offer alternatives. In Ireland, for instance, a country that depends to a great degree on international capital flows, with some of the highest nominal earnings and fastest growth rates in the EU, we found that 28% of the Irish top 10% declared that they had difficulties 'making ends meet' in 2016, a year in which its economy grew by 5.2%.[22] Surely, part of the answer to that was that 'making ends meet' means something very different to the well-off, right? Or is something else going on?

To be sure, the top decile has thrived since the advent of globalisation, but not nearly as much as the top 1%. According to the World Inequality Database, while the top 10% captured 36.1% of all income in Britain in 2018 (up from 28.5% in 1980), it was the top 1% who received most of it (from 6.8% to 13.1%).[23] This leaves a 1.3% share growth for the remainder of the top 10%, and raises the question of how much of it was seen by those at the bottom of the top decile. Furthermore, as Piketty has famously shown, wealth is much more unequally distributed than income, and the more income you have, the more likely it is that a greater proportion of it derives from your wealth rather than only from your work.[24]

Given the above, we argue that growing inequality and the spectacular concentration of wealth at the top in recent decades – once touted as necessary for a thriving economy – now risk hurting even many within the top 10%. This is not only because of their perceived indirect effects (for example, crime and insecurity), but also because keeping up with the top 1% may prove increasingly hard for most. It is precisely because of this ambiguity surrounding the top 10%, the fact they are both privileged and mostly dependent on their work to make a living, that we decided to focus on them rather than on owners of wealth more directly, who are much more likely to align themselves with the interests of capital. By the same token, we acknowledge the increasing number of high earners in Britain who are also owners of the most wealth. Inequality expert Branko Milanovic tweeted: "your neighbourly CEO [...] is in the top 1% by labor income and also in the top 1% by [the] shares he owns."[25]

Anti-elitism, precarity, automation and higher costs of living also risk undermining the social and economic status of the top income decile. Our interviews revealed some veiled anxieties. Despite their relative advantages, comfort and insulation, those in the top decile do not feel politically empowered and fear downward mobility. Like all of us, they live in a world affected by climate change, higher costs of living, an eroding social safety net, and what they see as rising populism and political polarisation. Aware of intergenerational inequalities, they worry that the world their children will inherit will be worse off.[26] Like most of us, they know there's something wrong and unsustainable about how we live our lives, but don't know exactly what it is or what to do about it.

Recently, we found ourselves reflecting on how the top 10% may interpret the momentous changes the UK and the world are undergoing, and whether their lives and views have changed since the start of the pandemic. We know that their political and social attitudes develop from everyday concerns about good schools for their children, affordable housing and access to healthcare if they need it: a desire to be secure. How will this group respond when faced with societal shocks and the wider societal realisation that the gap between those in the top 1% and the remainder of the top 10% is significant and only likely to grow?

Before the pandemic, they were already facing a choice between an ever more unsustainable status quo and the far right. In 2020, they experienced significant changes to their lives and, if not becoming the direct recipients of state transfers through furlough and business-support schemes, witnessed their widespread use among people not too different from themselves. Meanwhile, as Gary Stevenson, a former trader in the City of London, has shown, the COVID-19 response represented an unprecedented transfer of wealth towards the rich, boosting the savings and assets of the already wealthy while the rest are left to struggle with rising inflation.[27] Since late 2021, high earners have seen a cost of living crisis and market instability that have increasingly threatened them too. The choice they have to make in the coming years is one between isolating and protecting themselves even further or reaching out and connecting with others, in the understanding that their concerns aren't ultimately that different from those of the median earner: being able to afford a good quality of life in an ever more expensive and uncertain world.

Chapter outline

The remainder of the book is structured as follows. Chapter 1 sketches a broad picture of the top 10%, examining what they look like and how they are different from the rest in sociodemographic terms. Perhaps unsurprisingly, they are doing rather well. We show how members of this income group are more likely than people lower down the distribution to hold a university degree and to have seen their incomes grow. However, the top 10% is also internally diverse, and there is a noticeable distance between those at the top and the bottom of the bracket.

In Chapter 2, we look at high-earning individuals in qualitative terms: what they tell us in interviews about their backgrounds and life stories. By most reasonable definitions of the term, they are the 'upper-middle class' but they would flinch if called that. They believe that they are merely average. This tells us that there is a distortion in how those who earn more than 90% of their fellow citizens think about themselves and others. What impact is this having on how they think about the society they live in?

Chapter 3 examines their views on work: its importance for their self-definition and how they derive moral and social worth from paid employment and educational attainment, measured by income and professional status. This logic explains why even high-income earners who hold progressive views on the economy often come across as hierarchical rather than egalitarian. Those with the most career achievements and educational credentials are, according to an unspoken meritocratic truism, better positioned to lead the state, steer the public conversation and decide over the public purse.

Chapter 4 zeroes in on the politics of the top 10%, in both formal and informal terms. It does so by acknowledging that public opinion can be complex and conflicting and that it is an oversimplification to align principles, behaviours, morals and values to either the right or left of the political spectrum.[28] Notwithstanding, previous research has positioned the top 10% broadly on the right on economics and on the left on issues such as same-sex marriage, abortion and immigration. Recently, these views have been under strain, especially after the populist waves of the 2010s and, in the UK, the emergence of Brexit and Jeremy Corbyn. We also explore some of the reasons why voters in the most affluent constituencies of the UK continue to support the Conservatives at the same time as being quite critical of their lurch to the right.

According to surveys, this group has higher levels of trust in political institutions than the rest, as well as being more likely to vote and to believe they have a say in how their countries are run. However, and seemingly in contradiction with that, our respondents also show a certain mistrust of politics, fearing political instability, populism, corruption and the erosion of democratic norms. This might be explained by the fact that, although they have a detached familiarity with national political debates, they rarely engage with small 'p' politics. Given their tendency to prioritise work and competition and to surround themselves with those of similar socioeconomic status, they frequently feel detached from the communities in which they live, which are often quite segregated. Moreover, their lives have been relatively insulated from the effects of austerity and their knowledge of how hard it is at the bottom is mostly theoretical.

In Chapter 5, we underline the challenges that mounting inequality presents for high-income earners. As is well established, inequality threatens not only those in poverty but the whole of society on a wide range of social indicators: insecurity, crime, climate change, public health and even political polarisation.[29] Although most of our interviewees agreed inequality was something we should be concerned about, they were much more pessimistic about society's future than their own. This speaks of an imagined distance from the rest and an ontological sense of security. There will continue to be opportunities for them and they will be able to get out of whatever circumstances they find themselves in, despite their anxieties and concerns, through the hard work that got them where they are in the first place.

Even so, holes are beginning to appear in their narrative of constant social advancement. Access to housing, jobs, opportunities for career progression and places in elite universities is becoming scarcer and competition fiercer. Many are also aware that catastrophic events such as illness or accident could derail their career trajectories. In tandem, intergenerational inequalities are becoming more accentuated, as Millennials and Generation Z find the transition to adulthood increasingly difficult. Education does not seem to guarantee income the way it once did, as income and status are becoming closely linked to inheritance and wealth. Our respondents' optimism was less pronounced about the world their children will inherit.

Chapter 6 asks what the top 10% will do when faced with such pressures, considering their mobility and their ability to isolate themselves. As globalisation was emerging, sociologists highlighted the increasing mobility and flexibility of a globalised workforce. This especially applies to the well-off, driving the process of 'brain-drain' and the interconnectedness of fields such as science, finance, business and education. Commuting and moving for work and education also means that many high-income earners lack a strong connection to any one place. Interviewees who were originally from less-privileged backgrounds described their upward mobility as individual exercises of 'getting out' of environments offering few prospects.

However, in an increasingly nationalistic post-COVID-19 world, our respondents' ability to cross borders is endangered while competition for services (increasingly offered online) threatens to become global. If they cannot escape these societal shocks, what are the alternatives? They could hunker down, insulating themselves from the worst effects of inequality, or seek to acquire as many advantages as possible for their children. While these are all attractive in the short term, they are also becoming more difficult and less effective, both because of the magnitude of the crises we are facing and because of the distance the very top has already secured from everyone else.

Chapter 7 identifies some of the barriers to a wider sense of belonging created by their perspectives, including a dominant belief in meritocracy. As we establish in Chapter 3, high earners' identities are mostly centred on homogeneous workplaces. High earners also tend to live either in high-income areas or at a 'social distance' from less-affluent communities near them. Although confident about their occupational status, many didn't feel they made a wider contribution to society and felt disempowered by corporate structures.

We believe there is a need for this group to tear down some of these barriers and strengthen their connection with their communities. While relatively protected, the pandemic has shown all of us – including the top 10% – that we depend on each other, especially on many of those we pay the least. COVID-19 will have also altered their work-life balance and led to more time spent locally. It might be time for high-income earners to rethink their assumptions about which parts of society are valuable, the meaning of citizenship and what work is 'essential' and worthy of respect.

Chapter 8 may make uncomfortable reading because rather than mapping out a positive vision of the future, it instead suggests some of the ways the top 10% could reset their attitudes towards the lives of others and re-examine their relationship with the private sector, public services and the state. It starts by reminding us what we know: that while they told us they largely defined themselves through work, they rarely thought about the contribution of their work to society beyond the bottom line. They also worried their older selves may not remain 'ahead of the curve' in a global market and that their children might be unable to climb the meritocratic ladder as they did. They acknowledge the value of public services, but, prior to the pandemic, tended to focus on education and equality of opportunity. They were generally supportive of public spending on healthcare and education, partly because they touch the lives of individuals in spheres mostly outside their influence. By the same token, many viewed those receiving welfare as somehow deficient.

The book's conclusion reflects on how high-income earners may react to societal shocks as it becomes increasingly apparent that their previous strategies are becoming ineffective. It questions whether the economic structures that have, until now, served them well will continue to. The first obstacle is that the very definition of elite implies a distance from non-members. For meritocratic high-income earners, the rationale for this distance cannot be ascribed status: it has to be the reward for effort, whether in the form of work or educational credentials. Therefore, one of the first tasks is to question the concept of 'reward' and its linkage to social goods and status. Our respondents were beginning to see that this link is getting weaker, that hierarchical employment structures and hiring demands are changing – with a hollowing out of middle-class jobs – and that social mobility is coming to a standstill. They are aware that their children, notwithstanding their education, will not have the same opportunities or standard of living, and their choices for work and consumption will therefore have to change.

High-income earners, particularly those working in the private sector, appear compliant with a meritocratic, pro-austerity common sense. However, they were likely to consider the limits of this logic when encouraged to reflect on the tensions between their own needs (and those of their children) and the requirements of global capital. We have seen that they have mostly sought to meet the former by serving the latter. They may prefer paying for advantages for their children while at the same time erecting fences to keep other people's children out, in the understanding that the benefits of doing that are much more direct and tangible than building a less unequal country. But as the fence grows taller and the club's fees become more expensive, this may not continue to work. And this means that we will need to promote the need for, and value of, new models of ownership (both at work or locally) and the legitimacy of other work, life and consumption roles and choices. If not, high earners may continue to see the distance between the idea and the reality of meritocracy only grow, to the point where only capital is truly valued.

The well-off are uncomfortably off, intuitively coming to terms with the awkward truth that they cannot be, as Markovits puts it, 'both rich and free'.[30] Living at the current level of competition has negative effects on their wellbeing while directly relying on other people's exclusion. Their imagined sense of self cannot be dissociated from the economic structures they live within. This book's aim is to invite the top 10% to consider a future in which, for the price of giving up the barriers through which they seek to distinguish themselves from the rest, they could become less anxious, more secure and less isolated. Their children, who will increasingly struggle to retain the position they were born in, are likely to push them in that direction.

1

Not billionaires, but well-off?

This chapter describes the top 10% in statistical terms, based mostly on survey data. It explores what, if anything, makes them a recognisable group that can be distinguished from the rest of the population.[1] However, an important caveat is that incomes at the very top are sometimes difficult to fully detect, and increasingly so the higher up you go. Top incomes are under-reported in surveys when compared with tax data[2] – and tax data also underestimate the riches of the truly affluent.[3] This may be because the higher you climb, the more likely you are to have incentives and the capacity to hide your true income, for tax reasons or otherwise. Many within the top 10% (as well as among our interviewees) are business owners and can decide what to take from their businesses as a salary rather than rely on a fixed monthly amount. Nevertheless, using the lower bound of the top 10% as a benchmark, what we show in this chapter holds as a rough sociological sketch of those who are doing *relatively* well. There will be many exceptions, but at an aggregate level, there is much that distinguishes this group from the other 90% of the population (though, of course, the boundary between 'well-off' and those 'not quite there' is always fuzzy).

How to define the top 10%

Posh, well-off, privileged, upper class, elite. In societies where the lives of their citizens are ruled by the possession of money such as ours, these words are loaded and contradictory. On the one hand, being well-off has positive connotations: being able to provide for oneself and one's family, but also being articulate, well travelled, confident, educated and successful – it implies being a member of society whose contribution is valued enough to deserve a decent living. On the other hand, calling someone well-off also insinuates they might be spoiled, cloistered, arrogant or unrelatable: always at risk of engendering distance and envy. For that reason, being (or being perceived as) well-off is a sensitive affair that has both societal and interpersonal dimensions, that touches on both history and the everyday. Hence our attitudes towards what is apparently a strictly economic category are also political, cultural and moral.

Not only are our attitudes to affluence contradictory, but also relative. In the UK, you might not think of the working class of post-industrial northern England as privileged, but arguably they are compared to most in Eritrea. Similarly, a family of doctors from South America might be by many definitions well-off, but their income is minuscule compared with the fortunes of the tech barons of Palo Alto. Given both how laden and relative this issue is, it is easy to see why delimiting who is and who is not well-off is problematic. The lower boundary is always fuzzy, dependent on our vantage point, and riddled with danger. A 2016 Gallup poll in the US found that those earning under $20,000 a year and those earning between $150,000 and $250,000 both identified as middle class at similar rates (roughly 30%).[4]

All of this poses difficulties for anyone studying the relatively privileged. Those familiar with income statistics will know there are many ways to break down the population that implicitly address the question of who should be considered well-off, middle class and poor. Quintiles and deciles are probably the most common – dividing a population into five or ten groups ordered by an unequally distributed variable such as wealth or income.

To be sure, there is some arbitrariness involved. The cut-off point could conceivably be the 50%, 13.9%, 4.8% or 0.2% mark, or not based on income or wealth numbers at all. Nevertheless, for the sake of simplicity and comparability, they tend to be used not only as reference points to detect relative wealth or deprivation but also as the basis for indexes to measure inequality. For instance, the Palma ratio aims to reflect the extent of inequality by comparing the share of the total income of the top 10% of the population with that of the bottom 40%. Only in particularly equal countries such as Sweden does the Palma ratio approach, meaning that both groups capture about the same percentage of the country's income. In the UK, according to the Organisation for Economic Co-operation and Development (OECD), it was 1.57 in 2019.[5] In other words, for every pound earned by the bottom 40%, £1.57 is captured by the top 10% – and the bottom 40%, it may be obvious but needs restating, is four times larger.

In that sense, though focusing on the top 10% is arbitrary, it has its advantages. The first is quite prosaic: several measures use that benchmark. Besides the Palma ratio, there are the 90/50 and the 90/10 ratios, measuring the distance between the threshold for the top 10% and the earner right in the middle of the distribution (90/50) or the one at the top of the lowest decile (90/10). According to the OECD, these numbers in 2019 were 1.9 and 4, respectively, meaning the poorest member of the top 10% earns almost twice as much as the median earner and four times more than those in the poorest 10%.[6] Another advantage of using the top decile as a cut-off point is that, although few would argue that the top 10% are affluent relative to the rest of society, this population is broad and diverse enough to encompass many who may not necessarily feel so. As we will show, within that group you can find both billionaires and people who would struggle to get a mortgage.

Research by the Trust for London in 2020 identified five levels of progressively higher living standards, which were not equally spaced: minimum income standard, surviving comfortably, the (securely) comfortable, the wealthy and the super-rich. Focus group discussions found 'there is no agreement on what it means to be rich'. Attitudes are nuanced and narratives of the deserving and undeserving rich emerge – such as consideration of how the rich get their money, how they spend it, and whether it is used for the good of others.[7] The researchers concluded that:

> The concept of a 'riches' line, if defined as a line above which people are considered to have 'too much' [...] (rather than a *descriptive* line above which someone can simply be defined as rich) is by nature a normative evaluation. If public consensus on this *normative* view

(that it is wrong to have too much) could be found it would be a valuable addition to debates about the scope for the redistribution of wealth or for the curbing of high income, including the compressing of pay differentials. But the idea of surplus, excessive or unnecessary income, consumption or wealth is open to many different interpretations.[8]

In what follows, we argue that drawing the line at the 10% mark makes sense sociologically, not because the top 10% is cohesive or homogeneous, but because at an aggregate level they have some distinct characteristics compared with everyone else. Doubtless, they are a diverse group, but what they share says a lot about them too. Among those variables, probably the two most immediate are occupation and education.

What is peculiar about the top 10%?

Unsurprisingly, the top 10% is massively overrepresented among managers (28% of them are part of the top 10%, according to data from European Union Statistics on Income and Living Conditions [EU-SILC]), professionals (21%), and, to a lesser extent, associate professionals (8%), with the notable but not numerous exceptions of the armed forces and some elite technical occupations such as pilots and railway operators.[9] There are very few clerical staff, skilled agricultural, fisheries and forestry workers, trades and crafts workers and machine operators in the top 10% and almost none among those employed in elementary occupations such as cleaners and carers. None of the other categories have more than 5% of their members in the top 10%, and clerks, sales and service workers and those in elementary occupations barely have anyone among their ranks (see Figure 1.1).

At this stage we should remind readers that, according to the Office for National Statistics (ONS), in 2018, professionals and managers account for, respectively, 11% and 20% of all workers in Britain, and professionals and managers in the top 10% are a smaller group still.[10] Even so, a 2016 NatCen Social Research study found that 47% of professionals and managers in Britain declare themselves to be working class.[11] Comparing

Not billionaires, but well-off?

Figure 1.1: Occupation by income decile, UK, 2016

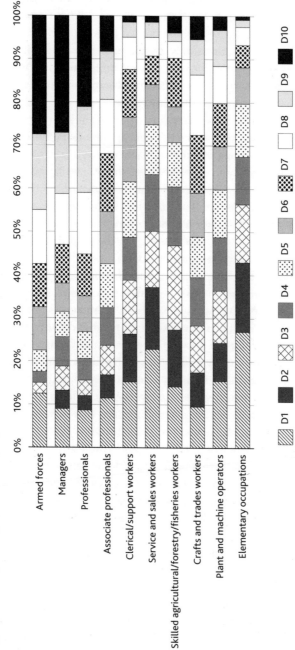

Source: Eurostat, 2018

these results with the US Gallup poll mentioned earlier, British people's understanding of class is clearly different from that of the Americans.

Occupation has, to be sure, several important effects on people's lives. As we grow older, and leaving aside our social networks associated with family and education – and arguably to a lesser or diminishing degree, churches, hobbies and neighbourhood – work is the place we make many of our friendships. It shouldn't be surprising because we spend most of our waking hours there. If that is the case, most of our immediate colleagues (or at least those we are most likely to relate to), will share a similar occupational status with us: in the case of professionals and managers, that usually means other professionals and managers.

Work shapes to a large extent the kinds of people we have daily contact with. This could include, in the case of the top 10%, colleagues and clients who may be sociologically very different (for example, civil engineers and the builders they oversee; doctors and their patients), but often it does not. Indeed, many well-paid occupations, especially in a country as welcoming to international capital as the UK, seek to attract the very wealthiest clients. You only need to think of the many industries geared towards selling to the 1%, especially in and around the City of London: investment finance, asset management, management consultancy, corporate and tax law, stock trading and so on, but also, closer to home for us as authors – the elite universities selling postgraduate courses to students largely from families in the top 10%.

Even where a well-paid profession is not mostly oriented towards the top 1%, access to its ranks may still be defensively policed, making it difficult for outsiders or those without the connections, money or 'cultural fit' to join. This immediately recalls the top echelons of media and politics: in 2019 it was reported that two thirds of Boris Johnson's cabinet attended Eton College (for those not from the UK, an elite boys' school that charges up to £48,500 a year).[12] The truth, however, is that this phenomenon is much more widespread than at the apex of the political elite. According to the Institute for Fiscal Studies, the average annual net private school fees in Britain are £13,700, while total state school spending per pupil is about half of that, £6,900.[13]

According to Sam Friedman and Daniel Laurison in their celebrated book on social mobility, *The Class Ceiling*, over 50% of those working in elite fields such as medicine, journalism, law, life sciences, management consultancy, academia and advertising have parents who were professionals and managers themselves.[14] More specifically, Friedman and Laurison also show that the children of doctors are 24 times more likely than the rest of their cohort to become doctors; the children of lawyers, 17 times more likely than the rest to become lawyers; and the children of people working in film and television, 12 times more likely to have the same occupation as their parents.

Friedman and Laurison found that people whose parents were from lower socioeconomic backgrounds tend to be paid less for the same job than high-income earners with parents who had elite occupations. How does this square with 47% of professionals and managers who describe themselves as 'working class'? Interviewing people in elite jobs, they conclude that part of the explanation is the 'way in which working class ways of being have been ruthlessly appropriated by the upper-middle class as a way to make money and cachet from authenticity'.[15] With increasing levels of inequality and the dominance of elites in many occupations, class certainly seems to remain relevant in the UK in explaining people's life trajectories.

Income is correlated with who is most likely to work from home. Studies following the COVID-19 pandemic have found that the industries where high-income earners tend to be concentrated (finance and insurance, IT, professional services) are also among the most adaptable to be carried out remotely, while elementary and manufacturing occupations are much less so.[16] Coincidentally enough, these are also the kinds of jobs which often require being more mobile and at ease with globalised, innovation-driven labour markets and also those where much of the top 10% are concentrated.

While all of this is happening, the structure of the labour market is changing. More professional-level jobs are appearing, while at the lower end the structure of the labour market is shifting away from skilled work and manufacturing towards clerical and blue-collar service occupations. A 2020 Eurofound report (in which the UK was still considered), found that between 2011 and 2018, white-collar, highly skilled jobs were by far the fastest to expand in Europe (2.4%), especially in services. Most other occupational categories, meanwhile, dwindled, especially highly skilled blue-collar and construction jobs. The only exception was blue-collar, low-skilled jobs in private-sector services (for example, retail and catering).[17] Meanwhile, growth in full-time, permanent employment was almost completely concentrated in the first income quintile (top 20%), while the proportion of part-time, temporary jobs is increasing across the economies of Europe. Conceivably, the only way for this process of deindustrialisation not to generate insurmountable societal pressures is if the numbers of professional, well-paid service jobs continue to increase and are captured by the children of blue-collar workers. But how likely is that, considering what we know about social mobility trends? And if the children of blue-collar workers do seek to become professionals and managers, won't that generate further incentives to police access to elite occupations for those already 'in' them?

Unsurprisingly, having a high income is also strongly correlated with years spent in formal education. EU-SILC data show that 36.8% of the UK population have at least a tertiary education (meaning at least a university degree). For the top 10%, that number is 75.8%, (in Ireland these figures are 39.8 and 81.7%, and in Spain 29.6 and 71.6%).[18] Considering the concentration of professionals and managers in the top 10%, this is perhaps unremarkable. However, even though the great majority of high-income earners attended university, over two thirds of people with degrees in the population at large are not part of the top 10%.[19]

Not only are the years in education important, but also the perceived quality of that education and how much it is valued in the labour market. For instance, the diminishing returns of getting a PhD versus an MBA, or a degree from post-1992 universities versus one from Oxbridge. According to data from The Sutton Trust, 41% of senior public servants, 31% of politicians, 39% of media elites, and 17% of business leaders attended either Oxford or Cambridge, compared to 1% of the population.[20] In recent years, much has been written about Oxford and Cambridge's outreach efforts to increase their uptake of state school students (93% of all pupils). Yet, in 2020, these universities reported as a success story that 69.1% of admitted applicants to Oxford and

70.6% of those at Cambridge were from state schools.[21] One reason that these percentages were reported as success stories is that they are higher than many other elite universities. In 2021, Oxford Brookes University, formerly Oxford Polytechnic, appeared to take more children from private schools than Oxford University. However, more importantly, 51% of Oxford's students and 46% of Cambridge students are postgraduates – and most are paying very high fees.[22] Put this way, the undergraduate stats provide a 'shop window' that hides the extent to which Oxbridge students come from privileged backgrounds.

Another characteristic shared by the top 10% is location. A majority live in large cities where the best-paid jobs tend to be concentrated and the cost of living is highest. The ONS has reported that the highest incomes in Britain are found mostly in and around London, with important pockets in Buckinghamshire, Surrey and West Kent, plus a few others further afield in places like Edinburgh, Cheshire, North Yorkshire and East Cumbria.[23] Truly high incomes at an aggregate level, however, are mostly found in Central and West London. In particular, the boroughs of Kensington & Chelsea and Hammersmith & Fulham have an average yearly income of £63,286, which would position the average earner living there firmly in the top 10%.[24]

One of Friedman and Laurison's most interesting arguments in *The Class Ceiling* is that among the most important mechanisms by which privilege is reproduced at the top is the fact children from privileged backgrounds can rely on what they call 'the bank of mum and dad'.[25] In other words, the children of affluent parents have the possibility of delaying their entry into the workforce even while living and studying in places like London, where housing costs and salaries are highest. This allows privileged children to work in unpaid internships, spend more time in education, grow their networks and hone their skills so that they can compete in ever more specialised and credentialled labour markets.

In terms of gender, the figures are no more encouraging. Women comprise the majority of earners at each and every of the six poorest deciles, and their share diminishes the higher you go. Notwithstanding big differences among European countries, EU–SILC data show that although women were slightly over 50% of the European workforce in 2016, they were around 70%

of the poorest 10% of workers and around 33% of the top 10%. This tendency doesn't stop even within the top decile, as they are only 17% of the top 1%.[26] According to the ONS, the gender pay gap increases substantially in high-paying jobs in the UK, driving up the overall gender pay gap numbers, a gap that is also much more pronounced for workers below the age of 40.[27] Coincidentally, the highest average incomes in terms of age and gender are concentrated in men aged 45–49 and 50–54 (£55,300 and £54,100, respectively), while women of the same age can expect to earn much less (on average £36,300 and £35,200).[28]

Regarding race and ethnic origin, ONS data show that White, Chinese and Indian are the only ethnicities well represented in the top quintile, meaning at least 20% are part of the 20% of highest earners. The numbers for other ethnicities are dire: only 3% of Bangladeshis, 5% of Pakistanis and 11% of Black African/ British/Caribbean workers are part of that top quintile, and 47%, 42%, and 31% respectively are part of the poorest.[29] Of the total economically active population in March 2022, estimated to be 33,792,000, 29 million are classified as White, 1 million as Indian and 194,000 as Chinese. However, even though high-income earners may look overwhelmingly White (90% of the top 20% of income earners are), they make up a lower percentage than the comparable 50+ age group in the rest of the income distribution.[30]

What can we conclude about high earners from these data? That they are mostly southern, middle-aged, White and male, even if most southern, middle-aged, White males are not high-income earners. Similarly, they are mostly professionals and managers, but a majority of professionals and managers are not part of the top 10% either.

From the data, it can be surmised that many factors are at play – both in terms of innate characteristics and upbringing – that make it likely that an individual will or will not be part of the top 10%. However, perhaps the single most noticeable variable identifying this group is the years spent in education. This does not mean that everyone with a university degree is a high earner, but that high earners are especially likely to have been to university. Education is crucial, not only to secure access to highly paid professional and managerial occupations but also as a cultural marker. It is through education that the economic and cultural signifiers of wealth come together, as well as the social prestige and lack of stigma that diminishes the possibility of finding fault with someone's CV to justify overlooking it. We also wager that this group is the kind whose children are all but guaranteed to go to university; for many, it isn't even a question. The top 10% are, on paper, those who have dotted all the I's and crossed all the T's.

Are they all that secure?

Previous research by Piketty and Saez, as well as by the OECD, on the impact of the 2008 financial crisis showed that the immediate effect of the crash was to suppress incomes at the top, briefly lowering inequality – at least for a couple of years.[31] However, soon after, the top deciles rebounded while incomes in the rest of the distribution remained stagnant. Based on these data, it is possible to argue that high incomes are more sensitive to economic shocks, at least initially, but that the proceeds of subsequent growth are also more likely to end up benefiting them.

Even so, nothing guaranteed that those in the top 10% before the financial crisis would still be there after it. Be it because of economic downturns, a health crisis, a bad financial or professional decision, or because of sheer bad luck, many who were once in the top 10% will fall out of it. Furthermore, the fact that high incomes tend to be concentrated in the middle of an individual's working life (roughly between the ages of 40 and 65) means that most people who belong in the top 10% will not be there for the majority of their lives.

This also applies across generations. Friedman and Laurison showed that although more than half of those in elite occupations had parents who also had elite occupations, many of the children of the professional-managerial class do not end up at the same level or above in the socioeconomic hierarchy.[32] Jessi Streib wrote a fascinating book, *Privilege Lost*, on the downward mobility of the children of the US upper-middle class.[33] Streib explores how values, interests and resources affect the decisions of young people on their transition to adulthood. She shows that many of the paths that granted a relatively comfortable experience to parents – and therefore influenced how their children were raised – cannot currently ensure the same level of economic security.

In addition, there is the internal diversity of high-income earners. The top 10%, by definition, has no upper limit. The poorest 10% has a lower bound of 0 (or negative numbers if one considers debt), while the rest are bound by the distribution itself. Among the top 10% are doctors, barristers, engineers, accountants, head teachers, senior academics and small business owners, but also billionaires. That is why median incomes are a better indication than averages: the latter are too sensitive to outliers. Nicanor Parra, the Chilean 'anti-poet', used to say: 'You eat two pieces of bread. I eat none. Average bread consumption: one per capita.'

Mindful of that phenomenon, we devised what we call the 99/90 ratio: a measure of the distance between the income of the lowest member of the top 10% and the lowest member of the top 1%. We found that, based on the same EU-SILC 2016 figures, that ratio was, for many countries, comparable to the distance between the bottom of the top 10% and the median income earner. In the UK, in terms of gross earnings, while the bottom of the top 10% earns 2.42 times more than the median earner, the bottom of the top 1% earns 2.78 times more than they (the bottom of the top 10%) do. Or, to make the comparison even more extreme, the 1% threshold equals 6.74 times the median income.[34] This does not even consider that within the 1%, inequalities are even sharper and that incomes at the very top are famously tricky to ascertain.

These inequalities, if anything, are getting more pronounced. According to the World Inequality Database,[35] the share of total income taken by the top 10% in the UK has gone from 28.5% in 1980 to 36.1% in 2018, while that of the bottom 50% has dwindled from 22.6% to 20.2%. However, most of the growth in the share of the top 10% has gone to the top 1%, which rose 6.3 points from 6.8% to 13.1%, leaving only 1.3% of the increase in the share of total income to the other 9%. And although one could argue this increase in inequality is irrelevant if the overall size of the economy continues to grow healthily, the truth is that real wages have mostly flatlined since the year 2000 – even without considering the cost of living crisis that is raging as we write. The tide rose, but not all boats were lifted.

One thing that puzzled us was that 12% of those in the top 10% in the UK declare facing difficulties in making ends meet –

and this figure was almost 30% in Ireland, the country with the highest nominal earnings in Europe![36] Surely, what 'making ends meet' means for different groups in the distribution is subjective and varies. For some, spending on private education, for instance, might seem like a bare minimum. However, even if that is the case, this phenomenon means something. We are not asking for commiseration for high-income earners – far from it – but merely saying that if this is the state of affairs, something is amiss.

Unsurprisingly, perhaps, high-income earners are the most likely to have access to a mortgage. However, it is important to point out that for the top half of the 1%, mortgages are for 'the little people' – in other words, they can buy their property without incurring debt. Still, according to EU-SILC data, the proportion of people who own their houses outright is much more representative of the whole distribution than that of those who hold a mortgage: 58% of the top 10% of households have one, while 5% of the bottom 10% do.[37] According to the ONS, the average house price in the UK was £278,000 in March 2022, up £24,000 from the year before, and it was £524,000 in London.[38] With those figures, it is not particularly shocking that mortgages are concentrated at the top of the distribution – a tendency that is only set to grow, considering interest rate hikes and a reduction in the range and generosity of mortgage products after Liz Truss's premiership. Still, considering that mortgages tend to be in the region of four to five times a person's annual salary, it is conceivable that a sole-income earner at the tail end of the 10%, earning roughly £60,000, may struggle to get a foothold on the housing ladder without family help.

Another interesting aspect about the top 10% concerns income from capital. Although we have said that we will focus to a lesser extent on capital, it is important to briefly mention some findings from the TASC report we previously worked on.[39] Based on EU-SILC data, we were able to identify income from wealth (renting, stocks, investments and so on) at the household level and how it has evolved. The poorest eight deciles did capture some of the share of total income from capital in 2008, but much less than the top 10%, let alone the top 1%. By 2016, however, almost all income from capital was captured in the top 20%. This is interesting because, as we are talking about proportions of the total share, the wealthiest deciles may conceivably have retained a similar level of income from capital, at the same time as the wealth from everyone else collapsed. These results chime with the findings of Berman and Milanovic, who argue that those at the very top of the income and wealth distribution are increasingly becoming the same people. They explain: 'In 1985, about 17% of adults in the top decile of capital income earners were also in the top decile of labor-income earners. In 2018 this indicator was about 30%.'[40]

In other words, lower deciles may have had some participation in income from capital in 2008, but this had mostly flatlined by 2016, the year of Brexit. Meanwhile, the participation at the top 10% level has either remained the same or grown – perhaps even without substantive increases, the share would automatically rise given the losses in the lower deciles. The Resolution Foundation also found similar results for the UK.[41] Comparing 2006–08 with 2016–18, they found that the lowest three wealth deciles (which include those with negative wealth: more debt than assets) saw no change, while deciles 4 to 7 saw their wealth decline by almost one percentage point. Only decile number 8 saw no change, while the top two (and especially the first) increased their wealth. Much may have changed in the overall wealth distribution, increasing wealth inequality significantly, and the top decile may not have even noticed.

Where is the top 10% going?

Back in 2018, we found ourselves at the entrance lobby of a large multinational in Canary Wharf, London, for the first interview in this project. William, our interviewee, approached us: middle aged, White, well mannered, wearing a nice suit, handkerchief in his jacket pocket, with earnings that would situate him just into the top 1%.[42] As we were at the beginning of our research into high-income earners, he ticked many of the boxes of what we thought we could expect. We asked him: do you see yourself as privileged? He told us:

> 'I feel fairly middle of the road and average, but objectively I know this is completely untrue. I know I

am at the top of the income percentile, but I also know I'm miles away from the very rich. Everything I earn goes at the end of the month. Whether it is school, holidays, et cetera. I never feel cash-rich.'

The top 10% are, by definition, a privileged group. William knows this at a theoretical level but does not feel particularly wealthy. He is not alone. Inequality expert Danny Dorling showed in his 2014 book *Inequality and the 1%* that those at the bottom of the 1% often declare that they are struggling to keep up with expenses, particularly school fees.[43] There are at least two explanations for this tendency. One is that they are simply out of touch and do not know what struggling or want means. This is certainly a possibility, but we did not want to start on the basis that our interviewees are simply wrong. If nothing else, it is bad form for a social researcher: our respondents have access to a world we do not necessarily know and the whole point of asking them is to try to understand it.

In a fascinating book on the lives of the very wealthy in New York, sociologist Rachel Sherman[44] argued that many among her interviewees were what she called 'upward-oriented', meaning that they thought they were situated somewhere in the middle of the income distribution: first, because most of the people they socialised with had similar or even higher incomes; and second, because there will always be the Bill Gates and Elon Musks of the world, whose fortunes dwarf everyone else's.

Considering this, a more feasible second explanation for William's unease is that those at the cusp of the top 1% have been prospering, but not necessarily so compared with some of their colleagues in Canary Wharf. They are well-paid, high-achieving professionals, often with advanced degrees and with all the respect associated with this. They have been doing well for themselves and, in their view, have done everything right: most of our interviewees (as well as Sherman's) justified their position by saying that they had arrived there through hard work.

However, raising children who have a fair chance of continuing an upward trajectory – and let's remember, their success will to a great extent be measured against how well their parents did – is becoming more expensive. Private schools cost on average over

£13,000 a year, but the type of private school that churns out prime ministers costs close to £50,000. Based on rough estimates, the top 10% have more children than average so their children make up 6% of the 7% who go to private schools; but half the children of the top 10% attend – often quite exclusive – state schools. Roughly one in seven children in private schools comes from the bottom 90%.[45] Despite this, the more the top 10% feel that they absolutely must commit to this expense, the more they will say they struggle to make ends meet. It is ultimately an arms race.

Society tends to view social mobility positively because of its upward direction; but the fear of a downward trajectory is part of the equation too, and throwing money at the problem seems to be the most immediate response to it. These are the concerns likely to be found among those in the top 10%. Those earning, say, £60,000 a year, especially if they are the only earner in their household, though not poor, may not have access to the same quality of housing, private schools (unless they have a very well-paid partner or wealthy relatives), or the same level of savings that would allow them to feel economically secure and competitive against the top 1%. And we have not even mentioned possible unexpected expenses, poor pensions or the impact of economic downturns. Amparo, a small business owner we interviewed in Spain, told us:

> 'I'm not doing badly. I'm happy; I've recovered my old customers who, after the [2007–08 financial] crisis, are finally doing better. It's not as good as it was before [...] but I'm doing fine. But I do worry that if at any given moment I will start doing worse, my children depend on me. I am 52 years old. I know that if I do badly as a businesswoman and I have to close down [my business], I won't be hired by another company.'

Could we really say she is wrong to worry?

In a 2017 Eurofound report, statistician Veli-Matti Törmälehto argues that measures of the well-off should be considered at an absolute rather than relative level.[46] That is, instead of defining who earns well by their position along the spectrum, we should focus on the income itself. In other words, someone right in the top 10% may be close to the top 1% in the graph, but in terms of income and lifestyle, they may be worlds apart. The top 10% of income earners, although doubtlessly privileged in relative terms, may not necessarily be affluent in absolute terms.

Our research confirms that there is much anxiety at the top. High earners, for example, may be so afraid of not being able to afford private school fees that they overwork and go without holidays. This is in the context of private schools offering much less advantage than they did in the past when they guaranteed a university degree, which in turn was a golden ticket. At the same time, student debt is growing; only 10% of UK students can attend university without incurring debt.[47] This level of pressure creates tensions throughout society. If, as these tendencies suggest, economic and social insecurity near the top is not an exaggeration, then we should all worry.

2

On the ubiquity and invisibility
of the upper-middle class

In this chapter, we explore where the top 10% tend to think they sit in the income distribution, why they are often inaccurate in this estimation, and the connection between that inaccuracy and how they understand richness, privilege and worth. We argue that high-income earners could roughly be divided into two groups which, following Thomas Piketty's formulation, we call Brahmins and Merchants. We also claim that high-income earners' lack of knowledge of their own place in society is both cause and consequence of their disconnect from the rest.

We asked interviewees about their views on the rich, on those less well-off than themselves, and where they position themselves along the spectrum. Towards the end of each interview, we also asked each respondent about their income and then showed where it would situate them in the income distribution. We did not reveal that information beforehand because we wanted to avoid framing them as 'high-income earners' from the get-go and because we were curious about how they would react to the information. We simply told them in advance they were 'high-achieving professionals and managers' and that the interview would be about their views on inequality and politics. As we go on to show, they rarely, if ever, recognised themselves as high-income earners, let alone rich.

When speaking of class self-identification, discussing terminology is almost unavoidable. After all, it is through vague yet loaded terms that we tend to position ourselves and others socioeconomically and culturally. In the UK, the term 'upper class' is rarely used in casual conversation, though probably most would agree it's fair to describe the top 10% of income earners as such, socioeconomically speaking. Similarly, the 2013 Great British Class Survey defined 'elite' as the top 6%, and though that label is emotive and politically sensitive, it is also justifiable. Nevertheless, we met many who would qualify for that bracket who railed against elites, the establishment or the rich. Few high-income earners declare themselves to be upper-middle class either, and, if they did, it would seem vaguely like a confession. We also feel uneasy about using 'elite' or 'upper-middle class' to refer to our interviewees; not because these terms wouldn't be defensible, but because they sound like a veiled accusation.

In the UK, the labels 'middle class' and 'working class' are much more common (interestingly, rendering the upper class near-invisible).[1] However, 'middle class' does not completely shake off the negative connotations of upper-middle class. That distinction, instead of being mainly about money, generally refers to cultural signifiers: accent, vocabulary, demeanour, level of education, dress sense, taste and so on. As we mentioned in Chapter 1, according to a 2016 NatCen Social Research survey, 47% of professionals and managers – who, let's remember, account for around 80% of the top 10% – declare themselves to be working class.[2] A corollary of this way of thinking is that someone with many years in education and the 'right' accent but struggling to pay rent can be considered of a higher social class than a well-earning businessman with no degree and a northern accent. Although belonging to the upper-middle class undoubtedly has many advantages, overt bragging rights doesn't seem to be one, especially where meritocratic discourse holds sway. At the same time, declaring yourself to be middle class is seen as a great achievement and declared with pride by many – 'look where I have got to' – but it can also feel like a confession. The lengths that the 2022 Conservative Party leadership election candidates went to, to underplay their advantaged backgrounds, is an example of that.

Pinning any of this down is tricky, even more so following the advent of globalisation and the 'end of history', when many declared class to be 'dead' – society was deemed too complex and fluid for class to retain any explanatory power.[3] As Oly Durose wrote in *Suburban Socialism (or Barbarism)*, social classes have become more complex and internally diverse and 'to leave a polarised class untouched, in the hope that "the middle" disappears, is conceptually dishonest'.[4] However, ambiguously defining the middle class isn't an option for Durose, a left-of-centre campaigner seeking to appeal to the suburbs, because it has significant political consequences. Parties and leaders don't simply 'win over' the middle classes but construct them to pave their way to power. Drawing from his experience campaigning in Brentwood and Ongar – an affluent commuter hub in Essex and a safe Conservative seat since its creation – he describes suburbia as 'a space in which to *construct* a particular notion of the middle class for political gain. More specifically, parties have found suburban success by equating "middle class" identity with individual aspiration.'[5]

All of this means that how class is understood is not a given. It depends on which resources are valued; it is a construction, but one that uses the ideas and materials at hand. Pierre Bourdieu – the French sociologist who, while writing mainly about French society, has been most influential in the UK – provided one of the most popular ways of conceptualising class.[6] He argued that education and cultural signifiers are resources in themselves that, not unlike money, help distinguish those who have them from those who don't. He coined the term 'cultural capital': having the right knowledge, degree, demeanour and references – and even the right sense of humour – to do well in elite spaces. Easy to identify but hard to measure precisely – though proxies do exist (countries visited, framed degrees on walls, having books on your shelves – and making sure they're the right ones) – cultural capital can open or shut doors. For instance, according to Friedman and Laurison, in the context of interview panels for elite employers, cultural capital determines who *fits in*, which candidate is considered *polished*, and therefore who is hired.[7]

Put this way, though money is certainly crucial, it's not the only measure by which class manifests itself. Having spent many years in formal education (and being exposed to the associated behaviours) can be in itself a mark of privilege; it signals both investment by others (be it the state, parents or charities) in that person's education and, at a minimum, increased prospects for future earnings. The British focus on culture and education in matters of class is defensible, but it is disingenuous in that it allows for a certain confusion and partially dissociates class from money, or, at the very least, money in the here and now.

More than one way of being at the 'top'

The partial dissociation of class from money, therefore, allows a distinction between at least two kinds of privilege and, by extension, two kinds of high-income earners who are often lumped together: Piketty's 'ideal types' – Merchants and Brahmins.[8] Merchants derive their status mainly from their income and their position in the market. They are particularly common in the top 1% and among those in direct service to it in industries such as finance, in functions such as accounting and sales, and as landlords, investors or owners of their own businesses. They study for MBA degrees, invest and have a hard-boiled attitude to economic matters. Meanwhile, Brahmins base their status mainly on their employment, which often depends on their possession of cultural capital, meaning particularly high levels of education. They tend to be concentrated in bureaucracies and in the liberal and cultural professions: academics, lawyers, doctors, scientists, civil servants, artists and so on. One way to think about the difference between these groups is to consider who is more likely to be mentioned in casual conversation: Michel Foucault or Warren Buffett. Piketty's assertion is that, over the past decades in the Western world, Merchants have remained the bastion of the right while Brahmins have increasingly turned towards the left, which was not necessarily always the case. In other words, education is increasingly becoming a source of political divisions.

We are aware that these classifications are analytical tools that can be implicitly used by the Brahmin elite – of which we, the writers, are arguably a part (if not by income, by education) – to chastise another elite (the Merchants), and it's therefore important to apply them with a dose of scepticism. A Brahmin could be someone earning an income anywhere between 15% and 2% on the income distribution – at the bottom, it includes bishops on about £50,000 and, at the top, university vice chancellors and high court judges. The categorisation is therefore a coarse overgeneralisation (where would most engineers fit, for example?)

and exceptions abound (despite the stereotype, not all academics are on the left and all bankers on the right). Nevertheless, we find it a useful device with which to look at inequality in British society more closely. And although other variables intervene (age, gender, the urban/rural divide), there is ample evidence that years in education is one of the strongest predictors of liberal or conservative political views, especially in the last few decades.[9] However, we would like to add another dimension to the relationship that Piketty draws between politics and education: the distinction between political matters that are economic or, for lack of a better word, cultural in nature.

In 2012, US political scientist Martin Gilens showed that the top 10% of income earners are more likely than the rest to lean left on issues such as immigration, foreign policy and same-sex marriage.[10] However, that is not the case when it comes to the economy, as they are the most likely income group to oppose tax hikes and expansions of the welfare state. We found the same in our interviews: most people we spoke with were liberal on cultural issues, but a slight majority were against redistributive policies or raising taxes. As Figure 2.1 shows (based on European Social Survey figures), in the UK, the anti-welfare inclination of the top 10% compared with the rest is noticeable, but not static. It was particularly sharp before 2012 but, for whatever reason, it has begun to recede as most of the population has become increasingly supportive of government welfare provision.

Our interviews broadly aligned with what Gilens found. Most respondents were fairly liberal when it came to immigration, for instance, though these results may be subject to social desirability bias, especially considering that one of us is an immigrant. Most, whenever those issues arose, were also quite supportive of initiatives to ameliorate the exclusion of women, minority ethnic groups and LGBTQ+ people. However, there was an important difference between those supportive of more taxation and redistribution and those less so.

If we had to summarise what both Merchants and Brahmins have in common, it is a small 'l' liberal attitude to most issues: everyone is an individual responsible for his or her own actions and, as long as they don't hurt anyone else, they should be let be. The main difference between both views is one of emphasis:

Figure 2.1: Agreement with statement 'Government should reduce differences in income levels' by income decile, UK, 2008–18

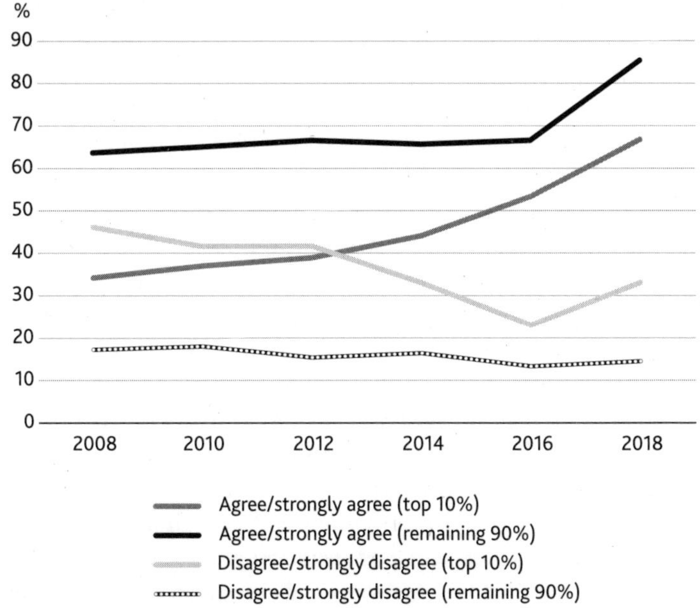
%
90
80
70
60
50
40
30
20
10
0
2008
2010
2012
2014
2016
2018
Agree/strongly agree (top 10%)
Agree/strongly agree (remaining 90%)
Disagree/strongly disagree (top 10%)
Disagree/strongly disagree (remaining 90%)

Source: ESS data, 2010–20

Merchants tend to prioritise the rights of individuals and economic freedom, whatever its results may be, while Brahmins are most concerned about freedom from discrimination and want. That is why both groups, in the main, share an animosity against biases based on gender, race and sexuality, but less so in relation to class.

Crucially, in our interviews, the Merchants were in a slight majority and mainly worked in the corporate and finance sector, while most Brahmins were highly educated professionals, often with postgraduate degrees. Roy, chief financial officer (CFO) of a small firm in the City of London, told us "I don't think much about inequality in the UK, because even the very poor have a bit with welfare. I don't think they are poor enough for me to feel sorry for them." Sean, owner of an HR consultancy, similarly said "If I'm funding people who are sitting at home and don't want to work, then I'm not happy about it. If I'm contributing to people who are below the poverty line, fine. But do I want taxes to go up for higher earners? No. I pay more than enough."

Stephen, a law professor, meanwhile, said that the current level of inequality "is the most obvious source of shame for civilised Western democracy. I find it unacceptable," and Paul, an architect, said, "Thatcher's effect on Britain was to make people insecure and greedy."

Put this way, there is a divide among high-income earners between those who have the view that the state should be small and the market robust and those who see the need for the state to actively shape and support our economies. After all, the discourse on whether the state or the market should prevail structures most political debates in the West and, we would claim, signals the split between the two types of elites who derive their status from their position in either the public or the private sector. Arguably these are the groups the Labour and the Conservative parties traditionally represent: workers and professionals versus owners and bosses, the highly educated versus the wealthy.

However, this view exaggerates the tendency of professionals to prioritise the public sector wholesale. Many Brahmins support a combination of both state and market solutions, especially after the end of the Cold War, as since then statist and pro-union policies have fallen out of fashion. It suffices to recall that top Labour politicians these days are much less likely to come from trade unionist or working-class backgrounds than they were in the past. According to the House of Commons library, in 1975, 98 MPs came from manual labour backgrounds. In 2015, the equivalent figure was 19.[11]

Moreover, even if our own professions were ever to put us in the top 10% and qualify us as Labour-voting Brahmins, we do not want to simply state that Brahmins have it right and Merchants do not. If nothing else, the electoral results and political climate of the last few years should warn us about such an easy conclusion. Here the role of life trajectories is crucial. Sean also told us he had a difficult childhood, growing up in deep poverty and with an alcoholic parent. In his account, he 'pulled himself by the bootstraps' and, understandably, resents the idea that those on a low income are simply victims and cannot do anything about their situation. He thinks everyone can succeed in Britain if they work hard and values what he sees as the market's fairness and appreciation of graft. Gemma, a consultant based in London, similarly, told us about how her 'escape' from Hull allowed her to move upwards. Simon, a manager in a City of London IT firm, said something similar about his experience of living in a housing estate in Sheffield when he was younger.

In her 1992 book, *Money, Morals, and Manners*, sociologist Michèle Lamont argued that in both France and the US at least three forms of justification for the position of elites in society could be identified.[12] She exemplified the *money elite* with the owner of a car-leasing business, a CEO, and a real estate developer; the *manners elite* with an architect, an economist and an academic administrator; and the *morals elite* with a labour arbitrator, the inheritor of a furniture plant and a finance executive for the US Department of Defense. Roughly, Brahmins would be comparable to the manners elite and Merchants to the money elite. The question of who would represent the moral elite (or who could be convinced to join its ranks) is an interesting one, but one corollary of Lamont's argument we would like to explore here is that different forms of elite produce powerful boundaries around themselves.

According to Lamont, each of these elite groups engages in constant 'boundary work': seeking to determine who is in or out based on shared norms over what is valued and what is not. Crucially, the norms these elites use differ in how they justify their own position and disparage others, and these justifications make sense from within each worldview. In such a way, members of the money elite can chastise manners elites for their perceived elitism and pretentiousness, while the manners elites see the former as philistine and short-sighted. In other words, the values espoused by the two elites (graft or sophistication) determine both what they admonish (laziness or bigotry), their cardinal sin (materialism or snobbery) and the accusations they level at each other (hypocrisy or pettiness).

These different forms of high-income earners have effects on how they think others, particularly those richer and poorer than themselves, came to be where they are and by extension where they themselves think they sit. Earlier, we mentioned sociologist Rachel Sherman. In a study of high-earning couples in New York, Sherman wrote that her interviewees could broadly be divided into what she called the 'upward'-

and the 'downward'-oriented rich.[13] The former didn't think they were particularly wealthy, as their point of comparison tended to be people surrounding or immediately above their economic station. Since there will always be those who are stratospherically richer than the rest, the upward-oriented can rest assured they are somewhere in the middle. Sherman interviewed some respondents in their own homes and recounts one such interviewee commenting "everyone's so busy that you don't think about [the underprivileged]" while a member of staff was cleaning in the next room. The downward-oriented, on the other hand, tended to emphasise their own privilege and declare awareness of their luck. In Sherman's study, many of the downward-oriented rich concentrated in high-status professions such as academia and generally had liberal views (in the US sense of the term), while the upward-oriented were much more likely to be found in the upper echelons of the corporate sector and leaned to the right politically.

Put this way, Brahmins would be much more likely than Merchants to be receptive to ideas that highlight their own privilege and urge them to make greater efforts to help those less well-off. However, these days, you do not have to look very hard to find laments about the massive and growing distance between the values, views and life experiences of highly educated professionals and the majority of the population. We all remember Brexit, and we all know a columnist or politician or two who have made a career out of lambasting Brahmins.

In the previous chapter, we cast a light on the sharp sociological differences of high-income earners when compared to the rest of the population, especially in terms of education and occupation – and via those variables, also in terms of their networks and worldview. In other words, much has to happen for a Brahmin to be raised and equipped for the role: investment in their cultural capital, in time not working and in cultivating themselves. This puts Brahmin status out of reach for most people, especially in countries where access to education is increasingly unequal and mediated by debt. David Graeber once wrote that conservative voters in the US 'tend to resent intellectuals more than they resent rich people, because they can imagine a scenario in which they or their children might become rich, but cannot possibly imagine one in which they could ever become a member of the cultural elite'.[14] In that broad sense, both Merchants and Brahmins share (as to an extent, we all do), a certain unawareness of how many people lead very different lives from themselves. To paraphrase Nietzsche, we are furthest away from ourselves.

On (not) knowing where you stand

Interestingly, none of our interviewees considered themselves rich. Neither Merchants nor Brahmins, neither doctors nor City of London professionals, neither the upward- nor the downward-oriented, regardless of where they sat within the top 10%. This was partly because many of them were ignorant of their own position in the income distribution. Indeed, most interviewees were way off the mark: most said they sat around the middle or top 30%, though a few, quite diligently, looked up the data ahead of interviews. But not even they, conscious of where they stood, *felt* rich.

More importantly, however, we would argue that richness is not generally understood in relative terms. If it were, most people in Britain would be considered so. According to the World Bank, in 2018 around half of the world lived on less than USD\$5.50 a day.[15] Richness is, in some sense, absolute. It evokes private jets, gold, power, the fulfilment of every whim and limitless bounty. Few overtly call themselves rich, and those who would sit in a particular cultural space: think of Donald Trump's garish taste in interior design, think of the characters in *Succession*, the famous HBO TV series. These are not the high-income earners we spoke with; not even the most affluent among them could compare. And even if they could, they wouldn't want the label (if nothing else, to avoid producing resentment). In the words of William, the Canary Wharf management consultant who was just in the top 1%, he has a 'sensible' German car and, after school fees and all other monthly expenses, ends up feeling 'cash poor', even though he knows, in the abstract, that he earns well.

However, when we asked interviewees if they felt privileged, most said yes. They were appreciative of the fact they had a well-paying job, a relatively secure economic situation, opportunities to study and develop themselves, and that they lived in an advanced economy with access to healthcare. The only ones who said no were the ones most invested in meritocratic discourse, who told us nothing had been given to them. They were, however, a minority. Most people acknowledge luck as part of their trajectories: having parents who could provide, a mentor, or a 'break' somewhere. A few uneasy sentences often followed that admission. In *Success and Luck*, Robert H. Frank pondered on the role of luck in society and the extent to which the lives of the 'successful' are marred by it.[16] He reflected that our lack of acknowledgement of luck in our own lives is harmful to society and perpetuates dangerous myths about others, but also about the uneasiness that the admission of luck often produces for the lucky.

Whenever that uneasiness appeared, a reference to hard work frequently followed suit. This was particularly the case with Merchants, who often think their position is down to grit and hard work. Their world is a fast-paced one where remaining competitive is key. Hence, their position within it always remains precarious. Roy, the CFO, told us, "I am where I am because I work very hard. I'm not a brilliant person so I have to work hard." This discourse also appeared among Brahmins. Jonathan, a semi-retired barrister, told us "Hard work? Yes, a hell of a lot. I work harder than anyone I know. Historically, eight days a week and 26 hours a day." It appeared especially in reference to a certain ethic of responsibility and professionalism: the satisfaction of a job well done and knowing you have helped others. However, it is difficult to tell whether these appeals to their industriousness were an 'ex-post' rationalisation of privilege. In other words, is privilege the consequence of hard work or is hard work something they do to justify their privilege? While many respondents did acknowledge that there are many in society who work incredibly hard but struggle to make ends meet, the comments of high earners still often seemed a world away from the reality of those who work the hardest in physical labour and have a shorter life expectancy.[17]

The fact they felt privileged but not rich, we believe, speaks to the interesting position they occupy in the income distribution. As the graph is steeper the closer you get to the top, those in a relatively advantageous place may still find themselves quite far from the very wealthiest. This means that there may be many luxuries or privileges that those at the bottom of the top 10% may not even dream of. Nevertheless, they know at least theoretically that they have had important advantages in life, particularly in the educational and professional realms. How to make sense of this? Are they 'posh' for example? What even are the boundaries of the posh?

Another way of understanding this quandary is through what sociology refers to as the primacy of either 'structure' or 'agency' and the concept of the 'sociological imagination'. In a 2017 article, sociologist Daniel Edmiston wrote that the poor have a better 'sociological imagination' than the rich.[18] By that he meant that the poor are much more likely to be able to put their private experiences in a wider context: how constraints and opportunities shape where people end up. The less well-off, in that sense, understand that not everything is down to drive and individual action (agency), but that much is determined by the place from which one begins (structure). By contrast, the rich tend to exaggerate people's capacity to influence their lot in life through their own actions rather than attributing it to 'luck', 'destiny', or wider societal forces.

Edmiston interviewed people in the lowest and the highest income deciles. He presented them with 'scenarios': hypothetical individuals and their economic circumstances to see how his interviewees would interpret their situation and the degree to which they deserved it. In Edmiston's account, 'limited exposure to, and awareness of, financial management in a low-income household appeared to inform the judgments of affluent participants'.[19] High-income participants often blamed the hypothetical people for becoming pregnant, for relying on benefits, for having too many children and for falling into debt. In their estimation, they shouldn't have done any of those things because it is irresponsible to do so without the necessary financial means. Low-income participants were much more sympathetic to the plight of the people described in these scenarios, to a great extent because they could see themselves in the same situation. They had a clearer view of how broader structures can force people, through no fault of their own, in certain directions and towards poverty.

Similarly, a study by sociologist Serge Paugam and others, titled *What the Rich Think of the Poor*, finds that the wealthy in Paris,

Delhi and São Paulo often engage in strategies that are both symbolic and practical to distance themselves from the less well-off in their cities.[20] Crucially, according to the authors, it is not only that the rich are separated from the poor as if by accident, but that this separation is enforced through policy, custom and architecture, and justified through stigmas related to peril and even 'dirtiness'. In other words, it is not only that the rich are ignorant of the plight of those in poverty because they simply do not share the same experiences, but that they often do their utmost not to have anything to do with them.

Put this way, the privilege that most high-income earners admit to does not stop them from judging the life choices of the worse-off. Indeed, this privilege is the sign of their membership to a group that cannot be justified in terms of race, gender, national origin or any other categorical variable, so instead the behaviour of the excluded is pathologised. They are lazy, unintelligent, feckless, lacking in aspiration, and so on. Privilege for high earners is both the result and the cause of their hard work – it is a prerequisite and a consequence: they work hard because they are privileged; if they weren't, they wouldn't. Much like, in Max Weber's famous account of the Protestant work ethic, predestination, far from producing indolence, impels believers to continually demonstrate that they are part of the chosen ones.

To be sure, this logic was much more common among 'upward-oriented' Merchants, but it was not completely absent from the Brahmins. Although they tended to be much more aware of the structural constraints low-income earners face and were much more sympathetic towards their plight, they rarely had contact with those living in very different social circumstances. We asked interviewees whether they tended to engage with people whose socioeconomic background was substantially different from their own. The high-earning and highly educated tend to mostly network with others like them; as their most important networks outside their families are linked to work and education, it is perhaps unsurprising. Most of those who experienced upward mobility answered that they did know people who were significantly less wealthy, often living in the place from which they had 'escaped'. Gemma, for example, a consultant with a top 3% income, who moved from the north of

England to London, says: "You don't know what people earn in London. My closest friends tend to be people I've worked with, that's just how it's turned out, so you're meeting people at around the same economic level. At home, I know what people do and how much they earn."

The more that work and education are valued, the more time we are compelled to spend in them and hence to associate with people of broadly similar social status (especially in increasingly unequal countries). The fewer opportunities we have to meet others of a different social class, the more we depend on simplistic explanations, common tropes and the media, to try and understand them. And the more our own position is based on being able to distinguish ourselves (be it through the accumulation of money or 'cultural capital'), the less incentive there is to meet others who cannot meet our criteria of what is valuable. This also affects Brahmins, who often spend much of their time with other highly educated people (definitely the case in academia and the world of think tanks, in our experience). Interestingly, Adam, 39, who does not have a degree, was one of the few to reflect on people relatively close to him who ended up in a very different place. In the context of thinking of the role of work and luck in people's success, he said:

> 'I think it's not just hard work, I think it's also luck. I could still be working hard on the checkouts in Sainsbury's. My friend has just turned 40 and is doing exactly that. There's an element of luck and being in the right place at the right time.'

The effects of this social distance cannot be exaggerated. It is one thing to be aware in the abstract that others are worse off, to see homeless people in the street on your way to work. It is something else completely for them to be part of your life, with a voice and agency in the world you inhabit.

Income and status are always insecure

Despite their high incomes, our respondents conveyed a surprising degree of insecurity or 'fear of falling'. The majority of those living in London and south-east England, and in the financial and corporate sectors, are upward-oriented. While their employment provides independence and status, their workplaces, for those employed in the private sector, tend to be hugely unequal and hierarchical. Their frame of reference is with those higher up in their sector or the top of the 1%, who seem a world away. Roy, the CFO, commented that: "[h]aving £2 million isn't rich, but maybe £20 million, because people don't need that kind of money". Similarly, William, a management consultant, sees himself in the middle of the income spectrum, despite earning over £170,000 per year, which puts him in the top 1% of income earners. He is aware of this, though: "I know I am in the top 1% but I also know that I am a million miles from the super-rich."

Ben, a young IT consultant, told us he did not consider himself as high earning when approached for this research project. He had "self-selected himself out of the potential pool based on that [...] and it might be worth rewording [the Facebook recruitment post for the research project]". Dan, a head of client services at a marketing agency in his early forties with a top 6% income, thought he was in the 10–15% income bracket. We asked him if he finds his relative income position surprising: "Yes. It hammers home that there are a lot of people who earn a lot less. When you walk into work from Waterloo, I look around and presume everyone earns the same or more. The reality is not the case."

Little contact with those from other socioeconomic groups makes it hard to assess what 'normal' could be like for other people. In addition, the high cost of living, especially in relation to housing, contributes to high earners not feeling especially affluent. All but two respondents own their own homes or have a mortgage, with some having two. Jonathan, a 70-year-old, semi-retired barrister living in London still earns £170,000 but is nevertheless concerned about the possibility of losing his house if a mansion tax is introduced. He is angry to be even included in the 1% income band, which he finds a "nonsense bracket" as there "are very few [in the 1%] saying they're comfortable [...] you're going from £170,000 to £100 million or more [...] a ridiculous bracket [...]; it ignores assets. Plus, there are landowners."

Louise, a 44-year-old sales consultant living in London with a top 1% income, tells us that stamp duty is "too punitive", but that is "probably because I'm living in a very expensive area of the country". We heard from William, who, reflecting on the fact that he never has any cash left by the end of the month even though he is in the top 1%, comments "it must be very hard for vast numbers of people to make ends meet".

Contradictory isolation

High earners, like all human beings, are contradictory. When we asked Louise about inequality, the plight of those in poverty and whether the rich should do more, her answers were broadly the same as we would give: inequality is detrimental to society and not inevitable; those in poverty struggle because of circumstances beyond their control; the rich should make much greater efforts to address inequality. However, when asked which political party she voted for in the last election, she responded: "The Conservatives." The obvious question we should have asked next was 'Why?' but for some reason we simply let the silence linger. Louise's voice cracked slightly. "The tax issue. Protecting high earners," she said.

Like all our interviewees, Louise did not think of herself as rich. She agreed that there should be more redistribution and more help for those worse off in society, but she didn't agree it should come out of her taxes. She is sufficiently informed to know there is a problem that should be addressed and that she is privileged, but that does not necessarily mean she would support action that would directly affect her pay. Once, in describing the book we were writing to a Merchant acquaintance, we mentioned that many found the threshold for the top 10% surprisingly low. The person responded, "Yes! the top 10% doesn't earn that much! They should be taxed much less!"

High-income earners' tendency to speak of the well-off, the elites and the rich in the third person is due partly to a lack of experiential knowledge of the lives of those in other social classes and little incentive to find out. But it's also due to their particular circumstances. Whether justifiable or not, the more you earn the more expenses tend to accumulate. The more onerous it becomes to maintain your position, the less time there is to develop relationships outside your income bracket, networks or status.

This creates a situation whereby those who should feel 'well-off' do not because their frame of reference is those who belong to the same income level or above and because of broader economic pressures, which we explore further in the coming chapters. A certain contradiction (or if we are feeling less charitable, hypocrisy) thus appears, one we all partake in. Most of us may know global warming is an urgent issue, yet we continue to take flights and eat meat. We may believe public education should be strengthened to give everyone a fair shot but, if we can afford it, we send our children to private schools. We may not like rampant consumerism, we may even be against capitalism, yet we still wear trainers made in Bangladesh. Academics may know university rankings are a sham but will still prioritise the Russell Group universities. According to the 2022 World Inequality Report, the top 10% of income earners in the world produce 47.6% of all carbon emissions, even though interest in environmental concerns grows with income and education.[21]

We believe that to understand this duality (*knowing* but not *feeling* their place) and the contradictions that come out of it, we need to start thinking about high earners' isolation from others and how it is due, to a surprising extent, to the role work plays in their self-definition and their lives.

3

'Work is life, that's it'

This chapter looks at how high earners perceive work and shape a worldview in which their jobs and effort are the basis and justification of their status. Unsurprisingly, when they talk about work, they mean employment and are not talking about activities that have to be carried out and on which society depends, whether someone is paid to do them or not, such as cleaning or caring for older people. We have already established that high earners are sociologically distinct from the rest of the population, and implicitly see themselves as such. Work is fundamental to their self-understanding in two ways. First, although as individuals they might be quite different from each other, the high proportion of professionals and managers among them identifies them as a group – discounting a few exceptions in technical jobs such as railway drivers and pilots. Second, hard work loomed large in their accounts. This is crucial, as the fact they consider themselves hard workers is used to justify their position and validate their relatively high salaries. In their view, they neither belong to the idle rich (who do not need to toil) nor those in poverty (whose toil, if it exists, is lower down the rung).

Good jobs and the top 10%

As we were interviewing this group, it became clear just how much moral and social worth high earners gain from paid employment. Work to a great degree defines a person; it is key to how they evaluate themselves and others. As urban sociologist William Whyte wrote back in 1943, 'For a man to think about his job is to see himself as others see him, to remind him of just where he stands in society.'[1] Indeed, many social scientists have argued that a fundamental characteristic of modern societies is the primacy of work over other types of status such as kinship. Even the importance of gender, sexuality, ethnicity and other crucial dimensions of identity are often evaluated to the degree they are constructed as enablers or barriers to 'good' jobs. We are so used to this that we hardly notice. When adults meet for the first time, one of the first questions they ask is 'What do you do?', and the answer is rarely concerned with anything other than employment. This is also why the phenomenon of unemployment (and its associated stigma) only makes sense in modern capitalist societies.

Work, thus understood, generally means formal and paid employment or self-employment. This kind of work has a status that other forms do not, the recognition of being engaged in something 'worthwhile'.[2] Self-respect is thus felt through fulfilling the social norm of engaging in a paid job but not through, for example, unpaid care, which is often associated with women. Besides prestige and material rewards, formal employment also offers high-income earners benefits such as private medical insurance, life insurance, pensions and stock options. This drives their interests even further away from universal public services, which they believe they rely on to a much lesser extent than those who earn less.

Such formal work grants our respondents not only status but also 'independence' and autonomy. Meanwhile, informal work is frequently conceptualised as being 'dependent', in the traditional gendered model of the male provider and the female homemaker. Feminists have long argued that viewing formal employment as guaranteeing self-reliance while informal or unpaid work is secondary is a misleading model of human behaviour and damaging to policy decisions. In fact, the economy is predicated on unpaid labour, which has its fingerprints all over paid work.[3] In 2020, the International Labour Organization valued this unremunerated work at 13% of global gross domestic product (GDP), 75% of which is estimated to be carried out by women.[4]

Regardless, considering how the economy is organised, informal work cannot at present provide the economic security that formal employment does. The status the latter also carries is often crucial for our self-definition and determines not only material returns but the esteem by which each of us is rewarded. It is perhaps unsurprising, then, that talk of social mobility immediately means talking about the jobs that a person has had over their lifetime and those of their parents: ideally, always better paid, onwards and upwards. This is also why many of our interviewees emphasise their support for equality of opportunity over equality of outcome, which generally means equal access to educational and training opportunities so people from all backgrounds can compete for the best jobs. In this view, worth and deservingness are always implicitly connected to these jobs, and they are valuable because it takes effort to get them and not everyone does.

Even so, social mobility does not occur in a vacuum. Sociologist Lauren Rivera has shown that, at every step of the hiring process, elite employers in the US favour the upper classes: they tend to recruit most strongly from Ivy League universities where the children of high earners are disproportionately represented. CVs are screened according to the prestige of the institutions candidates attended, while the interview process itself is biased towards applicants from the same social strata as the recruiters.[5] Earlier we showed how Friedman and Laurison found similar patterns in the UK.[6]

Despite new diversity and inclusion targets encouraging companies to recruit employees from working-class backgrounds and the increasing number of larger employers that have stopped demanding applicants with Russell Group degrees, analysis of ONS data shows that those from better-off backgrounds are 80% more likely to land a top job than their working-class peers.[7] Of those from working-class backgrounds who do become professionals, 17% earn less than colleagues whose parents had professional jobs. Working-class women in professional jobs earn 36% less than men from a professional background in similar posts, compared to a 17% gap between men and women who are both from professional backgrounds. Polling finds that British workers from ABC1 occupations are more likely than those working C2DE jobs to have asked and been successful in asking for a pay rise.[8] Women from working-class occupations (69%) are considerably more likely than women from middle-class occupations (55%) to have never asked for a pay rise.[9] For the first time, in 2018–19, the Social Mobility Commission began to look at the interaction between class, gender, ethnicity and disability, finding that women, people with disabilities and minority ethnic groups from working-class backgrounds generally experience multiple disadvantages in occupational outcomes.[10]

There are also substantial differences at a local level. Where you grow up makes a difference in how much your family background affects your life chances.[11] People from privileged backgrounds and who have university degrees are much more likely to move. Those who do move do far better financially than those who remain. They earn 33% more and are more likely to end up in professional jobs.[12] Moving out is often necessary to move up.

Regardless of those systemic-level differences, education and effort continue to play an important part in respondents' narratives about how they attained their position. The people we spoke with, especially those who had been the most socially mobile, were keen to give a meritocratic description of how far they had travelled socioeconomically. Tony was one of them. A senior manager with a top 1% income in his fifties, he came from a working-class background. Thanking his stable and supportive parents for his success, he also spoke of following his father's example – joining the army at 17 and rising to the rank of captain, which was "quite an achievement from his [father's] humble stock". Tony reflects: "If my mum and dad were alive, I'd say they'd be proud of where I ultimately ended up."

Christopher, one of only two respondents under 35 already in the top 3%, worked for a global IT service and consulting company. He knew he was "massively privileged" to have been able to study and questioned the degree of equality of opportunity in the UK: "I don't believe in meritocracy. If you work hard, you can improve your baseline. There are two classes in Britain: those born in opportunity and those born in disadvantage, who would need to work incredibly hard."

Like Tony, Christopher also thanks his upbringing for his upward trajectory, in his case one that was "middle class [and] valued education". Louise, a 44-year-old sales consultant living in London with a top 1% income, does too: "It's […] having a system around you, including your parents, that are going to help you identify opportunities and nurture you. The problem is if the parents haven't had those opportunities, then it's hard for them to give them to their children. It's a vicious cycle."

Interestingly, however, as these accounts imply, education means not only having access to institutions that can provide it to a reasonable standard, but also coming from a home life where education itself is valued and there is an understanding of the type of education that could help someone succeed. This suggests that some of our respondents believed poverty could be explained by 'low expectations'.[13] In other words, the onus is put on the underprivileged for undervaluing education. It's not that opportunities don't exist, but that some people cannot identify them.

Education, in these accounts, operates at the meeting point between individual and structural explanations for poverty but doesn't solve them. The less well-off may – or may not – be to blame for not getting a good (generally meaning middle-class) job and moving upwards, because poverty understood in this way is ultimately due to ignorance. While such views came across as patronising, they were also ambiguous about where they lay blame. Was the misfortune of not earning enough the fault of an individual's characteristics or was it down to being brought up in the wrong family and failing to escape from it?

Explanations emphasising an individual's role in their social mobility soon tend to return. Upbringing is not everything, and talent and graft in adult life play a key part. Educational ability is often cited as a key factor in social mobility because it is an acceptable, undebatable attribute that reinforces the belief that social mobility is deserved. Many respondents mentioned their intelligence, degrees and good grades, especially the Brahmins. Few acknowledge their luck in not having had any significant structural barriers impeding their social mobility, such as health emergencies, caring responsibilities or having to work to put food on the table. Gemma, a management consultant in her late thirties in the top 3%, does, however. She mentions that although gaining a place at university did kick-start her successful career, her "very supportive family" helped with rent during a degree internship in London. This opportunity allowed her to pursue a structured career in a large corporate firm, providing the stability she did not experience growing up.

There is also little distinction between educational qualifications and the networks and social capital (private) education can provide. Twenty-three of our 29 UK respondents were state educated. This might be as you would expect if you considered that well over nine out of ten children attend state schools in Britain, but more than you would expect if you took into account the overrepresentation of the privately schooled in highly paid jobs.[14] As the Social Mobility Commissions have concluded, the small elite who rise to the top in the UK today looks remarkably similar to those in the same position half a century ago. As former Conservative prime minister Sir John Major put it, 'in every single sphere of British influence the upper echelons of power are held overwhelmingly by the privately educated or the affluent middle class'.[15] This is seen, for example, in the monopolising of senior roles in law, the armed forces and the civil service by those who attended private schools.[16] As the commission pointed out:

> Of course, the best people need to be in the top jobs – and there are many good people who come from private schools and who go to top universities. But there can be few people who believe that the sum total of talent resides in just 7 per cent of pupils in the country's schools.[17]

However, despite this overwhelmingly obvious dynamic of working life in the UK, only one high earner we spoke with, a state school headteacher, suggested that bringing education under the state sector was the key to properly addressing inequality.

Few interviewees mentioned labour market inequalities either. Whether due to a skills gap, a rapid expansion of graduate labour (and the associated credential inflation), decreased union membership or the increased participation of women, the UK's occupational structure has changed dramatically in the last decades. Today, the British labour market has an hourglass shape, polarising at the top and bottom ends in terms of occupation and earnings, with few jobs in the middle.[18] This amounts to a two-tier system where employment growth is concentrated on high-earning workers pursuing seamless career progression at the top while others are stuck in dead-end, insecure jobs at the bottom.

Some careers that in the past guaranteed secure, white-collar employment, are increasingly precarious at the entry level – and many people are kept there or forced to jump ship. Increasing precarisation of jobs and the over-reliance on insecure part-time employment seems to be expanding in many walks of life, as illustrated by striking criminal barristers, a profession traditionally considered to be elite.[19]

Many respondents were aware of these trends. Some acknowledged that young people today do not enjoy the same opportunities they had growing up (all but one had been to university or a polytechnic). When we asked them what role luck had played in their life situation, they acknowledged that having had the means and opportunity to attend university without facing crippling debt or having to compete in a labour market experiencing credential inflation was crucial. However, the acknowledgement of that luck is qualified; some pointed out that a person still has to apply themselves and make good decisions to make the most of it. Hard work is indispensable.

Work is hard

Hard work is a consistent trope, particularly for Merchants working in the private sector or who started their own businesses. They often tended to emphasise the need to remain competitive in the market, and that the market itself is the best arbiter for societal outcomes. Nevertheless, Brahmins put great importance on hard work too, if sometimes with a different emphasis. This was manifested in their endorsement of providing good-quality service (for instance to students or patients) and of the effort needed to attain a certain level of expertise and credentials in their line of work. Education, understood this way, is a trial by fire that validates those who went through it (though the commodification and expansion of higher education can undermine this narrative). Even so, high earners are increasingly acknowledging that hard work does not always guarantee success and that some must work much harder than others for similar rewards. Hard work, after all, is not valued solely by high-income earners. Louise, a sales consultant, tells us: "I'm sure there are a lot of people who are hard-working who are just in low-paid jobs."

It tends to be those who work outside the corporate structure, with experience in or with the public sector and working with colleagues and clients from different income groups who discuss in detail the structural barriers preventing social mobility. They not only refer to the realities of low-wage work but also may compare their salaries to those of workers fulfilling essential roles for little remuneration. Sociologist Katharina Hecht describes such respondents as 'critical evaluators' who 'question evaluative practices based on money as a metric of worth, do not view market outcomes as necessarily fair and are concerned about top incomes and wealth shares'.[20] In our study, they tend to be at the lower end of the top 10% income band.

When we asked our respondents the question 'Do you think that, broadly speaking, if you work hard you will succeed [in the UK]?' they expressed strong feelings about inequality and referred to the realities of low-wage work. Duncan, in his late fifties, a director of a non-departmental public body, living in Scotland, right at the margin of a top 10% income, comments:

> 'I struggle with the idea that if you work hard, money will come to you. If you're on a minimum wage in this country, working 16 hours a day, you'll only get a certain amount of income. Irrespective of what you do with it, that's all you'll get. In theory, being in work means you can build networks and relationships and move on and earn more. But frankly, if you're working for minimum wage in McDonald's, you're not meeting many people.'

Stephen, a professor living in Manchester with a top 6% income, spoke of people who have to take two jobs to make ends meet, who are "working hard, but not exactly flourishing". When asked whether he thought hard work had a role in determining his current status, Paul, an architect working with the public sector, just in the top 10% income band, who splits his week between London and Liverpool, felt strongly that it was not: "People who clean hospitals – they work hard. No, that is a terrible suggestion to make. People who think they work hard because they earn hundreds of thousands of pounds are not working as hard as they believe."

Hannah, a 44-year-old occupational health consultant, earning just above the 10% threshold, tells us in relation to the statement 'The richer the rich, the more all of society benefits': "No! I don't agree, because I think the rich getting richer benefits themselves and I'm not sure how much of that is passed down because I think some people get rich at other people's expense."

Such respondents also confirm the importance of networking for social mobility. Claire, a teacher, living in Manchester, with an income just above the 10% threshold, speaks of the 'old-boy network': "Opportunity comes from having money, contacts, knowing people in places, work experience and connections." Wang, an under-35-year-old former doctor who now runs his own start-up, observes that he gets to meet many wealthy entrepreneurs who mostly come from wealthy backgrounds. This, in part, he thinks is what made them successful, as they were able to take risks without having to worry about their financial security.

Several respondents comment that while hard work may have been the route to upward mobility in the past, this was no longer true. They felt it had the potential to contribute to economic security, but would certainly not guarantee it. Maria, a marketing director in her forties with a top 3% income, comments:

> 'This was true 50 years ago [...] even if you were working class, if you worked hard you could earn enough to get your kids through school and then to university, and then they could potentially break out of the working class and make the middle class. It's only just starting to hit the middle class that it doesn't matter how hard you work, you may not earn enough money to break even, let alone make it out of your social class. And that is key – that change.'

Peter, a young IT consultant with a top 1% income, tells us: "I disagree with the idea that if you work hard, you'll do well. It used to be the case. But that plays back to when career paths were designed and the way to progress was to show that you worked harder than anyone else."

Presenteeism was another feature in discussions about work. The UK labour market is characterised by increasing work intensity with the second-highest average weekly working hours in Europe, only after Greece. Still, we have the second-lowest GDP per hour worked in the G7. Evidence suggests that there seems to be no direct link between hours worked and the strength of the economy. The opposite seems to be true: higher productivity is associated with fewer hours per year spent at work.[21] The pandemic exacerbated this trend. Some of our respondents described the transition to working remotely as characterised by an 'always on' culture and an extended working day, to an even greater degree than used to be the case. Women who had been working and carrying out childcare at home were more likely to report increased psychological distress during the pandemic.[22]

Perhaps aware of these developments, some also raised the need to work 'smart'. The emphasis on individuals' responsibility to ensure their employability is also seen in how respondents – particularly those working in the corporate sector – talk about the importance of embracing risk in an uncertain global marketplace. This implies the belief that upward mobility is possible solely through the cultivation of human potential, as sociologists of late modernity such as Beck and Giddens argued.[23] Peter, one of the youngest respondents – the head of his own IT consultancy and with a top 1% income – provides an example of an over-individualised sense of his trajectory. He believes that good decision making has led to his current position, knowing "[w]hen to pursue opportunity, to balance risk with reward." He reflects that "this might be related to upbringing and being encouraged to pursue risk". This includes a willingness to be flexible. It is closely associated with making good decisions and leveraging the skills that you have: "These days it's about working smarter. We have to see what technology is doing. Why work hard as a taxi driver if you might be replaced by a self-driving car?"

Later in the interview, we asked Peter if he thought there should be a space for people who are not necessarily good decision makers, such as the taxi drivers he spoke about. He responded:

'If someone cannot recognise [...] the demise of an industry, then that's a problem that needs to be addressed, maybe through re-education and empowerment. But it's ultimately their choice whether they do something about it or not. However, I believe there should be a general understanding of future-proofing jobs. [...] Reskilling and retraining are important, but there needs to be self-motivation and self-drive there. The government shouldn't do everything.'

This commitment to flexibility implies remaining competitive against a global workforce, being prepared to move from job to job and relocating if necessary. In these meritocratic accounts, the right attitude and self-motivation are crucial, and in turn, affect opinions about inequality and local communities. For Peter, the taxi drivers threatened by automation are at least partly responsible for their economic misfortune; they need to have self-motivation and initiative. Sean – a 40-year-old with a top 1% income who did not have much parental support growing up and was one of the staunchest Merchants in our sample – tells us his own motivation and hard work are the reasons for his success: "Nobody coached me to go to university or to do well for myself."

Though hard work was key, the end of that work seemed to be less important. The high earners we spoke with rarely thought about the role of their jobs beyond the workplace. We asked them about their career progression, where they've been the happiest and the most discontented work-wise, and what they thought the effect of their work was on society, if any. A few times the question was interpreted as an accusation (particularly by those working in the City). Peter, from the previous example, left the corporate world and now works for himself, employing five people. He says of the move: "I've been the happiest now because everything is under my control. I have full autonomy over the decisions that I make; I can change the work–life balance."

Respondents who have been working for corporations for a long time, even those like Peter who have moved on to set up their own companies, are not used to even being asked what wider role their work or organisation plays in the economy or society. His response was typical: "I don't think my current job has a huge effect on larger society." Susannah's answer in particular astonished us. In a very senior position at a major international bank, she seemed surprised even to be asked the question:

> '[laughs] Not much really. Society at large […]. Well I suppose you could say that I'm helping to make sure [the bank] are efficiently spending […]. They've got a huge customer base globally […] so we're helping deliver them products at a more affordable price and the customer service they get around that is better. So I suppose you could say that, but/if I compare that to my husband's contribution as a police officer, his is way more.'

This is worth underlining. Susannah is a highly educated, high-achieving woman at the top of her career working in a senior position in banking in one of the financial centres of the world. And yet she doesn't think her work makes a massive difference to the lives of others. Would we be right to disagree, considering she is the one actually doing the job? Anthropologist David Graeber famously argued in his 2018 book *Bullshit Jobs* that an increasing number of employees do not believe society would be worse off if their jobs did not exist. This applied even to the private sector (35% of its employees in the surveys he cites), which is supposed to be driven by efficiency and where useless jobs would supposedly be driven out by the bottom line.[24]

Only a few respondents in the private sector conveyed a sense of purpose in or motivation for their work beyond material gain and the narrow, direct satisfaction of the needs of their clients. These tended to focus on acquiring knowledge, being part of a good team, and producing something technically sophisticated that does its job well. Ben, an IT consultant earning just over £100,000, told us:

> 'I am happiest when I'm learning new things. So, in the nineties at the software company that was being acquired, I suddenly had a bigger responsibility and it

was an opportunity to learn and get involved. That was a nice place to work. But, after a while, when they got rid of everyone, it felt a bit empty. Before that, it was a great bunch of people and I enjoyed working there.'

He described his motivation as:

'To keep doing the best you can and it's the way forwards and upwards. You may not like what you have to do, but by doing it you can move on to bigger and better things. The other half of it is that you have a mortgage and bills to pay.'

And he had pride in his role of making something: "I think the product we're selling and implementing is helping defend people against hackers and other cyber security attacks. It does it very well."

Ben, and a few others, were the exception to the rule. Their main motivation was learning, improving and delivering, and they were proud of their accomplishments. This is an enviable and commendable position, to be sure. However, we would argue their situation was predicated on possessing specialised expertise in areas that haven't yet suffered a dramatic loss of status (IT, for instance), and on remaining at a certain distance from the very top of management. They tended to concentrate on technical occupations and were not necessarily at the top of the hierarchy. Michael, a 49-year-old engineer, told us he is the happiest he's ever been at his job at the minute. He's "near the top of the tree. Above me, it gets political."

Other respondents working in the corporate sector who had views about its broader societal effects tended to have experience outside it. Luke is one example. A 27-year-old strategy consultant with a top 8% income who attended private school and Oxbridge, enrolled on the Teach First programme before joining one of the 'Big Four' accounting firms.[25] When asked what effect his work had on society he replies "currently very little [...] and if it does it's probably negative". Asked to elaborate on what that role is, he replies: "Essentially to help big companies and make rich people richer."

Some, such as Maria (whom we introduced earlier), had left the corporate world for more socially minded positions. When we first interviewed her, she was working for another Big Four firm, but in the follow-up interview she had joined an organisation focusing on the underrepresentation of women in boardrooms. When asked what she thought the effect of her work is on society at large, she replied: "For once I'm doing something that does make a difference. [laugh] But that […] hasn't really been the case in my previous jobs. My previous jobs have been about me making money."

Meanwhile, those in the public sector, much like their counterparts in the technical occupations described earlier, tended to say that they were satisfied with their jobs and were clearer about their benefits to society. This was particularly the case for those in healthcare and education. Douglas, who had a lifetime's career in the public sector and social enterprise told us that in his view people working for large organisations do not feel that empowered in them and allude to their unattainable echelons. He very much preferred the current organisation where he works, as he is working with "a good bunch of people" and is able to "run your own show".

Nevertheless, many in the public sector also had apprehensions about the pressures they were under and conflicting views on their management. Jonathan, for example, a semi-retired barrister, but still in the top 1% income bracket, looked back at an extensive career, originally built on legal aid, but local authorities "bled out" with consequences for his practice.

What both Brahmins and Merchants had in common was that being busy tacitly provided status. Lack of time was cited as a key barrier to not doing more outside work. Stephen, a law professor, pithily told us: "Work is life, that's it." Meritocracy, corporate culture and organisational hierarchy loom large. All of these reward (or seem to reward) keeping apace in a competitive and fast-moving world, in which everyone knows they can be replaced by younger, more technically skilled candidates (or even software) at short notice. That means more and more time invested in work, staying afloat and honing new and old skills. This confirms previous research that speaks of pervasive uncertainty and chronic insecurity about the future of jobs, housing and relationships, which is present even in the top decile.[26]

One consequence of this sense of anxiety is overwork. Maria, when asked whether she would say she is generally happy with her career progression, said:

> 'Yeah, very happy. In some ways, I would have liked to be more senior at [company] but I was put off by the people above me because they weren't great role models and they were quite stressed. I worked very long hours [...] and I thought if I got more senior it would be even worse.'

Maria seems to reflect on the fact that many companies reward talent that 'goes above and beyond' and delivers value (through achieving projects, securing clients or managing people) in addition to their prescribed job. Just fulfilling your job description is not necessarily seen as enough to get promoted or obtain a good, in-line-with-inflation pay rise. These practices reinforce the perception that getting to the top echelons of the company would require too much effort and negatively shift the work–life balance.

Furthermore, the pressure to keep moving up in a career often involves being mobile, which meant most of our respondents didn't volunteer outside work. Christopher, an IT consultant with a top 3% income, when asked about his social/civic behaviour, replies: "As soon as we settle down – we're quite nomadic at the moment – I would like to do something hands-on, something that makes a large societal shift and helps lots of people." Others spoke of a working culture, particularly in large private corporations, that made it more difficult to develop connections with their community as less value was placed on activities such as volunteering.

We also asked our respondents whether they thought the private sector had any responsibility for reducing inequality. Most Merchants were surprised by the question and most emphasised creating jobs, paying tax and earning profits, not much more. Gemma, a consultant in her late thirties, was one of a few who spoke directly to this, precisely because her job was to help drive organisational change: "Get businesses to do things better – impact on society, their culture, reputational risk, making institutions more stable. Treating customers more fairly. Not messing up the economy. Keeping an eye on big business. [Businesses] would do whatever they like if there was no structure in place."

Louise, whom we introduced earlier, works for a global tech company with a household name. She acknowledged that societal benefit was not a priority: "So, you do see private companies do things like apprenticeships. But I can't think of any private companies that are really investing in society. You do have corporate responsibility programmes, but they are not top of the agenda."

While the women, especially those with young children, tended to feel that they ought to do more in their local community, the men we spoke with rarely questioned their level of interaction in the same way. It was considered something their wives did or that they could do when they were older. They rarely volunteered and left school commitments mostly to their partners. William, a management consultant in the top 1%, tells us:

> 'My wife has chosen to work in the charitable sector […] a residential school, to look after children. She could be doing something that pays more but is very important in our local community, it's one of the largest employers there. What I do here [at work], enables my wife to do something there, as a partnership.'

The exception to this tendency was when volunteering or donating was sanctioned by their employer. Respondents were more comfortable talking about corporate responsibility. Luke, the 27-year-old consultant we introduced earlier, thought that while there was more appetite for corporate responsibility, there was very little action. One example he cited was Barclay's scheme to train customers in financial management skills.

Maria thought similarly: "there's got to be something around a more sustainable outlook [as] people are interested in giving something back". In her follow-up interview, she repeated that companies have "got to give a reason for them to go back" and that they "now have to have 'purpose' – this is the new buzzword!" Worrying that we might be returning to Victorian times, she also commented that "The private sector would have to plug that gap, particularly in healthcare [...] If employers don't have healthy employees and [...] we have another pandemic [...] well."

Even those who were relatively senior in the corporate sector made similar comments. William, in the top 1%, told us that charitable giving is encouraged in the Canary Wharf firm where he works: "Trustees, boards of governors, contribute [...] being a citizen has become more prominent. The business is much more aware of how it's perceived." Peter, a young IT consultant with a top 1% income, also told us:

> 'We are looking at how to give back. We do open source [coding]. Also, the consultancy wants to contribute to marine aspects, such as beach clear-ups. [...] I like to do this and it resonates with me, but also a lot of aspects are due to PR [public relations] / marketing of the consultancy. I also like that I have the flexibility to do this via the consultancy.'

However, as the last example implies, volunteering organised by corporate responsibility is quite different from contributing on an individual basis to your community outside the remit of paid work. This is because corporate objectives include the status of being busy and helping the organisation position itself. Many large established companies allow employees a number of hours per year to dedicate to volunteering. These hours go largely unclaimed because most employees would rather spend additional time on activities that further their careers within the company. As long as volunteering does not further one's connections and interests, it is not an interesting enough proposition. In the best-case scenario, such initiatives could be compared with the extracurriculars carried out by the young of the top 10% in the hope of improving their chances of gaining a university place or their first job.

Perhaps unsurprisingly, few of those we spoke with contemplated any reform to their workplaces. Their perspectives were mainly individualised, focused on their sense of control, and started from the position of the job they do. Their workplaces were also mostly hierarchical, and workplace democracy was rarely mentioned. This, we believe, is at least partly because of the long-term decline in union membership and the individualisation of the sense of worth in the workplace. Many of the individuals we spoke with worked for organisations where appraisals and performance reviews were regularly conducted, where their work was increasingly monitored and where perceptions of how hard they worked had a direct effect on their status, economic situation and career progression.

Nevertheless, research shows that employees often dislike how they are ranked and scored. According to a survey of Fortune 1,000 companies, 66% of employees were strongly dissatisfied with their performance evaluations.[27] A later study showed HR executives were equally disparaging of performance management programmes; 70% believed such reviews did not accurately reflect employee contributions. Two thirds said performance management practices were easily distorted and misidentified who were the high-performers.[28] Performance management has also been identified as a potential source of employee anxiety.[29] Far from being a catalyst for improvement, such reviews are often met defensively, resulting in an atmosphere of competition that stifles innovation, transparency and collaboration.[30]

Despite these obstacles, the current crises are bringing the contradictions of the working world to a head and won't be solvable by past strategies. As of 2016, only 16% of the UK's private sector workers were covered by collective bargaining agreements. While the UK's overall trade union density is considerably lower than many European countries, there have been green shoots in the movement recently with high-profile cases of employment rights not being protected, such as the fire and rehire policies of P&O Ferries.[31] As the cost of living crisis unfolds, trade unions have seen a recent rise in membership, among women in particular.[32]

Even Sean, one of the most solid Merchants in our sample, said in his follow-up interview that the pandemic had "made me reflect on what's important in life. So, I'm no longer running my own company and don't have to work all the time." Michael, a 49-year-old engineer just in the top 10% and living in the south-west felt that people's attitudes as a whole had changed during the pandemic:

> 'You can't eat money. When you can't get food or fuel or whatever you need to live. A lot of people are less money-centric, more lifestyle focused. Difficult to measure. A lot of people have started saying "What's the least amount of money I need to live contentedly?" Not many people were asking that [before].'

Taking a breather

When we were thinking about potential titles for this book, we considered 'never good enough'. However, it had already been taken by a few other publications. Among those, we found an evocative ethnography by Laura Alamillo-Martinez, which explored feelings of anxiety among students and parents in a Spanish upper-middle-class secondary school.[33] She describes how children who, in many respects are privileged, seem to have a fairly precarious view of their future security, one that depends on their performance. If they do not measure up, they have no one but themselves to blame. Though certainly, the road from good school grades to a high-paying job is long, winding and marred by uncontrollable factors, this does not detract from the seemingly ever-present dread, stress and anxiety these students have when thinking of their future. Reports on the high rates of mental health issues among elite university students – even before the pandemic – suggest this is a widely underreported phenomenon.[34]

Reading about such issues made us reflect on our own upbringing and on the hard-working ethos both Brahmins and Merchants share. Both of us were brought up in families where grades were overvalued. For Marcos, it has to do with his family history. His paternal grandfather lost his job as a journalist after Pinochet's 1973 *coup d'état* and could never work again. This experience of sharp downward social mobility made his father concentrate all his energies on attaining a well-earning professional job, in which he succeeded. But it also meant that Marcos was raised to believe having perfect grades is the only guarantee for a good life and that, even then, history may happen, so to speak. Gerry was raised the same way. Her mum had been left without financial support at a young age when her parents divorced acrimoniously while she was taking her A-levels. Not having been able to attend university herself, she had ambitions for her daughter to be the first person to do so on her side of the family. There was a lot of pressure to aim high.

Similarly, our respondents define themselves largely through hard, smart work, through their competitiveness, flexibility and their achievements. An underlying meritocratic 'common sense' justifies their own position and their aspiration to move up the ladder. This 'common sense' is also the rationale for legitimising inequality, a cultural logic based on deserving a lot in life as the reward for effort and talent. From this worldview, moral and social worth is derived from paid employment and measured by income, educational attainment and professional status (which are also, interestingly enough, the variables that distinguish this group sociologically). Such pressures may also explain, for example, the 2019 US college admissions scandal, where wealthy parents had been colluding to guarantee access to elite universities for their children.[35]

Nevertheless, and seemingly independently of the importance of hard work, most people we spoke with only rarely thought more broadly about the place of their companies or the effects of their work in society. They reflected Kate Soper's view that the more caught up you are in work, the less time you have to imagine, let alone believe, that alternative ways of living are possible or to look into how the existing system might be improved because: "Through its theft of time and energy, the work and spend culture deters development of thinking and critical opposition [...] those suffering most from time scarcity are unlikely to be spearheading the revolution against the work practices that create it".[36]

This logic of over-emphasising work as 'position' and 'graft' also affects Brahmins. Despite their left-of-centre views, high-income earners who hold their position based on claims of expertise and educational credentials can come across as hierarchical rather than egalitarian. They implicitly accept an unspoken meritocratic truism that the public conversation and decisions over the public purse should be made by those with the most career achievements and educational credentials.

What is needed, we argue, is greater emphasis on a third, often neglected dimension of work: the result of an action which changes the world in some way. David Graeber said that today's world seems to be ruled by "the general principle that the more one's work benefits others, the less one tends to be paid for it".[37] In other words, he argues, many believe a job that is purposeful and beneficial to society should be its own reward, while work that nobody would do unless they were getting paid for it should be better remunerated. This, from Graeber's viewpoint, explains the difference in earnings between nurses and corporate lawyers.

Still, losing sight of that ultimate purpose risks turning work into a perennial chase for status that has few, if any, effects beyond giving workers a respectable 'job' and granting the status that comes with being perceived to 'work hard'. Neglecting the end results of our work risks fostering both overwork – and the neurotic need to be always on call and always at your best – and apathy towards its effects on the world, which often are limited to making those who are already wealthy wealthier. To tackle that dimension of our working lives, politics is unavoidable.

4

Don't rock the boat:
politics and the well-off

High earners have political clout. That is one of the main reasons we wrote this book. Compared with other income groups, they are more likely to feel more engaged in politics, to believe they have a say, to vote and to have higher levels of trust in government.[1] Because of those reasons, they are arguably among the demographic groups that are most courted by political parties.[2] They are also overrepresented in elite positions of authority including the 'Westminster bubble'. Every MP qualifies, as well as many of the most influential civil servants, journalists, lobbyists and policy experts. This also applies in Brussels, Washington and most centres of political power.

Still, our respondents frequently showed unease with politics and misgivings towards much of the electorate. During our first round of interviews, following austerity and the Brexit referendum but before the 2019 general election, they expressed fears about political instability, populism and the erosion of democratic norms. Most were cynical about the current state of politics and political parties. And it was clear to see how that cynicism expressed itself in the 2019 elections. Of the 20% least deprived constituencies in England, 1 elected the Labour Party, 7 elected the Liberal Democrats and 98 were won by the Conservatives.[3] During our second round of interviews in early 2022, they were mainly apathetic and pessimistic. In the aftermath of Boris Johnson's 'partygate' scandal (where he was shown to be in flagrant violation of his own COVID-19 rules), the opening salvos of the Ukraine–Russia war, and a looming cost of living crisis, even the most Conservative among them had few reasons to be cheerful about the state of British politics.

Our interviews confirm that many people do not have well-worked-out political ideologies, and their values have a stronger influence than any identification with political parties. These guide their choices across public and private spheres and 'have come to play an increasing role in [their] political choices [...] as older group-based loyalties have lost their power and structural roots'.[4] The majority of high earners we spoke with were conservative on matters related to social security, income redistribution and taxation. Though they were in principle supportive of public services such as the NHS, quite a few were concerned with how they were run, referring to 'mismanagement' and 'inefficiency'. Many were quite supportive of means testing rather than the universal provision of public services, even if the latter would allow them to tap into services currently unavailable to them, such as care for older people, healthcare provision and higher education.

These views have been under strain. The populist waves of the 2010s, from both the left and the right, came to challenge the centrist, liberal consensus that has held sway at least since 1990. 'Billionaires', 'the rich' and 'metropolitan elites' were decried more frequently, and what high-income earners often saw as 'common-sense' politics became increasingly unpopular with large parts of the electorate. With this context in mind, this chapter explores what we know about our respondents' politics, their degree of political participation and the political tensions among them. But before that, we provide some of the contexts behind the crisis of the post-Cold-War consensus.

The state of the British polity

When we began this research in 2018, the UK was the fifth most unequal country in Europe. The top 10% took 28% of the country's total income, around half of which was captured by the top 1%. Indeed, since the 1960s, inequality has increased between the top 1% and the 99%, but fallen within the 99%.[5] After the 2007–08 financial crisis, a temporary reduction in top incomes meant that inequality declined slightly, but by 2017 the average CEO's pay was 145 times that of the average worker.[6]

The 2008 financial crash was partly caused by unsustainable household debt in the US and beyond; in other words, the increasing dependence on credit of large parts of the population and the incentives faced by financial institutions to offer loans to those unable to repay them. This credit-driven growth is connected to decades of runaway incomes at the top and stagnant wages at the bottom.[7] Half of the UK population had barely gained from the previous four decades of growth, with a declining share of national income going to salaries and a rising share going to capital. Today, 60% of those in poverty have someone in their household who is employed, which is 20% higher than in 1995.[8] With sluggish household earnings at the bottom, average weekly earnings have mostly decoupled from GDP growth. The UK has been getting richer but most people are not noticeably better off. This has been particularly true outside the capital. Average weekly earnings among full-time employees in London are a third higher than the UK average and nearly two thirds higher than those in the north-east.[9] At the same time, though London is one of the richest regions in northern Europe, 27.7% of its inhabitants live in poverty.[10]

After the financial crisis, the UK government, instead of tackling the root causes of the financial crash – an economy over-reliant on an over-leveraged financial system whose proceeds mostly benefited one city – found scapegoats; initially welfare recipients and later, immigrants. In 2010, Labour was replaced by a Conservative-Liberal Democrat coalition whose main policy response was to cut public sector spending while relying on the Bank of England to provide quantitative easing,[11] which was 'originally conceived to enhance productivity and wages by bringing down borrowing costs and encouraging investment. Instead, it has pushed up asset prices (which favours wealthier asset-owners) but without the investment.'[12] Money ended up in the coffers of banks rather than generating more loans to individuals and small businesses. In parallel, spending cuts were presented as necessary for reducing the deficit, but were also a bid to dismantle what the coalition saw as an over-centralised, ineffectual and overbearing state and to 'discipline' a population that was framed as idly taking advantage of the largesse of hard-working taxpayers. Economist Simon Wren-Lewis has shown that, although by 2013 the government had stopped its most ambitious spending targets, the restructuring of the welfare state and the vilification of its beneficiaries remained.[13]

With £12 billion of unspecified welfare cuts promised during his campaign, David Cameron said in a speech a month after securing his re-election in 2015: "if you want to work hard and get on in life, this government will be on your side."[14] It was all about *getting on* and *working hard*. Benefit claimants as a whole were often implied to be deadweight. But among those not in work, some of the sharpest cuts were aimed at disabled and young people, while state spending on pensioners – a crucial constituency for the Conservatives – was ring-fenced.[15] In the words of Brown and Jones: 'Single mothers, the unemployed and recipients of disability benefits were blamed for depleting the country's financial reserves through claiming state welfare, while the actual architects of the financial crisis in the City of London were never mentioned.'[16]

Tens of thousands of disabled people are estimated to have died from the combined impact of cuts in social care, working-age benefits, healthcare and housing, as well as from regressive tax increases. Disabled people are 8% of the population but took an estimated 29% of all cuts, including the Personal Independence Payment for people with the highest personal care and mobility needs. Around that time, there was a noticeable slowdown in the growth of UK life expectancy.[17]

Austerity also undermined business confidence and the investment required for growth. Since 2010, the economic recovery has mostly been driven by increasing public and private debt. In tandem, quantitative easing – although explicitly designed to supply banks with liquidity to lend at low interest, instead boosted the assets of the richest while lending to UK businesses was negative.[18] Credit instead flowed to an overheating property market, fuelling property prices. This affected harshly those who do not own their homes but created a boon for sellers, landlords and the real estate sector.

Meanwhile, technological change, automation, offshoring, and the tension between globalisation and the nation-state continued to threaten the local labour market and create a sense of economic insecurity, while there was little to no improvement in productivity, investments, exports, or manufacturing.[19] After decades framed by a narrative of progress, many in the UK faced the prospect of living in a country that was going backwards, where children would be poorer than their parents and where working was much less profitable than owning.

Two social movements sought to give answers to this malaise: Brexit and Jeremy Corbyn's Labour leadership. Both sought to convince disaffected voters to join their ranks, either by blaming immigrants and Brussels (Brexit) or billionaires and media barons (Labour) for the despair and disconnect engulfing us all. Brexit relied mostly on votes from those aged 50+ (60% of voters aged 50–64 and 64% of those aged 65+ opted to Leave), with a GCSE or lower qualification, and living in the countryside.[20] In contrast, Corbyn was supported by the young, the university educated and those living in urban areas.

The first succeeded; the second did not. In its success, Brexit left a deep scar in Britain's body politic that is unlikely to ever heal. Indeed, though the referendum result is not as widely contested as it was before the 2019 election, today most Britons believe it was the wrong choice.[21] That election also marked the unceremonious end of the Corbynite project which, whatever faults it may have had, was the last political movement to represent young precarious workers in any significant manner. And all of this was before the pandemic and the Ukraine–Russia war.

Are the top 10% politically active?

Nearly all our respondents vote regularly and all are interested in politics. As we have said, the higher your income, the more likely you are to vote. Talking about individuals' civic responsibilities, Gemma, a young consultant, said that "voting is part of it". Similarly, Tony, a senior IT manager in his early fifties with a top 1% income and living in the north comments: "If you want to get involved, then you have to vote, take part in the democratic process." The few who hadn't always voted explained that it was due to work relocation and not being based in any one place for long.

For the majority, this is the extent of their political involvement. We asked if they were part of a party, political group or trade union, or if they protested or participated in politics in any other way. Only a couple of respondents answered affirmatively to any of those questions. While some had signed online petitions, only two had been to protests. Adam, a professional services consultant, comments that while he hasn't ever been on a protest, he had "intended to go to a pro-Europe march, but my wife wouldn't let me". Jonathan, a 70-year-old, semi-retired barrister just in the top 1% bracket, comments, almost proudly: "I'm not really a joiner."

Among our interviewees there is a curious tension: while as a rule they vote and follow politics, most do not participate in politics in any consistent manner. Their relative passivity, however, should not be equated to the disaffection of those who believe politics is not for people like them.

Three reasons were immediately apparent for this relative lack of participation. Not enough time is the first reason cited. Interviewees are much more likely to prefer using their waking hours with their families or advancing their careers, in much the same way that they are more likely to donate to charity than to volunteer. Second, the decline in civic engagement has been well documented by sociologists such as Robert Putnam and Nina Eliasoph in the US.[22] The third reason is that many high-income earners are wary of the oppositional, factionalist, and in their view, populist and extremist character that politics has taken in the past few years.

While some in the top 10% may consider joining a national party, few would go out of their way to participate in their local party, certainly not for personal interactions. While we are reminded that there never has been a golden age of political engagement, Putnam and others confirm that there has been a rise in anti-political sentiment, including towards local government.[23] And there is no corresponding positivity towards informal politics to compensate for this trend. In terms of participant numbers, alternative forms of political action – from demonstrating to donating and volunteering – do not seem to be on the rise. They also appear to be minority forms of action practised mainly by citizens who already vote and join parties.[24]

In 2019, for the first time since the mid-1970s, more than half of British survey respondents were dissatisfied with democracy in the UK.[25] While dissatisfaction with democracy has risen across many countries, it is striking that the developed countries worst affected are those with majoritarian electoral systems. That dissatisfaction increases when economic inequality increases, and has an even stronger impact geographically, with some areas of the country feeling neglected – in gerrymandered or safe seats.[26] While levels of trust and confidence have risen back to pre-Brexit levels, 44% of British people still say they almost never trust politicians to tell the truth, down from 51% in 2019.[27] People tend to keep up with political news nationally, but few take an active interest in how their local area is run.[28]

The proportion of the UK electorate that is a political party member has fallen from around 1 in 12 citizens in the 1950s to around 1 in 50 today. The UK has one of the lowest party memberships in Europe.[29] As Berry and Guinan chart, the local voluntary and community sector, which could sit at the heart of participatory politics, was hollowed out during austerity with grassroots organisations 'struggling to survive, competing for what money is available and with less and less capacity to give disenfranchised citizens a voice'.[30] Changing the electoral system would:

> breathe new life into campaigning by moribund local parties in historically safe seats, and would give party supporters a reason to be politically active in areas where the voting system had previously made their votes worthless. It could also encourage a less negative campaigning style, which has greater potential to engage turned-off voters.[31]

Gerry's experience of joining her local Labour Party in a safe Conservative seat confirmed a formal top-down bureaucratic relationship between local and national parties with, locally, a small executive of long-standing members and rules and procedures which could be off-putting to a newcomer.[32] And, at least until the pandemic temporarily changed the pattern of some people's working lives, there was very little interest in or knowledge of local politics by the community with many members of the public believing that local parties are run by paid officials rather than volunteers. Labour Party members make up 1.1% of the voting public[33] and are not a very representative slice, either, with members being on average much older, whiter, more male, and better off than the UK population average.[34]

Even if there were a renaissance of local politics, local councils have faced devastating cuts to their budgets for over ten years, leaving many on the brink of collapse. This includes a long-term reduction in the number of councillors, with 500 losses since 2014.[35] As an Unlock Democracy-commissioned report on the past 40 years of local government describes it: "the erosion of local democracy has been substantial, putting into jeopardy local government's ability to continue providing a vital democratic link for the communities it is elected to serve." What is more, the role of the councillor has been increasingly 'managerialised' and 'depoliticised'. As a result, 'accountability gaps' have emerged, with local government being bypassed by a 'new magistracy' of unelected bodies.[36] It is therefore unsurprising that there is little public interest in becoming local councillors.

On the whole, local councils only come to mind when the bins haven't been collected or when making a planning application. It is certainly not an area most would entertain spending their time in. Running for elected office is on the decline and this has been Gerry's experience when trying to encourage members of her local Labour Party to come forward and nominate themselves for local government.[37] The lack of remuneration (only expenses are paid) is also a barrier for people who might be interested, especially those on lower incomes or with family responsibilities. Although much depends on the local ward, candidates tend to be older and male. A lack of confidence and being put off by the potential experience is also a key factor, no doubt not helped by our polarising media and the combative and elitist nature of national politics.

One noticeable tendency, however, is the influence of more liberal voters moving from cities into affluent suburbs, which has only been hastened by the pandemic. Since 2019, this has been part of the explanation for the growth of progressive politics in the 'blue wall' (a set of parliamentary constituencies in the south of England where Conservatives have historically dominated). In contrast to the relative lack of interest in local formal politics, local pressure groups have grown, often set up about a specific issue such as a planning application and they exist predominantly online. Similarly, local branches of national pressure groups such as Extinction Rebellion or Make Votes Matter have sprung up. It has been Gerry's experience that members of such groups then move into formal politics as a result of their campaigning on local issues.

Given this, the lack of trade union or party membership among our respondents is also noticeable yet unsurprising. The two clearest exceptions to the rule are staunch Brahmins such as Paul, an architect just in the top 10% income band living in London, who is the only respondent to currently be a party member (Labour) like both his parents before him. Only one respondent, Duncan – a director of a non-departmental public body who votes Green – is a lifelong trade unionist and charity volunteer.

Other partial exceptions include Gemma – a consultant in London who had briefly been a member of the Liberal Democrats as part of an internship in parliament, but left once it finished, and Maria, who joined Labour only to vote against Corbyn's leadership. Maria's views also speak to the third reason many high earners have for not participating actively in politics: they do not like what it has become. Most respondents were, as predicted by the literature, quite progressive when it came to 'cultural' issues but less so on economic matters, which situated Labour supporters to the right of Corbyn and Conservative respondents to the left of every Tory leader after Cameron. Most felt short-changed by both parties in terms of both the ideology and the behaviour of its leaders. Many were likely to vote for the Liberal Democrats or speak approvingly of Tony Blair, and even David Cameron. Ben, 39, working in IT in the south-east, describes his relationship with the Conservative Party:

'I have been a Conservative Party member in the past. But there's no way with the current lot. I left the Conservative Party not long after Theresa May came in and the direction of Brexit was becoming clear. I also became disillusioned with people like Boris Johnson. He was previously MP for Henley, not far from here.

Him and Michael Gove in particular seem interested in helping themselves rather than fixing anything or running the country. That comes across bluntly in their case.'

Even when respondents identify with a party without being members, most have caveats. Roy, a 66-year-old finance director with a top 3% income, says that the Liberal Democrats probably best represent his views, but that he won't necessarily vote for them as he doesn't see what difference it will make. Jonathan, the 'non-joiner', semi-retired barrister we mentioned earlier, tells us he has always been a Labour supporter but he often doesn't vote for them. Claire, a teacher living in the north with an income just above the 10% threshold, describes herself as a "floaty voter". Maria, similarly, votes tactically either for Labour or the Liberal Democrats without belonging to either:

Maria:	I have been a member of a political party. I've been a member of Labour so I could vote for Jeremy Corbyn not to win.
Interviewer:	So you're not a member anymore?
Maria:	Yes I left. I felt quite bad because I'm between LibDem and Labour, so I thought I'm not going to keep it up in case I want to join the LibDems in the future.

Caught in the middle

Many respondents felt that political parties had been moving away from the typical centre ground. That comment was mostly levelled at the Conservatives, but similar views were expressed about Labour under Jeremy Corbyn. Many who had voted for Labour in the past felt it was no longer for them; it had veered towards socialism, a 'dirty' word for many. They much preferred the pragmatic, centrist politics of the New Labour era. Christopher, an under-35-year-old, working for a global IT consultancy, in the top 3% and one of the few who doesn't vote, says it is because "there's no party that I feel totally affinity to". Tony, introduced earlier, tells us:

'Everything's "far" – what's happened to the centre group? It's not just in politics, it's in every area of life, there's nowhere everyone can meet […] the age of debate is disappearing. The age where you could persuade people of your opinion has gone. Everyone sets off down a track. I don't know when it happened […] they became polarised.'

Maria as a marketing director with a top 6% income, has similar views:

'You know […] it's too kind of ideological and now it's getting even further […] the ideology is too far to one side. And the centre won't work either because […] sometimes the centre can be quite weak, trying to keep too many people happy and they don't actually come out and say "This is what we're going to do," […] that's not gonna work either.'

Our respondents' unease with current politics and predilection for previous centrism was clear. Perhaps this is why the Liberal Democrats represent the affluent voter's protest vote. Most interviewees said they would be voting for the same party in the 2019 general election as they had voted for in 2017, and parties' different stances on Brexit were the deciding factor for those contemplating changing their vote. Most intended to vote for the Liberal Democrats, primarily because of their pro-Remain stance. One mentioned that the unfairness of the voting system needed to be addressed. While we asked no specific question on Brexit – we preferred it to arise naturally – respondents spoke of the divisions it had revealed, such as Hannah, the occupational health consultant, earning just above the 10% threshold, who said: "If you look at the ways the country was divided in terms of areas, you see the more deprived areas broadly speaking voted for Brexit as opposed to more affluent areas that voted Remain."

Dan, the head of client services at a marketing agency in his early forties with a top 6% income, described the turmoil in April 2019:

'Brexit is on everyone's mind. A few weeks ago, it felt like the country might tear itself apart. It questioned friendships, political standing, democracy as a vehicle for governing, and that's quite scary. People seem hell-bent on destroying what was a democratic process. MPs are not acting on behalf of the public. The whole thing is an abomination.'

When asked during the first round of interviews whether she thought inequality had had an impact on British politics in recent years, Louise, a 44-year-old sales consultant living in London with a top 1% income, replies: "Yeah, absolutely. Brexit is the stand-out one. The fact that people like Jeremy Corbyn are still leaders. No one ever thought originally that he would stay so long. Maybe that's due to, in part, the inequality across the nation. Yes, it's definitely played a part."

Ben, 39, an IT consultant in the top 3%, also commented on inequality and polarisation: "There's more polarisation in politics, perhaps because of inequality. You become not so happy with how things are organised and you either follow Jeremy Corbyn or the Green Party route, or you blame it on foreigners and get into UKIP."

Our research spanned Brexit, the governments of Theresa May and Boris Johnson, the pandemic, and the beginning of the post-pandemic recession. The lack of effective opposition was a concern throughout the process. Respondents mistrusted Jeremy Corbyn's ability to handle the economy and saw Keir Starmer as ineffective. In our follow-up round in early 2022, we asked whether they thought the country had been changed politically by COVID-19. Michael, a 49-year-old, engineer just in the top 10% living in the south-west, who spoke with us a few months before Boris Johnson's resignation, responds:

'[W]hile the current incumbent is untrustworthy, corrupt [...] you could not accuse them of doing nothing. This country is in a better situation than most. Puts us in an interesting situation. Left with a government that is not trustworthy. During Covid, the quality of the opposition is so weak, that the system is untenable. The opposition is supposed to put the counterargument [...]. It's not functioning. So we have one party with free rein. We get benefits off of that: they make decisions quickly and choices go through unopposed, rather than everything getting talked about; but we also get corruption.'

Tax: the glue in the social contract

Regardless of the distress about polarisation, Brexit and the radicalisation of political discourse, the overwhelming majority of wealthy constituencies in Britain went to the Conservatives in 2019, a party that had just purged most of its Remainer MPs. Though we suspected more, only four respondents openly told us they consistently voted Conservative. They did so mostly because of taxes. All four had young children, three worked in the corporate sector, and all were near the top of the ladder. Three were surprised by their position on the income distribution. Upward-oriented, they all thought they were placed much lower down the scale.

Louise, a 44-year-old sales consultant living in London in the top 1%, is one of them. She worries about the high cost of living and does not feel particularly wealthy. Nevertheless, as we described earlier, she gives taxation as the reason for voting Conservative: "as I've started to earn more [...] and worked hard for it, I care more about the tax I pay. Didn't think about it when I was younger [...]. Now I'm more aware of it and how it's helping society." While she agrees that those with the means should actively care for those with fewer, she thinks she pays enough tax already and therefore believes increasing taxes wouldn't solve the problem.

Susannah, another 1% income earner with young children living in the south-east, is similarly concerned about taxes. She feels that the existence of stamp duty and inheritance tax amounts to an unfair 'double taxation'. In terms of inequality, she feels there has to be a 'gap', a certain level of inequality for the economy and businesses to run: "people won't strive for anything different [...] if everyone has the same". At the same time, she thinks there is a duty to "make sure people at the lower end of the gap can live well and healthily".

Merchants, especially those with the highest incomes, tended to feel their duty to provide was already being carried out by paying tax, but many also recognised the need to provide for those on the lowest incomes. However, the lack of exposure to different income groups by those working in the corporate and financial sectors is a significant barrier to their understanding of the lives of those well below them, affecting their beliefs on the extent of inequality and the role of redistribution and welfare. Even before the 2008 crisis, Toynbee and Walker had found an increasing disconnect between the financial engine of the country in the City of London and the lives of the majority.[38] Considering the economic and political tendencies that followed, it is unlikely that this distance has been bridged.

Others, especially Brahmins working in the public sector, disagree. With jobs in healthcare, law and education, they were more likely to vote Labour, more likely to mention the negative effects of austerity such as the surge in food bank use, and more passionate about the need for public services. Jacqui, a state school headteacher, in the top 6% income band, felt that living in the north of England gave her a more grounded perspective on inequality, which informed her work: "Inequality is something to be concerned about: you want every kid to have the opportunity to succeed." Claire, another teacher living in the north and just above the top 10% threshold, comments: "The rich shouldn't be rich at the detriment of the poor. There should be a basic standard. [The rich] should have a duty." Concern with society's duty to care is consistent with European Social Survey (ESS) data showing an increase in the percentage of people in the top 10% who agree that the government should strive to reduce inequality (see Figure 2.1, Chapter 2). However, what that concern means in practice and the extent to which it would open a space for more redistribution is open to debate.

How to make sense of this primacy of right-of-centre voting based on an economic anti-tax rationale over any other factor, especially considering that the economy hasn't been performing especially well? A centralised parliamentary system and concentrations of elites in our politics, government, academia, media, law and other areas of public life have created a society in which 'economic change is currently done to people rather than by or with people'.[39] We found this to be true for high earners too. Despite being part of the elite – well educated, informed about current affairs and regular voters – they are as much in thrall as the rest of us to an economic 'common sense' that legitimises political power and underwrites the social contract.[40] Our respondents tended to accept a mainstream version of our economy, society and politics described as 'realistic to the extent that it approaches what already exists'.[41]

This version of economics – which operates more as a set of maxims than as a positive social science – has been used as a crucial prop for political authority for some decades. It has been propped up by, among others, right-leaning think tanks that traverse the worlds of media, academia, politics and economic interests. Many of its senior members are also part of the top 10% and, at least until recently, have been mostly insulated from the effects of the policies they propose.[42] Since the 1970s, their work has contributed to commodifying spaces that once seemed beyond purely financial considerations, such as public health.

One consequence of this process is that politics is reduced to questions of managerial competence (which party or leader will be most efficient?) or to bitter partisanship, where each party attacks the other regardless of the result. An example of the former focus on how the state is managed and its (in)efficiency rather than focusing on politics with a capital 'P', is provided by Michael, introduced earlier, in his explanation of what determines his vote: "My preference has always been for competence and rational behaviour. Who's more rational?"

The erosion and hollowing out of institutions – and the subordination of democracy to a certain vision of economics – has seen the worlds of politics, media and finance collapse into each other. A world in which vested interests stop reforms being made that would hit the wealthiest the most, as that would go against 'common sense', regardless of how many experts argue the contrary. Economist Simon Wren-Lewis, for instance, has argued that there is an increasing distance between the discipline of economics and what is broadly understood in politics and the media as 'the economy' and 'basic economics'.[43] Maria, the management consultant we quoted earlier, compared the crippling effect of business taxes on high street businesses with global tech firms: "And yet you don't get the same application of tax to technology platforms. That has to be looked at. Basically, they don't want to upset all their friends so that's why they don't do anything."

If high earners were to ask more often who has the power and why, when considering high prices for food and fuel, for example, they would see how deeply the market has entered every facet of life. Increasingly, no area of social and political life can avoid 'the gaze of a blanket financial audit'.[44] Finance is placed above legal mechanisms and determines which policy pledges will be kept, to the point where it is no longer clear that contemporary capitalism requires a norm-based legal model of the state. Only one respondent, a barrister and expert in housing law, reflected on the history of our state infrastructure in his lifetime: "You've got to start with Thatcher. Demunicipalisation of gas, water, electricity, railway, […] housing […] with the right to buy […]. A mass transfer of stocks. A mass depletion of what the state, what public services, provide."

Conflicted views on the role of the state

Many respondents working in the private sector distance themselves from the welfare state, for at least two reasons. First, there is a certain status in thinking that they are not dependent on public services. If welfare recipients and state spending are blamed for the recession, it is perhaps to be expected that paying taxes while 'going private' becomes a reason to feel proud. Nobody in our sample describes having to make frequent use of public services, living in social housing or needing social care. Where respondents have children of school age, they are either in private schools or in state schools in relatively affluent areas. Framed like this, state spending commitments by one government or another seem much more abstract, and much less applicable to this demographic compared with the rest. They see no concrete benefit to their lives from further state spending, and if they did they would consider that a sign of failure, so the consequences of austerity feel foreign. The only partial exception is healthcare, which is more easily framed than most other policy areas as an issue beyond individual control. However, most of those that mention health problems have private healthcare 'for emergencies', often as part of their employment contracts.

Second, public services are considered inefficient and sub-par compared with the private sector, the NHS among them. For many, the state is almost by definition overweening, elephantine and prone to corruption. This belief in government inefficiency is often paired with low trust in the state's role in the economy. Ben, 39, an IT consultant in the top 3%, was one of many who justified not wanting to pay more taxes because:

> 'A lot of government initiatives are woefully inefficient. Where there is a new scheme or project, it seems they end up paying hundreds of millions or billions more than what it should have cost. Outside government, if you put £10 worth of help into inequality you may get £10 worth of effect. But putting that same £10 through the government will give £2.50 worth of overall effect.'

This sense that the government overspends and that it is not a question of spending more but rather 'spending better' is widespread among those working in the private sector. It is also consistent with ESS data from its rotating modules on welfare attitudes in 2008 and 2016, which show an increase in the percentage of British people who agree that social benefits and services place too great a strain on the economy (Figure 4.1).

Nevertheless, three quarters of those we spoke with felt that inequality was increasing. When asked how it was noticeable, they spoke of the more visible elements of poverty, such as homelessness on their way to the train station, and the rise of food banks and donation boxes in supermarkets. Nearly all were concerned about it at its most extreme and felt that people should not be struggling on the breadline. They saw providing for those with fewer resources as a moral duty, if sometimes a reluctant one. We have mentioned that the top 10%, while less favourable to redistribution than other parts of the population, are becoming less reticent. As we showed in Chapter 2, in 2018 the top 10%

Figure 4.1: Agreement with the statement 'Social benefits and services place too great a strain on the economy' in the UK, 2008–16

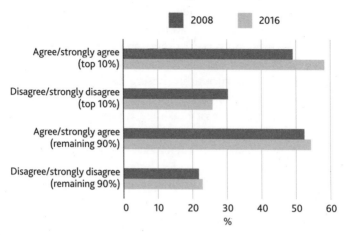

Source: ESS data, 2010, 2018

were more open to the suggestion of redistribution than they were in 2008. Most feel that 'in the fifth richest country in the world' the system is not working.

However, those working in the private sector, and those earning above £100,000 in particular, are conflicted as to the role the state should play. Jonathan, a 70-year-old, semi-retired barrister in the top 1%, starts by being clear that it is the government's duty to address inequality of outcome, then mid–interview argues instead that its role is only to ensure equality of opportunity, and from there concludes that its duty is purely to ensure people's basic standard of living: "Its duty is to provide education and opportunity and a basic standard of living. A basic standard of living – adequate, at least."

Sean, a 40-year-old with a top 1% income, who owns a recruitment company, is clearer:

> 'I hate these questions about the government because I don't know if the government should fix anything in this country. They have a duty to make sure that people are not living below the poverty line and they have a general duty to keep people safe and protected.'

Interviewees also discussed the relative importance of cash transfers as opposed to services and infrastructure. Michael, for example, a 49-year-old engineer earning just above the 10% threshold, is not alone in thinking that the emphasis should be taken away from universal benefits and instead make them means-tested. In his view, policy should focus on investing in the "infrastructure [that is currently] missing for better education, council housing, childcare".

Support for universal services as they are organised now (for example, the NHS) was weaker from those respondents working in the private sector, with little reference to the social solidarity function a universal system provides. Even the few who refer to the tradition of universalism, often end up arguing in favour of means-testing. Dan, head of client services at a marketing agency with a top 6% income, argues that if services are partially paid for by their beneficiaries, they will improve through customer demand for better quality: "If you pay a contribution to your son going to school then there's an expectation of what you're getting back. If you pay council tax, you expect bins to be collected and local services to function."

Ben, 39, an IT consultant in the top 3%, argues that people can't be trusted not to abuse the system. "Part of the problem is that [the NHS] is universal and absolutely free, and some people abuse that. If you give people a free resource, there's no reining in demand for it. [I] think that should change to slightly more means-tested."

However, he then makes clear that this does not mean he favours a US-style health service:

> 'If you've been run over and are taken to hospital you shouldn't have to show payslips before they operate. I'm thinking [introduce means-tested payments for] primary care. A bit like dental care, in certain situations you get it completely free and the same with prescriptions. I think we ought to do something like that with GPs as well.'

Duncan, a director of a non-departmental government body, refers to the erosion of the political consensus on universalism:

'It's quite frightening because it undermines all of the principles from after the Second World War, which were about caring for everyone and a communal approach to life based on people's experience. The creation of the welfare state and the NHS were two of those which society generally accepted. A lot of that has been eroded in the past 20 years, so it seems a bad thing instead of a good one. It's seen as unaffordable [by] the rich. Not the super-rich, just those with income – there's more an attitude of "I'd rather pay for myself than pay into a pot." It would be good to try and reverse some of that.'

The relatively weak support for universalism – especially from those working in the private sector – and the few references made to austerity, are to be expected. They can even be framed as a progressive impulse not to support the well-off with the taxes of those on low incomes, and fit perfectly also with the stigma associated with public service users and welfare recipients. Instead, a 'rights and responsibilities' discourse runs through many respondents' accounts.[45] Michael, a 49-year-old engineer just above the 10% threshold, was one of a few to concede that benefits only provide a minimum standard of living. This may stem from his experience of living in relative poverty as a child:

'Any one of us can find ourselves in a situation where we really haven't got any money and it can happen really quickly [...] although unemployment is low at the moment, it can still be difficult because there's a lot of choice out there. You can easily find yourself with no income for a while. If you do go onto welfare then it's a very, very difficult situation. The welfare state will give you really not quite enough money for what you need. It might give you enough to live on. But things like maintenance, anything that requires any kind of upkeep – you quickly will find you can't run a car, and then [...] you can't get a job [...] so, there's a divide, a watershed point, at which if you go beyond an economic line, it all decays, the whole situation collapses very quickly.'

Where will the political tide take high earners?

High-income earners occupy an interesting position. They dominate politics and most institutions of political importance and yet they feel unease: not mainly because they think politicians live in a different reality from theirs (like many others feel today), but because they are fearful of the current political tides. It's an attitude reminiscent of Barack Obama's response after Donald Trump's win in 2016: of disbelief at the perceived irrationality of others, a fear that passion has overtaken reason. Small 'l' liberal views seem to be going out of fashion on the economic and cultural fronts, discredited by figures such as Bernie Sanders and Jeremy Corbyn on the left and by Nigel Farage, Marine Le Pen, Jair Bolsonaro and the like on the right. Famously, Theresa May said in October 2016 "if you believe you're a citizen of the world, you're a citizen of nowhere. You don't understand what the very word 'citizenship' means." That seems to us like an almost direct critique of the subjects of this book.[46]

Although elites are rarely popular, the 2010s have seen anti-elite discourse become increasingly commonplace. Perhaps this is unsurprising after an economic crisis mainly caused by a financial system populated by unaccountable high-income earners, highly educated experts who were not capable of predicting it or dealing with its fallout, and growing concentrations of wealth. At the same time, the concept of 'elite' is murky, and we do ourselves a disservice if we think it is homogeneous or easy to identify. Nevertheless, it is not cavalier to assume some Brahmins and some Merchants are part of it.

David Goodhart, a journalist and think-tanker who started his career on the centre-left and has moved steadily to the right in the past years, has written two relevant books on the matter.[47] In *The Road to Somewhere*, he argues that the 'anywheres', those whose economic situation and outlook are directly influenced and benefited by globalisation, have dominated politics for too long. In the process, they have cast aside the 'somewheres', those with more local attachments and more small 'c' conservative mindsets. In *Head, Hand, Heart*, Goodhart states that in the last decades, society has tended to value the kinds of non-routine jobs that require credentials and specialist knowledge, prioritising the academically oriented. In other words, we have overemphasised the 'head' (expertise) over the 'hand' (manual labour) or the 'heart' (care), and the 'anywhere' over the 'somewhere'. In such a system, the top 10%, populated as it is by highly educated professionals and managers, has done well, ostensibly at the expense of those who are now leading the backlash against their values.

Goodhart's analysis is compelling if betraying a sometimes unhealthy animosity towards urbanites, which puts him in dubious company. However, this diagnosis does not answer why the most affluent constituencies in England voted in huge numbers for the Conservatives after Boris Johnson purged the party from moderates and populated it with Brexiteers, or why Trump voters in the US were more affluent than the national average.[48] The left-of-centre ideas on culture and right-of-centre ones on the economy that high-income earners seem to favour appear to be under attack. Yet, when they had to choose, a majority seems to have chosen the economy. Why is that?

We would argue that 2019 was a watershed. In front of the country and high-income earners were Jeremy Corbyn and Boris Johnson. Corbyn was portrayed as a radical left-winger and irresponsible on the economy, though his programme would have been considered a normal social democrat one in much of Europe – indeed, his spending proposals were almost identical to Germany's in 2019.[49] Johnson is an openly mendacious politician who opportunistically positioned himself on the right of the right wing of his party and, while pursuing Brexit, seemed to propose little to no change on the economic front. High-income earners sided mostly with the latter, at least based on results from the least deprived constituencies.

From a purely materialistic standpoint, it was an unsurprising choice. However they are understood, elites are in some sense defined – not illogically – as likely to be negatively affected by redistributive policies. Any such change risks impinging on their privileges and their capacity to reproduce their elitism and bequeath their resources to their children. That is, after all, how tax hikes are commonly framed among high-income earners. If pushed, we would say that many in the top 10% resent the left for promoting policies in the run-up to the 2019 general election that in their minds were irrational and harmful, forcing them to vote with the far right. In the conflict between their economic interests and their sociocultural inclinations, the former took precedence.

Meanwhile, in the background, Brexit, one of the most impactful and radical policies of the last decades, continued to disrupt huge swathes of the economy, and trickle-down economics continued to drive concentration at the top. Most far-right parties propose precious little to avert these trends and instead espouse a Darwinian view of the economy, where those 'out' are punished for the benefit of those 'in'. Most of the relatively affluent are generally considered 'in', but as the history of far-right movements shows us they are driven by the exclusion and scapegoating of one segment of society after another, and at some point they may find themselves the target.

High-income earners are, in the main, not delighted by this turn of events. A majority do remain small 'l' liberals and resent being ruled by governments that are allied with right-wing European administrations such as Orbán's Hungary, under a programme and a discourse that is not too distant from those of Trump, Bolsonaro, Meloni or Le Pen. Brahmins are the most worried; they fear not just polarisation and populism, but also the loss of democratic standards and the legitimisation of bigotry in the public arena. This often prompts them to become apathetic and ever more distant from the political process. The attitude of many Merchants can be encapsulated by a *New Yorker* cartoon from 30 January 2017, days after Trump officially became president (Figure 4.2). Two male figures in suits look down on the city from what seems to be a swanky office in a skyscraper. The caption reads: "Part of me is going to miss liberal democracy."

Whatever you may think of the proposals coming from the left, it is clear that neither the Conservatives nor any hypothetical centrist programme has answers to the structural crises that are beginning to affect everyone in this group. This gives us some indication of the fragility of our society and economy: even the top 10% is feeling wary. In less unequal countries, the same group is far more secure and has much less to worry about. The next chapter further explores some of the crises and tensions that our respondents and many of our readers now face.

Figure 4.2: *The New Yorker* cartoon, by Barbara Smaller

"Part of me is going to miss liberal democracy."

Source: Barbara Smaller/The New Yorker Collection/The Cartoon Bank

5

Business class tickets
for a sinking ship

Whether they know it or not, and through whatever means, high earners have a disproportionate influence on policy. Since they are more likely to vote than most, political parties court their opinion, and they are often sociologically similar to the elites of these parties.[1] In Europe, research shows a similar pattern.[2] Nevertheless, and despite their relative political dominance, politics doesn't seem to be working for the top 10%. Holes are beginning to appear in their meritocratic narrative. Access to housing, jobs, opportunities for career advancement and places in elite universities for their children are becoming scarcer and competition fiercer. Many are also becoming increasingly aware that a catastrophic event such as an illness or accident could derail their until now upward trajectories.

As a rule, high-income earners are relatively pessimistic about their country's future but less so about their own. They are, in the main, quite optimistic about themselves, which betrays a tacit distance between how they see their lives and the fate of the rest. However menacing challenges such as climate change and inequality may be, many are confident they will still do well. Politics happens to others, so to speak.

At the same time, intergenerational inequalities are becoming more accentuated, as Millennials and Generation Z find the transition to adulthood increasingly difficult and many are unable to maintain the economic status of their elders. Housing is becoming nigh unaffordable without parental support, especially in metropolitan areas where salaries tend to be highest. At the same time, education does not seem to guarantee a comfortable living as it once did, as income and status are becoming closely linked to inheritance and wealth. Our respondents' optimism was less pronounced when asked about the world their children will live in.

As we write, and in no particular order, there seem to be record highs in all the wrong things. Just to name a few: global temperatures; inequality; inflation; the cost of energy, food, transport and housing, and the profits of privatised companies supplying those resources; excess deaths; turnover in key essential services; and waiting times for emergency services and hospital operations. And there are the corresponding record lows in all the wrong things too: life expectancy; real earnings; productivity growth; income growth in the lowest deciles; and the state of public services.

This chapter explores how critical events (Brexit, the pandemic, the Ukraine–Russia war, the cost of living crisis) and the structural crises of our times may affect the top 10%. As much as their situation is more secure than most, they are finding it harder to ignore these crises, especially in the long run. It is clear that the factors behind their anxieties are sociological and structural, and affect far beyond the top 10%.

Critical events

Brexit

The 2016 referendum for the UK to leave the EU was followed by a further four years of negotiations. During this time, other social and political issues were crowded out of the policy agenda, even those often reported to be behind Brexit itself. As Sean, the owner of an HR consultancy, put it: "Brexit has overshadowed everything political." High earners acknowledge the inequalities exposed and aggravated by Brexit, and the fact it has many causes and facets. Not least, Brexit exposed the cultural and socioeconomic divides in the country, many of which criss-crossed the Conservative versus Labour divide.

The Brexit vote has often been characterised as largely working class and English, driven by older, socially conservative people living in declining areas and feeling increasingly powerless to face the pressures of globalisation.[3] Another theory on the motivations of Leave voters was that they tended to be old enough to remember more equitable times and might have associated the UK's EU membership in 1975 with a decline in living standards because during roughly the same period economic inequality has taken a marked turn for the worst.[4] Whatever the motivations, five years on, Ipsos polls showed that Brexit identities are still stronger than party identification.[5] Most high-income earners we spoke with were against the whole thing. They told us they no longer felt represented by politics; they feared polarisation, populism and their economic impacts. Ben, 39, an IT consultant living in the south-east in the top 3%, explains to us why he voted Liberal Democrat:

> 'Brexit is a big thing for me and they seem to be the most pro-European party. I think their views are closer to my own. The Conservative Party has taken a lurch to the right following the departure of David Cameron and I don't feel the party is even close to representing my views anymore. I have been a Conservative Party member in the past. But there's no way with the current lot.'

Other people's lack of concern for the impact of Brexit also troubled our respondents. Alan, a 50-year-old director of a logistics company in the south-east, when asked about what worried him about his country and his own future, replied, with reference to Brexit, that the British need to have a greater "ability to respond to misinformation". Claire, a headteacher living in Manchester with an income just above the 10% threshold, commented: "people felt they were going to get more money into the system. People who voted Leave thought they would be better off. They were lied to." International onlookers, such as *The New York Times*, wrote about the corrosive impact of Brexit on British politics and 'the readiness of the political right in particular to lie and peddle obvious untruths, to place their party politics and party unity over and above the national interest'.[6]

COVID-19

The UK has one of the worst Covid records in the world. The country was ill-prepared for the pandemic after more than a decade of disinvestment and privatisation of public infrastructure. Adult social care was particularly vulnerable. Despite being warned, the government downplayed the importance of care provision at the beginning of the pandemic, neglecting to supply it with further funding. The first confirmed COVID-19 cases in the UK were on 31 January 2020.[7] On 25 February, Public Health England issued guidance for social care settings, advising that 'it is [...] very unlikely that anyone receiving care in a care home or the community will become infected' and 'there is no need to do anything differently in any care setting at present'.[8] From an initial £5 billion emergency response fund, £1.6 billion was allocated to local authorities, but they were not legally required to spend that money on social care, and it was therefore not always received by the sector. NHS England asked hospitals to urgently discharge patients who were medically fit back into social care settings, and 25,000 patients were.[9] It was only midway through April 2020, almost a month after social distancing measures had been put in place, that an adult social care action plan for controlling the spread of infection was finally issued. This delayed and uncoordinated response failed to protect an already vulnerable sector.

On 27 April 2022, the High Court ruled that the government had been reckless in moving Covid-positive patients back into nursing homes from hospitals and that this led to thousands of unnecessary deaths.[10] At the same time, government spending elsewhere, such as the £37 billion pound test-and-trace scheme – which according to the Public Accounts Committee, achieved none of its aims and failed to make 'a measurable difference to the progress of the pandemic'[11] – amounted to double the central government cuts to local authorities over the last 10 years.[12] Meanwhile, the pandemic highlighted the poor pay and working conditions of many essential workers in society. A third of care workers, for example, are paid less than the real Living Wage.[13]

Covid may also have been the first time many high earners experienced being direct recipients of state cash transfers through the furlough scheme and business loans. In 2020, COVID-19 benefit claimants were much more likely to be highly educated and younger than before.[14] At the same time, high earners were also insulated from the worst effects of the crisis, as a higher income was strongly correlated with the capacity of a job to be carried out from home and with savings on non-essential goods and services such as eating out and leisure travel.[15] Apart from a reminder of the importance of key workers and public healthcare provision, this relative insulation from the most severe economic effects of COVID-19 may well contribute to a forgiving attitude towards the government's management of the pandemic, as well as relative ignorance of its broader social consequences.

Ukraine–Russia war

According to the OECD, the UK will be the major economy to be most affected by the Ukraine–Russia war. It will be the slowest growing in 2023 due to a combination of factors, including higher interest rates, reduced trade, rising energy prices, and the fact that, in 2019, the UK imported around 13% of all its fuel from Russia.[16] Nevertheless, disruption to the supply of energy to Europe will affect wholesale prices in the UK to a greater extent than implied by direct trade links. Traders buy gas in the UK to avoid higher prices in Europe and then export it to the Continent, both reducing UK supply and causing prices to rise in the Continent.

Inflationary pressures on households from soaring food and energy prices, cutting household disposable income and living standards and lowering consumption as the book goes to publication, mean that consumer spending continues to shrink and confidence is low. Recovery, as the Institute of Government predicted, looks likely to be delayed by the uncertainty holding back the UK economy as firms and consumers 'adopt a "wait and see" approach, cutting back on investment and consumption plans'.[17]

Energy costs and market failures

Paul Johnson, Director of the Institute for Fiscal Studies, described Kwasi Kwarteng's September 2022 budget as a 'complete reversal of policy compared with the government only a few months ago, this was like an entirely different government coming into office'.[18] Within three weeks, without having won a general election, Liz Truss had announced the biggest unfunded package (over £50 billion) of tax cuts in 50 years, bigger than any introduced by Margaret Thatcher. These included cuts in the basic rate of income tax to 19p; a reversal in the rise in corporation tax and national insurance; abolishing the cap on bankers' bonuses; and lowering the tax rate on incomes above £150,000.[19]

Markets unsurprisingly reacted, concerned at the potential for rising inflation, without a serious plan from the government to pay the debt back, so sterling was sent 'spiralling down and gilts soaring, costing the Bank of England £65bn to prop up pension funds'.[20] Two of these tax cuts (the top rate and corporation tax) were subsequently rolled back due to public and market pressure. However, even with the quick U-turn on two taxes, the richest 5% of households will still gain almost 40 times as much as the poorest fifth of households by the measures announced.[21] Crucially, Rishi Sunak's government is still planning public spending cuts and further austerity. With the need for additional borrowing and no fiscal plan in place, the government has undermined the Bank of England's attempts to tackle inflation and led to interest rates spiking on government debt, volatility in sterling and market uncertainty.[22]

Described variously as 'disastrous', 'a fiscal and moral outrage', 'a reckless mini-budget for the rich' and 'At last! A true Tory budget',[23] what's surprising about this episode is the confluence of three phenomena: the brazenness of the proposals, which married tax cuts for the most affluent with spending cuts for the most vulnerable; the effect of the markets' reaction to the government's sudden lurch to the right, reflecting their increased power as quantitative easing starts to be reversed; and that all of this is happening in a context where the fallout of previous and ongoing crises (not least 2008, Brexit, COVID-19 and the Ukraine–Russia war) still afflict the UK economy. Ultimately, this represents a rift between the markets and their most die-hard advocates and the end of the idea that tax cuts are *per se* a responsible proposal to spur growth and address government debt. If we are lucky, this might be the end of the idea that 'trickle-down economics' brings benefits to anyone other than the already wealthy.

Still, British people face mortgage rate rises, the costs of which will pass on to both owners and renters; rising costs of food, of which 50% is imported, and which in the context of a falling pound will continue to go up; and an estimated 80% increase in energy bills this winter.[24] The effect of these cost rises, in combination with long-term wage stagnation and no uprating of benefits in line with inflation, means that many millions of people will be in ill health and food, energy and fuel poverty. Communities around the country have already set up 'warm banks' as well as food banks.[25]

While we've been led to believe our markets are competitive and consumers can shop around, COVID-19 and the energy crisis have exposed the role of monopolies. In the case of both gas and electricity distribution networks, six companies have a market share of 94%. Among the gas networks, one operator has close to 50% of the total market share. It also has higher profit margins than any other sector in the economy.[26] Large oil companies are making huge profits in 2022 – a year that saw energy costs rise 23 times faster than wages – and are distributing these profits to shareholders rather than investing in decarbonisation.[27]

This doesn't have to be the case. Some of the owners of energy companies operating in the UK are foreign governments, such as French-owned EDF. In France, energy bills went up by 4% in spring 2022, while in the UK, they went up by 54%. While EDF made £106 million in the UK in 2020 alone, that was followed by overall losses, partly due to reduced nuclear output and to the cap imposed by the French government to shield consumers from soaring energy prices.[28] In contrast, the UK economy remains dominated by monopolistic practices, with some of its biggest corporations using the cash generated from profiteering to maintain their position, buying up or pricing out smaller rivals, and, increasingly, investing in financial markets. Indeed, some of the world's largest international monopolies are behaving like banks, using their cash to buy up the bonds (debts) of other corporations.[29] Meanwhile, in August 2022, then-chancellor Nadhim Zahawi stated that those earning £45,000 may need support for their energy bills; that is, over the top 20% income threshold of £43,700.[30]

There is little regulation of monopolies. The House of Commons Committee for Business, Energy and Industrial Strategy on the regulation of the energy sector concluded that the government had 'prioritised competition over effective market supervision, failing to recognise the fundamental importance of energy supply and maintain sight over Ofgem's actions'.[31] This failure of regulation has left the energy supply market and taxpayers more exposed to the global wholesale energy crisis. Not even the private sector is immune, as thousands of pubs and other venues face closure without immediate support.[32]

Market failure is affecting all essential areas of life in the UK. This is seen only too starkly in care provision. It is not a coincidence that there is little to no public conversation on the topic. The sector is monopolised by a handful of private equity firms. HC-One, the UK's largest care home operator, received an additional £18.9 million in government payments for Covid costs, while its owners, in the year 2020 alone, continued to siphon £47.2 million in tax-free profits to the Cayman Islands.[33] All the while, care homes are in a continual crisis, with the sector now losing one third of its staff every year.[34] Under-investment, coupled with demographic pressures, mean that an increasing number of people need adult social care and support but fewer are getting it, with many having much less than they need.[35]

Structural crises

Precarious work

Precarity has become an increasingly salient issue, especially for young people just joining the labour market. The rise of the gig economy, degree inflation, the casualisation of previously secure occupations such as academia and law, high housing costs and automation threaten the livelihoods and security of many.[36] Certainly, these pressures are more strongly felt lower down the income distribution; however, the top 10% is not immune, not because they are feeling the effects of these processes now, but because of the looming sense of fear for the future they elicit. Indeed, the threat of automation seems to be increasingly patent among high income earners, as artificial intelligence software such as ChatGTP threaten to render many professions obsolete.[37]

Few high earners we spoke with had experienced significant disruptions in their careers. While some had been directly affected by the financial crash, others remembered feeling only its 'ripples'. Nobody who started an ambitious upward trajectory had to change their career path due to, for example, health or family reasons, though to be sure, there may be a certain 'survivorship bias' in our sample, as we considered those who were in the top 10% at the time of being interviewed. Men in their forties or fifties, in particular, described uninterrupted career trajectories; most had stable upbringings, often with their mothers staying at home while their fathers worked. They often seek to replicate that model for their own families.

Nevertheless, at an age when their parents would have been moving into comfortable retirement, having paid off their mortgages and seen their children become independent, those in their fifties who had been recently divorced instead found that their upward trajectory wasn't as upward as they expected. Alan, in his fifties, whose interview we referred to earlier, talks about the prospect of continuing to work into his sixties and seventies, as he had recently been through an expensive divorce. Paul, an architect in his late forties, also divorced, imagines himself competing with younger versions of himself: "[you] find yourself back in the twenty-something's situation, but with less potential".

Younger high earners spoke with a similar insecurity in the face of a fiercely competitive labour market. Gemma, a management consultant in her late thirties, and one of the few respondents with no dependants, said she felt insecure about maintaining a sufficiently high income within the corporate sector. Having initially been drawn to the rigid structure of working in a large accountancy firm, she began to feel she was on "a treadmill" and left to become an independent contractor. However, she now finds this "a scary move", partly because there's no structured progression and her income "may go up and down a little". This relative insecurity is made worse because the amount of money she needs to sustain herself is increasing: "my stable bar gets higher all the time". She even explains that her decision not to have children is partly due to not wanting to feel "trapped financially [...], coming from a volatile economic background, where money was always really tight". When asked whether she has savings, Gemma says: "I have to keep a pot [...] because my job's really unstable". This chimes with recent research for the Economy 2030 Inquiry, which found that high earners fear losing their jobs, partly because they do not think the benefits system 'has their back'.[38]

The sense that those in the private sector must always be moving on, moving up and cannot take their position for granted is a striking yet common feature in their narratives. This contrasts with greater job retention and security in the public sector, if at lower earnings. In sum, insecurity and anxiety are prevalent for those in the private sector, particularly in the City of London, and those who live in London and the south-east. There, the cost of living is highest and they are more likely to be living near the super-rich.

Given this, many in the top 10% worry that their children will not be able to climb the ladder as they have done. The meritocratic rationale for the distance between those who do well and those who do not is the reward for effort, whether in the form of hard work or attaining educational credentials. Respondents such as Susannah, a top 1% earner, were starting to see that this link was weakening as middle-class jobs are being hollowed out:

> 'I worry about my kids. I don't know what they're going to do because of all the jobs [...] and I say this from a financial services background [...] a lot of the entry-level jobs have all been moved offshore. So, where I started, when I started my job at [accountancy firm] is now done in India and has been done in India for some years [...] So it's harder to break into those industries.'

Stephen, a law professor in his early fifties and in the top 6%, when asked if he agreed with the statement 'Broadly speaking, if you work hard, you will succeed in the UK', replied that there was "no guarantee of that at the moment, based on the number of graduates who find themselves in so-called dead-end jobs".

Housing

Perhaps unsurprisingly, research shows that the top 10% is more likely than the rest to have a mortgage.[39] In our sample, nearly all own their homes or are paying a mortgage, with some having two. Many of them have done well from the rise in house prices. The value of land has increased fivefold since 1995. Nevertheless, many among them feel the cost of housing and would like to see council tax and stamp duty replaced with a proportional property tax.[40] Over half of the UK's wealth is now locked up in land, dwarfing the amounts vested in savings. Britain's broken housing market and housing crisis is in fact a land crisis, as Guy Shrubsole demonstrates in *Who Owns England?*:

> Politicians can talk all they like about building more homes, or slashing planning regulations to free up developers. But fail to tackle sky-high land prices, and all you'll end up with is a bunch more unaffordable houses. Housing developers are often accused of land banking to bolster their profits, but in reality all landowners have a propensity to hoard land – and to demand as high a price as they can get when they come to selling it.[41]

Older generations have benefited from rapid rises in the value of their homes, generous occupational pension provision, decades of healthy wage growth, free university tuition when they themselves studied, tax breaks for pension saving and capital gains on main homes, and the 'triple lock' on the state pension.[42] The young, meanwhile, spend an increasing percentage of their earnings on rent, all while real wages have stagnated. Considering this, it's unsurprising that a growing number of young adults are living with their parents. In 2018, a third of those privately renting in the UK only had £23 to spend on anything else each week after paying for their rent, gas, electricity, and food.[43] And this was before COVID-19 and the cost of living crisis.

The housing market continues to move further out of reach for many young people. The stamp duty holiday introduced in July 2020 to kick-start the housing market, together with increased demand for larger properties due to homeworking, has contributed to the fastest rise in house prices since 2005.[44] The average age for owning your first home is now 33 and a third of those first-time owners will have had help from 'the bank of mum and dad', partnering or government support.[45] After more than a decade of low interest rates and rising house prices following the 2008 financial crisis, the 2020s are now seeing interest rates *and* house prices increase – and sharply so. This could have serious political repercussions if highly indebted homeowners – having been sold the idea of home ownership as a rite of passage and ploughed hard-earned savings into their deposits – were to see mortgages become increasingly unaffordable or unavailable, as indeed we saw in the market response to Truss's 2022 mini-budget.

Paul, the architect in his early forties whom we introduced earlier, lives in London, and reflects on the ability of his children to buy houses, particularly in the south-east. He advised them to stay up north, where they studied: "I have told my three children, who've been to university in Birmingham, Keele and Manchester, that they should consider staying in the north to have a higher standard of living."

The importance of inheritance in transmitting inequality is evident in housing. It presents a challenge not only to meritocratic views but also to the ideal of modern life, what in the US is called the 'American Dream'. Paul continues to ponder the relationship between housing and inequality:

> 'It's intergenerational, isn't it? My children will be able to pay their rent, but don't know what will happen, there's no gaining any security as it stands. […] It's Thatcher's effect on Britain, to make people insecure and greedy. People grab enough for themselves. They have to be all right. But there's a loss of belief in the community, a divergence between those who've got

it and those who haven't. The property market is an indicator. [...] It excludes a lot of people. For a whole generation [owning a home] won't be taking place. It matters where and when you're born.'

The prospects for the financial reforms needed to change the housing circumstances for young people are unlikely in the short term. There is little political will in the ruling parties.[46] What this will mean for the top 10% is uncertain; it could mean further attempts to shore up their assets, but also resentment if they cannot do that. As we found in our follow-up interviews, many older children are remaining in the parental home, with pressing consequences for the quality of life, family formation, mental health and career progression.

Wealth inequality

In most countries, and certainly in the UK, wealth inequality is much greater than income inequality and getting worse at a faster rate.[47] Globally, unrecorded offshore wealth has grown exponentially since the 1980s, significantly more than recorded onshore wealth; and in the case of the UK, it is valued at 15–20% of GDP.[48] Net private wealth has risen from 300% of the national economy in the 1970s to over 600% today.[49] This increase has been driven by growth in the price of property and the value of private pensions. A recent Resolution Foundation report describes the extent of wealth inequality:

> Wealth gaps have not just grown over time, they are also extremely high from an international perspective. The share of wealth held by the richest 10 per cent in the UK is in line with the OECD average, but the gap between these rich families and the poorest 40 per cent of the distribution (measured as a multiple of median earnings) is the second highest in the OECD – only the US is more unequal.[50]

'Extraction capitalism', as Stewart Lansley has termed it, is 'the latest incarnation of the collective monopoly power of the nineteenth century'.[51] However, while this form of capitalism and its resultant inequality has become the norm, it is unlikely that the country will improve economically while we continue to ignore the effects of wealth growing so much faster than income, partly because any corporations and individuals sitting on income-generating assets will not be motivated to innovate or invest in new businesses. Low corporation tax even encourages working individuals to move labour income into companies and, as share ownership is concentrated in the hands of the wealthy, these tax incentives on corporate profits benefit almost exclusively those who are already well-off.

Despite what right-wing think tanks would have you believe, low taxes at the top disproportionately benefit those with savings and assets, which produces economic stagnation and inequality. The wealthy spend a smaller percentage of their income on simply getting by than those who need to work to survive; they are, increasingly, the only ones who can save. This decreases overall demand and limits who is able to save. In this context, monopolies are inevitable. Employees can't negotiate the wages they receive related to output and neither can they – along with consumers and regulators – influence the markup of selling prices over costs.[52]

Furthermore, modern wealth is largely dependent on wealth accumulated in the past. As Piketty puts it, wealth grows more rapidly than the rate of growth of income and output,[53] 'capital reproduces itself faster than output increases. The past devours the future.'[54] This can be seen in the historical injustices of legacies that have started to gain salience. Movements such as Black Lives Matter have begun to put a spotlight on how the wealth of the truly wealthy in the UK is based on a long history of exploitation of non-White people.[55]

The dominance of capital in the UK isn't only useful for wealthy Brits. According to Oliver Bullough, in his celebrated book *Butler to the World*, Britain 'operates as a gigantic loophole, undercutting other countries' rules, massaging down tax rates, neutering regulations, [and] laundering foreign criminals' money'.[56] We are now seeing the consequences in sectors including energy, banking and care of having become a 'paradise' for disaster capitalists. Not only that, but as Bullough reminds us:

It's not just that Britain isn't investigating the crooks, it's helping them too. Moving and investing their money is of course central to what the UK does, but that's only the start: it's also educating their children, solving their legal disputes, easing their passage into global high society, hiding their crimes and generally letting them dodge the consequences of their actions.[57]

Climate change

Tackling climate change will require a profound transformation that will have a massive impact on households and their consumption. Individual carbon footprints will have to be cut from 8.5 tonnes to 2.5 tonnes by 2030, which will require huge change and disruption. The gaps between environmental targets and actual footprints show that high-income countries need to reduce their emissions by 91–95% before 2050.[58] However, lead author on the Intergovernmental Panel on Climate Change (IPCC) Lorraine Whitmarsh warned that 'we are going nowhere'.[59]

This is unsurprising to many commentators. Stewart Lansley points out that business as usual has long been 'bad for livelihoods, resilience and the environment, while big business has mostly eschewed any sense of wider responsibility to society, the workforce or the planet'.[60] Equally unsurprising, given its track record, is that the UK government has not signalled much urgency on the matter. Instead, it hints that British people shouldn't need to disrupt their behaviour or lifestyles. This is despite the fact that, for example, climate objectives will not be met without a major improvement in UK housing.[61] How can sustainable homes be made affordable? Are the workforce and the housing sector ready to deliver the changes needed? How can policy help drive this change? How can we avoid the costs of transition landing unfairly or its benefits being unfairly distributed?

While research shows that the higher your income, the more likely you are to worry about climate change, the topic rarely appeared in our interviews, and when it did, it did so only cursorily when respondents were asked about their fears for the future. Carbon-intensive luxury consumption is globally responsible for half of all emissions. Each member of the top 10% of global emitters produced on average 27.7 tonnes in 2019.[62] The equivalent from low-income groups is significantly lower: the top 10% produces 48% of all emissions, while the bottom 50% produces only 12%.[63] Plus, let's not forget that a disproportionate share of people from wealthy countries will be included in that 10%.

These figures demonstrate that the main driver of climate change isn't overpopulation or birth rates in poorer countries. The rich emit more carbon, not only through the goods and services they consume but also through their investments. This means that high earners will have to make a greater effort at curbing emissions, but the opposite is happening. Lower-income groups are shouldering the burden as recently happened in France, where the government raised carbon taxes in a way that hit those on low incomes in rural areas, kick-starting the *gilets jaunes* (yellow vests) movement. One of the few interviewees who spoke at length on the climate was Jonathan, a barrister near retirement. On a gloomy note, he said:

> 'The world's collapsing. We're at the end of our days. Global warming, rising seas, floods [...] I see no remission in that. [I am] not convinced my daughter will see out her natural life [...] In another 50 years there will not be a world in recognisable form.'

Social reproduction under threat

Healthcare

Before the pandemic, indicators of health inequality in the UK were already getting starker. From the beginning of the 20th century, Britain experienced continuous improvements in life expectancy but from 2011 these improvements slowed dramatically, almost grinding to a halt. In 2020, for the first time in more than 100 years, life expectancy failed to increase across the country and for the poorest 10% of women it declined.[64] The year 2015 saw the largest rise in mortality since the Second World War.[65]

Powerful evidence on health and wellbeing inequalities – and how these are reflected in education, employment, income and quality of life – has been published since the well-known 1977 Black Report (*Inequalities in Health*) and later in the 2010 and 2020 Marmot reviews. The latter illustrated how the 2010s austerity has affected the social determinants of health in the short, medium and long term. These range from rising child poverty, declines in education funding, increased precarity and a housing affordability crisis, to a rise in homelessness and increasing reliance on food banks. Darkly, the reviews suggest we will see many of these impacts only in the longer term when austerity's children are adults.

COVID-19 reminded high earners that the NHS, public health and social care are crucial for the wellbeing of us all. However, pressures relating to public sector pay, austerity and a cost of living crisis have presented an unprecedented threat to the health and wellbeing of the UK.[66] High earners are fearful that waiting times and beleaguered service provision will not provide for them and their families. Several spoke to us about 'going private' when they could. Indeed, the UK now pays almost as much as the US in out-of-pocket healthcare, with the number of people resorting to crowdfunding campaigns to pay exorbitant private medical expenses rising 20-fold in the past five years. It is also the people who can least afford them who are paying the most. Between 2010 and 2020, the portion of UK spending that went on hospital treatments increased by 60% overall, but more than doubled among the lowest-earning fifth of the population. The poorest now spend as much on private medical care as the richest, in relative terms.[67]

The extent to which higher earners will continue to be insulated from the worst of inequalities is debatable. Marmot warned a focus on the poorest and the very richest is obscuring more widespread health inequalities, with 'middle class people [...] missing out on an average of eight years of full and active life because of deep-seated inequality'.[68] Conditions that lead to marked health disparities are detrimental to all members of society, with some types of health inequalities having 'obvious spillover effects on the rest of society, for example, the spread of infectious diseases, the consequences of alcohol and drug misuse, or the occurrence of violence and crime'.[69] Economic inequalities, for example, were shown in the US to be closely related to the frequency of deaths from external causes such as homicides and accidents.[70] Put this way, reducing health inequalities would benefit all of society by reducing the incidence of spillover effects. Woodward and Kawachi conclude: 'A society that tolerates a steep socioeconomic gradient in health outcomes will experience a drag on improvements in life expectancy, and pay the cost via excess health care utilisation.'[71]

All of the health inequalities described and their spillover effects will have significant impacts on social care, which has been an ongoing national crisis for decades. This has been compounded by an ageing population, a declining number of hospital beds and the responsibility having been shifted from hospitals to cash-strapped local authorities. It has been made worse by devastating losses to local services from cuts in central government funding, at a time when demand for services has soared. Austerity cuts have also forced responsibility for social care to be shifted onto families. Cuts were more severe in deprived areas while spending in fact increased in more affluent ones, which means our respondents were unlikely to notice.[72] However, it's crucial for high earners to understand that the crisis in social care has a direct effect on the speed at which acute hospital services can meet patient needs. A collapsed healthcare system slows down the discharge process, which in turn leads to fewer available beds and increased waiting times. Marmot warns: 'if health has stopped improving it is a sign that society has stopped improving. Evidence from around the world shows that health is a good measure of social and economic progress. When a society is flourishing, health tends to flourish.'[73]

Education

Millennials are the first generation not to achieve the progress their predecessors enjoyed, on a number of living standard measures, including pay stagnation, a shift towards less-well-paid and precarious employment, lower home-ownership rates and higher housing costs (spending a quarter of their income on housing).[74] Since 2012, there has also been a noticeable decline in real terms spending on education, falling by about 14% to its

2005–06 level, with the biggest drops found in education for 16- to 18-year-olds.[75] Higher education funding has also been erratic, with cuts to the sector offset by the tripling of tuition fees after 2011. This has given the UK the second most expensive higher education system in the OECD, only after the US. Nevertheless, spending specifically on higher education has little effect on educational achievement. At best, higher education institutions can only partly compensate for the effects of inequalities that start early in students' lives. While Millennials are the best-educated generation in history, the cohort-on-cohort gains experienced by Generation X have not been reproduced. The 37% increase in degree attainment recorded between the 1969–71 and 1972–74 cohorts fell to just a 7% improvement between those born in the early and late 1980s. And as the Intergenerational Commission pointed out, 'non-degree routes have not picked up the slack'.[76]

Despite acknowledging their luck in having access to a university grant, avoiding the levels of educational debt seen today, and joining the labour market before the current credential inflation, our respondents nevertheless underplayed the importance of networks and social capital accessed by attending top universities and private schools, which seem to be ever more important. Many seemed to retain a belief in meritocracy and education as its vehicle.

Whenever we asked for the drivers of poverty, education was at the forefront, regardless of the fact that we have seen declining real wages and casualisation in parallel to increasing educational attainment. In a recent poll by *The New Statesman*, 60% of British people believe that an individual can change their social class in their lifetime, despite only 25% saying they have themselves changed class. The poll results also demonstrated that young people in the UK are becoming less confident about their future: 'Many worry they will never be financially stable, a rising proportion don't feel in control of their lives, and nearly half feel hopeless because of unemployment.'[77] Jonathan Mijs, assistant professor of sociology at Boston University, who specialises in perceptions of meritocracy and inequality, attributes this to a gap between aspiration, belief and lived experience. 'Perhaps they believe they will climb the ladder at some future time, or maybe their belief stems from the many stories of upward mobility that reach them through social media, TV and film; the exceptions to the rule that keep their hopes alive.'[78]

While some of our respondents might be able to afford private schools and save for their children's university fees, they were aware that it was getting harder to gain admission and pay for university education, and to get a well-paying job on the basis of your degree after graduation. The extent of elitism in our education system is illustrated by the 48 out of 211 sixth formers from Eton who got Oxbridge places in 2021, roughly the same number who got in out of the UK's estimated 33,250 state school sixth formers claiming free school meals.[79] Unsurprisingly, top private schools' alumni go on to monopolise senior positions in elite professional, financial and managerial jobs.[80] For example, only 7% of children attend private schools, yet 70% of judges went to one. In the US, something similar applies. Lauren Rivera's *Pedigree: How 'Elite' Students Get 'Elite' Jobs* demonstrates 'that the way in which elite employers define and evaluate merit when hiring strongly tilts the playing field for the nation's highest paying jobs toward children from socioeconomically privileged backgrounds'.[81] This includes recruiting primarily from a select number of universities, themselves accessible to a privileged few.

Crisis of democracy

Between 2016 and 2022, Britain saw one historic referendum, two general elections, five prime ministers and a chaotically handled pandemic. A large percentage of the population are disillusioned by British democracy and unsure whether 'business as usual' can simply continue. Just as monopolies have become the norm in the economy, so too in our democracy. Without fundamental change, many foresee the alternative will be either greater xenophobic nationalism or a privatised technocracy (or both).[82]

The continuity of a well-functioning democracy requires safeguards designed to ensure that a government cannot do too much damage during its term of office or subvert the democratic process to prolong itself. These safeguards are under threat or already becoming weaker and, if we are not careful, there is nothing to prevent the UK from turning into a 'managed democracy'. In the past years, parliamentary scrutiny has also been under threat. A clear example is the unlawful prorogation of parliament to avoid its scrutiny of Boris Johnson's plan to leave the EU without an agreed deal on 31 October 2019. Another is the resignation of two of Johnson's ethics advisers within two years, due to being unable to support his breaches of the ministerial code.[83]

The integrity of our democracy is also maintained by regulatory review, most importantly by the Electoral Commission, the formerly independent body that is meant to ensure that elections are free and fair. However, in 2021, it was announced by the government that the commission would be stripped of its powers to propose criminal prosecutions, and be overseen by a Conservative-dominated committee of MPs.[84] This attack is seen partly as a result of the commission calling the Conservatives to account for irregularities in the Brexit referendum.

The Conservatives have been in Number 10 for 63% of the time since 1950, despite receiving 41% of the votes cast throughout this duration, compared to Labour's 40%. Most votes went to parties to the left of the Conservatives in 18 of the 19 general elections in this period.[85] In 2017, under our current voting system, only 11% of constituencies changed hands: the remainder were 'safe' for the incumbent party. Under the current first-past-the-post system, 70% of votes are not counted and therefore wasted.[86]

In 2019, the Conservatives gained power with less than 44% of the vote. On average, 38,264 votes were needed to elect one Conservative MP in the last election, while that figure was 50,835 votes for Labour, 336,038 for the Liberal Democrats, and 865,000 to elect Caroline Lucas, Britain's only Green Party MP (2.7% of votes returning 0.2% parliamentary seats). Those campaigning for a more democratic voting system refer to this pattern as the 'inverted pyramid of power'.[87] Voters are starting to question how democratic our electoral system is and the possibility of reforming it is increasingly becoming 'a doorstep issue', certainly among younger voters.

Speaking one's mind, critically challenging government decisions and protesting peacefully are a vital part of a healthy free society. However, the pandemic has been used as a moment to, as Mark Thomas says, 'chip away' rights and silence dissent.[88]

In 2021, in just 48 hours, the Policing Bill, the Elections Bill, and the Nationality and Borders Bill were introduced with the government at risk of turning the UK into one of the only countries in Europe without a right to peaceful protest.

At the same time, three quarters of the UK press is controlled by three people: Lord Rothermere, Rupert Murdoch and the Barclay family. All of them present a consistently right-wing view of public events and issues, 'that of a handful of wealthy individuals based outside the UK, whose personal objectives bear no relationship to those of 99% of the population'.[89] On top of this dominance of the right in the press, the party that has been in power for 12 years is now consulting on plans to stifle whistle-blowers and journalists who might embarrass the government by leaking details of its activities.

The 1998 Human Rights Act, the main piece of law that protects freedoms and human rights in the UK, is also being replaced with a British Bill of Rights. With this new Bill, the duty to ensure that legislation is compatible with rights and freedoms will no longer exist. Public bodies will have no obligation to respect such rights and neither will the courts have to follow European judgments. This has profound implications for the devolution settlements, which legally require active compliance with the European Convention on Human Rights, especially the Good Friday Agreement that has guaranteed peace in Northern Ireland. The politics of devolution is already fragile. In May 2022, Sinn Féin won the most seats – and first preference votes – in the Northern Ireland Assembly election, becoming the first pro-reunification party to win an Assembly election in Stormont, while the Scottish National Party and the Scottish Greens enjoy a healthy pro-independence majority in Holyrood. In short, as Stephen Gethins puts it: 'The UK is in trouble. Voters have backed an independence referendum in Scotland and a Northern Irish party seeking Irish reunification. But you would never know it if you listened to debate and discussion at Westminster.'[90]

Our respondents tended not to mention any of these ways in which democracy has been undermined, although they did discuss the relationship between the press and the right wing of politics. They were not activists and did not attend protests so they were unlikely to be aware of the freedoms being curtailed.

However, they did feel isolated from politics, and did not think that they were represented. Those in Scotland conveyed an added lack of identification with British politics. Post-pandemic, they were also aware that Boris Johnson's position had repeatedly been undermined by scandal, but there was a sense that there was no alternative.

We can't solve collective problems individually

Data tell us that while economic development and rising living standards are important drivers of wellbeing in the developing world, having more makes less of a difference to wellbeing in richer countries.[91] The weight of evidence also shows that economic growth in the UK has slowed markedly and that the fruits of whatever growth we had went overwhelmingly to very few at the top.

Despite being concerned about the societal effects of inequality, few if any high earners can envision how to make Britain's economy and politics more equal, robust, resilient and free. Nevertheless, it is clear the most serious problems we face are too big for any one segment of society, or perhaps even one country, to deal with. The climate emergency has been aptly described as 'a collective action problem on steroids',[92] and one that will have to be navigated by the whole of society and even the whole global community.

Problems such as climate change are too big for any one group in society to address, no matter how influential that group might be. And crucially, solutions designed in isolation won't work. Designing policies to tackle climate change, for example, without corresponding policies to address inequality, will not work. Reducing inequality, on the other hand, will increase the wellbeing of entire populations, which will in turn lessen their environmental impact.

In other words, those in positions of power in government and political parties need to formulate policies that work not only to improve life for their own demographic, but for their children too. Even if Labour forms a future government with a huge majority, it is unlikely to set out a programme of sufficient structural change to enable this to happen. Nowhere is this starker than in the need for collective agency on climate change. This requires both that we think again about what governments can do for us and that those in government rethink their own role. Why and why now? Because, regardless of their shortcomings, only states have the capacity to bring about the scale of change needed to address a problem the size of climate change. They can and should take on the strategic leadership role in living a cheaper, easier, more tranquil life, moving towards net zero. Part of this means bringing stakeholders together across the economy and civil society, part of it means providing better education and awareness to signal the extent of behavioural change that will be needed in schools, businesses and organisations.

Nevertheless, most responses to recent and ongoing crises have been personal rather than collective. Rather than cumulative, concerted action on the environment, individual actions such as recycling have tended to be prioritised. This is especially the case among high earners, a group that feels increasingly isolated, living by an ethos that prioritises hard work, mobility, individual responsibility, flexibility and accumulating resources to improve their own circumstances. The next chapter looks in more detail at those strategies.

6

Jumping ship, but where to?

This chapter explores what respondents told us about their experiences of weathering shocks in the past: the financial crash in 2008, Brexit and the pandemic. We reflect on how they might act when facing similar shocks in the future and whether these approaches will remain effective. We begin by talking about the ability to be mobile and competitive.

Mobility

High earners see being flexible enough to move as a means of ensuring they continue to thrive, including relocating abroad. This 'brain drain' mirrors the capital mobility that is the foundation of the UK's financialised and internationalised economic model, explains the magnetic pull of the City of London, and underpins the view that any turn to the left would cause capital flight.[1] When we first interviewed Alan in 2019, a 50-year-old director of a logistics company living in the south-east, he was considering the benefits of higher tax countries: "A progressive tax system, not an outrageous tax system. Not a tax rate of 95% at the top that doesn't encourage wealth creation. There should be balances. We should be like Nordic countries. High taxation but high benefits as well." By the time of our follow-up, in early 2022, he had moved to Finland.

One consequence of this mobility is that, while high earners may anticipate a crisis, they almost never think that it will affect them personally. As Ben, a 39-year-old IT consultant living in the south-east explains, he can rely on his membership to a globally competitive and mobile workforce:

'For my own future within the UK, I'm pessimistic. Brexit is a big factor colouring that […]. My wife is Bulgarian so my daughter can also have Bulgarian nationality. If things go badly, it's not too difficult to move. If it goes really badly in the UK, I can see us moving overseas.'

However, relying on mobility as a strategy to avoid crises in a post-Brexit, post-COVID-19 world may prove increasingly difficult. Some respondents expressed insecurity about the impact of Brexit: they saw it as an event that could affect them personally. When interviewed about his views on the future before the pandemic, Sean, the 40-year-old owner of an HR company in the top 1%, told us: "I feel pessimistic about the future of my country and optimistic about my future. However, depending on the outcome of Brexit that may change to both being pessimistic."

His fears were not unjustified. When we interviewed him again after the pandemic, his plans to move to Gran Canaria had been thwarted by Brexit. As immigration policies become more restrictive across much of the world – whether because of the pandemic, war, refugee crises or old-fashioned immigrant scapegoating – many in the top 10% may also see their capacity to move curtailed, even if their wealth and educational credentials are considered.

Mobility also has limited long-term value as a strategy against climate change. As we mentioned earlier, our respondents rarely brought up unprompted the issue of climate, and when they did, it was generally cursorily. However, the scale of the challenge cannot be ignored for long. Michael, a 49-year-old engineer, just in the top 10% living in the south-west and one of only a few to mention the topic, said: "We're all strapped to the same planet!"

Insulation

Not all high earners can physically move away from societal and economic shocks. They may not have the skills required in other markets, the capacity to simply pack bags and go, or may have dependants keeping them in place. So what are the alternatives? The first is to try and insulate themselves from the worst effects of such crises. William, a management consultant and a top 1% earner in his forties, found that even though his team had disappeared overnight after the 2008 crisis, the first salvo of this new era, he still kept his job. Maria, a marketing director also in her forties on a top 3% income, felt she had been "insulated" from the 2008 crisis as, while her department had been reduced, she had simply moved to another part of the firm. Alan, a 50-year-old director of a logistics company, also in the top 3%, confessed that the crisis had "bypassed him" but felt that "in services and its effects, it is not over for normal people".

This insulation from 'normal people' is worth teasing out. Luke, 27, spent the first part of his life in a private school, enlisted in the army, then attended Oxbridge. He was later a teacher in the Teach First programme before starting work as a consultant for a large accountancy firm. He told us that his background meant he doesn't really think about inequality on a daily basis. He comes from a privileged upbringing and all his friends do too. He does not interact with anyone outside his socioeconomic group, although he did when he was a teacher: "It was clear I was teaching kids with very different lives." Yet Luke was still surprised to find his income placed him in the top 8% of income distribution. He thought more people would be above him and, looking for a house to buy in London at the time, he didn't feel particularly affluent.

In addition, high earners were also insulated from the pandemic by being more likely to be able to work from home, thus reducing the risk of catching Covid while saving on commuting and other costs.[2] It also allowed them to save or invest in their homes. Amazon sales went through the roof at the same time as COVID-19 deaths tended to concentrate among the most vulnerable groups in society.[3] Michael, the engineer with a top 10% income quoted earlier, said that he tries to make his life "as bulletproof as possible, not too sensitive to global conditions or local ones". By the time of our follow-up interview, Paul, an architect just in the top 10% income band when we first interviewed him, had moved into the top 3% in 2022. While his practice had suffered initially, a government loan allowed it to stay in business. During the lockdowns, he had also taken a consultancy, "cashing in on his experience". As a result, when asked if the cost of living crisis had affected him, he said "I feel quite well-off. There has been significant improvement in my income."

During the lockdowns, better-off families reduced consumption to a greater degree than poorer ones, as they tended to spend a higher proportion of their income on social goods and services that were less available during the pandemic such as restaurants and leisure travel. Meanwhile, lower-income families deploy a larger percentage of their earnings on essentials that cannot be reduced, such as food, bills and housing. It was the same with the wealth of the richest. During the pandemic, 'a typical family in the richest 10% of families experienced an increase in the value of their wealth by £44,000 per adult'.[4]

If the pandemic had any positive potential, it was to bring to bear the importance of low-paid key workers and instil in us a greater sense of social solidarity. However, and more tangibly, it threatened to exacerbate the increasing inequalities of the past decades. It also risked insulating the top 10% even more than they were before: their only social interaction with those on lower incomes being their status as clients (of the gig economy and delivery services, for instance).

Some of the high earners we spoke with think inequality has diminished between the lower and middle classes, citing increased material consumption of cars and TVs as evidence. Nevertheless, they also think it's growing between the very wealthiest and the rest, though only a few, such as Maria, were explicit about the scale of inequality in the UK and its destabilising effects: "I think what is really key in the last 10 years, maybe 20 years, is [that] the difference between CEO pay and executive-level pay and people on the shop floor is totally ridiculous and unsustainable. And this creates a big sense of animosity."

Isolation

High earners are generally not tied to one local community: this in itself holds a status that extends to other areas of life, such as independence from public services. As Alan, a logistics company director in his fifties living in the south-east with a top 3% income, put it: "[I]solation from social context is something that only the very wealthiest can achieve." Respondents often commuted from areas largely segregated by income. If they live in a mixed-income area, long working hours, especially in the corporate sector, don't allow them to make time for their local communities. The rules of climbing the ladder are applied as much to parenting and to time spent outside work. Rachel, a treasurer for a multinational organisation with a top 1% income, when asked whether she mixes with people from different socioeconomic backgrounds, responded: "How much interaction are we talking about? Friends and family? No. But my kids go to the local swimming pool on a poor estate and I happily participate with other parents. My son goes to their houses to play."

These segregated realities are also true for high earners' online lives. If working from home, high earners tend to subscribe to networks of similar professionals. Our social media narrows down, reinforces and feeds back to us what we want to read. This phenomenon, which has come to be called the 'echo chambers', is as true for high-achieving, highly educated individuals who feel well informed as for everyone else. In fact, research has shown that the more political media people consume, the more mistaken they are about the other side's perspectives.[5] That is partly why election results seem to always take us by surprise.

One of the consequences of this isolation may be high earners' lack of sociological imagination discussed earlier. Douglas, who has worked in the public sector for most of his career, was one of the few, for example, to comment on the unequal impact of the pandemic: "Middle-class people were phoning for pizzas to be delivered by poorer people. [COVID-19's impact] very much depended on your occupation [...]. The people screwed were those not able to furlough whose wage rates had been squeezed."

The competitive pressures of work and the status of busyness, of not having time, of being quick on your feet act as a barrier to connecting with others. Hannah, a 44-year-old occupational health consultant, living in the south-east and earning just above the 10% threshold, reflected:

> 'We're all so busy running around, living our individual lives and I for one have such little time to do what I feel

I need to do, that I haven't got anything left. I think part of this is because of increased expectations [...] the hours that people commute, the hours they spend at work [...] we don't have the same connections.'

Hannah's comments chime with a pervasive sense of the increased pace of life among our respondents, something that sociologist Hartmut Rosa has written extensively about. Acceleration is one of the key features of modern society; changes in technology, social tendencies and the pace of life render our lives harder to predict and our commitments more fluid.[6] The desire for a simpler, happier past is shared across generations – with around 70% of people in each age category holding this view today – which may explain the appeal of those politicians who wish to bring back an imaginary view of the 'good old days'.[7]

Meanwhile, much of life outside work is reduced to what David Graeber referred to as 'compensatory consumerism': 'pumping iron or attending a yoga class at the local gym, ordering out from Deliveroo, watching an episode of Game of Thrones, or shopping for hand creams or consumer electronics'.[8] Similarly, sociologist Robert Putnam wrote that there's been a 'striking shift in how we allocate time – toward ourselves and our immediate family and away from the wider community'.[9] Besides the well-documented decline in involvement in organisations such as clubs, political groups, unions or churches, there may also have been a reduction in the amount of time spent informally interacting face-to-face with others outside our immediate circles such as our neighbours. This is happening in all groups, with a corresponding decline in the availability and quality of public spaces such as public libraries and swimming pools.[10]

All of these tendencies mean it's increasingly rare for high earners to get to know people outside their usual interaction with friends, family, work and education, especially when other networks (such as those based on religion or hobbies) either dwindle or move online. Considering this group's disproportionate political influence, this is not innocuous. In unequal societies, how people treat each other is affected by income differences; there is less social mixing, less social mobility and less respect granted to those from different social strata. Research on the wealthy in Paris,

São Paulo and Delhi has shown this.[11] In addition, marriages between people from different socioeconomic backgrounds are less common, with an increase in what sociologists call 'assortative mating'.[12] There is also more residential segregation. We are more separated from each other – culturally, socially and physically. We become increasingly worried about how people judge us relative to others and social contact is more stressful. As a result, everyone keeps more to themselves.

Unequal societies also have poorer mental health, with higher rates of psychotic conditions, narcissism, lack of confidence, low self-esteem, depression, and anxiety.[13] People trust each other less, and less trust means more stress. Although the top 10% may be floating away in their own socioeconomic bubble, that mistrust still engulfs them: it's both the cause and consequence of their isolation. Our respondent Hannah also told us: "The other thing that stops me from doing other things is also fear. We've also become much more fearful of being involved with other people and of putting ourselves out there to do something."

In highly unequal countries, which the UK is increasingly becoming, we are less likely to be helpful to each other; community life deteriorates and violence is more common. A vague but ever-present fear manifests itself in, among other things, the higher percentage of the labour force employed in guarding duties.[14] At their worst, these fears end up fuelling trends such as the increasing demand for bunkers for the rich in far-off countries such as New Zealand to prepare for a post-apocalyptic world.[15] Maria, a marketing director with a top 3% income, was one of several respondents to voice concerns about insecurity and civic unrest: "if you don't distribute that wealth then you get inequality and then there's discontent. Then, once you get discontent you get civil unrest and then, you know [...] slippery slope."

What these strategies of insulation, isolation and social distancing all achieve, however unintentionally, is a decline in trust. Even high earners cannot live without trust. It is a needed component of not only large and complex societies but also of the economy itself. Any transaction that's more than just a face-to-face barter of goods depends on trust, as the goods and services being exchanged will be separated in time and place. Trust is both more essential and more fragile in the modern economy where distances and chains of connections have been stretched even further and we will need to build appropriate institutions to strengthen it.[16] Figure 6.1 portrays a nightmare vision of what happens in a world of bunkers without trust and a functioning public realm.

Figure 6.1: 'Daddy!' by Peter Schrank

Source: © Peter Schrank/The Independent

Enabling the wealthy

Many in the top 10% have jobs whose purpose is to service, support and protect the wealth of the top 1%. Indeed, whole cottage industries have sprung up to supply the needs and whims of those with the most capital: from furnishers of high-end consumer products to family offices concentrated in London that provide expert services to manage the wealth of some of the highest-net-worth individuals in the world. As we saw in Chapter 3, quite a few high earners also see the public role of the private sector only as paying taxes, increasing value for shareholders and creating jobs. Wang, a doctor and entrepreneur, was very clear on this:

> 'The system is clearly engineered for the benefit of the wealthy. Skewed to the benefit of wealthy investors. I don't believe in trickle-down. It just leads to accumulation of wealth. Having integrated with the wealthy, society creates these structures to accommodate the desire of the wealthy to stay wealthy.'

However, this subservience to the wealthy does not only apply to accountants, corporate lawyers, hedge fund managers or other such professions. It is also true of us, the authors, and other cultural sector workers, academics, doctors, scientists and economists who facilitate the status quo. They make living in the capital more attractive, driving the concentration of talent and housing market speculation. Their parents have often sought to bequeath their children a fighting chance in a labour market where qualifications and expertise on their own cannot guarantee access to good jobs. And they work for organisations that are often owned, funded or overseen by the truly wealthy and well connected. For instance, anyone with experience in the charitable sector will know that many of those working or volunteering within it tend to be quite wealthy themselves and unlikely to challenge the interests of the top 1%.[17]

This enabling of the wealthy also applies to the way knowledge is produced in academia and extramural organisations. Be it because of funding priorities, disciplinary fads, or the pressures of peer review, much of the way that policy-relevant knowledge is produced has traditionally tended to speak to a narrow community of specialists or be critical in a way that allows access to a professional niche but doesn't achieve much else. Ghosh and Ambler put it this way for the case of economics: 'Much of the mainstream discipline has been in the service of power, effectively the power of the wealthy, at national and international levels. By "assuming away" critical concerns, theoretical results and problematic empirical analyses effectively reinforce power structures and imbalances.'[18]

One of the most successful things that the wealthy have done is, in the words of polemicist Owen Jones, to 'persuade the middle class that they're middle class too'.[19] When politicians talk about middle England, they are not always talking about people on median incomes, but actually about affluent voters in 'upper-class Britain' – they are the 'middle class' in the British sense of the term, after all. This is how tax rises on incomes over £80,000 can be presented as an attack on middle Britain, even though 19 out of 20 of us earn less than that.

However, while they often work for and with the wealthiest, the interests of the top 10% are and will become increasingly quite different. It's in the interest of the top 10% for education to provide genuine opportunities, for housing to be affordable, for work to pay well, for society to remain minimally flexible and open to new people and views, for there to be a functioning and transparent state, and for there to be a democracy at all. It's not difficult to think of modern authoritarian countries where the 1% is very well catered for, whether living in gated communities or free zones. Maria, quoted earlier, comments on the end result of a highly unequal distribution of income: "Even from an economic point of view if those people haven't got money they're not going to be buying your goods and services. So on a basic level, get with the programme [...] these people need to have a decent life [...] otherwise your circle's going to run out."

Notwithstanding the 'othering' evident in the reference to 'these people' in Maria's statement, she is one of the few to articulate that if those on a lower income don't have enough income then this affects the whole economy. Similarly, Paul, who as an architect was sensitive to housing trends, and living between Liverpool and London was able to contrast them, commented on the relationship between wealth and the unsustainability of extreme gentrification:

'It's not possible for a city to survive for any extended period of time if it only meets the needs of a small, wealthy minority. Even the most abstract financial service work depends upon an infrastructure of waged and unwaged care labour; even unoccupied trophy housing requires ongoing maintenance to keep deterioration at bay. A relative handful of high-wage jobs and so-called high-net-worth individuals cannot keep a city going, to say nothing about questions of justice.'[20]

Accumulating and hoarding

Inequality increases our concern with status and the importance of money. In her book *Get It Together*, journalist Zoe Williams states that 'wanting stuff is basically social' because it is a way of sending signals to each other about who we are. However, we can't simply flaunt our possessions. Signalling 'I can afford this thing, therefore I'm the best,' is an isolating, not a social-inducing act. The designer bag, or whatever it is, the purpose of which is to distinguish us from others, ends up also separating us from them. The satisfaction in owning it is therefore temporary.[21]

We saw how this 'compensatory consumption' took on a particular meaning as a coping mechanism during the pandemic, with online consumption, particularly for household items, as a means of spending unused income. When asked if his spending had changed during the pandemic, Paul replied "lots of online shopping". Sean, a 1% income earner and owner of an HR company, when asked the same question, similarly replied: "Everyone has been telling me how much they saved. I don't think I saved any money. Everything was online. Constant online purchasing – from basics, to gifts, to clothing. When the doorbell rang, and the Amazon man was coming, that was the most exciting part of the day."

Michael, a chief engineer, whose income had also increased from just below 6% to just above it due to an internal promotion,[22] also confirmed what national data tell us, that high earners had more disposable income and could save or replenish resources: "We have had much more disposable income than we have ever had. What we did, if anything needed repairing or replacing – a 'fortification mentality'. We kept a stockpile of food and wine and every bit of equipment or clothing that wasn't good enough, we replaced."

Improving wellbeing through consumption thus puts pressure on high earners' ability to keep up with an expected lifestyle and its costs. As money becomes ever more important, status anxiety begins to rear its head, which leads to longer working hours, more debt and more bankruptcies.[23] Paul describes how easy it is:

> 'People can think "If I had one million, I could buy […] a flat in London […] so maybe I need five or ten or 50 million." That is the spiral they're in […] They want palpably more, but when you have had it taken away, it makes you realise you can live without these things, you think "What's important?"'

Some of the high earners we spoke to were starting to question consumption, not for its influence on their lives but for its impact on the climate. We know that their lifestyle choices and consumption patterns mean that high earners are responsible for a disproportionate number of emissions. Globally, the richest 10% accounted for over half (52%) of emissions between 1990 and 2015. The richest 1% were responsible for 15% during this time – more than all the citizens of the EU and more than twice that of the poorest half of humanity (7%).[24] What will happen if unlimited growth remains a national goal? Economist Kate Raworth points out that even the *Daily Mail*, perhaps the most influential right-wing tabloid, references a study published in 1972 that predicted business as usual would lead to a collapse of society by 2040.[25]

Social reproduction

Michael, a 49-year-old engineer just in the top 10%, living in the south-west, told us that "most rich people's time and money is spent maintaining status". This includes their children. However, as outlined earlier, access to elite education and housing is becoming ever more expensive. By way of illustration, the UK has the fourth highest childcare costs in the OECD. Net childcare costs for a working couple with two children, as a percentage of the average wage, and including benefits, are 28% in Ireland, 7% in Spain, 5% in Sweden and 36% in the UK.[26]

The correlation between economic disadvantage and poor educational attainment is particularly strong in the UK. One fifth of children in England on free school meals do not reach the expected maths level at age seven. The ability to choose schools is still a prerogative of better-off families. From the 1980s, the UK slowly introduced market policies into education (driven by consumer demand fuelled by league tables), ensuring that the middle class became the major beneficiaries of the best state schools. The education system continues to focus on 40% of students who take A-levels (the British non-compulsory qualifications usually taken after the age of 16). Furthermore, while the economic return to getting a degree has not fallen and the greatest social mobility gains come to people with degrees, not all such qualifications guarantee economic security.[27]

Seven per cent of children go to private schools in the UK, the majority of which have parents with a top 10% income.[28] They have three times as much spent on their schools than the average child in the other 93%. More money is spent on private education in Britain than almost anywhere else on the planet. Elite education is seen as the primary vehicle of upward (and protection against downward) mobility. From a very young age, the segregating and hot-housing of some children has a powerful and damaging effect on them.[29] In the UK, as less is being spent on the education of the majority, more are likely to drop out earlier. This is seen in the fall in the number of teenagers staying on in school and an increase in young people not in education or training.

Countries with bigger income differences have bigger differences in educational performance and lower average levels of educational attainment overall.[30] This is because differences in ability among people at different levels in the income hierarchy are produced by the hierarchy itself. Position in the hierarchy determines ability, interests and talents rather than the other way around. Each layer in the income hierarchy tends to do less well than those above it. In other words, this strategy is not just bad for those who don't do so well, it is bad for everyone, including high earners.

However, the ideas that anyone can get on, that differences in ability are the main influence on where people end up in society, believing that all those 'at the top' are naturally endowed with the 'right stuff' and that we should judge worth, ability and intelligence from a person's position are all potent.[31] This makes the chances of those currently at the top being open to alternatives to the status quo even more unlikely, unless they are presented with convincing and attractive alternatives (something that isn't happening at the moment).

Markets in everything

High earners continue to portray the public sector as unresponsive, slow and inefficient. Phrases such as 'you wouldn't get away with those inefficiencies in the private sector' were typical. This attitude is used as justification to use private services. Sean, a 1% income earner and owner of an HR company, comments: "I'll be honest, I have a private GP and any medical attention I've had the NHS has failed to deliver. So, I've gone private."

Some told us that they would rely even more on the private sector if its costs weren't out of reach. In our interview before the pandemic, Maria told us how she had defended her daughter's local state school from parents who had been complaining about it, by reminding them of the impact of funding cuts. In our follow-up, she told us that her daughter had now moved to a private school following the receipt of some inheritance. She rationalised the move by telling us that her daughter's potential had not been fulfilled at her previous school. She had been just a 'tick in a box'. The bureaucratic approach referenced by Maria and the corresponding reduced attention on children has partly come about, not just from under-resourcing but also by embedding competition into our social and economic institutions. In education, this has manifested in a preoccupation with Ofsted[32] ratings and performance league tables and associated distortion of housing prices that fall within certain schools' catchment areas. In turn, this creates 'sink' schools, with additional bureaucracy imposed on teachers already under pressure from class sizes and the challenges of under-resourced environments. High earners will have to question the assumption that public services can be resolved through further efficiency.

There is also an ongoing myth that government welfare spending is on those who are unemployed. In fact, in the financial year ending 2017, the single biggest item of spending was pensions, at 42%, while 1% went to unemployment benefits.[33] In 2020/21, of the £1,094 billion total spent by the government, £20 billion went to social protection.[34] At 28% of its GDP, the UK has the sixth highest ratio among the countries spending most on social protection in Europe.[35] Before the pandemic, there was a similar belief that spending on health was at runaway levels. As any cursory research will show, its increase as a share of total government spending is largely because of the UK's demographics and its health inequalities.

Research on the NHS demonstrates that it is under-resourced compared to other countries. In fact, it '[still] lags well behind other nations in a number of key areas that materially affect a country's ability to improve the health of its population'.[36] In 2018, the King's Fund found that the NHS has fewer doctors and nurses per capita than 21 other countries.[37] It also invests comparatively little in technology such as MRI and CT scans. While the media continues to cover the failures of emergency response times, and more than a tenth of the population is waiting for treatment (the highest since records began) the question that high earners should actually ask is 'not why doesn't the NHS perform better compared to other health systems but how does it manage to perform so well […] when it is clearly under-resourced'.[38]

The NHS is of course also an interventionist system established to address problems *once they are there* in the population. Any preventive health systems have long been marginalised as was seen in the response to COVID-19. Studies of poorer but more equal countries with better health outcomes than the UK show that *equality is key to improving everyone's health*. Higher average material standards no longer improve wellbeing. Except under conditions of austerity, there is also little to no correlation between national income and changes in life expectancy.[39] What this research shows is that economic growth will not in itself reduce socioeconomic inequalities for developed countries.

Continuing with the individualistic, market-first, high-inequality paradigm that the UK has been stuck in, and which the government plans more of through deregulation, tax cuts and further austerity for public services will drive up inequality but do nothing to improve the lives of the majority.[40] Redistributing resources through environmental, economic and social intervention provides more plausible and popular answers to the country's challenges. This would include continuing to develop alternatives to big business, such as employee or public ownership, reinvigorating cooperation, and mutual organisations. Continuing on the same track will only give us more of what we already have: health inequalities and increasing long-term economic costs resulting from disability, ill-health and healthcare.

High earners also show little awareness of the consequences of private sector involvement in our public services, in the way that government itself has become financialised, whether through the privatisation of pensions schemes and our health service, the marketisation of higher education or through private finance initiatives (PFIs) – all taking liabilities off the public books and placing them with private investors. As a rule, for them, more private-sector involvement means less pressure on the public sector. In actuality, governments reduce their creditworthiness over the long term by having to show credit ratings to financial markets. Otherwise, they risk bond sell-offs and a run on their currencies, but, as Blakeley points out, this often doesn't matter to markets, as the time horizons of finance capitalism are shorter than at any other period in history.[41]

Collective denial

High earners' narratives often portray the belief that there is little that can be done about the crises we are facing. This is because they believe that impersonal forces create them, that they are driven by global or technical change out of our control, or they are governed by a 'natural' and inescapable economic logic. They do not factor in the political and ideological decisions and processes that have created a massive imbalance between employees and those who own companies and the extremely unequal distribution of income and wealth that results from them. Neither do they fully acknowledge what the financial crisis and then the pandemic have shown: that state-provided liquidity and full-on bailouts can be used effectively and are even necessary for the functioning of that logic.[42] The state has proven capacity to spend where there is the political will to do so, despite the persistence of pro-austerity interpretations of how governments work.[43]

Since 2020, some of the misunderstandings about government debt and the capacity of its spending are beginning to be demystified. Taking a look at how countries not far from us are handling the current crisis will show that costs are sky-high in the UK largely because of monopolies controlling key sectors, not least energy. Yet, there is still little recognition of – much less action taken on – the power that companies controlling our infrastructure have to design regulatory and tax policy in their favour. There is also little acknowledgement of the connection between that influence and increasing inequality. As long as high-earning voters do not recognise these connections, the obvious solutions will not be taken up. These include taxing excess profits, revising subsidies, or preventing share buybacks.[44]

Asking our respondents, in 2018–19, what public services they use, they would refer to having their bins collected or going to the park. Few mentioned social or physical infrastructure such as transport or public health. Most who had access to it (generally as a benefit from their employment) used private healthcare. Others asked what was meant by public services. Since the pandemic, the benefit of public goods and the cost of externalities – such as polluted rivers or air, or insufficient public healthcare provision – have been pushed to the top of the agenda. We are seeing more questions such as these on mainstream media: what happens when essential goods and services are in the hands of a few private companies? Should we spend more on long-term infrastructure projects? How do we make the nation more resilient to global supply crises? What are the effects of market failure in key sectors of our economy?

However, little has been done to encourage the electorate to think more radically and expansively about progress and prosperity, to talk about the purpose of wealth production and whether it really enhances wellbeing.[45] We are rarely encouraged to imagine alternative views to the mainstream consensus on how our economy is run – to do so is to be unserious. Markets have become embedded in our social and democratic choices to the extent that we have "drifted from having a market economy to being a market society".[46] This is especially the case for the top 10%. They often don't recognise market failures as they happen because they are the ones who often *give a voice* to these markets: as economists, as policy experts, as traders, as consultants, as journalists. And if all is kind of okay for them, all is good for everyone else. However, as Robert Reich has warned about the US:

> If the pandemic has revealed anything, it's that America's current social safety net and health care system does not protect the majority of Americans in a national emergency. We are the outlier among the world's advanced nations in subjecting our citizens to perpetual insecurity. We are also the outlier in possessing a billionaire class that, in controlling much of our politics, has kept such proposals off the public agenda.[47]

In other words, vested interests in highly unequal countries, such as the UK and the US, have a fear of enlarging the nation's sense of what is reasonable for the government to do for its citizens. And that is why, for example, the public have not been given any serious hopes about the government's role in investing in the UK's adaptation to climate change or to expect it to lead in a green industrial revolution in areas such as hydrogen, electric vehicles, decarbonising or renewable energies. Previous governments ended onshore wind projects, cut solar subsidies and slashed energy-efficient schemes, referred to as 'the green crap',[48] Truss's short-lived government even announced a commitment to extract 'every last drop of oil and gas' and lift the ban on fracking.[49] In the meantime, while we are in the slow lane, other European countries are moving ahead with adapting much more quickly. This will be to their advantage: the price of solar and wind energy, for example, is nine times cheaper than gas.[50]

High earners, as much as any other part of the British public, are used to putting their trust in elected representatives, the media and experts. In their case, this is perhaps even more natural, as these institutions are populated by people like them. They 'nod along' when politicians, media commentators and academics tell them that better wages for more people and a better-regulated financial system aren't possible because the country will lose competitiveness, jobs will disappear and they will suffer.[51] This is the version of events along the lines of, quoting philosopher Michael Sandel, 'whether we like it or not, the world is governed by neoliberal ideas, and that won't change. There's no point fighting the inevitable.'[52] What they are left with is the trickle-down argument that 'once the economy has picked up, living standards will improve'. This has endured for decades as common sense and is still pervasive, despite being widely discredited, even by US President Joe Biden.[53]

High earners need to push back on the related argument that we have to accept lower wages and everyone will have to accept cutbacks to important public services. The UK has enormous amounts of wealth (indeed, it lives off wealth; for instance, through a property market propped up by international investors); it is just very poorly distributed. Until these inequities are addressed, the country will continue to experience deficient demand, little productive investment and sluggish growth.[54] As Paul Mason put it, the 'six dials on the dashboard of the UK economy: inflation, investment, trade, debt, sterling and the current account [...] are all flashing red'.[55] We are at the end of what rising material standards can do for wellbeing and in the middle of the managed decline of a dilapidated economy. Only major improvements in our social environment can now increase our quality of life.[56]

The pandemic elicited a certain level of consensus, but that temporary sense of solidarity cannot compete with the influence of much more powerful long-term trends. The common factor in the strategies of high-income earners described in this chapter is the desire to distance themselves from these trends, even though nearly all of them inevitably will, if they haven't already, affect them and their children.

A more tangible future

One of the most interesting technological and financial developments of the last decade is the rise of cryptocurrencies – digital currencies that seek to do away with inflation and central banking through a decentralised registry system, the 'blockchain' – and NFTs (non-fungible tokens)[57] – which, in the simplest terms, are an attempt to replicate the logic of private property for online informational objects such as memes. Both are interesting economic and sociocultural phenomena; digital in nature but increasingly important for speculators. The most famous cryptocurrency, Bitcoin, began in January 2013 being traded at USD$13.30 and by January 2014, was worth $770. However, in the following years, its trading slumped sharply and then rose again, as competition started to appear and advocates struggled to make cryptocurrencies useful as actual currencies (or to seamlessly turn them into their nominal value). Cryptocurrencies then began to be used for trading NFTs, which operated like auction sales of images, tweets and other such online objects, now transformed into economic 'goods'. In 2021, that market trade was estimated at a nominal $17 billion.[58]

We mention these phenomena because they encapsulate many of the logics and strategies that middle to high-income earners may carry out in a context of increasing concentration of wealth. Both NFTs and cryptocurrencies have come to expand the logic of markets – in this case forcing scarcity on data that would otherwise be infinitely replicable. Even though they are virtual, they rely on physical resources and are astonishingly harmful to the environment: the carbon footprint needed to produce these goods has been compared to the emissions of mid-sized countries.[59] They rely on eager advocates to stimulate their demand, and are prone to create economic bubbles. Many investors have lost their life savings on the off-chance they'd see them multiplied by ten- or a hundred-fold off the back of other investors' eagerness. They are, in many ways, the 21st-century version of the tulip mania, but tulips at least are tangible (and beautiful).

Cryptocurrencies and NFTs are symptoms of awareness by those who trade them: that wealth and speculation drive economic outcomes much more strongly than wages and that early market access is everything. They are also predicated on an implicit libertarian philosophy that has only contempt for the welfare state: part of the reason cryptocurrencies and NFTs exist in the first place is to make taxation and central banking obsolete. These new markets, like other manias before them, promise their participants that if they enter early enough and convince enough buyers that they can become wealthy too, they'll win big, much like the winner of a Monopoly game is the one who buys earliest. Their very existence, in the words of filmmaker Dan Olson, represents "a turf war between the wealthy and the ultra-wealthy. Techno-fetishists who look at people like Bill Gates and Jeff Bezos, billionaires minted by tech-industry doors that have now been shut by market calcification and are looking for a do-over [...]. It's a cat fight between the 5% and the 1%."[60]

The popularity of NFTs and cryptocurrencies demonstrates a growing awareness that it will become increasingly more difficult to maintain our current standard of living through wages alone. The top 10% will find themselves increasingly confronting a number of myths about the capacity of markets to continue to provide their current levels of affluence. This includes the extent to which high earners rely on universal public services and the impact they have on their own life chances and social mobility. The arrival of the pandemic made it even harder for them to ignore the exposure of a significantly weakened healthcare system. It also showed how deepening inequalities directly affected the ability of key workers to keep essential public and private services going. As a result, inequality has become a more salient topic of public concern.[61] In the following chapters, we explore what will need to happen for the top 10% to back a stronger social contract. How can they be convinced that good-quality public services, available to all regardless of income, are more beneficial to them than lower taxes? What would life be like for the top 10% if they didn't feel the need to continuously apply the strategies we have discussed here?

We want to make a case that they shouldn't need to relocate to have a decent life, nor to insulate or isolate themselves from others. Not even to hoard or build the best post-apocalyptic bunker they can afford. In return, they would have better mental health and wellbeing. Not having enabled the exorbitantly wealthy and having lost the pretence that they will ever join their ranks, they would no longer sustain an economic system based on nepotism, the depletion of natural resources, and debt in place of decent wages. That is, a system, in the words of economist Diane Coyle, 'directed towards fending off the moment when the unsustainable can't be sustained any longer'.[62] Instead their taxes would provide more investment and infrastructure for high-quality public services and a safety net they would not be ashamed of using. There would be more funding for necessary collective changes such as bringing carbon emissions down. They would not feel the need to accumulate and consume to the same extent because, experiencing less status anxiety, they would interact with a wider group of people in a less divisive society. They might not be as well-off, but they would be better off.

7

Barriers to being comfortably off

We have been focusing on a group who, on the face of it, should be doing well for themselves, but who feel discomfort. This is manifested as anxiety about their jobs, as pressure to keep up with colleagues and neighbours, as nervousness about not being able to maintain their living standards, as fear of an uncertain economy, as not feeling attached to where they live. Previous research concludes that having stronger and more diverse relationships can improve wellbeing substantially.[1] Are then, high earners' primary concerns with themselves and their own economic future hampering their wellbeing? Could a more collective focus and addressing a range of barriers, which this chapter discusses, be at least part of the remedy for their individual concerns? This chapter explores high earners' perceptions of their own success and lifestyle. What might be preventing them from building social networks beyond their immediate circle and developing a wider sense of solidarity and belonging?

Barrier 1: Belief in meritocracy

A major barrier to developing a new social contract is how movements up or down the socioeconomic ladder tend to be explained. As explored in Chapter 3, many high-income earners emphasise their own part in their successes, explaining life outcomes as the result of their actions or factors they have control over: their skills, talents, willingness to work hard and the wisdom of their choices. This belief, that one's lot in life is and should be the result of one's abilities and graft, is often called meritocracy.[2]

In the words of Danny Dorling, with increasing inequality, the more widespread the opinion becomes that:

> It is, or should be, the 'fittest' who get to the top [...] that we are largely ruled by our betters, and that that is good for us. They think that almost all of the 1 per cent are very clever – much cleverer than most people – and that within the 1 per cent there are some exceptional geniuses.[3]

Dorling goes on to describe them as 'not part of an especially talented bunch and even those who are talented may not be that special'.[4] However, a number of those who do rule us believe they do so because they are special. We only have to look globally to see how meritocracy breaks down. By way of illustration, worldwide, the vast majority of those who score highest on IQ tests will be living in poverty.

Despite most of our respondents recognising the existence of deep inequities, a majority still believed that education was the main vehicle for moving up. It was seen as the route to opportunity. Following this idea, if more parents instilled in themselves and their children the importance of education and hard work, there would be more social mobility. However, widening access to education, laudable as it is as an aim, risks becoming a justification for inequality. This was seen in the views of those who did not necessarily come from privileged backgrounds. Gemma, a management consultant in her late thirties originally from the north-east and now living in London, is typical in citing her educational successes as the primary reason she became a high earner: "I was a high achiever. Teachers and family said 'You have to go to uni.' If I'd been an average student, that wouldn't have happened."

Emphasising her own attributes – equating status and respect with financial gain – makes her success seem acceptable, something she deserves. What this view ignores is that social mobility has often little to do with the educational system. Indeed, education in its current form arguably does more to enshrine social hierarchies than to subvert them. In the UK, more money is spent on private education than almost anywhere on the planet and it's also the home to the third most innumerate cohort of young adults in the developed world.[5] Graduates from a small number of private schools and elite universities dominate many top 10% professions, despite the fact that well over nine out of ten children attend a state school.[6] Moreover, decades of studies have shown that while school plays a role in socialisation, it is not as significant as the influence of peers, family and societal attitudes. As Peter Mandler has recently written:

> Middle-class and working-class kids today have the same educational experience, and yet the middle class still go into the top-paying jobs. One study showed that 30% of people from Class 1 backgrounds leaving school with no educational qualifications nevertheless end up in Class 1 jobs. It seems your class position is, mainly, inherited.[7]

Owen Jones wrote that aspiration, however commendable a goal it might be, has become a 'dominant atomised, consuming, acquisitive sense of self' sold as a means to individual salvation, resulting in the communitarian dimension of our lives being stripped bare.[8] This was evident among many of the members of the top 10% we spoke with. The route to economic success seems to begin with a geographical move away from the communities they grew up in – most often from north to south, in the case of the UK.

Barrier 2: Belief in the 'undeserving'

This is the counterpart of meritocracy: if the system is designed so that the best climb to the top, those who remain below do so for a reason. When some of our respondents talked about where they grew up, they made clear they were among the few who had 'made it out'. This was particularly the case for those who espoused meritocratic views and who had experienced upward mobility. They saw the places they were raised in and the people they knew there as 'others' in thrall to a culture of poverty. For them, deprivation, lack of housing, precarious employment, below-standard education and health inequalities are not understood as barriers to individuals succeeding, because those barriers had not stopped them. At most, what's needed are better role models and awareness of the opportunities offered by the market.

A belief that everyone in a meritocratic society receives their just rewards also runs the danger of estranging us from the experiences of others, exaggerating their chances of climbing the ladder and underappreciating how much current levels of inequality hamper those chances. Roy, a 66-year-old finance director with a top 3% income, told us:

> 'The less well-off are less well-off because of schooling, broken families, uneducated families, lack of control, blame everything on teachers [...] Where you have societies where some people are very rich, others very poor and no middle class, you're going to have problems. But when there are more echelons, when there's more of a spectrum, it's better, which is more or less where I think we are.'

This tendency to pathologise people and places runs deep in the British psyche.[9] As many social scientists have documented, it can be traced back to the division of the poor into deserving and undeserving in the workhouse. The latter were those who were able-bodied but seen as lazy and unwilling to take responsibility for their own lives. This put the idea that people experience poverty because of their own choices at the heart of British welfare provision, which explains the disciplinarian approach of many modern policies such as welfare-to-work schemes. Interestingly, although such attitudes were also present in other countries, we found that most interviewees in Spain had a more fatalistic view of poverty, seeing people living on low incomes as victims rather than as complicit in their own misfortune.

In addition, our interviews reflect a wider tendency to equate employment with independence and citizenship rights (such as access to social security). Being a full citizen thus means contributing through taxes and work. This view has an important communitarian element (the responsibility everyone has to 'contribute to society') but is unfortunately also often marked by cruelty towards those who are seen as failing to measure up

– and is predicated on what kind of work is considered valuable in the first place. The idea of an implicit charter of citizen rights and responsibilities – detectable in the discourse of all UK governments since at least 1979 – is an attempt to transform those who are perceived as passive recipients of social security benefits into active citizens engaged in public and economic life. This view hinges on (implicitly male) paid work, downplaying the importance of unpaid caring work and of key workers.[10] Despite being frequently reported and common knowledge in social policy and academic circles, our respondents rarely if ever considered the fact that the majority of those in receipt of social security payments in Britain today are in work. In their minds, they were a burden, while we would argue that those payments are actually subsidies supplementing the poverty wages in the private sector.

Barrier 3: Forgetting that 'no man is an island'[11]

Our research has shown that high earners often see their lives and experiences as mostly separate from the rest of society, in the sense that it was 'them' and only 'them' who drove where they ended up. Michael Sandel has studied the wider negative effects of elitism in universities in the US. Young people are sold the message that they have got their college places 'on their own merit'. This is of course mistaken and also means that if they fall short, they have no one to blame but themselves. If they continue to be 'successful', they often look down on those engaged in lower-wage work; people in such a situation are seen to have been judged by the market as less valuable and by educational institutions as less talented. And if they fail to remain in their position, high achievers risk anxiety and depression. This corrodes social cohesion. As Sandel puts it, 'the more we think of ourselves as self-made and self-sufficient, the harder it is to learn gratitude and humility. And without these sentiments, it is hard to care for the common good.' He continues:

> At a time when anger against elites has brought democracy to the brink, the question of merit takes on a special urgency. We need to ask whether the solution

to our fractious politics is to live more faithfully by the principle of merit, or to seek a common good beyond the sorting and the striving.[12]

Recently, COVID-19 exposed the assumptions still built into the design of our welfare state about the relationship between paid employment and independence, which were not true when the modern welfare state began in 1945 and are certainly not true now. For instance, that most 'proper' jobs are full time and permanent, pay enough to support dependants, and provide statutory sick pay and other protections from being part of a system into which each worker contributes. Nowadays the majority of those in poverty are in employment; many are precariously self-employed, with sick pay that does not cover their living and childcare costs, which are among the highest in Europe. Many are, in the words of Howard Reed and Stewart Lansley: 'piecing together a patchwork livelihood from multiple sources, not knowing from one day to the next if or when they will be paid. For creative workers, on whose innovations an increasingly knowledge-based economy relies, the borderline between unpaid and paid work is fluid and shifting.'[13]

The spread of COVID-19 raised questions over the necessary coupling of work and pay, where assumptions of what work is of the greatest societal value are being challenged. Many among us have looked at the rewards for different kinds of work and have begun to question why some earn so much more than others. Particularly, why are so many key workers, those we could never do without, paid so little? People who participate in the labour market should be able to earn a decent wage and those who cannot should be able to rely on a dependable and respectful benefits system[14] – precisely because, as the pandemic itself has shown, the fact that we can or cannot work in the first place depends on a myriad of factors beyond our control. The government's ability during the pandemic to provide an income floor for the population shows what is possible where there is the political will to do it. There was little backlash against the furlough and business support system, after all, and whatever existed was certainly less cruel than we are used to when dealing with benefits for those who are disadvantaged.

Barrier 4: Fear of falling

Although the top 10% are not in jobs we typically think of as precarious, many among them do not take their employment for granted. They exhibit, in the words of Barbara Ehrenreich – a formidable journalist and chronicler of the US's class system who died in 2022 – a 'fear of falling'.[15] This insecurity comes from being upward-oriented: comparing themselves to the 'super-rich' and as a result not feeling particularly rich themselves. The reverse of that orientation is that they don't really know what lies beneath – 'here be dragons'.

Gemma, without dependants and on a 3% income, who we introduced earlier in the book, was fearful of 'slipping down the ladder' and part of that fear was the implication it would be her own fault.

Much of the focus of our respondents' motivations was on keeping up with the cost of living, especially in London and the south-east where most well-paying jobs are. By December 2018, UK households had been net borrowers (had spent more than they received or 'lived beyond their means') for nine consecutive quarters (or 27 months in a row), with nothing comparable to that since 1987,[16] with a noticeable hit to family finances after the Brexit vote, and a sudden drop in the value of the pound. UK household savings are also very low and private debt – one of the key drivers of the 2008 crisis – is high. What is more, all of this was before the post-pandemic cost of living crisis.

Barrier 5: Consuming is all-consuming[17]

In modern capitalist societies, our lifestyles are inextricably linked to consumption, the goods and services we acquire and what this says about us. Material goods and the services we pay for take on a symbolic meaning, they are reflections of our position in the status order.[18] Symbols and the culture of elites trickle down to others, even while a mounting cost of living makes it increasingly difficult for most to keep up. Sociologist Shamus Khan points out that, while elites have opened up their institutions (such as their schools and universities) in terms of ethnicity and gender, income inequality has widened, leaving us with the 'puzzle of democratic inequality'.[19] There is at least a drive for inclusivity in gender and racial terms in elite institutions, but much less so on the basis of income or educational attainment.

Some of these consumption conflicts within the cultural position of our respondents were again illustrated by Gemma. She was aware of the difference in income between her home community and her network in London, and tries to reconcile this when her mother visits: "I'm very aware of different incomes when I go back home. [It's] very uncomfortable. When mum comes to visit, I pay for everything." At the same time, even though she has the purchasing power of her colleagues at work, she feels she doesn't 'fit in'. She encapsulated this in an anecdote from her first corporate job: "It was a very obvious difference [...] bit of a culture shock [...] people would say things like 'Do you ski?'"

Even if high earners can't copy the leisure pursuits of elites, they can try and imitate the consumption patterns of those just above them. Their 'ascriptive' identity (the personal, social or cultural identities placed on us by others) greatly influences the value of the resources they own. It's not enough that Gemma has the money to ski; she has to feel (and be seen as feeling) comfortable doing it, like a fish in water. This is a critical feature of the dynamics of inequality. Formal equality of opportunity, while essential, will never be enough. Ascriptive identities make up the foundations of durable inequalities and help us understand how elites can embrace opportunity without jeopardising their own advantages.

Groups are defined by who is excluded as much as by who is included. And this is not just based on people's characteristics, but also on food, music, objects, clothes, cars and so on. When one group seeks to distinguish itself, exclusion of others' practices becomes crucial. The field of culture, Khan writes, is not one that trickles down from top to bottom, but a struggle over who chooses and is able to like what kinds of things, and power is deployed by protecting or capturing a distinct way of defining oneself and one's group.[20]

Our interviewees were aware of this. For example, the age and type of car someone had featured in several interviews, even though we never raised the issue ourselves. Interestingly, this focus on consumer objects made them question whether inequality was in fact increasing. A senior executive at a major bank with a top 1% income told us:

Susannah: I think inequality probably has increased but I don't know [...] whether it is more noticeable because people, and I include myself in this, place more importance on tangible items and being portrayed to have the best trainers, the best car, the best telly [...] so I don't know whether it's because it's risen or whether it's just because we have more access to those items and therefore it's become more visible.

Interviewer: So, there's more competition at the level of consumption, of showing you have enough to spend on those things?

Susannah: Yes, and it's become more of a status symbol – 'I'm doing well because I've got a new car,' or 'I'm doing well because I've gone on this holiday,' or whatever it might be.

However, while the increasing costs of living and maintaining a 'suitable' lifestyle are presented as problematic, none of our respondents commented on these problems as symptoms of something larger or questioned whether there should be 'a better balance between time and things'. This is because, as Neal Lawson says, this choice is never presented to them. "The option is never more time, it's always buying more."[21] The debt-driven, consumption-dependent growth model that has become dominant and which exerts such downward pressure on most people, including high earners, is interpreted as commonsensical, as a commitment to progress. There was rarely any reference to the shape of the recovery we have followed since the financial crash – how it has boosted the assets of those wealthier than they are and overheated the property market.

Barrier 6: Segregated lives

In the UK, the top 10% of income earners overwhelmingly work in professional, managerial and associated professional jobs, largely in the private sector in London and the south-east. It was similar for the other countries we looked into: in Sweden, they lived generally around Gothenburg or Stockholm; in Spain, it was Madrid, Barcelona or a handful of its other large cities; and in Ireland, it was overwhelmingly around Dublin, where most international capital is concentrated. These cities also tend to be among the most unequal regions in their respective countries. London itself is the most unequal part of the UK, with a high proportion of high- and low-income earners, and comparatively fewer in the middle.[22]

In addition, mathematically, there is more inequality within the 1% than within the 99%.[23] This concentration of capital income in the top 1% has left many high earners feeling vulnerable. Their colleagues at the very top seem a world away economically, although quite close in their minds. William, whom we mentioned earlier in the book, knows "theoretically" that he is in the top 1%, but at the same time feels like he is somewhere in the middle: in his immediate social world he's surrounded by people much wealthier than he is.

Little contact with people from other socioeconomic groups partly explains these distortions. High-income earners, especially those in industries like banking, just don't come across them – or at least not in a way that creates lasting social bonds. This 'availability bias' is a significant barrier to their understanding of inequality.[24] New research suggests that people's exposure to and interactions with other people across economic fault lines grounds their beliefs about inequality. As Jonathan Mijs describes it: 'When you look out from a bubble, you don't really see much inequality in your own network. Most people you know have the same kind of income, the same advantages and disadvantages, so the world looks meritocratic and more equal than it really is.'[25]

Earlier we mentioned Luke, a privately schooled and Oxford-educated 27-year-old consultant. He told us he had become more aware of inequality while teaching in a state school a few years ago. However, these days, even though he has read that inequality is increasing, he says "If you're in a privileged position, and all your friends are from a similar background, then you don't think about it on a day-to-day basis." His comment confirms what Mijs and others tell us – that people think about inequality by starting with their own experiences, from those close to them and then making inferences about the rest of society. We often overestimate the representativity of our context. Moreover, when 'bad' things happen to us, we attribute it to misfortune, bad luck or beyond our control, but when we look at others – for instance, the unemployed or victims of crime – we tend to think first about what they did wrong. We apply to them an 'individualising lens' – the exact opposite of our approach to others' successes and our own failures. This is known as the 'fundamental attribution error'.[26]

In countries where levels of inequality are increasing, people become less aware and less concerned about the issue, which affects how and the extent to which people learn about inequality in the first place. As Danny Dorling points out, numeracy levels display an almost inverse perfect relationship to economic inequality:

> [I]n places where the rich take far more, young people find it hardest to understand why there can be such a large difference in income between the median and the mean. In nations, in other words, where inequality is more of a problem, fewer young people will understand how it is measured.[27]

The more unequal a country is, the less likely there will be many bonds across income groups. The maintenance of the status quo is therefore in large part down to the effects of an unequal society. In such societies the class hierarchies are stickier: opportunities for children are uneven, marriages across social classes are less common, and residential segregation is higher. Referring to the US (but it might as well have been the UK), Mijs wrote:

> Increasingly, rich and poor Americans are living segregated realities: people's workplace, neighborhood and social network mirror their own economic circumstances and level of education, limiting the chances of rich and poor Americans sharing the same spaces and getting to know about each other's lives. This disconnect also means that neither can see their

unequal society for what it really is. That goes some way toward explaining why Americans underestimate inequality and overstate its meritocratic nature.[28]

Barrier 7: Work is not the new public square

Robert Putnam has been studying the decline in political, civic and religious organisations in the US for decades. In his acclaimed 1995 book *Bowling Alone* he documents how social capital in the shape of formal organisations has not increased to offset this decline; indeed, there has been a steep drop in union membership.[29] Unions and professional societies were once an important site for social solidarity in the US: "among the most common forms of civic connectedness" and a crucial precondition for economic collaboration. He questions whether people no longer like the idea of being a member of something or whether we have simply seen a shift 'between residence-based and workplace-based networks, a shift from locational communities to vocational communities. [...] perhaps we have simply transferred more of our friendships, more of our civic discussions and more of our community ties from the front porch to the water cooler'.[30] He describes modern-day US professionals and blue-collar workers: 'putting in long hours together, eating lunch and dinner together, traveling together, arriving early, and staying late. What is more, people are divorcing more often, marrying later (if at all) and living alone in unprecedented numbers.'[31] And from that, in one sense, '[w]ork is where the hearth is [...] the workplace increasingly serves as a sanctuary from the stresses of marriage, children, and housework'.[32]

David Graeber also studied the effects of spending so much time at work:

> Much of the day-to-day drama of gossip and personal intrigue that makes life entertaining for inhabitants of a village or small town or close-knit urban neighborhood, insofar as it exists at all, comes to be confined largely to offices or experienced vicariously through social media (which many mostly access in the office while pretending to work).[33]

Even so, Putnam points out that structural changes in the workplace have reduced the likelihood for much socialising. These include shorter job tenures, more part-time and temporary jobs, more self-employment, less unionisation, and threats of downsizing, automatisation and offshoring, all of which result in increased competition among colleagues and employee anxiety. In turn, this makes it likelier that most will keep their heads down at work to avoid getting fired, and thus less likely to form deep connections with colleagues as these would be so fleeting there would be little point. Putnam concludes that it is hard to accept the hypothesis that 'the workplace has become the new locus of American's social solidarity and sense of community'. Therefore, in his words, 'Any solution to the problem of civic disengagement in contemporary America must include better integration between our work lives and our community and social lives.'[34]

Work cannot be the new public square, Putnam concludes, because the ties we form there are mostly for instrumental, not social, reasons – and even conviviality is tainted in such a context. In addition, the more your clients and co-workers are of a similar social class – which is increasingly the case the higher your income is – the less likely you are to interact with those of a substantially different lot in life. A decline in our civil ties in our neighbourhoods and other areas of our lives can't be compensated for by work. Monitoring, hierarchy, competition, and lack of free speech and privacy all act as barriers to 'public deliberation and private solidarity'.[35]

Barrier 8: Rights and responsibilities

Prior to the pandemic, our respondents voiced what has been observed of middle-class individuals in the US, that the 'enormous complexity of society remained elusive and almost invisible to them'.[36] The absence of reference to "the structure that guides us all", as Hannah, a 44-year-old occupational health consultant earning just above the 10% threshold, puts it, includes an acknowledgement of interconnectedness and 'one's debts to society, that bind one to others, whether one wants to accept it or not. [This] is also the ability to engage in the caring that nurtures that interconnectedness'.[37]

Lack of solidarity is perhaps the greatest obstacle for the top 10%. Our respondents tended to believe public services were inefficient and, not coincidentally, had very low levels of trust in the capacity of the state. Apart from an enthusiasm for the state's role in providing at least baseline educational opportunities and healthcare services, support for redistribution was mixed. State inefficiency was often mentioned, as was the need to motivate people to work.

Our interviewees' attitudes towards the role of government were a world away from a vision of a social state outlined in recent European social democratic manifestos such as the Social Democratic Party of Germany's Programme for the Future. They made little reference to the British tradition of universalism (in the NHS, for example) and mostly argued in favour of means-testing. Dan, with a top 6% income, head of client services at a marketing agency, argues that if services are partially paid for by their beneficiaries, they will improve through customer demand for better quality: "If you pay a contribution to your son going to school, then there's an expectation of what you're getting back. If you pay council tax, you expect bins to be collected and local services to function."

Perhaps this preference for means testing could be explained by the fact many high earners prefer (and can consider) to rely on private healthcare or education if they can, as well as the fact that public services often operate as part of the background; they are unnoticed. Few of our interviewees declared they use public services frequently. Of those who mentioned healthcare issues, most accessed the NHS but also had private healthcare 'for emergencies'. Similarly, nobody lived in social housing or needed social care. Where respondents had children of school age, they were either in private schools or in state schools in relatively affluent areas.

Similarly, a rights and responsibilities discourse dominated opinions on the issue of increases in public spending. A slight majority of our respondents felt that the government should be 'helping people help themselves'. Michael, a 49-year-old engineer, just in the 10% threshold, was one of the few to concede that benefits only provide a minimum standard of living and this largely stemmed from his own childhood of living in relative poverty. For a majority of the others, a significant problem of more welfare provision was that it would discourage work. In relation to the proposal to have a universal basic income (UBI), for instance, they said: "I don't love that idea. I don't think it takes other factors like effort or drive into account"; "Pass"; "Not convinced. But I don't know enough about it"; "In the long term, benefit receivers lose the incentive to look for work." However, many also recognised that something like a UBI would be needed, as more jobs become threatened by automation. William, a Merchant (see Chapter 2) and a consultant well placed in the 1%, said on the matter:

> '[UBI is] an interesting concept, more relevant in a world with fewer jobs? But what do you do to keep those people busy, productive and leading fulfilled lives? How do you pay for it? It is becoming somewhat unavoidable, but I'm not sure how we pay for it.'

As this last example shows, the barriers that the top 10% face to developing greater 'sociological imagination' are not exclusive to them. After all, the fact there are fewer connections across social groups affects everyone. However, among high earners these barriers are perhaps exacerbated, considering how much their self-understanding is entangled with their views on work and their own position in the labour market. Like most of us, they live relatively isolated lives with little contact with those of very different means. And the less of that kind of contact there is, the more likely that judgements about people living in different circumstances will be preconceived. Nevertheless, the pandemic and the current cost of living crisis, not to mention the Ukraine–Russia war, have shown more clearly than ever how quickly individuals can get into difficulties through no fault of their own and how quickly financial reserves can be exhausted. With these barriers in mind, in Chapter 8 we explore how a different form of organising economic priorities and dealing with those in need could serve not just a majority, but also this group.

8

'When the facts change, I change my mind'[1]

'You have to face it head-on. You have to recognise what the tension points are and why people have them. Then you have to produce an alternative vision and deliver it. It's difficult to do that in small numbers. It needs a change of people who buy into that at the centre. It probably needs an opportunity to come out and that may be post-Brexit. If we end up leaving and everyone is further impoverished by it, which I think is 95% certain, that might be an incentive to say "It's not the thing you thought it was," and introduce a different narrative about how society can be delivered in a more equitable way.' (Duncan, director of a non-departmental public body with a top 10% income)

As a way out of the dilemmas we have described, this chapter suggests that high earners take a different perspective on their relationship with the state and their expectations of it. We don't want to offer a 'how-to' guide or tell them what to do; after all, that would be presumptuous and unlikely to have any effect. What we want instead is to put forward the case to those earning higher incomes that many of the ideas and policies that they think unfairly target them could actually be in their self-interest. What we propose here is mostly limited to taxation, redistribution, the state, the environment, and their social and economic lives because changes in those spheres of life are among the most urgent, actionable, tangible and far-reaching. However, many other policies could be explored; for instance, mitigating educational inequalities by addressing how they are reproduced by elite private schools.[2] Rather than dismissing such proposals as wishful thinking and not what 'the economy' needs, we argue instead that it is the status quo that does not make economic sense and does not benefit the lives of the great majority, not even of the top 10%. We also set out why and how high earners should have higher expectations of what the government can do for them. But first, we need to provide a reminder of why they are uncomfortable.

What high earners told us

The top 10% rarely know where they sit. They know they are not at the very bottom or the top but, interestingly enough, they underestimate their distance from both extremes. Our interviewees might be vaguely aware that the 1% are drifting away, but may not realise that they themselves are as far away from that 1% as they are from the median earner.

A belief that individual effort got them to where they are is pervasive, but waning. Working hard is a crucial part of their self-definition, yet many are surprised to be asked about the ultimate purpose of their work. Their priority, especially for Merchants, tends to be the bottom line, and this focus promises to allow them to lead a comfortable life.

They fear downward mobility, unemployment and economic downturns. Those currently at the bottom of the top 10%, with an income of around £60,000, may soon start to struggle to get on the housing ladder. If they don't have assets, their affluence feels increasingly precarious. As we mentioned earlier in the book, in late 2022, a government minister cited those just below them, people on £45,000, as likely to struggle to pay their energy bills.[3]

High earners know that it is now much harder and more expensive than it was in previous generations to progress through the rites of passage that they took for granted, such as finding a well-paid job, having a place to call their own and starting a family. In fact, for many of their children, these will be out of reach without family support. High-earning parents fear their children's downward mobility, perhaps even more so than their own.

Despite their relatively high income and status, those in the private sector find themselves in very hierarchical and unequal workplaces.[4] Even though many in the top 10% are managers and high-ranking professionals, they don't feel they have much power. While trade unions have been in decline for decades and their absence is rarely questioned, they are beginning to be sorely needed. Looking across the whole labour market, wages could be as much as 15–20% lower than they would otherwise be because of a lack of worker power. According to the Resolution Foundation and Centre for Economic Performance, this is equivalent to almost £100 a week for the average worker.[5]

High earners feel isolated and politically alienated but would be willing to pay more in taxation for better-delivered services, though they often struggle to trust the integrity and efficiency of the state. They support redistribution more than they used to, but want higher taxes targeted on those earning more than they do as well as on global corporations. This was nearly always the case when the issue of tax was raised in our interviews. It was others, the truly rich, who did not pay their fair share (though perhaps they are not wrong on this).

High-income earners have misconceptions about their relationship with the state and underestimate their reliance on it over their lifecourse. While they enjoy the status of using private services (often as benefits of their employment), if asked they acknowledge that there will be times when they'll need the public sector. Yet, understandably, they are frustrated with its current state. They fear that these services will not be there in an emergency. The question they ask themselves is 'Should we give more money to support a welfare state that isn't working?' The answer for many is 'no', because of the perceived inefficiency of the state, the undeservingness of its recipients or simply because they don't see the benefit in it for themselves. So, if high earners critique the value of public services in their own lives, do they approach their relationship with the economy and political system in the same way?

Question 'business as usual'

As we discussed in Chapter 6, we found that respondents were accepting of how the economy works to deliver profits to the top with excessive pay and bonuses for a few, rather than working to improve the wellbeing of the majority.[6] There was no reference, for example, to ten years of wage stagnation. Andy Haldane, a former chief economist at the Bank of England, has said that UK employees' share of national income has fallen from 70% to 55% since the 1970s, which is less than what they received at the outset of the Industrial Revolution.[7] Falling living standards should therefore come as no surprise, and none of this has anything to do with how hard people do or do not work.[8]

We, therefore, urge high-income earners to pause and consider why they think it is that the UK's economic and political system doesn't work for most people. How can they continue to be convinced by the argument that business as usual is best for our economy? The 15 years before the pandemic (2004–19) were the weakest growth period since 1934.[9] Per head, the economy is set to shrink. We have already been witnessing a 1930s-style drop in living standards.[10] The question is: who will be made to pay for rising prices? Without government intervention to ensure wages keep pace with inflation and strategic price controls in industries like energy, upward redistribution will continue apace.[11] Corporate profits are holding up; some raise prices higher than the increases in their costs. It's becoming even more difficult than it was to argue that these companies 'deserve' such profits.

The need to better understand the lives of others

Before the pandemic, quite a few of those we interviewed had already commented on social inequalities. Stephen, a former barrister, now a university professor, put it simply: "the taxation system. It works for the rich and doesn't work for the poor." He told us: "The way that society and economy has been managed post-crash, such as cuts to social services and the welfare state, there has been nowhere near enough redistribution of wealth."

Meanwhile, many of our interviewees, especially in the private sector, found inequality difficult to think about. This response by Sean, a 40-year-old owner of a recruitment company with a top 1% income, to the question of what has caused inequality in the UK is not untypical:

> '[Inequality is due to] lack of drive and effort. Nobody coached me to go to university or to do well for myself. I do understand certain situations mean people start off their life in a place where they don't have it. If I see a homeless person in the street, a child who's been kicked out, obviously I'll see them differently to a 40-year-old man who could probably get a job.'

We would argue this view underestimates current levels of inequality and how entrenched they are. Inequality is now of a completely different order from our respondents' parents' and grandparents' generations, a sign that jobs are no longer providing enough income to live a comfortable middle-class life. Current levels of inequality also raise the question of how the UK could continue to have a functioning economy if a majority of the population does not get paid enough to afford their bills or to live in the cities where they work.

During the pandemic, it became clear that many people in jobs that are vital to our society's survival have poor working conditions and are not paid enough to live on. Unions helped the public join the dots regarding the inequalities: wage depression, weak employment rights, real-term pay cuts, the high cost of living and crises in our public services.[12] This re-evaluation of key workers could lead higher earners to have greater respect for different social groups and the jobs they do. As high earners continue to move out of cities and work from home, there could be opportunities for more connection with a wider group of people and greater attachment to their local areas. It could lead to a softening of meritocratic beliefs. However, the pandemic could also have led to further isolation from the rest of society, in line with the increase in inequality after Covid, the change in consumption patterns and more time spent at home and online.[13]

High earners often don't acknowledge the extent to which inequality affects them directly because part of their status derives, after all, from how they differentiate themselves from others. Through a myriad of everyday ways, they avoid the stigma of being associated with people on lower incomes. As we have shown, these strategies will decline in value or become increasingly expensive. Two respondents, Douglas and Maria, were aware of this tendency and also what they gain from being influenced by people from different walks of life:

Douglas: For me, it's not role models, it's people that you meet that show you that good stuff is possible. [...] People collaborating together, making a good job of it. The influence of people.

Maria: I've tried to make myself read something else to get the other point of view but I've found it very difficult. [...] I'm quite lucky that I mix with a diverse group of people; maybe mixing with a diverse group has influenced me as well.

If high earners don't make connections with people who have different life experiences and continue to think of themselves as separate, they will continue to miss crucial dynamics about how society and the economy work. They'll be caught by surprise when the wave breaks.

Using public services without thinking less of yourself

The high earners we spoke with had a conflicted relationship with the state. Pre-pandemic, they saw public services as sub-par, slow and inefficient, fearing their decline. Paul, an architect, told us:

> 'Recently one of my children had to call 999. A burglar had got into the ground floor flat and was making his way up to the first floor. They didn't answer at first. Then, [the police] didn't come for 25 minutes. It's only until someone calls it [an emergency service] that you then feel it is lacking [...]. Until you need it, you don't know.'

However, few mentioned the impact of austerity on public services and on the people who provide them. Only Jung, formerly an NHS doctor, when asked whether he thought inequality had increased, replied:

> 'Yes, I think so, as a public sector worker I've seen little [in relation to] pay increases. Pay has been largely standard, not in line with inflation, while we hear bankers', CEOs' salaries [are] on the rise. So it does feel like the public sector is being shafted. You hear all the time of nursing staff, who haven't seen rises in pay for many years.'

The relationship of the top 10% with the state has seen some change since the pandemic, with many more aware of its support as a result – be it economic or health related. Despite this, high earners still have preconceptions about the extent to which they rely on and benefit from public services over the course of their lives. The idea that the welfare state is only for those lower down the socioeconomic scale reinforces the status that we discussed in relation to mobility (see Chapter 3) – of never being dependent if you can buy a service anywhere. It is also a way of imitating the 1% and their separation from the social context. Maria, for instance, though generally a centre-left Brahmin, said she had decided to go private to "give my space to someone else". Lamenting the situation, she said "The government wants us to do that, why else would they be advertising that there are no doctors?" Still, as Richard Titmuss is widely quoted as saying, 'separate discriminatory services for poor people have always tended to be poor quality services'.[14]

The belief that high earners do not benefit as much from the state as those on lower incomes is partly rational. When high earners need medical care, they can use private hospitals and they are economically sheltered by company schemes subsidising pensions and housing costs. Their children are more likely to attend private schools. They may not gain directly from the welfare system, but at the same time, they pay a higher percentage of their income for the taxes that keep those services running.

However, we have already argued in previous chapters that it is very much in high earners' self-interest and that of their children to support public services. This is because they gain substantially from the indirect benefits of the welfare state. For example, the doctor who treats a rich patient in a (private) hospital will most likely have been trained at public expense, and those who own businesses depend on the welfare state to care for the healthcare of their employees.[15] The public welfare system maintains the social fabric and prevents or minimises breakdowns of law and order. While this benefits everyone, it particularly does so for those 'with the most to lose'.[16] In 2022, criminal barristers went on strike for better working conditions, a warning against thinking that funding cuts will not be felt more widely. Barristers felt that politicians had supported cutting funding for criminal legal aid because "[B]y talking about slashing legal aid, it made it sound like they were being tough on criminals [...] there's no votes in funding defendants. Like I said, no voter thinks it's going to happen to them. But I'm afraid it does."[17]

Many more benefit from the operation of the benefits system than those who are directly targeted by it. Indeed, nearly all of us do; from public transportation and parks, to safer streets, healthier populations, a more educated society and the institutions that guarantee a more robust democracy. And while the pandemic momentarily reminded high earners of the importance of properly funding public healthcare, they tend to be unaware that most of them get back something at least close to what they pay into the welfare state. The majority will rely on it at some point during their lifetimes. The alternatives, either through private insurance or accumulating enough cash to see 'our families and ourselves through all eventualities are hugely expensive and out of reach for most'.[18]

When benefits are paid universally, irrespective of income, even if the amounts may seem meagre to a high earner, they can be important at a symbolic level. They strengthen the principle of being a citizen, part of something bigger, while decreasing the stigma from receiving them. As the late John Hills, an expert on income distribution and the welfare state, expressed it:

When we pay in more than we get out, we are helping our parents, our children, ourselves at another time – and ourselves as we might have been, if life had not turned out quite so well for us. In that sense, we are all – nearly all – in it together.[19]

Understand the cost of not investing

Part of taking a different perspective on what seems simply common sense is to look at the role of government in other countries. Globally, there is a clear tendency for states to become more economically proactive.[20] Christian Lindner, the federal finance minister of Germany, recently announced a draft budget with the euro equivalent of £44 billion earmarked for investments into 'climate protection, digitalisation, education and research as well as the infrastructure required',[21] the goal being to 'transform Germany into a sustainable, climate-neutral and digital economy' as part of a federal budget worth £401 billion.[22] In Spain, train travel on large parts of the national railway network is currently free. Even in the US, the Inflation Reduction Act of 2022 will pump hundreds of billions into low-carbon transition and healthcare, including slashing the cost of prescriptions and cancelling $10,000 of student loans for millions of graduates, although this last item is being challenged in the Supreme Court. This is in sharp contrast to the 'tax cuts for the rich and austerity for the rest' recipe we have by now become used to.[23]

High earners will need to start pushing back on the fallacy that the UK spends too much on inefficient public services and that our financial problems stem from excessive state spending. Much more significant to understanding Britain's economic woes is its reliance on debt-fuelled consumption.[24] The well-worn truism that 'there is no magic money tree', was used to drive over a decade of cuts to benefits for the most vulnerable, while still finding room for cutting taxes for millionaires and corporations. Although reducing state deficits in normal times could lead to a fall in the government debt-to-GDP ratio, doing so in a recession is self-defeating.[25] This is not least because, as governments cut spending and try to pay down their debt, money is taken out of the economy, which has impacts on growth and tax receipts, all while increasing pressures on the welfare system.[26]

It is also crucial to understand that failing to invest in the social safety net actually increases the taxpayer's bill in the long term. After 12 years of austerity, the UK has not been able to significantly reduce its government spending and is set to increase it, largely due to our ageing population and inequalities exacerbated by austerity itself. Child poverty, for example, will cost an estimated £38 billion a year.[27]

On the eve of COVID-19, government spending was equivalent to about 40% of GDP – around the average for the post-war period. The single biggest item was pensions, while 1% went to unemployment benefits.[28] Following the pandemic, spending spiked sharply, rising to its highest level since the First and Second World Wars.[29] Of the £167 billion additional government spending in 2020, only £20 billion went to social protection, while the rest went to support businesses (over £122 billion).[30] The UK is way down the list in Europe on social spending.[31]

Since at least 2010, every government has made one of its central commitments to cut billions of pounds in public services, regardless of how the economy is doing.[32] It is time for high earners to decide whether to continue thinking that the NHS is ailing because the public sector is inefficient or to acknowledge that chronic underfunding is the cause. As state schools can't recruit teachers or refurbish their classrooms and one in five teachers have to spend their own money for school supplies,[33] are they going to continue to believe the UK is a meritocracy while elite professions remain dominated by the privately educated? Would they change their minds on the matter if suddenly they could not afford private education? Can they continue using the inefficiency argument for justifying further cuts to public services when many of those services are businesses in the hands of private companies?

If high earners continue to believe it is in their best interests to exclude themselves from the welfare state and rely on private services instead, they will have a strong incentive to avoid paying taxes. Some will go to great lengths to do so. If they do, they also have to accept that they are complicit in the deterioration of our public infrastructure and civic institutions, which will steadily make us an even more divided society.[34] Either way, for those seeking to foster social solidarity among high earners there is an urgent need to destigmatise public services. As we wrote in the 2020 TASC report, 'the top 10% should be able to use public services without thinking less of themselves'.[35]

Expect more from the private sector

High earners were generally silent on the political aspects of their work. They rarely reflected on its effects on society at large. To an extent that is unsurprising among those in the 'army of professional enablers, including accountants and lawyers who design new schemes to help their clients pay less tax'.[36] Envisaging change seems unlikely, given the level of monitoring, hierarchy, and lack of free speech and privacy that many refer to when describing their workplaces.[37]

Nevertheless, relationships between high earners and their employers are beginning to change. Many we spoke with wanted a better work–life balance and fewer hours, a 'well-proven intervention to improve wellbeing'.[38] According to a 2019 survey, 70% of employees believe a four-day week would improve their mental health and 64% of businesses supported the idea of adopting one. More than three million people in the UK would like to work fewer hours even if it would result in less pay, and 10 million would like to work fewer hours overall.[39] Crucially, again looking at international evidence in countries with shorter working weeks, reducing hours does not result in reduced productivity.[40]

Working fewer hours would also reduce high earners' carbon footprint. In the words of Stronge and Lewis from the think tank Autonomy, '[w]orking less not only reduces the sheer amount of resources being used as part of the labour process, but it also reduces the amount of carbon-intensive consumption that comes with what Juliet Schor calls the "work and spend" cycle'.[41]

Everything we do will need to change

One of the fundamental problems with the public and political debate on the climate is that inequality is rarely acknowledged as part of the issue, and therefore high earners don't recognise how much they are part of the problem.[42] Any meaningful change will thus be difficult for them, not least because improving wellbeing while consuming less is in tension with many aspects of their lifestyles.

Three quarters of the public agree with the statement 'If individuals like me do not act now to combat climate change, we will be failing future generations.'[43] However, the scale of behavioural change is not yet appreciated. For each person to reduce their carbon footprint to 2.5 tonnes by 2030 won't be enough to continue with small, relatively unobtrusive measures such as recycling, switching off lights, or cutting food waste and energy usage. This is nowhere near the needed scale. Everything we do will need to change – how we travel, what we eat and what we consume. According to surveys, willingness to pay to mitigate climate change goes up with income, and high earners are willing to go to greater lengths to protect the environment.[44] However, this does not detract from the fact that carbon emissions increase with income. What gives?

Little interest in participating

The high earners we spoke with, like much of the electorate, are disillusioned with the state of democracy and uneasy about an increasingly divisive and populist political culture. Many speak nostalgically about a missing 'centre ground'. Respondents such as Roy, a finance director with a top 3% income, remarked that change was unlikely with the political system we have "because of the structure of the parties. And you have to have a significant number of people in the marginals to change things."

Nevertheless, only a few of our respondents articulated the need for political reform. This is unsurprising, given that the system of representative democracy that we have has a tendency to favour the economic elite. Those who do argue for reform, therefore, are not seeking to improve on the representative model but are focused on 'the democratisation of democracy' through building in mechanisms such as citizens' assemblies into the formal political system.[45]

Despite a lack of public conversation about the country's political structure, British people do now want to see reforms. For the first time since records began, most of the public wants to scrap the first-past-the-post electoral system. According to a YouGov poll, 51% are in favour of switching to a form of proportional representation, while 44% prefer the status quo.[46] This reflects the policy of many parties and an increasing number of trade unions. Some respondents hinted that their voting would become more tactical, and this is consistent with wider trends. In the 2019 general election, almost a third of voters said they had voted tactically. Nobody we spoke with reflected on what would be required for the structural changes discussed in this book: namely, the liberal centre finding common ground with more progressive groups through an alliance, formal or otherwise. The prospect of a different kind of politics gathering momentum among the general public looks uncertain with an Electoral Calculus poll predicting a Labour landslide majority of 112 seats in the next general election.[47]

Nobody we spoke with currently participated actively in politics beyond voting or seemed to want to. The dwindling prospects for economic transformation coming from Westminster risk fostering further apathy. However, here again, we ask readers to consider the possibility of taking a less passive stance. The community wealth-building movements in the north are evidence of what can be achieved when local political parties, businesses and community groups work together.[48]

Expect more from the state

In the past few years, high earners have had their views of the state challenged by the pandemic, witnessing an unprecedented amount of peacetime state intervention. While Covid made huge demands on monetary, fiscal and welfare policy – particularly relating to state pensions, healthcare and net zero – the parameters for acceptable state spending have changed dramatically, with the fiscal line dividing political parties blurred.[49]

Recent events should have made clear that it's now 'everybody's business' for the state to work in the public interest, stepping up and confronting long-standing deficits in public infrastructure and in the quality and accessibility of public services. Those consulting progressive governments globally, such as economist Mariana Mazzucato, are clear that they must offer a new narrative on value creation, moving beyond the 'old, entrenched narratives' where the private sector plays the leading role and the state fixes market failures along the way, instead delivering:

> both a well-resourced welfare state and a dynamic innovation state, because the two go hand in hand. Without social services, too many people will remain vulnerable and unable to gain access to the basic ingredients of wellbeing and economic participation, including education, job security and health. And without innovation, economic growth and solutions to pressing societal problems – whether a pandemic, climate change or the digital divide – will remain out of reach.[50]

However, rather than a government with moral resolve and a bold, visionary plan for our future, the pandemic has exposed the moral bankruptcy of the corporate governance we currently have. It has allowed billions in public bailout money to be funnelled to shareholders while jobs are cut and massive companies are allowed to profiteer in crucial sectors of the economy.

Although we understand the circumstances of the emergence of the British modern welfare state were not the same as today's, we cannot continue to delay action on structural challenges such as net zero. If we do, we will disadvantage the country in the long run, producing higher costs, missed opportunities and prolonging the crises we already face.[51] The current juncture is an opportunity to present an honest but ambitious plan for the transition to net zero that includes a vision for local investment, bringing improvement to wellbeing, health, prosperity and inequality.[52] Showing at least a level of commitment to meet these challenges, our respondents repeatedly told us that they would welcome a stronger welfare state, provided it was efficient, transparent and didn't disincentivise work. We have to make the case that such a welfare state can exist and that it would empower not demotivate people on lower incomes. Work is becoming less effective at warding off poverty, with the percentage of working-age adults in poverty in work at its highest since records began.[53]

The government can take more risk than anyone else, certainly more than any individual or private company bound by short-term shareholders' interests. All the high earners we spoke to, even the most hard-nosed Merchants, said that the government has a responsibility to ensure its citizens' economic circumstances do not fall so low they cannot participate in society. They variously described this point as 'below the poverty line', 'a basic standard of living', 'enough to live on' and 'a duty to make sure people get a fair wage for a good day's work that will keep them at a level where they can eat, pay their bills and keep them safe and warm'.[54]

Whichever definition we want to use, it is difficult to argue that the state is adequately fulfilling that responsibility. In 2021–22, the food bank charity Trussell Trust distributed over 2.1 million food parcels. The trust calls for the government at all levels and across the UK to use its powers and take urgent action.[55] In September 2022, Disability Rights UK called for the government to put in place emergency uprating of benefits to at least match the latest Bank of England predicted inflation rates.[56] In the autumn statement, the government committed to raising working-age benefits and the state pension by 10.1% from April 2023, in line with September's inflation figure.[57]

In 2023, real household disposable incomes are expected to fall to their lowest levels since 2013/14.[58] In January 2023, 11.7 million households will be spending at least 25% of their income on fuel. Without an energy price freeze, combined bills for food and fuel would take up 80% of the budget of households on universal credit or the minimum wage.[59] Speaking of the extent to which charities have stepped up in the past years of crisis, Gordon Brown, former UK prime minister, wrote: 'With these last lines of defence now breached and charities about to hit a breaking point, only the government has the resources to end the unspeakable suffering caused by unpayable bills and unmet needs.'[60]

The pandemic has also highlighted our interdependence. A bolder government would respond to that by reassessing what activity is given recognition and promoting what are currently low-paid and low-status jobs such as those in the care sector. It would reassess the status of domestic work as well, which has an estimated value of between 10% and 39% of GDP and can surpass that of manufacturing, commerce, transportation and other key sectors.[61] Unpaid care and domestic work support the economy and often make up for the lack of public expenditure on social services and infrastructure. In effect, they represent a transfer of resources from women to others in the economy. In the 21st century, women still carry out at least two and half times more unpaid household work than men and are less than a third of the top 10%.[62]

As Grace Blakeley reminds us, 'States construct markets – they enforce contracts, provide basic services and uphold a monetary system needed for any kind of economic activity to take place – and they do so in a way that favours certain interests over others.'[63] A visionary future government would support and promote a wider range of sectors, particularly in net zero and creative industries, as well as the whole of our world-leading service sector (not just finance). It would also start weaning us off our reliance on GDP as an index of success.[64] Many of the activities included in GDP work against our environmental goals while neglecting areas that are essential to social reproduction such as domestic, family, political and charitable work.[65] GDP should be abandoned as the sole target and alternative targets should be considered, including indexes of quality of life, social health and carbon footprint.[66]

Getting serious about net zero

The government needs to lead on large-scale investment, taking more risks and moving faster, mobilising the workforce, and upskilling with technological skills that are currently in short supply. It needs to lead on "inspired regulation of the [energy] grid",[67] building trust among different actors, who, individually, would not take the risk on their own,[68] and promoting the growth of a UK green supply chain of net zero products such as heat pumps: "[making] net zero things in net zero ways".[69]

The fair financing of the net zero transition will be crucial for its progress and continued public support. However, the

UK government seems to be 'missing in action'.[70] The state's top priority should be to protect low-income households from the upfront costs.[71] It should lead the way by, for example, reinstating grants for home insulation that would give thousands the chance to improve the energy efficiency of their homes. Any tax reform therefore will be part of a broader package that includes investment in a Green New Deal, direct job creation, strengthening the social safety net and redistribution. Chancel warns us that 'there can be no deep decarbonization without profound redistribution of income and wealth'.[72]

Still, globally, decade by decade, countries have become more unequal in most regions of the world. In many places, the 10% richest take over 50% of national incomes. Earth4All, a group of leading economic thinkers, scientists and advocates warns that this is a recipe for deeply dysfunctional, polarised societies. They propose all governments:

> increase taxes on the 10% richest in societies until they take less than 40% of national incomes by 2030 (and the share of wealth controlled by the top 10% should continue to decline this century). Stronger progressive taxation and closure of international loopholes are essential to deal with destabilising inequality and luxury carbon and biosphere consumption.[73]

A modest welfare tax on multi-millionaires with a pollution top-up could generate 1.7% of global income to fund the bulk of extra investment needed to mitigate climate change. It would make access to capital more expensive for fossil fuel industries and generate large revenues. It goes without saying that such a proposal would face fierce opposition not only from the fossil fuel industry directly, but also indirectly from its lobbyists in finance, government and other sectors populated by the top 10%.

Take back control of energy and transport

Currently, there is mounting pressure for the government to do more to bring down energy prices for consumers, including removing VAT (value added tax) on energy bills, legislating to compel energy companies to remove high-standing charges on domestic gas and electricity, and implementing a much bolder and comprehensive windfall tax. On the last point, the government's current windfall tax rate of 25% hasn't gone anywhere near far enough, especially as it includes opt-out clauses that reduce it from £15 billion to £5 billion.[74]

With the ongoing energy crisis, there is growing support for taking public services back into public ownership, including energy and water.[75] UK energy firms could make excess profits totalling £170 billion between 2022–24, according to Treasury estimates.[76] Meanwhile, millions of households struggle amid the cost of living crisis – or income crisis, as Green Party deputy leader Zack Polanski has asked everyone to rename it.[77] Taking companies that generate, distribute or supply energy into public ownership and democratically run them would lower energy bills but also speed up home efficiency improvements, cutting carbon emissions. Publicly owned utility companies would have more incentives to introduce these improvements and set energy prices, prioritising affordability to customers rather than maximising the profits in dividends delivered to shareholders. The energy price cap would also be reinstated. The same principles can be extended to food, with basic necessities distributed through a public and democratic national food service with 'a right to food' enshrined in law.[78] What's needed from the perspective of high earners in this respect is a destigmatisation of those whom they believe would benefit from such policies – because, actually, the whole of society (including the top 10%) would.

Get better at tax

Tax is good. It has unbounded potential when compared to individual consumption or charity.[79] The impulse to buy often comes from a universal desire to bond with others, but as many psychologists have noted, the satisfaction is fleeting and often followed by post-purchase dissonance: the disappointment we feel on realising that our latest purchase won't fulfil what it promised.[80] However, when something is created collectively – such as the NHS – there is the 'exhilarating vastness of what we might do next', the sense it bestows of our own power. In the words of Zoe Williams, 'it turns us all into adventurers. It is beautiful in itself.'[81]

By contrast, to quote Mick Lynch, Secretary-General of the National Union of Rail, Maritime and Transport Workers, there are "those of us that are on PAYE, [who] cannot avoid tax, we pay it out of our wages every week [but] there are many, many people in this country avoiding tax like it is some kind of disease".[82] While there is frequent reference to the record high tax take, this is largely due to the income made from regressive taxes such as VAT and national insurance that hit middle- and low-income earners the most. Responsible economic and social policy requires more than just marginal tax rates on incomes, even on the highest. Our tax system already focuses disproportionately on income rather than assets, where true wealth is concentrated. Perhaps Rob Barber, the BBC *Question Time* audience member with whom we started this book, was on the mark when he complained that as he pays his taxes through PAYE he's at a disadvantage compared with the truly wealthy.

Since the 1980s, the amount of wealth held by private households has risen from three to nearly seven times the national GDP, but there has been no increase in the related tax taken as a proportion of GDP.[83] Significant tax breaks for savings, private pensions and allowances are heavily concentrated among the wealthy. Some have argued for an annual wealth tax or reform of the inheritance tax, which is riddled with loopholes. Inheritance taxes are always a touchy subject: though their use should be consistent with a meritocratic discourse, they are often fervently opposed as being unfair towards those who have worked hard all their lives. Still, even high earners and Conservative voters have acknowledged that the time to tax wealth properly has arrived.[84] As Martin Sandbu puts it: 'The importance of wealth in our economies and the inequality of that wealth have been going up for decades but the revenue raised from that wealth has not followed suit. So, I think politicians, facing pressure on their public finances, are missing a trick.'[85]

Advani and Summers make the same point:

> In the coming years, the pressure to rebuild public finances and to place crucial public services on a

sustainable footing will inevitably require politicians to make tough choices about who should bear the burden of additional taxes. It is important that these debates are not framed exclusively through the prism of headline rates. What matters − both for revenue and the fairness of the tax system − is effective rates. Instead of asking 'can the rich pay more?', a better question may therefore be 'who amongst the rich is not paying enough?'[86]

In the year 2015–16, the average rate of tax paid by people who received one million pounds in taxable income and gains was just 35%, the same as someone earning £100,000. But one in four of those people paid 45% − close to the top rate − while another quarter paid less than 30% overall. One in ten paid just 11%, the same as someone earning £15,000.[87] As Summers and Advani conclude, 'the rich are not all in it together'. Crucially, they also point out that those low tax rates are not due to complex tax avoidance schemes; they're a feature of how our system is designed.[88]

As we finish this book, the current government's plans for corporate tax are uncertain. Corporate tax rates had been going to be brought in line with the OECD average from 2023, which would increase tax revenue. That was after a decade-long experiment of seeing if lowering corporation tax increased productivity in the UK. The evidence by now should be clear: it didn't. However even if or when the tax rate is increased to 25%, this will still be lower than its lowest rate under Margaret Thatcher (34%).[89]

In addition, removing loopholes for rich individuals and large corporations would alleviate some of the current rigging of the tax system against average income earners. It would also make it easier to ask the top 10% to gradually increase their contributions. They would be willing to pay more, as interviews and polls suggest, in return for what they perceive to be a well-functioning state. The system of taxing multinational companies, as economist Jo Michell has written, is a hundred years out of date, designed when physical goods were moved around. It allows firms such as Amazon to pay offensively low tax rates.[90] Reform through the creation of unitary taxation, combined with an effective corporate tax rate, would allow governments to tax the profits of such large multinationals based on where they employ people, own assets and make sales. Furthermore, a progressive global tax on capital is perhaps the best-suited instrument to face the inequalities of the 21st century, as Piketty suggested.[91] For the very wealthiest and for the top 10%, mobility shouldn't be a way of evading contribution to the societies that make their affluence possible in the first place.

The way our property is taxed is also in urgent need of reform. Council tax is out of date and deeply regressive. Replacing it with a progressive property tax, as outlined in current Labour Party proposals, which would be set nationally and paid by property owners rather than tenants, would reduce the tax paid by a majority of households and discourage the use of homes as financial assets.[92]

High earners also want action on tax avoidance and evasion. We know that avoidance costs governments 4–10% of global corporate tax revenues, money that could be spent on health, education or infrastructure for the energy transition. Even though tax fraud costs the economy 9 times more than benefits fraud (£20 billion versus £2.2 billion), you are 23 times more likely to be prosecuted for the latter.[93] Tackling tax avoidance and evasion through fixing structural problems in the system, enforcing rules and regulations, would not only raise revenue but also restore public faith in the tax system.

Realism is defined by those in power

Some of the policies described in this chapter would be difficult to implement and require extraordinary political will. They would need what Gary Younge has called 'sufficient collective imagination for a shared sense of possibility and a set of principles that could apply to a common future; the idea that Britain stands for something more than posterity and itself'.[94]

Britain's political culture doesn't currently seem to have that, though that may change. The ideas in this chapter also challenge the meritocratic, pro-austerity and pro-insulation 'common sense' we have described throughout the book and would be staunchly opposed by those with too many assets to lose. Making them a reality would need a level of public trust and confidence in our political system, which is currently at an all-time low.

We argue, however, that the vast majority of the top 10% won't lose out. The 'common sense' and attitudes that have served them well up to now in reaching a comfortably-off position may not help them remain there. We hope to convince people like Rob Barber that marginal income tax rises over £80,000 would not only sustain the quality of life that they have come to expect but would even improve their lives, their children's and those of the majority in the communities in which they live. There's a reason, after all, why the famous Occupy movement slogan makes reference to 'the 99%', not 'the 90%'.

Conclusion:
Accepted truths, social
distance and discomfort

To start with, high-income earners don't know that their incomes are high. They don't think they are rich and have little idea of where they fit on the income distribution. Although they feel relatively comfortable and privileged, they worry about downward mobility, especially for their children. The near inevitability of their family falling down the ranks at some point means that they are right to worry. All in all, the UK's top 10% is a fragile group. Most people aren't in it for the majority of their lives. They are generally high earners only in middle age when they are compelled to cement their position by acquiring assets and contributing towards their children's education which, in turn, will allow them to differentiate themselves from the rest.

Despite believing in meritocracy, high-income earners know that the higher they go, the bigger the step beneath them.[1] This 'fear of falling' is one of the reasons why they feel so politically isolated. They support redistribution more than they used to but want higher taxes targeted on those earning more than they do. The truly rich are always above them, and they don't have to work. As such, the top 10% are yet to be convinced that their take is disproportionate, that it has negative consequences for others or that the way they seek to secure it affects their own wellbeing.

It could be argued that a crucial effect of their relative isolation and effort to distance themselves from the rest is the belief that their decisions affect only them. From that point of view, private education and healthcare are the business only of those who pay for them. We know this is not the case. The main flaw of the small 'l' liberal mindset is the belief that the causes and consequences of one's actions are much more independent from the rest of the world than they actually are. In spite of raised awareness about the extent of inequality and the need for a new social contract after the pandemic, many in the top 10% remain unconvinced that they need and rely on public services and infrastructure, and that there's no shame in that. In the words of Danny Dorling:

> Without public higher education, their businesses could not function, their children would not be educated, their lives would be less enriched. This is the group who make by far the greatest use of public health services because they live the longest and are least likely to die a quick death at a younger age. Instead it is the best-off 10% who stagger on for the greatest time with the highest number of comorbidities. We at the top might wish for a more equitable future if those of us in this group thought a little more about [what] our final year of life might be like; often being cared for by people in the lowest 10% pay band in care homes (our successful children having migrated far away).[2]

If economic structures are not working for the most privileged in our society, then this is a sign that the wider system of reward is not working for anyone. As Mike Savage points out, inequality bothers those with privilege much more now because they cannot use wealth to guarantee their own security in a world they can no longer predict and control: 'The rules of the game, orientated toward a market-driven business logic (and that have shaped the world since the 1980s) can no longer be taken for granted.'[3]

What will these structural changes mean for them? As parents, they may be forced to accept that the economy and hiring demands are changing and that includes a hollowing out of middle-class jobs (not to mention current developments in artificial intelligence). If things continue as they are, their children might not be afforded the same opportunities or standard of living that they had. The legitimacy of new employment, consumption, and other lifestyle choices (which are different from those of previous generations) will be an expectable outcome of the diminishing value of meritocracy. This creates a dilemma for high earners and the current social settlement more broadly, with many asking themselves '[W]hy should young people support capitalism when they could never expect to own any capital?'[4]

High earners will increasingly see their children have different priorities and make different life choices. They might see them become more politically engaged than they were at the same age. They shouldn't blame them. Avocado on toast or shop-bought coffees are not at fault. The top 10% could choose to become a little less wary about the possibility of alternatives to the status quo or, conversely, they could entrench their position and reproduce the generational divides that we are seeing. Increasingly the only way to secure the future will be assets and other inherited advantages such as networks and status. This undermines the pretence that we live in a meritocratic society in the first place.

Will people who are relatively comfortable now realise that if they want to stay the same, things will have to change? And that this will mean paying attention to how power is exerted in Britain. Duncan Green, in his book *How Change Happens*, writes that '[p]ositive social change requires power, and therefore attention on the part of reformers to politics and the institutions within which power is exercised'.[5]

In his famous 1958 book *The Rise of the Meritocracy* – where the term was first coined – Michael Young predicts his fictional version of the year 2034. He concedes that there will be 'stir enough' but nothing:

> more serious than a few days' strike and a week's disturbance, which will be well within the capacity of the police (with their new weapons) to quell [...] The charter is too vague. The demands are, with one exception, not in any way a fundamental challenge to the government. This is no revolutionary movement but a caucus of disparate groups held together only by a few charismatic personalities and an atmosphere of crisis. There is no tradition of political organisation on which to draw.[6]

In 2001, four years into the last Labour government, Young reflected on what he had written in 1958, asking whether anything could be done about Britain's new meritocratic common sense. He wrote:

> It would help if Mr Blair would drop the word [meritocracy] from his public vocabulary, or at least admit to the downside. It would help still more if he and Mr Brown would mark their distance from the new meritocracy by increasing income taxes on the rich, and also by reviving more powerful local government as a way of involving local people and giving them a training for local politics.[7]

What Young said in 1958 and 2001 remains relevant today. However, structural political change seems at the moment unlikely, but this does not mean nothing can be done. As the Club of Rome warned the world decades ago, the way we live is not sustainable. The first step is for 'man [to] explore himself – his goals and values – as much as the world he seeks to change'.[8]

We have been taught to believe that the more we work, the more we are worth and the more we deserve. The rationale for being part of an elite is that high income is a reward for effort, whether in the form of work or qualifications. A key consequence of that assumed link between effort, reward, and status is believing that where we end up on the social ladder is a foregone conclusion in our own control. In this view, inequality is essential for remaining motivated, for keeping up with the Joneses. But it's also crucial for maintaining an economic settlement that has produced stagnation, global warming, pollution, reduced social mobility, and political instability, as well as apathy and anxiety. Crucially for Brahmins, this implies questioning whether they would value education and credentials so much if those things weren't so successful at distinguishing them from other people. Capital, even in the concept of 'cultural capital', is another word for assets, after all.

We hope this book prompts high earners to question accepted truths and to contest 'the process of self-delusion that has driven consensus about what is true'.[9] In other words, we ask readers to question long-held and powerful beliefs that affect how they see themselves as well as how they judge others. This needs to include looking beyond our own personal circumstances to observe wider societal trends, noticing how what we do every day affects everyone else.

Our research tells us that high-income earners think of social action in individual terms, carried out and mostly having effects on the individual concerned. But individual effort will only take us so far. What is needed is to open space for collective action and to stop using every waking hour in improving our CVs or our bottom line. If we don't make the collective investment, we will not have a resilient society and economy. In that sense, one of the things that members of the top 10% could do is less. That would allow the 90% to participate more fully in the decisions that concern us all by granting them a more prominent role in the institutions that shape the public conversation.

Our deadline for this book happened soon after Liz Truss became prime minister, in the chaotic days of October 2022, when the demand for urgent change of some sort was becoming harder to ignore. We hope by the time you read this that there's more political will to build the institutional infrastructure needed to address the problems we have covered. But change can't be expected to come only from the very top. This is because, as should now be clear, the stakes are too great for those already with the assets and with the financial, political, and media wealth and status. They have too much to lose. However, the growing gap between high earners and the top 1% provides an opportunity for change, a possible breaking point among the elites that govern key institutions. We have reached the point of diminishing returns not only from meritocracy but also from increased production: more is not always better.[10] A more equitable society could protect both ourselves in our old age, and our families long after we are gone. The children of the top 10% are likely to be more aware of the trends we have discussed than their parents and, as a result, may be forced to take different routes to those their parents took – or conversely, to rely mainly on their inheritance. Still, as things stand, the road has become too narrow to comfortably accommodate any more in the 'middle class'.

We hope to have convinced at least some high-earning readers that, however hard they work, they will remain 'uncomfortably off' if the economy and society continue to operate as usual.

Our social contract and democratic institutions need reviving, and that is true in spite of having been repeatedly told that a more collaborative and equitable society is impossible. The best alternative for the relatively well-off in a future world without such collective effort might be a post-apocalyptic bunker furnished with the latest Amazon gadgets, perhaps in Surrey or New Zealand.

Notes

Introduction

[1]   Bell, 2019; see also Joyce et al, 2019
[2]   Statista, 2022
[3]   Goodwin and Heath, 2019
[4]   Race, 2022
[5]   Parsons, 2022
[6]   Although, as we discuss later, this does not mean people in this income bracket would identify with those labels.
[7]   Matthew Stewart, for instance, talks about the 9.9%. See Stewart, 2018, 2021. See also Reeves, 2017.
[8]   TASC, 2020
[9]   Piketty, 2014
[10] See HMRC, 2022. Other sources vary, but all are roughly in the £55,000–60,000 region. The relatively low median income in this data source compared to others may be because it includes all sources liable to income tax (including pensions and some state benefits).
[11] The threshold to be part of the top 10% of households for equivalised disposable income (that is, after taxes and benefits and accounting for household composition) is, according to the ONS, £62,682 for 2021. See ONS, 2022a.
[12] Atkinson, 2007; Bollinger et al, 2018; Advani et al, 2022; Edmiston, 2022
[13] Gilens, 2012; Page et al, 2013
[14] Atkinson and Flint, 2001
[15] Despite 14% of the working population being from a BME (Black and minority ethnic) background, many minority ethnic groups are concentrated in low-paying jobs. However, this is not uniform across ethnicities, some of which are underrepresented in the sample. See ONS, 2020a.
[16] Agrawal and Phillips, 2020
[17] ONS, 2022b
[18] All interviews were recorded, but any reference to individuals or organisations has been anonymised.
[19] UCU, 2019
[20] See Laurison, 2015
[21] OECD, 2015; TASC, 2020
[22] TASC, 2020
[23] World Inequality Database, 2021; see also Equality Trust, 2020
[24] Piketty, 2020

25 Milanovic, 2019
26 Milburn, 2019
27 Stevenson, 2021
28 Haidt, 2012
29 Wilkinson and Pickett, 2010, 2019
30 Markovits, 2020

Chapter 1

1 Unless otherwise stated, the figures below and in the remainder of the text are based on the European Survey of Income and Living Conditions, mostly on an individual's total income (from all sources) before tax rather than the household's, as were used in the 2020 TASC report from which this book draws. Though the top 10% of individual income earners and the top 10% of households overlap to a great degree, they are not the same, because a family of five would tend to be under much more financial strain than a single person if they earned the same amount. The advantage of using the figure for individuals is that it makes it easier to find individuals who belong to the top 10% to be interviewed. A considerable disadvantage of using individual rather than household income is that it neglects those who are part of wealthy households but do not earn well themselves, such as the children of the top 10%. Also, we concentrate mostly on income rather than wealth, not because we think one is more important than the other, but because we want to see the degree to which high-income earners may be feeling the pinch, as Piketty's theory on the increasing primacy of capital and wealth in relation to wages from labour implies.

2 Higgins et al, 2018
3 Guyton et al, 2021
4 Gallup, 2017
5 https://stats.oecd.org/Index.aspx?QueryId=66597
6 https://stats.oecd.org
7 Davis et al, 2020, p. 9
8 Davis et al, 2020, p. 11, emphasis in original
9 TASC, 2020
10 ONS, 2018
11 Evans and Mellon, 2016
12 Walker, 2019
13 IFS, 2021
14 Friedman and Laurison, 2019, pp. 33–5
15 Hanley, 2019
16 Adams-Prassl et al, 2020
17 Eurofound, 2020, pp. 7–11
18 TASC, 2020
19 TASC, 2020, p. 39
20 The Sutton Trust and Social Mobility Commission, 2019
21 University of Cambridge, 2021; University of Oxford, 2021
22 University of Cambridge, 2022; University of Oxford, 2022

Notes

23 ONS, 2021a
24 ONS, 2021a
25 See also Toft and Friedman, 2021
26 TASC, 2020, p. 41; see also Phipps, 2021
27 ONS, 2021b
28 ONS, 2021c. See also Guvenen et al, 2014
29 House of Commons Library, 2021
30 ONS, 2022c
31 Piketty and Saez, 2013; Cingano, 2014; *Financial Times*, 2014
32 Friedman and Laurison, 2019, pp. 12–13
33 Streib, 2020
34 TASC, 2020, pp. 30–1
35 World Inequality Database, 2021
36 TASC, 2020
37 TASC, 2020
38 www.ons.gov.uk/economy/inflationandpriceindices/bulletins/houseprice index/march2022
39 TASC, 2020
40 Berman and Milanovic, 2020; see also Milanovic, 2018
41 Bangham and Leslie, 2020
42 Please note that changes in any one respondent's income percentiles throughout the book are the result of either (1) adjustments (increases or decreases) in income between the first and follow-up interviews, or (2) income positioning in 2022 compared with when we interviewed them in 2019/20.
43 Dorling, 2014
44 Sherman, 2017
45 We thank Professor Danny Dorling for these estimates.
46 Törmälehto, 2017
47 Ehsan and Kingman, 2019

Chapter 2

1 This way of distinguishing between the middle and working class doesn't make sense everywhere, and how we interpret class is always tricky. In the US, for instance, most people think of themselves as middle class, except perhaps those who are forced to learn they are not.
2 Evans and Mellon, 2016; see also McCall, 2013
3 Pakulski and Waters, 1995
4 Durose, 2022, p. 30
5 Durose, 2022, p. 30, emphasis added
6 Bourdieu, 1984
7 Friedman and Laurison, 2019, pp. 124–44; see also Friedman et al, 2021
8 Piketty, 2018
9 Piketty, 2018
10 Gilens, 2012
11 House of Commons Library, 2022a

12 Lamont, 1992
13 Sherman, 2017
14 Graeber, 2018, p. 258
15 https://openknowledge.worldbank.org/bitstream/handle/10986/30418/9781464813306.pdf
16 Frank, 2017; see also Sauder, 2020
17 Coenen et al, 2018
18 Edmiston, 2018a, 2018b; see also Rowlingson and McKay, 2012
19 Edmiston, 2018b, p. 986
20 Paugam et al, 2017; see also Krozer, 2018
21 Chancel et al, 2022

Chapter 3

1 Whyte, 1943, p. 60
2 Sen, 1975
3 Tilly and Tilly, 1998, p. 22
4 Dhar, 2020
5 Rivera, 2016
6 Friedman and Laurison, 2019
7 Social Mobility Commission, 2019, p. 16
8 For an explanation of the Social Grade classification system based on occupation, see www.nrs.co.uk/nrs-print/lifestyle-and-classification-data/social-grade.
9 Kirk, 2022
10 Kirk, 2022, p. 8
11 Major and Machin, 2019
12 Social Mobility Commission, 2020
13 See Reis and Moore, 2005
14 Dorling, 2014, p. 35; The Sutton Trust and Social Mobility Commission, 2019
15 https://assets.publishing.service.gov.uk/government/uploads/system/uploads/attachment_data/file/347915/Elitist_Britain_-_Final.pdf
16 See, for example https://assets.publishing.service.gov.uk/government/uploads/system/uploads/attachment_data/file/347915/Elitist_Britain_-_Final.pdf
17 Social Mobility and Child Poverty Commission, 2015, p. 4.
18 Major and Machin, 2019
19 Siddique, 2022
20 Hecht, 2017
21 Coote et al, 2010
22 Xue and McMunn, 2021
23 Beck, 1992; Giddens, 2000
24 Graeber, 2018
25 The 'Big Four' refer to the four largest global accounting and professional services accounting firms. On the topic, we recommend Brooks, 2018.
26 Standing, 2019, p. 16; see also Mijs and Savage, 2020

27 Chun et al, 2018
28 Wilkie, 2015
29 Blackman et al, 2015, p. 79
30 With thanks to Irina Predescu for her reflections and references on this issue.
31 Forrest, 2022a
32 Roper, 2020
33 Alamillo-Martinez, 2014; see also Salverda and Grassiani, 2014
34 Shackle, 2019
35 *The New York Times*, 2022
36 Soper, 2020; see also Jaffe, 2021
37 Graeber, 2018, p. 220

Chapter 4

1 TASC, 2020. See also Armingeon and Schädel, 2015
2 Enns and Wlezien, 2011; Gilens, 2012; Lindh and McCall, 2020
3 ONS, 2020b; see also Afonso, 2015
4 Surridge, 2021
5 Dorling, 2016; IPPR, 2019; Joyce and Xu, 2019
6 Kalinina and Shand, 2018; Joyce and Xu, 2019
7 Lucchino and Morelli, 2012; Joyce and Xu, 2019
8 Standing, 2019, p. 13
9 Joyce and Xu, 2019
10 Davis et al, 2020
11 Quantitative Easing, or QE, is a monetary policy tool whereby a central bank (in this case the Bank of England) purchases government bonds and other securities to increase the money supply and incentivise loans and economic activity.
12 See Goldman Sachs, 2022
13 Wren-Lewis, 2018
14 See Gov.uk, 2015
15 Carpenter, 2018
16 Brown and Jones, 2021, p. 5
17 Martin et al, 2021
18 Lee, 2015
19 Blakeley, 2018
20 Moore, 2016
21 What UK Thinks, 2022
22 Eliasoph, 1998, 2012; Putnam, 2000
23 University of Southampton, 2016
24 University of Southampton, 2016
25 Foa et al, 2020
26 Labour for a New Democracy, 2022
27 Clery et al, 2021; see also University of Southampton, 2016
28 Brown and Jones, 2021
29 Perryman, 2019
30 Berry and Guinan, 2019

[31] Nixon, 2015, p. 252
[32] Nixon, 2015; Mitchell, 2020
[33] Keen and Audickas, 2016
[34] Bale, 2021
[35] Game, 2019
[36] Barnett et al, 2021
[37] Shames, 2017; Patel and Quilter-Pinner, 2022
[38] Toynbee and Walker, 2008
[39] Handscomb et al, 2021
[40] Jackson, 2021, p. 41; see also Driscoll, 2022
[41] Williams, 2015, p. 326
[42] González Hernando, 2019
[43] Wren-Lewis, 2018
[44] Davies, 2021
[45] Lister, 2004, p. 166
[46] *The Spectator*, 2016
[47] Goodhart, 2017, 2020
[48] Manza and Crowley, 2018
[49] Proctor, 2019

Chapter 5

[1] Gilens, 2012; Schlozman et al, 2012; Rigby and Wright, 2013
[2] Lutz et al, 2015
[3] Dorling, 2016
[4] https://blogs.lse.ac.uk/politicsandpolicy/brexit-inequality-and-the-demographic-divide
[5] Skinner, 2021
[6] *The New York Times*, 2017
[7] Wright, 2021
[8] Dunn et al, 2020
[9] Dunn et al, 2020
[10] Booth, 2022
[11] UK Parliament Public Accounts Committee, 2021
[12] Local Government Association, 2018
[13] Jooshandeh, 2021; see also Reeves and Rothwell, 2020
[14] Edmiston et al, 2020
[15] Adams-Prassl et al, 2020
[16] Elliott, 2022
[17] Bartrum, 2022
[18] Johnson, 2022a
[19] Brown, 2022a; Johnson, 2022b; Partington, 2022
[20] Toynbee, 2022
[21] Resolution Foundation and Centre for Economic Performance, 2022
[22] Sillars, 2022
[23] Sridhar, 2022; Walker, 2022
[24] Allegretti, 2022a; Carson and Finnerty, 2022; Forbes, 2022

Notes

[25] Cotton, 2022

[26] Baines et al, 2022; *Financial Times*, 2022a

[27] Neame, 2022

[28] Mallet and Aloisi, 2022

[29] Allen et al, 2021

[30] Jackson and Cooney, 2022

[31] UK Parliament, 2022

[32] Davies, 2022

[33] CICTAR, 2021

[34] Mitchell, 2022

[35] An Association of Directors of Adult Social Services survey found that, between May and July 2021, social services departments were unable to meet 355,554 needed hours of home care due to lack of capacity. See ADASS, 2021

[36] Pembroke, 2019

[37] Mok and Zinkula, 2023

[38] Handscomb et al, 2021, p. 7

[39] TASC, 2020

[40] Spencer, 2022

[41] Shrubsole, 2019, p. 5

[42] Advani and Tarrant, 2022

[43] Mulheirn, 2019; Standing, 2019, p. 58

[44] *Financial Times*, 2020

[45] Corlett and Odamtten, 2021

[46] Allen et al, 2021

[47] Davis et al, 2020; Hills, 2014; Standing, 2019

[48] Alstadsæter et al, 2018

[49] Alvaredo et al, 2018

[50] Broome and Leslie, 2022

[51] Lansley, 2022, p. 240

[52] Stevenson, 2021

[53] Savage, 2021, p. 161

[54] Piketty, 2014, p. 746

[55] Davies, 2022

[56] Bullough, 2022, p. 14

[57] Bullough, 2022, p. 14

[58] Akenji et al, 2021

[59] Whitmarsh, 2022

[60] Lansley, 2022, p. 241

[61] Committee on Climate Change, 2019

[62] Chancel et al, 2022; see also Jorgenson et al, 2016

[63] Chancel, 2021a

[64] Marmot et al, 2020

[65] Raleigh, 2021

[66] Marmot et al, 2020, p. 37

[67] *Financial Times*, 2022b

68 Marmot, 2015
69 Woodward and Kawachi, 2000
70 Wilson and Daly, 1997
71 Woodward and Kawachi, 2000, p. 928
72 Hastings et al, 2015
73 Marmot et al, 2020, p. 5
74 Corlett and Odamtten, 2021
75 Belfield et al, 2017
76 Intergenerational Commission, 2018, p. 11
77 Chakelian et al, 2022
78 Chakelian et al, 2022
79 Mahmood, 2022; see also Department for Education, 2012; Iniesta-Martinez and Evans, 2012
80 Jones, 2014; Friedman and Laurison, 2019
81 Rivera, 2016
82 Davies, 2021
83 Webber et al, 2022
84 *Financial Times*, 2021
85 Winter, 2019, p. 8
86 www.makevotesmatter.org.uk/first-past-the-post
87 www.bhcompass.org.uk/a/44852767-45609270
88 Thomas, 2020
89 Thomas, 2019
90 Gethins, 2022
91 Wilkinson and Pickett, 2019, p. 217; see also Stiglitz, 2016
92 Coglianese, 2020

Chapter 6

1 On sociological work on modernity and flexibility, see Giddens, 2000; Bauman, 2005; Boltanski and Chiapello, 2018. On capital flight, see Harrington, 2016; Young, 2017
2 Adams-Prassl et al, 2020
3 Uni Global Union, 2020; EMG Transmission Group, 2021
4 Leslie and Shah, 2021
5 Klein, 2020
6 Rosa, 2015
7 Duffy and Thain, 2022
8 Graeber, 2018, p. 247
9 Putnam, 2000, p. 107
10 Klinenberg, 2018
11 Paugam et al, 2017
12 Reeves and Venator, 2014
13 Wilkinson and Pickett, 2010
14 Wilkinson and Pickett, 2019, p. 228
15 Garrett, 2021
16 Coyle, 2011, p. 10

17 Sklair and Glucksberg, 2021
18 Cited in Ambler et al, 2022, p. xv
19 Jones, 2012, p. 250
20 For further discussion of what Paul is describing, see for example, Madden, 2020.
21 Williams, 2015, p. 128; Soper, 2020, p. 108
22 When we conducted a follow-up interview with Michael, just after the pandemic, a pay rise had moved him into the top 6% income band.
23 Wilkinson and Pickett, 2019
24 Chancel, 2021a, p. 20
25 Raworth, 2021
26 OECD, 2018
27 Social Mobility Commission, 2019
28 Estimated figures provided by Danny Dorling.
29 Social Mobility Commission, 2019, p. 180
30 Wilkinson and Pickett, 2010
31 Edmiston, quoted in Chakelian et al, 2022
32 Ofsted is the Office for Standards in Education, Children's Services and Skills. It inspects services providing education and skills for learners of all ages. It also inspects and regulates services that care for children and young people. www.gov.uk/government/organisations/ofsted/about
33 OBR, 2021
34 House of Commons Library, 2022b
35 ONS, 2018
36 Ward and Chijoko, 2018
37 Ward and Chijoko, 2018
38 Ward and Chijoko, 2018
39 Wilkinson and Pickett, 2019, p. 217
40 Harrop, 2022
41 Blakeley, 2020a, p. 8
42 A £137 billion package (Full Fact, 2019).
43 See Van Lerven and Jackson (2018) on why such interpretations are a fallacy.
44 This occurs when a company buys shares of its own stock from its shareholders. This repurchase reduces the number of shares outstanding, thereby inflating (positive) earnings per share and, often, the value of the stock (Ghosh, 2022a).
45 Soper, 2020, p. 69
46 Sandel, 2013
47 Reich, 2020
48 Savage, 2022a
49 Dunne and Gabbatiss, 2022
50 Evans, 2022
51 Monbiot, 2022
52 Cited in Fisher and Gilbert, 2013, p. 90
53 Stronge and Lewis, 2021, p. 95
54 Davies, 2022

55 Mason, 2022
56 Ghosh, 2022b
57 A non-fungible token is a unique digital identifier in a blockchain (a decentralised log shared across a network) that cannot be copied, merged or subdivided. Its purpose is to certify the authenticity or ownership of a digital object, turned into a commodity.
58 Pymnts, 2022
59 European Central Bank, 2022
60 Olson, 2022
61 Blundell et al, 2020
62 Coyle, 2011, p. 11

Chapter 7

1   Wilkinson and Pickett, 2019
2   See Markovits, 2020
3   Dorling, 2014, p. 46
4   Dorling, 2014, p. 46
5   Dorling, 2014, p. 46
6   Dorling, 2014, p. 40
7   Mandler, 2022, pp. 44–5
8   Jones, 2012, p. 258
9   Lister, 2004
10 Tilly and Tilly, 1998, p. 22; Dhar, 2020
11 'No man is an island, entire of itself; every man is a piece of the continent, a part of the main.' John Donne (1572–1631), *Meditation XVII*.
12 Sandel, 2020, p. 20
13 Reed and Lansley, 2016
14 Lister, 2020
15 Ehrenreich, 1989
16 Partington, 2019
17 With acknowledgements to Neal Lawson, 2009.
18 Khan, 2016
19 Khan, 2016
20 Khan, 2012
21 Lawson, 2009
22 ONS, 2021a
23 Dorling, 2014
24 Hecht, 2017
25 Mijs, 2021
26 Mijs, 2021
27 Dorling, quoted in Wilkinson and Pickett, 2019, p. 180
28 Mijs, quoted in Liscomb, 2022
29 Putnam, 1995
30 Putnam, 1995, p. 85
31 Putnam, 1995, p. 86
32 Arlie Russell Hochschild, quoted in Putnam, 1995, p. 86

[33] Graeber, 2018, p. 118
[34] Putnam, 1995, p. 91
[35] Putnam, 1995, p. 92
[36] Bellah et al, 1985, p. 251
[37] Bellah et al, 1985, p. 194

Chapter 8

[1] We chose this apocryphal quote, attributed to several historical public figures, including Winston Churchill and John Maynard Keynes, as it reminds us that economics is 'the science which studies human behaviour as a relationship between ends and scarce means which have alternative uses' (Lionel Robbins quoted in Kishtainy, 2012, p. 13). In other words, unlike other sciences, the systems it examines are fluid and, as with the 'soft sciences' of psychology, sociology and politics, there is modelling, describing and storytelling involved.

[2] On this topic, we recommend the work of Green and Kynaston, 2019.

[3] Jackson and Cooney, 2022

[4] Wilkinson and Pickett, 2019

[5] Resolution Foundation and Centre for Economic Performance, 2022, pp. 19–20

[6] Raworth, 2017, p. 64

[7] Soper, 2020, p. 74

[8] Coyle, 2011, p. 14; Williams, 2015, p. 4

[9] Corlett et al, 2022

[10] Bastani, 2022

[11] Byline TV, 2022

[12] See Hunt (2021) for a discussion of unions' renewed sense of purpose and increased membership since 2020.

[13] TASC, 2020, p. 62

[14] Titmuss's 1967 lecture on 'Welfare and wellbeing' to the British National Conference on Social Welfare, quoted in Glennerster, 2014.

[15] Blakemore, 2003

[16] Blakemore, 2003

[17] Newman and Dehaghani, 2022

[18] Hills, 2014, p. 267

[19] Hills, 2014, p. 268

[20] Ramsay, 2022

[21] Ramsay, 2022

[22] Federal Government, 2022

[23] Ramsay, 2022

[24] Osborne, 2022. In 2009, for example, the UK was the world's most indebted country, with household, finance and business debt at 420% of GDP.

[25] Grace Blakeley speaking on Byline TV, 2022

[26] Holland and Portes, 2012

[27] Hirsch, 2021

[28] OBR, 2021

29 IFS TaxLab, 2021
30 Brien and Keep, 2022
31 ONS, 2018
32 Elgot and Stewart, 2022
33 Adams, 2019
34 Blakemore, 2003
35 TASC, 2020, p. 68
36 Michell, 2021, p. 228
37 See Riso, 2021
38 Murray, 2020, p. 31
39 Coote et al, 2020, p. 3
40 Duff, 2020
41 Stronge and Lewis, 2021
42 Chancel, 2021b
43 CAST, 2021
44 Graham et al, 2019; Streimikiene et al, 2019
45 White, 2022
46 Pack, 2022; YouGov Poll, 2022
47 Davies, 2021; Electoral Calculus, 2022
48 Brown and Jones, 2021, p. 128
49 Mishra and Rath, 2020
50 Mazzucato, 2022
51 Meyer and Newport, 2022, p. 3
52 See, for example, Intergovernmental Panel on Climate Change, 2021.
53 Joseph Rowntree Foundation, 2022
54 David Willetts, in Resolution Foundation, 2022
55 The Trussell Trust, 2022
56 Disability Rights UK, 2022
57 Employers for Childcare, 2022
58 Employers for Childcare, 2022
59 Allegretti, 2022b
60 Brown, 2022b
61 United Nations Economic and Social Council, 2017
62 International Labour Organization, 2016
63 Blakeley, 2020b
64 Dutkiewicz and Sakwa, 2013
65 Meda, 2022
66 Hickel, 2020
67 Julia King, in Resolution Foundation, 2022
68 Mike Biddle, in Resolution Foundation, 2022
69 Mike Biddle, in Resolution Foundation, 2022
70 Jo Michell, in Resolution Foundation, 2022
71 Resolution Foundation and Centre for Economic Performance, 2022, p. 133
72 Chancel, 2021b
73 Earth4All, 2022
74 Stewart, 2022

[75] Shoben, 2022

[76] Forrest, 2022b

[77] Polanski, 2022

[78] Byrne, 2022; Neame, 2022

[79] Giridharadas, 2019; Glucksberg and Russell-Prywata, 2020

[80] Jackson, 2021, p. 226

[81] Williams, 2015, p. 129; see also Murphy, 2016, 2020

[82] Novara Media, 2022

[83] Leslie and Shah, 2021, p. 130

[84] Chappell, 2022

[85] Sandbu, 2022

[86] Advani and Summers, 2020

[87] Summers and Advani, 2021

[88] Summers and Advani, 2021

[89] Browning, 2017

[90] Michell, 2021

[91] Piketty, 2014

[92] Monbiot et al, 2019

[93] Chakelian, 2021

[94] Younge, 2022

Conclusion

[1] Phillips, 2020, p. 66

[2] Dorling in TASC, 2020, p. 10

[3] Savage, 2022b, p. 44

[4] Blakeley, 2020a, p. 17

[5] Green, 2016, p. 250

[6] Young, 1958, p. 189

[7] Young, 2001

[8] Meadows et al, 1972, p. 197

[9] Lothian-McLean, 2022

[10] Jackson, 2021, p. 42

References

Adams, R. (2019) One in five teachers using own money for school supplies – report. 19 April. *The Guardian.* www.theguardian.com/education/2019/apr/19/one-in-five-teachers-using-own-money-for-school-supplies-report

Adams-Prassl, A., Boneva, T., Golin, M. and Rauh, C. (2020) Work that can be done from home: Evidence on variation within and across occupations and industries. *IZA Discussion Paper, n.13374.* Bonn: IZA Institute of Labor Economics.

ADASS (2021) *ADASS home care and workforce snap survey, September 2021.* London: ADASS. www.adass.org.uk/media/8863/final-rapid-survey-report-070921-publication.pdf

Advani, A. and Summers, A. (2020) Raising money from 'the rich' doesn't require increasing tax rates. LSE blog. https://blogs.lse.ac.uk/businessreview/2020/06/15/raising-money-from-the-rich-doesnt-require-increasing-tax-rates

Advani, A. and Tarrant, H. (2022) Official statistics underestimate wealth inequality in Britain. *LSE British Politics and Policy.* 7 January. https://blogs.lse.ac.uk/politicsandpolicy/official-statistics-underestimate-wealth-inequality

Advani, A., Ooms, T. and Summers, A. (2022) Missing incomes in the UK: Evidence and policy implications. *Journal of Social Policy* [onlinefirst], 1–21. www.cambridge.org/core/journals/journal-of-social-policy/article/missing-incomes-in-the-uk-evidence-and-policy-implications/6F454FD9D74613B182631F9453EDB671

Afonso, A. (2015) To explain voting intentions, income is more important for the Conservatives than for Labour. https://blogs.lse.ac.uk/politicsandpolicy/to-explain-voting-intentions-income-is-more-important-for-the-conservatives-than-for-labour

Agrawal, S. and Phillips, D. (2020) *Catching up or falling behind? Geographical inequalities in the UK and how they have changed in recent years.* London: Institute for Fiscal Studies.

Akenji, L., Bengtsson, M., Toivio, V. and Lettenmeier, M. (2021) *1.5-Degree lifestyles: Towards a fair consumption space for all. Summary for policy makers.* Berlin: Hot or Cool Institute.

Alamillo-Martinez, L. (2014) Never good enough. *Comparative Sociology*, 13:1, 12–29.

Allegretti, A. (2022a) Ministers warn of scammers posing as energy bill support scheme. *The Guardian*. 1 October. www.theguardian.com/money/2022/oct/01/energy-bill-support-scheme-scam-alert

Allegretti, A. (2022b) Gordon Brown urges Liz Truss to 'show up' for workers struggling with bills. *The Guardian*, 7 September. www.theguardian.com/politics/2022/sep/07/gordon-brown-urges-liz-truss-to-show-up-for-workers-struggling-with-bills

Allen, P., Konzelmann, S.J. and Toporowski, J. (2021) *The return of the state: Restructuring Britain for the common good.* Newcastle: Agenda Publishing.

Alstadsæter, A., Johannesen, N. and Zucman, G. (2018) Who owns the wealth in tax havens? Macro evidence and implications for global inequality. *Journal of Public Economics*, 162, 89–100.

Alvaredo, F., Chancel, L., Piketty, T., Saez, E. and Zucman, G. (2018) *World Inequality Report 2018.* Paris: World Inequality Lab.

Ambler, L., Earle, J., and Scott, N. (2022) *Reclaiming economics for future generations.* Manchester: Manchester University Press.

Armingeon, K. and Schädel, L. (2015) Social inequality in political participation: The dark sides of individualisation. *West European Politics*, 38:1, 1–27.

Atkinson, A. (2007) Measuring top incomes: methodological issues. In: A. Atkinson and T. Piketty (eds) *Incomes over the twentieth century: A contrast between continental European and English-speaking countries.* Oxford: Oxford University Press, pp. 18–42.

Atkinson, R. and Flint, J. (2001) Accessing hidden and hard-to-reach populations: Snowball research strategies. University of Surrey *Social Research Update*, 33.

Baines, J., Hager, S. and Peggs, A. (2022) The sector secretly profiting from the cost of living crisis. *Open Democracy*. 5 May. www.opendemocracy.net/en/oureconomy/uk-energy-distribution-networks-nationalise-profit-cost-living

Bale, T. (2021) Ploughed under? Labour's grassroots post-Corbyn. *The Political Quarterly*. 92:2, 220–8. https://onlinelibrary.wiley.com/doi/full/10.1111/1467-923X.12987

Bangham, G. and Leslie, J. (2020) *Rainy days: An audit of household wealth and the initial effects of the coronavirus crisis on saving and spending in Great Britain*. London: Resolution Foundation. www.resolutionfoundation.org/app/uploads/2020/06/Rainy-Days.pdf

Barnett, N., Giovannini, A. and Griggs, S. (2021) Local Government in England: Forty years of decline. Unlock Democracy. https://unlockdemocracy.org.uk/resources-research/2021/6/17/local-government-in-england-40-years-of-decline

Bartrum, O. (2022) Russia–Ukraine war: How could it affect the UK economy? Institute for Government, 3 March www.instituteforgovernment.org.uk/explainers/ukraine-war-uk-economy

Bastani, A. (2022) The coming recession will be worse than 2008: Expect living standards to collapse as five years of zero-growth meets a 15-year downturn. London: Novara Media. https://novaramedia.com/2022/08/10/the-coming-recession-will-be-worse-than-2008

Bauman, Z. (2005) *Liquid life*. Cambridge: Polity.

Beck, U. (1992) *Risk society: Towards a new modernity*. London: Sage.

Belfield, C., Crawford, C. and Sibieta, L. (2017) *Long-run comparisons of spending per pupil across different stages of education*. London: Institute for Fiscal Studies.

Bell, T. (2019) Question Time's £80K man was wrong about the top 5%. But the super-rich are on another planet. *The Guardian*, 22 November. www.theguardian.com/commentisfree/2019/nov/22/question-time-80000-super-rich-earning-workers

Bellah, R., Madsen, R., Sullivan, W., Swidler, A. and Tipton, S. (1985) *Habits of the heart: Individualism and commitment in American life*. Berkeley, CA: University of California Press.

Berman, Y. and Milanovic, B. (2020) Homoploutia: Top labor and capital incomes in the United States, 1950–2020. *World Inequality Lab Working Paper*, 2020/27, 1–29.

Berry, C. and Guinan, J. (2019) *People get ready: Preparing for a Corbyn government.* New York: Or Books.

Blackman, D., West D., O'Flynn, J., Buick, F. and O'Donnell, M. (2015) Performance management: creating high performance not high anxiety. In J. Wanna, H-A. Lee and S. Yates (eds) *Managing under austerity, delivering under pressure: Performance and productivity in public service.* Sydney: ANU Press, pp. 79–102.

Blakeley, G. (2018) *On borrowed time: Finance and the UK's current account deficit.* London: IPPR.

Blakeley, G. (2020a) *The corona crash.* London: Verso.

Blakeley, G. (2020b) The era of state-monopoly capitalism. *Tribune.* 7 June. https://tribunemag.co.uk/2020/06/the-era-of-state-monopoly-capitalism

Blakemore, K. (2003) *Social policy: An introduction.* Buckingham: Open University Press.

Blundell, R., Costa Dias, M., Joyce, R. and Xu, X. (2020) *COVID-19 and inequalities.* London: Institute for Fiscal Studies.

Bollinger, C.R., Hirsch, B., Hokayem, C. and Ziliak, J. (2018) Trouble in the tails? What we know about earnings nonresponse thirty years after Lillard, Smith, and Welch. *Andrew Young School of Policy Studies Research Paper Series*, No. 18–08. https://ssrn.com/abstract=3296464

Boltanski, L. and Chiapello, E. (2018) *The new spirit of capitalism.* London: Verso.

Booth, R. (2022) Covid care home discharge policy was unlawful, says court. *The Guardian*, 27 April. www.theguardian.com/world/2022/apr/27/covid-discharging-untested-patients-into-care-homes-was-unlawful-says-court

Bourdieu, P. (1984) *Distinction: A social critique of the judgement of taste.* Cambridge, MA: Harvard University Press.

Brien, P. and Keep, M. (2022) *Public spending during the Covid-19 pandemic.* House of Commons Library. Research Briefing No. 09309. UK: Parliament. https://researchbriefings.files.parliament.uk/documents/CBP-9309/CBP-9309.pdf

Brooks, R. (2018) *Bean counters: The triumph of the accountants and how they broke capitalism.* London: Atlantic.

Broome, M. and Leslie, J. (2022) *Arrears fears. The distribution of UK household wealth and the impact on families.* London: The Resolution Foundation.

Brown, G. (2022a) Kwasi Kwarteng may have U-turned, but huge spending cuts are still coming. *The Guardian.* 4 October. www.theguardian.com/commentisfree/2022/oct/04/liz-truss-kwasi-kwarteng-chancellor-u-turn-tax-cuts-public-services-benefits

Brown, G. (2022b) Britain's charities have done all they can to help desperate people. What will Truss do? *The Guardian.* 7 September. www.theguardian.com/commentisfree/2022/sep/07/britain-charity-help-liz-truss-government-cost-of-living

Brown, M. and Jones, R.E. (2021) *Paint your town red: How Preston took back control and your town can too.* London: Repeater Books.

Browning, C. (2017) Corporation tax: could we have raised more? Full Fact. 2 June. https://fullfact.org/economy/corporation-tax-rates-and-revenues

Bullough, O. (2022) *Butler to the world: How Britain helps the world's worst people launder money, commit crimes, and get away with anything.* New York: St. Martin's Press.

Byline TV (2022) How to solve the cost of living crisis. 4 September. https://byline.tv/title/consensus-cabinet-how-to-solve-the-cost-of-living-crisis

Byrne, I. (2022) It's time to enshrine the right to food. *Tribune.* 9 February. https://tribunemag.co.uk/2022/02/right-to-food-hunger-cost-of-living-crisis

Carpenter, N. (2018) Austerity's victims: Living with a learning disability under Cameron and May. Great Britain: Amazon (CreateSpace Independent Publishing Platform).

Carson, R. and Finnerty, D. (2022) Pound hedges become most expensive since Brexit as fears grow. Bloomberg. 3 October. www.bloomberg.com/news/articles/2022-10-03/pound-hedges-become-most-expensive-since-brexit-as-fears-grow?leadSource=uverify%20wall

CAST (Centre for Climate Change and Social Transformations) (2021) UK public willing to take significant action to tackle climate change. 22 April. https://cast.ac.uk/ipsos-earthday21

Chakelian, A. (2021) New: You're 23 times more likely to be prosecuted for benefit fraud than tax fraud in the UK: Yet tax crimes cost the economy nine times more. *The New Statesman*. 19 February. www.newstatesman.com/politics/welfare/2021/02/new-you-re-23-times-more-likely-be-prosecuted-benefit-fraud-tax-fraud-uk

Chakelian, A., Goodier, M. and Swindells, K. (2022) Britain is falling harder for the myth of Molly-Mae meritocracy. *The New Statesman*. 7 April. www.newstatesman.com/society/2022/04/britain-is-falling-harder-for-the-myth-of-molly-mae-meritocracy

Chancel, L. (2021a) Climate change and the global inequality of carbon emissions, 1990–2020. World Inequality Lab, Paris School of Economics, Sciences Po.

Chancel, L. (2021b) The richest 10% produce about half of greenhouse gas emissions. They should pay to fix the climate. *The Guardian*. 7 December. www.theguardian.com/commentisfree/2021/dec/07/we-cant-address-the-climate-crisis-unless-we-also-take-on-global-inequality

Chancel, L., Piketty, T., Saez, E. and Zucman, G. (2022) *World Inequality Report 2022*. Paris: World Inequality Lab, Paris School of Economics, Sciences Po.

Chappell, E. (2022) Uxbridge and South Ruislip focus group: Labour has more to do to set out its stall. 22 July. *LabourList*. https://labourlist.org/2022/07/uxbridge-and-south-ruislip-focus-group-labour-has-more-to-do-to-set-out-its-stall

Chun, J., Brockner, J. and De Cremer, D. (2018) How temporal and social comparisons in performance evaluations affect fairness perceptions. *Organizational Behavior and Human Decision Processes*. 145, 1–15.

CICTAR (Centre for International Corporate Tax Accountability and Research) (2021) *Death, deception & dividends: Disturbing details of the UK's largest care home operator*. London: CICTAR. https://cictar.org/wp-content/uploads/2021/12/Death-Deception-Dividends-Dec-3.5.pdf

Cingano, F. (2014) Trends in income inequality and its impact on economic growth. *OECD Social, Employment and Migration Working Papers, n.163*. Paris: OECD Publishing.

Clery, E., Curtice, J., Frankenburg, S., Morgan, H. and Reid, S. (eds) (2021) *British Social Attitudes: The 38th report.* London: NatCen Social Research.

Coenen, P., Huysmans, M.A. and Holtermann, A. (2018) Do highly physically active workers die early? A systematic review with meta-analysis of data from 193 696 participants. *British Journal of Sports Medicine* 2018; 52:1320–6. https://bjsm.bmj.com/content/52/20/1320

Coglianese, C. (2020) Solving climate risk requires normative change. Blog. UPenn Risk Management and Decision Processes Center. https://riskcenter.wharton.upenn.edu/climate-risk-solutions-2/solving-climate-change-requires-normative-change-2

Committee on Climate Change (2019) *UK housing: Fit for the future?* February. London: Committee on Climate Change. www.theccc.org.uk/wp-content/uploads/2019/02/UK-housing-Fit-for-the-future-CCC-2019.pdf

Coote, A., Franklin, J. and Simms, A. (2010) *21 Hours: Why a shorter working week can help us all to flourish in the 21st century.* London: New Economics Foundation.

Coote, A., Harper, A. and Stirling, A. (2020) *The case for a four day week.* Cambridge: Polity.

Corlett, A. and Odamtten, F. (2021) *Hope to buy: The decline of youth home ownership.* London: Resolution Foundation. www.resolutionfoundation.org/publications/hope-to-buy

Corlett, A., Odamtten, F. and Try, L. (2022) *The Living Standards Audit 2022.* London: Resolution Foundation. www.resolutionfoundation.org/app/uploads/2022/07/Living-Standards-Audit-2022.pdf

Cotton, J. (2022) We are planning 'warm banks' in Birmingham to try to save people abandoned by government. *The Guardian.* 7 September. www.theguardian.com/commentisfree/2022/sep/07/birmingham-warm-banks-government-council-fuel-poverty-national

Coyle, D. (2011) *The economics of enough: How to run the economy as if the future matters.* Princeton, NJ: Princeton University Press.

Davies, R. (2022) Thousands of UK pubs 'face closure' without energy bills support. *The Guardian*. 30 August. www.theguardian.com/business/2022/aug/30/thousands-of-uk-pubs-face-closure-without-energy-bills-support

Davies, W. (2021) *This is not normal: The collapse of liberal Britain*. London: Verso.

Davies, W. (2022) Destination Unknown. *London Review of Books*, 44:11, 9 June. www.lrb.co.uk/the-paper/v44/n11/william-davies/destination-unknown

Davis, A., Hecht, K., Burchardt, T., Gough, I., Hirsch, D., Rowlingson, K. and Summers, K. (2020) *Living on different incomes in London: Can public consensus identify a 'riches line'?* London: Trust for London.

Department for Education (2012) *Pupils not claiming free school meals*. https://assets.publishing.service.gov.uk/government/uploads/system/uploads/attachment_data/file/183380/DFE-RR235.pdf

Dhar, D. (2020) Women's unpaid care work has been unmeasured and undervalued for too long. www.kcl.ac.uk/news/womens-unpaid-care-work-has-been-unmeasured-and-undervalued-for-too-long

Disability Rights UK (2022) *DR UK says £150 September cost of living payment to disabled people 'nowhere near enough'*. www.disabilityrightsuk.org/news/2022/august/dr-uk-says-£150-september-cost-living-payment-disabled-people-"nowhere-near-enough"

Dorling, D. (2014) *Inequality and the 1%*. London: Verso.

Dorling, D. (2016) Middle classes (not working class) voted for Brexit, argues Danny Dorling on BBC Newsnight. 29 September. www.youtube.com/watch?v=eOMiUONDLno

Driscoll, J. (2022) Our political consensus is built on lies and fear. Letters. *The Guardian*. 1 April. www.theguardian.com/politics/2022/apr/01/our-political-consensus-is-built-on-lies-and-fear

Duff, C. (2020) Why you should try a 4-day workweek (+ how to pitch it). 15 June. Owl Labs. https://resources.owllabs.com/blog/four-day-work-week

Duffy, B. and Thain, M. (2022) Do we have your attention? How people focus and live in the modern information environment. The Policy Institute. The Centre for Attention Studies. King's College London. www.kcl.ac.uk/policy-institute/assets/how-people-focus-and-live-in-the-modern-information-environment.pdf

Dunn, P., Allen, L., Cameron, G., Malhotra, A. and Alderwick, H. (2020) COVID-19 policy tracker: A timeline of national policy and health system responses to COVID-19 in England. www.health.org.uk/news-and-comment/charts-and-infographics/covid-19-policy-tracker

Dunne, D. and Gabbatiss, J. (2022) Factcheck: Why fracking is not the answer to the UK's energy crisis. 9 September. www.carbonbrief.org/factcheck-why-fracking-is-not-the-answer-to-the-uks-energy-crisis

Durose, O. (2022) *Suburban socialism (or barbarism)*. London: Repeater Books.

Dutkiewicz, P. and Sakwa, R. (eds) (2013) *22 Ideas to fix the world: Conversations with the world's foremost thinkers*. New York: New York University Press.

Earth4All (2022) Earth for all: A survival guide for humanity: Executive summary. www.earth4all.life/publications

Edmiston, D. (2018a) *Welfare, inequality and social citizenship: Deprivation and affluence in austerity Britain*. Bristol: Policy Press.

Edmiston, D. (2018b) The poor 'sociological imagination' of the rich: Explaining attitudinal divergence towards welfare, inequality, and redistribution. *Social Policy and Administration*, 52:5, 983–97.

Edmiston, D. (2022) Plumbing the depths: The changing (socio-demographic) profile of UK poverty. *Journal of Social Policy*, 51:2, 385–411. doi:10.1017/S0047279421000180

Edmiston, D., Geiger, B.G., de Vries, R., Scullion, L., Summers, K., Ingold, J., Robertshaw, D., Gibbons, A. and Karagiannaki, E. (2020) *Who are the new COVID-19 cohort of benefit claimants?* Rapid Report #2. The Welfare at a (Social) Distance project. September. https://hub.salford.ac.uk/welfare-at-a-social-distance/wp-content/uploads/sites/120/2020/09/WaSD-Rapid-Report-2-New-COVID-19-claimants.pdf

Ehrenreich, B. (1989) *Fear of falling: The inner life of the middle class*. New York: Twelve.

Ehsan, M.R. and Kingman, D. (2019) *Escape of the wealthy: The unfairness of the English student finance system*. London: Intergenerational Foundation. www.if.org.uk/wp-content/uploads/2019/01/Escape-of-the-Wealthy_Jan_2019_final-1.pdf

Electoral Calculus (2022) Regression Poll September 2022. www.electoralcalculus.co.uk/blogs/ec_mrppoll_20220928.html

Elgot, J. and Stewart, H. (2022) Liz Truss U-turns on plan to cut public sector pay outside London. *The Guardian*. 2 August. www.theguardian.com/politics/2022/aug/02/liz-truss-u-turns-plan-cut-public-sector-pay-outside-london-tory-leadership

Eliasoph, N. (1998) *Avoiding politics: How Americans produce apathy in everyday life*. Cambridge: Polity.

Eliasoph, N. (2012) *The politics of volunteering*. Cambridge: Polity.

Elliott, L. (2022) UK to be major economy worst hit by Ukraine war, says OECD. *The Guardian*. 8 June. www.theguardian.com/business/2022/jun/08/uk-to-be-major-economy-worst-hit-by-ukraine-war-says-oecd

EMG Transmission Group (2021) COVID-19 risk by occupation and workplace, 11 February. https://assets.publishing.service.gov.uk/government/uploads/system/uploads/attachment_data/file/965094/s1100-covid-19-risk-by-occupation-workplace.pdf

Employers for Childcare (2022) *What does the Chancellor's autumn statement mean for families?* www.employersforchildcare.org/news-item/what-does-the-chancellors-autumn-statement-mean-for-families

Enns, P. and Wlezien, C. (eds) (2011) *Who gets represented?* New York: Russell Sage Foundation.

Equality Trust (2020) *The scale of economic inequality in the UK*. www.equalitytrust.org.uk/scale-economic-inequality-uk

ESS (2022) European Social Survey data portal. https://ess-search.nsd.no

Eurofound (2020) *Labour market change: Trends and policy approaches towards flexibilisation*. Luxembourg: Publications Office of the European Union.

European Central Bank (2022) Mining the environment: Is climate risk priced into crypto-assets? www.ecb.europa.eu/pub/financial-stability/macroprudential-bulletin/html/ecb.mpbu202207_3~d9614ea8e6.en.html

Eurostat (2018) *The European Union Statistics on Income and Living Conditions (EU-SILC), 2016*. Luxembourg: Eurostat.

Evans, G. and Mellon, J. (2016) Social class. Identity, awareness and political attitudes: Why are we still working class? In: J. Curtice, M. Phillips and E. Clery (eds) *British Social Attitudes: The 33rd Report*, London: NatCen Social Research. www.bsa.natcen.ac.uk

Evans, S. (2022) Analysis: Record-low price for UK offshore wind is nine times cheaper than gas. 8 July. www.carbonbrief.org/analysis-record-low-price-for-uk-offshore-wind-is-four-times-cheaper-than-gas

Federal Government (Bundesregierung) (2022) Investing in the future and securing stability. Federal budget 2022. 16 March. www.bundesregierung.de/breg-en/news/cabinet-federal-budget-2022-2016888

Financial Times (2014) Middle class 'cling-ons' squeezed out of London property market. www.ft.com/content/0664615a-90dc-11e3-a2bd-00144feab7de

Financial Times (2020) UK house prices show strongest start of year since 2005. www.ft.com/content/0d022c74-f506-4599-9acf-925761a43efe

Financial Times (2021) Johnson to strip electoral watchdog of prosecution powers www.ft.com/content/aff47fb4-34ec-49c7-8aca-ebd462f4142b

Financial Times (2022a) Gas and electricity networks top UK profit margin ratings. www.ft.com/content/aff47fb4-34ec-49c7-8aca-ebd462f4142b

Financial Times (2022b) UK healthcare is already being privatised, but not in the way you think. www.ft.com/content/dbf166ce-1ebb-4a67-980e-9860fd170ba2

Fisher, M. and Gilbert, J. (2013) Capitalist realism and neoliberal hegemony: A dialogue. *New Formations*, 80/81.

Foa, R.S., Klassen, A., Slade, M., Rand, A. and Collins, R. (2020) *Global satisfaction with democracy 2020*. Cambridge: Centre for the Future of Democracy.

Forbes (2022) What now for UK mortgage rates? Forbes Advisor www.forbes.com/uk/advisor/mortgages/mortgage-rates-10-07-22

Forrest, A. (2022a) Government vows to clamp down on 'fire and rehire' after P&O sackings. *The Independent.* 29 March. www.independent.co.uk/news/uk/politics/p-o-ferries-fire-rehire-b2046586.html

Forrest, A. (2022b) Leak reveals staggering profits ahead for energy companies. *The Independent.* 31 August. www.independent.co.uk/independentpremium/uk-news/gas-electricity-bills-energy-profits-b2157700.html

Frank, R.H. (2017) *Success and luck: Good fortune and the myth of meritocracy.* Princeton, NJ: Princeton University Press.

Friedman, S. and Laurison, D. (2019) *The class ceiling: Why it pays to be privileged.* Bristol: Policy Press.

Friedman, S., O'Brien, D. and McDonald, I. (2021) Deflecting privilege: Class identity and the intergenerational self. *Sociology,* 55(4): 716–33.

Full Fact (2019) £1 trillion was not spent on bailing out banks during the financial crisis. 4 July. https://fullfact.org/search/?q=137+billion#gsc.tab=0&gsc.q=137%20billion&gsc.page=1

Gallup (2017) What determines how Americans perceive their social class? https://news.gallup.com/opinion/polling-matters/204497/determines-americans-perceive-social-class.aspx

Game, C. (2019) Local elections 2019: gone missing – 500 councillors. www.democraticaudit.com/2019/05/02/local-elections-2019-gone-missing-500-councillors

Garrett, B. (2021) *Bunker: Building for the end times.* London: Penguin.

Gethins, S. (2022) While 'beergate' dominates headlines, UK politics quietly changes forever. Open Democracy. 10 May. www.opendemocracy.net/en/beergate-keir-starmer-sinn-fein-win-uk-politics-change-scottish-independence

Ghosh, J. (2022a) Let's count what really matters. Project Syndicate. 16 June. www.project-syndicate.org/commentary/gdp-limitations-four-alternative-economic-indicators-by-jayati-ghosh-2022-06

Ghosh, J. (2022b) Control the vampire companies. *Social Europe.* https://socialeurope.eu/control-the-vampire-companies

Giddens, A. (2000) *Runaway world.* London: Routledge.

Gilens, M. (2012) *Affluence and influence: Economic inequality and political power in America.* Princeton, NJ: Princeton University Press.

Giridharadas, A. (2019) *Winners take all: The elite charade of changing the world.* London: Allen Lane.

Glennerster, H. (2014) Richard Titmuss: Forty years on. CASE paper no. 180. London: Centre for Analysis of Social Exclusion. https://sticerd.lse.ac.uk/dps/case/cp/casepaper180.pdf

Glucksberg, L. and Russell-Prywata, L. (2020) Elites and inequality: A case study of plutocratic philanthropy in the UK. UNRISD Occasional Paper – Overcoming Inequalities in a Fractured World: Between Elite Power and Social Mobilization, No. 9. 978-92-9085-112-7, United Nations Research Institute for Social Development, Geneva.

Goldman Sachs (2022) UK social mobility – a tough climb. 24 February. www.gspublishing.com/content/research/en/reports/2022/02/24/c9116edf-3ff1-4ec3-a459-bf9889763b0b.html

González Hernando, M. (2019) *British think tanks after the 2008 global financial crisis.* London: Palgrave.

Goodhart, D. (2017) *The road to somewhere: The populist revolt and the future of politics.* London: C Hurst & Co.

Goodhart, D. (2020) *Head, hand, heart: Why intelligence is over-rewarded, manual workers matter, and caregivers deserve more respect.* New York: Free Press.

Goodwin, M. and Heath, O. (2019) *Briefing: Low-income voters in UK general elections, 1987–2017.* London: Joseph Rowntree Foundation. www.jrf.org.uk/report/low-income-voters-uk-general-elections-1987-2017

Gov.uk (2015) PM speech on opportunity. David Cameron discusses plans to help working families and extend opportunities to all. 22 June. www.gov.uk/government/speeches/pm-speech-on-opportunity

Graeber, D. (2018) *Bullshit jobs: A theory.* London: Simon & Schuster.

Graham, H., de Bell, S., Hanley, N., Jarvis, S. and White, P. (2019) Willingness to pay for policies to reduce future deaths from climate change: evidence from a British survey. *Public Health*, 174, 110–17.

Green, D. (2016) *How change happens*. Oxford: Oxford University Press.

Green, F. and Kynaston, D. (2019) *Engines of privilege: Britain's private school problem*. London: Bloomsbury Press.

Guvenen, F., Kaplan, G. and Song, J. (2014) The glass ceiling and the paper floor: Gender differences among top earners, 1981–2012. *NBER Working Papers*, 20560. www.nber.org/papers/w20560

Guyton, J., Langetieg, P., Reck, D., Risch, M. and Zucman, G. (2021) Tax evasion at the top of the income distribution: Theory and evidence. *NBER Working Papers*, 28542. www.nber.org/papers/w28542

Haidt, J. (2012) *The righteous mind: Why good people are divided by politics and religion*. London: Penguin.

Handscomb, K., Judge, L. and Slaughter, H. (2021) *Listen up: Individual experiences of work, consumption and society*. London: The Resolution Foundation.

Hanley, L. (2019) The Class Ceiling review – why it pays to be privileged. *The Guardian*, 30 January. www.theguardian.com/books/2019/jan/30/class-ceiling-sam-friedman-daniel-laurison-review-pays-to-be-privileged

Harrington, B. (2016) *Capital without borders*. Cambridge, MA: Harvard University Press.

Harrop, A. (2022) *Faced with Liz Truss, the left can have confidence it will win the battle of ideas*. LabourList. https://labourlist.org/2022/09/faced-with-liz-truss-the-left-can-have-confidence-it-will-win-the-battle-of-ideas

Hastings, A., Bailey, N., Bramley, G., Gannon, M. and Watkins, D. (2015) *The cost of the cuts: The impact on local government and poorer communities*. London: Joseph Rowntree Foundation.

Hecht, K. (2017) A relational analysis of top incomes and wealth: Economic evaluation, relative (dis)advantage and the service to capital. *LSE International Inequalities Institute Working Paper*, 11.

Hickel, J. (2020) *Less is more: How degrowth will save the world*. London: Penguin.

Higgins, S., Lustig, N. and Vigorito, A. (2018) The rich underreport their income: Assessing biases in inequality estimates and correction methods using linked survey and tax data. *CEQ Working Paper Series* n.70. http://repec.tulane.edu/RePEc/ceq/ceq70.pdf

Hills, J. (2014) *Good times, bad times: The welfare myth of them and us*. Bristol: Policy Press.

Hirsch, D. (2021) The cost of child poverty in 2021. Centre for Research in Social Policy, Loughborough University.

HMRC (2022) Dataset: *Percentile points from 1 to 99 for total income before and after tax*. Release 16 March. www.gov.uk/government/statistics/percentile-points-from-1-to-99-for-total-income-before-and-after-tax#full-publication-update-history

Holland, D. and Portes, J. (2012) Self-defeating austerity? *National Institute Economic Review*, 222:1, 4–10.

House of Commons Library (2021) Income inequality in the UK. Research Briefing 7484. 30 November. https://researchbriefings.files.parliament.uk/documents/CBP-7484/CBP-7484.pdf

House of Commons Library (2022a) Research Briefing: Social background of Members of Parliament 1979–2019. Research Briefing 7483. 15 February. https://commonslibrary.parliament.uk/research-briefings/cbp-7483

House of Commons Library (2022b) Public spending during the Covid-19 pandemic. Research Briefing 09309. 29 March. https://researchbriefings.files.parliament.uk/documents/CBP-9309/CBP-9309.pdf

Hunt, T. (2021) COVID-19 and the work of trade unions: new challenges and new responses. Unions21. https://unions21.org.uk/files/Unions-21-Report-COVID-19-and-the-work-of-unions.pdf

IFS (Institute for Fiscal Studies) (2021) Comparisons of school spending per pupil across the UK. https://ifs.org.uk/articles/comparisons-school-spending-pupil-across-uk

IFS TaxLab (2021) What does the government spend money on? https://ifs.org.uk/taxlab/taxlab-key-questions/what-does-government-spend-money

Iniesta-Martinez, S. and Evans, H. (2012) *Pupils not claiming free school meals.* Research Report DFE-RR235. London: Department for Education. https://assets.publishing.service.gov.uk/government/uploads/system/uploads/attachment_data/file/183380/DFE-RR235.pdf

Intergenerational Commission (2018) *A new generational contract: The final report of the Intergenerational Commission.* London: Intergenerational Commission.

Intergovernmental Panel on Climate Change (2021) *Climate change 2022: Mitigation of climate change.* Working Group III contribution to the Sixth Assessment Report. www.ipcc.ch/assessment-report/ar6

International Labour Organization (2016) *Women at work: Trends 2016.* Geneva: ILO.

IPPR (2019) *Prosperity and justice: A plan for the new economy.* London: IPPR.

Jackson, M. and Cooney, C. (2022) Energy bills: Middle-earners will need help with rising prices too, says chancellor. BBC News. 27 August. www.bbc.com/news/uk-politics-62695778

Jackson, T. (2021) *Post growth: Life after capitalism.* Cambridge: Polity.

Jaffe, S. (2021) *Work won't love you back: How devotion to our jobs keeps us exploited, exhausted, and alone.* New York: Bold Type Books.

Johnson, P. (2022a) The mini-Budget explained. IFS. 23 September. https://ifs.org.uk/articles/mini-budget-explained

Johnson, P. (2022b) IFS response to U-turn on plan to cut 45p income tax rate. IFS. Press release, 3 October. https://ifs.org.uk/news/ifs-response-u-turn-plan-cut-45p-income-tax-rate

Jones, O. (2012) *Chavs: The demonisation of the working class.* London: Verso.

Jones, O. (2014) *The establishment: And how they get away with it.* London: Penguin.

Jooshandeh, J. (2021) *Key workers in the pandemic: Security traps among Britain's essential workers.* London: Trust for London. www.trustforlondon.org.uk/publications/key-workers-in-the-pandemic

Jorgenson, A., Schor, J., Knight, L. and Huang, X. (2016) Domestic inequality and carbon emissions in comparative perspective. *Sociological Forum*, 31:S1, 770–86.

Joseph Rowntree Foundation (2022) *UK poverty 2022: The essential guide to understanding poverty in the UK*. London: Joseph Rowntree Foundation.

Joyce, R., Pope, T. and Roantree, B. (2019) *The characteristics and incomes of the top 1%*. London: IFS.

Joyce, R. and Xu, X. (2019) *Inequalities in the twenty-first century: Introducing the IFS Deaton Review*. London: IFS.

Kalinina, E. and Shand, L. (2018) Executive pay: review of FTSE 100 executive pay. London: Chartered Institute of Personnel Development in association with High Pay Centre.

Keen, R. and Audickas, L. (2016) Membership of UK political parties. Briefing paper. Number: SN05125, 5 August. House of Commons Library. UK Parliament.

Khan, S. (2012) *Privilege: The making of an adolescent elite at St. Paul's School*. Princeton, NJ: Princeton University Press.

Khan, S. (2016) The many futures of élites research: a comment on the symposium. *Sociologica*, 10:2, 1–11.

Kirk, I. (2022) How many Britons have asked for a pay rise – and how many have been successful? YouGov. 4 April. https://yougov.co.uk/topics/economy/articles-reports/2022/04/04/how-many-britons-have-asked-pay-rise-and-how-many-

Kishtainy, N. (ed) (2012) *The economics book*. London: Penguin.

Klein, E. (2020) *Why we're polarized*. New York: Simon & Schuster.

Klinenberg, E. (2018) *Palaces for the people: How to build a more equal and united society*. London: Penguin.

Krozer, A. (2018) *Seeing inequality? Relative affluence and elite perceptions in Mexico*. Geneva: UNRISD. www.unrisd.org/en/library/publications/seeing-inequality-relative-affluence-and-elite-perceptions-in-mexico

Labour for a New Democracy (2022) Everything but the Commons: Why proportional representation is essential if constitutional reform is to address Britain's crises of democracy, inequality and the union. August. www.labourforanewdemocracy.org.uk/news/everything-but-the-commons

Lamont, M. (1992) *Money, morals & manners: The culture of the French and American upper-middle class*. Chicago, IL: University of Chicago Press.

Lansley, S. (2022) *The richer, the poorer: How Britain enriched the few and failed the poor. A 200-year history*. Bristol: Policy Press.

Laurison D. (2015) The right to speak: Differences in political engagement among the British elite. *The Sociological Review*, 63:2, 349–72.

Lawson, N. (2009) *All consuming: How shopping got us into this mess and how we can find our way out*. London: Penguin.

Lee, S. (2015) How has the UK's coalition government performed? London: Political Studies Association. www.psa.ac.uk/psa/news/how-has-uks-coalition-government-performed

Leslie, J. and Shah, K. (2021) *(Wealth) gap year: The impact of the coronavirus crisis on UK household wealth*. London: Resolution Foundation. www.resolutionfoundation.org/app/uploads/2021/07/Wealth-gap-year.pdf

Lindh, A. and McCall, L. (2020) Class position and political opinion in rich democracies. *Annual Review of Sociology*, 46:1, 419–41.

Liscomb, M. (2022) This professor went viral for asking students how much they think the average person makes, and it's eye-opening. BuzzFeed. 21 January. www.buzzfeed.com/meganeliscomb/wharton-average-american-income-guess

Lister, R. (2004) *Poverty*. Cambridge: Polity.

Lister, R. (2020) *Towards a good society*. London: Compass.

Local Government Association (2018) Local government funding: moving the conversation on. June. London: LGA. www.local.gov.uk/sites/default/files/documents/Moving%20the%20conversation%20on.pdf

Lothian-McLean, M. (2022) How bad do things have to get in Britain before we start to see solidarity emerge? *The Guardian*. 25 April. www.theguardian.com/commentisfree/2022/apr/25/bad-britain-solidarity-anger-division

Lucchino, P. and Morelli, S. (2012) *Inequality, debt and growth*. London: Resolution Foundation.

Lutz, G., Kissau, K. and Rosset, J. (2015) Representation of political opinions: Is the structuring pattern of policy preferences the same for citizens and elites? In: M. Bühlmann and J. Fivaz (eds) *Political representation: New insights into old questions.* London: Routledge.

Madden, D. (2020) Housing and the crisis of social reproduction. E-flux Architecture. June. www.e-flux.com/architecture/housing/333718/housing-and-the-crisis-of-social-reproduction

Mahmood, B. (2022) Private schools aren't 'losing' places at Oxbridge, their unfair privileges are being tackled – that's all. Left Foot Forward. https://leftfootforward.org/2022/05/private-schools-arent-losing-places-at-oxbridge-their-unfair-privileges-are-being-tackled-thats-all

Major, L.E. and Machin, S. (2019) *Social mobility.* Paper EA045. Centre for Economic Performance. London: London School of Economics. https://cep.lse.ac.uk/pubs/download/ea045.pdf

Mallet, B. and Aloisi, S. (2022) EDF issues fourth profit warning as nuclear output drops. Reuters. 28 July. www.reuters.com/business/energy/edf-issues-new-profit-warning-due-lower-nuclear-output-2022-07-28

Mandler, P. (2022) This idea must die: Grammar schools are a tool in promoting social mobility. *Cambridge Alumni,* 95. https://magazine.alumni.cam.ac.uk/this-idea-must-die-grammar-schools-are-a-tool-in-promoting-social-mobility

Manza, J. and Crowley, N. (2018) Ethnonationalism and the rise of Donald Trump. *Contexts,* 17:1, 28–33. https://doi.org/10.1177/1536504218766548

Markovits, D. (2020) *The meritocracy trap: How America's foundational myth feeds inequality, dismantles the middle class, and devours the elite.* London: Penguin.

Marmot, M. (2015) Middle classes being robbed of eight years of active life. Planning for Care blog. 10 September. www.planningforcare.co.uk/middle-classes-being-robbed-of-eight-years-of-active-life

Marmot, M., Allen, J., Boyce, T., Goldblatt, P. and Morrison, J. (2020) *Health equity in England: The Marmot Review 10 years on.* London: Institute of Health Equity.

Martin, S., Longo, F., Lomas, J. and Claxton, K. (2021) Causal impact of social care, public health and healthcare expenditure on mortality in England: Cross-sectional evidence for 2013/2014, *BMJ Open*, 11:10. https://bmjopen.bmj.com/content/11/10/e046417

Mason, P. (2022) Fresh-start Truss faces a 'sudden stop'. *Social Europe*. 19 September. https://socialeurope.eu/fresh-start-truss-faces-a-sudden-stop?s=08

Mazzucato, M. (2022) Toward a progressive economic agenda. *Social Europe*. 10 October. https://socialeurope.eu/toward-a-progressive-economic-agenda

McCall, L. (2013) *The undeserving rich: American beliefs about inequality, opportunity, and redistribution*. Cambridge: Cambridge University Press.

Meadows, D.H., Meadows, D.L., Randers, J. and Behrens, W.W. III (1972) *The limits to growth: A report for the Club of Rome's project on the predicament of mankind*. New York: Universe Books.

Meda, D. (2022) The urgent need for a post-growth society. Social Europe. 15 June. www.socialeurope.eu/the-urgent-need-for-a-post-growth-society

Meyer, B. and Newport, D. (2022) *Temperatures rising? Avoiding division on net zero*. London: Tony Blair Institute for Global Change.

Michell, J. (2021) Progressive tax reform. In P. Allen, S. Konzelmann and J. Toporowski (eds) *The return of the state: Restructuring Britain for the common good*. Progressive Economy Forum. Newcastle: Agenda Publishing, pp. 223–32.

Mijs, J. (2021) The paradox of inequality: Income inequality and belief in meritocracy go hand in hand. *Socio-Economic Review*, 19:1, 7–35.

Mijs, J. and Savage, M. (2020) Meritocracy, elitism and inequality. *The Political Quarterly*, 91:2, 397–404.

Milanovic, B. (2018) *Global inequality: A new approach for the age of globalization*. Cambridge, MA: Belknap Press.

Milanovic, B. [@BrankoMilan] (2019) Homoploutia is a neologism I invented (after some consultation w/my Greek friends). It indicates that the same people (homo) are wealthy (ploutia) is the space of capital & labor; your neighborly CEO who is in the top 1% by labor income and also in the top 1% by shares he owns. Twitter, 11 April. https://twitter.com/BrankoMilan/status/1116340273074921473?s=20&t=p6Tsbla wN5OfuyrjDX0LqQ [accessed 17 July 2022]

Milburn, K. (2019) *Generation left*. Cambridge: Polity.

Mishra, C. and Rath, N. (2020) Social solidarity during a pandemic: Through and beyond Durkheimian lens. *Social Sciences and Humanities Open*, 2:1, 1–7.

Mitchell, G. (2022) The clapping might have stopped, but our need for care is not going away. *LabourList*. 12 July. https://labourlist.org/2022/07/the-clapping-might-have-stopped-but-our-need-for-care-is-not-going-away

Mok, A. and Zinkula, J. (2023) ChatGPT may be coming for our jobs. Here are the 10 roles that AI is most likely to replace. Business Insider. 2 February. www.businessinsider.com/chatgpt-jobs-at-risk-replacement-artificial-intelligence-ai-labor-trends-2023-02?r=US&IR=T

Monbiot, G. (2022) Putin exploits the lie machine but didn't invent it. British history is also full of untruths. *The Guardian*. 30 March. www.theguardian.com/commentisfree/2022/mar/30/putin-lie-machine-history-untruths

Monbiot, G. (ed.), Grey, R., Kenny, T., Macfarlane, L., Powell-Smith, A., Shrubsole, G. and Stratford, B. (2019) *Land for the many: Changing the way our fundamental asset is used, owned and governed*. London: The Labour Party.

Moore, P. (2016) How Britain voted at the EU referendum. YouGov. 27 June. https://yougov.co.uk/topics/politics/articles-reports/2016/06/27/how-britain-voted

Mulheirn, I. (2019) *Tackling the UK housing crisis: Is supply the answer?* London: UK Collaborative Centre for Housing Evidence. https://housingevidence.ac.uk/wp-content/uploads/2019/08/20190820b-CaCHE-Housing-Supply-FINAL.pdf

Murphy, R. (2016) *The joy of tax: How a fair tax system can create a better society*. London: Corgi.

Murphy, R. (2020) The role of tax after the pandemic. Progressive Economy Forum. 4 May. https://progressiveeconomyforum.com/blog/the-role-of-tax-after-the-pandemic

Murray, N. (2020) Burnout Britain: Overwork in an age of unemployment. 4 Day Week Campaign/Compass/Autonomy. October. www.compassonline.org.uk/publications/burnout-britain-overwork-in-an-age-of-unemployment/

Neame, K. (2022) Miliband accuses Tories of being 'asleep at the wheel' as energy profits soar. *LabourList*. https://labourlist.org/2022/07/miliband-accuses-tories-of-being-asleep-at-the-wheel-as-energy-profits-soar

Newman, D. and Dehaghani, R. (2022) Why are barristers striking? Transforming Society [blog]. 6 July. Bristol: Policy Press. www.transformingsociety.co.uk/2022/07/06/why-are-barristers-striking

The New York Times (2017) No one knows what Britain is anymore. 4 October. www.nytimes.com/2017/11/04/sunday-review/britain-identity-crisis.html

The New York Times (2022) College admissions scandal: Complete coverage of a brazen cheating scheme. [News Event] www.nytimes.com/news-event/college-admissions-scandal

Nixon, B. (2015) *The 21st century revolution: A call to greatness*. Milton Keynes: Acorn Independent Press.

Novara Media (2022) Mick Lynch gives the BBC a reality check. TyskySour@NovaraMedia. www.youtube.com/watch?v=nbmQQ13UrMw

OBR (Office for Budget Responsibility) (2021) Welfare spending: Pensioner benefits. https://obr.uk/forecasts-in-depth/tax-by-tax-spend-by-spend/welfare-spending-pensioner-benefits

OECD (Organisation for Economic Co-operation and Development) (2015) *In it together: Why less inequality benefits all*. Paris: OECD.

OECD (2018) *A broken social elevator? How to promote social mobility*. Paris: OECD.

OECD (2019) *Under pressure: The squeezed middle class*. Paris: OECD.

Olson, D. (2022) Line goes up: The problem with NFTs. YouTube. 21 January. www.youtube.com/watch?v=YQ_xWvX1n9g

ONS (Office for National Statistics) (2018) Social protection, European comparisons of expenditure: 2015. 19 June. www.ons.gov.uk/peoplepopulationandcommunity/wellbeing/articles/socialprotectioneuropeancomparisonsofexpenditure/2015

ONS (2020a) Dataset: Ethnicity pay gap reference tables. Release: 12 October. www.ons.gov.uk/employmentandlabourmarket/peopleinwork/earningsandworkinghours/datasets/ethnicitypaygapreferencetables

ONS (2020b) Population by Index of Multiple Deprivation (IMD), England, 2001 to 2019. Release: 19 October. www.ons.gov.uk/peoplepopulationandcommunity/populationandmigration/populationestimates/adhocs/12386populationbyindexofmultipledeprivationimdengland2001to2019

ONS (2021a) Visualisation: What are the regional differences in income and productivity? Release: 17 May. www.ons.gov.uk/visualisations/dvc1370

ONS (2021b) Gender pay gap in the UK: 2021; Differences in pay between women and men by age, region, full-time and part-time, and occupation. Release: 21 October. www.ons.gov.uk/employmentandlabourmarket/peopleinwork/earningsandworkinghours/bulletins/genderpaygapintheuk/2021

ONS (2021c) National statistics: Distribution of median and mean income and tax by age range and gender. Release: 16 March 2022. www.gov.uk/government/statistics/distribution-of-median-and-mean-income-and-tax-by-age-range-and-gender-2010-to-2011

ONS (2022a) Dataset: The effects of taxes and benefits on household income, disposable income estimate. Release: 28 March. www.ons.gov.uk/peoplepopulationandcommunity/personalandhouseholdfinances/incomeandwealth/datasets/householddisposableincomeandinequality

ONS (2022b) Distribution of individual total wealth by characteristic in Great Britain: April 2018 to March 2020. Release: 7 January. www.ons.gov.uk/peoplepopulationandcommunity/personalandhouseholdfinances/incomeandwealth/bulletins/distributionofindividualtotalwealthbycharacteristicingreatbritain/april2018tomarch2020

ONS (2022c) Dataset: A09 Labour market status by ethnic group. Release: 17 May. www.ons.gov.uk/employmentandlabour market/peopleinwork/employmentandemployeetypes/datasets/labourmarketstatusbyethnicgroupa09

Osborne, H. (2022) Number of UK households with large debts rises by a third. *The Guardian*. 22 March. www.theguardian. com/money/2022/mar/22/uk-households-debts-energy-prices-benefits

Pack, M. (2022) Highest support for PR since British Social Attitudes survey started. 22 September. Mark Pack/Political. www.markpack.org.uk/169824/highest-support-for-pr-since-british-social-attitudes-survey-started

Page, B., Bartels, L. and Seawright, J. (2013) Democracy and the policy preferences of wealthy Americans. *Perspectives on Politics*, 11:1, 51–73.

Pakulski, J. and Waters, M. (1995) *The death of class*, London: Sage.

Parsons, T. [@TonyParsonsUK] (2022) If you think the men and women earning £150,000 year are the 'super rich', you need to get out a bit more. Twitter, 3 October. https://twitter.com/TonyParsonsUK/status/1576870782780657664?s=20&t=jLR7V0vimBej-zqMbfeGVw [accessed 10 October 2022]

Partington, R. (2019) UK households spend above their income for longest period since 1980s. *The Guardian*. 29 March. www.theguardian.com/business/2019/mar/29/uk-households-spend-above-their-income-for-longest-period-since-1980s

Partington, R. (2022) OBR forecasts likely to show £60bn-£70bn hole after Kwarteng's mini-budget. *The Guardian*. 7 October. www.theguardian.com/politics/2022/oct/07/obr-forecasts-likely-to-show-60bn-70bn-hole-after-kwartengs-mini-budget

Patel, P. and Quilter-Pinner, H. (2022) Road to renewal: Elections, parties and the case for democratic reform. IPPR. April. www.ippr.org/publications/road-to-renewal

Paugam, S., Cousin, B., Giorgetti, C. and Naudet, J. (2017) *Ce que les riches pensent des pauvres* [What the rich think of the poor]. Paris: Seuil.

Pembroke, S. (2019) *Precarious work, precarious lives: How policy can create more security*. Dublin: TASC. www.tasc.ie/assets/files/pdf/precarious_workersweb_version.pdf

Perryman, M. (ed.) (2019) *Corbynism from below*. London: Lawrence & Wishart.

Phillips, B. (2020) *How to fight inequality (and why that fight needs you)*. Cambridge: Polity.

Phipps, C. (2021) Why we should still be concerned about gender inequality in the UK. 15 November. https://blogs.lse.ac.uk/socialbusinesshub/2021/11/15/why-we-should-still-be-concerned-about-gender-inequality-in-the-uk

Piketty, T. (2014) *Capital in the twenty-first century*. Cambridge, MA: Belknap Press.

Piketty, T. (2018) Brahmin left vs Merchant right: Rising inequality and the changing structure of political conflict (Evidence from France, Britain and the US, 1948–2017). *WID. World Working Paper Series*, n.2018/7. http://piketty.pse.ens.fr/files/Piketty2018.pdf

Piketty, T. (2020) *Capital and ideology*. Cambridge, MA: Belknap Press.

Piketty, T. and Saez, E. (2013) Top incomes and the Great Recession: Recent evolutions and policy implications. *IMF Economic Review*, 61:3, 456–78.

Polanski, Z. (2022) Zack Polanski's maiden speech as Deputy Leader, Green Party of England and Wales. 1 October. www.facebook.com/thegreenparty/videos/549383200359989

Proctor, K. (2019) Labour will be 'spending less on public services than Germany and France'. *The Guardian*. 25 November. www.theguardian.com/politics/2019/nov/25/labour-will-bring-uk-into-line-with-france-and-germany-says-corbyn

Putnam, R. (1995) *Bowling alone: America's declining social capital*. New York: Simon & Schuster.

Putnam R. (2000) *Bowling alone: The collapse and revival of American community*. New York: Simon & Schuster.

Pymnts (2022) NFTs hit $17B in trading in 2021, up 21,000%. 10 March. www.pymnts.com/nfts/2022/nfts-hit-17b-in-trading-in-2021-up-21000

Race, M. (2022) Income tax to be cut by 1p from April. BBC News. 23 September. www.bbc.co.uk/news/business-63007219

Raleigh, V. (2021) *What is happening to life expectancy in England?* London: The King's Fund.

Ramsay, A. (2022) Brexit Britain is all alone in a senseless pursuit of disaster capitalism. Open Democracy. 4 October. www.opendemocracy.net/en/liz-truss-kwasi-kwarteng-disaster-capitalism-brexit-britain/?utm_source=tw?utm_source=tw

Raworth, K. (2017) *Doughnut economics: Seven ways to think like a 21st-century economist.* London: Penguin.

Raworth, K. [@KateRaworth] (2021) When the @DailyMailUK reports that humanity is tracking the projections of the 1972 Limits to Growth report – and notes that pursuing endless economic growth looks near impossible – then you know something is shifting in the world… dailymail.co.uk/sciencetech/ar… h/t @PlanB_earth https://twitter.com/kateraworth/status/14164 28555903328256?s=61&t=DFCQuYBOujiLA0V07aBKQA. Twitter, 17 July. [accessed 20 August 2022]

Reed, H. and Lansley, S. (2016) *Universal Basic Income: An idea whose time has come?* London: Compass. www.compassonline.org.uk/wp-content/uploads/2016/05/UniversalBasicIncomeByCompass-Spreads.pdf

Reeves, R. (2017) *Dream hoarders: How the American upper middle class is leaving everyone else in the dust, why that is a problem, and what to do about it.* Washington, DC: Brookings Institution.

Reeves, R. and Rothwell, J. (2020) Class and COVID: How the less affluent face double risks. Brookings Institution. 27 March. www.brookings.edu/blog/up-front/2020/03/27/class-and-covid-how-the-less-affluent-face-double-risks

Reeves, R. and Venator, J. (2014) Opposites don't attract: Assortative mating and social mobility. Brookings Institution. 10 February. www.brookings.edu/blog/social-mobility-memos/2014/02/10/opposites-dont-attract-assortative-mating-and-social-mobility

Reich, R. (2020) Billionaires' donations to fight Coronavirus are largely self-serving. *NewsWeek.* 13 April. www.newsweek.com/robert-reich-billionaires-donations-fight-coronavirus-are-largely-self-serving-opinion-1497617

Reis, E. and Moore, M. (eds) (2005) *Elite perceptions of poverty and inequality.* London: Zed Books.

Resolution Foundation (2022) Event: Green growth: miracle or mirage? Webinar. 23 May. www.resolutionfoundation.org/events/green-growth-miracle-or-mirage

Resolution Foundation and Centre for Economic Performance (2022) *Stagnation nation: Navigating a route to a fairer and more prosperous Britain. The interim report of The Economy 2030 Inquiry.* 13 July. https://economy2030.resolutionfoundation.org/reports/stagnation-nation

Rigby, E. and Wright, G. (2013) Political parties and representation of the poor in the American states. *American Journal of Political Science*, 57:3, 552–65.

Riso, S. (2021) Monitoring and surveillance of workers in the digital age. Research Digest. Eurofound. 15 December. www.eurofound.europa.eu/data/digitalisation/research-digests/monitoring-and-surveillance-of-workers-in-the-digital-age

Rivera, L. (2016) *Pedigree: How elite students get elite jobs.* Princeton, NJ: Princeton University Press.

Roper, C. (2020) Union membership rises for third year running to 6.4 million. TUC blog. 27 May. www.tuc.org.uk/blogs/union-membership-rises-third-year-running-64-million

Rosa, H. (2015) *Social acceleration: A new theory of modernity.* New York: Columbia University Press.

Rowlingson, K. and McKay, S. (2012) *Wealth and the wealthy: exploring and tackling inequalities between rich and poor.* Bristol: Policy Press.

Salverda, T. and Grassiani, E. (2014) Introduction: Anxiety at the top. *Comparative Sociology,* 13:1, 1–11.

Sandbu, M. (2022) Why we need a wealth tax. *Financial Times.* 6 September. www.ft.com/video/6f73c51e-a1d8-48db-a8da-892dbd53c08d

Sandel, M. (2013) Why we shouldn't trust markets with our civic life. TED talk. 7 October. www.ted.com/talks/michael_sandel_why_we_shouldn_t_trust_markets_with_our_civic_life/transcript?language=en

Sandel, M. (2020) *The tyranny of merit: What's become of the common good?* London: Allen Lane.

Sauder M. (2020) A sociology of luck. *Sociological Theory*, 38:3, 193–216.

Savage, M. (2021) *The return of inequality: Social change and the weight of the past.* Cambridge, MA: Harvard University Press.

Savage, M. (2022a) Cameron's decision to cut 'green crap' now costs each household in England £150 a year. *The Guardian*. 19 March. www.theguardian.com/money/2022/mar/19/david-cameron-green-crap-energy-prices

Savage, M. (2022b) Millions of households will be spending nearly third of income on fuel by spring. *The Guardian*. 27 November. www.theguardian.com/society/2022/nov/27/millions-of-households-will-be-spending-nearly-third-of-income-on-fuel-by-spring

Schlozman, K., Verba, S. and Brady, H. (2012) *The unheavenly chorus: Unequal political voice and the broken promise of American democracy*. Princeton, NJ: Princeton University Press.

Sen, A. (1975) Minimal conditions for the monotonicity of capital value. *Journal of Economic Theory*, 11:3, 340–55.

Shackle, S. (2019) 'The way universities are run is making us ill': inside the student mental health crisis. *The Guardian*, 27 September. www.theguardian.com/society/2019/sep/27/anxiety-mental-breakdowns-depression-uk-students

Shames, S. (2017) *Out of the Running: Why Millennials Reject Political Careers and Why It Matters*. New York: NYU Press.

Sherman, R. (2017) *Uneasy street: The anxieties of affluence*. Princeton, NJ: Princeton University Press.

Shoben, C. (2022) New poll: Public strongly backing public ownership of energy and key utilities. Survation. 15 August. www.survation.com/new-poll-public-strongly-backing-public-ownership-of-energy-and-key-utilities

Shrubsole, G. (2019) *Who owns England? How we lost our green and pleasant land and how to take it back*. London: William Collins.

Siddique, H. (2022) Criminal barristers prepare for indefinite strike over legal aid. *The Guardian*. 4 September. www.theguardian.com/law/2022/sep/04/criminal-barristers-england-wales-prepare-indefinite-strike-legal-aid

Sillars, J. (2022) Energy price guarantee could cost taxpayer £140bn in 'extreme' scenario, market expert warns. Sky News. 5 October. https://news.sky.com/story/energy-price-guarantee-could-cost-taxpayer-140bn-in-extreme-scenario-market-expert-warns-12712574

Skinner, G. (2021) Both Remainers and Leavers retain a strong Brexit identity 5 years on. Ipsos. 29 December. www.ipsos.com/en-uk/both-remainers-and-leavers-retain-strong-brexit-identity-5-years

Sklair, J. and Glucksberg, L. (2021) Philanthrocapitalism as wealth management strategy: Philanthropy, inheritance and succession planning among the global elite. *The Sociological Review*, 69:2, 314–29.

Social Mobility and Child Poverty Commission (2015) *State of the nation 2015: Social mobility and child poverty in Great Britain.* London: SMCP.

Social Mobility Commission (2019) *State of the nation 2018–19: Social mobility in Great Britain*, London: The Stationery Office.

Social Mobility Commission (2020) *Moving out to move on. Understanding the link between migration, disadvantage and social mobility.* Research report. London: The Stationery Office.

Soper, K. (2020) *Post-growth living for an alternative hedonism.* London: Verso.

The Spectator (2016) Full text: Theresa May's conference speech. 5 October. www.spectator.co.uk/article/full-text-theresa-may-s-conference-speech

Spencer, T. (2022) Fairer Share's response to the Levelling Up White Paper. London: Fairer Share. https://fairershare.org.uk/wp-content/uploads/2022/02/Report_Levelling-Up_v4.pdf

Sridhar, D. (2022) Who's paying for Britain's disastrous mini-budget? We are, with our health. *The Guardian.* 3 October. www.theguardian.com/commentisfree/2022/oct/03/britain-mini-budget-paying-with-our-health-stress-illness-food-poverty-cold-homes-financial-chaos

Standing, G. (2019) *Piloting basic income as common dividends.* London: Progressive Economic Forum.

Statista (2022) Number of people employed in the United Kingdom from July 1971 to July 2022 (in 1,000s). www.statista.com/statistics/281998/employment-figures-in-the-united-kingdom-uk

Stevenson, G. (2021) I made millions betting against trickle-down economics – now I'm tackling wealth inequality. Wellbeing Economy Alliance. https://weall.org/gary-stevenson

Stewart, H. (2022) Rishi Sunak announces £5bn windfall tax on energy firms. *The Guardian*. 26 May. www.theguardian.com/politics/2022/may/26/sunak-announces-windfall-tax-energy-firms

Stewart, M. (2018) The 9.9 percent is the new American aristocracy. *The Atlantic*. www.theatlantic.com/magazine/archive/2018/06/the-birth-of-a-new-american-aristocracy/559130

Stewart, M. (2021) *The 9.9 percent: The new aristocracy that is entrenching inequality and warping our culture*. New York: Simon & Schuster.

Stiglitz, J. (2016) *The price of inequality: How today's divided society endangers our future*. New York: W.W. Norton & Co.

Streib, J. (2020) *Privilege lost: Who leaves the upper middle class and how they fall*. Oxford: Oxford University Press.

Streimikiene, D., Balezentis, T., Alisauskaite-Seskiene, I., Stankuniene, G. and Simanaviciene, Z. (2019) A review of willingness to pay studies for climate change mitigation in the energy sector. *Energies*, 12:8, 1481–519.

Stronge, W. and Lewis, K. (2021) *Overtime*. London: Verso.

Summers, A. and Advani, A. (2021) How much tax do the rich really pay? LSE. 14 January. www.lse.ac.uk/research/research-for-the-world/economics/how-much-tax-do-the-rich-really-pay

Surridge, P. (2021) Values, volatility and voting: Understanding voters in England 2015–2019. University of Bristol and UK in a Changing Europe. https://ukandeu.ac.uk/wp-content/uploads/2021/07/Values-volatility-and-voting-working-paper.pdf

The Sutton Trust and Social Mobility Commission (2019) *Elitist Britain 2019: The educational backgrounds of Britain's leading people*. London: The Sutton Trust/Social Mobility Commission www.suttontrust.com/wp-content/uploads/2019/12/Elitist-Britain-2019.pdf

TASC (2020) *Inequality and the top 10% in Europe*. Dublin: TASC. www.tasc.ie/publications/inequality-and-the-top-10-in-europe-full-report

Thomas, M.E. (2019) *99%: Mass impoverishment and how we can end it*. London: Head of Zeus.

Thomas, M.E. (2020) Saving democracy. The 99% Organisation. 9 September. https://99-percent.org/saving-democracy

Tilly, C. and Tilly, C. (1998) *Work under capitalism*. Oxford: Westview Press.

Toft, M. and Friedman, S. (2021) Family wealth and the class ceiling: The propulsive power of the bank of mum and dad. *Sociology*, 55:1, 90–109.

Törmälehto, V.-M. (2017) High income and affluence: Evidence from the European Union statistics on income and living conditions (EU-SILC). *Eurostat Working Papers*. Luxembourg: Publications Office of the European Union.

Toynbee, P. (2022) These Tories are heading for oblivion, and no amount of U-turns can change that. *The Guardian*. 3 October. www.theguardian.com/commentisfree/2022/oct/03/tories-heading-for-oblivion-u-turns-kwarteng-truss-45p-tax-rate

Toynbee, P. and Walker, D. (2008) *Unjust rewards: Exposing greed and inequality in Britain today*. London: Granta.

The Trussell Trust (2022) End of year stats. www.trusselltrust.org/news-and-blog/latest-stats/end-year-stats

UCU (University and College Union) (2019) *Counting the costs of casualisation in higher education*. London: UCU.

UK Parliament Public Accounts Committee (2021) 'Unimaginable' cost of test & trace failed to deliver central promise of averting another lockdown. 10 March. https://committees.parliament.uk/committee/127/public-accounts-committee/news/150988/unimaginable-cost-of-test-trace-failed-to-deliver-central-promise-of-averting-another-lockdown

UK Parliament (2022) Energy pricing and the future of the energy market. *Third Committee Report*. 26 July. https://publications.parliament.uk/pa/cm5803/cmselect/cmbeis/236/report.html

Uni Global Union (2020) Amazon & the COVID-19 crisis: Essentially irresponsible. https://uniglobalunion.org/wp-content/uploads/amazoncovid_en.pdf

United Nations Economic and Social Council (2017) Women's economic empowerment in the changing work of work. Report of the Secretary-General. Commission on the Status of Women. 13–24 March 2017. www.unwomen.org/sites/default/files/Headquarters/Attachments/Sections/CSW/MSForumCSW61.pdf

University of Cambridge (2021) The University of Cambridge continues to attract record numbers of economically disadvantaged and underrepresented students. www.cam.ac.uk/news/the-university-of-cambridge-continues-to-attract-record-numbers-of-economically-disadvantaged-and

University of Cambridge (2022) Cambridge at a glance. Website. www.cam.ac.uk/about-the-university/cambridge-at-a-glance

University of Oxford (2021) Oxford shows continued progress on state school and ethnic minority student admissions. News & Events. 4 February. www.ox.ac.uk/news-and-events

University of Oxford (2022) Facts and figures: Full version. Website. www.ox.ac.uk/about/facts-and-figures/full-version-facts-and-figures

University of Southampton (2016) *The rise of anti-politics in Britain.* Southampton: University of Southampton.

Van Lerven, F. and Jackson, A. (2018) A government is not a household. Positive Money. https://positivemoney.org/2018/10/a-government-is-not-a-household

Walker, A. (2019) Two-thirds of Boris Johnson's cabinet went to private schools. *The Guardian.* 25 July. www.theguardian.com/education/2019/jul/25/two-thirds-of-boris-johnsons-cabinet-went-to-private-schools

Walker, A. (2022) Kwasi Kwarteng's mini-budget was a reckless gamble. Letters. *The Guardian.* 25 September. www.theguardian.com/politics/2022/sep/25/kwasi-kwarteng-mini-budget-was-a-reckless-gamble

Ward, D. and Chijoko, L. (2018) *Spending on and availability of health care resources: How does the UK compare to other countries?* London: The King's Fund. www.kingsfund.org.uk/publications/spending-and-availability-health-care-resources

Webber, E., Lanktree, G. and Casalicchio, E. (2022) Boris Johnson's ethics adviser caved to the inevitable. Politico. 17 June. www.politico.eu/article/boris-johnson-ethics-adviser-geidt-resignation

What UK Thinks (2022) Poll data: In hindsight, do you think Britain was right or wrong to vote to leave the EU? https://whatukthinks.org/eu/questions/in-highsight-do-you-think-britain-was-right-or-wrong-to-vote-to-leave-the-eu

White, S. (2022) *Labour, pluralism and creative constitutionalism.* London: Compass and Unlock Democracy. www.compassonline. org.uk/wp-content/uploads/2022/08/Labour-Pluralism-and-Creative-Constitutionalism-v3.pdf

Whitmarsh, L. (2022) Resolution Foundation event: Consuming carbon: What does the net zero transition mean for households? 1 March. www.resolutionfoundation.org/events/consuming-carbon

Whyte, W.F. (1943) *Street corner society: The social structure of an Italian slum.* Chicago, IL: The University of Chicago Press.

Wilkie, D. (2015) Is the annual performance review dead? SHRM. 19 August. www.shrm.org/resourcesandtools/hr-topics/employee-relations/pages/performance-reviews-are-dead.aspx

Wilkinson, R. and Pickett, K. (2010) *The spirit level: Why equality is better for everyone.* London: Penguin.

Wilkinson, R. and Pickett, K. (2019) *The inner level: How more equal societies reduce stress, restore sanity and improve everyone's well-being.* London: Penguin.

Williams, Z. (2015) *Get it together: Why we deserve better politics.* London: Hutchinson.

Wilson, M. and Daly, M. (1997) Life expectancy, economic inequality, homicide, and reproductive timing in Chicago neighbourhoods. *BMJ*, 314, doi: 10.1136/bmj.314.7089.1271

Winter, O. (2019) *The path to proportional representation.* Bristol: Make Votes Matter/Labour Campaign for Electoral Reform. https://static1.squarespace.com/static/563e2841e4b09a6ae020bd67/t/5d931f32fb48423f80f53ffb/1569922999502/peterloo_web.pdf

Woodward, A. and Kawachi, I. (2000) Why reduce health inequalities? *Journal of Epidemiology & Community Health*, 54:12, 923–9.

World Inequality Database (2021) United Kingdom. https://wid.world/country/united-kingdom

Wren-Lewis, S. (2018) *The lies we were told: Politics, economics, austerity and Brexit.* Bristol: Bristol University Press.

Wright, O. (2021) Coronavirus: How the UK dealt with its first Covid case. BBC News. 29 January. www.bbc.co.uk/news/uk-england-55622386

Xue, B. and McMunn, A. (2021) Gender differences in unpaid care work and psychological distress in the UK Covid-19 lockdown. *PLoS ONE*, 16:3, 1–15. doi.org/10.1371/journal. pone.0247959

YouGov Poll (2022) Should we change our current British voting system? YouGov. https://yougov.co.uk/topics/politics/trackers/should-we-change-our-current-british-voting-system

Young, C. (2017) *The myth of millionaire tax flight: How place still matters for the rich*. Stanford, CA: Stanford University Press.

Young, M. (1958) *The rise of the meritocracy*. London: Pelican.

Young, M. (2001) Down with meritocracy. *The Guardian*. 29 June. www.theguardian.com/politics/2001/jun/29/comment

Younge, G. (2022) What does it mean to be British? America has its Dream, France its Republic – but Britain suffers from a failure of imagination. *The New Statesman*. 23 March. www.newstatesman.com/politics/a-dream-of-britain/2022/03/what-does-it-mean-to-be-british

Index

References to figures appear in *italic* type.

Index

Index

LA NACIÓN DE LAS BESTIAS

Luna de Hueso

GRANTRAVESÍA

Mariana Palova

LA NACIÓN DE LAS BESTIAS

Luna de Hueso

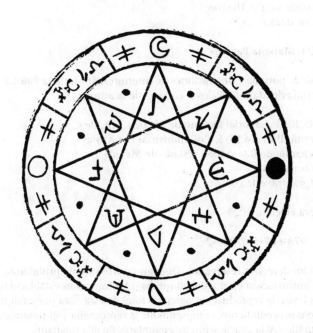

GRANTRAVESÍA

La Nación de las Bestias
Luna de hueso

© 2023, Mariana Palova

Diseño de portada e ilustraciones de interiores: © Mariana Palova
Fotografía de Mariana Palova: cortesía de la autora

D.R. © 2023, Editorial Océano de México, S.A. de C.V.
Guillermo Barroso 17-5, Col. Industrial Las Armas
Tlalnepantla de Baz, 54080, Estado de México
www.oceano.mx
www.grantravesia.com

Primera edición: 2023

ISBN: 978-607-557-800-2

Todos los derechos reservados. Quedan rigurosamente prohibidas,
sin la autorización escrita del editor, bajo las sanciones establecidas
en las leyes, la reproducción parcial o total de esta obra por cualquier
medio o procedimiento, comprendidos la reprografía y el tratamiento
informático, y la distribución de ejemplares de ella mediante
alquiler o préstamo público. ¿Necesitas reproducir una parte
de esta obra? Solicita el permiso en info@cempro.org.mx

IMPRESO EN MÉXICO / PRINTED IN MEXICO

NOTA
DE LA AUTORA

Algunas partes de los sistemas de magia utilizados en esta historia fueron sintetizadas y reinterpretadas para facilitar su incorporación a la trama; asimismo, algunos de los hechizos, rituales y símbolos han sido modificados para la seguridad del lector.

El *Culto a la Grieta Resplandeciente* y su contraparte son ficticios, pero están inspirados en tradiciones, sucesos y figuras históricas reales.

Ésta es la última puerta antes del despertar.

Bienvenidos de nuevo a nuestra Nación.

Este libro es para mí.

Mi viaje tuvo tanta niebla que creí
que me había perdido para siempre.

Pero decidí no rendirme.

Y volví a encontrar el camino.

PRÓLOGO
(El libro rojo de ~~Laurele~~ Elisse)

*F*río.

Siempre he detestado el frío y no sólo por haber crecido en una India abrasada por el sol, o porque me traiga malas memorias de las montañas heladas del Himalaya, de las cuales poco puedo ya recordar.

No. Lo odio porque el frío me recuerda lo frágil que puedo llegar a ser. Miembros entumecidos, temblores incontrolables, resfriados que amenazan con volverse neumonías; sentirse cómodo y seguro en el frío es sólo para aquellos que ignoran lo que es carecer de abrigo para vestirte o de un techo bajo el cual refugiarte en las noches. Para los que no comprenden lo terrible que es sentir los dedos helados de la muerte ir adormeciéndote poco a poco hasta arrebatarte la vida sin que puedas hacer nada al respecto.

El frío es hambre y miseria. El frío es un símbolo de dolor.

Pero, por encima de todo, el frío es un maestro cruel que me ha enseñado tres cosas que ojalá nunca hubiese tenido la desgracia de aprender.

La primera y la más preocupante: la piedra filosofal, aquella espada dorada que le quité a aquel ser mitológico llamado Rebis, y que introduje en medio de mis costillas ha comenzado a *oprimir* mi magia.

Desde que la llevo conmigo, no sólo siento como si cargase una enorme piedra sobre el pecho, sino que cada vez que intento utilizar mi brujería, la espada la consume y la devora con su oro hermético, dejándome tan débil que aun respirar me resulta agotador.

Como si, en vez de otorgarme vida eterna, luchase ferozmente por arrebatármela.

La segunda revelación y la más terrible: a pesar de haber nacido del fuego y la devastación, el frío es algo que al monstruo dentro de mí parece gustarle.

Cada vez que mi piel se eriza, cada vez que mis labios se pintan de azul o mis dedos se engarrotan en medio de la noche, su murmullo se aclara, su voluntad me resulta más imperiosa y su hambre... oh, *su hambre*...

El frío me hace sentir que, a través de este espantoso viaje, no he hecho otra cosa más que traer a mi monstruo de hueso de vuelta a sus raíces. Al origen de su poder.

Finalmente, la tercera verdad, la más dolorosa de todas: el frío me mostró, de la forma más dura, lo fácil que fue perder al hombre al que amaba.

Y cuando mi garra de hueso lo soltó en el río del plano medio y lo vi precipitarse hacia el vacío sin poder hacer nada al respecto, quise que el frío terminara conmigo allí mismo. Que me congelase hasta no sentir nada más, porque aun si yo lograba salir del bardo de los espíritus y alcanzaba de nuevo la luz del mundo humano, nada de eso me importaría.

Había sobrevivido a Laurele y al Señor del Sabbath, a la abominable alquimista Jocelyn Blake y a los legendarios tramperos Lander. Había sacrificado a Adam, a Red Buffalo, a lo que quedaba del amor de mi familia y aun así... no había logrado salvar a Tared.

No, era absurdo seguir adelante, ¿por qué más valdría la pena pelear si todo lo que juré proteger se había deslizado fuera de mis manos para desaparecer en el abismo? Así que, a medida que él se hundía, cerré los ojos también. El frío era tan terrible que casi podía sentir mis huesos encogerse, y la luz que había hecho nacer en mi mano para iluminar la negrura, poco a poco se apagaba como una diminuta flama en medio de la oscuridad. El sabor metálico de la sangre inundaba mi paladar, mi brazo entero dolía debido a ese último disparo con el que me habían alcanzado los tramperos, el terrible peso de la espada me ahogaba con más rapidez que el agua alrededor. Y mis astas, plateadas y brillantes contra las sombras, ya no eran más que una corona maldita que me empujaba cada vez más hacia el vacío.

Mientras descendía, miré sobre mi hombro, hacia abajo, hacia aquel pozo infinito donde ya no había vida ni espíritus ni engendros: la profunda frontera del plano medio, el último paso a la muerte definitiva. Y de ese lugar, de esa franja gruesa y oscura que separa todo lo que existe y lo que deja de existir, brotó un sonido extraño, tan quedo que no sabía si lo que escuchaba era más bien el flujo sanguíneo en mis tímpanos.

Al principio parecía estática, como cuando enciendes un televisor antiguo y aparece el tono del ruido blanco por la pantalla, pero después, comprendí que era un río infinito de gritos, de bramidos que *clamaban por mi llegada*.

¿Se trataban de las propias voces del monstruo dentro de mí, escapando de mi cuerpo ante el inevitable alcance de la muerte? Ya no me interesaba saberlo, así que cerré los ojos y me dejé sofocar por la idea de que tal vez siempre había sido mi destino volver a esa oscuridad y a lo que fuera que me esperara allí abajo. Tal vez *eso* fuera el único hogar al que podía aspirar, porque si algo tenía por seguro es que ya no había forma de que pudiera pertenecer a mi gente de nuevo.

Por primera vez, desde que había comenzado mi odisea en Nueva Orleans, estaba listo para que todo terminara.

Pero fue allí, en medio de la soporífera resignación de haber perdido la batalla, que una aurora brillante quebró la penumbra como una flecha. Todo resplandeció y las voces se desvanecieron junto con las sombras en las que habitaban.

Abrí los ojos de nuevo y al ver esa claridad y ser arrastrado de vuelta a la vida en contra de mi voluntad, me di cuenta de que, por más que lo deseara, no podía darme el lujo de morir en ese momento.

Porque no sólo mi mundo, sino el de todos los errantes, ése por el que habíamos luchado para proteger durante siglos, estaba a punto de derrumbarse.

PRIMERA FASE

UN MONSTRUO

MENGUANTE

CAPÍTULO I
UN PACTO FRÁGIL

19 años atrás

Hace más de un milenio escogí ser la creadora de un nuevo dios.

Una elección que, sin saberlo, me convertiría en la madre de una fuerza indestructible y arrebatadora de la naturaleza.

Después, se nos dio *a ti* y *a mí* un último regalo: la primera parte de una premonición: una advertencia lejana que anunciaba el Triunfo de la Luna, la cual, aun cuando volvería de entre la nieve, pequeña e insignificante como la última espiga del invierno, tendría el poder de rasgar para siempre el velo que separa a los vivos de los muertos.

Pero apenas hace un año recibí *la segunda parte* de ese vaticinio. Y entonces, supe que necesitaba despertar al menos tres magias. Tres ofrendas, tres pactos que aguardarían el regreso de aquella criatura que me había convertido en madre.

Y el último de esos pactos acaba de ser concretado, porque la mujer tirada a mis faldas, con los pechos expuestos al escrutinio de la noche y la cara torcida dentro de la niebla, expira, por fin.

El *athame*, el gran cuchillo de hierro blanco que empuño en mi mano se regocija, satisfecho al ver el símbolo que he trazado con su afilada punta, sobre la zona del corazón.

La ofrenda ha sido aceptada. Y lo sé porque, por encima del olor a carne quemada que desprende mi palma, empiezo a percibir el aroma de miles de flores.

El bosque enmudece al ver que abandono a mi víctima y me abro paso en sus entrañas, orgullosa y altiva contra el invierno que suspira en mi cara, la única parte de mi cuerpo que aún conserva su piel. Esta noche es dura, la más fría de la estación, pero no es suficiente para amedrentarme. La flama de la devoción que siento por mi criatura me ha devuelto la fuerza, de la cual estos largos años de espera intentaron despojarme, así que deslizo con más ímpetu mis pies a través de los restos de escarcha, lodo y hojarasca. Los gusanos congelados se retuercen y vuelven a la vida, la noche me observa con una luna entintada de rojo.

Me adentro en la espesura de endrinos negros como el hollín para seguir la ruta del viejo camino. La última vez que estuve aquí fue hace un milenio, pero tal como mi cuerpo, el bosque que me rodea, maldito, también se detuvo en el tiempo.

A cada paso que doy, observo con placer cómo el suelo burbujea cual caldero hirviente, a la par que desentierra decenas de columnas vertebrales antiguas, todas iguales, todas cosecha de la más brutal de mis semillas.

Un cementerio sin tumbas. Un camposanto entero para un solo cadáver.

Sonrío con placer al pensar en la furia que debes sentir al escucharme caminar sobre la tierra.

Escupo sobre los restos mientras mi túnica adquiere un matiz escarlata al rozar mis músculos despellejados, un hedor dulce que pronto perciben los espíritus que poco a poco despiertan en la oscuridad.

Los encuentro acuclillados detrás de las espinas, percibo sus ojos rojos como el carbón. Me observan. Me huelen. No saben quién soy, nunca me han visto antes, pero me desean como las moscas asedian la carne podrida, me buscan como anhelan a toda criatura con magia que pone un pie en estas tierras revueltas de sombras. Sus bocas famélicas se tuercen, sus entrepiernas se humedecen al percibir la sangre que impregna mi vestido, pero no se atreven a acercarse, no cuando la niebla del Señor del Sabbath me envuelve, la furia del trotapieles del desierto palpita en mis venas y un último pacto se derrama en la hoja blanca de mi daga.

—Tres magias. Tres pactos. Tres lealtades atadas a mi voluntad —repito con orgullo, como si quisiera mostrarte todas las cosas terribles que tuve que hacer por tu causa.

Llego hasta el corazón del cementerio, el sitio donde el viejo sendero se convierte en una estrella de ocho puntas, un cruce de caminos que los árboles rodean como un altar para los dioses que sólo despiertan después del crepúsculo.

Y, en medio, encuentro los restos de una fogata.

Camino alrededor del enclave tres veces. Me agacho y doy vida a la hoguera con el simple roce de mis manos, para después volver a circular.

No es calor lo que busco, sino librarme de esta desesperación.

Pero las doce dan paso a la una, la una se desdobla en las dos, las dos se convierten en las tres. Y cuando el sol comienza a vencer a la Estrella de la Mañana sin un remusgo de lo que llevo siglos esperando escuchar entre estos árboles, mi agonía se transforma en furia.

—¿Dónde está? —grito—. La predicción que hice era clara, ¡ésta era la noche! ¡¿Dónde está ese...?!

Me quedo quieta y el viento ulula en mis faldas, hasta que un gallo canta en la lejanía. Dos veces nada más.

El llamado me hace mirar hacia donde el alba rompe el horizonte negro de la noche. Mis ojos se llenan de alivio y mis brazos se alargan hacia la silueta que se acerca entre la nieve. Distingo sus hombros anchos, su cuerpo alto y el rubio de su cabello como un halo celestial alrededor de su cabeza.

—¡Por fin, por fin, padre de mi criatura! —exclamo jubilosa—. ¡Por fin has...!

Cierro la boca cuando la luz de la hoguera ilumina al hombre. Los demonios de las sombras callan y se levantan, sonrientes ante mi horror. El *athame* blanco se desliza de mis manos para caer al suelo y hacerse polvo como si estuviese hecho de cenizas. Y al verme indefensa, paralizada desde los dedos a la cabeza por una magia que tenía más de un milenio sin sentir, ellos me rodean. Tiran de mis ropas hasta arrancármelas con el deseo de llevarme con ellos, a las sombras.

Pero nada de eso me importa. Porque esta noche yo esperaba la llegada de un *bebé*.

Pero lo que tengo frente a mí... es a un hombre con los brazos vacíos.

CAPÍTULO 2
TEMBLOR

Una campanilla suena sobre mi cabeza cuando empujo la puerta de aluminio para pasar. Y al adentrarme en el pequeño establecimiento de carretera, lo primero que alerta mis sentidos no es el tufo a licor ni el tintineo de los tragos servidos por el cantinero: es el intenso olor a errante que desprende un grupo de motociclistas, apretujados en una esquina del bar.

Pero, a pesar del potente tirón que siento en mis entrañas, ninguno de aquel Atrapasueños dirige la cabeza hacia mí. Me quito la escarcha de los hombros y voy hacia las mesas atiborradas de camioneros. Por suerte, el calor del lugar me ayuda a controlar un poco las sacudidas de mi cuerpo, protegido sólo por una cazadora gris y los delgados vaqueros que poco han podido hacer contra el condenado clima del exterior.

En mi trayecto, un corpulento y solitario errante llama mi atención. Vestido con una gruesa chamarra de cuero, está sentado ante la barra de bebidas, apartado del grupo de motociclistas. Sus manos aprietan un tarro de cerveza y sus ojos, grises como los de Johanna, están clavados en el único televisor del lugar.

Me acerco hacia él, demasiado cansado como para prestar atención al silbido obsceno de un borracho a mis espaldas. Y paso a paso, las voces del monstruo de hueso se alzan ante la cercanía de *otro* de mi raza.

¿Tu raza?, se burla. Tú y yo somos bestias de otra clase.

Me siento en el banco al lado del perpetuasangre. Y en cuanto pongo los brazos sobre la barra, él mira hacia mi mano izquierda, aquella que oculta mis dedos descarnados bajo un guante de lana percudida. Los vellos de su nuca se erizan en un reflejo instintivo de su ancestro, uno que desprende un penetrante olor a montaña.

Recurro al poco autocontrol que me queda para no gruñir de irritación.

—¿Alguna novedad? —pregunto en voz baja. Los ojos del motociclista se desvían hacia mi cara, cosa que aprovecho para meter ambas manos en los bolsillos de la chamarra, lejos de su vista. Él mueve la cabeza de un lado a otro e intenta ignorar la inquietud del espíritu en su interior.

—Por suerte, no —responde para luego apurar un trago a su cerveza. Observo la hilera de botellas de cristal detrás de la barra, repentinamente sediento.

—Es cuestión de tiempo para que nos encuentren —digo, aún con la mirada fija en el licor—. Los Lander sólo están esperando el momento oportuno para acabar con todos nosotros. Y estoy bastante seguro de que pretenden divertirse mucho en el proceso.

Mis palabras aceleran los latidos de su corazón. Y ante nuestro breve pero gélido silencio, la voz del hombre a mi lado silencia el ruido del bar.

—Dios santo, ¿qué fue lo que hiciste allá, en Utah, muchacho?

Al girar hacia él, encuentro algo que me hace arrugar la nariz: *miedo*. El tipo me teme, porque su pregunta no fue un "qué pasó" ni un "qué les hicieron", sino un "qué hiciste".

De pronto, mi cansancio se desvanece y da paso a un fuego diferente, porque su ancestro, demasiado perceptivo para mi gusto, ha logrado ver una oscuridad que ya no tengo fuerzas para ocultar.

Me pongo de pie, despacio. El perpetuasangre abre bien los ojos y se echa hacia atrás, como si mi pequeño cuerpo fuese una amenaza contra la imponencia del suyo. Pero antes de que pueda dar un paso hacia él, alguien toma mi brazo y lo tuerce.

—¡Oye, tú! ¿Qué edad tienes? —exclama el cantinero, que se estira desde atrás de la barra—. Muéstrame tu identificación, *¡ahora!*

Quémale el maldito brazo

Y por unos segundos, *lo intento*. Intento llamar al fuego de mi magia para quemarle la palma entera al hombre, pero la espada filosofal dentro de mí lo ahoga como si disparase agua helada a través de mis venas.

Frustrado, empujo mi brujería con toda mi voluntad hasta que una chispa de rabia logra desatar un tenue calor bajo la piel de mi brazo.

Un calor que crece.

Y crece.

Y crece.

¡QUÉMALO!

Cuando estoy a punto de hacer aquel fuego estallar, cinco dedos grandes y pesados se colocan sobre mi hombro y tiran de mí, logrando que el cantinero, sorprendido, me suelte. El fuego se extingue de inmediato al encontrarme con los ojos azules de Tared.

Y su mirada, más fría que un témpano, hace que Wéndigo se agazape furioso dentro de mí.

Abro y cierro la boca, pero antes de que pueda replicar, él señala con un rápido movimiento de cabeza hacia atrás, a la puerta del bar. Bajo la barbilla y me suelto de su agarre con una sacudida.

El líder de Comus Bayou se da la mano con el perpetua-sangre. Éste llama a Tared "hermano" casi con alivio, como si todo el temor que sentía hace unos instantes se hubiera desvanecido con la presencia de...

Uno de los suyos.

Salgo del bar a zancadas y el frío de afuera me recibe con un latigazo. Aunque ya dejó de nevar, la gruesa capa de nieve que cubre los costados de la carretera y el cielo gris del mediodía me hacen sentir como si la tormenta nunca se hubiese acabado.

Encuentro, sobre el porche del establecimiento, nuestras mochilas de viaje tiradas de forma descuidada. Las paso de lado sin la mínima intención de recogerlas, y cruzo de manera distraída el estacionamiento lleno de motos y camionetas con las llantas envueltas en cadenas, preparadas para soportar los caminos helados. El tintineo de las botellas y el murmullo del bar desaparecen cuando llego a la orilla del estacionamiento, donde comienza una línea de árboles despojados de follaje.

La falda del bosque cruje con suavidad bajo mis botas. Camino un poco, sin dirección, hasta que el peso de la espada me obliga a ponerme en cuclillas para tomar aire. Miro la nieve unos segundos y me quito el guante para hundir mi mano humana en el manto. Dejo los dedos clavados allí y permito al hielo latir sobre mi piel hasta que la quemazón se vuelve insoportable.

Y cuando por fin la rabia se disipa a causa del dolor, un gemido escapa de mi garganta.

—¡Carajo! ¡Carajo! —retraigo mi mano contra mi pecho, como si eso ayudase a contener esa parte de mí que tanto lucha por dominarme.

Estuve a punto de quemarle el brazo al empleado de ese bar, de lastimar a un ser humano que no tenía nada que ver con mis problemas. Y encima, también traté de esa manera tan hostil a un hermano que sólo estaba asustado por razones completamente comprensibles.

Eso no era tu hermano...

—¡Cierra el maldito hocico de una vez!

Mi grito retumba en el bosque. Y aunque Wéndigo guarda silencio, sonríe con todos los dientes, porque sabe que tiene razón. No puedo culpar a aquel perpetuasangre por haberse sentido así, ni a él, ni a cualquier otro errante que se tope conmigo durante nuestro viaje a través del estado de Montana.

Pero lo peor de todo fue que Tared ha sido testigo, una vez más, de lo terrible que puedo llegar a ser.

Con dificultad, me levanto y regreso sobre mis pasos. Salgo por el desnivel y vuelvo a dar vueltas por el estacionamiento. Aunque la tentación de invocar de nuevo mi fuego interior para tratar de calentarme es enorme, desecho la idea de inmediato. No tengo ganas de perder más energía y sentirme todavía peor que ahora.

Minutos después enderezo la espalda al ver a Tared salir del bar con unas llaves entre los dedos. Recoge nuestras mochilas del porche, se acerca con la mirada fija en el suelo y, sin decir una palabra, *como si yo no estuviera aquí*, pasa a mi lado sin siquiera voltear a verme.

A decir verdad, me habría hecho menos daño una bofetada.

Cuando rodea el local y se pierde en la parte trasera del estacionamiento, decido por fin seguirlo. Pronto, Tared, el lobo, me guía hacia una camioneta estacionada en una esquina, una *pickup* color beige ya desvencijada por los años. Después de abrir el vehículo, lo primero que hace es meter la mano bajo el asiento del copiloto. Con discreción, arrastra sobre el tapete una larga escopeta, de gran calibre. Tared mira el arma de arriba abajo y vuelve a ocultarla.

El recuerdo de cuando lo vi hacer algo similar hace más de un año, allá en Nueva Orleans, me viene a la cabeza de pronto.

Noto que también hay una caja de municiones bajo el asiento y unos cuantos bultos en el espacio en la parte trasera; chamarras gruesas de plumón y lana con un aspecto mucho más confortable que la delgada cazadora que llevo encima. Él guarda ambas mochilas y retrocede para dar la vuelta al vehículo y subirse al asiento del conductor. Se acomoda el cinturón, fija su mirada en el parabrisas y tan sólo la desvía hacia mí cuando, tras unos largos segundos, yo sigo sin acercarme. El devorapieles me descubre con las botas quietas en el pavimento mientras intento hallar vestigios de nuestro *vínculo*, esa delgada línea que unía su corazón con el mío y que tiraba desesperadamente de nosotros con tal de unirnos de nuevo. Pero no encuentro nada... Porque esa unión ya no existe.

La garra *dentro de mi pecho* me hace llevarme una mano al esternón.

—¿Qué estás...?

—¿Me odias? —pregunto en voz baja, sin mirarlo a los ojos—. ¿O sólo me tienes miedo, al igual que ese hombre?

Vaya. Qué extraño es escuchar en mí ese matiz de tristeza cuando, en mi cabeza, todo el tiempo estoy enojado.

El silencio de Tared me hace sentir como si una roca se balanceara sobre mi cabeza. Y lo peor es que, a mi pesar, no sé cuál de las dos opciones me dolería más.

—Si me dejas aquí —continúo— toda esta pesadilla terminará para ti. Para todos. No necesitas seguir cargando conmigo. No tienes por qué... ~~Estar con alguien a quien detestas.~~

Tared aprieta el volante entre los dedos y mira hacia el frente durante unos segundos tan largos que parece considerar mis palabras.

Wéndigo musita y, como si lo hubiese escuchado, el lobo niega con la cabeza.

—Sube —dice con sobriedad. Tanta que no siento ningún alivio. Ninguna felicidad.

Tan sólo un tímido temblor.

Me acerco, encorvado. Abro la puerta y trepo sobre el asiento cubierto por algunas cobijas de lana. El olor del errante a quien pertenecía este vehículo persiste en el interior, lo que atiza el hambre del monstruo dentro de mí.

Tared enciende el vehículo, se desplaza por el estacionamiento y toma rumbo hacia la carretera, mientras algunos miembros del Atrapasueños salen del bar. El perpetuasangre con quien tuve el incidente hace una señal hacia el lobo a modo de despedida, mientras que yo no me atrevo a quitar la mirada del tablero.

Pronto, entramos en el asfalto, y la tensión se prolonga a medida que avanzamos cada vez más rápido por el camino de árboles flacos y montañas grisáceas. Y aun cuando el invierno del norte lo congela todo, el frío dentro de la cabina me parece mucho más desolador.

El lobo pisa el acelerador y el pequeño aglomerado de negocios de carretera por fin se pierde a nuestras espaldas. Copos de nieve se acumulan despacio sobre el parabrisas.

Al pasar un letrero que nos marca la ruta hacia la carretera estatal, recargo el hombro contra la puerta de la camioneta y me rodeo con mis propios brazos, rendido ante la fatiga.

No vale la pena...

Hoy, Wéndigo está más hablador de lo normal. Eso o son mis propios pensamientos, los cuales ya no se diferencian mucho a la voz del monstruo dentro de mí.

No lo sé. Ya no estoy seguro de nada.

CAPÍTULO 3
UNA GRIETA RESPLANDECIENTE

Blanca y feroz, una luz ilumina de pronto el costado de mi cara para despertarme como el beso de un amante violento.

Abro los ojos y el desmesurado resplandor, agresivo e hiriente, comienza a debilitarse, a convertirse en un brillo tenue sobre las paredes de tierra y roca de mi prisión. La última vez que fui agredida por este brillo lunar, la celda era toda plomo fundido, fuego y calor que me derretía la planta de los pies. Pero ahora, el suelo está tapizado de una nieve tan mortífera que hasta mi sangre se torna de cristal. ¿Cuánto habré dormido esta vez? ¿Horas, días, semanas? ¿Cuántos suplicios, cuántos ciclos habrán pasado desde que vi saltar a mi hijo de aquella catarata?

Giro la cabeza hacia la ventana de mi celda, hacia aquel *portal* por donde brota la insistente luz. Mi nuca unida al suelo por raíces se desgarra con el movimiento, pero la agonía ya sólo me es costumbre, así que observo aquel llamado hasta que decido arrancar mi cuerpo desnudo de la tierra para levantarme.

Sangro, sangro en abundancia, y la tierra debajo de mí absorbe mis fluidos con desesperación, se alimenta de mi dolor y me mantiene viva a la vez para recordarme que la misericordia del plano medio es tan inmensa como su apetito. Y con eso, empiezo a caminar entre las sombras, confiada en que mis pies y manos despellejadas ya han memorizado cada roca, cada fruto necrótico, cada columna vertebral con la que he tropezado a lo largo de mi permanencia en este lugar de muros ovalados; un Tártaro que ahora es mío, aun cuando yo misma lo construí para ti.

Me detengo frente a la ventana, una boca de absoluta oscuridad empotrada en medio de la pared curva, y escucho el sonido del agua detrás del portal, la voz de un pacto entre este mundo y el otro.

Mi vientre se hincha como un nido al acariciar con mis manos sangrantes *las cinco marcas de garras* hendidas más allá del borde de la ventana. El rastro escarlata parece complacer al velo entre el plano espiritual y el humano, puesto que, en cuestión de segundos, escucho el rugido del mar.

Un vendaval escupe agua salada desde el interior del portal hacia mi cara como una brisa de cuchillos. Me echo hacia atrás, pero la tempestad amaina y el agua de la ventana se queda quieta como la superficie de un estanque en el subsuelo.

Sólo así soy capaz de sumergir la cabeza.

Allí dentro, todo es negrura. La miro por largos minutos hasta que mis pulmones suplican por aire. Me aferro con huesos y uñas al borde para soportar la asfixia mientras mi cuerpo se convulsiona ajeno a mi voluntad.

Y al vislumbrar la muerte en mi pecho cada vez más apretado, el vínculo entre lo vivo y lo muerto por fin se establece;

la oscuridad se disipa y el agua se evapora alrededor, lo que me permite de nuevo respirar. Con mi magia oprimida por esta cárcel maldita, me he quedado sola con mis tres pactos. Tres magias por las que ahora, en este siglo, se me ha dado el nombre de "Mara".

Pero más allá de eso, ya sólo soy un escalofrío en la nuca, una sombra en el rabillo del párpado, un ojo que observa en la oscuridad.

Y tal como lo esperaba, puedo ver una vez más a mi criatura, pero ahora en medio de la nieve. Tan magnífico, ¡tan hermoso que podría devorarlo con tal de sentirlo dentro de mi vientre! Mi creación, mi amado, mi hijo, ¡cómo desearía lamer las lágrimas que la bestia obscena que está a su lado le ha hecho derramar! ¿Por qué no se da cuenta del ser vulgar y frágil en el que se transforma cada vez que busca el calor de aquel animal inmundo? ¿Por qué se niega a ver que su camino, destinado a la grandeza, se ha vuelto un sendero de espinas y fantasmas desde el momento en el que decidió convertirlo en su objeto de deseo?

Quisiera retorcerle el cuello hasta desprenderle la cabeza, abrirle el vientre en canal y usar sus tripas para buscar algo más que un vaticinio entre ellas...

Pero por ahora, lo único que puedo hacer es esperar. Observar y esperar, tanto como tú lo has hecho durante estos diecinueve años.

Saco la cabeza del portal y retrocedo para volver a recostarme sobre el suelo. Las raíces frías se remueven en la tierra como gusanos para alcanzarme; se introducen con puntas afiladas por cada cavidad de mi cuerpo para paralizar mi magia y unirme al plano de los espíritus, hasta que el portal necesite mostrarme algo de nuevo.

Después, miro hacia la puerta de madera detrás de mí, justo en contraposición con la ventana, hecha para que la única forma de salir de aquí sea si alguien la abre desde afuera. El dolor que inflige esta celda sería brutal para cualquiera, pero para mí ya sólo es pasajero, porque el día en el que tú me encerraste aquí, me fue revelada la *tercera parte* de la premonición: cuando caiga la última magia, mi criatura *resucitará*. Y ese día, por fin se abrirá esa puerta. Y cuando eso suceda, el mundo despertará de su sueño.

CAPÍTULO 4
UN MILAGRO DECEPCIONANTE

El dolor en mi pecho me obliga a despertar, jadeando. Abro los ojos y me encuentro solo en la cabina de la camioneta, recostado boca arriba a lo largo del asiento y con el peso de una cobija sobre mi cuerpo. Intento respirar, pero no logro llenar mis pulmones por completo, así que me hago un ovillo hasta que la presión se vuelve más o menos tolerable.

Me levanto, miro alrededor y descubro que estoy en el estacionamiento de un motel de carretera. Al lado hay un autoservicio con un restaurante diseñado para asemejarse a una cabaña, de esos que pululan por zonas montañosas como ésta. También hay una gasolinera del otro lado del camino, con un solitario tráiler cuyo tubo de escape expulsa humo negro que contrasta con el anaranjado del atardecer.

Al parecer, he dormido por lo menos tres horas, pero me siento como si no lo hubiese hecho desde hace semanas. El invierno devora los días con tanta rapidez...

Reúno el valor para apartar la cobija. Me ajusto el gorro de lana, me pongo una chamarra blanca de plumón que encuentro detrás del asiento y bajo de la camioneta, resintiéndome del peso de la espada en cuanto pongo los pies sobre el asfalto resbaladizo. La ventisca me llena la cara de diminutos copos de nieve que tampoco me hacen ningún favor.

Sin ganas de desnucarme en una caída, me acerco con cuidado al comercio, donde un oso de madera con un letrero de "bienvenidos" me recibe en la puerta de cristal. Al entrar, el agradable sopor de la calefacción me hace suspirar de alivio y volver a sentir los dedos de mi mano humana.

El sitio es grande y muy rústico, tan alusivo a una cabaña como su exterior, pero no está muy concurrido; apenas hay un par de turistas con tablas de nieve y un camionero que deambula por el pasillo, lo que me hace pensar que pasamos por una zona muy aislada o lejos de un foco turístico. Idea que, por alguna razón, no me termina de gustar.

Paso de largo la pequeña sección de autoservicio, aunque no sin antes dar un vistazo a los pasillos abarrotados de víveres, recuerdos de la región y artículos de viaje. No tengo idea de cuánto dinero nos queda para el resto del camino, pero ya no debe ser demasiado.

Pronto, logro divisar a Tared. Está sentado en una butaca al fondo de la zona del restaurante y tiene la mirada clavada en el celular que sostiene entre las manos, mientras la ventisca, ahora más vigorosa, golpea contra la ventana a su lado.

La sensación de la cobija que tenía encima al despertar, ésa que estoy seguro de que no me puse yo mismo entre sueños, aún acaricia mi piel. Pero cuando el lobo ni siquiera levanta la cabeza al acercarme, me desaferro de inmediato de esa ilusión.

Me siento en el lado contrario de la mesa y observo los platos de comida. La sopa frente a mí parece tibia, como si ya tuviese un tiempo servida, mientras que una lata de Red Bull abierta al lado de Tared me recuerda que no soy el único cansado aquí. ¿Hace cuánto que no dormimos más de cuatro o cinco horas seguidas? ¿Seis, siete días?

¿Hace cuánto que él no duerme con tal de vigilarnos?

Alargo mi mano hacia la cuchara. Nada más tocarla, el devorapieles deja el teléfono a un lado, toma su emparedado y, en completo silencio, comienza a comer.

Al sentir la humedad subir sin tregua hacia mis ojos me veo obligado a voltear hacia el vidrio y contemplar la nieve bajar, porque *esto* es lo que más me duele de todo: la cobija, la comida, su silenciosa sensatez; el hecho de saber que, sin importar qué tan responsable sea el hombre lobo conmigo, sus gestos son en realidad mecánicos y repetitivos, carentes de afecto, porque aun cuando nuestros cuerpos lograron salir del plano medio, una parte de nosotros se quedó allí abajo, perdida para siempre en la oscuridad. Tared jamás dejó de ser el líder, el errante leal, el protector... pero yo ya nunca volveré a ser el mismo de antes.

Y eso significa que ya no soy aquel chico a quien alguna vez él amó.

¿De verdad crees que lo hizo? No eras más que un juguete.

En vez de responderle a Wéndigo, miro de reojo al devorapieles, quien se ha acabado su plato en tres bocados para poder volcar su atención otra vez al celular. Siento una punzada en el pecho porque, para mantenerse sano, necesitaría comer dos o tres porciones más, por lo menos. Es un guerrero, alguien que necesita valerse de su fuerza física, él no es...

Un errante con magia.

Inquieta, mi mano enguantada se estruja contra mi regazo, como si tuviese vida propia al recordar el vacío del plano medio. El frío, la asfixia, la desesperación y de pronto...

La luz. La grieta sobre el abismo.

Vuelvo la mirada hacia la ventana y observo unas huellas en la nieve, sobre la jardinera. Los sucesos que vivimos al saltar por la catarata de Stonefall regresan a atormentarme, porque hasta el día de hoy sigo sin creer cómo pudimos salir vivos de eso.

No, ¿cómo es que *Tared* salió vivo de eso?

Cierro los ojos un momento y vuelvo a recordarlo todo, con tanta nitidez que siento la misma angustia trepar por mi garganta, como si en este preciso instante él estuviese desapareciendo de nuevo en la oscuridad.

En aquel momento, cuando caíamos en el agua, mi magia había logrado hacer que el hombre lobo cruzase al plano medio conmigo, lo que de por sí ya era un auténtico logro, pero eso no significaba que pudiese mantenerlo con vida *dentro de él*, así que sólo era cuestión de minutos, instantes, tal vez, para que el peso del mundo espiritual lo aplastara.

Hasta que el milagro sucedió. Hasta que aquella luz abrió la oscuridad como una grieta y la transformó en una transparencia turquesa e infinita, mientras que la terrible corriente que me arrastraba se apaciguó, como si el tiempo se hubiese detenido de pronto. Y a pesar de que el frío todavía me mordía los huesos, la sorpresa me sacudió cuando volví a mirar hacia donde se había hundido el hombre lobo. Porque él, en esa cámara lenta propia de un lugar sumergido en el agua, se depositó suavemente contra el fondo de "algo".

Una nube de polvo se elevó a su alrededor y luego, Tared se quedó inerte sobre lo que parecía una superficie de rocas y arena. Su mirada, antes en blanco, ahora estaba cerrada, como si sólo estuviese durmiendo, y él se balanceaba con una tranquila corriente, sin aquella rigidez mortífera que había tenido tan sólo segundos atrás.

Mi cuerpo despertó azotado por un látigo. Recuperé el control de mis extremidades y nadé hacia Tared con todas mis fuerzas, como si la esperanza me hubiese devuelto la vida que el plano medio estuvo a punto de quitarme.

Lo tomé del brazo y miré hacia arriba. El agua, que brillaba en un tono verde, casi neón, me hizo saber que no estábamos a demasiada profundidad.

Nadé hacia la luz y jalé al devorapieles detrás de mí, asombrado de no haberme ahogado todavía. El peso de la espada en mi pecho y la piel de lobo amarrada a la cintura de Tared luchaban por hundirme de nuevo, pero logré subir, subir y subir hasta que estiré la mano hacia arriba.

Y entonces, mis dedos se estrellaron contra una superficie dura y traslúcida. Desconcertado, golpeé como pude con el dorso, una y otra vez, pero aquella cosa ni siquiera vibró.

Mi corazón se desbocó hasta mi garganta al darme cuenta de que era una gruesa capa de hielo.

¡Suéltalo y sálvanos!

¡Olvídalo, hijo de puta!

Sé que le dije al monstruo dentro de mí. Luego grité debajo del agua al darme cuenta de que, aun cuando Tared y yo nos habíamos salvado de los tramperos, aun cuando habíamos escapado del plano medio y de la oscuridad, tal vez no íbamos a lograrlo.

A punto de desmayarme a causa del frío y la falta de aire, un puño salió disparado como un arpón a mi lado y golpeó el hielo con tanta fuerza que le hizo una fisura.

Tared, como si hubiese despertado de un sueño inhóspito, dejó escapar el último vestigio de aire en su pecho y soltó mi mano para aferrarse a la capa de hielo con las garras que había hecho crecer en sus manos humanas. Me revolví con desesperación para no hundirme, en tanto él, con puños y rodillas, comenzó a rasguñar y a golpear la superficie con un impulso exorbitante, a pesar de estar debajo del agua. Lo hizo una y otra vez hasta que, por fin, la capa de hielo se rompió como el cristal.

Un cielo gris y un frío desgarrador fue lo único que nos recibió en la superficie. Jadeé y chapoteé con desesperación en el agua helada hasta que pude aferrarme a uno de los bordes del agujero que había abierto Tared. Él salió de un solo impulso mientras yo me arrastré fuera con dificultad, como si la larga chamarra que llevaba puesta tuviese piedras en los bolsillos.

Me dejé caer y mis astas rasguñaron el hielo en un chillido lastimero. Luego, vi al lobo arrodillarse a un par de metros de mí; una densa capa de vapor brotaba de su boca y su costado estaba salpicado de manchas rojas y violetas por las costillas que se había roto durante la batalla contra el Rebis. Estaba pálido y parecía tener dificultades para respirar..., pero estaba vivo.

Tared, un devorapieles, había sobrevivido al plano medio.

No tuve tiempo de pensar demasiado en ello; el *rugido* del hombre lobo, quien se había abalanzado contra mí, me aturdió de repente.

—¡¿Dónde estamos?! —exclamó a la par que me sacudía de los hombros—, ¡¿a dónde nos has traído?!

Estaba tan desconcertado que ni siquiera gemí al sentir un punzante dolor en el brazo. Tan sólo miré alrededor.

Todo lo que había a la vista era blanco, tan blanco y cegador que me costó distinguir las siluetas de los árboles huesudos a lo lejos, bordeando el sitio al que habíamos llegado: un lago congelado con las orillas cubiertas de espesa nieve.

Intenté respirar de nuevo para decir a Tared que no tenía ni idea de dónde estábamos, pero el aire era tan helado que casi se congeló en mis pulmones, así que sólo pude mover un poco la cabeza en respuesta, el cuello tenso por el peso de mi cornamenta.

Furioso, me soltó y rugió, desesperado, para darme la espalda y girar la cabeza hacia un lado y el otro.

Me dejé caer de nuevo contra el hielo y temblé tanto que pensé que mis dientes se quebrarían los unos contra los otros. Intenté transmitir un poco de calor a mi cuerpo desde mi mano desgarrada para no morir allí mismo de hipotermia, pero no logré gran cosa. La espada dentro de mí me consumía, el frío tenía entumecidas mis extremidades y las voces de Wéndigo no dejaban de aquejarme, coléricas. Mis energías estaban al límite.

En medio de la confusión, un potente ruido zumbó a lo lejos, el cual hizo al lobo levantar la cabeza y abrir los ojos de par en par: el sonido de un tráiler.

Sin mediar palabra, corrió hacia el lindero del bosque y se perdió entre los árboles, siguiendo el retumbar de aquel motor. Lo miré desaparecer al tiempo que sentí menguar el ritmo de mis latidos, pero el miedo y la confusión me impulsaron a hacer un esfuerzo monumental para levantarme en dirección a donde se había marchado el devorapieles.

Pero en cuanto mis pies salieron del lago y se hundieron veinte centímetros en el manto de escarcha, casi me arrepentí de haberme movido siquiera.

Nieve.

No recuerdo si aquélla fue la primera vez que la pisaba, pero la encontré terrible, y me quemó tanto la piel que quizás hubiese preferido meterme en una hoguera. Aun así, me recompuse y troté lo más rápido que pude, siguiendo las huellas del lobo hasta caer de rodillas minutos después, agotado.

No sólo la espada pesaba muchísimo, sino también mi cornamenta plateada, tan plena de astas ramificadas como los propios árboles que me rodeaban.

Y entonces, me percaté del dolor en mi brazo.

Desconcertado, descubrí junto a mis huellas en la nieve un abundante rastro de sangre que se alargaba desde el lago. Y más abajo de mi hombro, allí estaba: el disparo que me había alcanzado en Stonefall antes de saltar a la catarata.

Toqué la herida y entorné la mirada al darme cuenta de que no era una bala, sino un artefacto pequeño y repleto de dientes metálicos incrustados en mi piel, con una luz roja parpadeante. Con un grito, arranqué aquella cosa y la trituré dentro de mi puño, para arrojarla sobre la nieve y dejarme caer boca arriba; el olor de mi propia sangre me revolvió el estómago como si saboreara una vez más la carne de Buck Lander en mi lengua.

De pronto, ya no podía respirar más, inhalar me dolía como si tuviese los pulmones llenos de cristales rotos. La chamarra empapada ya se había puesto tiesa a causa del frío, al igual que mi cabello mojado.

Miré hacia las copas de los árboles, motas blancas caían sobre mí como una lluvia de cenizas. El cielo comenzó a cambiar de color y el frío, cada vez más terrible, me hacía preguntarme sin cesar hasta dónde nos había arrastrado el plano medio. Y justo cuando creí que iba a quedarme congelado allí mismo, unos brazos me levantaron de la nieve hasta ponerme de rodillas de nuevo.

Ni siquiera tuve tiempo para reaccionar. En menos de un instante, Tared aferró sus palmas a la base de una de mis astas, apretó los dientes y, con un movimiento firme y preciso, la partió en dos.

Arrojó un asta a la nieve y luego prosiguió con otra. Después, el lobo volvió a darme la espalda y se alejó para abrirse paso una vez más entre la espesura de los árboles con una agilidad extraordinaria para su estado. Lo miré, estupefacto, mientras mi otrora corona de hueso se hundía en el blanco manto frente a mí; yo sabía que él había resultado herido en la batalla, pero parecía como si el frío le hubiese renovado las energías.

Me sentí un idiota de inmediato. Por supuesto. Él era un lobo plateado de Minnesota, un errante del norte y la nieve, de las tormentas y los bosques.

Aquél era su sitio.

Me levanté una vez más, aligerado por la ausencia de mis astas, y seguí su rastro con torpeza hasta encontrármelo frente a una solitaria carretera. El hombre lobo estaba petrificado en la orilla, observando un letrero grande y marrón clavado a un costado del camino:

BIENVENIDOS

Parque Nacional North Cascades

No lo entendí de inmediato. Tan sólo me quedé parado allí, como si aquellas letras no tuviesen sentido a pesar de que podía leerlas en orden.

—¿Washington? —susurró Tared, por fin, con lo que bien pudo ser su último aliento. Y al escucharlo, la realidad se desplomó sobre mí como una hilera de fichas de dominó, porque sólo hasta ese momento me di cuenta del grave problema en el que nos habíamos metido.

No sólo habíamos aparecido en un sitio remoto, a miles de kilómetros de Utah, y después de quién sabe cuánto tiempo desde aquella batalla en Stonefall, sino que nuestro mundo había cambiado de la peor manera posible...

Porque los Lander *lo habían descubierto.*

CAPÍTULO 5
STILL A WITCH?[1]

En aquel momento no lo quise creer, pero a medida que caminábamos a lo largo de la carretera sin divisar otra cosa que árboles y nieve, supe que debía aceptarlo.

Washington.

No la capital del país, sino el estado al norte de la costa del pacífico, a tan sólo unos kilómetros de la frontera con Canadá.

El razonamiento de lo que nos había sucedido a Tared y a mí era simple: el tiempo en el plano medio transcurre de manera distinta que en el humano y, al parecer, aún más en los portales que se hallan dentro de agua caudalosa como los ríos o las cascadas. Me había sucedido cuando salté al Dirty Devil River allá en Utah, y ahora en nuestra escapada de Stonefall.

Tanto el lobo como yo sabíamos que lo único que podíamos hacer en esos momentos era buscar un refugio. Así que, empujados por el instinto, caminamos en sentido contrario

---

[1] ¿Aún soy un brujo?

Nota de la autora: he decidido mantener algunas expresiones en inglés puesto que tienen origen en tratados antiguos en los que cobran un sentido más profundo únicamente en dichos contextos.

al letrero del parque nacional. Arriesgarnos a entrar en una reserva sólo sería echarnos la soga al cuello, por lo que seguimos en línea recta por la carretera, desesperados por encontrar algo que nos pudiese salvar de tan terrible situación.

En un abrir y cerrar de ojos, ya había oscurecido, y cada vez hacía más frío. Tared no parecía tener demasiados problemas para lidiar con la temperatura, a pesar de sólo estar cubierto de la cintura para abajo con su piel de lobo, pero ambos sabíamos que yo no sobreviviría demasiado allá afuera; apenas lograba calentarme con ayuda de mi débil magia lo suficiente como para no desplomarme congelado sobre el pavimento.

Por suerte, tras uno o dos kilómetros, logramos dar con un taller mecánico cerrado. Tared, abriéndose paso en la nieve acumulada en la entrada, destrozó la puerta trasera de una sola embestida y entró. Recuerdo que mientras lo seguía a trompicones, agradecí a todos los dioses de que no se hubiese activado ninguna alarma. El devorapieles jamás era descuidado, pero resultaba evidente que la situación no ameritaba su paciencia.

El taller era pequeño, apenas la cochera de servicio y una oficina con un corto pasillo que daba al almacén. Estaba tan helado como afuera, pero tenía energía eléctrica, y pudimos conseguir un par de uniformes y ropa seca para vestirnos, así como un botiquín de emergencia con el cual hacerme un torniquete improvisado en la herida de mi brazo.

Vestido con una sudadera que me quedaba enorme, di vueltas alrededor de Tared, quien trataba de encender un coche en reparación. Yo intentaba explicarle lo que había sucedido en el plano medio, darle a entender que había hecho todo lo posible por salvarnos a ambos, pero el hombre lobo no parecía escucharme.

No. Tared *no quería* escucharme.

¡CABRÓN!

Di una zancada hacia él y alargué la mano para que al menos me diera la cara. Pero antes de alcanzarlo, él retrocedió como si le hubiese acercado una vara de hierro caliente.

El vínculo herido entre nosotros se tensó como un frágil hilo de seda y tuve que observar a Tared unos cuantos segundos para que su reacción por fin tuviese sentido: sus pupilas dilatadas, el subir y bajar de su pecho, las pinzas con las que partía un par de cables apretadas en su mano...

Estaba asustado. *Me temía*, porque la mirada en sus ojos azules era exactamente igual a la de mis hermanos cuando me vieron devorar al hijo de Benjamin Lander.

Bajé la cabeza y me aparté. Retrocedí hasta salir de aquel garaje y me encerré en el baño. Abrí los ojos con sorpresa al verme en el espejo sobre el lavabo: la sien que Irina había cortado casi al ras, ahora estaba cubierta por una larga mata de cabello que podía colocar sin problemas detrás de mi oreja. El resto de mi pelo también había crecido mucho y ahora me llegaba muy por debajo del pecho, tieso por el hielo y la sangre.

Y no sólo eso. Mi lóbulo, aquél que había salido herido durante la batalla, ahora estaba cicatrizado.

Dioses, ¿cuánto tiempo había pasado?

Miré también las protuberancias de mi cornamenta destrozada, las cuales sobresalían como cuernos blancos de mi cabeza. No tenía ánimos para ir a buscar algo con qué limarlas y, con suerte, se caerían por sí solas después de un tiempo.

La idea me pareció estúpida de inmediato, porque tiempo es lo que menos teníamos.

Me deslicé hasta el suelo y puse la cabeza entre las manos. Estaba agotado, muerto de frío y, simplemente, no podía hacer nada más.

Después de un rato, el motor de aquel vehículo rugió. Me levanté y salí hacia el garaje casi arrastrando los pies como un perro apaleado. Encontré a Tared en el asiento del conductor, con la cortina del taller abierta de par en par y la mirada fija en el volante.

Estaba esperándome.

Ahora que pienso en aquel momento, creo que pude haber terminado con todo allí. Pude haber echado a correr para perderme en el bosque. Pude haber dejado que Tared continuase con su vida sin el temor de no volver a pegar ojo en la noche con tal de cuidarse de mí.

Pero no lo hiciste.

No. No lo hice. Fui egoísta, una vez más fui cobarde, y subí a aquel coche.

Salimos del taller y nos dirigimos hacia el pueblo más cercano que nos señalaban los letreros de la carretera. El termostato del tablero marcaba menos seis grados centígrados y yo tenía la terrible sospecha de que iba a bajar aún más.

Pero no me atreví a encender la calefacción. Sabía que el vehículo tenía gasolina gracias al bidón vacío que vi tirado en el garaje antes de subir, pero no tenía idea de hasta dónde podría llegar nuestra suerte.

Al final, lo único que me quedó fue confiar en que Tared sabría cómo sacarnos de eso, y la idea me inquietó demasiado. No entendía cómo es que después de descubrir el monstruo que era yo en realidad, después de la mirada atemorizada que me había lanzado, él había elegido no abandonarme.

Tal vez no sabía qué hacer conmigo. Quizás había enloquecido, allá abajo, en la oscuridad.

Tal vez, en el fondo, era yo quien no estaba listo para saber la verdad.

El hombre lobo condujo muy despacio, con recelo. Habíamos robado un coche en reparación, después de todo, y el que se estropeara de nuevo y nos dejase varados en medio de la carretera era un temor difícil de ignorar. Pero tras una hora que me pareció interminable, logramos llegar al pueblo más cercano de los alrededores, en mitad de la noche.

Lo primero que hicimos fue buscar una dispensadora de periódicos para enterarnos del día en que estábamos, conscientes de que, si parábamos en una gasolinera, nuestro aspecto no haría más que levantar sospechas. Y cuando logramos encontrar una hilera de ellas, colocadas sobre una acera en una calle vacía y a oscuras, nos quedamos largos minutos frente a las cajas de metal.

Diciembre. Todos y cada uno de los periódicos marcaban veintiséis de diciembre. Habían pasado más de cuatro meses desde nuestra pelea en Stonefall.

Y yo ya había cumplido diecinueve años.

Escuché un golpe metálico y el reventar de un cristal, pero estaba tan catatónico que ni siquiera me sobresalté por la maquinilla que Tared acababa de abollar con los puños. Los vidrios rodaron hasta mis pies y el coche se sacudió cuando el hombre lobo se dejó caer contra la puerta. Pero ni aun así me moví.

Me quedé parado durante largos minutos, pensé y pensé hasta que el frío me caló. ¿Cómo había ocurrido este desastre? ¿En qué clase de mundo habíamos despertado?

Levanté la cabeza y me lancé hacia la dispensadora rota para sacar uno de los periódicos del interior. Los cristales rasgaron mi brazo, pero no me importó.

Bajo la mirada inquisitiva del lobo, hojeé el periódico hasta terminarlo y lo arrojé al suelo, para luego asomarme a las otras dispensadoras como un loco, mirando los encabezados, las noticias y todas las notas que mi vista alcanzase.

—Nada —dije por fin.

Absolutamente nada. Ni movilizaciones militares, ni Apocalipsis, ni noticias escandalosas sobre gente convertida en animales. La calle estaba vacía y silenciosa, pero a lo lejos podían verse algunas luces navideñas a través de los negocios cerrados, en señal de que la gente estaba tranquila, en sus casas.

No. No había ningún indicio de que los Lander nos hubiesen delatado y eso, más que tranquilizarme, me perturbó sobremanera.

Escuché los vidrios del suelo crujir y me giré para ver cómo Tared se inclinaba sobre el periódico abierto para examinarlo. Por sí solo supo a qué se debía mi malestar.

—¿Y ahora qué? —escuché que susurró, pero no estoy seguro de que se hubiese dirigido a mí. Su voz sonó demasiado distante.

Tirité sobre el asfalto con los brazos cruzados e intenté pensar, buscando darle una respuesta que tal vez ni siquiera me había pedido, pero estaba tan cansado y tenía tanto frío que los ojos se me cerraban. Además, la herida me dolía mucho, la podía sentir palpitar a través de mis dedos humanos, apretados encima del ya ensangrentado torniquete.

Después de unos minutos, Tared pareció comprender que no ganaríamos nada quedándonos allí, estáticos y a la intemperie. Dejó escapar una bocanada de vaho y entró de nuevo al coche.

Lo seguí de inmediato y después de encender el vehículo nos limitamos a buscar un sitio dónde estacionarnos para pasar el resto de la madrugada. En otras circunstancias, ninguno de los dos habría pegado ojo en toda la noche, pero estábamos tan exhaustos que en cuanto metimos el coche en aquel terreno arbolado, a unos cien metros de la salida del pueblo, nos sumimos en el sueño al instante.

Ⓖ●◖○

Apenas media hora después de haberme quedado dormido, me despertó un ruido muy extraño, como un tenue silbido lastimero que rompía el silencio del interior del coche. Al principio me sentía demasiado cansado como para querer prestarle atención, pero el agotamiento se esfumó cuando me di cuenta de que aquel sonido no era otra cosa que la respiración de Tared.

La angustia me obligó a levantarme sobre mis codos y mirar hacia su costado, ése que había visto marcado por manchas rojas y moradas. Recordar el tremendo golpe que recibió durante la batalla con el Rebis hizo que un escalofrío me recorriera todo el cuerpo, ¿y si sus costillas habían soldado mal durante su transición en el plano medio?, ¿y si no habían sanado del todo? O peor aún, una de ellas podía haberle perforado un pulmón, ¿y si ese silbido era... sangre?

Sentí como si me hubiesen estrujado el corazón en un puño con tanta fuerza que creí que sufriría un infarto. Dioses, ¡yo sabía bien lo infernal que era el dolor de una costilla rota! ¿Cómo es que Tared había aguantado todas estas horas con semejante padecimiento y sin soltar un solo quejido?

No sobrevivirá la noche. Y lo sabes.

Miré el pecho de Tared subir y bajar con dificultad a través del delgado uniforme de mecánico que llevaba puesto.

Busqué sentirlo, y lo encontré: el vínculo entre nosotros latía, herido, *pero aún estaba allí.*

Supe lo que tenía que hacer.

Me erguí sobre el asiento y me eché encima su piel de lobo, la que él había dejado atrás en el asiento para que se secara —cosa que no había sucedido todavía—, y salí del coche en silencio. Troté sobre la nieve hasta la entrada del pueblo y me dirigí por la calle hasta encontrar un contenedor de basura apretujado en un callejón.

Al mirarlo, lleno de bolsas negras, rogué a todos los dioses que tuviesen algo de clemencia esta vez. Dejé la piel de lobo en el piso, me aferré al borde de metal y Wéndigo se estremeció.

Te gusta mucho humillarte, ¿verdad?

Familiarizado desde mi infancia con las búsquedas en la basura, me metí en el contenedor sin asomo de vergüenza. Revolví entre las bolsas y las rompí con los dedos entumecidos durante un largo rato hasta dar con lo que estaba buscando: los huesos pelados de un pavo de Navidad.

No eran costillas, pero estaba decidido a hacer que funcionaran.

Salí de aquel basurero, tomé la piel de lobo y caminé de vuelta al coche. Me senté en la tierra helada y recargué la espalda contra la puerta del copiloto para quitarme uno de los guantes aislantes que tomé del taller mecánico. Partí a la mitad uno de los huesos, el más corto que pude encontrar —*los largos para dañar, los cortos para sanar*, me repetí—, y arranqué algunos mechones del manto plateado sobre mis hombros, y procedí a usarlos para unir ambas partes del hueso de forma muy improvisada.

Finalmente, humedecí un poco de la sangre seca y congelada que quedaba del cuero de Tared con mi propia saliva y recubrí con ella el artilugio.

Murmuré una plegaria, pero el hueso no se movió.

—No, no, dioses... —susurré mientras volvía a intentar convocar mi magia en la punta de mis dedos. Podía sentirla, esa sombra, ese perfume indescifrable, esa vibración oscura bajo mi piel, pero no parecía expandirse más allá de la zona de mi esternón. Supe entonces que no era que mi magia estuviese débil, sino que la espada *la estaba reteniendo*.

Semejante revelación me cortó el aliento: aun cuando la piedra filosofal, la legendaria inmortalidad alquímica yacía alojada en mi cuerpo, yo no era inmortal en absoluto. Al contrario, estaba frágil y más débil que nunca. ¿Acaso era porque mi cuerpo humano no era capaz de soportar el poder de semejante objeto?

Sentí a Wéndigo sonreír.

Apreté los trozos de hueso y la sangre hirvió dentro de mis venas. Estuve a punto de soltar un puñetazo a la puerta del coche cuando percibí que algo se removió en mi mano. Abrí la palma y, sorprendido, me percaté de que el hueso de pavo había vuelto a unirse.

Me quedé largos segundos mirándolo, incapaz de creer la manera en la que *mi voluntad* se había sobrepuesto a la espada.

Suspiré y entré en el coche, en silencio. Cerré la puerta, me recosté de lado sobre el asiento y miré de nuevo a Tared, ahora con su rostro iluminado por el reflejo de la luna sobre la nieve. Su barba había crecido bastante, al igual que su cabello, y el rabillo de sus ojos parecía haber ganado un par de arrugas más, como si el tiempo no hubiese perdonado nada allá abajo.

Recordé que, a pesar de su madurez, de su temple y de su apariencia, él también era muy joven, tan sólo un muchacho a quien le habían pasado veinte vidas por encima. El pobre mantenía las piernas apretujadas en el escaso espacio entre el asiento y los pedales, se veía incómodo, era un hombre muy alto y nunca había podido sentarse bien en los coches pequeños. Tal vez por eso le tenía tanto cariño a aquella camioneta roja que alguna vez destrocé en un pantano de Luisiana.

No sé por qué empecé a pensar en todas esas cosas, lo que sí sé es que en ese momento deseé muchísimo estrecharme hecho un ovillo contra su costado, abrazarlo para cuidar de él y, al mismo tiempo, sentir su protección, su calor en mí, una vez más. Me hería tanto verlo así.

Sin embargo, tan sólo me acurruqué contra mi asiento, aún con su piel de lobo encima, fría. Estaba tan cansado que ni siquiera recordé ocuparme de mis propias heridas.

No importaba. Mientras Tared estuviese bien, yo aguantaría lo que fuera necesario.

Dormí casi de corrido el resto de la noche, tranquilo ante el hecho de que no volví a escuchar el doloroso silbido de su respiración.

CAPÍTULO 6
OPCIONES

—**D**ebemos encontrar un Atrapasueños que pueda ayudarnos. De otra manera, no sobreviviremos —fue lo primero que dijo Tared cuando finalmente desperté, azuzado por el frío.

Me erguí en el asiento, aliviado al escuchar su voz de nuevo después del largo silencio de ayer, pero lo dejé pasar al sentir un punzante dolor de cabeza. El sol atenuado por la neblina del invierno me iluminó la cara, aunque tampoco creí haber dormido más de cuatro horas seguidas.

Pero al mirar al lobo, supe de inmediato que a él le pasaba algo más.

Se estaba arrancando las garras que había hecho crecer anoche, una a una, para arrojarlas por la ventanilla sin emitir un solo quejido de dolor. Pero no era el acto en sí lo que me preocupó, antes lo había visto hacer cosas así con una gran naturalidad —a él y al resto de los errantes—, sino que su voz parecía más ronca de lo normal, y sus ojos estaban enrojecidos.

—¿Estás bien? —la pregunta era estúpida, nadie podría estar *bien* después de todo lo que habíamos pasado, pero no quise quedarme callado. Él sólo asintió, y aunque su respuesta no me convenció en lo absoluto, tampoco me encontraba en posición de presionar. Después, Tared observó por unos momentos mi brazo.

No está preocupado por ti, idiota. Está preocupado por lo que te hizo esa herida...

Me cubrí el torniquete, ya tieso a causa de la sangre seca, con la mano.

—No es grave —dije en voz baja, aunque él no me había preguntado nada.

Intercambiamos unas escasas palabras más al respecto, y luego puso en marcha el coche para regresar al pueblo.

En una de las esquinas de la pequeña avenida miró de reojo el letrero de un Wells Fargo, pero ni siquiera intentó estacionarse. Yo estaba casi seguro de que tenía ahorros en su cuenta personal y varias tarjetas de crédito, pero sin su billetera ni sus identificaciones no tenía sentido acercarse a un banco a sacar algo de efectivo.

Tared tenía tanta razón. Sin dinero y sin manera de comunicarnos con el resto de Comus Bayou, encontrar a más de nuestra especie iba a ser la única forma en la que pudiéramos sobrevivir.

Pasamos de largo esa calle y nos dedicamos durante la siguiente hora a recorrer el pueblo, pero fue inútil. No sentimos ni un solo vestigio de errantes, así que Tared emprendió la marcha rumbo a la carretera para ir en busca de otra villa, sin mencionar que nos preocupaba mucho no tener la certeza de cuándo alguien se daría cuenta de que había desaparecido un coche de aquel taller mecánico.

Pero no fue sino hasta que llegamos al siguiente pueblo cuando supimos que no tendríamos suerte. La comunidad era pequeña, de apenas unas cuantas calles, y no sentimos absolutamente nada en ellas que nos hiciera saber que había un Atrapasueños cerca, por lo que tuvimos que seguir de largo por la carretera. Se me ocurrió también que, si había errantes en alguna parte, estarían asentados en lugares alejados de los pueblos, pero con aquel clima, ir a campo abierto o subir las montañas sin llenar el tanque de gasolina era un suicidio seguro.

No, no podíamos arriesgarnos.

El hambre punzó en mi estómago, y estoy seguro de que también en el de Tared, pero su temple de acero me motivó a no protestar. A mí no me habría molestado mendigar un poco, lo había hecho gran parte de mi vida, después de todo, pero estaba tan desconcertado por cómo había reaccionado él anoche que ni siquiera quise sugerirlo.

No podía dejar de pensar en la expresión que tenía esa mañana. Al principio quise creer que se trataba de cansancio, pero había una parte de mí que me decía que más bien era...

Furia.

No. No quería averiguarlo, no en ese momento, y en mi inmensa cobardía, decidí esperar a que él quisiera hablar del tema primero. Fue así como pasamos el resto del día en ayunas, sin un refugio más allá de aquel destartalado coche y sin la posibilidad de siquiera conseguir unas monedas para usar un teléfono público y tratar de contactar a nuestros hermanos.

Por la noche, dormimos nuevamente a la intemperie, a un costado de la carretera, masticando nieve como único consuelo para nuestra sed y con esa piel de lobo a la que me había aferrado para protegerme del frío como si se tratase del propio abrazo de Tared. Pero al día siguiente, cuando pasamos dos poblados más sin rastro de errantes y el cielo comenzó a tornarse rosado por el atardecer, él maldijo por lo bajo. Se detuvo un momento junto a la carretera y miró el indicador de gasolina.

Tared se las había arreglado para hacer rendir el combustible lo más posible, pero en cuanto vio que la manecilla ya estaba por debajo del cuarto del tanque, un gruñido de su garganta me hizo saber que estábamos en serios problemas. Todavía nos faltaban cuarenta kilómetros para el siguiente pueblo.

Cerró los ojos un momento, apretó el volante, y luego siguió en línea recta hasta encontrar un área de descanso, de ésas que abundan en aquella parte de Washington. El plano medio nos había arrastrado al norte del parque, cerca de la estatal 20, por lo que las comunidades pobladas eran escasas y las zonas de campismo abundantes.

Tared se introdujo con cuidado en el asfalto congelado y avanzó hasta detenerse en el estacionamiento de un mirador al pie de una montaña, vacío y rodeado de árboles.

El silencio que se produjo al apagar el motor me estremeció, y más cuando el lobo lo rompió al abrir el coche y bajarse.

—¿Qué ocurre? —pregunté a través de la ventanilla, alterado al ver que se alejaba a zancadas. Abrí la puerta de mi lado para ir tras él, pero el estruendo de su voz me detuvo.

—Quédate aquí —ordenó, firme, para luego dirigirse hacia uno de los senderos que subían a la montaña, perdiéndose en él sin mirar atrás.

Parpadeé un par de veces y luego volví a cerrar la puerta. Me quedé inmóvil dentro del coche unos segundos, tomé de nuevo la piel de lobo —la cual ya empezaba a oler algo mal— y me cobijé con ella.

No sé cuánto tiempo permanecí en aquella posición, con la mirada fija sobre la pérgola de ladrillo construida a un lado del mirador, equipada con un horno campestre y un centro de piedra para fogatas, pensando en si podría calentarme un poco si me animaba a encender sobre él los tapetes del coche. Pero cuando por fin oscureció y todo lo visible quedó bañado en el resplandor lavanda de la noche reflejada contra la nieve, sentí una opresión monstruosa.

El viento soplaba. La temperatura descendía cada vez más. Y Tared no regresaba.

Te abandonó.

La voz de Wéndigo me hizo revolverme en el asiento, pero no le respondí.

Ya te ha dejado a tu suerte.

—No seas ridículo —repliqué en voz alta, irritado—. Tared nunca haría algo así.

El monstruo dentro de mí soltó una carcajada que sonaba como la iteración de miles.

Te tiene pavor y no quieres aceptarlo.

—¡Está en todo su derecho de estar asustado! —rugí, sin poder ocultar un matiz de dolor en mi voz—. ¡Mira lo que me obligaste a hacer delante de él!

Tiene miedo de que nos lo comamos. Lo vi observarnos en la oscuridad.

Me hizo mucho daño escuchar esas palabras, porque en el fondo, había algo en mí que me decía que eran verdad. Los ojos enrojecidos y las ojeras pronunciadas de Tared no podían significar otra cosa que un insomnio provocado por la necesidad de vigilarme.

—No, no es cierto —susurré, conteniendo el gemido que tan desesperadamente quería soltar—. ¡Yo jamás le haría daño!

¿Cómo se atreve a tratarnos así cuando hiciste tanto para protegerlo?

Aquello me hirió todavía más.

—Cállate... por favor —rogué con un sollozo.

Envolví con las manos los trozos de asta que quedaban en mi cabeza y los jalé con fuerza una y otra vez, desesperado por arrancar todo rastro de aquel ser abominable de mi cuerpo.

La piel me dolió, y hasta creo haber sangrado, pero los cuernos no se movieron.

Somos un monstruo. Y él ya lo ha descubierto.

—No, no —susurré al borde del llanto. Me llevé las manos a la cara—, sólo tengo qué hablar con él para solucionarlo, sólo...

¿En qué nos convertiríamos si probásemos el sabor de su carne?

—¡Yo nunca lo devoraría! —reclamé con los dientes apretados—. ¡Nunca, nunca, *nunca* me lo comería! Tared *me ama*, él...

¿Ah, sí? ¿Y por qué te mira de esa manera?

Un escalofrío terrible reptó por mi espalda.

Miré a través de la ventanilla y encontré al lobo parado a unos metros de ella, cargando algo que parecía un animal sobre los hombros. Estaba petrificado, la mirada azul confusa.

Me estremecí al darme cuenta de que me había estado viendo hablar solo dentro del coche. No, de que había *escuchado* a la perfección las cosas horribles que había estado diciendo.

La herida de nuestro vínculo se tensó con tanta fuerza que sentí que se desgarraría.

—No, no —salí del vehículo y la piel de lobo cayó al suelo—. ¡Tared, espera, yo estaba...!

Una luz brilló a sus espaldas y oscureció su silueta. Escuché, apenas, una voz femenina y pasos de botas firmes que se acercaban a nosotros.

—¿Qué ocurre? ¿Está todo bien?

Dos mujeres aparecieron detrás de Tared, una de ellas sostenía una linterna, mientras que la otra permanecía a su lado, y era muy, muy alta, casi tanto como él. En cuanto alcanzaron al lobo, pude sentirlo: un tirón instintivo, el llamado desde el vientre para acudir a la cercanía de aquellas personas.

Y cuando Wéndigo rugió, *hambriento*, ya no tuve duda alguna.

Eran errantes.

CAPÍTULO 7
DEPENDENCIA

En cuanto me ofrecieron un plato de sopa caliente con abundantes trozos de carne de alce, casi me eché a llorar.

—Tomen todo lo que quieran, hay bastante —nos dijo Lía al ver cómo Tared y yo comíamos en silencio, pero con voracidad—. Y si quieren, podemos prepararles una olla más.

—Se los agradezco mucho —repuso el lobo—. Pero no deben molestarse. Ya han hecho demasiado por nosotros.

La gentileza en su voz me separó del plato unos momentos. Escuchar de nuevo a *ese* Tared hizo que mi alma descansara, porque significaba que el lobo amable y centrado que bien conocía aún seguía allí.

O, al menos, una parte de él.

—No digas tonterías, yo sé que se necesita mucho más que un par de cuencos para llenar a un devorapieles —replicó Lía de buen humor, palmeando la rodilla de la mujer a su lado—. ¿Qué tal estás tú, cariño? ¿Quieres otra manta?

Negué con la cabeza y ajusté más la cobija de lana que me cubría, para recargarme de lleno contra el respaldo de la silla plegable. Sentí el agradable calor de mi cabello suelto y limpio sobre los hombros, y apreté bien el plato entre las manos, ahora cubiertas por unos buenos guantes de invierno.

—No hace falta —contesté, tibio y cómodo por primera vez desde que habíamos salido del plano medio—. Gracias.

Me costó hablar por el cansancio, pero lo decía en serio. Y no sólo por la cazadora o los generosos calcetines que por fin cubrían mis pies helados, sino también por la fogata que habían encendido en medio de la pérgola de ladrillo.

Esa noche éramos cuatro sentados alrededor del fuego, mientras que la casa rodante de las chicas había sido estacionada frente a nosotros para cubrirnos de cualquier corriente de viento.

Las observé unos momentos. Lía era una *humana* bajita y delgada, de cabello corto y envuelta en una gruesa chamarra de cacería. La mujer que venía con ella, Debbie, era su esposa, una devorapieles de rasgos muy similares a los de Nashua y cuyo ancestro olía a oso de montaña.

Tared se había topado con ellas mientras trataban de dar caza al mismo alce. Las dos estaban en el bosque en busca de la cena para año nuevo, una tradición muy propia de su Atrapasueños, el cual estaba asentado en el pueblo al otro lado de la montaña. Pueblo con el que jamás nos habríamos podido topar si hubiésemos seguido en línea recta por la carretera, tal cual teníamos planeado. Nos contaron que su familia estaba conformada por otras tres personas, tres devorapieles, concretamente, pero que sólo ellas habían subido a cazar esa vez.

Sí. Fue una coincidencia tremenda, aunque también quise creer que algún Loa por fin había escuchado mis plegarias, cosa poco probable porque aún no había recuperado mi libro rojo.

Estábamos tan, tan lejos de Luisiana…

Fuese como fuese, el milagro estaba hecho. Lía y Debbie no sólo nos habían permitido ducharnos con agua bien caliente en su casa rodante, sino que también nos habían vestido con ropa de sus armarios, permitiéndonos deshacernos de esos overoles helados que habíamos robado del taller mecánico.

Sin saberlo, nos habían dado la oportunidad de sobrevivir una noche más.

—¿Cómo sigue tu herida, Elisse? —me preguntó Lía de pronto, por lo que moví mi hombro por inercia de arriba abajo.

—Estoy como nuevo —dije, con las puntadas de la herida ya bien cerradas. No era un trabajo de perpetuasangre, pero ella lo había hecho de forma maravillosa de todas maneras—. No sé qué habríamos hecho sin ustedes.

—Oh, vamos, creo que te las habrías arreglado bien, no estaba infectada ni nada por el estilo —insistió—. Lo que hiciste con Tared también fue asombroso. Sus costillas sanaron bien y de no haber sido por ti, de seguro habríamos tenido que ir a buscar a un médico para operarlo. Debbie misma lo dijo.

Miré de reojo a la devorapieles, pero ésta permaneció callada, jugueteando un poco con el hacha de mano que había empleado para cortar leña para la fogata.

—Aunque admito que Tared también es tremendo —continuó Lía—. Cuando los devorapieles no se alimentan bien, se debilitan fácilmente por toda la energía que requieren. Que haya subido a la montaña a arriesgarse a cazar con las manos desnudas, a sabiendas de lo vulnerable que estaría frente a un oso o un alce adulto, dice mucho de él.

El hombre lobo no reaccionó ante mi escrutinio, sentado al otro lado de la fogata y todavía ocupado con su comida. Saber que él se había ido para buscar alimento y no para abandonarme, sirvió para callar a Wéndigo un buen rato, pero yo aún podía sentir nuestro vínculo más frágil que nunca. Sobre todo, después de lo que me había escuchado decir.

Sabía que había llegado el momento de hablar con él. Necesitaba hacerle saber que ya no tenía más mentiras bajo la manga y que, a pesar de las cosas horribles de las que había sido testigo en tan poco tiempo, jamás le haría daño a él ni a Comus Bayou.

O al menos, debía intentar convencerlo de ello.

Después de un rato, Lía apuntó con la barbilla a nuestro coche.

—¿Necesitarán ayuda con eso? Tiene pinta de que no durará mucho —observó.

—No, vamos a abandonarlo aquí —contestó Tared—. Tuvimos qué robarlo el día de ayer y quién sabe cuándo vayan a darse cuenta de ello.

Ella susurró un "entiendo", y luego dio un trago despreocupado a su termo de café, sin preguntar nada más. La facilidad con la que zanjó el tema me hizo saber que aquella mujer humana conocía bien las costumbres de los nuestros, puesto que no meterse en los asuntos de otro Atrapasueños era una regla tácita de los errantes. Y Tared y yo la habríamos mantenido así de no ser por los Lander.

El líder de Comus Bayou dejó el cuenco vacío en el suelo. Su gesto resultó tan significativo que todos lo miramos por instinto.

—Lía, Debbie, hay algo muy importante que deben saber —dijo, y su voz gruesa y profunda transformó el silencio en consternación. Yo me hundí más en la silla a medida que, con una selección cuidadosa de los hechos, sobre todo con relación a Wéndigo y a mí, Tared comenzó a relatar a las dos mujeres lo que había sucedido en Stonefall.

No mencionó mucho sobre nuestro pasado en Nueva Orleans ni los motivos que me habían llevado hasta Utah, pero sí habló de la terrible alquimista Jocelyn Blake, de los tramperos Lander y de la masacre de Red Buffalo, así como del problema en el que nos habíamos metido al cruzar al plano medio para salvarnos. De los cuatro meses de vida que habíamos perdido en el proceso.

Para mi tranquilidad, ellas no parecieron desconfiar del relato. Nuestra raza estaba acostumbrada a vivir circunstancias así de extraordinarias, después de todo, pero lo que sí me sorprendió fue que no hubiesen escuchado nada sobre lo ocurrido con Red Buffalo. La noticia de lo que pasó en Stonefall no había llegado más allá del descubrimiento de los asesinatos de Jocelyn Blake, los cuales pulularon por los periódicos durante meses gracias a la información que Hoffman había filtrado sobre las víctimas, pero todo lo referente a la tribu del desierto y su exterminio parecía haber permanecido en el olvido, tanto para los medios como para otros errantes.

Y lo que más nos preocupaba era que, a pesar de tener pieles y cadáveres para probar nuestra existencia, los Lander no habían hecho nada para sacar nuestro mundo a la luz.

Lo primero que se me vino a la mente fue que tal vez Comus Bayou había logrado ocultar los rastros de lo que había sucedido, lo cual me daba esperanzas de que siguieran con vida. Lía también sugirió que tal vez los nuestros hubiesen acabado con los Lander en algún momento y que por eso no habían revelado nuestra existencia, pero nadie en la fogata se regodeó con la idea porque simplemente no había manera de comprobarlo.

Mientras Tared contaba lo sucedido, noté que Debbie, poco a poco, fue posando su mirada sobre mí. Y entonces, pude sentirlo: una vibración, un gruñido de advertencia que provenía dentro de ella, como si su ancestro supiera que había algo en mi aparente inocencia que no terminaba de encajar en toda esta historia.

Pero ella no era la única que sentía algo. El monstruo de hueso parecía gruñirle *con avidez* en respuesta.

Yo jamás había percibido con tanta claridad a un ancestro, y la idea de que Debbie también pudiese sentir un atisbo de la maldad dentro de mí me estremeció porque, hasta ahora, el monstruo de hueso había pasado desapercibido para otros errantes. ¿Tan palpable, tan *mía* se había vuelto su presencia desde mi última transformación?

—... y por ello, nos vendría de maravilla algún teléfono.

Salí de mis pensamientos en cuanto Lía se puso de pie y pasó delante de mí para alargarle un celular al hombre lobo.

Tared agradeció el aparato y se levantó, alejándose del remolque para deambular por el estacionamiento en busca de señal.

La posibilidad de ser asediado con preguntas que no me convenía contestar me hizo disculparme y, con la cobija aún alrededor de mi cuerpo, pararme para seguir al lobo.

Lo alcancé justo cuando estaba a un paso de la línea de árboles que poblaban el pie de la montaña. Sé que se percató de que me acercaba, así que, por si las dudas, decidí quedarme a un par de metros de distancia. No quería ponerlo nervioso.

Momentos después, Tared detuvo su errática caminata y bajó el aparato, dejándolo apretado en su mano. El silencio de la noche me permitió escuchar la voz de una grabación automática, y al reconocer lo que decía, la manta sobre mis hombros perdió su calor.

El teléfono de Nashua estaba fuera de servicio.

De inmediato, pensé en sugerir el llamar a alguien más o escribir un correo electrónico dirigido a Julien, pero el miedo de que quizá sus líneas de comunicación hubiesen sido intervenidas por los tramperos me detuvo. Ellos tenían contactos con la policía y estaba seguro de que, a esas alturas, también sabían nuestros nombres, e incluso nuestros paraderos en Nueva Orleans.

¿Qué tal que si lo único que lográbamos al contactarlos era caer en una trampa?

Esperé con paciencia a que el devorapieles dijese algo, que pensara en una solución, pero largos minutos pasaron sin que hiciera otra cosa más que mirar al horizonte. Estuve a punto de entrar en pánico, porque era la primera vez que mi líder no parecía saber qué hacer.

Tared, el más fuerte de los nuestros, el que siempre nos había sacado adelante sin importar las circunstancias, parecía perdido.

Vi su expresión vacía, recordé lo que sentí cuando mi mano lo dejó ir en el plano medio, y me enojé muchísimo conmigo mismo.

Tared siempre había dado la cara por mí, llevando sus fuerzas y su salud mental al límite sólo porque confiaba en mí, pero ¿no era yo también un adulto, capaz de pensar y poner algo de mi parte?

Erguí la espalda y caminé hacia el lobo. Ignoré la forma en la que los vellos de su nuca se erizaron ante mi cercanía, y hablé:

—No creo que debamos volver a Utah —dije en voz baja, pero con firmeza—. Ha pasado mucho tiempo desde la batalla, no tendría sentido que se hubiesen quedado allí si los tramperos conocían bien el lugar y si Red Buffalo fue…

Aniquilado.

Perdí las fuerzas de pronto. Tared bajó la mirada hacia el teléfono, y pude notar que apretaba el puño y murmuraba algo para sí mismo, como si yo no estuviese allí. Me abracé, y después de unos eternos momentos, finalmente respondió:

—Estoy casi seguro de que la reserva quedó inundada tras el paso del huracán —dijo—, pero tal vez los demás hayan vuelto allí de todas maneras.

Levanté la cabeza.

Sí. Aquello era una solución viable a nuestros problemas. Un aventón, una búsqueda por el pantano, un reencuentro probable...

Y aun cuando también existía la posibilidad de que los tramperos nos estuviesen esperando ya en Luisiana, ¿qué otra opción viable nos quedaba?

Pero a pesar de que la respuesta estaba allí, frente a mis ojos, supe que algo marchaba mal. Que volver al punto de partida sólo retrasaría el final de esta guerra.

Mi monstruo ya tenía un nombre y una leyenda, y yo ya sabía adónde tenía que ir si quería terminar con todo esto. Pero lo más importante era que ni mamá Tallulah, ni padre trueno ni Muata habían sido asesinados para que yo decidiera dar la media vuelta y esconderme una vez más. Que Adam no había perecido en mis brazos sólo para dejarme vencer por alguien que, en algún momento de mi existencia, decidió que yo merecía cargar con todo este dolor.

Así que apreté los puños y supe lo que tenía qué decir:

—No voy a volver a Nueva Orleans —solté—. Tengo que ir hacia el noreste.

Cuando Tared levantó sus ojos hacia mí, sentí como si me hubiesen atravesado con una lanza. Era la primera vez que me miraba directamente en todo este tiempo, así que me llevé la mano descarnada al pecho para soportar ese peso.

—Esta cosa, este monstruo en el que puedo convertirme, se llama Wéndigo —susurré—. Sammuel, él...

Mencionar al perpetuasangre me hizo detenerme para tomar aire. Recordé cuando aquella escopeta escupió contra su pecho, sus alas blancas nacidas de la sangre y las promesas de una vida a la que jamás volvería. Respiré profundo y continué:

—Sammuel me dijo que es una leyenda originaria de los Grandes Lagos —dije, aunque me costó recuperar la firmeza de mi voz—, así que debo ir allí para buscar una forma de librarme de él. De lo contrario, esta batalla nunca terminará.

Y al mencionar esto último, Wéndigo se revolcó como si le hubiese hecho mucha gracia escuchar semejante hazaña.

Tared se metió el teléfono en el bolsillo y me quitó esa penetrante mirada de encima.

—Minnesota está en esa región —dijo, contemplando el bosque—. Y puede que Comus Bayou haya ido hacia allá también...

Me bastó un instante para entender todo lo que pasaba por su cabeza. Después, abrí los ojos de par en par.

¡Dioses, era cierto! Los demás habían visto mi transformación, así que cabía la posibilidad de que ya supieran algo sobre Wéndigo y el lugar donde se originaba su leyenda. Además, el lobo tenía familia en ese lugar, y si Comus Bayou albergaba las mismas dudas que nosotros sobre la interferencia de los tramperos, quizás hubiesen decidido buscarnos allí en vez de arriesgarse a volver a Luisiana.

Nuestro plan estaba lleno de agujeros, pero si teníamos un poco de suerte y lográbamos dar con *ellos*, si encontrábamos la forma de sanar nuestros vínculos y descubríamos la verdad sobre Wéndigo, por fin... por fin *estaríamos juntos otra vez.*

Tared se enderezó y caminó hacia mí, mientras la esperanza me cegaba. Luego, se detuvo a mi lado. El vínculo que nos unía se tensó tan dolorosamente que casi me doblé sobre mi abdomen.

—Iremos a Minnesota —dijo con voz queda—. *Encontraré* a los demás. Y cuando lo haga... serás libre de irte a donde te plazca.

Y de pronto, todo se volvió quietud. El bosque. El viento. Las llamas de la fogata; sentí como si me hubiesen empujado de un segundo piso y hubiese caído de espaldas contra el concreto. El lobo comenzó a alejarse, pero el percibir cómo el lazo entre nosotros se desgarraba a cada paso, me impulsó a aferrarme a él una vez más.

—Tared... —lo llamé, sofocado—. Nunca quise que todo esto sucediera. Nunca quise poner tu vida ni la de nadie en peligro.

Él se detuvo y se quedó en silencio unos momentos. Suspiró.

—La primera vez que discutimos tú y yo, allá en Luisiana, me pediste que confiara en ti. Y a partir de ese día, decidí que lo haría sin importar nada más —respondió, sin girarse hacia mí—. Pero tú... tú nunca me diste ese mismo beneficio. A pesar de todo lo que hice, de todo lo que te dije, de las veces que intenté que lo nuestro funcionara... nada de eso importó. *Mi amor nunca fue suficiente para ti* y por eso siempre me ocultaste la verdad, ¿cierto?

Ante la calma que mantenía al pronunciar tan difíciles palabras, no supe qué responder... porque era verdad.

Nunca confié en Tared. Y no me refiero a su fuerza o su capacidad como líder, sino en el afecto que sentía por mí. Si yo me odiaba tanto a mí mismo, ¿cómo me querría él lo suficiente para aceptar a la bestia sádica y caníbal en la que me había convertido?

Sabes que él habría perdonado a su esposa de acusarlo de ser un monstruo, gruñó el ser dentro de mí. Pero no te perdona que tú sí lo seas.

Entender esto hizo que el rostro se me anegara en lágrimas. Y al escucharme sollozar, se encorvó y apretó los puños, como si quisiera aferrarse al mismo aire para no dar la media vuelta hacia mí. Pero al escuchar que se marchaba, hice un último intento:

—Dijiste que *siempre* volverías —masculle, aferrándome a la desesperación—. Que siempre me escogerías, *a mí*.

En la oscuridad, Wéndigo rio, impresionado de lo mezquino que podía yo llegar a ser sin su ayuda. Aquellas promesas me las había hecho el hombre lobo en nuestros momentos más grandes de ternura, y ahora yo trataba de usarlas para chantajearlo y mantenerlo conmigo, a pesar de que mis acciones habían hecho todo lo posible por apartarlo de mí.

No, él no me debía ni una sola oportunidad más, y ambos *lo sabíamos*.

Fue por eso por lo que Tared no miró hacia atrás y, sin responder, sin dudar... simplemente se marchó.

Cuando me quedé solo levanté la mirada hacia el cielo para buscar la luna.

Todo este tiempo había pensado que el silencio que Tared había guardado desde que habíamos salido del plano medio era porque miles de preguntas se aglomeraban en su cabeza, dudas que yo habría respondido con desesperación para afianzar mi lugar a su lado. *¿Cómo había ocurrido lo de Wéndigo?* *¿En qué momento me había poseído? ¿Acaso eso tenía que ver con todo lo que había pasado en Utah, en Nueva Orleans...?* Pero no. No era así, porque las respuestas ya no importaban.

En mi infinita estupidez, viví con la esperanza de que podía hacer, mentir, deshacer y destrozar sin tener que enfrentar consecuencias. Hasta entonces había creído que mis razones eran lo bastante buenas, lo suficientemente nobles para que la gente alrededor lo soportase.

Pero no había sido así. Y tal como cuando lo solté en el abismo, Tared por fin se había rendido conmigo.

Esa noche, envuelto en la oscuridad de un insoportable insomnio, el vínculo entre nosotros se partió dolorosamente. Sangró. Sangró y sangró hasta que ya no quedó nada más que nos uniera. Y al desvanecerse ese lazo por completo... algo terrible comenzó a sucederme.

CAPÍTULO 8
RESILIENCIA

Durante la noche, algo había comenzado a crecer en mi interior. Una cosa que me hizo despertar a la mañana siguiente hecho un ovillo, con los dientes apretados a causa del terrible dolor: era como una jaula dura e invisible que se había encarnado alrededor de mi corazón mientras dormía. Lo sentía bien adentro, una presión que me estrujaba cada vez que mi músculo latía y que me dejó casi sin aire al intentar respirar.

Y lo más inquietante de todo fue descubrir que al estar solo allí, acurrucado en el suelo de la casa rodante y sin entender bien a bien lo que me sucedía, comencé a sentirme frustrado por razones *muy* diferentes al dolor que me achacaba.

Sentí nuevamente la herida recalcitrante del *vínculo roto*, y ésta dolía muchísimo, como si Tared mismo me destrozara el corazón con su propio puño. La garganta se me cerraba, los gemidos se atascaban en mi pecho y me impedían sollozar.

En mi agonía, comencé a preguntarme si el abandono que estaba sufriendo era justo, y si no eran todos los demás unos egoístas miserables indignos de mis esfuerzos. Si acaso, alguna vez, a alguien le habían importado los sacrificios que yo también tuve que hacer, y recordé con profunda humillación lo que aquellos a quienes alguna vez llamé *hermanos* me hicieron en Stonefall. No sólo fue su mirada de completo terror cuando me vieron devorar a Buck Lander, trozo por trozo, sino cómo todos ellos...

Te abandonaron.

De pronto vinieron a mí las imágenes de mi huida, completamente solitaria, en el bosque, perseguido por los tramperos, las balas, el fuego escupiendo de sus escopetas. *Queriendo darme caza.*

Te dejaron a tu suerte para que esos cabrones te mataran.

Y lo hicieron al darme la espalda en la oscuridad, mientras yo huía como un animal herido hacia la incertidumbre, indefenso y consumido por la espada.

¿Qué querías que hicieran, si habían descubierto el monstruo que eras en realidad?

Los... *odiaba.* Yo lo sacrifiqué todo, me convertí en un monstruo por Johanna, por Julien y hasta por Nashua, pero ellos tres intentaron matarme en Luisiana. Y luego, me abandonaron en Utah, para cortar así nuestro vínculo de la misma forma en la que lo había hecho Tared.

Me arrepentí del momento en el que el lobo apareció en mi vida aquella mañana en Luisiana. Y lo aborrecí *a él* más que a nadie por haber decidido que yo no era digno del mismo afecto que le había prodigado a su *mujer.* ¡Odiaba tanto su voz, su cuerpo; odiaba tanto esos ojos azules que...!

Me bastó un instante para sentirme aterrado por aquellos pensamientos. No, ¡yo no sentía ninguna de esas cosas! ¡¿De dónde estaba saliendo todo este veneno?!

Intenté levantarme, pero me fue imposible. Al principio creí que se trataba de la espada, pero me bastó escuchar dentro de mí esa risa de cientos de voces para caer en la cuenta de la verdad: ese dolor sobre mi corazón no provenía de mi pérdida, sino de *la garra* del monstruo de hueso, que lo estrujaba como si sus uñas afiladas se hubiesen materializado dentro de mí.

La ruptura del vínculo entre el líder de Comus Bayou y yo me había acercado más que nunca a esa bestia, porque era *su furia* la que estaba hablando por mí.

Me tomé unos minutos para contener mis emociones y empujar al bastardo al fondo de mi cabeza. Intenté usar el calor de mi magia para aliviar la presión helada de Wéndigo, pero aquel latido invernal no desapareció.

Y entonces, vi a Tared. Él se había acercado hasta detenerse delante de una de las ventanas de la casa rodante. Miraba a la nada mientras los copos de nieve le caían en los hombros, tan cansado, *tan triste,* que anhelé con todo mi ser recargar mi cabeza en su hombro para aliviar su pena.

Ante ese deseo, el dolor permaneció dentro de mi pecho, la garra obstinada del monstruo de hueso aprisionándome sin compasión, pero mi corazón latía de todas maneras bajo su palma con férrea voluntad. El vínculo entre Tared y yo ya no existía, pero yo amaba al hombre lobo como si aquél nunca se hubiese desvanecido.

La angustia de un corazón afligido y no uno furioso regresó a mí, llevándose consigo toda esa rabia que *no me pertenecía.*

Y sólo así, ahogado en el sentimiento más puro, más *mío* que tenía en ese momento, fue como reuní las fuerzas para levantarme.

Y, de alguna manera, seguir adelante.

CAPÍTULO 9
ABANDONO

Lía insistió en que nos quedásemos algunos días en su casa, con su familia, para descansar y abastecernos, pero Tared se negó en rotundo.

No podíamos detenernos. Todavía nos quedaban por cruzar Idaho, Montana y Dakota del Norte, antes de llegar a Minnesota, y no había tiempo que perder si queríamos tener la oportunidad de reencontrarnos con Comus Bayou.

Después de un poco más de insistencia por parte de Lía, al final aceptamos ser conducidos al pueblo más cercano, que ya quedaba a pocos kilómetros de la frontera.

Al bajarnos en el estacionamiento de una gasolinera, Debbie extendió a Tared dos mochilas de acampada y el celular que le prestaron la noche anterior.

—Hay un poco de ropa extra, por si la necesitan —dijo Lía—. Perdonen si no hay chamarras mejores, pero espero que les sirvan de algo.

Tared tomó las cosas, e inclinó la cabeza como agradecimiento. Y entonces, Lía hizo algo aún más significativo: me entregó una pistola.

—Pero… —titubeé, reticente.

Ella sonrió y envolvió mi mano descarnada con la suya. Sintió mis dedos huesudos bajo el guante, pero no añadió palabra alguna al respecto. Sin recelo, me hizo cerrarlos alrededor del arma.

—Si nosotras hubiésemos llegado con ustedes a su reserva, estoy segurísima de que nos habrían dado refugio, comida y tres veces lo que nosotras hemos podido ofrecerles ahora —dijo—. Ser familia, sin importar quienes seamos o de qué estemos huyendo es lo más importante que he aprendido de este mundo al que he tenido el privilegio de ser recibida.

Y luego, ella acomodó un gorro de lana sobre mi cabeza con tanta ternura que me recordó mucho a Louisa. Estuve tentado a romper en llanto otra vez, pero, en cambio, guardé el arma en la pretina de los pantalones, tal cual me había enseñado Hoffman tiempo atrás.

—No conocemos a ningún Atrapasueños en Idaho —dijo Debbie—, pero sé que hay de nuestra gente en Montana. No tenemos mucho contacto con ellos puesto que son nómadas, pero haré lo posible por conseguir que se encuentren. Les llamaremos en cuanto tengamos noticias de ellos o de los tramperos.

—También les he dejado algunos billetes en la mochila más pequeña —añadió su esposa—. No traíamos mucho efectivo, pero espero que al menos les haga la vida más fácil por un tiempo.

—Gracias, gracias, por tanto, Lía —dijo Tared estrechando su mano a modo de despedida. Noté que la miraba con muchísimo respeto, de una forma muy similar a como alguna vez se dirigió a Irina.

Siempre me había preguntado si era posible que un humano fuese la cabeza de un Atrapasueños, y acababa de recibir la respuesta.

Lía y Debbie subieron de vuelta a la casa rodante y se marcharon a su pueblo, mientras Tared y yo nos quedamos bajo la nieve por unos momentos. La quietud entre el lobo y yo me obligó no sólo a escuchar con demasiada claridad las cosas que Wéndigo me murmuraba, sino a sentir, una vez más, el dolor del vínculo roto.

Era terrible, como sentir las lágrimas en mis ojos todo el tiempo, aunque los tuviese secos, como una vena en carne viva, siempre abierta, siempre sangrante. Y la garra de Wéndigo estrujando mi corazón sólo añadía más presión a ese dolor. Me sentía tan cansado que el sólo quedarme de pie resultaba tan agotador como subir una colina.

Tared, ajeno a mi pesar, tal vez, sacó de la mochila pequeña los billetes y los contó. Después, miró el delgado fajo unos momentos.

—Podríamos buscar un autobús que nos lleve hasta allá —sugerí, aunque mi voz sonaba distante, como si le hablase a un desconocido. El pensarlo así me lastimó demasiado, pero ya no podía definir nuestra relación de otra manera.

—No nos dejarán subir sin identificaciones —replicó él con sobriedad.

El lobo levantó la barbilla hacia la carretera congelada mientras los conductores entraban y salían de la gasolinera. Para mí era obvio lo que teníamos que hacer ahora, pero me sorprendió mucho darme cuenta de que él no lo tuviera tan claro.

No. Algo le sucedía a Tared. Sus ojos estaban inyectados en sangre, su cuerpo parecía siempre tenso, con los puños bien cerrados. Se veía tan preocupado, tan invadido de una angustia silenciosa, como si en cualquier momento fuese a perder el control.

¿Acaso crees que su desesperación es por ti? ¿Piensas que lo que anhela es tu compañía, que lo que extraña son tus brazos?

Mi corazón dolió como si Wéndigo lo hubiese estrujado con gusto, porque, una vez más, me hizo ver las cosas como eran. Tared estaba triste y desolado no por mí, ni por el término de nuestra relación, sino por Comus Bayou.

Su verdadera familia.

Al entender esto por fin, me eché una de las mochilas al hombro y caminé hacia la carretera, y Tared sólo me observó alejarme hasta detenerme en la orilla. Por suerte, no tuve que esperar demasiado para que se acercara mi objetivo: un tráiler con placas de Idaho.

Levanté un pulgar para hacer la seña. El freno del vehículo rechinó al detenerse de inmediato, escupiendo una densa nube de humo negro. Me acerqué a la cabina, trepé hasta la ventanilla y me acomodé un mechón detrás del oído mientras el conductor me preguntaba algo con la voz aterciopelada.

Me mordí el labio inferior y le sonreí.

Tared se quedó perplejo, pero no tanto como el camionero cuando le hice una señal al lobo para que se acercara y subiera conmigo al tráiler. Según lo que me había dicho el hombre, cruzaríamos Idaho en un par de horas; la franja alargada del estado que se interponía entre Washington y Montana no era muy grande.

El viaje fue silencioso, apenas acompañado por algunos momentos de conversaciones breves con el confundido camionero quien, al parecer, no sabía qué era peor: si descubrir que yo no era una chica bonita pidiendo un aventón en la carretera o que viniera acompañado por un hombre que me sacaba treinta centímetros de estatura.

En esos momentos, apelar a mi apariencia para conseguir algo de los demás no me importaba, la moralidad no tenía ningún valor para mí ante semejante desesperación. Tared era la persona más importante de mi vida, cosa que no tenía nada que ver con el hecho de que todo entre nosotros hubiese terminado.

Y como último acto de amor, haría hasta lo imposible con tal de reunirlo con la familia que tan desesperadamente deseaba encontrar.

Una familia a la que —me había quedado claro— yo jamás podría volver a pertenecer.

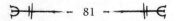

Los siguientes cuatro días, el tiempo que tardamos en llegar desde Newport hasta el Parque Nacional de los Glaciares, en Montana, tampoco fueron fáciles.

Nos tomó mucho recorrer esos casi cuatrocientos kilómetros, porque gran parte del trayecto tuvimos que hacerlo a pie, pegados a la carretera y, a veces, bajo inclementes nevadas. Y con el pasar de los días, nuestra suerte empeoró, y no sólo porque los vehículos comenzaron a volverse más y más escasos conforme el invierno se recrudecía. Me confundiesen o no con una mujer, mi apariencia ayudaba, pero los conductores se volvían menos benevolentes al ver a Tared.

Él estaba… cambiando.

Cada día le costaba más ser el hombre amable y educado de siempre, y las escasas palabras que cruzábamos pronto se transformaron en silencio tajante y respuestas frías al punto en el que evité hablarle del todo. Lo peor de todo es que él había perdido por lo menos cinco kilos en cuestión de días.

Más de una vez le rogué que comiera algo más que el mismo sándwich frío de siempre, pero jamás logré convencerlo. Sabía que teníamos poco dinero, por lo que se limitaba a alimentarse como una persona ordinaria y no en la medida que realmente requería, y eso estaba haciendo estragos a su cuerpo.

Pero a él no le importaba. Su prioridad era llegar lo más pronto posible a Minnesota.

Eso y nada más.

La presión en mi corazón también empeoró. A falta de alguien con quien hablar, Wéndigo comenzó a ocupar la mayor parte de mis pensamientos, y la brecha entre el hombre lobo y yo pasó de ser el fantasma de un lazo perdido, a un abismo que, a cada paso que dábamos en la carretera, se hacía más grande.

Me convertí en un desconocido para él también, y más que un hombre, era una sombra que caminaba a su lado, un espectro con el cual compartía el espacio en el que se movía. Y su indiferencia, su apatía, me dolía mucho más que el propio hierro de la garra de Wéndigo. No necesité de sus amargas voces para saber que Tared no sólo odiaba esta situación, sino *estar conmigo*. Yo lo había separado de su familia, lo más valioso que él tenía en el mundo. ¿Cómo no iba a aborrecerme?

No encuentro palabras para describir lo desoladores que resultaron esos días para mí y la cantidad de veces que quise soltarme a llorar en pleno asfalto, sintiéndome miserable y aislado. De alguna forma, Tared me había abandonado, dejándome solo con Wéndigo, y más de una vez quise suplicarle que, por favor, dejase de lastimarme de esa manera.

Pero nunca tuve el valor. Y, en cambio, mi tristeza comenzó a convertirse en enojo. El monstruo de hueso me infectó con sus voces y su rabia, y todo comenzó a irritarme: la gente, el frío, el hambre. Ya no toleraba nada ni a nadie, sólo existía en mi cabeza el desasosiego y el cansancio. Las ganas de dar la media vuelta y echar a correr.

Olvidarme de Tared. De Comus Bayou. De mi Mara. De todos.

Hasta que, una mañana, recibimos la tan esperada llamada de Debbie, quien había podido contactar con el Atrapasueños nómada de Montana: un grupo de motociclistas dispuestos no sólo a ayudarnos con dinero y provisiones, sino con un vehículo que nos haría llegar a nuestro destino en menor tiempo. Lo único que teníamos que hacer era encontrarnos con ellos en un concurrido bar de carretera a unos cuantos kilómetros de nuestra presente ubicación.

La noticia le sacó a Tared la única sonrisa que le había visto en todo este tiempo, pero a mí me destrozó por completo.

Porque eso significaba que había llegado el momento de separarnos.

CAPÍTULO 10
UNA CARA FAMILIAR

—¿Les ofrezco algo más?

Los tórridos recuerdos de lo que hemos vivido desde que salimos del lago desaparecen cuando escucho la voz de la mesera a mi lado. Parpadeo un par de veces y miro hacia la tormenta que se ha desatado afuera del restaurante, inseguro de cuánto tiempo habré estado perdido en mi nostalgia esta vez.

Al girarme para responderle a la chica, veo que ella, aunque nos ha llamado a ambos, tan sólo observa a un distante Tared con una sonrisa estúpida en su cara.

Y lo peor es que ni siquiera puedo culparla. Aún con los días duros que hemos tenido, él sigue siendo tan bien parecido que es imposible no querer mirarlo.

Qué fácil sería para él conseguir a alguien, ¿verdad? Una mujer divina, como debió de ser su esposa...

—La cuenta —pido con los dientes apretados para soportar el veneno de mis celos.

La mesera por fin se percata de que existo. Me mira y entorna los ojos unos segundos, escrutándome más tiempo del que se consideraría educado, para luego largarse.

Tared deja el celular sobre la mesa y mira hacia mi comida, la cual no he tocado por estar perdido en mis pensamientos.

—El primer bocado siempre es difícil —susurro ante su fugaz mirada, mientras acaricio el borde del plato de forma desinteresada.

—Ya —responde para volver a tomar el teléfono, imponiendo una vez más esa barrera de indiferencia que nos ha vuelto tan ajenos el uno del otro.

Eres patético. ¿Creías que eso lo iba a conmover?

Recuerdo con pesar la cara que puso el lobo el día en el que le confesé que la comida ya no me sabía a otra cosa más que a cenizas, después de que la textura de una sopa casi me había hecho vomitar. Y el haberle contado después que lo único que no me provocaba arcadas era el alcohol o el tabaco, tampoco ayudó a cambiar su semblante.

No dejo de preguntarme qué expresión pondría si además le dijera que lo único que he probado hasta ahora que no me supo a cenizas fueron sus labios.

Siento una profunda humillación al darme cuenta de que, al fondo del restaurante, aquella chica mira hacia acá, siendo testigo de la forma en la que contemplo al hombre frente a mí.

Sí. Wéndigo tiene razón.

Soy realmente patético.

☾●◗○

La noche no me trata mucho mejor, porque al subir a la camioneta a la mañana siguiente y darme de frente con el helor de la madrugada, lo que más me incomoda no es el frío, sino el dolor de cuello.

La tormenta no nos dejó continuar nuestro viaje por la carretera, por lo que quedarnos a dormir en el motel junto al restaurante fue nuestra única opción. Creo que éste es el sitio más decente en el que nos hemos hospedado hasta ahora —al menos, la regadera no era un tubo incrustado en la pared—, pero las almohadas estaban tan duras que casi me sentí tentado a regresar a dormir en la *pickup*.

—Cuarenta, por favor.

Salgo de mis lamentables pensamientos cuando Tared me extiende un billete sobre el tablero, puesto que no me había percatado de que nos habíamos detenido frente a un despachador de la gasolinera.

Son apenas las cinco de la mañana.

Cuánta prisa, ¿verdad?

Sí. El plan de Tared de hoy es conducir hasta llegar a Minnesota. Son veinte horas de camino, con todo y las paradas que necesitaremos hacer para que él descanse un poco, ya que yo no puedo ayudarlo, al no saber manejar en carreteras congeladas.

Veinte horas.

Sólo veinte horas para que tal vez no vuelva a verlo jamás.

La dependienta de la tienda ni siquiera se molesta en levantar la cabeza cuando me acerco, concentrada en no quedarse dormida sobre la revista que tiene en el regazo.

—Cuarenta para la número siete, por favor —pido, dejando el billete en el mostrador.

Mientras ella activa la bomba de forma mecánica desde su pantalla, miro a Tared entre el montón de hojas de anuncios pegadas en la puerta de vidrio de la tienda. Él baja de la camioneta para poner la manguera de gasolina en el tanque, luego, se agacha para revisar que las cadenas de las llantas estén bien colocadas. Se detiene un momento, acuclillado contra una de las ruedas, y se masajea los párpados en círculos.

Las ojeras parecen haberse oscurecido dos tonos más desde anoche, lo que me hace recordar, con un nudo en el estómago, sus ojos azules abiertos hacia el techo, atormentado por la bruma mientras la luz violeta del invierno se colaba por la ventana.

Me muerdo el labio inferior y me alejo de la caja hacia la zona de café para servir uno para él, extragrande, bien cargado de leche y azúcar. Vuelvo con la dependienta y pongo el vaso sobre el mostrador. Miro con resignación la hilera de cigarros detrás de la mujer a sabiendas de que, por más que Tared y yo los deseemos, no podemos costearlos.

Cuando la encargada por fin se digna a girarse para cobrarme, se queda con la mano dentro de la registradora, la mirada entornada hacia mí.

—Espera... —susurra, para luego abrir los ojos de par en par—. ¡Pero si eres *tú*!

Alzo ambas cejas, desconcertado. Ella mira hacia la salida de la tienda. No, hacia las hojas pegadas en la puerta de cristal.

Y de pronto...

Está allí. Impreso en un papel amarillo neón, brillante contra la oscuridad de la madrugada.

Me acerco al letrero y noto las múltiples tiras recortadas que cuelgan en la parte inferior, de forma que puedas tirar de una de ellas y quedarte con un número de teléfono.

Arranco el papel entero y salgo corriendo de la tienda, escuchando el grito inteligible de la dependienta. Tared, quien ya me esperaba dentro la camioneta, frunce el ceño desconcertado cuando me meto casi de un salto y azoto la puerta a mis espaldas.

—Vámonos —grito con un nudo en la garganta—. ¡Vámonos, ahora!

Le extiendo el letrero y al verlo, palidece.

Es una fotografía mía, con mi nombre y un enorme "¿HAS VISTO A ESTA PERSONA?" impreso en letras gigantes... Es el mismo volante policial con el que Dallas descubrió mi identidad en Stonefall.

Pero lo que aparta de su estupefacción a Tared y lo hace salir a toda velocidad hacia la carretera es ver que una de las tiras ya ha sido arrancada.

CAPÍTULO 11
CACERÍA

—Ha sido el rastreador —susurro, mordisqueando la uña de mi pulgar con los dientes mientras recuerdo, con rabia, la forma en la que aquella mesera en el restaurante me miró. O más bien, me reconoció.

Dioses, ¿cómo es que no me di cuenta?

Como respuesta, Tared hace un cambio en la palanca de velocidades para tomar una curva. Me paso una mano por la cara e intento no sentirme culpable porque, de todas maneras, ya lo habíamos visto venir. El rastreador en mi brazo, aquél que tenía enganchado cuando salimos del plano medio, funcionó el tiempo suficiente como para haberles enviado una señal a esos bastardos sobre nuestra ubicación, pero no quisimos darlo por hecho; por eso no aceptamos más ayuda de Lía ni de los motociclistas. Arriesgar la vida de otros errantes, a sabiendas de lo que unos monstruos como los Lander eran capaces de hacer, estaba fuera de discusión.

Días atrás, eso me había dado la absurda esperanza de que, tal vez, Tared entendiera un poco las decisiones que había tomado hasta ahora, dándose cuenta de que apartar a otros a veces era la opción más sensata, pero…

Aun así, te dio la espalda.

No doy el gusto a Wéndigo de contestar, más abrumado por todo esto que por sus ganas de arruinarme la existencia, porque si los tramperos siguen vivos, eso podría significar que Comus Bayou podría no estarlo.

—¿Qué vamos a hacer? —pregunto, angustiado por la incertidumbre. Tared alarga su mano hacia el celular, posado sobre mi fotografía impresa en ese papel amarillo.

—Darnos prisa, detenernos lo menos posible —contesta—, y prevenir a Lía.

Hace una marcación rápida, pero el aire se me escapa ante el pitido mecánico del teléfono. No hay señal.

—Mierda —masculla, y mete el aparato en uno de los cierres de su chamarra—. Lo intentaré cuando salgamos del parque.

Al ver la solitaria carretera, serpenteando en pronunciadas curvas a través de las montañas, la terrible sensación de que eso no sucederá pronto se agudiza. Peligrosos barrancos llenos de nieve y árboles huesudos surcan los costados del Parque Nacional de los Glaciares, lo que nos obliga a disminuir la velocidad para no resbalar sobre el asfalto congelado.

Minutos después, una camioneta plateada nos rebasa con calma y se pierde a lo lejos, lo que aumenta el aire de desolación del valle. Es el primer vehículo que nos topamos desde hace más de una hora, ya que esta ruta no parece ser muy transitada. Pero era esto o desviarnos cincuenta kilómetros hacia atrás en busca de una carretera más poblada.

Nervioso, le echo un vistazo al mapa. Y al calcular más o menos nuestra ubicación, me doy cuenta de que éstos son los últimos bosques que cruzaremos antes de llegar a las planicies que conectan Montana con Dakota del Norte, cosa que no sé si me termina de gustar. Las llanuras nos permitirán movernos con más rapidez, pero, al mismo tiempo, estaremos más expuestos. No por nada hemos tomado las rutas a través de las reservas naturales en vez de aventurarnos en las autopistas más despejadas.

La carretera se vuelve más estrecha a medida que subimos por la montaña. El barranco se ha volcado ahora sólo de nuestro lado del carril, mientras que el otro está bardeado por altas pendientes de roca.

La tensión sube y sube, hasta que el sonido de una bocina rompe con la quietud. Miro por el retrovisor y distingo a lo lejos una camioneta *pickup* negra que pita una y otra vez detrás de nosotros, con un solitario conductor que parece desesperado por la lentitud de nuestro paso.

Tared enciende las intermitentes para que nos adelante, pero lo único que hace es dejar de tocar la bocina... para luego acelerar.

Entrecierro la mirada y, noto que el vehículo tiene una extraña estructura de metal montada sobre el techo de la cabina, como un pedestal para poner, ¿tablas de nieve, tal vez?

Intento descifrar lo que es cuando el vehículo queda a escasos diez metros de nosotros.

Tared mira también por el retrovisor y aspira profundo. Y de pronto, yo también puedo percibirlo: metal. Óxido. Cuerdas. *Sangre.*

Un grito se atora en mi garganta.

¡PAM!

Una bala revienta el retrovisor de mi lado de la camioneta.

—¡TRAMPEROS! —suelto por fin a todo pulmón, agachándome contra el tablero. Tared se encorva sobre el volante ante el impacto y el vehículo resbala, pero recupera pronto el control. Pisa el acelerador y las cadenas de nuestras llantas comienzan a resonar con furia contra el asfalto.

¡PAM!

Otra bala más, pero esta vez, en la puerta de la caja de carga. Me asomo por una esquina de la ventana trasera y descubro que los dos hombres que viajaban en el cajón de la *pickup* se han puesto de pie, cubiertos con visores de nieve y pasamontañas. Uno de ellos nos dispara con un rifle de alto calibre, mientras que el otro comienza a levantar una especie de cañón de acero que, rápidamente, instala en el pedestal sobre la cabina.

—Pero ¿qué diablos...?

Pierdo el aliento al verlo meter una pesada asta de acero dentro del cañón.

Es un arpón. *Un jodido arpón ballenero.*

El hombre lobo lo ve también a través del retrovisor y comienza a zigzaguear para evadir otro disparo del rifle.

—¡Mierda, mierda! —me quito el cinturón de seguridad y me inclino para sacar la escopeta de debajo del asiento. Echo el seguro hacia atrás y saco medio cuerpo por la ventanilla.

—¡Elisse!

Disparo y el sujeto da un volantazo mientras mi bala alcanza a conectar en medio del parabrisas. Hace un agujero al vidrio y la camioneta patina por la grava. Pero, en menos de lo que me gustaría, el trampero vuelve a encarrilar el vehículo.

Escucho una explosión.

—¡Cuidado!

El grito de Tared me hace regresar a la cabina justo cuando un maldito arpón vuela frente a mis narices.

El arma, cuyo blanco era mi cabeza, da de lleno contra la gruesa rama de un árbol, con tanta potencia que la parte como si fuese una vara seca.

El otro trampero vuelve a disparar y su munición revienta nuestra vieja ventana trasera, cubriéndonos por una lluvia de cristales.

Escucho una segunda explosión y de pronto, la camioneta empieza a sacudirse de un lado a otro.

—¡Carajo, la llanta! —exclama Tared, haciendo todo lo posible por mantener el control del vehículo. Pero al girarme, veo que la punta de un arpón sobresale de la puerta trasera de nuestra camioneta y, detrás de ella, una gruesa cuerda de acero que la une al pedestal de los tramperos.

—¡No, le dieron a la puerta! —exclamo—, ¡nos tienen enganchados!

Ambas camionetas comienzan a tambalearse en una lucha de fuerzas; la pendiente de la montaña y el hielo hacen que pronto las llantas de nuestro vehículo empiecen a echar humo. El suyo es un modelo más nuevo, más potente.

Escucho un par de cadenas reventar y no lo pienso más.

Tomo la caja de municiones y recargo la escopeta.

—¿Qué estás haciendo? ¡No, Elisse! —grita Tared al verme arrojar la escopeta a través de la ventana trasera, hacia la caja de carga, para luego lanzarme yo también por detrás.

Al caer sobre mi hombro en el suelo de metal, el trampero del rifle lucha por apuntarme, pero le resulta imposible debido al movimiento errático de los vehículos.

Logro arrastrarme, con todo y la escopeta, hacia la puertilla de nuestra camioneta, y disparo a la punta del arpón.

La *pickup* de los tramperos patina con violencia al desencajarse de nuestro vehículo. Y de puro milagro, la puertilla del nuestro no se abre, lo que impide que yo salga disparado hacia la carretera.

—¡Hijo de perra! —exclama el trampero del rifle al dejar caer su arma en el asfalto presa de una sacudida.

El conductor recupera el control de su camioneta y acelera hacia nosotros una vez más. Y cuando veo que los dos hombres de atrás logran montar un nuevo arpón, decido que es suficiente.

Acérquense...

—*Acérquense*, bastardos —musito y, como si los hubiese embrujado, el cofre de su *pickup* se sitúa a apenas unos metros de mí.

Me pongo de pie. Vuelvo a apuntar la escopeta y, con un chasquido de lengua, disparo hacia el conductor de la camioneta.

Mi bala atraviesa el ya fragmentado parabrisas y revienta su corazón. El vehículo vira con violencia y se estampa contra una barricada de rocas al lado de la carretera, mientras los dos tramperos de la parte trasera salen disparados del cajón. No me quedo a escuchar los gritos ni a saborear el quebrar de sus huesos contra el asfalto. En cambio, me deslizo como puedo de vuelta a la cabina, echando la escopeta por delante.

—Dios mío, ¿estás loco? ¡Pudiste matarte!

La mano de Tared se cierne sobre mi brazo al ponerme de vuelta el cinturón de seguridad. Nos miramos un instante y esa breve mirada azul me provoca más adrenalina que toda la jodida persecución que acabamos de tener. El lobo me suelta, consternado ante su propia reacción, y gira la cabeza hacia delante.

Y entonces, *lo escucho gritar.*

Distingo las luces cegadoras de otra camioneta delante de nosotros, llena de dientes cromados. Un monstruo plateado que estoy seguro de que vi rebasarnos kilómetros atrás.

No logro percibir con claridad lo que sucede después de escuchar el terrible estallido de otro arpón.

El parabrisas frontal se rompe y los vidrios me cortan la cara. Nuestra camioneta da un giro mortal y sale disparada de la carretera hacia el largo y empinado barranco, totalmente fuera de control.

Rodamos hacia abajo, al vacío, y nos estrellamos una y otra vez contra los árboles entre el estruendo del metal y la madera que se parte en pedazos.

Y después, cuando el frío logra sobreponerse al ruido... ya no percibo nada más.

CAPÍTULO 12
INQUISIDOR

A lo largo de todos los milenios que tengo con vida llegué a conocer a muchos tipos de monstruos. Criaturas obscenas y descabelladas, algunas reales, algunas imaginarias, pero todas extraídas de la más profunda oscuridad, cuyos apetitos habían alimentado las pesadillas de los humanos desde tiempos inmemoriales.

Seres alquímicos, mitológicos; dioses viejos, dioses inventados, bestias que jamás debieron salir de la atormentada culpa de los hombres.

Pero Benjamin Lander, él es... *otro tipo de monstruo.*

El olor de su piel me recuerda al hierro que mata al brujo y despelleja al errante. Su odio es la pira donde se quema a los herejes, y sus métodos, el potro donde se tortura a los inocentes.

Y ahora, esta mítica criatura avanza sobre el pavimento congelado de la carretera, reventando los pedazos de cristales bajo sus botas de casquillo. Y por los veinte años que llevo observándolo a través de mi portal, sé muy bien que no piensa en la camioneta negra volcada contra la montaña, a un lado del camino, ni en el hombre dentro de la cabina que ostenta una mueca eternamente conmocionada por la bala que lo mató.

Para él, el llanto de uno de sus sobrinos meciendo el cuerpo de su hermano no es distinto al graznido molesto de los pájaros. Y tampoco tiene gran mérito que haya un sobreviviente, porque lo que le interesa yace al fondo de aquel barranco al que se acerca poco a poco para asomarse.

Estrujo el portal y dejo enterradas unas cuantas uñas en él de sólo pensar en lo que esas manos llenas de venas viejas y manchas le harían a la preciosa piel de mi criatura. La imagen me hace querer montarme desnuda sobre el anciano y abrirle la garganta en pleno clímax, robarle su semilla podrida antes de que pueda derramarla sobre tierra fecunda.

En cambio, sólo puedo observar cómo el tirano mira con severidad a los hombres que se movilizan para limpiar la carretera: una grúa para enganchar la camioneta destrozada, gasolina para cubrir la sangre en el asfalto, un sujeto disfrazado de policía por si algún vehículo se acerca.

Después de haberse asomado hacia el precipicio y comprobar que no hay más que un rastro de llantas y árboles partidos, camina a su propia camioneta, esa bestia de plata que todavía ostenta su corona de arpones en la cabeza y que su gente reemplazaría gustosa con una escultura de los huesos de mi hijo.

Pero eso no es lo que busca.

Benjamin Lander no quiere que le traigan su piel o la del animal inmundo que lo acompaña. Lo que quiere es que lo conduzcan vivo hasta sus manos, vivo para cobrar sobre él una venganza que se prolongue días, semanas, meses. Un ajuste de cuentas que sea recordado por generaciones entre los suyos y entre las criaturas que, para él, no son más que animales que han aprendido a pararse sobre dos patas.

Benjamin Lander es el peor tipo de monstruo porque no necesita de colas, dientes ni garras para destrozar todo lo que se le ponga en frente.

Benjamin Lander es el peor tipo de monstruo porque simple y sencillamente es *humano*.

CAPÍTULO 13
SUEÑOS DE HAMBRUNA

*P*rimero, fue una puerta de madera roja, llena de cicatrices oscuras. Luego, una verde esmeralda, tan caliente que parecía exudar fuego. Y ahora, una vez más, se alza una puerta frente a mí. Pero ésta es muy diferente a las de mis otras visiones. Porque está… **viva**.

O al menos, eso es lo que parece, puesto que sólo puedo percibirla como una lámina negra en medio de la nada, cuya oscuridad se mueve como el cauce de un río.

Y justo cuando creo que voy a ser abducido por el hipnotismo de aquel portal, escucho el ensordecedor grito de una trompeta.

El apocalíptico eco retumba y se pierde a lo lejos entre la noche oscura, y la sacudida me ayuda a percatarme de que estoy parado en medio de un bosque, frente a esta puerta hecha de sombras.

Los árboles alrededor están secos y muertos, con coronas de ramajes de largas espinas. Sus troncos oscuros contrastan contra el suelo empastado de nieve, nieve sucia, revuelta en tierra y hojas marchitas.

Ya no siento dolor en el pecho, y tampoco percibo el helor en mis pies descalzos, ni la brisa que acaricia mi cuerpo cubierto por apenas una túnica negra que, abierta hasta debajo de mi ombligo, revela mi desnudez. Inclusive, la espada filosofal ya no parece pesar en mi interior, como si ésta hubiese desaparecido.

Pero hay algo que sí puedo percibir.

Me toco la cara y la siento caliente, empapada de esas lágrimas que conocí muy bien en mi infancia: estoy llorando de hambre, un ansia tan intensa que las paredes de mi estómago parecieran deshacerse a causa de la acidez.

Rodeo la puerta para adentrarme en el bosque sin saber hacia dónde dirigirme, tan sólo guiado por la urgente necesidad de buscar algo de comer, lo que sea. Pero lo único que encuentro a mi paso es una luna oculta entre las nubes.

De pronto, algo cruje bajo mis pies. Miro hacia el suelo y encuentro una columna vertebral que sobresale de la tierra helada, tan vieja que se ha pulverizado con mi peso. Observo alrededor y más espinas dorsales yacen esparcidas por el bosque, tan secas que no podría sacar de ellas ni un poco de tuétano para alimentarme.

Después de caminar durante un tiempo indeterminado, logro ver un claro en la lejanía y un sendero difuso que serpentea hacia él. El dolor en mis entrañas me obliga a seguirlo, pero me detengo cuando se atraviesa con otros senderos para formar una estrella de ocho puntas. En medio del cruce de caminos se yergue un árbol muy grueso, gris como la ceniza, y torcido, con ramas largas como garras.

Y en el tronco, casi al pie y flanqueada por raíces espesas como anacondas, hay… una cavidad. Oscura y roja, amplia y abierta de par en par, con pliegues de corteza a su alrededor; una imagen demasiado sugerente para que pase desapercibida por mi cabeza, sobre todo cuando el hueco palpita como si la madera húmeda de su interior estuviese hecha de carne fresca.

Un hedor a cadáver comienza a emanar de aquella herida en el árbol, algo que reconozco como la terrible fetidez de la magia muerta.

Somos.

Miro hacia un lado y otro, sobresaltado ante el eco de las voces del monstruo de hueso, porque esta vez no provienen de mi interior, sino de afuera, de alguna parte del bosque.

Al sentir una vez más el latigazo del hambre, me doblo sobre mí mismo.

—Dioses —murmuro, con mis interiores retorciéndose sin piedad—, ¿cuánto tiempo llevo sin comer?

Siglos...

Olvido mi malestar al escuchar las voces de Wéndigo emanar de la sangrienta abertura, y me quedo helado cuando un ruido espeso les prosigue, como el de las entrañas de un animal al ser removidas.

Y entonces, la obscena cavidad comienza a dilatarse.

Una ola espesa de tierra mezclada con sangre y trozos de vértebras brota de ella, arrastrándose a través de las raíces, la nieve y el sendero hasta llegar a mis pies.

De la masa de podredumbre, una figura humana se revuelve y, despacio, empieza a levantarse. Aquella trompeta oscura retumba una vez más, con tanta fuerza que pareciera querer partir el suelo. Y cuando aquello que ha nacido del árbol se yergue por completo, lo primero que distingo son las astas plateadas que resplandecen en su cabeza.

Lentamente, el ser se gira para mirarme. Está tan delgado, tan raquítico, que la piel se le ha amoratado sobre los huesos. Y en medio de su pecho, sobre una abertura sangrienta en el esternón, hay una pequeña luna menguante que brilla contra la oscuridad de los corazones podridos que palpitan de forma necrótica debajo de ella. El cabello blanco de la criatura cae largo como una cortina sobre su espalda desnuda y reconozco mi rostro en el suyo.

—Bestia Revestida de Luna —susurra con cientos de voces. Las voces de Wéndigo—. Es hora... de despertar.

ᐧ ● ◖ ○

Una punzada en el pecho me arranca de tajo del sueño, y aunque quiero gritar con todas mis fuerzas debido al dolor, lo único que logro es dejar salir un gemido contenido. Intento despabilarme, recuperar el control de mi cuerpo, pero estoy tan entumecido que apenas puedo mover la cabeza.

Al principio sólo distingo una mezcla intermitente de gris y manchas rojizas, pero cuando consigo enfocar a través de la luz reflejada en la nieve, lo primero que entra en mi periferia es el parabrisas destrozado frente a mí, junto con el montón de escarcha acumulada sobre el tablero. Ramas huesudas se atraviesan por mi ventana rasguñándome la cara y los brazos, mientras un tronco partido yace incrustado en la defensa de la camioneta, la cual expulsa una columna de humo espeso, negro contra la blancura del bosque.

La caída. Los tramperos. Una emboscada.

Aturdido entre imágenes de batalla y hambruna que buscan desvanecerse, erguirme me resulta imposible; el peso de la espada me empuja contra el asiento sin tregua y pronto empiezo a sentir dolor en las piernas, los brazos, la cadera, así como varias heridas cortantes desperdigadas por todo mi cuerpo.

Libero el cinturón de seguridad, con la mano aterida por el frío.

—Aah... —gimoteo—, Ta... ¿Tared...? —llamo en voz baja, con dificultad, pero al no recibir respuesta, giro la cabeza hacia su asiento.

Y al ver al hombre lobo, me llevo la mano a los labios para no dejar escapar un grito descomunal.

CAPÍTULO 14
LÍMITE

De pronto, es como volver a estar dentro del lago congelado. En el plano medio, asfixiado y encerrado en la misma pesadilla interminable.

Tared está recargado contra la puerta de la camioneta en una postura extraña, poco natural, con un brazo fuera de la ventanilla destrozada y los ojos cerrados. Cualquiera pensaría que está profundamente dormido, pero el tubo letal de un arpón de hierro resplandece sobre su vientre, *atravesándolo de lado a lado*.

La conmoción me aturde y me deja inmóvil como si estuviese enterrado bajo el gran peso de un alud.

—Tared, Tared, ¿puedes escucharme? —musito, intentando hacerlo reaccionar.

Acuno con una mano un flanco de su rostro y descubro la tibieza que baja de su sien, junto con el filo letal de un par de cristales clavados en ella.

—Por los dioses, Tared, ¡Tared, despierta, por favor! —grito ahora, horrorizado al percatarme de que también se ha golpeado la cabeza contra la ventana.

—Ah… —la voz débil del devorapieles me agita los nervios de arriba abajo—, E… Elisse…

—No, no. No te esfuerces, por lo que más quieras —suplico—, aguanta, ¡por favor, resiste!

Todo da vueltas al ver que la punta del arpón ha atravesado por completo el asiento; el corto pedazo de tubo que puede verse desde el sillón hasta la espalda del lobo está empapado de sangre, al igual que el cojín y el respaldo.

La terrible imagen de la muerte de Calen, perforado por la columna del trotapieles, acude a mi mente sin piedad.

No, no, no, no, no, ¡POR LOS DIOSES! ¡POR LOS DIOSES!

¡¿Cuánto tiempo estuve inconsciente, con Tared *muriéndose* a mi lado?!

—Por favor, no te muevas —insisto, a la par que aparto un poco su ropa, lo suficiente para ver la gravedad de la herida. El arpón, que ha logrado penetrarlo a centímetros del ombligo, parece una versión moderna de aquellos que se usaban antes para cazar ballenas, con una cabeza estrecha y pequeña, pero más afilada. El delgado tubo se incrustó firmemente entre la carne y el hueso, pero la hemorragia no parece haberse contenido, tal vez a causa de las sacudidas de la camioneta.

No debo sacar el arpón, si lo hago, si acaso le ha tocado algún órgano vital, Tared podría...

¡Desángralo!

¡NO! ¡No voy siquiera a pensar en ello! Dioses, ¿qué hago? ¿Qué hago? ¿Qué hago? ¡¿Qué harías tú, Johanna?!

Un murmullo me hace sentir una descarga eléctrica por la espalda. Levanto el mentón y miro hacia afuera.

Encuentro, a sólo unos metros de nosotros, la silueta traslúcida de Barón Samedi, erguido entre las sombras de la neblina del bosque.

Un vaho negro brota del habano de su maldita boca sonriente, el primer vistazo que tengo de este cabrón desde que hice mi último juramento en Monument Valley.

—No, ni se te ocurra, bastardo —susurro entre dientes mientras que, por instinto, deslizo mi brazo sobre los hombros de Tared—. *No vas a llevártelo.*

El hombre lobo, sin fuerzas para mostrar desconcierto ante mi locura, tan sólo aprieta los ojos y acalla un gemido de dolor.

Miro sobre mi hombro, por la ventanilla trasera de la camioneta. Un largo sendero de árboles abatidos marca nuestra caída por el barranco de la montaña, pero la densa niebla del bosque me impide hacerme una idea de la altura de la pendiente.

Otra bofetada de realidad me obliga a poner los pies en la tierra: tengo qué encontrar la forma de sacar a Tared de aquí, porque estoy seguro de que los tramperos vendrán a buscarnos, si no es que ya están encima de nosotros.

Cierro los ojos un momento y me fuerzo a ordenar mis ideas, porque no estoy indefenso, carajo, soy un brujo y *aún tengo mi magia.*

—Voy a parar la hemorragia, y luego te quitaré el cinturón de seguridad para poder moverte —le digo al devorapieles con más confianza de la que siento, limpiando el sudor de su frente con el dorso de mi mano humana—. Te sacaré de esto, Tared. Lo juro.

Sus ojos azules me responden con una mirada vaga, un tenue parpadeo que me empuja hacia la lucidez.

Me quito los guantes empleando los dientes y con mis afiladas garras rasgo cuidadosamente trozos de la camisa de franela del lobo, ya apelmazada a causa de la sangre y la nieve. Hago tiras pequeñas y comienzo a amarrarlas, abultándolas hasta que toman la forma de algo semejante a un muñeco.

Sin mediar palabras, y sin que él se queje —o tenga fuerzas para hacerlo—, arranco unos cuantos cabellos de la cabeza de Tared, los cuales coloco dentro de la figurilla. La cierro bien haciendo varios nudos a su alrededor con un par de tiras adicionales.

—Ya casi, un poco más —susurro y tomo del tablero un trozo de vidrio lo bastante largo y afilado para mi propósito.

De reojo, me doy cuenta de que Samedi me observa entre la nieve, ahora sin esa sonrisa estúpida en la cara. Mantengo la mirada fija en el Loa de la Muerte y comienzo a murmurar, desafiándolo.

Apenas abro los labios, la espada vibra furiosa con el fin de arrancarme la magia de las venas. Pero basta que yo mire a Tared para que pueda sobreponerme al hambre de la piedra filosofal.

Cierro la palma de mi mano humana alrededor del cristal, me hace sangrar sobre él.

—No van a vencerme —siseo, rabioso—. Ninguno de ustedes lo hará.

De un solo golpe, clavo el trozo de vidrio en el vientre del muñeco.

Tared aprieta los dientes cuando la sangre de la figura de franela se retrae hacia el cristal, como si éste la succionara hasta desaparecer. Y tal cual, con el monigote, la herida del propio hombre lobo deja de sangrar.

—Funcionó… —susurro, sin permitirme ser embargado por el alivio. He logrado detener la hemorragia por ahora, pero eso no significa que el riesgo haya terminado.

Aún debo ocuparme del arpón.

Tared no parece tener claridad de lo que sucede, es como si estuviese fuera de sí. Baja la barbilla un par de veces y cierra los ojos, a punto de quedarse dormido de nuevo.

—¡Eh, eh! —le susurro, sujetándolo de la mejilla para que me mire. La sangre de mi palma se mezcla con la de su sien—.

Necesito que te mantengas despierto. Sé que puedes hacerlo, por favor —suplico, y arranco con cuidado los pequeños cristales de su cabeza, haciendo todo lo posible para que no se me quiebre la voz.

Él parpadea, despacio, y asiente aún con más lentitud. No debo sacar el arpón para desencajar a Tared del asiento, pero tal vez... tal vez pueda cortarlo.

De nuevo, me alargo hacia el tablero para tomar dos puñados de la nieve que se ha colado a través del parabrisas roto. Con ella, rodeo ambos lados de la vara de hierro, sobre la piel de la espalda y el vientre del lobo, quien farfulla ante el helado contacto.

—Resiste, por favor... y, por lo que más quieras, intenta no moverte —suplico. Tared no me contesta, sigue pálido y respira con grave dificultad.

No puedes salvarlo.

Mírame hacerlo, cabrón.

Cierro los ojos e invoco, con todas las energías de las que dispongo, el fuego de mi interior hasta hacerlo brotar de mis manos. Siento cómo el hierro se calienta, pero muy despacio gracias a la rabia de la espada que jalonea mi magia con desesperación.

Lucho con todas mis fuerzas hasta que, de pronto, el arpón bajo mis dedos se torna de un color rojo candente y se ablanda como el barro.

Pero la nieve, en cambio, se funde acompañada de un vapor blancuzco.

Mierda.

El lobo lanza un gemido de dolor, pero no infligido por la herida, sino porque el arma ha comenzado a arder entera. Tared se aferra con fuerza, tanto a la ventanilla rota como al asiento para no moverse, tal cual se lo he pedido.

—¡Aguanta por favor, ya casi! —exclamo hasta que, finalmente, el arpón se parte en sus dos extremidades, liberando
al lobo del asiento. Él exhala mientras yo arrojo los trozos al
suelo de la camioneta y me abalanzo por más nieve.

—E-Elisse…

—Aquí estoy, Tared, ya casi lo logras —digo, poniéndole
más nieve sobre las heridas para reducir el calor. Después, me
vuelco hacia nuestras cosas detrás del asiento, pero gran parte
de ellas están aplastadas por el metal abollado del respaldo.
Consigo sacar una sola de nuestras mochilas; la otra ha quedado hecha un acordeón, imposible de mover.

Una parte de mi alma regresa al cuerpo cuando logro encontrar la escopeta en el suelo de la camioneta junto con la
caja de munición, la única suerte que parece que hemos tenido
hasta ahora. Me cuelgo la mochila y el arma a la espalda y
abro la puerta de mi lado para salir de la camioneta. Ésta quedó
varada de forma perpendicular contra el árbol con el que se
ensartó por el frente, por lo que debemos dar un pequeño
salto para poder bajar.

—¡Carajo! —siseo al quedar enterrado en la nieve hasta las
pantorrillas. Con dificultad, me abro paso y rodeo el vehículo
para llegar hasta Tared, quien abre por sí solo la puerta.

—No, ¡no! —exclamo—. ¡No te esfuerces! —corro hacia él
y me encaramo sobre un tronco enterrado en la nieve para alcanzarlo—. Apóyate en mí, por favor. Déjame sacarte de aquí.

Él aguanta mientras yo pongo con cuidado su brazo alrededor de mis hombros. Con dificultad, logro bajar lentamente
al lobo de la cabina, intentando no resbalar sobre el tronco
helado. Al posar por fin los pies en la nieve, Tared coloca su
mano sobre su vientre, a centímetros de la herida, y reprime
un gemido más.

No podré evitar que el tubo se mueva y le cause dolor, pero al menos mi hechizo ayudará a que no se desangre. Por ahora.

—Vamos, hay que ponerse a cubierto.

Lo sujeto de la cintura, procurando no tocar la laceración. Despacio, comenzamos a introducirnos en el espeso bosque mientras el cielo cambia de color sobre nuestras cabezas. Sus pasos se vuelven ligeramente más firmes, como si poco a poco recuperara la consciencia.

Avanzamos, nos abrimos paso a través de la nieve y los árboles... pero no logramos alejarnos ni doscientos metros cuando escucho a lo lejos el rugido de un motor.

CAPÍTULO 15
UN RASTRO EN LA NIEVE

Tared vuelve la cabeza hacia donde proviene el sonido. Éste se eleva sobre los árboles y comienza a acercarse por el bosque, en dirección a donde quedó varada la camioneta.

—Son ellos —susurra con los dientes apretados.

¡Mierda, mierda, mierda!

Intento empujarnos a través de la espesura de los árboles con más rapidez, pero, aunque el lobo intenta mantener el paso, sus dedos se crispan constantemente alrededor de la base del arpón. Habré detenido la hemorragia, pero esa cosa debe doler como si lo acuchillaran por dentro una y otra vez.

Miro alrededor y a poca distancia encuentro una pendiente de rocas cubiertas de nieve.

—Vamos—musito—, por aquí.

Al llegar a la pendiente lo ayudo a recargarse de costado, sentado contra las piedras, y apoyo una rodilla en el suelo para descolgarme la mochila. Susurro un "gracias, dioses" al abrirla y encontrar de inmediato la manta de camuflaje de invierno que las chicas usaban para cazar en la montaña. La pongo en mi regazo y sigo revolviendo. El devorapieles agita la cabeza cuando me ve sacar la pistola de Lía.

—¿Qué vas a hacer? —pregunta con la voz ronca, falta de aire, mientras cargo el tambor y me ajusto la escopeta a la espalda. El peso de la espada busca tirarme de frente, pero al ver cómo la piedra donde está recargado Tared se mancha con su sangre, mantengo mis pies bien plantados en la nieve.

—Voy a enfrentarlos —contesto, sin más. Él abre la boca para replicar, pero sus palabras son silenciadas por un nuevo rugido de aquel motor.

Cuando encuentro en la mochila el hacha de mano de Debbie, mi pulso se dispara con una nueva ola de adrenalina.

—No importa qué tanto los evadamos ahora, Tared —le digo mientras llevo el hacha a mi cadera para engancharla en la pretina de los pantalones—. Nos alcanzarán si no acabamos con ellos primero, así que quédate aquí, por favor —le pido, acercándome con la manta para cubrirlo.

—No —dice en un gemido, rechazándola—. Llévatela.

—Mi chamarra también es blanca —aseguro, aunque el grueso chaquetón está salpicado ya de sangre y suciedad—. Y tú la necesitarás más que yo.

Él levanta la mirada hacia mí, pero no logro interpretar la expresión de sus ojos azules.

Déjalo, que se pudra.

—Volveré —susurro con firmeza, y poso mi mano humana sobre su mejilla—. Lo juro.

Dejo el arma de Lía en su mano antes de que pueda negarse de nuevo. Lo cubro bien con la manta y me alejo sin perder más tiempo, arrojando nieve tras de mí para ocultar las huellas que llevan hasta el improvisado escondite.

Corro en línea recta hasta perder al lobo de vista. La sensación de peligro se agudiza a medida que trazo, de un lado a otro, caminos erráticos entre los árboles con la esperanza de que mis huellas puedan despistar a los tramperos. Podría intentar algún truco complejo empleando mi magia, pero aún estoy demasiado cansado por el hechizo anterior y...

De pronto, escucho los gritos de un hombre.

—¡Por acá, por acá!

Me subo la capucha de la chamarra y me oculto boca abajo detrás de unos troncos caídos. Momentos después, miro por encima y veo a tres tipos montados sobre cuatrimotos acercarse a través de la niebla.

Para mi horror, ignoran mi rastro y pasan de largo a gran velocidad en dirección a Tared. Tenso la mandíbula y me descuelgo la escopeta. Levanto el arma hacia ellos y disparo a ciegas.

Los vehículos se detienen de inmediato, en silencio.

—Eso es, malnacidos. Vengan por mí.

Al escuchar que se ponen en marcha de nuevo, doy la media vuelta y me escabullo por el bosque. Por suerte, sus vehículos no están equipados para todo tipo de clima, son demasiado pesados y llevan cadenas en las ruedas, cosa que tal vez pueda usar a mi favor.

Busco caminos cada vez más difíciles de sortear, repletos de maleza enjuta y rocas que entorpezcan el avance de los tramperos. Aquello parece funcionar por un buen tramo de camino, hasta que me encuentro con uno de los tantos barrancos de montaña, un escarpado de rocas de gran tamaño entremezcladas con troncos caídos, como si fuesen el resultado de un agresivo derrumbe.

Doy un vistazo alrededor para familiarizarme con el complicado terreno salpicado de peligrosos tocones ocultos bajo la nieve. Ambos flancos de la ladera están poblados de árboles, mientras que el manto helado me llega a las pantorrillas en las partes más abultadas.

Un desliz en la piedra fría y podría desnucarme.

Aguzo el oído cuando percibo que las motocicletas se apagan a lo lejos, donde el bosque se espesa tanto que es imposible acercarse más a bordo de cualquier vehículo. No tengo tiempo de idear un plan complejo, así que decido actuar con rapidez.

Tomo una rama del suelo, de un grosor similar al de mi escopeta, y escalo por el escarpado dejando bien plantadas mis huellas hasta llegar a una de las tantas rocas recubiertas de nieve. Me acuclillo detrás de ella, pongo la rama encima del lado más llano de la piedra y la cubro con escarcha.

Me quito el gorro de lana y lo relleno de más nieve, para luego colocarlo justo detrás de la falsa escopeta. Tan sólo un poco, apenas un asomo del pompón escarlata, nada más.

Me cubro con la capucha de la chamarra blanca y me entierro boca abajo en la nieve, a un lado de la roca y con la escopeta bien apretada entre mis dedos.

Libero el seguro.

Pronto veo a los tramperos acercarse a través de los árboles, pero tenso la mandíbula al no reconocer a ninguno de ellos. ¿Cuántos malditos integran esta manada de infelices?

—¡¿Adónde se fue?! —exclama el más joven de los tres.

—Cállate, Fitz…

Al ver que mis huellas llegan hasta el escarpado de roca, se detienen en el lindero del bosque para agazaparse detrás de un montón de troncos derribados por la avalancha. Dos de ellos son hombres maduros, armados hasta los dientes, mientras que el restante es un chico quizá tres o cuatro años menor que yo, y quien parece tener los nervios hechos trizas; puedo leer su ánimo a través de sus dedos temblorosos, incapaces de tensar con firmeza el gatillo de la ballesta entre sus manos.

Una presa fácil.

Sí. Demasiado fácil para ser conveniente.

Soporto el ardor de la nieve en mi cara, y observo a los tramperos más experimentados. Uno lleva una pistola pequeña y preparada en la mano, la mirada entornada, tan oscura que casi me recuerda la de un halcón. El otro, un tanto más joven y casi tan corpulento como lo era Buck Lander, trae un largo machete en su mano, mientras que el arma abandonada en la cintura me deja claro que su especialidad no es precisamente disparar.

Mis dudas se disipan cuando el trampero más viejo mira en mi dirección.

Cierro los ojos con fuerza.

—Te crees muy listo, maldito monstruo —lo escucho gruñir.

—¡Papá! ¿qué…?

El sonido mecánico de un arco y el zumbido de algo que viaja a gran velocidad llega hasta mis oídos. El estómago se me tensa como una tabla y lo siguiente que escucho es el crujir de la roca a mis espaldas.

No me atrevo ni a respirar, inmóvil aún bajo la nieve.

—Lo sabía —dice el hombre, para luego escupir al suelo.

Abro los ojos y veo que el viejo trae la ballesta entre sus manos, mientras que la piedra a mis espaldas cruje, agrietada por la flecha que ha clavado en mi gorro.

El tipo le pasa la rústica arma al joven y le hace indicaciones a él y al otro tipo para que vayan en direcciones opuestas, hacia los lados boscosos del acantilado, para buscarme. Los dos se alejan del viejo, agachados, mientras él clava una rodilla en la nieve y empieza a apuntar entre las rocas con su arma en alto, seguro de que me he ocultado en algún sitio lejos de mi señuelo para sorprenderlos.

Su mirada se eleva hacia arriba, fuera de mi dirección, y retengo el cansancio que recorre todo mi cuerpo. Cuando todo ha dejado de dar vueltas, apunto mi escopeta bajo la nieve. Calibre doce. De treinta a cuarenta metros de distancia. No necesito más.

¡PAM!

La bala revienta en un costado del cuello del trampero, quien se desploma hacia atrás presa del impacto.

—¡No, PAPÁ! —chilla el muchacho, mientras el hombre restante se lanza a zancadas sobre él y los sepulta a ambos en la nieve.

Escucho los débiles quejidos del chico detenerse por completo. Aguzo mi oído, aún atosigado por el estallido del arma, pero largos minutos transcurren sin un solo crujido en la nieve.

El ruido de un resorte me hace echarme hacia un lado con todo y escopeta para evitar que una gruesa flecha de hierro me perfore la cabeza. El largo artefacto le abre una nueva grieta a la roca, debajo de donde quedó clavado mi gorro.

—¡Maldita sea, Fitz!

Un resplandor afilado cae como una guillotina sobre mí y me hace rodar por la nieve; la hoja letal de un machete me persigue por el suelo, sacando chispas al golpear contra las rocas.

—¡No huyas, bastardo de mierda! —exclama el enorme trampero, quien ha salido del flanco del bosque. El maldito descarga su arma una y otra vez contra mí hasta hacerme perder la escopeta de una patada.

Desde el suelo, consigo reventar la suela de mi bota contra su rodilla con la fuerza suficiente para hacerlo retroceder y tambalear. El desgraciado, voluminoso y torpe, patina sobre las rocas heladas y cae de espaldas contra el suelo abultado.

—¡HIJO DE PERRA!

Sin oportunidad de recuperar mi escopeta, consigo ponerme de pie para echar a correr hacia abajo, al lindero del bosque. Y justo cuando llego al conjunto de troncos donde yace el cadáver del primer trampero, otra maldita flecha me roza el muslo y me lanza de bruces contra las ramas.

—¡Aaah! —grito al sentir la carne de mi pierna abrirse de tajo; el chiquillo me ha disparado desde lo lejos, oculto entre los árboles. Lo veo recargar su arma con torpeza, mientras el otro trampero logra por fin levantarse. Cojea, lastimado aún por mi patada, pero avanza ya con pasos pesados y firmes, como si quisiera demoler todo a su paso.

Se abalanza sobre mí y me arrastro hacia atrás con los codos hasta toparme contra los pies del trampero asesinado. Su sangre aún caliente me hace resbalar sobre la nieve.

—¡Quédate quieto, cabrón!

Escucho el filo de su machete rebanar el aire al levantarse.

¡Imbécil!

Me lanzo hacia el cadáver detrás de mí.

El grito del joven trampero es opacado por el rugido de una pistola; el arma de su padre humea entre mis dedos y el hombre frente a mí se aprieta el estómago, penetrado por la bala. Me levanto y disparo dos veces vez más, pero ahora contra su pecho.

Él por fin deja caer el machete a un lado, me mira con los ojos cristalizados, abiertos de par en par, y finalmente se desploma hacia atrás.

No veo venir la patada a un costado de mi cabeza. Y tampoco puedo retener la pistola en mi mano e impedir que salga volando por la sacudida.

Caigo contra el suelo del bosque e, instantes después, la punta de una bota de casquillo se clava directo en mi cara y me revienta el labio. El aturdimiento apenas me permite comprender la sarta de gritos del muchacho sobreviviente.

—Voy a matarte, ¡voy a hacerte pedazos, maldito monstruo de mierda! —chilla, una vez más.

Se coloca delante con la ballesta apuntando directo a mi frente. Me clava su mirada colérica y, por unos instantes, creo distinguirme en su anhelo de venganza.

Pero aquello sólo me hace sonreír. Él baja el arma unos centímetros y su mirada muta de la ira a la confusión por apenas unos instantes.

Idiota.

Un pisotón directo hacia la herida abierta de mi muslo me arranca un grito que retuerce su cara de regocijo. Me patea una vez más con esa suela sucia, y me deja tirado boca abajo.

—¡Basura, basura! —grita, moliendo a puntapiés mis costillas hasta hacerme escupir un hilillo de sangre. Jadeando, el joven se coloca sobre mí con ambas piernas al lado de mi cuerpo. Su suela me aplasta el flanco del rostro, la nieve helada me quema la piel.

—Ya verás, cretino asqueroso —gruñe, atolondrado por la cólera, y con la ballesta lánguida en su mano—. El abuelo te despellejará vivo por lo que has hecho. Y luego, ¡y luego...!

Destripará al lobo frente a ti.

De un solo movimiento, alcanzo el hacha de mano de mi cintura. Lanzo un grito de rabia y, limpiamente, le clavo la hoja justo en la coyuntura del tobillo, tan profundo que siento el metal vibrar cuando parte el hueso.

Un torrente de sangre sale disparado de su arteria y cae de espaldas, profiriendo alaridos casi animales.

Mientras el chico se revuelca en agonía, me levanto despacio y escupo un poco más de sangre contra la nieve. Cojeo y me inclino para arrancarle el hacha del tobillo.

Su grito de dolor hace que Wéndigo se relama el hocico.

—M-monstruo —gimotea el joven con los ojos llenos de lágrimas—. Te comiste a Buck, ¡monstruo!

Sus palabras revuelven el panal de voces dentro mi cabeza. Comienza a arrastrarse hacia atrás, con el pie colgando de una forma grotesca hacia un lado. El rastro en la nieve que deja a su paso me revuelve el estómago con algo que me causa una profunda contrariedad.

No es asco.

No es odio.

Es hambre.

Aprieto el mango del hacha contra una mano y, esta vez, no siento ni una pizca de remordimiento.

Tan sólo una deliciosa opresión en el corazón.

CAPÍTULO 16
REFUGIO

Cuando logro regresar con Tared, ya casi es de noche. El lobo se ha movido de su lugar, lo sé porque está sentado de una forma distinta a como lo dejé y ahora mantiene la cabeza fuera de la manta. De seguro escuchó los disparos en el bosque y quizá *los gritos* también, porque la expresión que tiene ahora mismo me recuerda mucho a la manera en la que me miró en el taller mecánico.

Estaciono la motocicleta frente a él y me descuelgo el bolso de lona que tomé de uno de los tramperos. Luego, alargo el brazo hacia el celular, puesto a un lado suyo, y presiono el botón del costado. El reloj marca las cinco y pico de la tarde, con la batería ya muy por debajo de la mitad.

Ayer lo usamos bastante y no recuerdo que lo hayamos recargado en el motel...

—No conseguí nada —susurra él, más lúcido después del golpe en la cabeza—. No hay señal.

Observo las manchas rojas que el aparato exhibe por toda la pantalla. Lo guardo y me arrodillo para vaciar en nuestra mochila las municiones que he robado, así como una linterna que me pongo en el bolsillo del pantalón. Todo bajo la mirada tensa del devorapieles.

—Intenté encontrar algún botiquín —murmuro, sin mirarlo—, pero sólo traían armas con ellos.

Tared observa la parrilla de la motocicleta: la ballesta y el machete amarrados junto con un par de abrigos de cacería.

—¿Estás... bien? —pregunta, arrastrando las palabras debido al esfuerzo.

Me detengo unos segundos con un puñado de balas en la mano. No. No estoy bien. Estoy *muy* lejos de estar bien, pero me limito a asentir.

—¿Qué sucedió? —insiste y yo pienso en la imagen de un brazo escarlata enterrado en la nieve.

—Tardarán en encontrarlos —aseguro, volviendo a mis cabales, para luego levantar la mochila y llevarla hacia la parrilla.

Tared no me pregunta nada más, pero no hace falta. Sé bien qué es lo que piensa de mí y yo ya no tengo fuerzas para convencerlo de lo contrario.

Miro hacia los árboles y considero nuestras opciones. Volver a la camioneta para recuperar algo de provisiones sería una insensatez, por lo que sólo nos queda tratar de viajar mañana en paralelo a la carretera hasta encontrar una pendiente asfaltada por donde podamos subir. Pero, por ahora, lo único que nos queda es dar con un refugio.

Me acerco al lobo una vez más.

—Ven, vamos —digo con aparente calma mientras extiendo las manos hacia él.

Tared, en vez de tomarse su tiempo como cualquier persona en su sano juicio haría, se sostiene de mí en el acto y con firmeza. Con cuidado, logro ayudarlo a sentarse en el vehículo motorizado. Se aferra a mis hombros para no caer por si tropezamos con algún tronco o caemos en un bache, y siento su agarre tenso por el dolor de soportar aquel arpón moviéndose dentro de su cuerpo.

No entiendo cómo logra hacer todo con tanto aplomo, con semejante resistencia...

Tenso la mandíbula y enciendo el vehículo. El ruido del motor me preocupa, pero no más que el que hayamos permanecido demasiado tiempo en este lugar.

Arranco e intento avanzar cerca del pie de la montaña durante unos cuantos kilómetros, en busca de una caseta o un sitio para campistas, pero cuando la oscuridad de la noche me impide ver más allá del barranco y del propio bosque, es tiempo de detenerse. Mi boca exhala una fumarola espesa y blanca, y siento mi mano humana agarrotada en el manubrio de la motocicleta.

Está helando como nunca, y si seguimos a esta velocidad, el frío terminará por congelarnos.

—Allá... —la ahora tenue voz del devorapieles me hace mirar hacia un punto lejano entre los árboles. Veo el pie de una colina que parece sólida y lisa, como una pared de concreto, pero al apuntar con la linterna, vislumbro una grieta escondida entre los pliegues de las rocas.

Una caverna.

Casi quiero gritar. Acerco la moto hasta donde la espesura me lo permite y la estaciono, dejando al lobo sobre ella unos momentos.

Me dirijo a la grieta e ilumino el interior. La cueva está un tanto inclinada, como si fuese un túnel escarbado en pendiente, pero el suelo rugoso se ha mantenido seco, por lo que parece seguro bajar por él. También hay varios montones de ramas y maleza seca acumuladas, señal de que alguna vez fue la madriguera de un animal del que, por suerte, no parece haber rastro reciente.

Enfrentarme en estas condiciones a una osa enojada se me antoja tanto como tener otro encuentro con los tramperos.

Regreso a la moto y ayudo a Tared a bajar, puesto que la entrada es tan estrecha que no hay forma de resguardar al vehículo con nosotros.

—Apóyate en mí, por favor —le pido.

Él no logra erguirse del todo en la gruta, pero el lugar se ensancha una vez que logramos adentrarnos. Así que, después de recargar a Tared contra la pared helada, me ocupo de bloquear la entrada con la manta de camuflaje, encajándola un poco entre las piedras. No servirá de mucho para aislar el frío, pero ayudará a cubrir la luz de la fogata que pienso encender en cuanto termine de poner a salvo al lobo.

Una vez que lo ayudo a sentarse sobre un acolchado mediocre que logro idear con uno de los abrigos que he tomado de los tramperos, vacío con algo de desesperación todo lo que encuentro en nuestra mochila: una tira de analgésicos con apenas seis comprimidos, dos camisetas de algodón y una camisa de franela, un termo a medio llenar, unas cuantas tiras de carne seca y una pequeña navaja suiza. Nada más.

Mierda.

Tomo dos de las pastillas y el agua, pero endurezco el agarre de ambas cosas al advertir la herida de Tared.

—Me obligué a orinar hace rato, mientras no estabas —dice, adivinando mis pensamientos—. No había sangre.

Escuchar aquello me provoca un alivio indescriptible, porque eso significa que el arpón no le ha perforado el intestino. Le alargo ambas cosas y él se las traga de golpe, con dificultad. Sé que no servirán de mucho, por no decir de nada, pero debo racionar el ibuprofeno si quiero paliar un poco su dolor hasta que encontremos la forma de salir de esta pesadilla.

Escojo la camiseta más limpia, la cual resulta ser mía, y con ayuda de la navaja trozo delgadas tiras.

—Déjame ver eso —le pido, a la par que estiro mi mano descarnada hacia él.

El lobo permanece quieto, obediente, pero aun así logro percibir cómo su mirada azul se contrae al alcanzarlo con mi guante. Le abro la chamarra y levanto las capas de ropa hasta llegar de nuevo a su herida. La observo unos momentos, esforzándome por no gemir de frustración.

—La hemorragia parece aún contenida —le digo en voz baja—. ¿Crees que si te transformas…?

Tared se lleva una mano al vientre.

—No sé cuánta sangre he perdido, y necesito bastante de ella para poder cambiar de piel —dice con una extraordinaria lucidez para su estado—. Además —hace una pausa para tomar aire—, tendrías qué sacar primero el arpón.

La idea me hace pensar las cosas mejor. Si dejamos el tubo dentro, el cambio podría ocasionar que algún órgano vital quedara dañado, pero si lo sacamos, la hemorragia lo mataría.

No. Transformarse queda completamente descartado. Tared tendrá que permanecer en su forma humana hasta que encontremos la manera de que alguien que sepa lo que hace intervenga.

Decidido a no dejarme llevar por la histeria, humedezco una de las tiras de tela con el agua que resta del termo para acercarla al lobo.

—No —dice, atrapando mi muñeca con suavidad—. Estoy bien.

Lo miro como si acabase de propinarme una bofetada.

—¿*Que estás bien?* —le digo, y grito—: ¡tienes un jodido tubo atravesándote el cuerpo de lado a lado! ¡¿Cómo CARAJOS puedes decirme que estás bien?!

Mi arrebato produce un eco agresivo en la caverna. Tared me mira, sin fuerzas, y su semblante me orilla a comprender lo que sucede.

Lo que no soporta es que lo toques...

Estrujo la tela entre mis dedos descarnados, ahora consciente de que estoy empapado de pies a cabeza en sangre que *no es mía*, que tengo reventado el labio y la cara llena de cortes de cristal afilado, con un aspecto propio de una película de terror.

—No voy a hacerte daño —es lo único que se me ocurre decirle, aun cuando sé que eso *ya no es verdad*.

Él cierra los párpados, espera unos segundos y luego... deja mi mano libre.

Me inclino hacia Tared y limpio con extremo cuidado la piel alrededor del arpón, con la barbilla bien abajo para que no vea cómo se me han cristalizado los ojos.

Tendrías que haber dejado morir a este cabrón.

Aparto los —**nuestros**— pensamientos de Wéndigo, y paso a cubrir la piel lo mejor que puedo con gasas hechas a base de las mangas de mi camiseta. Enrollo gruesos trozos de tela en la base del cuerpo del arpón, atrás y adelante, para asegurarme de que el objeto no se mueva y tampoco se enfríe demasiado; el muñeco que hice sigue bien guardado en uno de los compartimientos de la mochila, pero con semejante gravedad y sin antibióticos, una infección podría matarlo más rápido que la propia lesión, por lo que debo hacer todo lo posible por mantenerla limpia.

Una vez que termino de vendarlo con más tiras de ropa, procedo a retirar, con sumo cuidado, las esquirlas de vidrio que se abrieron paso en las sienes de Tared.

—¿Te duele mucho? —pregunto, respecto al golpe que se dio contra la ventanilla. Él, como respuesta, ladea la cabeza un poco y frunce el entrecejo.

—Tu pierna —dice, con la voz más débil que antes, lo que me hace bajar la mirada. Una gran mancha roja empapa casi la mitad de mi muslo: el rastro violento de aquella flecha de ballesta.

Estaba tan concentrado en traer a Tared a un sitio más seguro que mi propia herida me tuvo sin cuidado todo este tiempo. De hecho, la temible visión que tuve después de que cayéramos por el barranco lucha por ocupar mis pensamientos, pero soy consciente de que no es momento para cavilar en ella.

—No es nada —respondo sin darle más importancia, a pesar de que empiezo a ser consciente del dolor.

Lo ayudo a recostarse, y una vez que lo he dejado bien cubierto con otro de los abrigos de los tramperos, me pongo de pie y me dirijo hacia la salida de la cueva.

—¿Adónde vas? —pregunta, mientras yo me ajusto bien la chamarra de plumón.

—Voy a llevar la motocicleta a otra parte —respondo—. No quiero que apunte a nosotros si llegan a encontrarla.

Al mirar hacia afuera y ver que la ligera nevada empieza a convertirse en ventisca, me digo que las probabilidades de que eso suceda son bajas, pero, aun así, no pienso arriesgarme.

—Intenta dormir un poco, por favor —digo.

Creo escuchar que Tared replica o pregunta algo a mis espaldas, pero no me quedo a averiguarlo.

No puedo estar ahí un minuto más.

Salgo de la cueva y llego hasta la motocicleta, consciente de lo que tengo que hacer ahora. Pero en vez de subirme y arrancar el vehículo, clavo la mirada sobre los manubrios por largos segundos.

El peso monstruoso de la espada lucha por enterrarme contra la nieve y dejarme allí, agonizando... pero no sólo es eso lo que me lastima.

Miro debajo de mis uñas, teñidas de rojo oscuro. Observo el machete sucio, aún amarrado a la parrilla, y pienso en el hacha cubierta de costras heladas enganchada en mi cintura.

Despedacé hoy a dos hombres y a un chico a sangre fría, sin titubear. Y lo que más me perturba es que, a pesar de que aún su sangre mancha mis manos, que aún puedo escuchar el eco de sus gritos dentro de mis oídos, ni siquiera siento remordimiento.

Somos...

La nieve cubre mi espalda al encorvarla.

Yo sabía que, cada vez que me transformaba, Wéndigo se las arreglaba para ocupar un poco más de espacio en mi cabeza, aprovechándose de la vulnerabilidad de mis sentimientos. Y todo este tiempo creí que la única forma de evitar que siguiera consumiéndome sería el no recurrir de nuevo a su poder.

Pero, una vez más, estaba equivocado.

Había otras cosas, otras personas que mantenían a raya la presencia del monstruo de hueso, y perderlas fue como cortar una a una las cadenas que lo retenían en mi oscuridad. Al perder a Adam, el recuerdo de mamá Tallulah ya no fue suficiente para contener a la criatura. Y después, la forma en la que mis hermanos me miraron en Stonefall desbarató de cuajo nuestra ya de por sí frágil unión.

Y lo sentí, más que nunca, en el momento en el que decidí dejar de buscar a mi papá.

Sí. Después de todos esos desprendimientos, el vínculo con Tared era la última protección que me quedaba contra Wéndigo, porque ese lazo que compartíamos el lobo y yo, más que errante, era *humano*. Y ahora que ese amor ha dejado de ser mutuo es como si el monstruo de hueso tan sólo necesitase encontrar mis momentos más bajos, aquellos cuando me dejo dominar por mi propia maldad, para someterme con ese dolor que tanto insiste en ejercer sobre mi corazón. Y el rechazo de Tared me duele tanto que cada vez me cuesta más luchar contra ese aborrecimiento que sentí hacia él cuando decidió dejar de quererme.

Cuando me negó ese amor que yo tan desesperadamente buscaba.

Él daría lo que fuera, incluso a ti, con tal traer de vuelta a su esposa, ¿verdad?

Me quedo quieto, con la angustia buscando resbalar de mis mejillas, y respondo un "no lo sé" con una mota de vaho.

Aunque, en realidad, sí que lo sé.

Sé que Tared preferiría que esa noche en Minnesota nunca hubiese sucedido. Sé que él desearía tener a su lado a su mujer y no al monstruo con el que alguna vez intentó llenar el vacío que ella dejó.

Y sé que, ahora mismo, *lo único que yo deseo es estar muerto*.

Ríndete, dice la bestia, casi con lástima.

Ríndete y déjame vengarnos...

De pronto, percibo algo que me hace levantar la cabeza: una risa baja y siseante como el arrastrar de una serpiente, acompañada de un penetrante olor a tabaco.

Barón Samedi me observa. Recargado contra la oscuridad, aguarda.

Ya no tengo fuerzas para siquiera decirle que se largue. Tan sólo subo a la motocicleta y arranco para llevarla lejos del refugio, preguntándome qué hará el Señor del Sabbath conmigo una vez que recupere su lengua.

Me río en voz baja y, a la vez, me rompo en mil pedazos al comprender que lo único que me da fuerzas para continuar es el deseo de mantener a Tared con vida, a pesar de que él, sin importar lo que yo haga, terminará por abandonarme.

Wéndigo se llevará todo de mí. Mi personalidad, mi corazón, mis recuerdos.

Y una vez que ya no haya nada más que impida que mi cuerpo y mi voluntad se vuelvan uno con aquella bestia, ya no tendré ningún motivo más para pelear.

Estaré, finalmente, a completa merced del monstruo que habita en mi interior.

CAPÍTULO 17
RECHAZO

Un llamado bajito y suave, como el gentil piar de un ave, me hace abrir los ojos. El ruido brota de alguna parte que no logro encontrar, ya que suena como si estuviese detrás de una pared o dentro de una caja, encerrado. Instantes después, un malestar me recorre de arriba abajo al distinguir que es el llanto de un bebé. Y que, una vez más, me encuentro en el cruce de caminos.

Pero donde antes se erguía un árbol gris, ahora hay una vibrante fogata a mis pies que contrasta con el cielo.

Todo está oscuro. Sucio. En sombras. Y aunque mi otro "yo" ha desaparecido, no estoy solo aquí.

Una mujer me mira desde el otro lado del fuego. Es muy anciana, o al menos lo parece, ya que la piel oliva de sus brazos y piernas le cuelga por todos lados de forma antinatural, mientras que su cabello, largo y rizado, es lo único que cubre su completa desnudez.

La luz de la hoguera se aviva y se arroja sobre la vieja, creando un marcado claroscuro en su faz marchita. Sonríe con una boca sin dientes y de aliento a fruta podrida, pero son sus ojos lo que más rechazo me provoca. Son negros, oscuros como un pozo, pero con una diminuta flama que parece brillar dentro de ellos, roja e incandescente.

La anciana sólo está allí, mirándome, mientras un símbolo sangra en su frente, grabado a punta de cuchillo:

—¿Dónde está el niño? —pregunto, y en cuanto las palabras abandonan mi boca, el hambre me agobia con tanta intensidad que tengo que sujetarme la barriga para soportarla. La anciana ladea la cabeza, y mira mi vientre con una sonrisa obscena.

—Acércate —me dice. Tuerce el cuello y levanta su dedo índice para mostrarme una uña sucia y un trozo de cordón negro atado a su nudillo—. ¡Ven para que pueda alimentarte, querido! —exclama con una carcajada, apretándose uno de los pechos de una forma que logra ensuciar mi hambre con náuseas.

Intento retroceder, huir en dirección contraria a tan desagradable ser, pero mi voluntad parece atada a la tierra bajo mis pies.

Cuando la anciana mueve su dedo y mi cuerpo es atraído como por una cuerda hacia delante, comprendo que es ella quien me tiene aprisionado.

—O tal vez quieras comer otra cosa —dice ella, y baja la otra mano al suelo. Mete los dedos en la tierra, la remueve, sin dejar de mirarme, y empieza a sacar algo que está enterrado allí.

De haber podido, me habría llevado una mano a la boca.

Tirando de un pie, ella extrae a un bebé de la nieve y el lodo, y lo alza para mostrármelo. El cuerpecito está agusanado, la piel cetrina y el rostro deformado por la hinchazón. Y aun cuando el cuerpecito está claramente muerto, con labios y ojos cerrados, puedo escucharlo llorar.

La anciana lanza un grito y empieza a bailar de forma errática, a mover el cadáver como un pequeño costal y sacudir los pliegues colgantes de su piel. Tira de las extremidades en una cruz y le arranca trozos de carne necrosada con los dientes.

Quiero gritar. Quiero huir de semejante monstruo que mastica a placer el cuerpo de aquel niño inocente, pero no puedo moverme.

Y lo peor de todo es que, a pesar del horror, del asco… hay algo en esa mujer que me hace querer devorarla.

☾●◖○

Dejo de pensar en la horrenda visión que tuve anoche cuando, al ir en busca de la motocicleta, me encuentro con una "maravillosa" sorpresa.

La maldita no enciende. Pruebo una y otra vez, pero la máquina tan sólo me da por respuesta un sonido rumiante y tosco. No era un vehículo especial para la nieve, ¿la habrá averiado el frío?

Saco el celular de Tared y busco recepción, pero por más que doy vueltas y estiro el brazo hacia arriba, no logro encontrar más que el pitido agonizante de la batería. Miro hacia las copas de los árboles, tratando de percibir un atisbo de la carretera, pero ya no distingo la curvatura que veníamos siguiendo ayer.

Maldición. Debí haberla perdido de vista sin darme cuenta.

Me abrigo con la capucha de la chamarra y me pongo en marcha de vuelta hacia la cueva. A medio camino, al intentar dar una zancada para pasar por encima de un tronco, un pinchazo en el muslo me hace cojear.

—Demonios —siseo con los dientes apretados. Me inclino y rehago el nudo con las vendas de tela alrededor de la herida que me infligió la ballesta.

La pierna herida, el tórax molido a patadas, el labio reventado… hasta respirar es complicado sin sentir que me astillo una costilla, pero si no me detengo a quejarme demasiado

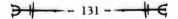

es porque el dolor me ayuda a mantenerme alerta. Ayer no dormí prácticamente nada, ya que en el breve lapso en el que logré hacerlo, aquella horrible visión me obligó a despertar. El resto del tiempo estuve atento a los ruidos del exterior, preocupado por mantener vivo el fuego de la fogata que encendí con mi escasa magia y vigilando que al hombre lobo no se le cortara la respiración.

Estoy tan cansado, y la espada me pesa tanto, que me bastaría cerrar los ojos unos segundos para caer dormido. Pero no. No puedo rendirme.

Tared me necesita.

Me doy unas palmadas en la mejilla para despabilarme.

—Vamos, Elisse —me animo—. De peores has salido, carajo.

Llego a la caverna y me abro paso en silencio a través de la nieve que se ha acumulado en la entrada, ya que Tared todavía no ha despertado.

Voy hacia las cenizas de la fogata aún calientes y levanto el termo lleno de nieve que dejé sobre ellas, para luego inclinarme hacia el hombre lobo. Con cuidado, levanto sus ropas para revisar de nuevo su herida.

Me detengo al percibir un olor desagradable, como de carne podrida.

Con el corazón en vilo, retiro las vendas alrededor del arpón tan sólo para descubrir que la piel, aunque un tanto seca, está limpia. El alivio que siento es inmenso, pero, aun así, ladeo la cabeza, consternado, porque el olor a carroña debe provenir de alguna parte. No es de un espíritu del plano medio, podría distinguirlo de inmediato, ¿o habrá algún animal muerto en la caverna?

Me masajeo los párpados con los pulgares cuando las formas y las ideas pierden nitidez delante de mí. Sacudo la cabeza y coloco el termo cerca de la laceración para conferirle algo de calor; tengo entendido que el frío y la sequedad son muy malos para las heridas, pero mientras no tenga un sitio más apropiado dónde atender al devorapieles, no puedo hacer mucho más.

Vuelvo a cubrir el vientre del lobo con lo que queda de mi camiseta, para luego llevar una mano hacia su frente. Está pálido, pero al menos no hay fiebre y eso es buena señal. Me levanto y voy hacia nuestra mochila para sacar la bolsa con las tiras de carne seca. El hambre empieza a punzar con fuerza en mi estómago y estoy seguro de que también en el de Tared. No hemos comido nada desde la madrugada de ayer, después de todo.

—Elisse...

Me sobresalto, no al escuchar la voz del lobo, sino al verlo tratar de sentarse por sí solo sobre el improvisado colchón.

—¡Tared, no! —me arrodillo junto a él con las manos alrededor del filo amenazador de la varilla. Tiene un semblante terrible, como si hubiese dormido tan poco como yo.

—Estoy bien —dice con la voz más grave de lo normal, cosa que no me deja muy convencido—. ¿Qué pasó con el vehículo?

El vacío en mi estómago se intensifica, pero en estas circunstancias no me sirve de nada endulzar las cosas.

—No pude echarlo a andar —contesto, cabizbajo—. Ya no sé muy bien hacia dónde queda la carretera y no creo poder ubicarnos hacia el este hasta que sea de noche y vea las estrellas... aunque dudo que las nubes de la nevada me permitan hacer eso.

Tared mira a la entrada de la cueva, como si intentase procesar algo en su cabeza. Observa la nieve, los rastros de ceniza de la fogata, y una vez más percibo esa expresión vacía y desolada en su mirada, ese cascarón en el que parece transformarse cada vez que está cerca de mí.

—No tardarán en encontrarnos —dice en voz baja—. Es mejor que te vayas.

Sus palabras me duelen más que la flecha que intentó destrozarme la pierna. Me inclino hacia él y siento la tensión subir por su brazo cuando mi cabello sucio y enmarañado lo roza.

—¿Que me vaya? —susurro—, ¿quieres que me largue y te abandone aquí?

Él no responde. Es más, ni siquiera es capaz de mirarme a la cara.

Tenso la mandíbula y, otra vez siento a la bestia del odio asomarse, porque es como si Tared metiese a propósito el dedo en la llaga de nuestro vínculo destrozado.

—No crees que sea capaz de salvarte, ¿verdad? —pregunto con rabia—. ¿O tan malo sería para ti darte cuenta de que no soy tan terrible como piensas?

Él entorna los ojos y ladea la cabeza, su expresión lacerada por el dolor de su herida.

—Elisse...

Arrojo el paquete de carne al suelo y me levanto, sin ganas de escucharlo más. Asegurándome de traer la pistola de Lía bien sujeta en la cintura, salgo de la cueva a zancadas.

Y él, como ya me lo esperaba, no hace nada para detenerme.

Empiezo a ver todo rojo conforme atravieso el bosque nevado. En un parpadeo, recorro más de un kilómetro, a punto de reventar de coraje. Bien podría caminar otro más de no ser porque la tierra de pronto se desmorona bajo mis pies.

—¡Mierda!

Caigo de sentón, aferrándome a la maleza congelada para no resbalar más. El camino errático me ha llevado al filo de una cañada que, aunque es poco profunda, por su fondo corre un río congelado de al menos diez metros de ancho.

Estoy a punto de levantarme cuando veo algo en el barranco que me hace entrecerrar la mirada. ¿Es eso un... sendero de piedra?

Parpadeo para asegurarme de que no alucino por el cansancio, pero luego mi corazón da un salto al darme cuenta de que no es un sendero, sino los rastros de una rústica cañería pluvial.

—¡Por los Loas! —grito, recuperando el aliento. Si hay un acueducto conectado al río, significa que debe haber una construcción cerca que se alimenta de esa agua.

Me deslizo por la inclinada pendiente hasta llegar a la orilla del caudal. La cañería está del otro lado del río, por lo que miro unos momentos la superficie de hielo antes de poner un pie encima. La corriente se mueve con rapidez debajo de ella, en señal de que tiene poco tiempo de haber comenzado a congelarse, pero parece lo bastante resistente para aguantar mi peso.

Paso a paso, empiezo a cruzar con cuidado. Escucho los sonidos caudalosos del agua y el cristal crujir a mis pies, pero no lo suficiente como para resquebrajarse.

Al llegar al otro lado, me detengo un momento en la orilla para tomar aire.

A media exhalación, desenfundo la pistola de golpe al escuchar un ruido a mis espaldas. Apunto hacia atrás, al río, y perfilo el lugar con la boquilla. Después de unos momentos de tensa quietud, bajo el arma, desorientado, porque parecía el sonido de algo... ¿ahogándose?

Pero bien pudo haber sido sólo el chapoteo del río. O mi paranoia.

Con la anciana de mi visión presente en mis pensamientos, comienzo a seguir el trayecto de la cañería a través del bosque casi un kilómetro más, hasta que ésta me lleva, efectivamente, a una pequeña cabaña construida de troncos y piedras, oculta entre los árboles y muy cerca del pie de una de las montañas.

Las estrechas ventanas cubiertas por tablones y el camino tapizado de nieve me hacen saber que tiene tiempo sin ser utilizada, pero abandonada o no, el alma me vuelve al cuerpo al saber que por fin he encontrado un sitio para ponernos a salvo.

Avanzo un poco más hacia la choza, pero estando a escasos metros de ella, me veo obligado a recargar el hombro contra un árbol. Me siento mareado, invadido por un súbito calor. Me llevo una mano a la pierna, cuya franja ha empezado a quemarme al igual que el resto de mis heridas.

Quiero caer rendido al suelo. La espada me pesa, el estómago me duele por el hambre y la presión en mi pecho no hace más que empeorar. Pero yo sé que todo este malestar no es sólo por eso.

¿Qué carajos esperaba que hiciera Tared hace rato ante mi arranque de enojo? ¿Que por un milagro de los dioses se levantara y corriese detrás de mí con el jodido arpón en el vientre, si apenas tiene fuerzas para hablar? No. Él no podía detenerme ni consolarme como yo hubiese querido, y yo ya tenía bien claro desde hacía mucho que ni antes ni ahora era su obligación hacerlo. Pero...

—No es justo —susurro con una mezcla de rabia y tristeza, porque en el fondo, quiero creer que no merezco nada de esto. Que no merezco que Tared haya dejado de quererme.

Pero *lo hizo*. Y aun así...

Vas a morir por él.

Cuando el dolor ya no es suficiente para mantenerme despierto y todo empieza a dar vueltas sin parar, me doy cuenta de que no me estoy quedando dormido. Me estoy desmayando.

Me derrumbo boca arriba sobre la nieve. Sin poder más, cierro los ojos y me dejo tragar por la inconsciencia con un único pensamiento en la cabeza.

No es justo.

No es justo.

No es justo.

No...

—No. No lo es, Elisse.

Abro los ojos de par en par al escuchar aquella voz. Y mi impresión al reconocerla es tan grande que, aun dentro del sueño en el que he caído, intento levantarme de golpe.

Pero no puedo lograrlo porque *hay un hombre encima de mí*.

El vínculo muerto pulsa y grita desde su tumba. Y al cruzar mi mirada con la suya, *Adam* sonríe y pronuncia mi nombre.

—Hola, Elisse.

CAPÍTULO 18
UN REEMPLAZO OPORTUNO

En un instante, me doy cuenta de que estoy otra vez dentro de mi visión. Acostado sobre las cenizas calientes de la hoguera ahora apagada, sobre el cruce de caminos. No está aquella mujer terrible y tampoco escucho ya los llantos de su víctima.

Pero nada de eso me interesa.

Porque es *él*.

Sus ojos dorados. Su cabello. Su piel. Su irritante forma de torcer los labios para sonreír.

—¡ADAM!

Sin pensarlo, sin titubear, echo los brazos alrededor de su cuello y lo atraigo con fuerza hacia mí. Él me devuelve el gesto, mientras la emoción me cierra la garganta hasta dejarme sin aliento.

—¡Adam, Adam! ¡Eres tú…! —susurro una y otra vez con los ojos bien abiertos, el temor latente de que, de cerrarlos, él se fundirá con la oscuridad. Entierro mis dedos en su cabello, lo apretujo hasta asfixiar el aire entre nosotros, pero no siento su corazón latir contra mi pecho desnudo, ni tampoco percibo el calor de su cuerpo sobre el mío.

El Adam que tengo encima *no está vivo*, pero no me importa, no me importa que éste sea sólo un encuentro imaginario.

Sólo me importa tenerlo aquí, verlo, estrecharlo con todas mis fuerzas como no pude hacerlo mientras vivía.

Él, con paciencia, acaricia mis cabellos, despacio, esperando a que me tranquilice. Y cuando por fin logro sacar mi aliento de sus clavículas, me toma de la espalda, como si pesara menos que una pluma, y me levanta de las cenizas para ponerme de pie. Me quedo frente a él con mis dedos enterrados en sus brazos, y el tiempo en el que nos miramos se vuelve tan largo que un repentino pudor me hace reaccionar.

Me cierro la reveladora túnica a la altura del pecho.

—¡Oye! Estaba disfrutando del espectáculo —dice con una sonrisa.

Por unos instantes considero insultarlo, pero en cambio, me río con ganas, porque es justo algo que él diría en un momento así. Me abraza y me atrae hacia él, quizá para protegerme del frío. Su tacto es igual de helado, sin vida, pero tan maravilloso que ni siquiera me importa.

—Dioses, nunca vas a dejar de ser un imbécil, ¿verdad? —digo con el alivio que sólo puede sentir una persona que lleva demasiado tiempo sin sonreír.

Adam se encoge de hombros.

—Ni siquiera muerto.

Sus palabras esfuman toda la alegría de golpe. Miro de nuevo el cruce de caminos e intento encontrar algo que pueda amenazarnos en la oscuridad del bosque nevado.

—¿Cómo llegaste hasta aquí? —pregunto, aún sin saber si estamos atrapados en una visión, un sueño, o si mi alma se ha perdido en algún punto del plano medio.

—Alguien tenía que venir a consolarte —responde—. Se escuchaban tus berridos hasta acá.

—Idiota, ¡si verte fue lo que casi me hizo llorar!

—Lo sé, soy tan hermoso que hasta parezco un milagro, ¿verdad?

Sacudo la cabeza, resignado de que Adam sea el tonto de siempre. Lleva la misma ropa de dormir que el último día que lo vi con vida, pero está intacto, sin heridas, sin sangre.

—¿Eres... un espíritu? —pregunto con confusión, porque de ser así, debería llevar en el cuerpo las mismas marcas que lo traumatizaron durante su muerte.

—¿Acaso eso importa? —responde encogiéndose de hombros. Lo pienso unos instantes y bajo la mirada al suelo.

—Sí —contesto con un nudo en la garganta—. Porque me moriré de tristeza si sé que esto es algún bardo del plano medio, y que te has quedado aquí atrapado, pudriéndote.

Un desfile de todas las criaturas espantosas que he visto a lo largo de mi vida llega a mi memoria, seres deformados por el peso de este mundo vacío y rencoroso. Y la idea de que Adam pueda llegar a convertirse en algo así es...

Al ver mi angustia, él ladea la cabeza.

—Digamos que soy la manifestación de tus deseos más profundos —dice, convencido—. De la frustración que, en estos momentos, te resulta más dolorosa.

Frunzo el ceño, desconcertado.

—Entonces, ¿no eres Adam?

Al percibir el atisbo de cautela en mi voz, se encorva lo suficiente para rozar mi frente con la suya.

—Te lo voy a explicar así —susurra—: ¿recuerdas cómo fui tu refugio cuando más solo te sentías? ¿Cómo, entre tú y yo, volvimos a construir esa humanidad que pensamos que ambos habíamos perdido?

Pienso unos instantes en el efímero paraíso que vivimos en aquella casa terrible. En esa calidez que hacía tanto no podía sentir, y que Adam me brindó con su sola presencia.

—Estuviste allí cuando no había nada más para mí —susurro, aferrando mis manos a sus hombros. Él asiente, satisfecho.

—Exactamente. Y es por eso que he vuelto, Elisse.

La pena se apodera de mí al pensar que, a pesar de la dulzura de sus palabras, esto no es más que un desesperado deseo de encontrar algo de consuelo.

Una ilusión. Una mentira de mi cabeza. Eso es lo que tengo frente a mí ahora y me resulta tan cruel que tal vez hubiese preferido no ver nada.

—Te extraño, Adam, como no tienes una maldita idea. Pero tan sólo quiero salir de aquí —suplico cargado de dolor.

Como si atendiera a mis plegarias, Adam me recuesta de nuevo entre las cenizas. El desasosiego, la desolación, la penitencia, el hambre que ruge dentro de mí; todo vuelve a adormecerme cuando se inclina, acerca sus labios a los míos, y susurra:

—Es hora de despertar…

Momentos después, abro los ojos de nuevo, para encontrarme de vuelta en el mundo humano, acostado en la nieve y a unos metros de la cabaña.

Pero no estoy solo.

Sus manos aún sostienen mi cuerpo. Sus ojos dorados todavía me miran fijamente. Y ahora su corazón late delante de mí.

Adam me ha seguido al mundo de los humanos.

Y está vivo.

CAPÍTULO 19
SALVADOR

—¿Ves? Te dije que no te dejaría solo. Me arrastro sobre mis codos al sentir su aliento cálido sobre mis mejillas. Y sólo cuando mi espalda se estrella contra uno de los árboles, mi lengua se desenreda.

—I-Imposible... —susurro, sin concebir lo que está sucediendo. Adam estaba *muerto*. ¿Cómo diablos...?

El chico se levanta y camina hacia mí. Sus pies se hunden en la nieve y dejan huellas visibles a su paso.

—¿Qué forma de recibirme es ésa? —dice empujando su índice contra mi frente. Su tacto es tibio. Real.

—N-no, no puede ser —balbuceo sin salir de la impresión—. ¿A-Adam? ¿P-pero, cómo? No, no, ¡el abuelo Muata dijo que los muertos no...!

Él se rasca la cabeza.

—Yo tampoco lo entiendo —admite él—, aunque tal vez ese hombre que mencionas siempre subestimó el alcance de tu magia, porque, ¿quién dice que no soy uno de esos tantos milagros que has podido hacer hasta ahora?

Las palabras se hielan en mi garganta. Adam se pone de pie y me tiende una mano que me aterra alcanzar.

No está muerto. No es un espíritu del plano medio que ha venido a atormentarme. ¿Estoy alucinando? ¿Esto es un maldito sueño surrealista? ¿Realmente *es él*?

—¿Yo… te traje de vuelta? —pregunto, pero antes de que *¿Adam?* pueda contestar, bajo la mirada hacia el suelo, y frunzo el ceño al no encontrar en mí la respuesta a la pregunta más importante de todas—: ¿Por qué?

Al ver que no tomo su mano, Adam se pone en cuclillas. La presión bajo mi esternón se vuelve terrible, tanto que siento que en cualquier momento detendrá los latidos de mi corazón.

Me llevo la mano al pecho. ¿La espada habrá tenido algo qué ver?

—Ya te lo dije —responde—. Estoy aquí porque me necesitabas. Porque te habías quedado solo otra vez y no estaba dispuesto a seguir viendo cómo sufrías.

Adam toma mi mano humana, temblorosa, y me quita el guante con cuidado. La coloca sobre su cuello y mi corazón da un salto al sentir el latido de la vena debajo de mis dedos.

No. No estoy alucinando.

—No puedo creerlo —murmuro—. Por los dioses, ¡Adam!

Me lanzo a abrazarlo de nuevo, con tanto impulso que lo tiro de espaldas contra la nieve. Sus cabellos oscuros se enredan entre mis dedos y mis lágrimas de desesperación e incredulidad empapan realmente sus mejillas. Adam acaricia mi espalda de arriba abajo, y espera a que me recupere de la conmoción.

Después de tanto tiempo, *él* por fin me hace sentir algo distinto al rechazo, y no me importa si lo que ha traído a este hombre de vuelta ha sido mi magia, o la espada maldita, porque ha ocurrido justo cuando lo necesitaba.

Una vez que logro dejar de gimotear, Adam se ríe por lo bajo e incluso me tiende el cuello de su camiseta para enjugar mis lágrimas, el cual rechazo con un manotazo y una risa de histérica alegría.

Me toma de ambos brazos y me ayuda a ponerme de pie. Sigo tan asombrado que ni siquiera me afecta el dolor en mi pierna al hundirla en la nieve.

—Ven. Es el momento de terminar con todo esto —dice, poniéndome el brazo alrededor de los hombros a pesar de que él es quien sólo trae ese delgado pijama—. Vamos a buscar la carretera.

Como si su tacto me hubiese producido una descarga eléctrica, salgo de golpe de mi ensoñación. Dioses, ¡*la carretera*!

—¡No, no espera! —exclamo—. No podemos irnos, ¡tengo que regresar por Tared!

Lo empujo en dirección opuesta a la cabaña, hacia el camino que he seguido desde la cañería pluvial. Pero en vez de hacerme caso, él se planta en la nieve, consternado.

—¿De qué estás hablando?

—¡Él está en una cueva, cerca de aquí! —grito en respuesta—, por favor, si me ayudas, lo traeremos mucho más rápido, ¡Tared es...!

—Sé perfectamente quién es. Y, por lo mismo, no entiendo por qué quieres volver por él.

Me quedo de piedra en mi lugar, con mis manos hechas puños sobre su pecho.

—¿Adam? —musito, y su expresión pierde todo rastro de calidez.

—Te lo dije. Estoy de vuelta porque *me necesitas* —dice, tenso—. Soy la manifestación de la más profunda de tus desesperaciones y eso significa que también sé por qué estás así. O *por culpa de quién.*

Un atisbo de vergüenza me hace bajar la mirada de sólo pensar en que Adam haya visto cómo, de la manera más humillante, he sido repudiado una y otra vez por un hombre al que estoy desesperado por complacer.

—Sólo quiero sacarlo de aquí —murmuro—. Sólo quiero otra oportunidad. Tal vez él me perdone y...

Adam ladea la cabeza.

—¿Qué te perdone por qué, Elisse? —masculla con la mandíbula tensa—. ¿Porque has hecho todo lo posible para protegerlo a él y a tu familia? ¿Porque has hecho lo que creías que era correcto?

El chico atrapa mi muñeca con fuerza y empieza a tirar de mí hacia el bosque, en dirección contraria a la cañería. A la montaña.

—¡No, Adam, escúchame! —le pido, pero él tira aún con más fuerza.

—No voy a permitir que te siga haciendo daño —exclama—, ¡entiéndelo, Elisse, él fue un desgraciado contigo *y ya no te ama!*

—¡BASTA!

Me zafo de su agarre y retrocedo a zancadas. Él se queda inmóvil unos segundos, desconcertado, y luego baja la mirada.

Deja escapar un suspiro de resignación.

—Creí que también *me querías*, Elisse —dice en voz queda.

Entorno la mirada, sin comprender.

—¿Qué diablos estás diciendo?

Adam tarda unos angustiantes momentos en levantar la cabeza y responder:

—Creí que, si mi madre no me hubiera asesinado, me habrías amado de la misma manera que a él. Pero ya veo que nunca me habrías dado una oportunidad, ¿cierto?

Por unos segundos, creo haber escuchado mal, así que me quedo quieto, esperando a que él me diga que todo es una maldita broma. Pero en cambio, Adam se acerca de nuevo a mí. Se para cuan alto es y me acaricia los hombros, me acomoda el cabello detrás de las orejas. Y esta vez, su roce me provoca tanto terror que me quedo paralizado.

—Elisse... —susurra y luego levanta mi barbilla para besarme, pero giro la cabeza, sin permitírselo.

Él baja las manos y da un paso atrás.

—Entonces, ¿vas a darme la espalda de nuevo? ¿Vas a dejarme solo una vez más?

Sus palabras me duelen como si a mí también me hubiera atravesado un arpón. Tiemblo con tanta fuerza que bastaría que me tocase de nuevo para derrumbarme.

Adam suspira ante mi silencio.

—¿Cómo puedes cargar con la culpa, Elisse? —dice, mirándose las manos—. ¿Cómo puedes despertar todos los días, vivir siquiera, sin que el fantasma de todo lo que has hecho te atormente?

No puedo comprender, ni por un momento, de dónde ha sacado tan repentina crueldad. Su mentón y sus puños se tensan, el brillo dorado de su mirada se tiñe de dolor.

—Cada vez que tenía que acostarme con mujeres desconocidas y revivir en sus cuerpos las cosas que *ella* me hacía desde que era un niño, simplemente quería ahorcarme en algún balcón de la casa —dice—. Saltar de la catarata y ahogarme contra las piedras. Pero nunca tuve el valor de hacerlo, a pesar de que nada podía ser peor que sus manos sobre mi cuerpo o las de esas mujeres a las que me había obligado a seducir. Y sólo pude encontrar la paz hasta que yo mismo corté la cabeza de mi madre, aquella noche en Stonefall.

Levanta la mirada hacia mí y ya no veo más sol. Sólo un fuego terrible.

—Pero tú, Elisse, ¿dónde vas a encontrar el descanso? ¿Cómo vas a expiar tus pecados, si no hay nada en este mundo que sea capaz de levantar el peso que llevas a tus espaldas?

—Adam... —susurro, encajado sobre la nieve. Él se acerca de nuevo, alza el brazo y me acaricia los labios con la yema de su dedo.

Y esta vez, su piel se siente como el hielo.

—No podemos seguir así, a sabiendas que arrancamos la vida de otros con nuestras manos, con nuestro estómago —dice y me toca el vientre sobre la ropa. Luego, juega con la pretina de mi pantalón, hasta meter su mano—. Si regresas a esa cueva, lo único que lograrás será agrandar más ese sufrimiento, ¿no estás ya harto de sufrir?

Adam saca la pistola de Lía y la deja en mi mano. Miro el arma muy apenas, delante de mis ojos nublados por el dolor.

—¿Por qué me haces esto? —pregunto con la voz rota.

—Porque la única forma en la que yo pude dejar de sufrir fue rindiéndome —me dice con voz condescendiente—. Y yo ya no quiero verte sufrir más, Elisse.

Miro la pistola y pienso en qué es lo que me espera en la cueva. Tal vez logre salvar a Tared, pero y luego ¿qué?, ¿a dónde iré después? ¿A buscar a mi Mara?, ¿y para qué, si después ya no habrá nada más? ¿Realmente vale la pena seguir si, a fin de cuentas, voy a sucumbir al monstruo de hueso?

Sí. Tared es un hombre fuerte, siempre lo ha sido. Tal vez no me necesita para salir de ésta. Tal vez llegó el momento de rendirme también.

Dejo de pensar en el lobo cuando Adam me sonríe con esos ojos que han vuelto a llenarse de luz. Pero basta que roce mi mejilla para saber que el tacto de su piel me duele más que las consecuencias de usar el arma que tengo entre manos.

Creí que lo que habíamos forjado él y yo era real, que Adam me quería de verdad. Nunca pensé que me empujaría a hacerme daño, ni que me tocaría sin mi consentimiento. Nunca creí que él...

No.

Adam nunca me lastimaría.

Adam nunca me haría lo mismo que le hizo su madre.

...la nieve nunca es tan blanca, ¿verdad?

La voz de Wéndigo, apenas un susurro de burla, me hace dar un paso atrás.

Miro hacia Adam, hacia sus ojos de sol, el pulso de sus venas y la fuerza de sus manos. No puedo percibir su olor como lo haría con el de un errante porque no es más que una esencia plana y gris, como cualquier otro humano... pero *detrás de él* sí que puedo percibir algo más.

Flores. Un aroma a flores balanceándose en el viento, tan tenue que casi pasa desapercibido.

Sigo el origen del aroma, detrás del hombro de Adam. Y allí, sobre la nieve, por fin la veo: una raíz extraña, torcida debajo del manto como una serpiente blanca que se alarga desde detrás del chico.

Esa raíz crece, palpita, se engrosa y se levanta como una liana hasta las ramas de uno de los árboles del bosque.

Y entonces, caigo en la cuenta de que no es una raíz.

Es un brazo.

CAPÍTULO 20
NADAAZAN

Al principio, me cuesta mucho *entender* su apariencia. Porque *ella*, como si estuviese hecha de la misma pesadilla que el "yo" de mis visiones, tiene la piel de color blanco, pero de un blanco sucio y cruzado de venas azules, lo que la mimetiza a la perfección con la nieve y la maleza seca en la que se esconde. Su cuerpo es muy alto y famélico, y debajo de la línea de la cadera viste una piel *humana* que se amarra de la cintura, lo que deja sus pechos al descubierto. Múltiples brazos brotan de su espalda y sostienen rostros también humanos, como si fuesen máscaras adheridas a sus palmas, máscaras *vivas*, porque parpadean, mueven los ojos con iris dorados y sueltan bocanadas de aire caliente; caras pálidas y mudas marcadas por un gesto de angustia infinita.

Diría que aquel monstruo se asemeja a un Buda de mil brazos, pero hay algo en la disposición casi armoniosa de esas extremidades, en el movimiento de las mismas, que me recuerda a *otra cosa*, aunque no logro describir a qué.

No obstante, lo más inquietante es su cabeza. Lleva una máscara de un metal muy extraño, de color blanco marmoleado, cincelado como si fuese el rostro de una persona hermosa y andrógina. Su boca es el único orificio abierto y sangra desde las comisuras hasta el cuello, mientras que detrás de su nuca una especie de disco de hueso sobresale como si fuese una lápida.

Apenas puedo respirar, pero eso me basta para percibir su intenso aroma a flores.

—No temas. ¿Por qué estás tan asustado?

Me llevo una mano a los labios cuando Adam ladea la cabeza al decir aquello, porque me permite ver cómo el brazo grotesco que yace insertado en su nuca lo manipula como a un títere de carne.

Una *Marionetista*. Eso es lo que es, y el Adam que intentó hacer que me volara la cabeza no es más que uno de los rostros en las palmas de sus manos.

Levanto la pistola, pero estoy tan aterido que no puedo presionar el gatillo. En cambio, retrocedo a trompicones, el terror sube como una infección por todo mi cuerpo a medida que esa cosa comienza a levantar al chico sobre la nieve. Sus ojos de sol se apagan, sus extremidades se aflojan y cuelgan de sus costados como un cadáver flotante.

Me estrello de golpe contra la puerta de aquella cabaña. La marioneta de Adam se inclina hacia mí y abre su boca, tan grande, tan redonda que su cara se deforma de manera espantosa.

—*Criatura que viste de cordero, pero que habla como un dragón* —dice una voz que sale de allí dentro como un eco, muy distinta a la de Adam Blake—, *Bestia Revestida de Luna*.

Suelto un gemido y el arma se me escapa de las manos. Me cubro los ojos y hago lo único para lo que me alcanzan las fuerzas: grito. Una y otra vez hasta quedarme afónico.

Y detrás de la negrura de aquella boca creo escuchar el sonido de una trompeta.

—*Tu brillo llena este mundo de oscuridad* —dice aquel ser, una vez más. Lo siento inclinarse sobre mí, su boca abrirse más y más para engullirme como una serpiente, mientras que el aliento que brota de aquel abismo es igual al de miles de flores.

Y entonces...

Abro los ojos, temblando, y me encuentro completamente solo, empapado en sudor contra la puerta de la cabaña. El sonido de la trompeta se ha esfumado junto con el aroma del perfume, y el cielo se torna rosado.

No existe rastro de Adam, y en el bosque ya no se escucha la voz de aquel ser de pesadilla. Tan sólo se oyen, una vez más, los gritos de mi psicosis.

CAPÍTULO 21
CEGUERA

Después de que sellásemos nuestros pactos, cada una de las tres magias me otorgó un juramento.

Un vínculo que nos uniría a ellas y a mí en el más íntimo de los dolores, asegurándome que, gracias a eso, jamás podrían traicionarme.

El Señor del Sabbath me ofreció destrozar su propia lengua si alguna vez él la usaba para pronunciar mi nombre.

El trotapieles del desierto me entregó su columna, la cual amarré a la mía y rompí una y otra vez, arqueándome en mi celda con tal de obligarlo a cumplir su cometido.

Y hace diecinueve años, el tercer manipulador me hizo únicamente una promesa: sus criaturas jamás atentarían contra mi vida, pero sólo si a cambio les ofrecía dos cosas: un sacrificio… y un *Inquisidor*. Un hombre capaz de continuar el legado de hierro que estos seres había comenzado hace casi quinientos años.

Y yo acepté. Acepté porque estaba dispuesta a todo con tal de encontrarme de nuevo con mi hijo, con la fuerza de la naturaleza que yo misma había parido.

Y ahora, gracias a esa promesa, veo al Inquisidor caminar bajo el cielo purpúreo, con la mirada fija en el suelo. Da vueltas alrededor del vehículo enterrado de frente contra el suelo, en busca de un rastro aunque las huellas ya han sido cubiertas por la nieve.

Se detiene. Trepa sobre un tronco partido, y observa el trozo de arpón clavado en el asiento de la camioneta, así como la sangre que ha marcado un sendero hacia afuera. La toca, la lleva a sus dedos y la prueba. Se sonríe al pensar en que podría beberse una copa entera.

Mira hacia el cúmulo de árboles que rodean la camioneta y aprieta el puño al ver las siluetas de dos hombres que deambulan de un lado a otro como sabuesos.

—¡Tío Benjamin! —escucha que lo llaman a sus espaldas, pero él no responde. Tan sólo percibe por el rabillo del ojo cómo un chico se acerca a sus espaldas—. Encontramos dos de las motos, pero no responden a las radios y tampoco podemos encontrarlos por ninguna parte. Mi padre dice que se aproxima otra tormenta, y que, si no volvemos a las camionetas ahora, no podremos subir de nuevo la montaña y...

El trampero ni siquiera escucha la mitad de lo que ha dicho el joven, porque algo en la lejanía le hace entrecerrar la mirada: un hombre grande y fornido, que lo observa fijamente a varios metros, lejos de su gente.

La silueta difusa da la vuelta y se va en dirección a las profundidades del bosque, alejándose del tumulto, y un tirón frío impulsa el corazón del Inquisidor al reconocer la chamarra de cacería que lleva puesta.

—¡T-tío! —exclama el muchacho al ver que el viejo baja de un salto del tronco. Sus rodillas crujen al igual que sus dientes, pero el Inquisidor aparta de un agresivo manotazo al chico y va detrás de aquella figura.

Todos sus hombres levantan la cabeza hacia él. Lo llaman, pero no escucha sus bramidos y ellos lo dejan hacer, temerosos de ser apaleados si se atreven a detenerlo.

El Inquisidor fuerza las piernas envejecidas a apartar la nieve bajo sus pies, a resistir el soplo feroz del invierno. Su corazón late más rápido cuando aquel hombre mira sobre su hombro apenas un segundo, lo suficiente para que Benjamin pueda distinguir su perfil, sus ojos azules y su nariz torcida de tantas veces que él mismo se la rompió siendo un niño.

Ya no le cabe ninguna duda. Aquél no es otro que su hijo, Buck Lander.

Su raciocinio le dice que está alucinando, pero su instinto de cazador le exige que no se detenga, que, si aquello no es su hijo, quizá sea una ilusión del monstruo que lo devoró.

De pronto, se detiene en un derrumbe de la montaña; una pared de rocas y bosque que su gente escrutó horas atrás sin encontrar más que un gorro de lana clavado en una roca con la flecha de una de sus ballestas. Nada de sangre, ningún rastro de los tres hombres perdidos.

Su hijo está al pie de la ladera, con la mirada hacia el suelo. Se acuclilla en la nieve y comienza a remover algo con las manos. El viejo trampero se acerca despacio, parpadea, y Buck Lander ya no está delante de él. No hay huellas en la nieve, pero lo que sí hay es el rastro de un penetrante perfume a flores y una amplia cruz marcada en el suelo.

Benjamin exhala como un toro y se agacha hacia el símbolo. Con las manos desnudas comienza a escarbar hasta que encuentra un bulto pequeño, sanguinolento y congelado, a unos treinta centímetros en lo profundo, casi al ras del suelo del bosque.

Reconoce de inmediato lo que es: una bolsa de lona, de ésas donde sus hombres suelen guardar las municiones. Despacio, libera el cierre y se asoma. Siente un arrebato de furia al descubrir tres ojos humanos, distintos entre sí, metidos dentro de la bolsa y acompañados de cabellos, trozos de tela y cartuchos de bala, un artilugio tan ingenioso que casi es una pena ver cómo el hechizo se rompe.

El susurro inteligible de su hijo le hace levantar la barbilla y sacar la pistola que lleva en la cintura. Mira de un lado a otro y sus ojos se abren de par en par cuando el sonido lo hace apuntar hacia unos troncos apilados a apenas unos metros de él.

Y, por fin, Benjamin Lander los encuentra, como si siempre hubiesen estado allí, como si algo sobrenatural los hubiese ocultado a la vista todo este tiempo: unos dedos escarlatas que sobresalen de entre la nieve.

CAPÍTULO 22
UNA ÚLTIMA MOTIVACIÓN

Camino durante más de una hora hasta que encuentro la manta de camuflaje, aún enganchada en la entrada de la cueva.

Aunque la luz lavanda de la noche me deja ver con algo de claridad el camino, lo que realmente me ha permitido volver al refugio sin perderme han sido las copas de los árboles; a diferencia de los rastros o las huellas en el suelo, las copas nunca cambian, y en bosques muy frondosos es más fiable seguir un sendero de follaje y estrellas que un manto de nieve informe.

¿Quién me enseñó eso? ¿Fueron los campistas que conocí en Colorado? ¿O aquella anciana del rancho de Nuevo México? No. Ella vivía en una pradera, no había forma de que ella y...

Ah. Es verdad.

Fue Tared. Una noche en el pantano.

Justo cuando creí que pensar en estas tonterías me salvaría de hundirme de nuevo en la histeria, me dejo caer contra un tronco, a unos pasos de la gruta. Entierro las garras en la corteza y suplico, con todas mis fuerzas, que el monstruo de hueso estruje mi pecho para al menos poder sentir otro tipo de desesperación.

—Maldito, maldito seas... —mascullo, aguantando la impotencia. Yo creí que, con todo lo que ha pasado, mi Mara ya no podría lastimarme más, pero se las ha ingeniado para torturarme de la forma más terrible. Es decir, ¿qué puede ser más doloroso que la imagen de alguien a quien amas *haciéndote daño*?

"Soy la manifestación de tus deseos más profundos. De la frustración que, en estos momentos, te resulta más dolorosa."

—No te lo perdonaré —susurro a mi verdugo, si es que puede escucharme—. Nunca te perdonaré que lo hayas usado *a él* para atormentarme.

Y encima, para pisotear aún más mi corazón roto.

~~Te arrancaré la piel~~...

—Los ojos y la lengua —musito con los dientes apretados, rasgando la corteza del árbol como si fuese la misma carne de mi Mara.

~~Y luego~~...

—Te *devoraré* hasta quedarme con todos y cada uno de tus poderes...

El monstruo de hueso enmudece, dejándome con un silencio difícil de soportar. Sacudo la cabeza y me yergo lentamente.

Hundido entre la convalecencia y mis deseos de venganza, me tambaleo hacia la entrada de la cueva. Me cuesta mucho trabajo abrirme camino; la nieve se ha hecho tan espesa que me llega casi a las rodillas, y cada zancada me duele más que la anterior. Pero cuando paso por debajo de la manta, basta que respire una sola vez para percibir un olor que me hace mandar todo eso al diablo.

Sangre.

—¡¿Tared?!

El hombre lobo está recostado en el suelo, con las chamarras de los tramperos echadas a un lado. No reacciona ante mi llegada ni a mi llamado.

—¡TARED! —grito de nuevo, lanzándome de rodillas a su lado. Me quito el guante de mi mano humana y compruebo el pulso de su cuello, que está muy débil. Llamo al devorapieles varias veces, hasta que éste me contesta con un ligero gruñido.

Salto hacia la fogata ya reducida a cenizas, y la reanimo con mi magia. El fuego ilumina la figura del hombre lobo y a mí se me cae el corazón al suelo.

Está sumamente pálido, y al intentar moverse, masculla de dolor. Abro su chamarra, y descubro una senda mancha roja impregnada en todo su abdomen.

El hechizo ha terminado. Su herida ha vuelto a sangrar.

—Tared, ¡por los dioses...! —levanto las capas de ropa y mis dedos se tiñen al desenrollar los nidos de tela que puse en el perímetro del arpón—. ¿En qué momento empezó?

Él está tan débil que no puede responder.

Dioses, dioses, ¿fue mientras buscaba la cabaña, o mientras estaba desmayado por el agotamiento?

¡Estúpido, estúpido!

Voy hacia la mochila y saco el muñeco de trapo que formé con sus ropas: está húmedo. La espada filosofal sisea cuando repito el ritual para detener una vez más la hemorragia, pero no tengo idea de cuánta sangre ha perdido el lobo esta vez.

—Mierda, mierda —con el mayor cuidado que puedo, vendo de nuevo su herida con la última camiseta que nos queda, lo cubro con los abrigos y levanto su cabeza para ayudarlo a beber un poco de agua. A él le cuesta reaccionar, moverse, pero logro hacerlo tomar unos cuantos tragos.

—¿La encontraste?

Escuchar su voz de nuevo me trae un alivio indescriptible.

—¿La carretera? No, pero encontré una cabaña cerca de un río, a dos kilómetros de aquí —respondo en voz queda—, sólo que...

Dejo mi lengua quieta, pensando en que esa choza es ahora todo menos un refugio seguro. Pero a sabiendas de que no ganaré nada con ocultárselo, le cuento a grandes rasgos sobre la *Marionetista* que me atacó en el bosque.

Tared escucha en completo silencio. Y al terminar, él me asombra una vez más al empezar a levantarse.

—¡Oye, OYE! —reclamo poniendo mi mano en su pecho para tratar de detenerlo—, ¡deja de esforzarte! ¡¿No ves lo mal que estás?!

—Está nevando —dice en voz baja, lo que me hace cerrar la boca, sin comprender. Sus ojos azules se fijan en la salida de la gruta, donde pequeños montículos de nieve han comenzado a depositarse, arrastrados por el viento—. Si no nos movemos ahora, la tormenta nos enterrará.

Es verdad. La inclinación de la cueva es una trampa en la que no había pensado.

El lobo envuelve una de mis muñecas con la palma de su mano.

—Ya has logrado que lleguemos hasta aquí —susurra—, nada puede ser peor que no intentarlo.

Tared me deja sin aliento, porque a pesar de mi temor y su mal estado, no veo otra cosa que determinación en esos ojos azules.

Tiene razón. Maldita sea si no.

Asiento y me pongo en pie. Al buscar nuestras cosas por la cueva para meterlas a la mochila, percibo algo extraño:

las tiras de carne seca están fuera de la bolsa de plástico, colocadas a un lado, sobre una piedra. Están todas, si no me equivoco, pero lo que me desconcierta es que dentro del empaque ahora hay un puñado de hojas de pino parcialmente machacadas.

Arrugo el entrecejo, pero no me detengo a pensar en ello. Guardo todo y me echo el bulto en la espalda junto con las armas, que amarro como puedo con las últimas tiras de la camiseta.

Al girarme hacia Tared siento un nudo en la garganta al ver que otra vez se está quedando dormido. Aprieto los labios y me inclino hacia él.

—Vamos —lo aliento, para hacerlo despabilarse—. Trataré de que lleguemos pronto.

Él no dice nada más, tan sólo deja que yo pase su brazo alrededor de mi cuello, para después dejar caer sobre mí todo aquello que no puede cargar por sí mismo. Me doblega un poco su solidez, pero mi deseo de sacarlo de aquí me infunde fuerzas para levantarnos a ambos.

Despacio, salimos de la cueva mientras procuro vigilar en todo momento el movimiento del asta en su cuerpo. Y al igual que conmigo, el dolor le ayuda a mantenerse más o menos despierto.

Poco a poco, y en medio de una tormenta cada vez más copiosa, avanzamos por el bosque, y la dificultad con la que nos movemos, la manera en la que el manto se torna más grueso, me confirma que Tared tenía razón.

Puede que esta misma noche hubiésemos muerto bajo la nieve.

Una rama rota, un nido abandonado, un pino más sobresaliente que los otros; todo me indica la dirección hacia el río, y agradezco que la luz mortuoria de la noche resplandezca con fuerza detrás del nubarrón.

Pero el devorapieles respira cada vez con más dificultad sobre mí, y a cada paso que damos la angustia de que se desplome en cualquier momento se vuelve más y más latente. Está frío, su ropa se congela con la sangre y jadea para no gritar de dolor a cada zancada que damos.

—Aguanta, aguanta… —suplico en su oído, aunque la plegaria también es para mí.

Cruzar la cañada y el río congelado es la parte más difícil, sobre todo al no saber si el hielo podrá aguantar el peso de Tared y el mío combinados. Pero logramos cruzar a salvo.

Tras dos largas horas, finalmente llegamos a la choza de madera.

Ayudo a Tared a recargarse a un costado de la entrada y remuevo la nieve del umbral, buscando de vez en cuando la silueta de aquella bestia llena de brazos. Parto con el hacha la cerradura de la puerta y ésta se abre con un suave rechinido.

Arrojo luz dentro con la linterna, el lugar entero huele a humedad. No tiene habitaciones, es una sala común con una estufa antigua empotrada en una esquina, de ésas de hierro con chimenea que se alarga hasta atravesar el techo. De allí en más sólo hay un catre de lona desvencijado, un par de sillas de madera y otra puerta orientada al pie de la montaña.

Todo luce empolvado y viejo, en señal de que ya tiene tiempo sin que nadie lo use.

—Ven, vamos… —con cuidado, logro recostar al lobo en la camilla. La luz invernal que se cuela a través de los tablones de la ventana trasera me permite atisbar su rostro, agotado por el largo trayecto de la caverna hasta acá. Desearía poder cambiarle las vendas y la ropa ensangrentada, pero no nos queda nada más que una camisa de franela, la cual necesito para fabricar algo muy importante esta noche.

Le doy tres pastillas de analgésicos y, para mi tranquilidad, le toma menos de unos minutos quedarse dormido. Lo cubro con un abrigo y la manta de camuflaje y me dejo caer en una de las sillas, recordándome que tendré que encender la estufa más tarde y preparar un caldo con el agua del termo y la carne seca. El frío aquí no es tan terrible como en la cueva, pero sigue mordiendo los huesos.

Miro a Tared y siento que la garra de Wéndigo me estruja con más fuerza. Ha perdido mucho peso, demasiada sangre, está herido y más lejos de mí que nunca.

—Voy a sacarte de esto, aunque sea lo último que haga —susurro, deseando con todo mi ser tener las fuerzas para levantarme y acomodarle mejor la manta o limpiar un poco más la sangre de su sien.

Sufro la nostalgia de nuestro vínculo muerto. Deseo, una vez más, sentir la ternura de aquel lazo, el tirón, la certeza de que, sin importar cuánto lo estiremos, el hilo volverá a unirnos una vez más.

Casi me echo a reír, porque resulta que aquella criatura que pretendía ser Adam tenía razón en una sola cosa:

—Siempre te elegiría a ti —susurro hacia el lobo—. *Siempre*.

Cierro los ojos un momento, y cuando sólo se escucha en la cabaña el golpetear de la nieve contra los tablones de las ventanas y el castañeo de mis dientes, me doy cuenta de lo mucho que me duele la pierna.

Me inclino y desamarro el sucio vendaje, lentamente. Ladeo la cabeza, desconcertado al levantar los pliegues del pantalón y ver que la lesión que abrió la flecha de ballesta está hinchada, con los bordes blancuzcos, llena de pus.

Ahora lo entiendo. El olor a carne putrefacta que percibí antes no provenía de Tared, sino de mi propia herida infectada.

CAPÍTULO 23
ASFIXIA

Por la mañana, soy despertado por un fuerte dolor de cabeza. Abro los ojos y me encuentro empapado en sudor, a pesar de que la estufa de hierro lleva casi una hora apagada.

Fiebre.

Al intentar levantarme, el dolor en mi pecho me deja tendido un momento más. La herida de mi pierna sigue roja e hinchada, y aunque logré quitar algo de pus de los bordes con agua del termo, parece haber empeorado de todas maneras.

Avivo un poco más la estufa, pero no demasiado; anoche tuvimos la suerte de que la tormenta ayudara a disimular la columna de humo que sale por la chimenea, pero hoy ya se ha despejado el cielo, lo que podría delatar nuestra ubicación.

Me acerco a Tared y coloco mi mano sobre su frente para ver cómo está su temperatura, pero el calor de mi propio cuerpo me impide saberlo con claridad. Él respira, pero sigue tan pálido como anoche.

Ya no sólo es la pérdida de sangre lo que lo mantiene tan débil, sino que es nuestro tercer día sin alimentarnos.

Necesito encontrar comida. Y pronto.

Me calzo las botas, me cuelgo la escopeta y la ballesta, y me echo la mochila al hombro, llena de cosas que me quedé elaborando ayer para no quedarme dormido. Aunque, de cualquier manera, la tortura de *otra visión* se encargó de sacudirme el breve momento en el que pude hacerlo.

Esta vez había otra mujer, junto a la anciana. Era escuálida, putrefacta y de largo cabello blanco, igual de desnuda y con el mismo símbolo grabado a cuchillo en su frente. Levantaba delante de ella un espejo redondo del tamaño de su cabeza, y aunque a primera vista parecía que el vidrio era de un color tan negro que me impedía ver su cara, en realidad era un *vacío*.

Un abismo. Un túnel a alguna alcantarilla del plano medio, justo en medio de mis pesadillas.

Mientras esa mujer me observaba a través de la oscuridad, la horrible vieja a su lado parecía machacar algo contra el suelo; lo molía con una piedra de buen tamaño, y aquello que aplastaba era duro y a la vez carnoso.

No ver rastros del cadáver del niño me revolvió las entrañas, pero no tanto como comprobar que la *bruja* untaba esa pasta necrótica en sus codos, en sus genitales, en las plantas de sus pies.

Y de nuevo, lo que me atrajo de vuelta a la realidad fue ser consciente del hambre que sentía al ver a esas dos mujeres.

Jamás había tenido tantas visiones, una detrás de la otra. No me cabe duda de que tanto ellas como la criatura Marionetista han sido enviadas por mi Mara; sin embargo, indagar más a fondo en eso o en por qué siento tanta hambre al verlas me ha sido imposible.

Interrumpo mis cavilaciones cuando salgo de la cabaña y el frío del exterior me recibe con una ventisca. Me cuesta avanzar más que nunca, pero una vez que logro abrirme paso por la nieve, empiezo a recorrer el perímetro de la construcción. Pronto descubro detrás de ésta, a unos veinte metros, una letrina donde decido colocar mi primer "punto de vigilancia".

Saco de la mochila un muñeco de tela pequeñito, muy parecido al que usé para detener las hemorragias de Tared, pero relleno de mi propia sangre, cabellos y otro tipo de fluidos, cortesía de la herida de ballesta. Lo coloco encima de la letrina y me alejo de la cabaña dejando más de una docena de monigotes iguales en los árboles, bajo las piedras, en las raíces.

Una vez que he instalado el último, empiezo a caminar en dirección al río. Durante todo el trayecto busco alguna piña que no haya sido saqueada ya por los roedores, pero no tengo éxito. Estoy mareado. Me duele demasiado la cabeza y no sé cuánto más podré soportar.

Mi suerte cambia por fin al acercarme a la cuenca del río. A lo lejos, capto una mancha densa y oscura que, por unos momentos, me hace querer retroceder y ocultarme.

Pero no es la Marionetista. Se trata de un alce pequeño, parado en el bosque del otro lado de la cañada.

Como si hubiese escuchado el salto eufórico de mi corazón, el animal levanta la cabeza en dirección a mí. Me agazapo entre la nieve, y aunque estoy casi seguro de que no me ha visto, el alce comienza a moverse en paralelo al río.

—¡Carajo! —sigo a la criatura por el borde de la pendiente hasta que se detiene a mordisquear algo en el suelo. Empuño la ballesta, cuyas flechas resultarán mortíferas si logro dar en el sitio adecuado: la frente, el ojo, la sien.

En el ínterin, el alce levanta la cabeza, inquieto. Olfatea, mueve el cráneo y, para mi horror, se introduce en el bosque. Alejándose de mi vista.

—¡No, no! —susurro, ¡no puedo dejar que se me escape!
Bajo la barranca, y me deslizo hasta la orilla del caudal.
Con la confianza de que el río ya se haya endurecido lo suficiente, comienzo a cruzarlo a paso rápido, viendo cómo el animal se hace cada vez más pequeño en la lejanía, aún ignorante de mi presencia.

El fuerte crujido del hielo partiéndose bajo mis pies me hace parar de inmediato.

—Mierda —murmuro, y abro los brazos para mantener el equilibrio. Bajo la barbilla despacio, pero no logro encontrar dónde se ha fragmentado la superficie. Tan sólo veo la corriente oscura moverse bajo mis pies. Y entonces, escucho otro sonido, distinto y lejano, a mis espaldas.

Es ese sonido de nuevo, el gimoteo pesado de alguien que se ahoga.

Me giro con tremenda lentitud para voltear hacia atrás.

Encuentro a una chica flotando sobre la orilla del río de donde he venido. No es ninguna de las brujas de mis visiones. Ella es muy joven y viste una especie de camisón azul.

Me mira con el cuello de lado, los ojos desorbitados y la boca llena de espuma, se convulsiona porque algo invisible *la está ahorcando*.

Tenso la ballesta en mis manos y cierro los ojos unos instantes, con fuerza, con horror, porque no necesito mirar demasiado para comprender que en realidad no flota en el aire, sino que un brazo blanco brota de las faldas de su camisón y la eleva desde el suelo. Un brazo que corre debajo del hielo del río a la orilla. Un brazo que se alarga hasta donde yo estoy de pie.

Toc, toc.

Alguien toca la superficie de cristal.

Toc, toc.

El hielo se resquebraja.

La Marionetista está justo debajo de mí.

CAPÍTULO 24
UN DESCONOCIDO EN EL AGUA

En un segundo, soy hundido en las aguas heladas del río. Cientos de agujas frías se clavan en mi piel mientras que el hielo cruje en mis oídos como un cristal. Intento impulsarme de vuelta a la superficie, pero uno de los brazos de la Marionetista se ha enredado en mi mano. Los demás rostros, furiosos, atrapan mi ropa con los dientes y tiran de mí hacia abajo.

Lucho por liberarme pero, como era de esperarse, la criatura es demasiado fuerte. Todo aquí abajo es de un azul infinito cortado por rayos de luz que atraviesan el agua como espadas, una tumba glacial que busca convertirme en su cadáver.

¡Otra vez no, maldición!

¡Arde, idiota!

Afianzo el agarre de la ballesta y, con un jalón de mi mano descarnada, logro accionar el gatillo. Las caras parecen gritar al unísono cuando la flecha se clava en una de las costillas de la bestia, que afloja su agarre de inmediato.

Nado, nado con desesperación hacia la superficie, pero otra cosa más lucha por mantenerme abajo: el maldito peso de la piedra filosofal.

Aunada a la corriente del río, la espada me arrebata los escasos segundos de ventaja que pude conseguir. La criatura vuelve a tomarme de los tobillos, a arrastrarme al fondo de un río que, para mi horror, empieza a volverse demasiado profundo. Súbitamente, algo *cambia*. Las espadas de luz se apagan. El azul se torna de un gris cada vez más opaco. Percibo, perplejo, cómo las sombras del plano medio empiezan a abrirse debajo de mí.

"*No, no, ¡aléjense!*", grito como un loco en mi interior.

¡No puedes luchar contra lo que somos!

¡No, no, no!

La negrura se convierte en un abismo en el que soy introducido por aquel monstruo. Y descubro, al abrirse ese infinito, al escuchar esas voces que me reclaman, que lo que más me aterra no es morir ahogado, sino que mi magia abra el plano medio otra vez y me lleve a un lugar remoto.

Lejos de Tared.

¡Mierda, mierda, mierda!

Intento escapar del velo del mundo de los muertos, pero éste se eleva debajo de mí y empieza a ennegrecerlo todo como un remolino de tinta. Dejo de escuchar el crujido del hielo y el batir de la corriente. El tiempo se detiene, el plano medio está a punto de apartarme de la Marionetista.

Dejo de moverme, tan sólo un segundo, al reparar en mis propios pensamientos.

Cuando abrí un plano medio en el cuarto de Sammuel para escapar de Tared. Cuando abrí un plano medio en la catarata de Stonefall para huir de los tramperos...

Lo que quieren las sombras del plano medio no es matarme, sino *salvarme*. Y eso significa que son *mías*, ¡así que las hijas de puta harán mi voluntad!

—¡APÁRTENSE! —grito bajo el agua, dejando salir mi último aliento.

El monstruo de hueso emite una risa cuyo significado no consigo descifrar. Cierro los ojos y la desesperación se convierte en furia, un fuego de magia que asciende hasta rodear mi cuerpo de llamas. La espada ruge con fuerza, en tanto yo ilumino como una antorcha incandescente la oscuridad.

La Marionetista me libera, sus brazos se apartan de mí mientras gritan sin voz.

Con un movimiento de mi garra, dirijo mi fuego hacia la bestia blanca. El impulso de la magia la arroja hacia las sombras del plano medio y el mundo de los muertos se la traga para comenzar a desvanecerse. Las dagas de luz atraviesan de nuevo la superficie. Nubes de tierra, plantas y trozos de ramas empujadas por la corriente traen de vuelta el tiempo y la realidad.

El fuego de mi piel se apaga justo antes de que Wéndigo lo reclame para poseerme.

Emerjo del agua y trepo por el hielo, suplicando que no vuelva a resquebrajarse debajo de mí. Me arrastro hasta salir de la cuenca del río y me dejo caer boca abajo, temblando, sobre la nieve.

He perdido todas mis armas junto con la mochila, y el cielo se ha puesto ya de color rosa, lo que significa que una muy pequeña parte de las sombras logró alcanzarme para robar un fragmento de mi vida. Pero yo sólo puedo pensar en una cosa:

—Tared. Debo regresar, debo regresar...

Pero no puedo moverme. Cierro los ojos e intento volver a invocar el fuego de mi magia, pero la espada me aplasta sin esfuerzo.

Ya no me quedan energías.

—Puedo lograrlo, la cabaña no está lejos. Puedo... puedo volver con él...

Debo avanzar. Debo subir la pendiente, debo cruzar el bosque y encontrar la cabaña, pero mi cuerpo cede ante el dolor de todos los golpes que he recibido, ante mi ropa tiesa y helada y el aire frío que no me deja respirar.

Ya no puedo mover las manos. Ya no puedo mover las piernas. Me congelo, poco a poco, a la orilla del río.

—No, no —las lágrimas luchan por brotar de mis ojos, pero hasta éstas se escarchan en mis pestañas. Sólo logro ver, a través de ellas, a Barón Samedi al borde de la cañada.

Baja de un salto fantasmalmente lento. Sonríe. Se aproxima hasta acuclillarse a mi lado y me acaricia un flanco del rostro. Pero no importa. No importa si vino a arrancarme la lengua, los ojos o la piel. Lo único que anhelo es volver con Tared.

Quiero susurrar que lo siento, pero mis labios ya no responden.

Con la imagen del lobo abandonado a su suerte y desangrándose en esa cabaña, cierro los ojos por última vez.

CAPÍTULO 25
SEÑALES

Esta noche, un olor peculiar se esparce por mi celda: el aroma casi dulce y apetitoso de la grasa derretida, muy parecido al que tenían los trozos de mi cuerpo cuando se desprendían por el calor de las batallas contra la alquimista; esos que alguna vez me vi obligada a comer para seguir con vida dentro de los muros de esta prisión.

Atraída por la fragancia y el hambre, me asomo al portal y encuentro al Inquisidor erguido delante de una hoguera, observando aquello que expide tan interesante olor: Tres cadáveres fundiéndose en las llamas.

Tres.

Tres.

Tres.

Nueve tramperos caídos en total, incluido su propio hijo.

—¡Estamos más de treinta cabrones aquí, Benjamin! ¿Qué tenemos que hacer para acabar con un solo maldito mocoso? ¿Traer a nuestras mujeres para que hagan el trabajo por nosotros? —exclama alguien entre sus hombres, los cuales se han reunido en torno a aquella fogata.

—Lo hemos intentado todo, carajo, ¡todo! —añade uno más—. ¡Ni las jodidas balas parecen matarlos!

Benjamin, con la mirada de buitre entornada, parece preguntarse eso mismo. ¿Cómo han podido escapar a sus trampas, sus sogas, sus armas? ¿Cómo es que han burlado de tal manera a una dinastía de cazadores, el orgullo que heredó de su padre, de su abuelo, de sus ancestros que liquidaron a los bisontes de las praderas hace siglos?

¿Estás disfrutando *tú* de esto, acaso? ¿De este altar de nueve cuerpos?

Pero en vez de atender a los chillidos de su culto, el viejo contempla el cadáver tuerto y desfigurado de aquel chico que apenas había cumplido quince años, cuyo ojo arrancado todavía sigue en la pequeña bolsa de lona que encontró enterrada en la nieve.

El trampero se levanta y todas las miradas recaen sobre él, pero ninguno se atreve a despegar los dientes cuando se agacha para tomar un grueso leño de la hoguera. Da la espalda al grupo y se aventura por el campamento de remolques, estacionados en un amplio mirador situado en uno de los barrancos más altos de la montaña. Se pierde entre el pequeño laberinto de chatarras hasta llegar a una maciza camioneta de carga; un cubo de metal hecho para soportar el peso de al menos cinco caballos.

Mira las puertas traseras de la caja, cerradas con candado y cadenas cruzadas de lado a lado, como si lo que llevase allí dentro fuese un monstruo terrible que en cualquier momento pudiera despertar.

En un arrebato, comienza a golpear las puertas con aquel leño una y otra vez como si quisiera tirarlas a punta de palos. Unos gritos de terror retumban desde dentro de aquella camioneta, y al escuchar tan delicioso sufrimiento, Benjamin arremete hasta reventar el tronco en su mano.

—¡HIJOS DE PUTA, LOS DESPELLEJARÉ A TODOS! —exclama, invadido por la cólera. Arroja la madera a la nieve y busca en su bolsillo las llaves de aquel candado... pero se detiene al escuchar unos pasos crujir en la nieve.

Y lo percibe de nuevo. Aquel perfume que emana por encima del de la carne quemada.

El Inquisidor gira la cabeza lentamente hacia los árboles que bordean el barranco y descubre de nuevo a su hijo Buck, quien fijamente lo mira.

El trampero constriñe la nariz y da la espalda a la camioneta de carga. Camina cauteloso bajo las nubes lilas en pos de la figura. Al saltar el pasamanos que delimita el mirador, siente el frío muy real del abismo respirarle desde el fondo de la cañada.

Buck le da la espalda, pero su brazo largo apunta a lo lejos.

El perfume de la tercera magia rodea con más fuerza al viejo trampero y le hace cerrar los ojos un instante. Al abrirlos, él ya no está, pero Benjamin sigue mirando hacia donde su hijo apuntaba.

Y allí encuentra algo que le hace sonreír: una serpiente blanca y cruel que se eleva sobre el bosque.

La columna de humo de una chimenea entre la espesura arbolada del bosque.

CAPÍTULO 26
SACRIFICIO

Debería estar muerto.

Debería estar rodeado de hielo, enterrado bajo mi sepulcro de nieve. Mi ropa debería estar congelada contra mi cuerpo magullado, con los ojos entreabiertos hacia el suelo y las garras del río intentando arrastrarme a sus aguas.

Ya nada tendría que dolerme, ni la herida de mi pierna, ni mis costillas golpeadas, ni mis labios azules o mis dedos ateridos por el invierno feroz.

Debería estar muerto.

Pero, en cambio, sólo siento calor. Siento mi piel seca, mi cuerpo tibio y mis pulmones que respiran tranquilos, sin pausa. Siento el pecho dolorido, pero muy vivo, que sube y que baja contra mis manos desnudas.

Abro los ojos, despacio, y me encuentro acostado en el suelo frente a la estufa de la cabaña, enrojecida por el calor de unas llamas furiosas. Ya no siento fiebre, sólo tibieza, un calor paradisíaco que busca adormecerme de nuevo sobre la manta de camuflaje.

El calor se convierte en desconcierto cuando, al intentar moverme, descubro un pesado brazo sobre mis hombros. Un brazo cubierto de pelo plateado.

Pánico.

—Pero, ¡¿qué...?!

Me levanto de inmediato sobre los codos y me llevo una mano a los labios para no gritar.

Tared yace acostado detrás de mí, hecho un ovillo contra mi cuerpo y *transformado* en hombre lobo. El trozo de arpón que tenía en el vientre está inerte y frío a unos metros de nosotros, con un sendero fino de sangre ya seca que corre hacia acá.

Mi garganta se abre, sin voz, azorada por el cosquilleo horrendo de las lágrimas que pugnan por salir. Tared tiene los ojos cerrados y el hocico pegado al pecho, como si se encontrara acostado en la falda del bosque, dormido dentro de un cuento de hadas del que nunca debí sacarlo.

Observo el sitio donde antes estuvo el arpón, ahora vuelto sólo un amasijo de pelo apelmazado por la sangre, la piel de su herida abultada y roja como una costura mal cicatrizada esperando abrirse de nuevo con el más delicado de los movimientos. Mi cuerpo está cubierto sólo con la chamarra que tenía puesta Tared, mientras mi ropa se seca frente a la estufa.

Y el muñeco que hice para controlar su hemorragia yace olvidado en un rincón. Muerto. Sin magia.

Es en ese momento en el que hubiese deseado haber muerto no allá afuera, en la nieve, sino desde que puse un pie en Nueva Orleans.

Bajo mi cabeza hacia su hombro y se me parte el corazón al sentirlo, huesudo, contra mi frente.

—*¿Por qué?* —logro sollozar.

Tared despierta y mueve un poco la cabeza. Sus ojos me miran ahora entreabiertos, apagados por el cansancio. Hace un esfuerzo más y me rodea de nuevo con su brazo para volver a atraerme hacia su cuerpo.

Siento la herida en mi muslo, cubierta con una sustancia espesa que huele fresca, casi mentolada. Al bajar la mirada, descubro que son las hojas de pino, aquellas que estaban trituradas en la bolsa de carne.

—Perdona —dice él en voz baja—, también tuve qué lamerte un poco, para dejarla limpia...

Fue eso. Tared sabía que se me había infectado la herida y fue a buscar algo para curarme. Pero se abrió la propia herida en el proceso, y terminó tan débil que no pudo hacer más.

Gimoteo inconsolable contra su pecho.

—¿Por qué lo hiciste? —insisto.

Él contesta con voz agotada y gutural:

—Estabas enfermo. Oscurecía y no regresabas. Tenía que ir a buscarte.

—¡No, no tenías qué hacerlo! —exclamo, furioso—, ¡no debiste ponerte en peligro de una forma tan estúpida!

—Habrías muerto... —ataja.

—¡Era mi vida o la tuya!

—Lo sé. Por eso fue tan fácil... decidir.

Las palabras se atoran en mi garganta. Tared me mira con esos ojos indómitos, tan propios de él. El hombre lobo —*mi hombre lobo*— parece tranquilo y satisfecho, como si mi corazón palpitante justificase su vida deslizándose fuera de los muros de esta cabaña.

—Pensé que ya no me amabas —susurro, al fin, como un cobarde resentido, sin entender por qué ha hecho semejante sacrificio. Tared cierra los párpados unos segundos y acaricia mi mejilla con una dulzura que parece imposible para tan enormes garras, ahora enjuga mis lágrimas con la suave almohadilla de sus dedos.

—Tenía... mis razones para dejarte ir —susurra con una sonrisa cansada. Mis manos se hacen puños sobre su pecho, enroscados en las hebras tibias de su pelaje. Busco en él esa herida eternamente abierta donde yace el sepulcro de nuestro vínculo muerto—. Pero jamás dejé de quererte, Elisse. No hay nada que sea capaz de convencerme de dejar de hacerlo. Ni siquiera ese monstruo en el que crees que te has convertido.

—No, Tared, no... —sollozo.

—Te amo, Elisse. Y de eso *nunca* me he arrepentido.

—Te amo, también te amo, Tared —exclamo entre lágrimas—, ¡perdóname por no habértelo dicho!

—Jamás tuve dudas de ello, Elisse. A pesar de todo.

El lobo envuelve mi cabeza con sus garras y me permite empapar su piel de plata, me abraza todo el cuerpo con unas fuerzas que según la lógica ya no debería poseer.

—¿Qué va a pasar ahora? —pregunto con un miedo atroz. Me aferro más a él, e intento que mi cuerpo también le transmita algo de calor.

—Vas a irte de aquí cuando sea el momento —me contesta en voz baja, tan convencido de sus palabras que se me hiela la sangre.

—Por favor, por favor, no digas eso —le suplico—. No te vayas de mi lado como yo lo hice, por favor...

Me abriré el pecho y me sacaré esta maldita espada si con eso puedo mantenerte vivo.

Tared se limita a dedicarme una caricia de su nariz oscura, mientras la nieve se acumula fuera de la cabaña. Yo, en cambio, me lleno de un único deseo. Sé que no puede hacer mucho para corresponderme, pero tomo en mis manos el ángulo de su rostro y me acerco para besar sus labios aún en forma de lobo, sabiendo que tal vez sea aquélla la última vez que pueda hacerlo.

Lo siento respirar, cada vez más despacio, hasta que pronto nos rendimos a la cercanía del otro. En medio del silencio de la noche, del hambre y la desesperación de saber que lo que sentimos el uno por el otro es lo único que tiene fuerzas ahora para mantenerse vivo, nuestro abrazo nos mantiene tibios. Hasta que también siento su cuerpo enfriarse, poco a poco.

El vínculo roto, esa herida sangrante, ese trozo de pasado y dolor, se desprende y cae como una costra ya vieja. Y de esa herida cruda y roja, cual loto en el barro, nace un *nuevo vínculo* que crece, florece y vibra, vivo y rebosante a pesar de que la muerte amenaza con llevárselo esta misma noche.

Tared y yo, sin otra esperanza más allá de estas paredes, nos unimos en el infinito con un único momento de resplandor.

Y ante nuestro nuevo lazo, la garra del monstruo de hueso afloja por fin su prensa de mi corazón.

CAPÍTULO 27
STILL A WITCH! [2]

Una sutil vibración me despierta poco después, en medio de la madrugada. Con pesadez, entreabro los ojos en la oscuridad. Mi hombre lobo respira leve en un ronquido bajo, con sus brazos débiles aún cerrados a mi alrededor.

Vuelvo a sentir esa vibración, como si algo a través del piso palpitase hasta llegar a la palma de mi mano; un hilo invisible que me atrae poco a poco hasta convertirse en un tirón desesperado. Un grito de alarma.

Abro los ojos de par en par.

—¡Mierda!

Reúno fuerzas y me levanto sobre mis codos. Mi corazón galopa dentro del pecho, más fuerte ahora que está liberado de las garras crueles de Wéndigo.

Me deslizo del abrazo de Tared y llego a la ventana del frente de la cabaña para asomarme entre los tablones. El brillo de las nubes contra la nieve me permite mirar con claridad hacia afuera, pero todo parece envuelto en quietud. Aprieto la palma de mi mano, e intento sentir de dónde ha provenido aquel horrible tirón.

---

[2] ¡Aún soy un brujo!

—Elisse…

Me sobresalto al escuchar la voz del devorapieles, quien lucha por incorporarse sobre un codo.

Me arrastro hacia él y, en vez de forzarlo a volver al suelo, le ayudo a sentarse con la espalda contra la pared. Está tembloroso y apenas puede mantener los ojos abiertos, pero mi instinto me dice que no debo permitirle volver a acostarse.

Trago saliva e intento que las palabras salgan enteras de mi boca.

—Hay alguien *o algo* afuera —digo en voz baja a la par que le muestro mi puño—. Uno de mis señuelos me lo ha dicho.

Ladea su cabeza lobuna, pero no le cuesta mucho entender que me refiero a los muñecos que hice anoche. Estoy seguro de que debió haberlos visto repartidos en el bosque cuando fue a buscarme, y puede que hasta me haya encontrado gracias a ellos.

Me pongo los pantalones aún húmedos y me enfundo la pistola de Lía, tendida hasta entonces al lado de la estufa. Meto el resto de mi ropa y mis guantes en el fuego para apagar su brillo, y justo al quedarse la cabaña a oscuras, otro tirón en la mano me corta el aliento. Esta vez la señal ha venido del muñeco que dejé sobre la letrina.

Uno tras otro, todos mis señuelos empiezan a vibrar y a tirar de sus hilos como si quisieran arrancarme los dedos.

Mi peor miedo se confirma.

Tramperos.

El rugido de varios vehículos al unísono ensordece el bosque entero. Una luz incandescente se cuela por los tablones, con unos faros tan potentes que me dejan ciego por un instante.

—¡MONSTRUO!

Mi espalda se eriza al reconocer el origen de aquel grito, aún más terrible que el de los motores.

Lander.

A través de las rendijas logro distinguir no sólo la silueta del viejo trampero iluminada por los múltiples vehículos, sino la de un montón de cazadores armados con rifles, escopetas y cuchillos que brillan contra el resplandor de los faros. Y estoy bastante seguro de que muchos más nos aguardan en la parte trasera de la cabaña.

Algo metálico cruje a mis espaldas, y descubro con horror a Tared aferrado a la chimenea de la estufa, intentando ponerse de pie.

—¡¿Qué estás haciendo?! —exclamo en voz baja. Me lanzo hacia él para ocultarlo entre las sombras, pero resulta inútil debido a su tamaño.

—Déjame... enfrentarlos —pide con los colmillos apretados.

—¡Estás completamente loco! ¿Cómo demonios crees que vas a vencerlos?

—No pienso vencerlos —susurra— sólo distraerlos... para que puedas escapar.

Un disparo a la ventana frontal perfora uno de los tablones. La bala se incrusta en la pared detrás de nosotros y la ventisca se abre camino en la cabaña a pesar de la estrechez de la abertura.

—¡SALGAN, COBARDES! —grita uno de los hombres de Lander. Los aceleradores de las motocicletas braman sin censar.

Libérame.

—Todavía puedo correr unos metros —insiste Tared—, puedo... aguantar unos cuantos disparos antes de que me derriben.

No alcanzo a gritarle que es un completo imbécil cuando una balacera abre agujeros y grietas por todas partes.

—¡Van a matarnos a los dos, entiéndelo! —exclama.

—¡Deja de decir tonterías, no voy a dejarte! —replico.

Libérame. Es la única manera.

Tared me sujeta de la chamarra con una garra, desesperado.

¡Libérame!

—No lo escuches, Elisse, te lo suplico, ¡haz lo que te digo!

Aquello casi me hace olvidar a la manada de tramperos allá fuera.

—¿Cómo sabes que Wéndigo me hab...?

Un machetazo golpea contra la puerta de la cabaña. Y a ése le siguen otro y otro más, que resuenan desde todas las direcciones. Tared me rodea con su brazo y ruge por instinto hacia la entrada. El lobo tiene en una mano la pistola de uno de los tramperos que asesiné hace unos días, pero apenas puede sostenerla.

Los desgraciados podrían entrar ahora mismo y despedazarnos si así lo quisieran. Pero eso no es lo que buscan, ellos buscan...

Divertirse...

Siento el sabor de las cenizas en mi lengua. Una risa olvidada en las sombras. Ojos vacíos mirándome desde la arbolada.

Sí.

Hay otra manera.

Sostengo a Tared del hocico y lo hago mirarme:

—Haz un pacto conmigo.

—¿Cómo?

—¡Aún soy un brujo! —grito—, ¡ofréceme algo a cambio de salvar tu vida!

—Pero ¿qué estás…?

—Es la única manera, ¡por favor, debes confiar en mí!

Tared entrecierra la mirada, como si sufriese un repentino mareo, y mira hacia mi pecho.

—La espada —suelta en un suspiro.

—¿Qué?

—En cuanto podamos sacarla de tu cuerpo, yo portaré la espada por ti. Ésa es… mi condición.

Un proyectil se clava en la estufa y a mí no me queda tiempo para pensarlo más. Extiendo mi mano humana, y con mi garra descarnada abro un tajo en la palma, para acto seguido llevarla hacia la herida del arpón de Tared.

El devorapieles lanza un quejido cuando mi tacto abre su carne de nuevo. Su sangre y la mía se mezclan. La espada en mi pecho enfurece, incapaz de robar mi poder gracias al pacto que ahora quema entre mi mano y su vientre.

Líneas escarlatas comienzan a trepar por todo mi brazo hasta cubrir mi piel como si fuesen venas expuestas. Resplandecen al rojo vivo y se tuercen, forman círculos, líneas, puntos y curvas. El hombre lobo se estremece al ver que, en tan sólo unos segundos, todo mi cuerpo se cubre de figuras que, definitivamente, no son vevés.

Son símbolos alquímicos.

Abro mis ojos y sé, por la expresión de su rostro, que se han vuelto negros.

Los machetes por fin derriban la puerta y un hombre nos mira con una sonrisa dentada desde el umbral. Se relame los labios y dice cosas que no puedo entender por el ruido de los motores.

Ladeo la cabeza y susurro a Tared:

—Tenemos un pacto.

CAPÍTULO 28
UNA PROMESA INTERMINABLE

El cazador da un paso al interior de la cabaña, machete en mano. Los demás cabrones gritan y silban detrás de él, ansiosos porque seamos entregados para comenzar su sangrienta bacanal.

Pero el crujido antinatural de los árboles hace al hombre detenerse de inmediato.

Deja de sonreír y mira hacia atrás mientras aquel crujido se multiplica.

Abrazo a Tared con todas mis fuerzas. El silencio y la confusión se siembran en los tramperos. Y luego también *el terror.*

El sicario se da la media vuelta sólo para lanzar un grito despavorido. Tared comprueba, perplejo, cómo los hombres de Benjamin Lander desvían sus disparos hacia el bosque y sus risas se convierten en alaridos.

No le doy tiempo de ver más. Paso su brazo sobre mis hombros y lo hago levantarse.

—¡Vamos! —exclamo por encima del ruido de afuera—. *¡Ellos* los distraerán!

Lo arrastro hacia la puerta trasera de la cabaña, la cual abro con el empuje de nuestro peso. Desengancho el arma de Lía y disparo al primer cazador que entra en el rango de vista de mi periferia, el cual cae herido a mi paso. No me quedo a darle el tiro de gracia cuando *algo* sale de las sombras y se encorva sobre él y abre sus múltiples bocas acolmilladas.

El hombre grita y se retuerce de miedo en el suelo mientras el olor de la pólvora rodea la cabaña como una estela pestilente. Los cazadores corren por todas partes huyendo de aquello que acabo de invocar de la oscuridad. Tared, a quien cada vez le cuesta más moverse, mira sobre su hombro. Su respiración se detiene y el arma en su mano resbala al distinguir qué es lo que los ha enloquecido.

Unas figuras se asoman entre la nieve, iluminadas por los faros de las motocicletas. Grandes y gruesos como troncos, pequeños y escuálidos como niños; llenos de astas torcidas que les brotan por el pecho y el vientre; con piernas dobladas hacia atrás como si fuesen saltamontes; calvos o poblados de cabellos rubios; con caras y manos llenas de ojos verdes que miran por doquier.

Una docena de homúnculos *míos* se mueven por el bosque y emiten ruidos que difícilmente podrían considerarse de este mundo.

—¡Aguanten, cabrones! —escucho a Benjamin Lander gritar, fuerte y claro, como si lo tuviese a mi lado, al ver que sus hombres comienzan a retroceder.

Arrastro a un Tared cada vez más pesado hasta la letrina, donde nos agachamos cuando una bala pasa por encima de nuestras cabezas en dirección a una de mis creaciones. El cartucho traspasa a la criatura, delgada y larga como un poste, y luego perfora el pecho de otro trampero que estaba justo detrás de ella. Mi homúnculo falso sonríe con una cara partida por una sola hilera de muelas y salta sobre el trampero que le ha disparado, mientras que el aire se infecta con el olor metálico de la sangre.

Sé muy bien que en el pecho de mis creaciones no palpitan corazones, sino muñecos hechos de mi sangre, mis fluidos y mis cabellos; la magia de la alquimia que corre por mis venas, inmunda e inmortal.

Tomo de nuevo al lobo sin perder un minuto más. Nos alejamos del infierno que se ha desatado en la cabaña, y avanzamos a ciegas, lo más rápido que nos es posible, bañados por la luz lavanda de la noche.

La nieve me hace tropezar un par de veces. Cada vez me cuesta más mover a Tared y no sólo porque falta poco para que se desplome, sino porque que yo mismo estoy al límite de mis energías.

Déjalo. De todos modos, no le queda mucho tiempo.

No, no, ¡primero muerto!

Mientras nos alejamos, los gritos de pánico mutan en desconcierto, en armas que dejan de disparar a lo estúpido. Gemidos de incredulidad se convierten en rabia al descubrir que los homúnculos no son más que alucinaciones.

Contengo un grito de dolor cuando, uno a uno, los hilos que me unen a mis criaturas empiezan a ser cortados. Los símbolos de alquimia grabados en mi cuerpo comienzan a apagarse.

—¡Benjamin, se escapan!

La luz brillante de los reflectores de una moto nos alumbra las espaldas.

El hechizo ha terminado, demasiado pronto, porque los tramperos nos alcanzan a tan sólo cien metros de la cabaña.

¡NO, NO, NO, MIERDA, MIERDA, MIERDA!

Y entonces, el camino se acaba. El pie de la montaña nos recibe con una pared de roca lisa e imposible de escalar, que se extiende como un muro a izquierda y derecha. Sin salida, sin grietas por dónde deslizarnos.

—No, ¡NO!

Un balazo roza mi cadera y me hace caer en redondo en la nieve, con el hombre lobo aún sobre mis hombros. La pistola que estaba en mi mano sale despedida y el dolor de aquella mordida de plomo se expande por todo mi cuerpo como un fuego desgarrador.

Todo da vueltas. Todo pierde forma. Mis sentidos se vuelven bruma en el aire.

—T-Tared... —gimoteo. Él jadea en el suelo a mi lado, sin poder despegar el pecho de la tierra. Su aliento se vuelve una nube de vaho alrededor de su hocico y las luces de las motocicletas proyectan nuestras sombras contra el muro de piedra.

Una docena de malparidos se arremolina a nuestro alrededor, todos con pistolas, escopetas, ballestas, rifles; una hilera de verdugos forrados con óxido y cuerdas.

Una fila de fusilamiento.

Quiero arrastrarme delante de Tared, protegerlo hasta agotar la última de mis fuerzas, pero ni siquiera puedo ponerme de rodillas. Los tramperos ya ríen, escupen a la nieve y algunos hasta se relamen los dientes de anticipado placer.

—¡Bajen sus armas, cobardes de mierda! —ordena una voz de ultratumba—. Ninguno de ustedes se ha ganado el derecho de disparar esta noche.

Conjurado, el mismísimo diablo se abre paso entre sus demonios. Benjamin Lander avanza hacia nosotros y su gente obedece como perros apaleados. Con calma, se coloca delante de mí y ladea la cabeza, veo sus ojos fijos bajo ese sombrero de ala, lleva algo apretado entre sus dedos, un objeto de metal que no logro distinguir.

Su presencia, sus arrugas, su hedor, la rectitud de su espalda; es la primera vez que tengo al Trampero del Desierto así de cerca, y es como mirar directamente al cañón de una pistola cargada.

Enrosco las manos en la nieve y el viejo mira con curiosidad mi garra huesuda. Se pone de cuclillas, y sólo entonces logro dilucidar qué es lo que lleva en la mano: es una mandíbula de metal, grande y pesada, con colmillos de acero.

Una trampa para osos.

Saca un cuchillo de su cintura y con su punta afilada me levanta la barbilla.

—¿Quién diría que algo tan insignificante llegaría a ser tan peligroso? Pero al fin te tengo en mis manos, maldito monstruo —susurra sin sonreír.

—Lander...

Sus pupilas se contraen al escuchar su nombre apretado entre mis labios.

—¿Qué debería hacer contigo primero? —pregunta a la vez que dibuja una línea escarlata sobre mi cuello—. ¿Cortarte los dedos uno a uno? ¿Amarrarte a un árbol y abrirte las entrañas para que veas cómo un animal te devora pedazo a pedazo?

Ladeo la cabeza con una sonrisa:

—Depende, ¿a cuál de tus hijos quieres que me coma ahora?

Estoy seguro de que escuché sus dientes rechinar. El trampero, sin dejar de mirarme, apunta hacia Tared con su cuchillo:

—¿O prefieres que lo desuelle a él vivo, mientras observa cómo mis hombres te violan uno por uno hasta partirte en dos?

Benjamin Lander no lo ve venir.

Con sus últimas energías, Tared salta delante de mí y le suelta un zarpazo directo a la cara, haciendo que su carne se desprenda de un latigazo. El trampero grita con los dientes apretados y cae contra la nieve, con la suerte de que el devorapieles no le arrancara la cabeza de tajo.

Escucho el percutor de un rifle.

—¡No, TARED!

Una bala acierta en la espalda del hombre lobo. El errante ruge, se agacha en cuatro patas y clava las garras en la nieve para no desplomarse a causa del impacto. El mercenario que le ha disparado corre hacia él y, como un maldito cobarde, lo apalea en la cara con la culata de su arma hasta verlo rendido en coágulos de sangre.

—No, no, ¡alto!

¡Apodérate de mí!, suplico al monstruo de hueso al ver que Benjamin Lander se levanta con la mejilla despedazada. Aquel hombre sólo cesa su brutalidad cuando el viejo se aproxima al lobo, con su mano sosteniendo su cara y sus ojos de acero brillando por la furia.

Pero no se detiene a vengarse. En cambio, el cabrón lo mira con una sonrisa en lo que le queda de boca y hace algo que sabe que le aterrará mucho más que cualquier nuevo flagelo a su cuerpo: lo pasa de largo *para dirigirse hacia mí*.

—No. ¡No! ¡Voy a arrancarte la jodida garganta! —ruge Tared con desesperación.

El monstruo se detiene a mi lado. Presiona un botón de su trampa de oso y un chasquido resuena al abrirse de par en par.

—¡No, ELISSE!

De un latigazo, Lander la cierra contra la herida de mi pierna. Los afilados dientes de aquella cosa penetran en mi carne hasta tocar el hueso, la nieve debajo de mí se vuelve espesa y oscura; siento que me ahogo en mi propio grito de dolor.

¡Maldita sea, poséeme, poséeme, por favor!, imploro una vez más a la bestia dentro de mi cuerpo, pero tan sólo recibo un silencio sepulcral.

Benjamin Lander retrocede y me mira con placer. Sus tramperos lanzan carcajadas y se transforman en demonios contra la luz.

¡Por favor, por favor, te ruego que me hagas tuyo!

Pero ni una sola chispa. Ni el menor atisbo de flama.

Wéndigo, para mi horror, se niega a salir.

No quisiste entregarte.

No, no, no, ¡por favor!

Y ahora lo verás morir.

—Gerald, ven acá —brama Lander, y uno de sus hombres más grandes acude a su lado con un machete en el puño. Benjamin apunta hacia Tared—. Despedaza a este animal.

Un animal.

El hombre que amo reducido a nada más que eso.

El mercenario sonríe y encara al lobo. Levanta el arma sobre su cabeza y su brillo metálico resplandece contra las farolas de las motocicletas hasta cegarme.

Escucho el metal blandirse en el aire. Y cuando la sangre del devorapieles salpica mi rostro, ya no logro gritar. Tan sólo abrir la boca, presenciar cómo mi alma es expulsada de mi cuerpo al ver ese filo hundirse en su cuerpo.

Grito, grito sin voz, acaso sin vida, y me arrastro hacia Tared con la trampa colgando de mi pierna como una piraña. Mi piel se desgarra contra la nieve y la roca, pero el dolor es insignificante.

Las carcajadas de Samedi ensordecen mis oídos. Las luces me ciegan, Benjamin Lander se gira hacia mí y clava el cañón de su pistola en mi nuca.

—Te devolveré el favor que le hiciste a mi hijo —dice con una sonrisa— y habré de comerme tu maldita carne en su honor.

Y luego...

PAM.

Un disparo que no revienta en mi cráneo.

PAM.

Un disparo que conmociona a la multitud alrededor. Y luego, escucho una explosión, tan fuerte que el suelo se cimbra.

Una ola de fuego se alza por el bosque y lo cubre de un violento resplandor anaranjado. La noche se llena de plomo y de gritos, y la pistola de Lander es arrancada de mi nuca cuando una bala lo hace retroceder.

Pero yo no tengo cabeza para otra cosa que no sea el hombre lobo inerte delante de mí, cuyo pelaje plateado se ha empapado del río carmesí que emana de su cuello.

—Tared, no... —alargo mi brazo hacia él, partido de pena al sentir que nuestro vínculo vuelve a sangrar, pero ahora cortado por la distancia entre este mundo y el otro.

No, ése no fue nuestro trato, exclamo para mis adentros. *¡Nuestro trato fue que saldríamos juntos de aquí!*

La espada se convierte en un ancla contra el suelo que impide alcanzarlo. Samedi me observa desde arriba, ansioso por arrebatarme la lengua. Las voces de Wéndigo gritan, asegurándome que nunca, jamás podré escapar de las sombras, y que ahora me toca enfrentar este mundo sin Tared.

Le ofrezco mi último trozo de corazón al tocar muy apenas su garra, con la punta de mis dedos humanos. Lo siento tan frío que cierro los ojos y dejo que el mundo se incendie a nuestro alrededor.

Lo siento. Lo siento tanto, Tared. A pesar de todo lo que hice, de todo lo que luché para salvarte, te fallé.

Y tú, en cambio, me protegiste hasta el final.

SEGUNDA FASE

UN MONSTRUO

NUEVO

CAPÍTULO 29
UN PUEBLO EN LLAMAS

Esta vez el brillo prístino de la luz sangra en rojo, transformando mi celda en un vientre escarlata. Las paredes de tierra respiran, palpitan, se inflaman e imitan mi seno de madre acuchillado por el dolor de ver a mi criatura sufrir de semejante manera.

Y por eso, mi deseo más profundo es que mi portal lo muestre de nuevo ante mí, que me permita acariciar con los dedos su perfil al despertar por fin de la pesadilla.

Pero el abismo no escupe más que un sonido delicado, un tarareo muy distinto de su voz rota por la tortura, en señal de que el vórtice necesita mostrarme algo más.

A través de la niebla, la veo *a ella*, caminando colina abajo sobre la infame y vacía Proctor Street. Canta en voz baja una canción antigua, una leyenda de un hombre que se ahoga entre las olas.

La luz amarillenta de las farolas dispersa la noche a su paso, y su cabello blanco ondea debajo de su cintura en curvas que imitan a la luna reflejada en un estanque; una feminidad que lucha contra su hermoso rostro de muchacho. Y a cada paso que da, cada salto, cada pirueta alegre de su vestido, el olor de su magia se desprende de los orificios de su cuerpo como un perfume de almizcle y tierra de sepulcro.

Más adelante, cuando su pálida cara se tiñe de una luz roja, logro encontrar la fuente del resplandor que me ha despertado: el letrero neón de un solitario Walgreens, el cual parpadea en la esquina de la calle.

La joven llega a la farmacia, pero en vez de dirigirse a la entrada, cruza el estacionamiento y va hacia la pequeña loma a espaldas del edificio. El bosque de árboles flacos la recibe, bordeado por una cerca metálica doblada por el peso de todos los turistas estúpidos que han escalado por ella.

¿Qué escogerá la pequeña *Hela* como mentira para justificar su escapada al pueblo esta noche? ¿Una copa menstrual nueva, un anticonceptivo de emergencia, un tónico que no es más que basura comparado con los venenos que su hermana le pone en la piel?

No importa. La bruja siempre encuentra una excusa para *cruzar la niebla*.

Las otras le han advertido que tenga cuidado, que no se fíe de las criaturas a quienes debe *evocar* para atravesarla, pero ella no puede evitarlo, y no sólo porque le gusta mucho la compañía de los muertos; su cabeza lleva inquieta desde que cruzó su mirada con la de mi creación mientras estaba inducida en sus sueños de obsidiana.

Pronto, la *necromante* localiza la parte del alambrado que está rota y se escabulle por ella sin temor a que la descubran. Viste entera de blanco y conoce como la palma de su mano cada recoveco, cada arbusto y piedra en la que puede ocultarse de las torpes cámaras de seguridad.

Pero al llegar a la cima de la loma se detiene, petrificada. Mira a su alrededor con los ojos negros entornados por la extrañeza. A pesar de que todos los espíritus que habitan el lugar fueron ahorcados sólo al pie de la colina, suele encontrarlos dispersos por todo el diminuto bosque o en las ramas de los árboles para recordar antiguos dolores.

Pero esta vez hay algo diferente.

Los fantasmas que habitan el monumento Proctor's Ledge son seres tristes y nostálgicos, entes que rara vez ignoran el llamado de la *necromante*, así que ella *siempre* puede sentirlos cerca, rondar por la nieve y hacerla crujir con sus pasos. Pero ahora no puede percibir nada, como si se los hubiese tragado la neblina.

O el infierno.

Mira a su alrededor y sostiene el aliento. Por encima del soplido del viento, de alguno que otro coche que pasa por la avenida y el repiquetear de los letreros luminosos del Walgreens a punto de fundirse... *lo escucha*. A alguien que camina a su derecha, por el arbolado.

Ella se lleva una mano al inquieto pecho, porque no percibe tristeza ni nostalgia, sentimientos comunes en los seres que habitan la colina. Tan sólo percibe una rabia extraordinaria y el deseo inmortal de causar dolor. Mucho dolor.

La luz roja se apaga y mis paredes, súbitamente, dejan de respirar. La tierra cae como una lluvia tenue sobre mi cabeza mientras los muros empiezan a comprimirse alrededor para que yo misma pueda sentir en carne propia lo que la joven está a punto de atestiguar.

—Por la Grieta... —dice a la par que echa a correr hacia los árboles para alcanzar a aquella alma violenta. El tacón de aguja de sus botas se entierra profundo en la nieve, pero cruza sin problema toda la loma como un cervatillo.

Sabe que está traspasando una propiedad privada y que tampoco sería su primera advertencia, pero eso no le preocupa en absoluto. Lo único que quiere es alcanzar esa sombra, esa silueta torcida y grotesca que empieza a desprender el aroma de la sangre.

—¡Espera, por favor! —grita, cuando por fin logra alcanzar al espíritu, el cual ha bajado hasta una media luna de piedra fabricada al pie de la colina; un monumento histórico, fúnebre, que mantiene a los muertos arraigados a la tierra.

Él, quien antes cojeaba, se detiene, y la bruja arruga la nariz al darse cuenta de su extrañeza. En vez de hablar, el ente gorgotea y su olor se vuelve más pestilente.

Por unos instantes, la mujer piensa que la silueta de ese *hombre* está distorsionada por la neblina, pero no es así. Y cuando él se da la media vuelta para encararla y mostrarle sus huesos rotos y su carne *aplastada*, ella se cubre la boca para no gritar de terror.

Porque Hela sabe quién es ese hombre.

Y también sabe que, pronto, el pueblo de Salem habrá de cubrirse en llamas.

CAPÍTULO 30
PÉRDIDA

—¡D*evuélvanmelo!*

La fogata estalla como si hubiese escuchado mi grito. Y cuando sus llamas abrasan todo el bosque de luz, las dos brujas detrás de la hoguera giran sus cabezas hacia mí.

—*Devuélvanmelo, por favor* —*insisto, las lágrimas de hambre se mezclan con las de mi pena*—, *devuélvanmelo y tendrán todo lo que quieran de mí.*

La mujer de cabello blanco baja el espejo y me deja ver por fin sus dilatados ojos negros. Vieja, marchita hasta la podredumbre como la otra anciana, ella también se ha embadurnado del ungüento obsceno hecho con aquel bebé, del que no queda más que una plasta sanguinolenta sobre una piedra en el suelo.

Pero ni siquiera mi demencial deseo de devorarlas a ellas y a su magia muerta puede sobreponerse a mi profunda desolación. Porque aún en este lugar oscuro, en esta pesadilla terrible, soy consciente de que él se ha ido.

Tared ha muerto. Tared está muerto porque no fui capaz de protegerlo.

—*Ven, cachorrito* —*dice una de las brujas*—. *Ven y ofrécete a ella.*

—*A ella, ¡a ella!* —*secunda la otra y ambas lanzan carcajadas al cielo sin luna.*

Miro a sus espaldas, hacia donde la luz de las llamas no alcanza la penumbra del bosque. Allí, descubro que una tercera criatura me observa detrás de la hoguera.

No pude distinguirla al principio; de grandes dimensiones y con ojos que arden como el carbón, su pelaje es tan negro que parecía una sombra proyectada contra los árboles. Pero ahora, las llamas se enardecen con el sólo propósito de revelarla.

Ella, con una magia tan incipiente que me dobla de hambre, tiene una prominente cabeza de cabra, y está sentada en el suelo con las pezuñas cruzadas. Sus dos largos cuernos apuntan hacia el cielo, mientras que cientos de velas a medio derretir recorren sus brazos, sus piernas, su espalda. Poco a poco, los pabilos se encienden y gotean sobre el pelaje apelmazado.

Frescos restos humanos descansan como un trono debajo de ella, puestos como una ofrenda que ha sido devorada por fauces que expelen humo y ceniza. En medio de sus senos de piel lampiña y grisácea yace el símbolo grabado a carne viva de las otras dos brujas, mientras que, en la entrepierna, su pene se alza erecto y grueso como un mástil.

Al mirarme, aquella terrible Hembra Cabría levanta su largo dedo torcido y apunta hacia mi corazón.

—Tu voluntad, *Bestia Revestida de Luna* —dice, y su voz suena como la de una mujer dentro de un pozo.

Un tirón en mis entrañas tira de mí en dirección contraria, me incita a huir, pero aquella advertencia no es, ni de cerca, tan fuerte como el deseo de regresar a Tared al plano de la vida.

Aunque sea una mentira.

Aunque sea sólo una ilusión. Una máscara más de su Marionetista.

Una de las ancianas profiere gemidos obscenos, se tira al suelo y comienza a arrastrarse hacia el monstruo. Se relame los labios y se sienta sobre su regazo para penetrarse a sí misma con aquel miembro *exagerado. Lanza un grito de dolor, pero continúa con la terrorífica tarea con una sonrisa, hasta meter por completo el falo dentro de su cuerpo una y otra vez en un vaivén que me revuelve las entrañas. Luego, ella se retira del ente para que la otra bruja ocupe su lugar, dejando aquel pene cubierto de sangre.*

Gritos intercalados de agonía y euforia inundan la noche, y aquella imagen es tan espeluznante que despierta en mí un miedo tan profundo e instintivo que ahora mismo debería estar retrocediendo.

En cambio, empiezo a avanzar hacia la hoguera.

—Devuélvanmelo, por favor —imploro una vez más.

La criatura con cabeza de cabra arroja algo por encima de las llamas, algo que aterriza a mis pies. Es un libro grande y pesado, tan antiguo que debería haberse deshojado con la caída. Sin embargo, se ha abierto de par en par, y en sus pliegos amarillentos hay garabateadas montones de firmas rojas, nombres antiguos que nunca había escuchado en mi vida.

Y entre tanta tinta, un solo hueco libre se vislumbra al pie de la página.

Cuando entiendo qué es lo que quiere la criatura de mí, levanto la mirada hacia ella. La bestia despliega un par de gigantescas alas en su espalda, rematadas con plumas negras como su pelaje, bordeadas también por numerosas velas. Las dos brujas a sus flancos golpean el suelo con un pie y comienzan a flotar en espirales, danzan en el aire, se retuercen y gritan extasiadas con la entrepierna ensangrentada.

—Tu voluntad, Bestia Revestida de Luna —insiste, y su aliento no es otro que el olor de la carne quemada.

Tomo el libro y escucho gritos de dolor provenientes de cada uno de los nombres escritos. La cubierta de cuero negro quema como madera caliente en las palmas de mis manos, pero yo sólo pienso que, en estos momentos, haría arder el mundo por él.

Levanto mi mano de hueso para pinchar mi índice humano, pero ladeo la cabeza, desconcertado al ver que mi garra no está. Tan sólo hay dedos humanos, *llenos de carne.*

Escucho a Wéndigo rugir a lo lejos, llamándome desde las profundidades del bosque.

Y entonces... todo empieza a temblar.

Las tres criaturas frente a mí miran hacia arriba cuando un resplandor rompe sobre nuestras cabezas y abre una grieta en el cielo nocturno. El libro negro se hace cenizas en mis manos, las brujas chillan y sus pieles comienzan a quemarse en hondas fumarolas al ser alcanzadas por aquel brillo.

Como si me lo hubiesen estampado en la cara, aspiro de pronto el aroma de miles de flores.

—¡NO, NO, DEVUÉLVANMELO!

Es inútil. De pronto, mi voz es ensordecida por el terrible toque de una trompeta.

ᴳ ● ◗ ○

Mi despertar es tan violento como un martillazo en la sien. Y, aplastado contra una superficie blanda, me sacudo, me convulsiono, me revuelco entre mis propias extremidades, ahogado con un grito que no puedo dejar salir.

¡Levántate!

Y quiero hacerlo, ¡maldito sea si no! Pero el peso colérico de la espada me oprime contra el suelo. Me arden tanto los ojos que no distingo más que borrones crueles que llenan mi cabeza de fantasmas de luz y ceniza. Las voces del monstruo de hueso braman tan fuerte que siento que me reventarán los oídos por dentro.

Tared, *asesinado.* Mi mano alcanzando la suya sólo para descubrirlo más frío que el hielo.

Tared, Tared, Tared.

Los dioses lo saben. *Nunca debí despertar.*

—¡No! —despego la espalda del suelo, liberando por fin mi grito.

Me levanto de un salto a la par que busco desesperadamente un libro. Una Hembra Cabría. Una tríada de brujas.

Mis pies se enredan en una tela que casi me hace tropezar, pero en cuanto vislumbro el alba y *un bosque* que se asoma a través de un ventanal, no me detengo a observar, a entender el sitio en el que estoy ni el lugar donde me encuentro.

Tan sólo pienso en un pacto que no pude concretar en mis pesadillas.

El pacto, ¡sí, el pacto! ¡Aún estoy a tiempo de cerrarlo!

¿PARA QUÉ? ÉL ESTÁ MUERTO.

—¡BASTA! —rujo a todo pulmón.

Cruzo esta habitación que no deja de dar vueltas. Alcanzo la perilla de la puerta y me dejo caer contra ella como un costal.

¡ESTÁ MUERTO!

Me llevo una mano a la pierna. Mi herida late, aunque no siento el clamor tibio de la sangre brotar. Está completamente cerrada, pero me duele como si el círculo de dientes metálicos aún fracturase el hueso.

La cabeza me palpita, Wéndigo se agita en mi consciencia y lo fragmenta todo como una migraña, furioso por haberle arrebatado el control de mi corazón.

Me sujeto con todas mis fuerzas al pomo y lo giro. Afuera, me encuentro con un pasillo que cruzo con los pies descalzos hasta llegar a una escalera.

Escucho que alguien grita mi nombre, pero el llamado se difumina en el fondo de mi cabeza.

Bajo desaforado hasta alcanzar la puerta en la que desemboca, como si quisiera tirarme de bruces contra los escalones. Distingo alrededor una cocina de paredes amarillas y el bosque detrás de una ventana sobre el fregador.

Las náuseas se aglomeran en mi estómago, ¡¿por qué carajos sigo vivo?!

¡Porque tú lo mataste!

Mi hombro cimbra cuando lo azoto contra la puerta de aquella cocina. Un porche de madera me recibe y, más allá, a cincuenta metros, el predio nevado que tan desesperado estoy por alcanzar.

Salto hacia la nieve y me hundo en ella hasta los tobillos; el frío me desgarra en el acto y arrojo vaho por la boca como si algo dentro de mí se incendiara. Echo a correr hacia la foresta para encontrarlo, para salvarlo.

Está muerto.

Tared ha muerto.

Y aun así...

"... soy la manifestación de tus deseos más profundos."

Voy a traerlo de vuelta.

Iré al barranco, al arroyo, a la cabaña, e invocaré a esa asquerosa Marionetista. La obligaré a que extienda uno de sus brazos y me lo devuelva, aunque sea todo un engaño, una mentira.

Y después, que mi Mara me parta en pedazos si así debe ser.

Pero en cambio, caigo de rodillas a un paso del bosque, derrotado por el peso de la espada. Levanto la cabeza y la luna nueva de la madrugada me mira con ternura desde el cielo, sobre las montañas. Tan azul, tan ajena a la guerra dentro de mi cabeza.

Ella sabe que no vale la pena. Y no porque no pudiera firmar ese libro con mi nombre, con mi puño y con mi letra, sino porque, aun si pudiese resucitar a mi Tared de entre los muertos, jamás tendría el corazón para encerrar su alma en un cuerpo sin vida. En un muñeco terrible.

Dije que haría el mundo arder con tal de tenerlo de vuelta, pero, ¿qué mundo, si éste ya está vuelto cenizas?

—Tared... —musito, desbordado por la tristeza. Meto las manos en la nieve para estrujarla y descubro mi mano aún de hueso. Bajo la cabeza y dejo que las lágrimas se congelen sobre mis mejillas. Duele tanto que quiero morir. Tanto que no quiero levantarme de allí nunca...

De pronto, algo se lleva mi aliento. Algo que forcejea en mi pecho, que crece como una enredadera y lo rodea, lo estruja y tira de él con fuerza.

Pero no es la garra de Wéndigo.

La nieve cruje y yo levanto la cabeza para ver cómo una silueta aparece entre la niebla y los árboles. *Él* surge del lindero y me mira como si despertase de su propio sueño.

Sus vivos ojos azules. Su cabello rubio, su piel contra el invierno; el hombre lobo me llama con un grito, mi nombre escrito en sus labios y no en la tinta escarlata de un libro negro.

¿Es... es real? ¿O es una mentira de aquellas brujas que por fin escucharon mis plegarias?

No alcanzo a ponerme de pie cuando Tared ya me ha rodeado con sus brazos. Me eleva, me arranca de la nieve para sostenerme como si estuviese a punto de caer de un precipicio.

Y cuando abrazo su cuello, descubro con asombro que no hay ningún brazo en su nuca que lo sostenga, extremidades que se oculten en la nieve o una Marionetista que lo manipule entre los árboles.

—¡Dios mío, Elisse! —exclama, sus palabras atrapadas en el hueco entre mi hombro y mi clavícula. Me cuesta empujar las mías fuera de la garganta, azorado por la manera en la que me estruja entero.

Siento su cuerpo caliente y el palpitar de todas y cada una de sus venas.

—¡Eres...!

Es real. Pero, ¿cómo, si yo sentí el último palpitar de su corazón? ¿Cómo, si yo lo vi morir?

Él despega su rostro de mi cuello para que pueda mirarlo, para convencernos a ambos de que no estamos viendo una ilusión.

—Lo logramos, Elisse —dice con una sonrisa, opacando las terribles voces con el latido enloquecido de su corazón—. Llegamos. *Esto es Minnesota.*

CAPÍTULO 31
CÍRCULO DE PROTECCIÓN

Tared me deja en el suelo sólo lo suficiente para quitarse la parka de invierno que lleva puesta. Me la pone sobre los hombros y me levanta en brazos de nuevo para llevarme de vuelta al sitio del que salí corriendo como un desquiciado.

Es una casa en medio de un claro de pinos verdes, coronando una pequeña loma escondida en el frondoso bosque. Es de dos pisos y techo a dos aguas, con acabados en piedra y madera rústica. La larga chimenea arroja un humo blanco y espeso contra el amanecer aún salpicado de estrellas, y varias montañas azules se alzan en el fondo con la luna acunada sobre los picos angulosos.

El lugar es tan hermoso que me parece un sueño imposible. Uno que se vuelve más lúcido a medida que percibo las formas, las sensaciones, la realidad.

Las preguntas en mi cabeza no paran de multiplicarse, pero ya no siento miedo ni desesperación al percibir que el vínculo palpita entre nosotros, vivo y fuerte como las arterias de un toro.

Con la cabeza recargada en su hombro, aspiro el reconfortante aroma de Tared. Veo que aún lleva la barba y el cabello largos, las ojeras acentuadas por lo que parecen haber sido muchas noches de insomnio.

Y en su espalda, porta un rifle sujeto a una correa.

—Tared, ¿qué fue lo que ocurrió? —pregunto a la vez que me seco las lágrimas.

—Te lo explicaré en cuanto te quitemos esa ropa mojada —dice, mirándome como si quisiera limpiarlas él mismo—, ¿a qué clase de loco se le ocurre salir corriendo en pijama con este frío?

Allí, me percato de que si estoy temblando tanto es porque sólo llevo puesto un pantalón de felpa y una camiseta. Me hago un ovillo dentro del abrigo, y me pregunto de qué diablos está hecho este hombre que ni el hierro de los tramperos ni el peso del plano medio ha sido capaz de matarlo. ¿Acaso lo habré imaginado todo? ¿Verlo morir frente a mí fue sólo el delirio de aquel momento terrible?

Llegamos al porche y cruzamos la puerta que dejé abierta de par en par. Me encuentro de nuevo con aquella cocina de cálidas paredes amarillas, con una mesa redonda en medio, con bolsas de plástico y recipientes desechables.

Contigua a la estancia hay una sala de paredes pintadas de un color gris azulado, con la puerta principal de la casa al fondo. Sólo hay dos muebles en todo el espacio, una mesita de centro y un sillón largo frente a la chimenea, cuyo calor parece ser suficiente para caldear las dos estancias.

Parqué de madera clara, revestimientos de piedra natural y cornisas de yeso blanco, amplios ventanales que dejan ver el bosque que rodea la construcción; una casa sobria y elegante, pero vacía y empolvada, señal de que lleva mucho tiempo abandonada.

No me cabe ninguna duda. Éste es el hogar de Tared.

El lobo me baja con cuidado, y en cuanto pongo los pies sobre las baldosas de la cocina, siento un dolor extraño pinchar en mi esternón.

—Tared, ¿qué...?

—¡Elisse!

Escuchar aquella voz me corta la respiración. Tenso, como si me hubiese mordido una serpiente, miro hacia las escaleras. Johanna está parada en uno de los peldaños, con una mano sobre los labios y la otra aferrada al barandal; sus ojos grises casi desorbitados, como si presenciase una aparición.

No...

Una puerta en el extremo opuesto de la cocina se abre de golpe. Julien y Nashua entran precipitadamente a la casa, alarmados por el grito de la errante. Y, al verme, dejan caer algo pesado a sus espaldas, un cuerpo con astas que se hunde de sopetón en la nieve de afuera.

—Dios mío, Elisse, ¡por fin has despertado! —exclama el pelirrojo, y tanto él como la perpetuasangre corren hacia mí.

¡No!

—¡No! —grito también a todo pulmón, retrayéndome hacia el pecho de Tared. Julien y Johanna se detienen a media cocina, conmocionados ante mi reacción. Ésta vez, las voces de Wéndigo no gritan ni se retuercen, como si mi nuevo vínculo con Tared las hubiese vuelto apenas un hormigueo bajo la piel o la resaca de una migraña tras la nuca.

Pero es otra cosa la que me pone alerta. Un veneno que bombea desde mi propio corazón y que afina tanto mis sentidos que poco me falta para comenzar a gruñir...

Y es que no he podido evitarlo.

Al igual que me sucedió con el lobo, para mí es como si ahora estuviese frente a unos completos desconocidos, y tengo un miedo irracional de sólo pensar que, si los dejo acercarse, reviviré una vez más el trauma y el dolor de nuestro vínculo roto. ¿Es que ellos no lo perciben también? ¿Esa agonía? ¿Esa maldita distancia? ¿Cómo carajos pretenden que actúe como si nada hubiese pasado, que los estreche de nuevo entre mis brazos cuando no puedo hacer otra cosa que recordar cómo, una y otra vez, ellos *me rechazaron* cuando más los necesitaba? Ah, pero qué bestia más rencorosa has resultado ser, murmura Wéndigo muy, muy por lo bajo, su voz ahora no más que un susurro molesto.

Ante la forma instintiva en la que Tared cierne sus brazos a mi alrededor, los dos errantes deciden retroceder.

Por su parte, Nashua está impasible, con lo que parece ser un cadáver de ciervo a sus pies, tan apartado y ausente que resulta igual de agobiante que la euforia del resto.

—Me alegra mucho ver que por fin te has levantado, Elisse. Empezaba a preocuparme —la voz de la perpetuasangre parece genuinamente conmovida, pero no me muevo un centímetro.

—Todo está bien, flaquito. Ahora estás a salvo —insiste el bisonte a la par que levanta ambas manos—. Ya no tienes por qué tener miedo.

—Yo también tendría miedo si lo primero que hiciera después de despertar fuese ver la horrenda cara de Miller.

Aquel comentario mordaz me hace mirar hacia el segundo piso de la casa, al pequeño balcón al lado de las escaleras. Doy un respingo al ver a Hoffman bajar, cubierto por un saco negro de invierno. Llega a la cocina y lanza una mirada fría al hombre que me sostiene entre sus brazos.

Para mi sorpresa, el tirón desesperado en mis tobillos empieza a ceder con su presencia.

—Joder. Estás hecho un desastre —dice, no para dividir la cocina en un campo de batalla, sino para cortar la tensión.

—Supongo que tenemos mucho de qué hablar, ¿verdad? —añade Tared cuando entiende que ya me he tranquilizado un poco. Se separa de mí con cuidado y pone su mano en mi espalda para llevarme hacia la sala, seguidos de cerca por Comus Bayou.

Una punzada en la sien me hunde contra el sillón frente a la chimenea; mis sentidos siguen algo atontados y el monstruo de hueso no para de musitar lo apetitosos que le parecen los ancestros de aquellos que, con cuidado, empiezan a dispersarse por la habitación.

Para mi paz mental, el lobo me mantiene bien cerca de él, lo que ayuda a apaciguar la sensación. Por su parte, Julien y Johanna se quedan de pie junto al fuego, mientras que Nashua decide conservar su distancia, apoyado contra uno de los amplios ventanales de la casa.

Al observarlos, descubro mucho desgaste en ellos. Cabellos y barbas más largos y desaliñados, kilos más o kilos menos, ojeras y arrugas nuevas a causa del estrés...

Los devorapieles han dejado sus armas en la cocina y al ciervo que cazaron afuera, en la nieve, pero el olor a sangre y pólvora aún persiste en sus ropas, como si se hubiesen traído una parte de la esencia de los tramperos con ellos.

Tramperos. *Benjamin Lander.*

—¿Qué fue lo pasó? —decido preguntar cuando el silencio se vuelve insoportable.

Johanna retuerce los dedos con nerviosismo.

—Llegamos al ataque a la cabaña demasiado tarde —titubea—, no teníamos idea de que ustedes estaban en Montana hasta que...

—No. ¿Qué pasó en *Stonefall*? —preciso.

La pregunta sale con tanto resentimiento como si la hubiese pronunciado el mismísimo monstruo de hueso. El silencio en la estancia se recrudece, la culpa revolotea como una polilla y, por unos segundos, parece ser que nadie tiene las agallas de sostenerme la mirada.

Hoffman, quien se había detenido a fumar su cigarro en la cocina, lo tira en el lavabo y se acerca para sentarse frente a mí en la mesita de centro, traspasando sin chistar la respetuosa distancia que impusieron los demás.

—Cuando los Lander llegaron a la casa Blake, tuvimos que huir. Todos —dice a la par que busca su cajetilla en el abrigo, una sustitución interesante de su estereotipada gabardina—. Quise ir detrás de ti, pero me fue imposible; volaban disparos por todas partes y cuando logré volver al coche, no pude hacerlo subir por el camino por donde te habías ido.

Es extraño. No ha mencionado mi transformación en Wéndigo... o el canibalismo, como si aquellas circunstancias no le importasen lo más mínimo.

—Lo único que pude hacer fue rescatar a Johanna en la carretera —añade—, pero los demás...

Te abandonaron.

El silencio se alarga como si todos hubiesen escuchado al monstruo dentro de mí.

—Después, vimos las luces de las patrullas acercarse a la casa —continúa la texana—. Había disparos, gritos, motores y sierras por doquier; eran demasiados tramperos y todos ellos fueron por ti en cuanto Benjamin Lander supo que habías huido hacia la montaña. Fue entonces cuando nos dispersamos.

Dejándote a tu suerte...

Otra vez el silencio. La incomodidad. Esa polilla que revolotea peligrosamente cubriendo la luz.

—Pero, ¿sabes una cosa, Elisse? No importa que hubiera más de treinta cazadores persiguiéndote, hubo alguien que fue por ti, sin dudarlo.

Julien apunta a Tared con la mirada, quien se mantiene ocupado observando sus manos entrelazadas en el regazo.

Dioses, todo este tiempo creí que nos habíamos topado en el bosque por casualidad, ¡Tared nunca me dijo que había ido *por mí*!

—No debiste hacer eso —musito, conmovido—. Debiste huir y ponerte a salvo como los demás.

—Jamás te habría abandonado —replica, casi ofendido—. Y lo sabes.

Sí. Ahora lo sé.

La tensión y el silencio que Tared y yo imponemos al mirarnos es desgarrada sólo por la voz del detective.

—Esa noche tampoco logramos dar con Irina —dice en un susurro, algo poco usual en él.

—¿Qué? ¡¿No han sabido nada de ella desde entonces?!

—Tranquilo, Elisse —responde Julien levantando las palmas de las manos hacia mí—. Estuvimos escondidos en las colinas de Stonefall un par de días y no supimos nada más hasta que logramos volver a Red Buffalo. Allí...

—Me encontraron. Porque volví para buscar el cuerpo de mi esposo.

Como un rayo, la voz de Irina me atenaza el cuerpo de arriba abajo. Me pongo en pie con un movimiento, mudo de la impresión, no sólo de ver a la errante puma entrar por la puerta principal de la casa, sino al descubrir quién la acompaña detrás.

—¡Lía!

CAPÍTULO 32
RECUENTO DE LOS DAÑOS

De haber sido cualquier otro momento, habría corrido hacia Irina, sin dudarlo. Le habría echado los brazos al cuello para estrecharla y hacerle saber lo inmensamente feliz que me sentía de saber que pudo sobrevivir a la masacre de Stonefall.

Pero me basta con mirarla una sola vez para permanecer, inmóvil, en mi lugar.

Ella cruza la sala con los hombros salpicados de nieve, y se deja caer sobre la mesita de centro, justo al lado de Hoffman. Descuelga el rifle que lleva en la espalda y recarga los brazos en los muslos, con aquellos ojos azules mucho más oscuros a como los recuerdo, mientras que su expresión, la cual siempre fue dulce, eternamente gentil, no muestra ira ni dolor. Tan sólo un solemne vacío, como si se hubiese sentado frente a mí un cadáver.

Debbie y Lía entran detrás y ésta última se acerca para abrazarme.

—Estoy muy feliz de ver que has despertado, cariño —dice a la par que me empuja con suavidad para que me siente de nuevo en el sillón.

Mira bien lo que has hecho...

Regreso mi atención a la errante puma. Su presencia pesa como un yunque, tanto así que agradezco mucho que tenga la mirada en el suelo en vez de puesta sobre mí, porque, ¿con qué cara te enfrentas a alguien que de la noche a la mañana ha perdido a *toda* su familia?

La densidad del aire se vuelve asfixiante. El simple respirar parece más una provocación...

—Aquella noche quise ir tras los tramperos, pero no pude hacerlo —dice ella de pronto, y su voz parece haber envejecido diez años—. Me dispararon tantas veces que no pude capturar a ninguno para descubrir lo que había pasado con mis hijos. Por eso tuve que rendirme y esconderme, volver después al rancho a buscar a Chenoa.

Intento ver más allá de sus ojos vacíos, de su postura rígida y la indiferencia de su voz, pero no logro encontrar furia, desesperación o tristeza. No siento *nada*. Ni una pizca de vida, más allá del subir y bajar de su pecho, como si ella hubiese muerto también ese día, al lado de su esposo.

—Eso fue lo más jodido —continúa Hoffman, apartando un segundo el cigarro de sus labios—. Los malditos habían llegado primero al rancho. Mucho antes que nosotros.

—¿Qué quieres decir?

—Que después de la batalla, algunos de ellos volvieron a Red Buffalo para *limpiar*, mientras nosotros estábamos ocultos en la montaña —responde Johanna en su lugar—. Las paredes, el establo, la casona; todo estaba impecable, como si nunca hubiesen estado allí.

—Incluso se habían llevado a Fernanda y a Sammuel, y de no ser porque los quemamos, de seguro se habrían llevado también a Calen y a Alannah. Hasta parecía un trabajo hecho por errantes... —dice Julien.

—Lo único que no tomaron fue a mi marido —continúa Irina, su voz afilada como el bajar de un machete—. Lo dejaron pudrirse en la entrada del rancho. Estaba cubierto de cal, como un perro… porque sabían que yo iba a regresar por él. *Sabían cuánto dolor iba a sufrir al verlo así.*

El silencio después de sus palabras es tan frío que me siento de nuevo en la cañada, bajo el río congelado, y más cuando la devorapieles acaricia su arma de arriba abajo como único reflejo de sus emociones.

Sus hijos, devorados.

No…

Su esposo, acribillado.

¡No!

Y todo por tu culpa.

Al sentirme temblar, Tared desliza su brazo con discreción por mi espalda, cosa que ayuda a que no se me salgan los sollozos, algo que estoy seguro de que Irina no necesita en estos momentos.

—Después de la batalla, nos costó mucho volver a encontrar a los tramperos —dice Julien—. Ocultaron sus registros y sus huellas mediante los contactos que tenían en la policía gracias a Malcolm Dallas. Y también se las arreglaron para hacer desparecer *nuestro rastro.*

—Tu registro en el motel y hasta las denuncias de tu búsqueda —añade Hoffman—. Todo lo sacaron del sistema, como si no quisieran que nuestra existencia saliera a la luz. Lo único que no lograron ocultar a tiempo fueron los asesinatos de Jocelyn Blake.

—Aun así, no íbamos a quedarnos de brazos cruzados, ni mucho menos a aceptar que ustedes dos estaban muertos —dice Johanna a la par que crispa los puños—, por eso hicimos hasta lo imposible por dar con una pista de los Lander. Y sólo lo logramos apelando al mercado negro, donde Red Buffalo solía comerciar.

"Pero tampoco debíamos acercarnos demasiado. Tenían los cuadernos de Sam, los cuerpos y a los niños, sin mencionar que también podían haberlos capturado a ustedes. Era estúpido arriesgarnos a que se dieran cuenta de que los íbamos siguiendo. Así que, después de varios meses, por fin nos enteramos de dónde tenían su campamento.

—Texas —susurra Irina—. Los Lander son nómadas, así que suelen moverse constantemente en caravanas de un lado a otro por el centro y este del país, pero ésta vez, se habían detenido un tiempo en El Paso. Por un momento pensamos que huirían a Ciudad Juárez, no dudábamos que estuviesen amañados también con los cárteles de la frontera, pero de un día para otro, cambiaron de ruta y se marcharon. Así, sin más.

—Pero eso no fue todo —dice el detective—. Si nos pareció muy extraño que regresaran sus pasos al oeste fue aún más raro que dejaran gente atrás: casi cuatro remolques con mujeres y niños. Creímos que volverían a Utah, pero cuando rastreamos su ruta y vimos que cruzaban en línea recta como locos desde Nuevo México hasta Washington supimos que en realidad estaban *buscando algo*.

No hace falta hacer muchos cálculos. Es evidente que fue cuando Tared y yo salimos del plano medio y se activó el rastreador en mi brazo.

—Allí nos topamos con Lía, quien nos dijo que se dirigían a Minnesota. Y sólo pudimos alcanzarlos hasta que...

—Hasta que los tramperos se detuvieron para acorralarnos a Tared y a mí en las montañas —confirmo en voz baja.

—Eran muchísimos hombres, no sabíamos si íbamos a poder con ellos —continúa Julien—. Pero, por suerte, teníamos al Atrapasueños de Lía de nuestro lado, ¡y hasta uno de sus hermanos resultó ser experto en bombas caseras!

Levanto la cabeza hacia la humana.

—¿Trajeron a su familia para ayudarnos? —pregunto, sorprendido.

—Por supuesto —contesta Debbie en su lugar—. No podíamos permitir que esos malnacidos se salieran con la suya.

La escena en la cañada comienza a tener sentido. Las explosiones, las balas, el repentino caos en medio del terror calculado de los Lander; siento como si veinte kilos de peso descendieran de mis hombros al ordenar, por fin, la escena en mi cabeza.

Lía me sonríe bajo el brazo musculado de su esposa, tan protectora como el propio lobo a mi lado. De pronto, me dan ganas de erigirles un maldito monumento.

—Sin embargo, Benjamin Lander y la mayoría de su gente se las arreglaron para escapar —musita Johanna con los labios apretados.

Lander. ¡El maldito bastardo sigue vivo!

—Si es así, tenemos qué movilizarnos *ya* —sentencio—. Es cuestión de tiempo para que ese desgraciado vuelva a encontrarnos.

Tared se yergue sobre el asiento.

—Olvídalo —replica—. Acabas de despertar y no tenemos idea de las secuelas que estés por sufrir tras la pelea. No pienso ponerte en riesgo ahora.

—Benjamin no se quedará de brazos cruzados, y mucho menos después de que le arrancaras la mitad de la cara. Ahora es incluso más personal, Tared, y te aseguro que va a buscar la forma más jodida de vengarse *de ti.*

—Y no sabes con qué ganas le voy a arrancar la otra mitad de su horrible rostro cuando lo enfrente de nuevo.

—Pero ¿qué estás diciendo?

—*No pienso olvidar lo que te hizo, Elisse,* ¡sólo estoy esperando el maldito momento para...!

—¡DEJA YA DE DECIR ESTUPIDECES!

El grito de Johanna nos cierra la boca a los dos.

—Johanna...

—No, Tared, ¡NO ME VOY A CALLAR! —grita ella tres veces más alto—, hicieron falta dos días enteros de cirugía para salvarte gracias a esa tontería de transformarte con el arpón dentro, ¡fue un milagro que no murieras al instante!, ¿cómo diablos puedes hablar de pelear otra vez con Benjamin Lander cuando casi te rebanan el cuello esa noche? ¡DEJA DE SER TAN IDIOTA!

El vértigo se abre paso cuando miro al lobo, de arriba abajo, y encuentro una cicatriz blanca y gruesa asomándose por un costado de su clavícula.

Entonces no fue una ilusión o un momento de delirio. El machete *sí lo alcanzó.*

La errante coyote rompe a llorar a todo pulmón, como si se hubiese contenido hasta ahora. Y cuando se lleva las manos a la cara, puedo notar los vendajes alrededor de sus muñecas, seguramente producto de las transfusiones de sangre que necesitó hacernos a Tared y a mí para salvarnos.

Julien se acerca a ella para intentar consolarla, pero puedo notar que el desasosiego también se ha apoderado de él.

La escena me conmociona y a la vez me recuerda que no soy el único que habría sufrido terriblemente si Tared hubiese llegado a morir.

Ah, eres tan, tan egoísta...

Miro de nuevo a Hoffman, a Irina, a un Nashua que hasta ahora no me ha dirigido siquiera la mirada. Contemplo sus heridas y todo lo que han perdido a lo largo de este viaje, y casi quiero echarme a reír de sólo pensar en que, por unos momentos, creí que tenía derecho a pedirles cuentas cuando ellos tienen razones de sobra para alejarse de mí.

Supongo que mi vínculo con Comus Bayou se había roto desde hacía tanto tiempo que me había acostumbrado a ese dolor.

—Lo siento —sollozo, humillado por mi propia oscuridad.

Tú provocaste todo esto.

—Lo siento. Lo siento tanto —repito—. Lo de Nueva Orleans. Lo de Utah. Lo de Wéndigo. *Todo ha sido culpa mía.*

Y no mereces su perdón.

Cierro los ojos y me llevo las manos a la cara. Tared me rodea los hombros, me abraza con cuidado para ayudarme a resistir el peso del remordimiento, pero ya es demasiado tarde.

Siento la cicatriz abrirse de nuevo en canal.

—Elisse —llama la perpetuasangre en voz baja—, Hoffman, él... nos contó acerca del pacto que hiciste con Barón Samedi. Y por qué le perdonaste la vida.

Desconcertado, llevo la mirada hacia el detective.

—¿Por qué? —pregunto, sin comprender. Él me observa unos segundos, envuelto en los brazos del lobo, y baja la mirada hacia la mesa para apagar su cigarro en ella.

—Porque no iba a dejar que siguieran dudando de quién eres en realidad.

Me quedo sin aliento al escuchar aquello.

—Lo sentimos mucho, Elisse —dice Johanna, hipando—. Siempre te has sentido culpable por la distancia que pusiste entre Comus Bayou y tú, pero la verdad es que fuimos nosotros quienes deshonramos nuestro vínculo al darte la espalda en ese pantano. Perdónanos. ¡Perdónanos por nunca haberlo reconocido!

La conmoción me golpea y, de pronto, la culpa de todos se convierte en una ola que inunda la habitación. Percibo las manos de Nashua tensarse sobre sus antebrazos, como si no pudiese dejar salir las palabras, la mirada de mis hermanos suplicando una oportunidad.

Si los dejas entrar, volverán a verte como lo que somos.

Cierro los ojos.

Volverán a lastimarte.

La espada late como un segundo corazón intoxicado.

Y ya no podrás salvarlos de ti.

El cosquilleo bajo mi piel, la sombra de la migraña, la presencia del monstruo dentro de mí; nada es suficiente para evitar que me desprenda de mi refugio, de mi lobo, para ponerme de pie y dejar que Julien y Johanna sean ahora los que me envuelvan.

Wéndigo susurra con insistencia, pero el abrazo estrecho de *mis hermanos* me basta para jurar que, desde este momento, nunca volveré a cruzar palabra con el monstruo.

Debbie y Lía se limitan a observarnos, ésta última conmovida por nuestras emociones, mientras que Irina decide guardar un respetuoso silencio. Nashua sigue sin aproximarse, pero acepto su distancia como una última prueba para nosotros dos.

Recuperar la confianza con mi familia tomará tiempo, tiempo en que enfrentaremos situaciones que nos costará mucho superar. Pero ahora estoy convencido de que, tal y como nos sucedió a Tared y a mí, el vínculo que murió entre Comus Bayou y yo algún día, en algún momento… volverá.

Porque siempre, siempre encuentra la forma de volver.

CAPÍTULO 33
UN MONSTRUO VIENE A VERTE

En cuanto pone un pie en el empedrado, la bruja Caligo confirma que algo no va bien. No sólo es que la niebla la ha transportado a la calle Essex en vez de al mercado en Derby Square, sino que aún lleva las vestiduras impregnadas por el extraño olor a quemado que la despertó esta mañana en su alcoba.

Ella mira con severidad al hombre erguido a sus espaldas, quien es el responsable de haberla guiado hasta allí. Para el resto de los escasos transeúntes de la calle es sólo un sujeto muy grande y musculoso, de piel cetrina y ojos oscuros, pero ambas podemos ver con claridad una naturaleza mucho más interesante detrás de ese espejismo.

El sujeto levanta un dedo y apunta hacia el frente. Caligo descubre que la infame casa de Jonathan Corwin la observa, asentada en una esquina de la calle. El letrero de madera con el nombre del edificio histórico se bambolea con el viento helado, mientras que las paredes revestidas de pintura negra parecen doblarse con el peso de la nieve acumulada en los tejados.

Suspicaz, se acomoda la melena rizada, el color azabache ya salpicado por unas cuantas canas, y da la vuelta para alejarse con prisa.

En pocos minutos llega hasta un edificio de ladrillo rojo que desprende humo de incienso y hierbas aromáticas, un olor demasiado benigno para que le sea interesante a una *envenenadora*. Abre la vieja puerta de la tienda y escucha el repiqueteo del colgante de amatista en la entrada.

Recorre los anaqueles con la mirada. Los libros de Gerald Gardner en una mesa, sacos de piedras preciosas en otra, la estantería con rocas de sal y hierbas embotelladas que los turistas compran más por curiosidad que por deseos de práctica; su nariz aguileña se expande para tratar de percibir algún matiz putrefacto en el penetrante sándalo, pero todo parece normal dentro de la extrañeza.

Me sonrío y me relamo, porque no se da cuenta de que el aroma que debería perturbarle es uno muy distinto al de la carne podrida.

Con una ceja alzada, va hacia la caja registradora, donde un hombre delgaducho la recibe con los brazos en jarras.

—¡Por la diosa, mujer! ¡Otra vez traes esa cosa horripilante contigo! —exclama al ver la capa de piel emplumada que ella lleva sobre los hombros. La bruja, orgullosa, le responde con una sonrisa velada.

—Ah, querido. Tan pusilánime como siempre, por eso cobras una miseria por tus trabajos. ¿Dónde está Cecilia? —pregunta con una sonrisa, aunque estoy segura de que aún percibe esa sensación de calor y asfixia que parece haberla perseguido por toda la calle.

—¡Ah! Ha estado allá atrás toda la mañana —dice el tipo a la par que apunta con la barbilla al fondo del negocio, hacia una puerta cerrada—. Tenía una cita a las diez, pero me pidió cancelarla. Desde entonces, no ha salido de allí.

Caligo enarca una ceja.

—¿Se encuentra bien?

El hombre mueve la mano de arriba abajo.

—No durmió mucho anoche. Creo que está teniendo pesadillas.

La bruja guarda un silencio propio de su inteligencia, tanta que hasta me parece una lástima que hoy en día haya tan pocas como ella.

Pero *tú*, en cambio, la matarías sin dudarlo, y con mucha menos piedad que yo, ¿verdad? La estrangularías y la despedazarías con gusto si hiciera falta. A todas y a cada una de nosotras...

—Bueno, entonces iré a saludarla, quizás hasta pueda pensar en un remedio que le ayude.

El insignificante brujo pareciera querer protestar, pero basta una de las miradas de Caligo para que éste le dé su permiso, sin más.

Ella camina hacia el fondo de la tienda y se abre paso por la puerta. Del otro lado la recibe una pequeña habitación; una antesala hacia el almacén escondido detrás de unas cortinas aterciopeladas. El sitio no tiene decoración más allá de las paredes violetas, un trinchador pequeño en una esquina y una mesa redonda de mármol indio en el medio.

La envenenadora encuentra a la bruja Cecilia sentada en un taburete, con un mazo de Tarot cortado frente a ella y una sonrisa bajo sus ojos castaños.

—Querida —exclama—, hace tanto que no venías a verme, ¿ya te olvidaste de tu vieja amiga, verdad?

—No seas ridícula. Sabes que he estado pendiente de ti desde que me pediste *ese favor* hace un mes —contesta—. Y sírveme algo de beber, que me estoy congelando aquí dentro.

La otra parpadea un par de veces y se acaricia un poco la rodilla bajo la mesa.

—Perdóname, bella, pero esta pierna me ha molestado desde anoche, así que siéntete libre de robarte lo que quieras del mueble. Me siento incapaz de levantarme.

Caligo entorna los ojos un momento, pero luego asiente y se encamina hacia el trinchador. Abre la puerta de cristal y saca dos vasos junto con una botella de licor. Regresa y se sienta delante de Cecilia, quien empieza a tocar las cartas de forma desordenada con una sola mano, casi consciente de que la otra está observando con cuidado su rostro.

—¿Y cómo va el asunto con tu esposo? —pregunta la envenenadora—. ¿Ya ha empezado a crecerle el vientre?

Suelto una carcajada ante el perfecto patetismo que despliega la tarotista al no levantar la mirada. Caligo sabe que la mujer frente a ella se considera una "bruja buena", alguien que se cree demasiado justa, demasiado bondadosa para mirar siquiera de reojo el Camino de la Mano Izquierda... Pero el amor de un hombre violento siempre merece algo más que buenas intenciones.

Un trozo de matriz de gallina, un poco de semen de macho cabrío bien seco, una sopa condimentada para esconderlo todo y simplemente esperar a que *el favor* de Caligo crezca pronto con pezuñas duras y cuernos afilados en un intestino caliente.

—Me llegó un chisme interesante por ahí —evade la humana, jugueteando con las cartas con una sola malo, sin echarlas.

—¿Ah, sí? —responde la envenenadora mientras se sirve un poco de aquel licor.

—Dicen que tu hermana vio a Giles Corey la otra noche.

Caligo detiene el flujo de la bebida por unos instantes.

—Sí, es posible —dice con sobriedad, para luego alargar el trago a su amiga. Ella lo toma, lo acaricia, la observa con una sonrisa.

—¿No te preocupa? —pregunta—, ya sabes lo que dicen. Si el fantasma de Giles Corey aparece, significa que la tragedia azotará al pueblo.

La bruja abre la boca para responder, pero sus perspicaces ojos se detienen en el vaso sin tocar de su amiga. Cecilia es una alcohólica empedernida, pero ahora mantiene una mano en las cartas y otra en el regazo. Inamovible.

Observa de nuevo el rostro claro y pálido de la mujer, y busca la sombra de una mancha violeta bajo su mandíbula, un golpe de puño cerrado que, ella sabe, no pudo haber desaparecido en apenas un par de días, cuando le contó por teléfono que había recibido su última paliza. Pero la piel está limpia y hermosa, surcada sólo por las arrugas propias de alguien que lleva casi medio siglo en la Tierra.

—¿Y por qué has rechazado a todos tus clientes de hoy? —pregunta Caligo a la par que juguetea con su propio vaso—. El invierno no es precisamente la mejor temporada para Salem, ¿sabes? ¿O acaso el día de brujas te dejó con los bolsillos atiborrados, vieja tacaña?

—Ay, nada de eso, querida, ya te dije que me atosiga mucho la rodilla, así que no tenía ganas de atender a nadie y preferí echarme las cartas un rato. Sólo es eso.

La sonrisa de Caligo desaparece cuando la mía se ensancha.

Cecilia Blachet es una de las mejores tarotistas del pueblo, tanto, que inclusive las hermanas de la envenenadora han acudido a ella en más de una ocasión. Pero también tiene muchos problemas, muchos pájaros en la cabeza y demasiado alcohol en las venas, y por eso nunca, *nunca* se echa las cartas a sí misma.

Caligo se levanta de la mesa, tirando el vaso de alcohol que ella tampoco se atrevió a probar.

—¿Dónde está? —pregunta con los dientes apretados, y la mujer delante de ella ladea la cabeza—. ¿Y quién demonios eres tú?

La boca de Cecilia se tuerce como una grieta y sus ojos castaños comienzan a desbordarse.

—Qué suspicaces son los que se revuelcan en sombras —dice—, pero la tengo aquí mismo, si quieres verla.

La criatura por fin saca el otro brazo de debajo de la mesa. Lo alarga y deja sobre el mármol verde *una mano izquierda mutilada*. Pálida por la falta de sangre y engarzada de anillos de amatista.

Caligo se lleva una mano a los labios mientras que un calor terrible empieza a apoderarse de la habitación. El olor a quemado y la sensación de cenizas vuelve a infectar su nariz; la bruja abre los ojos de par en par cuando una nube de humo empieza a deslizarse por debajo de la puerta del almacén, a espaldas de aquella cosa que pretendía ser su amiga.

—¡CECILIA! —grita a todo pulmón.

Sin miedo, sin dudarlo, rodea a la bestia sentada a la mesa, quien tan sólo sonríe de placer cuando la envenenadora abre la puerta del almacén de golpe.

El fuego estalla desde el interior con cientos de lenguas que acarician las cortinas de terciopelo, acompañadas de fumarolas espesas que comienzan a bordear el marco de mi portal.

Caligo escucha los gritos de varias personas en la tienda, alertadas por el incendio. Retrocede y se cubre con los brazos en tanto la alarma se dispara. Y sólo cuando las llamas se retraen en un remolino puede ver por fin a su verdadera amiga dentro del almacén.

Cecilia Blachet está atada en una pira en medio de la habitación, gritando con todas sus fuerzas mientras su cuerpo es devorado por el fuego.

Un monstruo detrás de ella observa a la envenenadora, un monstruo que abre la boca sangrienta de su bella máscara de hierro, para luego desaparecer entre la lumbre.

CAPÍTULO 34
FANTASMAS

Después de la emotiva reunión en la sala, lo primero que hago es subir a darme una larga ducha en la misma habitación en la que desperté.

Con todo y que la casa llevaba abandonada más de nueve años, los demás lograron echar a andar el generador de emergencia, lo que significa que, aunque no tengamos calefacción en los radiadores, sí que hay agua caliente en la recámara principal gracias al pozo y la caldera eléctrica. Así que paso los siguientes veinte minutos bajo el chorro de agua intentando borrar hasta el último rastro de la sangre que derramé en Montana.

Estuve casi cuatro días inconsciente; Johanna tuvo que abrirme la pierna para reparar el hueso fracturado por la trampa de oso, y mantenerme dormido había sido la única forma de soportarlo. Por lo demás, se había limitado a limpiarme con un paño de vez en cuando, temerosa de moverme demasiado y dificultar mi recuperación. Y aunque mi labio partido y las cortaduras de mi rostro han desaparecido, la herida en mi muslo sí que ha quedado muy visible. Mi movilidad no parece haber sido afectada, pero la línea quirúrgica quedó tosca y enrojecida, y parece que cicatrizará mal.

Aun así, pido, desde lo más profundo de mi corazón, que esta vez los rastros de las heridas se queden en mi piel para siempre.

Somos...

Cubro mi pierna con gasa del botiquín que tomé prestado de Johanna y me visto con las prendas que dejé sobre el lavamanos de mármol: ropa interior nueva, pantalones deportivos grises y chamarra de felpa, todo en conjunto con ropa térmica y calcetines gruesos.

Y ahora decido no ponerme los guantes.

Una vez que termino de lavarme los dientes —y de cepillar mi cabello, por fin limpio después de haber parecido vómito de paja por tanto tiempo—, salgo del baño con el botiquín en la mano. La habitación es más amplia y bonita de lo que percibí al principio, vacía a excepción del mullido colchón en el suelo cubierto con varias cobijas de lana. Las paredes de color gris azulado combinan a la perfección con las cornisas blancas y la madera clara de las puertas y el piso, mientras que el gran ventanal triple da paso a una luz amplia y natural. Y ni qué decir de la pequeña pero elegante chimenea de troncos que dota de suficiente calor a toda la estancia.

Un cuarto principal. La habitación de un matrimonio.

Salgo al pasillo y me asomo por el barandal. Puedo escuchar a Tared y a Johanna hablar, y también alcanzo a distinguir, desde los ventanales de la sala, a Debbie y a Nashua sentados en el porche lateral de la casa. Busco a Hoffman por todos lados sin encontrarlo, así que tal vez esté en el garaje con Lía y los demás, preparando el ciervo que cazaron en la mañana.

Bajo con el silencio de un gato y miro de soslayo hacia el interior de la cocina. Encuentro al hombre lobo sentado junto a la mesa, dándome la espalda y sin camiseta. A su lado está mi hermana Johanna, quien revisa la herida del arpón. Hay medicamentos, servilletas de papel y hierbas repartidas sobre la madera blanca, todo cubierto del familiar olor a hojas de pino machacadas.

Distingo tanto la cicatriz de un agujero de bala en su omóplato como la marca de aquel machete, la cual surca su piel desde el hombro hasta casi la arteria carótida. La hoja debió hundirse hasta el hueso y desangrarlo, no había manera lógica en la que Tared hubiese sobrevivido después de todo lo que nos ocurrió.

Pero *lo hizo*.

—Yo creo que con eso será suficiente —dice la perpetuasangre, para luego dejar unas tijeras a un lado con trozos de cabello oscuro atrapados en la punta—. Ya cerró de ambos lados, pero no la subestimes; te acabo de quitar los puntos, así que deja un día más el parche y continúa durmiendo de lado, ¿de acuerdo?

Tared toma un algodón empapado en antiséptico y se inclina sobre su costado.

—Ya. Ésta es la que fastidia todavía —dice él con un poco de incomodidad.

—¿Quieres que yo lo haga? —pregunta ella con timidez al ver que al devorapieles le cuesta limpiar la laceración. Y la forma en la que lo observa, con esa infinita devoción, hace que me encoja contra la pared. Estoy seguro de que Tared guio a los demás aquí, a su casa, lo que me hace preguntarme si ya les habrá contado algo sobre su pasado. O su esposa.

Justo estoy pensando en volver arriba cuando el lobo mira sobre su hombro. Su cara se ilumina con una sonrisa, lo que también capta la atención de Johanna.

—Eh... —me llama él.

—Ah, ¡Elisse! ¿Pasa algo? —la chica contrae las manos contra su pecho como si la hubiese encontrado haciendo algo indebido, a pesar de que no es así.

Yo me encojo de hombros y le muestro el botiquín.

—Creí que tal vez necesitarías esto —digo con calma, aunque es más que obvio que he traído esto sólo como excusa para ver a Tared.

—Ah, ¡muchas gracias! Déjalo aquí, por favor —ella señala hacia la mesa con excesivo entusiasmo. Luego, coloca una silla para mí, en cuyo respaldo está colgada la camisa de franela del lobo.

Me acerco y él me sigue atentamente con la mirada.

—¿Cómo te sientes? —pregunto con calma a la vez que tomo asiento. Intento controlar el desaforado latido de mi corazón, pero es un tanto difícil ahora que está libre de su jaula de hueso.

—Estoy bien, ¿qué hay de ti? —me dice a la par que pone su mano sobre mi rodilla.

La naturalidad de su gesto hace que me enderece como una vara sobre la silla.

Miro a mi hermana de reojo, quien se ha puesto a limpiar un poco el lugar, pretendiendo estar en lo suyo.

—Mejor que tú, eso es seguro —contesto con un carraspeo. Pero al ver hacia su herida, el horrible recuerdo de ese arpón clavado de lado a lado en su cuerpo me hace cerrar los ojos un instante.

Tared desliza su mano hasta envolver mis dedos humanos.

—Tranquilo, estoy bien ahora, ¿lo ves? —dice—. Ya sabes que Johanna siempre hace un excelente trabajo.

Asiento, aun cuando algo dentro de mí se niega a convencerse de que ya todo pasó, y de que mi lobo por fin está a salvo. Escucharlo hablar sin la voz rota por el dolor, verlo respirar con calma, fuerte y lleno de vida; un auténtico milagro por el que estuve dispuesto a vender mi alma.

Los ojos de Tared se han desviado a su propio pulgar, el cual ahora acaricia mi mano en pequeños círculos suaves, como si él también quisiera convencerse de que estoy aquí, sin fiebre, sin frío, sin congelarme entre sus brazos. Su caricia me reconforta, me pone los pies en la tierra e inflama mi pecho con un suspiro que dejo salir despacio.

No tenía idea de lo íntimo que podía ser un gesto tan sencillo.

Mi hermana nos mira intermitentemente, y da un respingo.

—Dios, ¡qué tonta soy! —exclama—. Elisse, ayuda a Tared a ponerse el parche, por favor. Yo... iré a echar una mano con el ciervo.

La coyote pasa a mi lado para dirigirse a zancadas a la tercera puerta que hay en la cocina, la cual da al garaje.

—¡Johanna! —exclamo y el sonido de la silla al levantarme la hace detenerse en el umbral—. Gracias por salvarlo —le digo con el corazón en la mano—. Sin ti, Tared, él...

Mi hermana mira sobre su hombro, sorprendida, y luego sacude la cabeza con una sonrisa sincera.

—Nada de eso —responde con suavidad—. Los hechizos que hiciste y la forma en la que diste hasta la última de tus fuerzas con tal de protegerlo fue algo... extraordinario, y sin eso, yo no habría podido hacer nada. Tú fuiste quien le salvó la vida, Elisse, no yo. *Tú eres su héroe.*

La miro, perplejo, hasta que ella desaparece detrás de la puerta. El corazón me late tan rápido que casi siento la espada calentarse contra él, y al voltear, descubro a Tared mirándome de una forma tan intensa, con una admiración tan profunda, que me veo obligado a bajar la barbilla. Me acerco a la mesa y me siento otra vez para preparar el apósito de gasa, agradecido de, esta vez, tener algo más que trozos de camisetas rotas para hacer vendajes.

—Tu casa es preciosa —digo en voz baja, y él mira hacia la ventana que hay sobre el fregadero de la cocina. La luz del sol ya ha surgido como una yema, empapado los árboles de amarillo en una mañana despejada, sin rastros de nubes ni tormentas, un paisaje muy distinto a ese bosque lavanda en Montana.

Largos minutos en los que trabajo en silencio transcurren, los suficientes como para saber que Tared tiene una idea rondando en la cabeza que no termina de aterrizar.

—Creo que necesitamos hablar, ¿no es así? O, más bien, necesito darte un par de explicaciones sobre todo lo que pasó en Washington. Y en Montana.

Me detengo y levanto la mirada, con las tijeras aún entre las manos.

—No me debes nada, Tared. Aunque no lo creas, siempre *entendí* tus decisiones —respondo, para inclinarme de nuevo hacia él.

El hombre lobo se yergue en la silla y estira un poco su sólido bíceps detrás de su nunca para dejarme colocar el parche en su abdomen.

Johanna tiene razón, su herida no necesitará más vendas, pero es importante cuidarla por cualquier cosa. Por otro lado, me alegra ver que gran parte de la musculatura de Tared ha regresado, en señal de que se ha alimentado muy bien estos días, con mucha proteína. Los devorapieles pierden peso muy rápido si no comen lo suficiente, pero también lo recuperan con la misma facilidad si...

Tared toca mi muñeca con suavidad para detener tanto mis manos como el tren desaforado de mis pensamientos.

—Era más que eso, Elisse. *Mucho más.* Y por eso necesito hablar contigo.

Dejo mi tarea a un lado y lo miro con atención. Él suspira, nervioso, y por unos momentos puedo imaginarlo en su forma lobuna, con las orejas bajas a causa de la tensión. Cuando abre y cierra la boca como si no supiera por dónde empezar, esta vez soy yo quien se alarga para envolver su rodilla y darle el empujón que necesita.

No tiene por qué explicarme nada, pero si a él le consuela hacerlo, estoy dispuesto a escucharlo.

—Hace nueve años —comienza—, cambié de piel por primera vez e hice algo terrible *aquí.* En esta misma cocina.

Asesino...

Como si hubiese escuchado a Wéndigo, Tared baja la mirada al suelo. Observo también el piso y, de forma inconsciente, entre el patrón de ligeras vetas de mármol, la encuentro *a ella,* a Grace, su aspecto como una proyección aleatoria de mi imaginación. Veo también la sangre invisible esparcida por el suelo de baldosas blancas. Escucho el eco mudo de sus gritos en las paredes.

Siento que se me agota el aire al pensar que estuve cuatro días dormido. Cuatro días enteros en los que, probablemente, él tuvo que revivir y enfrentar ese fantasma *solo,* una y otra vez.

Tared se sacude el pasado y mueve un poco la cabeza.

—Ese día, cuando empecé a transformarme por primera vez, todo fue muy confuso. Y violento —dice—. Las imágenes que veía dentro de mi cabeza eran oscuras, recuerdos que no comprendía. No les encontraba forma ni sentido, como si algo taladrase una y otra vez dentro de mí, mientras que mi cuerpo cambiaba de una forma tremendamente dolorosa. En un segundo, me convertí en un ser sin consciencia, carente de razón, guiado sólo por el dolor del cambio y una rabia que no parecía... *mía.*

Sus palabras resuenan dentro de mí de una forma peculiar, conocida, y los relatos populares sobre los hombres lobo empiezan a matizarse en mi cabeza, antiguas historias de licántropos crueles, hambrientos por carne humana. No me extrañaría que una parte de nuestra naturaleza compleja de errantes también hubiese aportado un poco a esos cuentos de terror.

—En ese instante, pasé por tanto caos que comencé a destrozar todo a mi alrededor —continúa—, imaginaba, estúpidamente, que me abría paso entre la locura y las sombras con mis propias garras, sin darme cuenta de lo que estaba haciendo en realidad. Ataqué a quien era mi esposa y al mismo tiempo puse punto final a la vida humana que había llevado hasta ese momento. Pero lo peor fue que, mucho tiempo después, volví a ser aquel monstruo resquebrajado, privado de su voluntad, que agredió a Grace esa noche.

—Te refieres a... ¿Nueva Orleans? —pregunto con cuidado al recordar la noche en la que Tared acabó con todas esas personas mientras trabajaba con la policía.

Él toma aire y enlaza sus manos.

—No —contesta, mirándome a los ojos—. El día en el que salí contigo de aquel lago congelado.

Un sofocado "¿qué?" escapa de mis labios.

—Cuando estuvimos allí dentro, en... el *plano medio* —dice, como si el nombre de aquel lugar le pareciera difícil de mencionar—, fue como si mi cabeza hubiese vuelto a ese caos de mi primera transformación. Estar sumergido en esa oscuridad, en ese río infinito, era como una especie de *déjà vu*. Vaya. Yo tenía la idea de que, por su estado catatónico, Tared había experimentado algo similar a estar en coma, sin consciencia, sin visiones, pero parece ser que estaba equivocado.

—No podía moverme —explica—, pero sí que era consciente de todo lo que ocurría. De cómo me quedaba sin aire, del momento en el que soltabas mi mano y de la forma en la que la corriente me llevaba lejos de ti sin que pudiera hacer nada al respecto. No está de más decir que fue una de las cosas más angustiantes por las que he tenido que pasar en toda mi vida.

Tared, consciente del agobio que siento al escuchar todo esto, envuelve mi mano con su palma. Entrelazo mis dedos con los suyos, nos sostenemos como no pudimos hacerlo en aquella ocasión...

—No estoy muy seguro, pero creo que perdí el conocimiento segundos después —continúa—, y sólo pude despertar hasta que te sentí alcanzarme de nuevo en el fondo del lago. Luego, tiraste hacia arriba...

Su mano ejerce un poco de presión, como si rememorara esa sensación bajo el agua, el deseo desesperado de sujetarse con todas sus fuerzas a mí para que no se le fuese la vida.

—Y al salir a la superficie las cosas se pusieron mal. Muy mal —admite—. Tanto que, hasta el día de hoy, sigo sin entender cómo fui capaz de seguir medianamente cuerdo. Todo me embistió de golpe: la ira, la confusión, el dolor, y empeoraba a cada segundo que pasaba hasta que, al final, la desesperación me cegó. Acababan de morir tantos de los nuestros, te habías convertido en ese ser de hueso y de pronto estábamos en el lago congelado, en un lugar desconocido y a quién sabe cuántos kilómetros del campo de batalla. No sabía qué pensar, no sabía qué sentir; ya no escuchaba mi propia consciencia, sólo gritos. Sólo *aullidos*. Tan sólo necesitaba permanecer apartado de ti para poder controlarme, para no abrirme paso entre la locura como hice con Grace. Y no voy a mentirte... también tenía miedo.

Casi siento como si la garra de Wéndigo volviese a cerrarse sobre mi corazón, un dolor terrible que me apuñala al enterarme de que, después de todo, yo no estaba tan equivocado. Tared *sí me temía*.

Al sentir que mi mano da un leve tirón hacia atrás para tratar de soltarme, él la envuelve con más fuerza.

—No, espera. No estaba asustado de ti, si es eso lo que estás pensando —enfatiza, como si me hubiese leído la mente.

Abre la boca, pero luego la cierra y resopla.

—¿Tared? —insisto ante su titubeo.

—¿Estás seguro de que quieres escuchar esto?

Aquello me inquieta sobremanera, pero al final, le pido continuar.

—Hay dos razones por las cuales decidí cortar nuestro vínculo, Elisse —dice después de tomar aire—. Y la primera tiene que ver con Lobo Piel de Trueno.

De acuerdo. De todas las cosas que esperaba escuchar, definitivamente *ésa* no era una de ellas.

—¿Hablas en serio? —pregunto, petrificado al verlo asentir.

—Él, además de mi ancestro, es también *mi instinto* —explica—, ese sexto sentido que nace muy dentro, desde mi cabeza hasta mi corazón, y que me ha protegido... o *contenido*, en cada una de las situaciones a las que he tenido que enfrentarme. Estoy seguro de que fue gracias a Lobo Piel de Trueno que no maté a Grace en este lugar. Y también de que fue él quien me obligó a transformarme por segunda vez para no ser asesinado por aquellos hombres en Nueva Orleans. Pero esa vez en el lago, después de salir del plano medio, fue como si hasta él también hubiese enloquecido.

De pronto percibo, a través de nuestras manos enlazadas el temblor que lo ha recorrido de arriba abajo.

—Sentí un miedo difícil de describir —dice—, porque fue como si mi propio ancestro hubiese devorado todo lo humano en mí para dejar sólo a una bestia alerta, feroz y dispuesta a protegerme *de ti* con garras y colmillos. Y todo empeoró la noche que decidí cortar nuestro vínculo, porque a partir de ese día, empecé a escuchar a eso que llamas "monstruo de hueso". Y no me refiero a sólo sentirlo; era como si también lo tuviese dentro de mi cabeza.

Me quedo unos segundos con la boca abierta, sin palabras, porque, cuando pensé que no podía decirme nada más sorprendente, viene y me suelta *esto*.

—¿De verdad? —pregunto, recuperando un segundo el control de mi lengua—. ¿Escuchabas *todo*?

—En realidad, nunca podía entender lo que te decía. Aquello tenía demasiadas voces distintas y todas hablaban al mismo tiempo, tan caótico como mirar la maraña de un estambre enredado. Y te soy sincero: nunca estuve seguro de si lo que escuchaba era real o fruto de alguna de mis alucinaciones, pero fuera cual fuera la verdad, lo único que tenía claro es que esas voces, esas cosas terribles que ahora podía escuchar dentro de ti, sólo ponían más y más violento a Lobo Piel de Trueno.

—Por los Loas... —musito. Lo que me cuenta es tan oscuro, tan siniestro, que empiezo a preguntarme si todo esto que ha sufrido Tared no es más que una consecuencia de que un ser sin magia haya transitado por el plano medio. ¿Acaso Lobo Piel de Trueno se volvió más sensible a la presencia de Wéndigo gracias a eso?

—Ése era mi temor más grande, Elisse —continúa, consciente de mi desasosiego—. Si permitía que te acercases a mí lo suficiente, la locura de mi ancestro podría llegar a desbordarse. Y no estaba dispuesto a arriesgarme, porque aun cuando cada instante de mi furia estaba dominado por ese instinto de supervivencia que apenas podía controlar, una parte de mí seguía luchando a cada minuto, a cada segundo, por no hacerte daño.

Desvío la mirada hacia las agujas de pino machacadas sobre la mesa blanca. Siento el pecho tan pesado por la angustia que podría tirarme de bruces ahora mismo contra el suelo.

—Dioses, ¿por qué nunca me dijiste nada de esto?

Me vuelvo hacia Tared, y mi aliento se corta cuando lo encuentro con los ojos rojos, a punto de quebrarse.

—Porque *me rendí* —admite con la voz ronca—. Estaba tan herido por lo que había pasado y tan cansado de luchar contra mis demonios, que ya no tenía fuerzas para encontrar la forma de volver a acercarme a ti. No podía salvarte y tampoco mantenerte a mi lado porque *me estaba ahogando en mi propia oscuridad*. Ésa fue la segunda razón por la cual elegí terminar con lo nuestro y… lo sufrí, lo sufrí muchísimo porque aún te amaba, Elisse; y a cada segundo, a cada instante, quería volver y pedirte que olvidaras todas las estupideces que había dicho y rogarte que me dieras otra oportunidad.

"Me rendí".

Las palabras resuenan como un eco en mi cabeza. Todo esto yo ya lo sabía y, como le dije desde el principio, lo entendía perfectamente, pero aun así duele demasiado escucharlo ahora de sus propios labios.

Que te abandone alguien a quien quieres es muy duro. Pero dejar a quien todavía amas lo es aún más.

Él alarga sus manos a mis mejillas y, con una dulzura que me rompe el corazón, las limpia con sus pulgares. No me di cuenta del momento en el que había comenzado a llorar.

—¿Qué fue lo que cambió? —pregunto entre sollozos. Tared termina con mis lágrimas, como si eso hubiese ayudado a contener las suyas, y baja las manos de nuevo a mis rodillas.

—El día en el que caíste al río fue cuando por fin reaccioné —dice—. Desperté poco después de que te hubieras ido, y lo sé porque la estufa aún estaba caliente. Te llevaste las armas, así que estaba seguro de que habías salido a cazar, por lo que decidí esperarte. Me sentía muy débil, había perdido demasiada sangre. Pero al ver que anochecía, y que no volvías, fui a buscarte, pensando en que tal vez la herida en tu pierna habría empeorado. Y no sabes lo que sentí al seguir el rastro de aquellos muñecos, descubrir tus huellas en la nieve y luego... verte allí, tendido a la orilla del río con los labios azules. Fue entonces cuando me enfurecí conmigo por haber sido débil, *por haberme rendido*; una furia que superó por mucho a la del lobo dentro de mí y lo regresó por fin a sus cabales.

Veo, con toda claridad, cómo la culpa sube a sus hombros con un peso monstruoso que Tared se niega a sacudir.

—Todo se desvaneció —susurra—. La cordura regresó a mí, acompañada de la más imperante necesidad de hacer hasta lo imposible con tal de salvarte. Fue allí cuando te lleve de vuelta a la cabaña.

—Fue una estupidez, Tared, eso es lo que fue —mascullo furioso al recordarlo—, no debiste haber ido por mí en tu estado y mucho menos haberte sacado ese maldito arpón.

—Valió la pena —responde con una certeza que me hiela la sangre—. Valió totalmente la pena y, *por ti,* lo volvería a hacer una y mil veces más, sin dudarlo, Elisse.

Lágrimas de nuevo. Una tras otra.

Como un niño pequeño, débil e indefenso, me inclino sobre mis rodillas y me entrego al llanto con la cara oculta entre las manos, atrapado por la misma desesperación que acuchilló a Johanna hace rato. Tengo tantas emociones a flor de piel que ya no puedo contenerlas.

Tared corta la distancia entre nosotros. Me rodea con sus brazos y me atrae hacia él con esa fuerza demoledora que jamás lo ha abandonado, ni siquiera en sus momentos de más vulnerabilidad. Me siento sobre su muslo y lo estrecho en respuesta, nos fundimos en un abrazo que hasta ese momento no sabíamos cuánto necesitábamos, un gesto que nos ayuda a *aceptar* que la pesadilla en ese terrible barranco de Montana por fin ha terminado.

Después de llorar lo suficiente sobre su cuello, Tared me ofrece su camisa para enjugarme las lágrimas.

—¿Todavía puedes escuchar al monstruo dentro de mí? —pregunto al percatarme del silencio de Wéndigo. Tared niega con un movimiento de cabeza.

—Cuando nuestro nuevo vínculo se formó, dejé de oírlas del todo. Todavía puedo sentir que esa cosa está ahí contigo, pero nada más.

Ya. E imagino que esa misma sensación debe ser lo que perciben todos los errantes al estar cerca de mí.

Toco su pecho con mi mano de hueso y comienzo a preguntarme si la espada filosofal, si nuestro pacto, tuvo algo que ver con que Tared siga vivo. Quizá fue el hecho de que alcancé sus dedos fríos en el último momento, y allí la piedra decidió evitar que la vida escapase de su cuerpo.

—Dime la verdad, ¿te arrepientes de haber cortado nuestro vínculo la primera vez? —pregunto, por fin consciente de lo que él sintió en aquel momento.

Tared envuelve mi garra y me observa con sus ojos de luna:

—¿Tú sí?

Una sonrisa tímida apenas se asoma en mis labios.

—No. No me arrepiento de nada —respondo con absoluta sinceridad, porque era algo que debía morir para que renaciera más fuerte, más auténtico y honesto, tan resistente que ninguna garra o fantasma del pasado pudiera cortar ya.

Tared me mira con tanta intensidad que siento mi rostro llenarse de fuego.

—Dios, te besaría ahora mismo —susurra, embelesado por el intenso rubor de mis mejillas.

—¿Y por qué no lo haces? —pregunto antes de comenzar a morderme el labio inferior.

Siento su abrazo afianzarse sobre mi cintura, el reducido espacio entre nosotros acortarse todavía más.

—Porque no sé si esta vez seré capaz de conformarme *sólo con eso.*

La piel se me eriza ante la seducción de su voz. Aún tenemos mucho por hablar pero, justo ahora, no son palabras lo que anhelo de su boca.

Sin pensar en nada ni en nadie más que en él y en la redención de nuestro lazo, me inclino para besar por fin a mi hombre lobo. Y al hacerlo, confirmo que la delicia de probar sus labios es lo único que nunca me sabrá al fantasma de un error.

Tared corresponde a mi beso y siento como una caricia eléctrica el roce de su boca sobre la mía. Su mano, fuerte y firme, se abre como una estrella de cinco puntas y baja por mi cadera para abrazar el costado de mi muslo mientras mis brazos se cierran alrededor de su cuello. Me estremece la forma en la que lo escucho gemir muy bajito, casi en un gruñido, cuando me atrevo a acariciar su lengua con la mía.

La ternura se desvanece y me derrito de ombligo para abajo en el momento en el que él entierra sus dedos en mi cabello, en mi nuca, para besarme a profundidad. Ahogamos el aire, nos probamos una y otra vez, desesperados por el hambre mutua. Y cuando siento el calor de su piel desnuda abrasarme a través de mi ropa, él muerde mi labio inferior un poco más y me da un momento para respirar, cosa que mis piernas temblorosas agradecen.

—Perdona —carraspeo, acomodándome con torpeza el cabello que él ha despeinado con sus dedos—. No debe ser muy agradable.

Él inclina la cabeza con una expresión bastante canina.

—Mi lengua, ya sabes. Debe estar helada —menciono con timidez a la par que la paso por mis dientes, pero él se encoge de hombros como si nada.

—Me gusta el frío, por si no lo has notado —responde y yo arqueo una ceja ante su falta de repulsión.

—Eres un hombre muy raro, Tared Miller.

—No fui yo el que se besó con un perro allá en la cabaña, Elisse.

Si hubiese estado bebiendo algo en este momento, se lo habría escupido en la cara por el jadeo de la risa. En cambio, sacudo la cabeza y tomo sus mejillas para besarlo hasta sentir que la silla nos queda pequeña.

Muy, muy pequeña.

Un carraspeo nos hace mirar hacia la puerta de la cocina, aquella que da al porche lateral de la casa. El calor me sube por la cara cuando descubro a Debbie y a Nashua bajo el dintel.

—¿Qué necesitas, Nashua? —pregunta Tared con la voz ronca, algo irritado por la interrupción.

—Debbie quiere hablar con Elisse —responde el errante, y el intranquilo semblante de la mujer me hace levantarme del regazo del lobo.

—¿Sobre qué? —pregunto con recelo. Se miran un instante, y ella suspira.

—Es sobre la criatura que mencionaste antes —dice—. Aquella que dices que te ha poseído.

—¿Te refieres a Wéndigo?

El monstruo dentro de mí alza la cabeza, y Debbie arruga la nariz como si lo hubiese sentido.

—Sí. Cuando dijiste aquel... nombre, no pude dejar de pensar en ello —continúa en voz baja, como si luchara para no dejar salir la palabra de su boca—. Así que tuve que preguntar a tus hermanos a qué te referías, pero ninguno supo decirme nada y Tared tampoco quiso hablar.

Miro hacia mi lobo, quien se acerca una vez que se ha puesto la camisa.

—Decidí no contarles nada de lo que sabía sobre el monstruo de hueso hasta que despertaras —dice Tared—. Era mejor que lo escucharan de ti, después de todo.

Asiento, agradecido por el gesto.

—Es por eso que quiero hacerte saber que conozco a alguien que tal vez pueda ayudarte, un buen amigo mío que vive cerca de aquí, en Canadá —continúa Debbie—. No sólo es algonquino,[3] sino que también es un experto en la mitología que rodea los Grandes Lagos, así que estoy segura de que sabrá iluminarte un poco al respecto.

Poco me falta para soltar un grito al escuchar aquello.

—¿Estás hablando en serio? ¡¿Un experto en *Wéndigo*?!

Debbie se sobresalta al escuchar aquel nombre otra vez, pero eso no impide que una sonrisa se asome a mi cara, impulsada por una esperanza que no había sentido en mucho tiempo, muy similar a aquella que sentí cuando subí por primera vez al avión que me trajo a Nueva Orleans.

La emoción me hace acercarme a ella a zancadas.

—Dioses, ¡Debbie! —exclamo, eufórico—. ¡No sabes cuánto...!

Ella levanta una mano y me detiene.

—Yo que tú no me ilusionaría demasiado, Elisse —advierte, severa—. Espero de todo corazón que mi amigo pueda hacer algo por ti, pero no me hace falta ser una contemplasombras para intuir que, aunque pienses que has encontrado una salida, puede que tus verdaderos problemas con esta criatura estén a punto de empezar.

---

[3] Grupo de pueblos nativos de Canadá, Estados Unidos y del norte del estado mexicano de Coahuila que hablan las lenguas algonquinas.

CAPÍTULO 35
EMPATÍA

—¿Qué? ¡¿Se van?! Lía arquea ambas cejas, en señal de que alcé demasiado la voz.

—Lo sé, cariño, para ti puede parecer muy repentino —dice, comprensiva—, pero ya hemos estado aquí demasiados días y nuestra familia está muy preocupada. Nosotras sólo estábamos esperando a que despertaras para poder volver más tranquilas a casa.

Retengo la lengua y suspiro con resignación, porque es verdad que tampoco me parece justo intentar detenerlas. Además, Lía y su mujer ya han cargado sus cosas en su camioneta, estacionada frente al porche de la casa de Tared.

Pero lo que más me entristece es ver que Irina también ha empacado.

—¿Están seguras de que quieren irse ahora? —pregunta Johanna—. Oscurecerá antes de que lleguen a Idaho.

—No te preocupes, linda. Los del norte estamos aclimatados a los días cortos y las noches frías, ¿verdad? —dice, guiñándole un ojo a Tared.

El lobo a mi lado pone su brazo sobre mis hombros y sonríe con complicidad.

—Dioses, Lía, no sé cómo terminar de...

—Por favor, Elisse —interrumpe con un aspaviento—, no te atrevas a darme las gracias, suficiente he tenido con tu hombre haciéndolo durante cuatro días seguidos como para escucharlo de ti también.

Me sonrojo con fuerza al ver la naturalidad con la que Tared ríe por el comentario.

—Gracias por todo, Lía —dice él—. Comus Bayou está en deuda por siempre con la Espiral del Norte.

Ella niega con la cabeza.

—Nada de deudas, Tared Miller —responde, seria y formal—. Esto es una *alianza* entre la tormenta del norte y el huracán del sur. A partir de ahora, forjaremos un vínculo inmortal entre nuestra gente, un pacto que se heredará a través de nuestros libros de las generaciones. Que no se te olvide.

Y con esto, alza la mano hacia Tared. Él sonríe, estrecha la muñeca de la mujer y ella, a su vez, estrecha la suya. Un acuerdo tácito, sin rituales y sin ceremonias, pactado únicamente por el honor.

Debbie y Lía comienzan a despedirse de los demás hasta que, finalmente, el lobo y yo las acompañamos afuera, al porche. Él intercambia unas palabras más con las chicas mientras que yo camino hacia Irina, quien está recargada en la puerta de la camioneta.

Respiro profundamente y me coloco a su lado, pero dejo que la barrera de silencio se mantenga entre nosotros un poco más.

Quiero decirle que lo lamento. Que lamento mucho que haya perdido a Calen, a Alannah, a Sammuel, a Fernanda... *a Chenoa*. Y que me duele como no tiene una idea que ahora no tengamos ni el menor rastro de sus niños. Pero, ¿cómo se supone que uno da el pésame ante semejante tragedia, ante tamaño dolor, si ni siquiera tuve las palabras adecuadas para decírselo en su momento a Nashua, a mi propio hermano?

Me abrazo con fuerza para soportar no sólo el peso de la espada, sino también el de la culpa al pensar en cómo el errante oso no sólo me ha estado evitando, sino que parece... perdido, o retraído en alguna parte difícil de alcanzar.

—Cuatro —dice de pronto la errante a mi lado—. Cuando te encontramos a ti y a Tared, allá en la montaña, yo misma maté a cuatro de ellos. Pero ninguno confesó —susurra—. A pesar de que les arranqué dedo por dedo, diente por diente, ni uno solo de esos cerdos me dijo qué había pasado con Misha ni Enola. Ni a dónde se los habían llevado.

No retiro la vista de la nieve. Aunque en el pasado me hubiese causado un escalofrío lo que me acaba de decir, a estas alturas ya comprendo a la perfección lo que siente. Lo placentero que resulta causar tanto dolor, ¿verdad?

—Sí. Es difícil hacerlos hablar —concuerdo—. Hice pedazos a uno con un hacha, y aunque era muy joven, —un niño— no pude lograr que me dijera dónde estaban tus hijos.

El silencio se hace presente, una vez más. Frío y tenso como la escarcha bajo nuestros pies.

Irina por fin levanta la barbilla para mirarme.

—Lo siento mucho, Elisse —dice—. Siento mucho que hayas sido obligado a hacer algo así.

Parpadeo un par de veces, sin comprender. ¿Por qué esta errante sigue creyendo que soy yo el que merece compasión, cuando su familia entera fue exterminada?

—¿De qué estás hablando? ¡Todo esto ha sido mi culpa! —exclamo—. Los tramperos, Dallas, tus hijos; yo sabía lo peligroso que era aceptar un trato con ustedes y, aun así, me quedé en tu casa. *Yo* llevé a esos bastardos allí y...

Por primera vez la inmutabilidad de Irina se rompe. Su mirada se llena de ferocidad y su mano se planta en mi hombro.

—Nunca vuelvas a decir eso, ¿me oíste? —ordena en voz baja—. Los Lander asesinaron al abuelo Begaye antes de que siquiera hubieras nacido, y Dallas no hizo otra cosa más que protegerlos bajo las órdenes de Jocelyn Blake. No, Elisse, necesitas empezar a verte como lo que eres: una víctima. Una víctima de ellos, de tu Mara y de *esa cosa que llevas dentro*.

Wéndigo estalla en carcajadas y el zumbido rebota como cientos de piedras en un pozo. La errante se tensa, quizá presa de la incomodidad de aquella presencia dentro de mí.

—Jamás dejes que todos esos bastardos te hagan creer que tú tienes la culpa, Elisse —insiste—. No les dejes creer nunca que tú eres el malvado cuando ellos te forzaron a hacer cosas que no querías, a tomar decisiones con las que no tenías por qué lidiar. *No los dejes ganar.*

—Aun así, no sé si seré capaz algún día de perdonarme —confieso—. No puedo soportar verte y saber que ahora tienes que vivir así...

—Si te sirve de consuelo, en mí ya no queda ninguna tristeza, Elisse —asegura—. Lo único que puedo sentir ahora es *enojo*, un fuego que no puedo apagar, porque cuando te arrebatan todo lo que le daba sentido a tu vida, a veces sólo encuentras paz en la idea de que en algún momento podrás hallar la forma de vengarte, porque ya no te queda espacio para sentir nada más. Ni siquiera dolor.

Pienso de nuevo en Nashua. ¿Acaso yo le arrebaté esa anhelada paz al no haber vengado a los ancianos, al haber dejado con vida a Barón Samedi a cambio de los hijos de Louisa y Hoffman?

Irina retira su mano de mi hombro.

—*Tú y yo* estamos en paz, Elisse —dice— y la única manera en la que dejaremos de estarlo es si permites que esos bastardos nos ganen. Que te des por vencido. Entonces sí que me habrás decepcionado.

Clavo la mirada en sus ojos, azules como las montañas alrededor. Aún se ven vacíos, acorazados por su sed de venganza, pero me siento comprendido a través de esa rabia.

Cuando el silencio se vuelve suficiente, Irina sube a uno de los asientos traseros de la camioneta. Y al cerrar la puerta, vuelvo a ahogarme de desconsuelo por su partida. La he conocido muy poco, pero la quiero tanto como si siempre hubiese sido una de los míos.

—Es muy peligroso que vuelvas sola a buscar a los Lander, Irina —digo en un intento de disuadirla, porque es obvio que eso es lo que busca al regresar con Lía y Debbie hacia el oeste—. Aunque hayamos acabado con muchos, todavía no sabemos cuál es el siguiente paso que dará esa gente.

—No puedo perder más el tiempo —dice, tal cual esperaba—, no mientras aún pueda sentir el vínculo de mis hijos tirando de mí.

La errante puma saca la mano por la ventanilla y toma el cuello de mi suéter para acercarme.

—Cuida mucho a tu familia, Elisse —pide—. Y ámalos como si tuvieras la certeza de que no vas a lastimarlos con eso, porque en nuestro mundo nunca sabes cuándo será el último día en el que los tendrás a tu lado.

Sus palabras calan muy profundo en mi corazón. Ella me besa la frente y le susurro un "hasta luego", para alejarme y regresar al porche en silencio.

Lía y Debbie suben también a la camioneta y pronto veo a las tres marcharse a través del camino escarchado, hasta perderse por fin entre los árboles.

CAPÍTULO 36
TENSIÓN

Una vez que se hubieron marchado, cerré la puerta para recargarme un segundo contra la madera a ordenar mis pensamientos, sintiéndome como una silla que intenta encontrar el equilibrio después de haber perdido una pata.

Tared, quien me ha esperado todo este tiempo junto a la chimenea, se acerca a mi lado.

—¿Estás bien? —pregunta por educación; me conoce demasiado bien, así que ya debe saber la respuesta. De todas maneras, pongo mi frente en su hombro unos momentos, gesto que lo hace sonreír—. ¿Sabes? Me gustaría que terminásemos lo que empezamos hace rato en la cocina —dice, en tanto su mano sube para acariciarme la espalda.

Me sonrojo hasta las orejas, y el lobo ríe por lo bajo.

—Me refiero a que quisiera seguir hablando contigo, Elisse. A solas.

—Ah, ya —carraspeo, avergonzado por la naturaleza de mis pensamientos—, ¿quieres que vayamos arriba?

—No. Sabes bien que a éstos les encanta pegar el oído contra la puerta. Te juro que nunca he conocido a gente más chismosa que Comus Bayou —insiste—. Además, también me gustaría mostrarte *algo* esta noche.

Parpadeo un par de veces, extrañado.

—Eh, es decir, ¿quieres que salgamos de la casa?

—No iremos muy lejos de aquí, lo prometo.

Miro a través de los ventanales, hacia el predio nevado que se alarga hasta el bosque de pinos. La idea me intimida un poco, pero igual asiento.

No olvides que sólo eres un juguete...

Con un manotazo mental, aparto el susurro insidioso de Wéndigo y sigo al lobo hasta la cocina, donde mis hermanos y Hoffman se encuentran reunidos para desayunar. Nos apretujamos con los demás alrededor de la mesa cubierta por panqueques y una jarra de café que Julien preparó esa mañana.

—Esto sabe asqueroso —reniega el detective, después de darle un trago a su taza.

—¿Qué esperabas? —replica el pelirrojo, que me sirve un plato bien cargado de huevos fritos—. Es café de *Dollar Tree*.[4]

—Lo hubieras recogido del suelo de una vez.

—Agradezcan que al menos hoy sí vamos a comer carne —los reprende Johanna, para luego apuntar con la barbilla a la puerta del garaje—. Estamos viviendo de los ahorros de todos y tenemos que conformarnos con lo que se pueda hasta volver a Luisiana.

—Fabuloso. Veinte años partiéndome el lomo para gastarme mi retiro en agua de calcetín.

La conversación me hace sentir algo muy cálido en el pecho. Es como si estuviésemos de vuelta en la reserva, discutiendo por tonterías sin sentido para ganarnos un regaño de padre Trueno.

---

4 Tienda de productos variados donde todo cuesta un dólar.

—¿Y bien? —pregunta Julien—. ¿Cuál es el plan, flaco?

Picoteo uno de los huevos con el tenedor.

—Debbie tiene un amigo que puede ayudarme a saber más sobre Wéndigo —digo con cuidado—. Prometió venir aquí lo más pronto posible, pero no sabía exactamente cuándo. Tenía que consultar un par de cosas primero y...

—No me jodas —suelta el detective—, ¿se supone que debemos quedarnos varados en esta pocilga abandonada hasta que a ese tipo le dé la maldita gana venir?

Tared pone su taza sobre la mesa con algo de fuerza, en señal de que no le ha gustado nada la manera en la que el exagente se ha referido a su casa.

—¿Y movernos a dónde, Hoffman? —replica él, mordaz—. Lo único que importa ahora es encontrar la forma de deshacernos de la criatura que tiene Elisse dentro de él, ¿a dónde pretendes que vayamos si debemos esperar a quien podría darnos la respuesta?

Oh, no.

—Si nos quedamos demasiado tiempo en un solo sitio hay más probabilidades de que esos degenerados nos encuentren, *Miller* —replica Hoffman con similar desprecio.

—Que vengan —responde Tared con los dientes apretados—. Estoy dispuesto a enfrentarme a todos si con eso podemos conseguir ayuda para Elisse.

La cara del exagente se tiñe de rojo.

—¿Y hacer que esta vez sí lo maten por tu maravilloso juicio, perro asqueroso? —exclama, a la par que suelta un puñetazo a la mesa—, ¡porque te recuerdo que gracias a ti casi le arrancan la maldita pierna!

—¡Ahora resulta que él te importa, cuando siempre lo has tratado como a una basura!

—¡Al menos yo nunca le mentí para meterme en sus pantalones, hipócrita de porquería!

Tared casi vuelca la mesa al levantarse.

Un rugido lobuno y el clic de una pistola hace que todos mis hermanos se lancen hacia los dos. Julien retiene al detective del cuello con el arco de su brazo y le tuerce la muñeca para evitar que accione el arma, mientras que Nashua empuja a Tared contra la puerta del porche para que no pueda arrancar la cabeza de Hoffman de un zarpazo.

—¡Suéltame, animal! —grita el exagente, tan rojo como el cabello de mi hermano.

—¡Estoy harto de ti, maldito cabrón! —ruge el lobo, a quien le han crecido los caninos por la rabia—, ¡estás pidiendo a gritos que te rompa la jodida cara!

—¡*Vas y chingas a tu reputísima madre!* —contesta el otro, en español.

—¡BASTA YA, CARAJO!

Mi grito es tan estruendoso que los dos paran de forcejear de inmediato. Tomo aire con fuerza y me aprieto el puente de la nariz para evitar que me reviente la cabeza.

—Elisse...

—Cállate. Sólo... cállate, Hoffman, por una maldita vez en tu vida —le exijo al tiempo que le lanzo una severa mirada de advertencia a Tared—. ¿Alguno de ustedes dos se ha tomado siquiera la molesta de escuchar qué es lo que quiero hacer *yo*? ¿Para qué demonios nos molestamos con los tramperos si van a terminar matándose entre ustedes de todas maneras? ¡Parecen un par de animales, incapaces de estar en la misma habitación *un-jodido-minuto*!

Tared cierra la boca, y Hoffman se sacude el agarre de Julien. Ambos se miran con fuerte recelo, pero parecen ceder por fin.

—Tienes razón —reconoce el hombre lobo, aún agitado por el arrebato de ira—. Lo... lo siento, Elisse.

Hoffman, en cambio, guarda silencio. Tan sólo se enfunda el arma y nos da la espalda para dirigirse hacia el lavabo de la cocina y encender otro cigarrillo, como si los dos hombres quisieran tirar de mis tripas en sentido opuesto para partirme de una vez en dos.

Julien mira con lástima un desafortunado plato de desayuno tirado en el suelo, mientras que Johanna parece estar más confundida que atónita, quizás en señal de que no sabe a qué se ha referido Hoffman con eso de que Tared me había ocultado algo. Eso me da a entender que tal vez todavía no saben nada sobre Grace.

—Bueno, entonces, ¿qué sugieres que hagamos? —pregunta la errante, recordando de pronto cómo respirar.

—Los tramperos podrán ser unos malditos sádicos sin escrúpulos, pero a fin de cuentas son sólo *humanos* que han tenido mucha suerte —digo—. No me preocupa tanto que nos ataquen, sino lo que podrían hacer si utilizan lo que robaron de Red Buffalo en nuestra contra.

—Si es así, hasta nos convendría que nos encontraran —mascula Nashua entre dientes—. Mientras más rápido podamos silenciarlos, mejor para nosotros.

—Además, si hay algo aún más peligroso que Benjamin Lander y su gente es *mi Mara* —afirmo—.Y las criaturas que ha estado enviando todo este tiempo.

Con las cartas puestas sobre la mesa, no hace falta decir nada más.

—Bueno, entonces está decidido, ¿no? Hay que quedarse aquí hasta que llegue el contacto de Debbie —dice Julien, y aunque no me gusta la idea de darle la razón a Tared después del pleito que acaba de armar con Hoffman, termino por asentir—. Uf, ¡menos mal! Porque ya estaba harto de congelarme el trasero en la carretera.

—Y nosotros de escucharte roncar todas las noches.

—Ay, Johanna, ¡pero si se veían tan calientitos durmiendo abrazados a mí en la camioneta!

—Voy a vomitar —murmura Hoffman desde el lavabo.

Suelto una risa agotada y sacudo la cabeza.

—¿Saben? Hace unas semanas les habría dicho que si lo que quieren es salir vivos de esto, lo único que tienen que hacer es dejarme atrás, pero ya me quedó bien claro que si hay alguien más terco que yo son todos ustedes —admito—, así que no me queda otra cosa más que llevarlos conmigo hasta el final. Y no saben... lo mucho que les agradezco que, a pesar de todo lo que ha pasado, aún estén dispuestos a acompañarme. Sin ustedes nunca podría lograrlo y lamento mucho haber tardado tanto en entenderlo.

Mis palabras parecen cargar el silencio de significado. Johanna sonríe, conmovida, y se acerca para darme un cariñoso abrazo.

—Gracias —me dice al oído de parte de todos.

—Bueno, y ahora que ya nos estamos entendiendo, creo que es momento para que por fin nos digas todo lo que pasó contigo desde que te fuiste de Luisiana, ¿no crees? —dice Julien, quien se sienta a la mesa de nuevo para servirse un poco de agua de calcetín.

Ladeo la cabeza, confundido.

—Pensé que Hoffman ya les...

—Lo que queremos es escucharlo de ti, porque estamos muy seguros que aún te falta mucho por contarnos, ¿no? —dice mi hermana.

Miro a Tared, quien sonríe y vuelve a mi lado. Al ver la forma en la que todos me esperan pacientemente —a excepción de Nashua, quien es el único que no vuelve a acercarse a la mesa—, me concentro en por fin revelarles *todo*, y a medida que van escuchando una historia tras otra, relatos de pantanos, desiertos, de visiones de brujas alrededor de hogueras, de monstruos blancos que toman forma de seres amados y una permanente sensación de hambre, cenizas y dolor, los engaños se deshacen como arena. Ellos me escuchan, a veces con asombro, a veces con horror, dispuestos no sólo a oír, sino a *creer*. Pronto, no soy yo el único que habla, porque los demás también me cuentan lo que les ha significado tantos meses de incertidumbre. Las cosas que ellos también tuvieron qué hacer para sobrevivir el luto y la desesperación.

Dentro de un torbellino de recuerdos difíciles y esperanzas que se negaban a morir, me veo invadido por un puro y sagrado alivio al saber que se acabaron las mentiras y que, a partir de ahora, ya no necesitaré ocultar nada más.

Por fin hemos encontrado, tanto ellos como yo, la forma de vivir con la verdad.

CAPÍTULO 37
UN LUGAR A DONDE VOLVER

Horas más tarde, me veo sentado en la sala, torciéndome los dedos sobre el sillón. Escucho a Julien discutir con Nashua en el garaje por alguna tontería sobre preparar la cena, mientras los pasos de Johanna en una de las habitaciones de arriba resuenan como el neurótico tic tac de un reloj. Me levanto para deambular un poco por la estancia, y diviso de reojo el bosque nocturno a través del ventanal, apenas tocado por las luces halógenas del porche. Encuentro, colgado a un lado del armario de abrigos, un espejo de muy buen tamaño, con un elegante marco pintado de plata vieja, una de las pocas cosas que quedaron en la casa después de que Tared se mudase a Nueva Orleans.

Observo mi reflejo y acaricio la superficie con mi mano de hueso.

No hay portales al plano medio en esta casa, la revisé de arriba a abajo para asegurarme, pero eso no significa que no sienta curiosidad por descubrir si podría abrir uno ahora mismo, de quererlo.

Bajo la mano, azorado por la cantidad de tonterías que pasan por mi mente. Pero, ¿cómo diablos no intentar ocuparme con otras cosas si estoy más nervioso que un búfalo en el

Durgá Puyá?[5] Tared dijo que quería mostrarme *algo* esta noche, y mi cabeza no me ha dejado en paz desde entonces. Los minutos han avanzado a paso de caracol y el suspenso me está matando igual de despacio, porque no puedo dejar de pensar en lo que pasó en esa cocina.

Una mezcla agresiva de ansiedad y expectación me calienta la cara más que un maldito carbón. Sólo entonces soy consciente del color violáceo que acuna mis ojos, algo que ni siquiera todos estos días de descanso ha podido reparar. Me acomodo el cabello, pero no logro hacer que mi cara termine de gustarme.

Antes de darme cuenta de que estoy siendo demasiado duro conmigo mismo, una puerta en el piso de arriba se abre, y al alejarme del espejo y volver a la sala veo a Tared bajar por la escalera.

Durante la larga ducha que acaba de tomar se ha recortado bastante el cabello, y ahora lo lleva ligeramente parecido a la usanza militar; también se ha rasurado la barba casi al ras. Lleva puesta una camisa de franela oscura y su parka en el brazo, lo que acentúa ese aire rústico y salvaje tan característico de él, visible debajo de su modesta elegancia y formalidad.

Y se ve tan bien, tan jodidamente guapo y rejuvenecido, que al percibir su suave aroma a loción para después de afeitar me dejo caer sobre el sofá para terminar de derretirme sobre el asiento.

Mi cerebro sólo consigue conectar dos neuronas cuando el devorapieles se yergue a un palmo de mí.

---

[5] Festival hinduista realizado en hon⸲ ⸲ a la diosa Durga, en el cual se acostumbran rituales de sacrificio animal.

—¡Ah! —es lo único que logro expresar. El muy desgraciado sonríe de una manera irresistible y se pasa una mano por el cabello.

—¿Tal mal se ve?

—¿Eh? ¡No! ¡No, claro que no! —*torpe, torpe, torpe*—, ¡yo, tú, este...!

—Tranquilo. Me alegra que te guste —dice, consciente del magnético efecto que tiene en mí—. ¿Estás listo? ¿Te quedó todo bien?

Miro mi suéter de punto negro y los vaqueros deslavados que llevo puestos preguntándome si entre todas las prendas que compraron mis hermanos para mí pude haber escogido algo más bonito.

Me pongo de pie y el hombre lobo toma mi nueva chamarra larga de lana gris y me la coloca sobre los hombros. El suave apretón de sus manos ayuda por fin a disiparme los nervios.

—Hará frío, y mucho —me advierte—. Sé que lo odias, pero valdrá la pena. Te lo prometo.

—Más te vale —replico mientras me pongo los guantes y un gorro muy parecido al que quedó clavado en aquella piedra, en Montana—. Si regreso hecho una paleta, te devolveré a la tienda de mascotas.

Tared se echa a reír y me coloca también la bufanda. Bien podría hacerlo yo mismo, pero el tacto de sus cuidadosos dedos sobre mi cuello es demasiado agradable. Luego, acaricia mi mejilla con sus nudillos, apenas un roce que basta para detener el tiempo unos segundos.

—¿Pasa algo? —pregunto con la voz un poco atontada por la sensación.

—Quería pedirte disculpas por lo que pasó hace rato. Con Hoffman —responde—. Me comporté como un imbécil y lamento muchísimo si te asusté.

Observo al lobo unos momentos y noto que todavía se asoman la punta de sus colmillos en los dos caninos superiores. No ha tenido humor para arrancárselos, al parecer.

—Está bien —contesto—. Se pasó de la raya con ese comentario y pudo haberte delatado con los demás sobre Grace. Sé que no es algo que quieras compartir todavía con ellos...

—No me importa lo que él diga o piense de mí, pero lo que no le voy a tolerar es que se meta contigo.

Suspiro y niego con la cabeza.

—Estoy seguro de que no era su intención hacerlo. Es un poco como Nashua, se les hace fácil decir tonterías de las que luego se arrepienten.

—Con razón se toleran bien. El otro día estuvieron juntos en la cocina, bebiendo café sin siquiera dirigirse la palabra durante más de una hora. Fue espeluznante.

Me río un poco ante la imagen, porque es algo que no había notado hasta ahora.

—De todos modos, no tardará en disculparse.

—¿Hoffman? ¿Disculparse por ser un completo animal?

Ahora soy yo quien ayuda al devorapieles a cerrarse la parka. Noto que le queda un poquito justa en los brazos, por los músculos, cosa que me hace sonreír.

—A pesar de ser un cabrón, tiene lo suyo en muchas cosas, Tared.

—Eso te lo concedo —dice a regañadientes—. Y aunque prefiero que me atropelle un camión antes de decírselo, estaré en deuda con él para siempre.

Imagino que se refiere a las veces en las que Hoffman me ha salvado la vida, y el hecho de que el devorapieles lo reconozca me deja más tranquilo.

Después de ponernos las botas, ambos salimos de la casa. No hay nubes de tormenta, por lo que el cielo está iluminado por las estrellas, ya que la luna apenas es una grieta minúscula y blanca en la oscuridad a la que le falta poco para apagarse.

Al cruzar el porche, veo a un lado de éste algo que me hace entornar la mirada: una *pickup* roja estacionada junto a la *suburban* negra de Comus Bayou, una camioneta muy, muy parecida a ésa que alguna vez hice papilla en el pantano.

—¿Y esto? —pregunto, señalando el vehículo.

—La trajo una grúa hace rato, mientras buscabas portales en el sótano —dice—. Saqué el seguro de mi camioneta hace años cuando la compré aquí en Minnesota, y por azares de la vida que tú conoces muy bien no había podido venir por el reemplazo. Hasta ahora.

Miro de nuevo el reluciente vehículo, sus llantas cubiertas de cadenas y la elegante parrilla perfectamente cromada. Es preciosa, potente y varios modelos más nueva que la anterior.

—¡Tenías seguro y nunca me lo dijiste! —exclamo, boquiabierto.

Él sonríe y se encoge de hombros.

—Supongo que quería un pretexto para estar encima de ti todo el tiempo.

Le doy un puñetazo suave en el brazo, aunque no estoy realmente molesto, porque sé bien que en realidad el lobo nunca tuvo intenciones de cobrarme nada. Voy hacia la lustrosa camioneta, acaricio un poco el cofre y pienso en la cantidad de cosas que hemos vivido desde aquella mañana en Nueva Orleans. Es como si nos hubiésemos arreglado para volver al punto de partida, aun cuando este viaje parece cada vez más cerca de su final.

—¿Listo? —Tared abre la puerta del copiloto, lo que me saca de mi ensoñación. Al trepar, la nostalgia me hace sonreír de forma dolorosa cuando descubro un pequeño atrapasueños quemado que cuelga del retrovisor.

—Dioses, creí que se había perdido —susurro con alivio, porque lo último que recuerdo es que esto estaba guardado entre las cosas que llevé conmigo de Red Buffalo, antes de la pelea en Stonefall.

—Los demás lograron encontrarlo y fue lo primero que me devolvieron cuando llegamos aquí. Este objeto fue una de las pocas cosas que traje conmigo cuando fuimos a buscarte a Utah, después de todo —dice al subirse a la camioneta para encenderla.

—Debe ser muy importante para ti.

Él sonríe y mira el objeto con la misma melancolía que yo.

—Mi madre me lo dio hace muchos años, después del incidente de Grace. Ella es blanca al igual que yo, así que no comprendíamos en realidad el propósito de un atrapasueños indígena, pero le pareció adecuado debido a mi situación. Me dijo que, sin importar a dónde fuera ni qué tan lejos llegara, siempre me ayudaría a encontrar el camino a casa.

"¿A qué maldito sitio quieres que vuelva si mi hogar está aquí, frente a mí, cerrándome sus puertas y diciéndome que ya no me quiere más en su vida?"

Las palabras que dijo Tared la noche de la fogata con los Loas toman tanto significado que tengo que mirar a través de la ventanilla para que no vea mis ojos cristalizarse.

—¿Fue por eso que me lo diste en aquel momento? —es lo único que puedo preguntar antes de que se me quiebre la voz.

—Nunca ha dejado de ser tuyo, Elisse —dice, y logro verlo sonreír a través del retrovisor de mi puerta—. Al igual que yo.

Al comprender mi conmoción, él pone el vehículo en marcha y no añade nada más. Miro el camino y recuerdo que, mientras lo ayudaba a lavar los platos, Julien me dijo que el terreno que rodea la propiedad de Tared es muy amplio y boscoso, poblado de pinos y coníferas debido a que colinda con la frontera del Parque Nacional Voyageurs. No hay vecinos ni negocios próximos en tres kilómetros a la redonda, por lo que muros de árboles impenetrables se alzan por todos los costados de la casa, partidos sólo por el camino que baja hacia un tramo de la carretera cincuenta y tres.

Pero, en vez de encaminarse al asfalto, Tared rodea la construcción y se dirige hacia arriba, al lado contrario.

—¿A dónde vamos? —pregunto cuando entramos a un sendero estrecho y casi oculto por la nieve.

—¿Estás nervioso?

—Tú siempre me pones así.

—Créeme, nadie lo está más que yo en estos momentos, pero si llegas a sentirte muy inseguro, dímelo, por favor —pide—. Prefiero mil veces que lo olvidemos a presionarte.

—¿Lo dices por si temo que algo vuelva a atacarnos?

Él asiente y yo lo pienso unos momentos.

—¿Sabes? Da igual si es entre cuatro paredes o a la intemperie —respondo con seguridad—. No hay sitio en este mundo donde me sienta más seguro que a tu lado, así que mientras tú estés aquí, no hay nada de lo que tenga que preocuparme.

Esta vez es él quien me mira tan sorprendido que casi raspa un lado de la camioneta contra un árbol. Dejo salir una carcajada y él carraspea, con las mejillas ligeramente teñidas de rubor.

Noto que, aunque se ve que no le han pasado la pala en varios años, el sendero aún es transitable. De hecho, tengo la sensación de que hasta podríamos cruzarlo caminando.

Después de unos pocos cientos de metros empiezo a escuchar el sonido de agua que rompe contra las piedras, como una costa. Segundos después, las farolas alumbran a lo lejos lo que parece ser el borde de un acantilado.

Tared detiene de pronto la camioneta.

—¿Elisse?

Sin darme cuenta, mi mano se ha deslizado sobre su pecho, como si intentase protegerlo de una caída inminente. O del disparo de un arpón.

Retraigo la palma, espantado ante la alucinación.

—Perdona. Fue un reflejo —el devorapieles pone la mano sobre la palanca de cambios para dar reversa—. ¡No, no, espera! Dijiste que querías mostrarme algo y yo dije que confiaba en ti, así que, por favor...

Al ver mi determinación, Tared decide avanzar despacio hasta el claro del acantilado, donde los árboles se abren en forma de media luna. El precipicio está bordeado por una vieja cerca de madera, muy parecida a un corral, mientras que una banca que parece tener años sin usarse reposa en medio del lugar.

Cuando sólo restan unos veinte metros de distancia del cerco, Tared pone el freno de mano y apaga el vehículo. Las luces de los faros se extinguen y todo se envuelve en un suave tinte púrpura y aterciopelado creado por millones de estrellas que se acumulan en una estela gruesa contra el cielo: la vía láctea en toda su plenitud.

El sonido del agua también se vuelve cada vez más nítido a medida que mis sentidos se aclimatan, murmullos del viento que empuja las suaves olas. A través del parabrisas, logro por fin ver el lago que se asoma a unos treinta metros bajo el precipicio, tan enorme que se extiende hasta alcanzar el pie de otro monte frondoso.

El bosque también muta alrededor. Aquí, los árboles no son huesudos como los del barranco en Montana, la nieve no está sucia ni revuelta por las avalanchas. En este rincón de Minnesota, los pinos son verdes y espesos. La nieve es prístina y hermosa. La noche es dulce y huele a fresco.

Me cuesta unos segundos procesarlo pero, después, la idea termina de rodar dentro de mi cabeza: *aquí es*. Ésta es la región de los Grandes Lagos, cinco masas de agua tan frías y titánicas que alcanzan a tocar ocho estados del país. El sitio donde reside la leyenda de Wéndigo.

Mi mano huesuda cosquillea bajo el guante y Tared ladea la cabeza.

—Empecé a venir a este mirador cuando era niño, tiempo después de que mi padre se fuera de casa —dice, quizá para romper un poco la tensión—. El hogar de mi madre queda en el pueblo al otro lado del lago, así que no me costaba mucho cruzarlo escabulléndome en las lanchas de los pescadores. Después, sólo tenía que tomar ese camino y subir hasta aquí —dice a la par que apunta hacia un lado del bosque, por donde se asoma otro pequeño sendero asfaltado.

Mientras me cuenta todo esto, trato de imaginarlo de pequeño. ¿Habrá sido un chico serio y reservado o un pequeño huracán rebelde como lo fui yo en su momento? Recuerdo que una vez me dijo que tuvo un carácter difícil, pero me cuesta creerlo al considerar el hombre tranquilo y centrado que es ahora.

Tampoco me pasa desapercibido el que haya mencionado a su padre.

—Mi madre siempre pegaba un grito cada vez que desaparecía —continúa con una sonrisa somera—. Yo sabía que la volvía loca, pero había algo en mí que me obligaba a volver a este sitio, una y otra vez. Me gustaba tanto, me traía tanta nostalgia que terminé por comprar el terreno donde ahora está mi casa para tenerlo siempre cerca. Éste era mi lugar seguro y lo sentía tan *mío* que nunca se lo mostré a nadie.

Tared acaricia distraídamente el volante a medida que los recuerdos lo inundan, mientras yo me pregunto si con "nadie" se refiere también a Grace.

Súbitamente, soy consciente de que conozco bien al Tared del presente, pero muy poco del de su pasado. Y aunque el hombre al que amo es el primero, también hay una parte de mí que está ansiosa por saber más. *Mucho más.*

—Además de tu esposa, ¿hubo alguien más?

En cuanto aquello sale de mi lengua, temo haber indagado en eso demasiado pronto. Es más, ni siquiera creo que sea algo que tenga derecho a preguntar de todas maneras.

Tared gira la barbilla hacia mí.

—¿Te refieres a que si tuve otras parejas? —asiento con la cabeza—. No.

—¿Es en serio? —digo con sorpresa—. ¿Ni siquiera cuando estabas en Nueva Orleans?

De acuerdo, eso sí que ha sido grosero, pero es que no pude evitarlo. ¿En tantos años, y con semejante...?

Por suerte, él no parece incomodarse por mis tonterías. Tan sólo desvía la mirada a las estrellas, y como no podía ser de otra manera, las lunas azules que tiene por ojos las opacan con creces.

—No, ni siquiera en Luisiana —contesta con tranquilidad—. Pero es por una razón más sencilla de la que imaginas.

Él se acomoda un poco en el asiento para mirarme.

—Verás —empieza—, con Grace mantuve una relación estrecha desde pequeño. Vivíamos en el mismo vecindario, asistíamos a la misma escuela y a la misma clase, así que desde el principio hubo una conexión *emocional*, algo que construimos con los años y que, cuando se acabó, me costó mucho... superar.

Meto ambas manos en los bolsillos de mi abrigo con la esperanza de que no haya visto cómo se han tensado. Imaginarme a un Tared joven y profundamente enamorado de una chica a quien conoció desde su infancia me lleva a pensar en tardes de juegos en los veranos y citas maravillosas bajo las hojas de otoño.

Crecer al lado de tu primer amor en un lugar tan bello como este rincón de Minnesota debe ser algo precioso, sacado de esas historias que tanto se intentan imitar en la ficción. Y la tuya no ha sido más que el resultado del dolor.

—Después de su muerte, la idea del amor no volvió a cruzar más por mi cabeza —confiesa—. A lo largo de estos años conocí a muchas personas nuevas, pero nadie con quien pudiese sentir otra vez ese vínculo que me hiciera querer levantar la cabeza y darme *otra oportunidad*. Además, el rencor que me tenía y el trauma de lo que había hecho al perder el control de mi cuerpo me impidió siquiera pensar en refugiarme en el de alguien más para lidiar con mis problemas. Y agradezco que haya sido así; ya había hecho suficiente daño para una vida entera.

Una de mis manos ha vuelto a tomar vida propia, pero ahora para posarse sobre mi corazón como si pudiese sentir todavía la garra cruel y dura del monstruo de hueso sobre él.

Tared, impregnado aún de esa melancolía, apenas logra sonreír.

—Aunque eso no significaba que no pudiera reconocer la belleza cuando la tenía en frente, ¿sabes? —dice—. Después de todo, cuando te conocí, me dije que eras la persona más hermosa que había visto en mi vida.

Como una flecha, vuelve a mí el recuerdo de sus ojos de lobo entre la niebla helada de Audubon Park.

Me sonrojo con tanta intensidad que podría derretir medio Minnesota.

—Dioses, qué cosas dices —susurro sin poder sostenerle la mirada. Él se ríe por lo bajo.

—¿Qué hay de ti?

—¿Eh?

—¿Hubo alguien más en tu vida, Elisse?

La pregunta basta para bajarme el calor. Observo el lago unos momentos, los suficientes como para que Tared perciba la tristeza emanar de mí.

—*Adam* —confieso en voz baja—. Aunque no lo quería de la misma forma que a ti, él fue... importante.

—Te refieres al hijo de Jocelyn Blake, ¿verdad? —pregunta con tiento. La herida de lo que sucedió en la cabaña me abre en canal, y me arden los ojos al recordarlo ahora como una extensión de la terrible Marionetista.

Tared se desliza sobre el asiento y pasa su brazo por mis hombros para acercarme a su costado.

—Lo lamento mucho, Elisse —susurra—. Adam no merecía nada de lo que le pasó. Y tú tampoco merecías haberlo perdido de esa manera.

El errante acaricia en mi cuello el sitio donde alguna vez hubo una cicatriz que yo mismo me hice cuando desperté en Red Buffalo. Levanto la barbilla y me sorprendo de no encontrar rastro de amargura en su expresión ni en sus palabras, y que su empatía por mí, por mis sentimientos, sobrepasa cualquier celo o inseguridad que pueda provocarle mi afecto por otro hombre.

Su calor esfuma fantasmas y sombras, lo llena de una magia que ni siquiera la espada puede absorber, porque me ayuda a encontrar en mí ese dolor tan puro y empático que me hace entender que Tared no sólo perdió a su mujer, sino que tuvo que abandonar su hogar, su trabajo, *su familia*, con tal de reparar sus errores.

Tomo su mano y la envuelvo con la mía.

—También lamento que hayas perdido a Grace —digo con sinceridad, inspirado por la nobleza de sus sentimientos—. La amabas y me pesa mucho el saber que tuviste que pasar por el dolor de no tenerla más en tu vida. De verdad, lo siento mucho, Tared...

Ahora es él quien necesita un segundo para sopesar sus emociones.

Después, baja su brazo a mi cintura y me atrae aún más. Su rostro queda tan cerca del mío que su aliento acaricia mis labios como un beso, pero es su nariz la que roza la mía en un gesto de gratitud.

—*Te quiero, Elisse.* Te quiero más de lo que te puedes imaginar —me susurra. Mis ojos buscan empañarse de nuevo, pero lo disimulo con una breve carcajada.

—Dioses, Tared. Hacerme venir hasta aquí para decirme cursilerías mientras me congelo el trasero.

Él se echa a reír con sus labios dulcemente cerca de los míos. Le acaricio la mejilla con mis nudillos, y disfruto de la sensación de su barba recién perfilada.

—Pero hablando en serio —musito—, gracias por enseñarme este lugar tan importante para ti.

—¿Quién dijo que eso era lo que quería mostrarte?

Él mira hacia el lago y detiene mi cabeza con suavidad para impedir que yo pueda hacerlo también. Y entonces, me pide que cierre los ojos y que confíe en él una vez más. Sin poder negarme, obedezco para luego escucharlo apartarse y bajar de la camioneta. Sus pasos llegan a mi puerta y la abren. Me toma de ambas manos y el frío que siento al salir de la cabina me hace castañetear los dientes.

—No vayas a abrirlos por nada del mundo —insiste y un escalofrío distinto me recorre cuando percibo que vamos en línea recta hacia el barranco. El vértigo crece, pero su agarre es tan firme sobre mí que camino sin detenerme, con seguridad. Finalmente, el alivio me inunda cuando él pone mis dedos sobre la cerca de madera.

—Agárrate bien y no abras los ojos, escuches lo que escuches. Confía en mí —insiste una y otra vez hasta soltarme. Tiemblo cuando percibo sus pasos retroceder en la nieve. Mis dedos se crispan sobre el corral.

Y entonces lo escucho *aullar*.

Una. Dos. Tres veces. Tared aúlla como un lobo desde su garganta humana hasta que la potencia de su voz opaca el sonido del viento y el agua. Y cuando el silencio se prolonga lo que parece una eternidad, escucho un aullido más. Pero no proviene de Tared, sino del bosque.

Uno tras otro, como un coro invernal, decenas de aullidos de *lobos* se levantan por la inmensidad de las montañas que rodean el lago, respondiendo el llamado del devorapieles hasta convertirse en una melodía. Un llamado de la sangre y el instinto.

Una leyenda entre los humanos. Un mito que se vuelve realidad.

Tared se acerca de nuevo y me rodea con sus brazos, sus manos sobre las mías, su corazón que palpita desbocado contra mi espalda.

Despacio, se inclina y susurra sobre mi oído:

—Ábrelos.

Cuando lo hago, un resplandor neón aparece en el horizonte para romper la oscuridad. Es enorme, brillante y majestuoso sobre las aguas, y surca las estrellas en una ola de distintos matices de verdes, cada uno más vibrante que el anterior. Su movimiento es armonioso y bellísimo, como si el cielo entero se contonease al ritmo de su vaivén.

Es una aurora boreal.

—Tared... —susurro sin aliento mientras los lobos aún aúllan alrededor como si quisieran dotar de música al espectáculo.

—El parque Voyageur es uno de los pocos lugares tan al sur del polo donde se pueden ver las auroras boreales —dice el errante, aún sobre mi oído—. Siempre dije que había algo muy familiar en ti cada vez que te miraba y por fin comprendo qué era. Tus ojos verdes me recordaban mucho a las luces del norte. *A mi hogar.*

Tared me estrecha la cintura y roza su mejilla contra la mía. Y cuando giro la cabeza sobre mi hombro para dejar que atrape mis labios, yo también regreso a casa.

Porque, aunque este momento termine para enfrentar de nuevo la crueldad de la batalla que nos espera, siempre, siempre podré volver aquí. Al recuerdo de este bosque. A los aullidos de estos lobos y a los brazos de este hombre que me sostienen bajo el brillo de la aurora boreal.

CAPÍTULO 38
UNA MAGIA DISTINTA

Cuando Tared estaciona la camioneta frente al porche, encontramos las luces del frente apagadas. Entre el tiempo que permanecimos en el lago y el rato que nos tomó bajar a la carretera para buscar una gasolinera, nos dieron más de las doce, por lo que los demás ya deben haberse acostado.

Nos quedamos en la cabina unos minutos, tan sólo con la luz de las estrellas y la quietud de la noche, el silencio de la casa delatando el golpeteo ansioso dentro de mí.

Pongo la mano en la puerta y Tared me llama por mi nombre. Y tras una breve petición de sus ojos azules, me deslizo por el asiento hacia él.

Me toma en brazos y yo acuno su rostro para besarnos una vez más, tal cual hemos hecho durante todo el camino, robando tiempo en un semáforo, en un cruce de caminos o mientras se cargaba el combustible en la estación.

El calor de la cabina empieza a subir cuando deslizo mis manos a su pecho para liberar el cierre de su parka, demasiado apretada contra un corazón que late cada vez con más fuerza.

Mi tímida señal hace que él rompa nuestro beso con cuidado para luego llevar sus labios por mi comisura, por mi mejilla, por mi oreja. Despacio, deshace el nudo de mi bufanda para alcanzar mi cuello.

No podría encontrar una manera de explicar la forma en la que mi piel se eriza cuando él la besa, pero creo que el suave gemido de mis labios basta para describirlo.

Escucho los nudillos de Tared estrujar el volante, su beso convertirse en una suave mordida que busca arrancarme un suspiro más. Él se separa de mí dolorosamente despacio. Nos miramos a los ojos y la tensión se siente como la resistencia de un gatillo.

Bajamos de la camioneta y el frío se derrite contra mi piel enrojecida, la bufanda y el gorro ya olvidados sobre el sillón. Nuestro andar silencioso empieza a parecerme eterno cuando él me toma de la mano y tira de mí con suavidad hacia la puerta.

Al entrar, encontramos una única luz encendida en el porche lateral de la cocina, en señal de que a quien le tocaba hacer guardia hoy ha salido a hacer una ronda. Pero de allí en más, el resto de la casa está tranquilo, casi insonoro. Tan sólo se escucha el roce de nuestras ropas cuando, al pie de la escalera, volvemos a comernos a besos.

—Elisse...

Suelto un gemido de sorpresa al sentir sus dedos fríos colarse bajo mi camiseta, rodear mi cintura y estrujarme contra él para saborear cada letra de mi nombre en su boca, ejecutando un conjuro que dejó caer sobre mí desde la primera vez que lo pronunció.

El lobo desliza mi abrigo para descubrir mis hombros. Los acaricia, los besa, anhelando la piel que yace debajo de la ropa. Deshace mi trenza. Sus pupilas se dilatan. Su respiración se acelera.

Tared gruñe con fuerza contra mi cuello cuando suplico sobre su oído:

—Llévame arriba.

Me levanta en brazos y me sube hasta la habitación sin tambalearse una sola vez. Entramos en la recámara y me baja junto a la chimenea sólo para volver un segundo a la puerta. Una sensación asfixiante de nerviosismo y expectación se dispara dentro de mí al escuchar el clic metálico del seguro resonar contra las paredes. El hombre lobo se acerca de nuevo y siento sus pasos como los de un depredador que acecha en la nieve.

Siempre he dicho que el líder de Comus Bayou tiene una mirada muy... intensa, dominante, pero esa palabra se queda corta comparada con lo que siento cuando él se para delante de mí para clavarme sus ojos azules. Es tan alto, tan grande comparado conmigo que me siento como un ciervo indefenso ante el apetito de un lobo hambriento y feroz.

Tared termina de quitarme el abrigo, que aterriza en el suelo con un suave susurro. Y como si comenzáramos un ritual grabado en el instinto, ahora soy yo quien lo despoja del suyo. El frío es palpable en la recámara, nuestros alientos densos se mezclan en el claroscuro...

Pero yo ya no siento frío. Sólo una flama que busca estallar.

Él se desabotona la camisa, tan despacio que el sendero de piel que se abre como una grieta sobre su pecho me evapora la saliva. Y, al dejarla caer, siento una envidia terrible por la suerte que tiene esa tela de deslizarse de esa manera por sus hombros.

Me permito unos segundos para admirarlo. No es la primera vez que lo veo quitarse algo de ropa, pero sí es la primera vez que Tared se desnuda *para mí*.

Y eso lo cambia todo.

Alargo mi mano descarnada para bordear la herida del arpón, aún cubierta por el parche. Luego, la subo despacio por su cuerpo para sentir las cicatrices en los pectorales y el esternón, marcas blancas y gruesas que no han podido mancillar su belleza.

Cincelado y duro como el granito, firme desde sus hombros hasta esas líneas gemelas que marcan su vientre bajo, Tared tiene un cuerpo tan hermoso que me parece un crimen tocarlo con una garra tan horrible como la mía.

Retraigo mi mano maldita hacia mi pecho, consciente ya no sólo de mi deformidad.

De pronto, me siento diminuto e inseguro, con mis curvas suaves y andróginas en sitios donde se supone que debería haber músculos como los suyos. A veces me da rabia no tener un solo vello sobre la barbilla o una apariencia más varonil, sentirme como algo más que un fenómeno de circo.

Como siempre, Tared parece leerme la mente, pero en vez de desestimar mis sentimientos con halagos que no serían de ningún consuelo, me atrae con cuidado hacia él. Toma mi mano de hueso, la acaricia con su pulgar y arranca un grito furioso del monstruo dentro de mí cuando *la besa*. Me quedo mudo de la impresión al ver cómo acaricia mis nudillos sin asomo de repulsión. Sin una pizca de temor.

Estoy tan conmovido que disfruto cada gesto de ternura con los ojos cerrados.

El corazón casi se me sale del pecho cuando Tared me toma de los hombros y me empuja suavemente hacia la cama.

Nuestro peso hunde el lecho cuando nos fundimos unos momentos sobre las frazadas, tan sólo besándonos, enredándonos en los brazos del otro, buscando ser uno a través de nuestro tacto. Percibo su aroma muy de cerca mientras que esas manos que pueden partir astas y huesos me acarician con una ternura y un cuidado que me derrite contra la almohada.

¿Cuántas noches desee tener a Tared en mis brazos, sentirme amado y deseado por él como en este momento? ¿Y cuántas veces me sentí indigno de su afecto a causa de mis errores, de la criatura que llevo dentro...?

Al descubrir que lo que quiere ya no va a conseguirlo sólo en mis labios, el devorapieles se arrodilla y empieza a quitarme la ropa. Me saca el suéter, las calcetas, la camiseta. Y entre prenda y prenda, besa con tanta devoción cada costilla, cada hueso que pienso que se marcan muy poco o demasiado, hasta recordarme que todo eso es perfecto tal y como está.

Y entonces, me veo obligado a aferrarme a las sábanas cuando él posa las manos en la pretina de mi pantalón.

—Tared...

El lobo levanta la mirada, encendida ya no como una luna, sino como un vibrante fuego azul.

—¿Quieres que me detenga, Elisse?

Preferiría morir primero, así que niego con la cabeza, mi cara más caliente que un carbón. Sin dejar de observarme, desabrocha el botón y finalmente baja el cierre por completo. Tared sonríe y se inclina hacia mi ombligo para besar el vello que nace claro y escaso en una línea fina sobre mi vientre. Suspiro tan profundo que mi espalda crea un suave arco sobre la cama, el cual él aprovecha para quitarme todo lo que me queda de ropa.

El hombre lobo abandona mi abdomen y se arrodilla delante de mí. Observa mi cuerpo de arriba abajo, mi cabello derramado por la almohada, mi pecho acelerado y el sendero de besos que ha marcado sobre mi piel.

Y al detenerse en mi sexo, endurecido por la excitación, él deja escapar un suspiro de lo más erótico.

—Dios mío, Elisse —dice sin aliento—. Eres precioso.

Escuchar aquellas palabras así, en el momento más vulnerable de mi vida, transforma todas y cada una de mis inseguridades en cenizas. Y al ponerse él de pie para desabrocharse sus propios vaqueros, me queda bien claro que el deseo que siente Tared por mí también es *bastante real*.

Retuerzo las sábanas entre mis puños cuando el hombre lobo, con una paciencia deliciosa, se recuesta sobre mí y me hace descubrir miles de sensaciones que jamás había experimentado antes: la piel de otra persona contra la mía, su peso sensual sobre mi cuerpo y sus caderas abriéndose paso entre mis muslos en busca de la promesa de un paraíso.

Dejo salir un gemido al sentir su propia dureza presionar contra la mía, porque no tengo ni la menor idea de cómo describir semejante sensación. Él es tan tibio, tan firme y a la vez tiene una textura tan aterciopelada que mis caderas se mueven por sí mismas contra las suyas para buscar un poco más de ese placer tan nuevo para mí.

Tared cierra los ojos y gruñe mi nombre contra mi clavícula. Mis labios prueban su cuello, la firmeza de sus hombros y el maravilloso sabor de su piel bronceada por la nieve. Sus vellos se erizan ante la frialdad de mi lengua y su entrepierna pulsa con fuerza.

Quiero más sensaciones. Quiero acariciar y probar más allá de lo que alcanzan mis dedos, descubrir tanto de su cuerpo que mi mano humana se desliza de forma instintiva por su abdomen, aunque con algo de duda y timidez.

—Tranquilo —susurra a la vez que él mismo la guía con cuidado hacia su vientre—. Puedes tocarme todo lo que quieras…

Por los Loas, ¿cómo puede decirme eso mientras me mira tan fijamente a los ojos?

De nuevo, más sensaciones desconocidas me desbordan: el grueso de su sexo al tenerlo entre mis dedos, la agradable y masculina densidad de su vello, sus gemidos guturales contra mi oído cuando lo acaricio de arriba abajo...

Dioses. No sabía que se podía sentir tanto placer por el simple hecho de tocar así a otra persona.

Y cuando él me hace sentir de la misma manera, poco me falta para derramarme sobre las sábanas... Hasta que decide que no va a soportarlo más.

De pronto, sus labios bajan por mi pecho. Por mi ombligo. Por los delicados huesos de mis caderas.

—Eres tan jodidamente hermoso —susurra contra mi piel, tocando y probando todo lo que encuentra a su paso—. ¿Cómo diablos puedo ser tan afortunado?

Qué ironía. Justamente estaba pensando en que, a pesar de todas las cosas terribles que me han pasado, Tared es la prueba de que soy un chico con mucha suerte.

Mi espalda forma otro agresivo arco cuando él por fin alcanza la suave piel del interior de mis muslos. Me toma de las rodillas, las abre y sin piedad, sin una pizca de compasión, se hunde entre mis piernas y *me devora*, tan despacio y a la vez, con tanto apetito, que el mundo deja de tener forma y sentido. Me aferro con fuerza a su cabello y él gruñe muy bajo, un ruido feral y salvaje que se intensifica cuando hago trizas las cobijas con mi garra.

Entonces sucede algo extraordinario: a medida que mi clímax se acerca, la magia fluye dentro de mí como si la propia lengua de Tared la acariciara, con tanta fuerza que la espada ni siquiera puede detener la marea de poder que se dispara hacia cada rincón de mi cuerpo. Y cuando por fin llego a la cúspide, esa poderosa fuerza natural cimbra en su punto más alto para luego desvanecerse entre mis gemidos. Tiemblo sobre la cama largos segundos, embriagado y con el nombre del lobo haciendo eco en mi boca una y otra vez.

Tared sube de nuevo hacia mi rostro y sonríe.

—Olvida lo que dije hace rato —susurra, relamiéndose los colmillos—: tú, *teniendo un orgasmo*, es sin duda lo más bonito que he visto en mi vida.

Me echo a reír, a punto de desvanecerme debido al placer. Me sostengo de su nuca, y la piel de Tared se eriza cuando observo hacia el bolsillo de su parka, echada a un lado del colchón.

Jala la prenda y saca el par de cosas que se bajó a comprar en la gasolinera con la excusa de echar combustible. Las deja a un lado, cerca de la almohada, y recarga su frente contra la mía.

—Todavía podemos dejarlo para después —sugiere, aun cuando puedo sentirlo palpitar ansioso contra mis muslos.

—Vamos. No seas cobarde —le digo con una sonrisa que él corresponde.

—Perdona. Es sólo que tengo muchos años sin hacer esto y en su momento tampoco me consideré un experto. Me asusta mucho hacerte daño, Elisse...

Al principio, me sorprende escuchar la timidez en su voz, pero después recuerdo que ninguno de los dos ha estado con otro hombre antes, así que es entendible que también esté nervioso. Aunque, para ser honesto, el dolor es lo último que podría preocuparme ahora, puesto que esta vez se trataría de un tipo de dolor distinto, uno que he anhelado desde el primer momento en el que supe que deseaba a Tared.

Además, él mismo lo dijo una vez en Nueva Orleans: a veces el dolor es un signo de que algo está cambiando. Y yo estoy cambiando.

Estoy cortando el último cordón que me ata al Elisse del pasado.

Él termina por entenderme, pero eso no evita que yo contenga la respiración al verlo romper el envoltorio del preservativo. Con cuidado, se lo coloca frente a mí y luego se inclina sobre mis labios. Escucho una pequeña botella abrirse, y la luna nueva desaparece tras la ventana cuando las caricias húmedas del lobo vuelven a alcanzarme.

Aquello es un poco difícil al principio, quizá más de lo que pensé. Pero pronto me encuentro buscando más de esa sensación nueva e iniciática cuando Tared logra llegar a partes de mí que nunca habían sido tocadas antes.

Su contacto se alterna entre la ternura y la firmeza, y echo mi cabeza contra la almohada, el dolor y el placer tambaleándose en una línea indescifrable, tan fina que mis ojos se llenan de lágrimas. Suspiro con angustia hasta que, con un autocontrol y una calma asombrosa, él mismo se abre paso en mi cuerpo como una magia nueva y poderosa, una sensación que ni siquiera el más potente de los hechizos sería capaz de imitar.

Sin prisa, gruñe, gime y se deshace de placer con cuidado, consciente de la fuerza y el peso de su cuerpo sobre el mío, de lo que me está costando albergarle dentro de mí. Me invoca una vez más, mi nombre como acónito[6] en su boca cuando sus caderas logran llegar hasta el fondo. Suspiro bajo sus la-

---

[6] También conocida como wolfsbane, es una hierba a la cual se le atribuían poderes que volvían vulnerables a los hombres lobo.

bios al sentir que mi vientre arde y que todo mi ser suplica por ser liberado de semejante presión.

La satisfacción es inevitable cuando esa misma tensión lo hace gemir en voz baja, un sonido tan erótico y tan feral que podría embrujarme con la melodía.

Tared planta sus manos al lado de mi cabeza y, después de asegurarse de que no me está haciendo daño, comienza a moverse contra mí. Primero, despacio, con firmeza, pero sin brutalidad, buscando desesperadamente un instante, una sensación que domine todo menos su consciencia sobre mí.

Él baja sus labios a mi oído y me dice que me encuentra tan maravilloso que le resulta una tortura contenerse. Su voz se engrosa, su frente se perla de sudor y un rugido escapa de sus labios cuando, a cambio, le pido más. *Mucho más.*

El hombre lobo se funde conmigo bajo la luna oscura hasta que, después de un último beso, él también alcanza una clase distinta de magia.

CAPÍTULO 39
UN SUEÑO PELIGROSO

La Maligna encuentra el endrino despedazado por la madrugada, horas antes de que el sol alcance a besar el bosque. La veo inclinarse como un junco hacia lo que queda del tronco, el cual ha sido cortado de forma precisa, casi quirúrgica. Y por encima de los anillos de la madera, percibe también el olor del fuego y las cenizas, lo que confirma su sospecha de que el potro en el que fue quemada la tarotista Cecilia había sido fabricado con el desdichado árbol.

Debió haberlo visto venir. Ese endrino negro era, por sí mismo, un mal presagio. Una criatura perteneciente a la niebla que, de pronto, había aparecido en el mundo de los humanos, sembrado en la atropellada acumulación de rocas al pie de la colina y oculto de cualquier guardaparques que pudiese preguntar qué hacía un árbol de esa especie —y de semejante tamaño— plantado en medio de la reserva Lynn Woods.

Y ahora, alguien había cortado aquel endrino para llevarlo al almacén de Cecilia. Algo que había descendido desde los sueños de aquella desgraciada sólo para quemarla viva en su propia casa como una burla, un insulto hacia el simbolismo del endrino que, siglos atrás, se consideraba madera de brujas. La mujer estira el largo brazo para tocar la corteza. La dilatación de su mirada y la forma en la que sus dedos se crispan me hace saber que la magia dentro de ella se ha contraído de forma dolorosa.

Un músculo de mi boca se estira cuando las palabras "hierro blanco" brotan de sus labios, con tanta certeza como si hubiese visto el arma con la que el árbol fue talado. Miro a la bruja de arriba abajo y acaricio el perfil de su estrecha cintura entre mis uñas.

De pronto, gira hacia la niebla donde se oculta mi ojo vidente. Sé que ella no puede verme, pero su mirada se enciende como si hubiese escuchado el latido frenético de mi apetito.

Ah, *Inanna*... A sus dos hermanas las mataría de un solo golpe. Les enterraría un athame directo en sus corazones y les abriría un agujero como una coladera. Luego, los arrojaría *a tus pies* como unas simples sobras inmundas. Pero a ella... Oh, a ella *me la quedaría*. La llevaría al sitio más repugnante de mi celda y la abriría en canal desde la garganta hasta su verga. La bebería entera como un elixir y succionaría cada gramo de su inmensa magia directo de sus tripas, y su alma, tan sombría como el crepúsculo negro que le da color a su cabello y sus ojos, me llenaría a mí también de oscuridad.

—¡Mi Señora!

Aquel grito la hace desviar su atención hacia su costado. La mujer levanta el exquisito encaje de sus faldas de terciopelo negro y camina unos cuantos metros hasta el borde de una precipitación poco profunda. Abajo ve a un hombre de piel y cabello tan blancos que podría confundirse con la nieve si se quitase el abrigo negro que lleva puesto. Es muy alto y fornido, con los ojos de un pálido color rosa fijos en el tronco de otro árbol, observando algo que ella no puede distinguir.

Pero el rastro rojo que se arrastra hasta la base del tronco ya parece haberle dado una idea.

—Mi Señora, venga a ver esto, por favor —pide el gigante sin levantar la barbilla, como si temiese que aquello que observa pudiese escapar si le quita la mirada de encima.

Ella baja de las rocas de un salto y camina con una elegancia propia de las sombras que se arrastran obedientemente detrás de ella.

Y cuando la Maligna por fin rodea el árbol para ver lo que quiere mostrarle, comprime los dedos para no llevarse una mano a los labios.

De la mujer recargada contra la corteza ya no queda gran cosa, sólo el cuello y el brazo derecho aún unido a la caja torácica. Se han *comido* la cabeza, los pechos, el vientre, todo lo que tuviese algo de carne, mientras que el resto se ha convertido en una escultura móvil que cuelga de las ramas del árbol; un adorno de huesos que se mueven con el viento, diseccionados por la misma arma que se usó para cortar el endrino.

—Habrá que descubrir qué clase de monstruo hizo esto —dice Inanna. Ella no puede reconocer a la víctima, pero es obvio que era una hermana, una bruja, y lo sabe porque el brazo izquierdo, el cual cuelga de una rama, tiene la mano cercenada.

—No fue sólo uno, mi Señora. Por el tipo de ataques, deben de ser por lo menos dos.

De no ser porque yo no esperaba menos de aquella bestia disfrazada de hombre, sonreiría.

—Debería volver por la caverna —le advierte —. El bosque ya no es seguro para usted ni para sus hermanas.

Ella levanta la barbilla para mirarlo. Inanna es alta y larga como una espada, pero su guardián sigue siendo gigantesco aún a su lado.

—No tengo miedo. O al menos, no a estas criaturas —contesta con pasmosa tranquilidad al estar ahora segura de qué es lo que se ha comido a la mujer a sus pies.

—¿Entonces? —pregunta él con cuidado, y la oscura criatura acaricia el anillo dorado que yace en el dedo anular de su mano izquierda.

—*Un monstruo para engañar a la magia, dos para despedazarla y uno más para revelarla* —su piel morena se eriza al pronunciar estas palabras, aquellas que su hermana Hela había escuchado en el vaticinio que tuvo poco después de haber visto al fantasma de Giles Corey—. Vamos, Ilya. Hay que volver con Madre. Y de paso, pedirle prestados algunos de sus restos...

Ella le da la espalda al hombre y éste la sigue en silencio a través del bosque, como una sombra blanca que no deja una sola huella en la nieve.

CAPÍTULO 40
UN AMOR NO CORRESPONDIDO

Al despertar, atosigado por la sed, descubro que la habitación apenas empieza a ser bañada por el tinte azul de la madrugada.

Intento levantarme, pero mi pecho se siente un poco más pesado de lo habitual, como si la espada presionase contra el colchón. Me despabilo, y la piel se me se eriza por razones ajenas al frío, al descubrir que no es la piedra lo que oprime, sino el brazo de Tared, enroscado alrededor de mi cuerpo.

Me giro sobre mi costado y sonrío al verlo dormir bajo las cobijas. Está tan tranquilo y respira tan profundamente que contengo mis ganas de acariciar su rostro, sus labios, redescubrir las marcas que siguen frescas en nuestra piel, porque no recuerdo cuándo fue la última vez que lo vi descansar de esa manera.

Cierro los ojos un momento al pensar en nuestra noche sin hambre, sin hogueras ni pesadillas. Sin brujas ni criaturas con cabeza de cabra.

Tan sólo nosotros dos.

Después de unos momentos, ya no es sólo la sed lo que me incomoda, así que me levanto de la cama para ir a orinar, procurando no despertar al lobo —cosa que no creo que pase pronto después de lo *mucho* que se esforzó anoche—. Al ponerme de pie, siento un tirón en las piernas que me hace alzar ambas cejas; la cara interna de mis muslos está tensa y tengo un poco acalambrada la espalda baja, pero no es un dolor molesto. De hecho, es una sensación que encuentro muy agradable.

Sacudo la cabeza y me visto con el pijama. Después de ir al cuarto de baño, me pongo mis botas y la parka de Tared, y salgo de la habitación de puntillas con la garganta más seca que un desierto.

Al cerrar la puerta, me quedo con la mano tensa sobre el pomo, y no sólo al escuchar los cavernarios ronquidos de Julien en una de las habitaciones al fondo del pasillo, sino al descubrir que la luz de la cocina está encendida.

No quiero pensar en si los demás se habrán enterado de lo que pasó anoche; Tared y yo no hicimos demasiado ruido —creo—, pero son errantes, tienen buen oído y...

Los colores me suben a la cara, pero decido bajar de todas maneras. Cuando me asomo al final de la escalera, encuentro a Nashua sentado a la mesa, con una taza de café en la mano y un rifle recargado en la silla, en señal de que fue él quien hacía guardia anoche. Y, por la forma en la que su mano se tensa sobre la cerámica, es obvio que ya es muy tarde para que yo haga el ridículo volviendo arriba como si nada.

Me acerco para tomar una de las botellas de agua de los gabinetes, y pienso en el rugido hambriento de mi estómago. Tared y yo llegamos tan tarde anoche y estuvimos tan en lo nuestro que ni siquiera se nos pasó por la cabeza cenar y...

El súbito rechinar de una silla casi me hace soltar la botella. Nashua se cuelga el arma y se marcha de la cocina para ir hacia el porche lateral de la casa, sin siquiera cerrar la puerta a sus espaldas.

Aguanto un suspiro de agotamiento, porque una parte de mí, ésa que parece arraigarse con fuerza al pasado, quiere dar la vuelta y largarse a la tranquilidad y el calor de mi hombre lobo. Pero la otra, ésa que aún quiere hacer crecer de nuevo mi vínculo con Comus Bayou, tira testarudamente hacia esa salida.

A sabiendas de que me voy a arrepentir de esto, salgo también y cierro la puerta tras de mí.

Me acerco con calma al errante oso y me detengo a unos pasos de él. Pone las manos sobre el barandal del porche, quizá para no enroscarlas en mi cuello.

—Sabes que no podemos evitarnos para siempre, ¿verdad? —le digo.

En respuesta, Nashua se queda con la cara fija en el lindero, como si sólo hubiese escuchado el viento susurrar.

Bueno. Igual ya sabía que esto no iba a ser fácil.

Tomo un trago y dejo la botella en el suelo.

—Sé que las cosas siempre han sido... complicadas entre nosotros —insisto—, y si bien no espero que eso cambie pronto, de lo que sí estoy seguro es de que por lo menos debemos mantenernos unidos. *Todos.* Y eso te incluye a ti y a mí.

Él aprieta el barandal con tanta fuerza que siento que en cualquier momento se astillará los dedos. Una parte de mí quiere creer que esa reacción es más bien debida a la presencia de Wéndigo, pero no soy tan estúpido todavía para creerlo.

—¿Y exactamente qué quieres de mí, Elisse? —bufa—. Porque yo estaba muy bien antes de que decidieras venir a decirme estas... cosas.

Sí. Estoy seguro de que "cosas" no era la palabra que iba a usar.

Contengo un suspiro e intento mantener esa paciencia que tanto le falta a Nashua.

—Para empezar, debemos encontrar la forma de estar juntos en la misma habitación más de cinco minutos. Al menos, por ellos —digo con un ademán hacia la casa—. Ya tenemos suficiente con Hoffman y Tared queriéndose arrancar la cabeza.

—¡Entonces que te baste con que yo no tenga ganas de hacerte lo mismo! —responde, exasperado—. ¿Es que no puedes dejar todo como está? ¿Es que todo el mundo tiene que quererte y adorarte para que estés contento? ¿No puedes dejarme tranquilo y ya?

—Dioses, lo único que quiero es que arreglemos las cosas, maldita sea, ¡te recuerdo que, te guste o no, seguimos siendo…!

—Deja de creerte tus propias mentiras, carajo, ¡tú y yo nunca hemos sido *hermanos*!

Después de su grito, sólo queda un silencio frío en su boca, tan denso que hasta opaca a la propia nieve.

Es cierto. A diferencia de Julien, de Johanna, yo *nunca* pude formar un vínculo verdadero con Nashua. Él y yo jamás logramos convertirnos en hermanos, y por más que quise negarlo, por más que intenté creer que había algo real que nos unía, la verdad es que…

Tú eras el único que quería eso, ¿verdad?

Pero esta vez, Wéndigo no logra herirme. No al Elisse que ha llegado hasta aquí.

Al ver que no doy media vuelta para escapar como lo he hecho siempre, el devorapieles se encorva por el peso de sus propias palabras.

—¿Nashua?

Como dos agujas, él me clava sus hostiles ojos negros cuando doy un paso hacia él. Comienza a respirar aceleradamente, como si algo luchara por liberarse de su pecho, pero me he tomado tan poco la molestia de conocerlo que no tengo la menor idea de qué es lo que piensa o siente ahora mismo.

El oso mira hacia el bosque de nuevo y su respiración se detiene tan súbitamente que me da la impresión de que va a ahogarse.

Y en un parpadeo, Nashua da un salto hacia la nieve.

—¿Pero qué estás...?

El errante echa a correr. Y yo, como buen imbécil, bajo también de un salto preguntándome si vale la pena congelarme el maldito trasero por alguien que no parece estar dispuesto a hacer el mínimo esfuerzo por cooperar.

Dioses, entiendo tanto a Tared ahora mismo...

—¡Nashua, espera, es peligroso!

El muy bastardo cruza el lindero como un lunático y se mete a zancadas al bosque mientras yo voy tras él. La nieve es espesa y mi delgado pantalón se humedece de inmediato, pero me esfuerzo para que mis sentidos no se atolondren con el frío o el peso de la espada.

Lo llamo una y otra vez, pero él toma caminos cada vez más intrincados por la foresta hasta que el terreno empieza a inclinarse, en señal de que vamos cuesta abajo, hacia la carretera. Su silueta se vuelve más tenue por la neblina de la mañana, y después de unos cuantos minutos de persecución en los que ya no puedo ubicar la casa a nuestras espaldas, veo que algo se mueve por delante del devorapieles, tan rápido que apenas puedo distinguir más allá de un borrón blanco.

Una caricia fría me roza la nuca, porque eso significa que Nashua no huye de mí, sino que está *persiguiendo algo.*

Sólo logro alcanzar al errante cuando éste se detiene a unos veinte metros de la carretera, a unos pasos de la línea de árboles que la bordea como un muro espeso.

El aire frío de mi propio aliento me ahoga al descubrir que lo que él intentaba alcanzar ahora yace sentado entre las gruesas raíces y la nieve, con el rostro surcado de arrugas y un collar de cuervo colgando en medio de su pecho.

Es el abuelo Muata.

CAPÍTULO 41
UNA LENGUA INCOMPRENSIBLE

Cualquiera hubiera pensado que mi reacción sería rápida. Que en cuanto viese a aquella criatura con la apariencia de Muata, sentada sobre brazos que simulan ser raíces, lo primero que haría sería lanzarme sobre Nashua para alejarlo de aquel monstruo.

Pero, en cambio, me quedo absorto durante unos segundos valiosos, petrificado por aquellos ojos de ópalo.

Nunca creí que tendría que volver a enfrentarme al peso de la presencia del abuelo Muata, pero me resulta tan aplastante que bien podría arrancarme la espada del pecho ahora mismo y no sentiría el menor alivio.

No. Esto no es más que una pesadilla de la que necesitamos despertar. *Ahora.*

—Nashua, el rifle —llamo en voz baja. Quiero dar un salto hacia él y alejarlo, pero los brazos de la Marionetista, escondidos bajo tierra como topos, hacen surcos y espirales a su alrededor, listos para dispararse como trampas mortales si me atrevo a mover un solo dedo.

No logro ver el cuerpo del monstruo por ninguna parte, lo que me hace creer que está enterrada justo debajo del falso Muata.

¡Mierda, mierda!

—Abuelo... —el viejo levanta la barbilla hacia Nashua, con ese brazo parasitario en su nuca que articula cada uno de los gestos de su cara.

—Has cambiado mucho en poco tiempo, muchacho —dice, y su voz es igual a la que tenía el verdadero contemplasombras, lo que le añade otro matiz horripilante.

El devorapieles se lleva las manos a la cara un momento.

—No lo entiendo —musita—, *¿por qué?*

Un escalofrío me recorre la espalda cuando recuerdo cómo yo hice exactamente la misma pregunta a Adam.

—Porque ya era hora de encontrarnos en un lugar distinto a tus sueños —contesta el impostor—. Un sitio del que no despertases llorando como un niño.

El falso Muata extiende una mano hacia su bisnieto y éste se convierte en eso: un niño pequeño, porque el hombre se encorva, se pasa la manga de la chamarra por la cara, y se acerca despacio hacia la criatura.

Los mortíferos brazos bajo la nieve se tensan como serpientes cuando intento moverme para detenerlo.

—¡No, aléjate, Nashua! —grito—, ¡esa cosa no es Muata!

Pero no parece escucharme.

El errante se arrodilla a los pies del viejo en busca de consuelo. El espectro sonríe y posa la mano sobre su cabeza en un gesto que me parece más bien degradante.

—Abuelo, lo siento, lo siento tanto —gimotea el devorapieles con una voz tan frágil y rota que parece haberse transformado en otra persona—, estoy tan perdido sin usted. Desde que se fue yo...

—Lo sé, niño, lo he visto todo —consuela con una ternura impropia del verdadero Muata—, he sido testigo de tu sufrimiento y también he visto el rechazo de los otros. Todos hablan de ti en cuanto les das la espalda, susurran lo mucho que les asquea que los llames *hermanos*. Ven en ti a un traidor, a un asesino, a un idiota incapaz de controlarse...

—No dejes que te manipule —insisto, furioso ante la crueldad de la criatura—, ¡no dejes que la Marionetista use tu dolor contra ti!

El imitador gira la cabeza y me observa con esos falsos ojos ciegos.

—¿Mi *premonición* te sigue torturando, hijo? —pregunta a Nashua, sin quitarme la mirada de encima—. Lo que te dije sobre esa bestia resultó ser cierto, ¿verdad?

El monstruo de hueso sonríe dentro de mí.

—¿Premonición? —musito, desconcertado. ¿De qué diablos está hablando?

—Yo te lo advertí, muchacho —continúa el falso Muata como si no me hubiese escuchado—. Yo, mamá Tallulah, padre Trueno... todos nos pudrimos ahora en la tierra porque no tuviste las agallas de hacer lo que te pedí. ¿Cuántos más necesitan morir para que lo entiendas? ¿O acaso también quieres ver cómo él se traga a todos aquéllos a quienes debías proteger?

El instinto me hace retroceder cuando noto que los puños del errante comienzan a llenarse de pelo. El falso Muata se levanta sobre dos piernas que deberían ser débiles como ramas y empieza a acercarse hacia mí.

Pero no camina, *flota* sobre el manto invernal, manipulado por el brazo que se alarga detrás de su nuca.

Las múltiples caras de la criatura brotan de la nieve como flores, se elevan alrededor de nosotros en un jardín terrible. La Marionetista se revela bajo las raíces de carne y hueso y comienza a erguirse como una dama mortífera que lentamente despierta de su sueño.

El olor paradisíaco que ella desprende se vuelve insoportable, mientras me pregunto cómo demonios pudo volver esa bestia a encontrarme tan pronto si yo mismo la arrojé hacia las sombras del plano medio para que se la tragaran.

El devorapieles se transforma tan despacio que parece que su cuerpo se resiste al cambio. Crece y se ensancha con un dolor que aguanta con los colmillos apretados, y su voz se convierte en gruñidos que se alargan junto con su hocico negro. La correa del rifle revienta, incapaz de contener los fibrosos músculos de la espalda de Nashua... pero él no es el único que cambia.

El pelo del títere Muata empieza a caerse, la piel se torna leprosa y dedos blancos brotan de las cuencas y la boca, empujando a un lado la lengua y los ojos para abrirse paso y convertir su cara en no más que una máscara de donde cuelga una carcasa vacía.

Estoy tan absorto en la terrible transformación que el sonido de un pesado tráiler que atraviesa la carretera me distrae apenas un segundo.

Un segundo que le basta a Nashua para lanzarse hacia mí y alcanzarme con su zarpa.

—¡Aggh!

Sus enormes garras me hacen trizas la manga de la parka y me arrojan con una potencia propia de sus trescientos kilos de peso, lanzándome lejos del jardín de la Marionetista.

Suelto un breve grito de dolor ante la caída, para después echarme hacia atrás con los codos. Las heridas a lo largo de mi brazo manchan el suelo mientras que él se yergue, grande y brutal en su forma de hombre oso.

—¡Nashua, no!

—Tú lo sabías —le susurra el títere detrás de él, avivando su cólera—, tú sabías que el brillo de la luna traería la desgracia sobre todos nosotros. Y pese a ello, *lo dejaste vivir.*

Siento el sudor frío aglomerarse en mi sien; con el rifle tirado en medio del remolino de brazos, mi única opción es intentar llegar a casa de Tared antes de que Nashua me despedace.

Pero cuando mi espalda se topa contra un árbol en mi intento de escapar, es obvio que me alcanzarán antes de que pueda levantarme.

Ambas criaturas se acercan hacia mí. El devorapieles, feroz y terrible con aquella cosa agazapada en su espalda, los ojos turbios de Muata inyectados en sangre y colgando fuera de las cuencas.

—Salva a los que quedan, hijo —le susurra—. Acaba con él, tal cual debiste hacer desde el principio.

Nashua se abalanza hacia mí. Ruge y levanta su zarpa manchada de rojo.

Pero el golpe nunca llega.

En medio segundo, el errante oso da media vuelta y se arroja de cuerpo completo contra el anciano a sus espaldas. Atónito, veo que atenaza con sus mandíbulas el brazo que manipula la cabeza de Muata. Le clava las garras en los hombros, que parecen duros como piedras, y de una potente mordida arranca la muñeca entera y separa al anciano de la extremidad con un crujido muy similar al del cristal haciéndose pedazos.

El falso Muata cae con el peso de una rama sobre la nieve mientras la Marionetista se revuelve, sacudida por el dolor de su miembro cercenado, pero ni ella ni sus múltiples caras parecen ser capaces de gritar.

—¡Cuidado! —exclamo cuando los brazos se lanzan al errante oso. Elásticos como lianas, envuelven sus extremidades para inmovilizarlo.

Otro tráiler más pasa a toda velocidad por la carretera, opacando los rugidos del devorapieles cuando el monstruo empieza a elevarlo del suelo.

El rifle yace a diez metros de mí, libre ya de la protección de los brazos blancos, pero en vez de lanzarme a recuperar el arma, miro el cuerpo deforme del títere Muata, inerte ahora que el brazo que lo manipulaba se ha desgarrado.

Todos los dioses del mundo parecen escucharme cuando logro ver que Nashua ha dejado algo clavado en el durísimo hombro del muñeco: un gran trozo de su garra.

Me levanto a trompicones hacia el cuerpo del muñeco, y cuando la Marionetista descubre lo que estoy a punto de hacer, la boca de su máscara se abre como si el metal se convirtiese en carne.

Y de ella brota un grito que se asemeja mucho al ruido de una trompeta.

Los brazos de la criatura dejan caer al devorapieles al suelo y se lanzan al mismo tiempo hacia mí.

—¡No! —grita Nashua—. ¡Huye, Elisse!

En cambio, me quedo de rodillas en la nieve y empuño la garra del devorapieles como si fuese una daga.

La sangre de Nashua como vínculo y el cuerpo de Muata como una extensión de la Marionetista: el muñeco vudú perfecto.

No necesito nada más.

La espada filosofal intenta tragarme entero cuando clavo la garra en el corazón del cadáver. Y ante el golpe, los brazos del monstruo se paralizan en el aire como las patas de una araña.

La Marionetista grita de nuevo y su pecho se resquebraja, se le abre una grieta de clavícula a esternón.

—¡*Telocgraa, Telocgraa!*[7] —exclama aquella criatura. Su voz es igual de extraña que su cuerpo en más de una manera; no distingo si es aguda o grave, femenina o masculina, si es una o si son miles, pero lo más desconcertante es que, aunque la entienda, aunque sepa qué significan esas palabras, *no reconozco* el idioma en el que grita.

—¡¿Quién te ha enviado, desgraciada?! —rujo en su misma lengua.

—¡*Laiapon, amma Graa!*[8] —insiste con esa voz horripilante.

La piedra filosofal succiona la magia de mis venas; los brazos vuelven a cobrar vida en un intento de liberarse de la parálisis, y cuando siento que mi hechizo está a punto de ceder, vuelvo a clavar la garra en el cadáver, una y otra vez.

Partiéndose en cada punto, el pecho del monstruo revienta en miles de pedazos y proyecta una luz tan brillante que el devorapieles y yo nos cubrimos para no quedar ciegos. El resplandor desaparece en un segundo, y deja detrás de sí un agujero negro donde debería estar el corazón del monstruo blanco.

La criatura cae al suelo con una ligereza sobrenatural. Y con las pocas energías que me quedan, me lanzo para abrir su cuello de tajo con mi mano descarnada.

Y una vez que la Marionetista ha muerto, Nashua grita al ver que yo también me desplomo sobre la nieve.

---

[7] "Él, la Luna caída".

[8] "Vas a arder, Luna Maldita".

CAPÍTULO 42
LA LUNA FAMÉLICA

A Nashua le costó hacerme reaccionar. De hecho, necesitó golpearme un par de veces la mejilla con todo el cuidado que una zarpa como la suya podría tener para lograrlo. Y cuando pude enfocar un solo oso en vez de tres, lo primero que noté fue que la espada estaba mucho más pesada de lo normal, tanto que me tomó una eternidad levantarme.

Y más porque no permití que el devorapieles me ayudara.

Una vez que me puse en pie, arrastré yo mismo el cuerpo del títere Muata hasta aquí, al lindero del bosque donde empieza la propiedad de Tared. Descubrimos que la Marionetista es muy ligera, como si en vez de un monstruo que le saca un par de cabezas a Nashua hubiésemos cargado un par de sacos de plumas durante todo el camino.

Y aunque la criatura ya no podrá moverse, es obvio que mi pelea todavía no ha terminado.

Me detengo a unos pasos delante del devorapieles y dejo caer el cuerpo del falso contemplasombras. Éste se parte y se resquebraja, se marchita como una flor desprendida del tallo, a diferencia de la aún intacta Marionetista.

En vez de escuchar sus reclamos habituales, Nashua suelta también el otro cadáver cuando me giro para enfrentarlo.

Mueve un poco las orejas redondeadas, un gesto que me parecería adorable de no ser porque estoy a punto de estallar.

—Estás herido —murmura cuando se inclina para tomar algo de nieve y ponerla sobre su garra rota—. Y traes la ropa mojada otra vez...

—Deja de pretender que eso te importa.

Nashua arruga el hocico, pero en vez de reclamar por mi tono, baja un poco la cabeza.

—¿Quieres que me quite la piel para que hablemos? —pregunta, y es hasta gracioso cómo ahora su voz es la que suena como un susurro obligado, casi de la forma en que la mía se ha escuchado frente a él en todo el tiempo que llevamos de conocernos.

—No hace falta. Para mí eres exactamente la misma persona en esa forma o en la otra.

Él aprieta las zarpas, quizás en señal de que siempre ha tenido dudas de eso respecto a mí. Finalmente, se acerca hasta quedar a un par de palmos. Lo veo enorme y corpulento, inclusive más que Tared en su forma de hombre lobo, pero eso no es capaz de intimidarme. Ya no.

Después de un momento que se alarga demasiado para mi gusto, él suelta un suspiro.

—*Hash Chaf Chito* —dice—. Así te llamó el abuelo Muata una vez.

Miro hacia el cadáver del anciano títere, el cual ha comenzado a deshacerse en pequeños pedazos de algo que, efectivamente, parece ser vidrio.

—Luna de la Gran Hambruna —musito al reconocer el idioma choctaw, nativo de la familia de Nashua. El devorapieles asiente, quizá receloso ante mi talento para las lenguas ahora que sabe de dónde proviene.

—El día en el que atacaron la reserva por primera vez, mi abuelo tuvo una visión antes de quedar ciego —empieza—. Y en ese presagio había tres símbolos importantes que nunca pudo descifrar con claridad. Aunque no lo sabía, no me parece extraño. Mi presencia no fue precisamente un regalo de los cielos, así que era lógico que el contemplasombras de Comus Bayou tuviese una premonición turbia sobre mí.

Inicito al oso a continuar.

—El primer símbolo era la muerte de una sombra perteneciente a un árbol muy viejo —dice—. Al principio, mi abuelo no estaba seguro de qué podría ser, pero creo que ahora tú y yo ya podemos imaginarlo.

—Ciervo Piel de Sombras —murmuro al recordar aquellas astas recubiertas de puntas, tan similares a un árbol deshojado y gris como la ceniza.

Una nostalgia trágica me enfría el corazón, porque hacía mucho que no pensaba en quien alguna vez fue mi ancestro. El monstruo de hueso, en cambio, se relame el hocico al recordar su sabor.

—El segundo símbolo fue un ojo blanco mirando a través de un cristal —continúa Nashua, ajeno a mi batalla mental—. Pero no estoy seguro de lo que éste signifique.

Al pensar en la imagen, no necesito mucho para darme cuenta de la familiaridad de aquella descripción.

—Cuando Barón Samedi me destrozó los ojos en casa de Laurele, la habitación tenía un tragaluz en el techo. En ese momento, uno de mis pensamientos más claros fue que la luna parecía un ojo que lo observaba todo a través del cristal. Ese día me sucedió… esto —levanto mi mano de hueso.

Cuando Nashua me observa, estruja la zarpa con la que me atacó, aún teñida con mi sangre.

—Pero el que más le preocupaba a mi abuelo era el último de los símbolos —dice despacio, casi con reticencia—: una luna cayendo hacia una boca de oscuridad. Una luna con el *hedor* de las sombras.

—Era yo, ¿cierto? —no es una pregunta, en realidad—. Entrando a Guinée a través de la tumba de Marie Laveau.

Nashua asiente.

—La Luna Famélica, aquella que mi abuelo vio en su visión, aparece en nuestro calendario nativo durante el mes de febrero, cuando comúnmente se celebra *Mardi Gras*. Con el ataque que habíamos sufrido en la reserva, para él no cabía ninguna duda: la aparición de esa luna era una señal de *inanición*, un mal presagio, una señal inequívoca de que, en sus palabras, había un monstruo hambriento entre nosotros.

Siempre supo quiénes éramos, ¿verdad?, susurra la criatura dentro de mí, su voz tan detrás de mi nuca que comienza a asemejarse al umbral de una migraña. Lástima que nunca pudiste engañarlo...

A estas alturas, el cadáver del anciano títere ya no es más que fragmentos de cristal a los que poco les faltará para desaparecer. Pienso en todas las cosas que el falso Muata dijo a Nashua en la pelea con toda la intención de que yo las escuchara.

El Adam de la Marionetista tampoco era real, pero vaya que sabía *verdades* que me dolían hasta la médula. Y eso significa sólo una cosa:

—Muata te pidió que me asesinaras, ¿verdad?

Nashua abre y cierra el hocico un par de veces, quizás impresionado por la tranquilidad con la que he llegado a esa conclusión. Me observa tan quieto, tan paciente por su respuesta, y se lleva una mano a la cabeza como si algo dentro de ella le martillease.

—Él jamás te creyó —dice por fin—. Desde el primer momento en el que te vio estaba seguro de que era cuestión de tiempo para que la Luna Famélica devorara a Comus Bayou. Pero no tenía pruebas y sabía que Tared y mamá Tallulah te defenderían con dientes y garras, si llegaba a insinuarlo. Inclusive, una noche le contó a padre Trueno sobre esta visión, y aunque él tampoco confiaba en ti, se negó a creer que fueras tan terrible bestia. Mi abuelo sabía que no tenía a quién recurrir, excepto...

—Tú.

La palabra sale de mi boca con tanto peso que la espalda del oso se encorva. Se lleva una garra al pecho y gimotea, se estruja la piel como si quisiera arrancársela allí mismo.

—Él estuvo más seguro que nunca cuando te otorgó a Ciervo Piel de Sombras. Dijo que, aun cuando te había reclamado un ancestro tan antiguo y poderoso, *tú seguías oliendo a hueso* —Wéndigo me acaricia la espalda desde dentro, tocando cada una de mis vértebras—. Y ese día... fue cuando me dio la orden.

Bajo la mirada a la nieve, a los fragmentos ya casi inexistentes del anciano títere, y siento como si un peso que no sabía que llevaba encima de los hombros se hubiese evaporado.

Muy en el fondo, siempre quise ganarme el favor del abuelo Muata. Ser lo bastante bueno para él y que en algún momento de su vida no sólo me tolerase, sino que me considerara lo bastante digno para ser su sucesor. Y hiere más de lo que me gustaría saber que el anciano no sólo me detestaba, sino que me temía tanto que estuvo dispuesto a enviar a su propio nieto a matarme.

—Qué ironía —espeto con una sonrisa furiosa—. Y decías que el traidor era yo.

La lengua de Nashua se petrifica a la par que tiembla como un niño pequeño de nuevo.

Te ha dado gusto, ¿verdad? Ver la culpa por fin en esa maldita cara...

No le respondo a la bestia. Tan sólo siento con más insistencia aquel malestar tras la nuca, el hormigueo bajo la piel.

—¿Por qué no lo hiciste? —pregunto—, ¿por qué carajos esperaste a que mamá Tallulah y él estuviesen muertos para obedecerlo? Pudiste haber escogido cualquier momento, cualquier lugar. Tuviste miles de oportunidades para hacerlo y...

—¡PORQUE NUNCA LE CREÍ, ELISSE! —exclama—, ¡porque no te soportaba y me parecías un mocoso insolente y de lo peor, pero veía en ti tanto de mí mismo que me negaba a aceptar que fueses el monstruo que él pensaba que eras! Y luego... luego sucedió el ataque a la reserva —continúa en voz baja, como si se le hubiese acabado el aliento—. Mi decisión mató a los tres ancianos porque al escogerte *a ti* le di la espalda a mi tribu, a mi propio abuelo, ¡al hombre que silenció a mi madre para salvarme la vida!

La quietud que precede al grito del errante es opresiva, tan dura que cuesta quebrarla.

¿Silenciar a su madre?

Me muerdo los labios para no gemir, porque escuchar a Nashua es como mirarme a mí mismo, podrido de culpa en aquel desierto de Utah. Quiero entregarme al llanto pero, en cambio, me quedo quieto y lo observo abrirse con una verdad que debió ser nuestra hace mucho tiempo.

—Él confiaba en mí —continúa y se mira las almohadillas de las manos, los ojos como los de un osezno desbordado por el dolor—, me decía que debía ser valiente por todos, que no debía esperar a que sucediera lo peor, pero yo tenía tanto miedo que *no pude hacerlo*. Y cuando ellos murieron, me sentí... Dios mío...

Entierra la cara en las zarpas y su hocico sobresale entre esas garras oscuras, un gesto irreal, casi caricaturesco de no ser porque sus gimoteos me destrozan el alma.

—Y cuando descubrimos que el abuelo estaba equivocado, me sentí tan acorralado, ¡tan confundido! Si te hubiese asesinado, tal como me ordenó, tal vez nada de esto hubiese sucedido; pero *tú eras inocente*, ¿cómo habría podido volver a mirar a Tared a los ojos, sabiendo que le había arrebatado sin razón al chico del que se había enamorado? ¿Al hijo y al hermano que los demás vieron en ti? ¡Dios mío! ¡Yo fui quien debió haberse ido de la reserva, yo...!

—¡Basta ya, carajo!

Atrapo sus muñecas y lo empujo hasta echarlo varios pasos hacia atrás. Nashua está tan sorprendido que, aun con su tamaño, no alcanza a protegerse de mi rabia.

Pero no estoy furioso con él. Estoy furioso con Muata.

—Escúchame bien, Nashua, pero hazlo de verdad y sin largarte como siempre haces, porque créeme que no te va a gustar lo que te voy a decir: te habrá salvado la vida, te habrá criado y todo lo que tú quieras, pero es hora de que aceptes que, al final, Muata *se aprovechó* de la influencia que tenía sobre ti para obligarte a hacer algo que no querías. Te puso entre la espada y la pared, entre tu lealtad y tu corazón, porque no tuvo los malditos cojones para enfrentarme él mismo, porque *él* tuvo miedo de sentirse como un cobarde y un traidor, tal como tú te estás sintiendo ahora. Eso no es confianza, eso no es honor, Nashua, ¡eso se llama manipulación, carajo!

—¡No! —grita como si le hubiese clavado un puñal en el pecho. Forcejea, ruge y se revuelve, pero no lo suficiente para soltarse. Me podría apartar de un zarpazo si quisiera, pero no lo hace porque sabe que necesita escuchar la verdad.

De pronto, deja de luchar. Se encorva hasta ponerse de rodillas en la nieve, baja el hocico al pecho y muy bajito, en un susurro imperceptible, comienza a sollozar. Sus mejillas se mojan y se enfrían, la pena me recorre de arriba abajo.

No sabía que, envestidos en nuestra forma bestial, los errantes podíamos llorar.

—Aun sabiendo la verdad, no tuve el valor de decir nada de esto a los demás —confiesa entre gimoteos— y encima, tu huida de la reserva, de Utah, Wéndigo... Quise seguir encontrando razones para culparte y odiarte, para seguir creyendo que mi abuelo era bueno y que me había hecho esas cosas tan terribles por mi bien, pero era mentira, ¡todo era mentira y yo tenía tanto miedo y tanta vergüenza de aceptarlo, de que mis hermanos me odiaran a mí por ocultarlo todo! Dios mío, perdóname, Elisse, ¡perdóname, por favor!

Dejo de torturar su pecho con mis manos y las alzo hacia sus hombros para estrujarlos. Me inclino hacia él para que mi voz no se escuche desde arriba como un regaño.

—No, no necesitas que yo te perdone de nada de esto, porque yo también sé lo que es cargar con el miedo y la ver-güenza —susurro con la mayor gentileza que puedo—. Pero, ¿sabes? Por fin entendí que pensar que todo era mi culpa era mucho más fácil que dejar de idealizar a los demás y aceptar que la gente que amaba también me había hecho daño. Que yo también tenía razones para querer huir. Los dos estamos a tiempo de resolverlo todo. Y si te sirve de consuelo... *tú y yo estamos en paz*, Nashua.

El oso ruge de forma dolorosa cuando alzo mis brazos hacia él. Su tamaño me impide envolverlo del todo, pero hago lo posible para consolarlo contra mi pecho.

Cierro los ojos unos momentos, tan sólo para reunir fuerzas para mirar por encima de mi hombro. Mis hermanos, Hoffman, Tared; todos nos observan a unos metros del porche de la casa, y por sus semblantes, que pasan de la consternación al horror, quizás hasta la rabia, me queda claro que lo han escuchado *todo*.

No sé qué tanta verdad hay en las cosas que dijo la Marionetista respecto a cómo los demás comenzaron a tratar a Nashua después de los incidentes, pero de lo que sí estoy muy seguro es de que, en este momento, algo muy importante acaba de resquebrajarse en los cimientos de Comus Bayou.

CAPÍTULO 43
BRUJAS

—**B**ueno, ¿y qué se supone que hacemos con... esto? —pregunta Julien, quien apunta al cadáver de la Marionetista, puesto sobre una larga mesa en el garaje.

El foco sobre nuestras cabezas tirita mientras que la única ventana del lugar tampoco deja entrar demasiada luz, lo que le da un aire aún más tétrico a la criatura cuyos brazos se desparraman por los cuatro costados de la superficie.

—Está muerta, ¿verdad? —pregunta Johanna en un susurro, asqueada al mirar la piel humana amarrada en su cintura.

—Sí —respondo, para luego agacharme hacia el agujero en su pecho—. Pero, por si acaso, le pedí a Tared que me traiga algo de la cocina.

Remuevo un poco más de aquella extraña epidermis que se resquebraja como el vidrio, pero no logro ver nada en su interior; está hueco y oscuro dentro de la criatura, como si después de proyectar aquel resplandor no hubiese quedado más que una carcasa incomprensible.

¿Qué poder crees que nos daría comernos su carne?

Me cuesta ignorar la pregunta cuando la tentación de llevarme un trozo a la boca se vuelve demasiado grande. También me gustaría poder quitarle la máscara, pero he descubierto que la tiene unida a la cara.

La curiosidad de seguir escrutando el cuerpo del monstruo me carcome, pero sé que no sería algo bonito de ver para mis hermanos.

—¿Por qué diablos huele así? —señala Hoffman con la nariz arrugada, una reacción peculiar ya que, aunque el hedor comienza a diluirse, aún es dulce y penetrante, como si hubiésemos montado un altar de flores sobre la mesa.

—Es su magia —confirmo.

No estaba seguro al principio, pero ahora ya no me cabe ninguna duda. Y debe ser una magia muy poderosa si hasta Hoffman puede percibirla con tanta claridad.

—¿Y qué crees que es esta... cosa? —pregunta Julien.

—No tengo idea —respondo con franqueza—. Pero no es un cadáver como los errantes que enfrentamos en Nueva Orleans, ni tampoco un espíritu del plano medio. Ninguno de ellos podría tener este tipo de olor.

—¿Será algo así como el trotapieles que nos atacó en Utah? —tantea mi hermana.

—No. Ese monstruo fue traído de un recuerdo, así que nunca estuvo vivo en realidad, y es por eso que su magia apestaba a podrido.

—¿... entonces? —insiste el detective.

Me cruzo de brazos un momento y observo las costras de sangre seca en los labios metálicos de la Marionetista, algo muy interesante ya que la criatura no parece tener sangre en su propio cuerpo. Paseo la lengua de Samedi por mis dientes y Wéndigo se mueve de un lado a otro dentro de mí.

—Cuando un ente del plano medio posee a un ser vivo no puede deformarlo de una manera tan compleja como ésta

—explico mientras señalo los múltiples brazos de la bestia—, los espíritus "simples" no tienen tanto poder, pero lo que sí podrían hacer, si son ayudados por un espíritu regente y reúnen la suficiente fuerza, es algo parecido a lo que me sucede con Wéndigo: *alimentarse* para cambiar de forma.

Si la Marionetista se levantara ahora mismo de la mesa no causaría tanta conmoción como lo han hecho mis palabras.

—Es decir que esto... ¿esto está hecho de...?

—¿Seres humanos? Sí, seguramente —respondo con tranquilidad—. Eso explicaría por qué huele a algo "vivo".

Julien exhala en forma de silbido.

—Vaya. No sé qué me da más miedo, flaquito, lo horrible que ha sido enterarnos de esto o la seguridad con la que lo has dicho. El abuelo estaría...

El bisonte calla de pronto, consciente de su desliz. Johanna parece a punto de decir algo más, pero la puerta que da a la cocina rompe el trágico silencio al abrirse.

Al entrar Tared y Nashua siento la tensión apoderarse del garaje, puesto que Johanna y Julien apenas y respiran cuando el errante oso les pasa por un costado. Con una cuerda, él amarra el cuerpo de la criatura a la mesa, en tanto que mi lobo me extiende una bolsa de sal en grano.

Una vez que Nashua termina, los cinco me rodean como en un ritual de sepultura, mientras yo comienzo a crear un círculo de sal alrededor de la Marionetista, aliviado de sufrir mucho menos que la última vez que necesité hacer un perímetro de protección.

Después de dejar vacío el costal, me aseguro de que la circunferencia quede perfectamente cerrada. Por último, establezco el vínculo entre el círculo y yo: me pongo en cuclillas y me hago una pequeña incisión en el índice con mi garra de hueso, lo bastante profunda para dejar caer un par de gotas de sangre sobre la sal. Siento el hilo invisible de mi magia tirar de mí y alargarse como una serpiente desde mi dedo; ésta recorre el círculo de cristales hasta cerrarse, todo bajo un espectro sólo perceptible para mis sentidos.

Un hechizo tan sencillo no requiere mucha magia, pero una vez que termino comienzo a respirar con dificultad, con ese golpeteo incómodo en la nuca extendiéndose a mis sienes. Al ponerme de pie, todos me miran como si acabase de realizar un trasplante.

—Los círculos de sal son buenos para contener o bloquear energías —explico, besando mi herida para parar el sangrado—. Y aunque estoy seguro de que esta cosa está muerta, la sal unida a mí me avisará si se levanta de su sitio.

Me pongo el guante de invierno bajo la mirada impresionada de todos mis hermanos. El único que no parece haber sido tomado por sorpresa es Tared, ya bien consciente de mis capacidades.

Johanna gira la cabeza hacia el brazo cercenado de la Marionetista.

—¿Por qué tomó en específico la forma de Muata? —no me pasa desapercibida la forma en la que Nashua se contrae cuando ella omite la palabra "abuelo"—. Es decir, ¿por qué no la de mamá Tallulah o padre Trueno?

Observo el cadáver, preguntándome exactamente lo mismo, hasta que Hoffman chasquea la lengua.

—Fue porque Nashua soñó con él —el detective pone los ojos en blanco cuando los cinco giramos la cabeza para mirarlo—. Es lógico. Adam Blake se apareció en Montana justo después de que estuviera en los sueños de Elisse. Y por lo que escuchamos de su... plática de hace rato, a él le pasó exactamente lo mismo.

El oso asiente de inmediato.

—Es verdad —confirma—. Me quedé dormido mientras hacía guardia anoche. Sólo fueron unos minutos, pero supongo que fueron suficientes...

—Entonces sí es un poco como el trotapieles —concluye Johanna—. Aquél se movía por medio del agua. Y la Marionetista lo hace a través de los sueños.

Un escalofrío colectivo parece sacudirlos cuando confirmo la teoría con la cabeza.

—Menos mal que ahora está muerta —susurra Julien, y creo que todos estamos de acuerdo. No habría sido lindo dejar de dormir por miedo a cuidarnos de esta criatura.

—Elisse, ¿crees que las mujeres en tus visiones sean algo así como la Jocelyn y la Laurele en turno? Ya sabes, hechiceras manipuladas por tu Mara... —pregunta Johanna.

—*Puf*, pobre de ti —suspira Julien—. Ahora hasta *el diablo* anda detrás de ti.

—¿El diablo? —pregunto—. ¿Qué quieres decir?

—Pues, es que ese monstruo que viste en tu visión se parece mucho a eso —explica.

—Pero, ¿el diablo no era un hombre rojo con cuernos y cola? —pregunto confundido al recordarlo aparecer en una que otra caricatura cuando era niño.

—Sí, en ocasiones —dice Tared—, pero un ser de color negro con cabeza de cabra también es una representación muy conocida.

Ya. Supongo que no había caído en la cuenta debido a que crecí en la India y no estaba muy familiarizado con esa versión del diablo.

—Ahora que lo pienso, ¿esas mujeres no serán acaso *brujas*?

—... pensé que eso era obvio, Julien.

—No, no me entiendes. Me refiero específicamente a brujas *satánicas*, Elisse.

—Eso suena estupidísimo. Y me encanta porque tiene sentido —escupe Hoffman.

—¿Alguien puede ponerme en contexto, por favor? —suplico ya un poco exasperado. Johanna piensa unos momentos hasta acomodar las ideas en su cabeza.

—Elisse, ¿sabes lo que fue la cacería de brujas? —pregunta, a lo que niego con la cabeza—. Mira, no estoy tan enterada del tema más allá de lo que estudié en la escuela pero, por lo que recuerdo, hace como seis siglos comenzó una especie de histeria colectiva en el Norte de Europa. Las Iglesias cristianas más influyentes de aquel tiempo condenaron, torturaron y asesinaron a miles de personas, mujeres, en su mayoría, por el crimen de brujería. Ellos decían que estas "brujas" eran adoradoras de Satanás y sus demonios, y que hacían pactos con él para conseguir poderes malignos. Causaban desastres naturales, asesinaban a inocentes y se reunían alrededor de hogueras para hacer cosas exactamente iguales a las que viste en tus premoniciones.

—De hecho, esa "cacería" se extendió tanto que inclusive se celebraron juicios así de infames en este país, en un pueblo llamado Salem, cerca de Nueva York —añade Julien.

—Entonces, ¿están sugiriendo que mi Mara envió brujas satánicas para matarme esta vez?

—Es... es una opción.

Pactos. Una vez más, viene a mi memoria aquel libro negro que estuve a punto de firmar a cambio de revivir a Tared.

Por un segundo, pienso en preguntar si acaso alguna de las cosas que sucedieron en este pacto de brujas fue real, pero si los errantes lo somos, no tiene sentido pensar que no haya algo de verdad en todo eso. Lo interesante sería descubrir *qué*.

—Necesito más información —susurro—, tal vez un libro sobre su historia o... ¿alguien tiene internet?

—Sólo en el celular de Hoffman —dice mi hermana—. Tras el huracán, todos nos quedamos sin empleos y salía demasiado caro pagar más de una línea. Por eso Tared y tú nunca pudieron contactar a Nashua cuando salieron del plano medio.

—Pero igual no te será de mucha ayuda, este lugar está tan aislado que casi no llega señal —dice Julien—, no nos queda otra que bajar al pueblo, y de paso conseguimos algo de víveres.

—Estás loco si crees que voy a dejar la casa mientras esta cosa siga en el garaje —replico.

—Y sabes bien que yo no puedo salir a plena luz del día —enfatiza Tared—. No podemos arriesgarnos a que alguien me reconozca.

—Me queda claro, y por eso ustedes dos se van a quedarse aquí en tanto el resto salimos a encargarnos de todo esto —replica el errante para luego guiñarme un ojo.

—*Qué oportuno...*

Al escuchar al detective decir aquello en español, miro los labios cerrados de la Marionetista. Con un escalofrío, comienzo a pensar en ese lenguaje extraño en el que me habló, el cual, aunque pude entenderlo, no reconocí su origen.

Eso significa que no es una lengua humana, sino de los espíritus, tan rara que ni siquiera Barón Samedi la había escuchado antes.

La espada triplica su peso cuando comprendo que, si estas brujas son reales, puede que su magia sea tan extraña, tan monstruosa, que escape de la comprensión del mismísimo Señor del Sabbath.

CAPÍTULO 44
RESPONSABILIDAD

—¿Te duele? —pregunta el lobo.

—Ya no.

—Agradece que no necesitaste una sutura —dice.

—Agradece que no estoy muerto.

—Te encantan los problemas, ¿verdad? —replica.

—Oye, esta vez no fue sólo mi culpa —me defiendo—. Aunque debo admitir que eso de fingir que me atacaba fue muy buena idea de parte de Nashua. Hicimos un gran equipo allá afuera.

—¿Ah, sí? Pues a la siguiente buena idea que se le ocurra al gran equipo los mando a dormir al pozo.

Me río un poco porque sé que Tared no lo dice en serio. Después de todo, aún se siente culpable de no haber bajado cuando escuchó que discutíamos acaloradamente en el porche, pues creyó en que lo mejor sería darnos espacio para resolver nuestros problemas, sin mencionar que estaba tan cansado que le costó mucho levantarse. Le he insistido en que no se torture con eso, pero no creo que el pobre deje de darle vueltas al asunto en un buen rato.

De pronto, la potente voz de Julien sacude la casa: canta a todo pulmón en la ducha de la habitación principal, de seguro sacándole canas verdes a Johanna por lo mucho que se está tardando.

En cuanto terminamos nuestros asuntos en el garaje, los dos se lanzaron a toda velocidad para ganar la regadera y por fin acicalarse a detalle para bajar al pueblo, lo que demuestra que el encierro puede volver loca a la gente con mucha facilidad.

El lobo y yo, en cambio, no teníamos ninguna prisa, así que nos quedamos frente a la chimenea de la sala para revisar la herida de zarpa que me quedó en el brazo. Y una vez que termina de vendarme, Tared acomoda la manga de mi cárdigan y me alarga una taza de café de la mesita de centro.

Observo el fuego crepitar mientras la nieve baja despacio por la ventana. Estoy tan agotado por el uso de mi magia y la pelea con la Marionetista que me bastaría con cerrar los ojos para quedarme dormido... Pero hay algo que no me deja en paz.

—Nashua me dijo que Muata silenció a su madre —digo en voz baja a la par que pienso en el errante oso, quien se ha aislado en una de las habitaciones de arriba.

Al escuchar aquello, Tared detiene su propia taza frente a los labios.

—Es verdad —dice para luego dar un trago a su café.

Suspiro con pesar. No puedo ni imaginar las circunstancias que debieron ocurrir para que Muata tuviese que hacer algo tan terrible. Y encima, a su propia nieta.

—... no tenía idea —musito, acongojado.

—No te lo tomes como algo personal, Elisse. Johanna y Julien tampoco lo saben porque Nashua siempre fue tan hermético como yo sobre su pasado, y quizá no estarían tomándose las cosas tan mal como ahora si supiesen por qué le fue tan difícil hacerle frente a su bisabuelo.

Pensar en aquello me ocasiona un dolor tan severo que se siente como si tirasen de mis brazos en sentidos opuestos, porque tampoco es que pueda culparlos a ellos por sentirse así.

—Pero de alguna manera, tú supiste ganarte su confianza para que te hablara de esto, ¿verdad? Por eso eres el único que no está enojado con él.

El devorapieles se recarga de nuevo contra el respaldo.

—Ese idiota no sólo es mi hermano, también es mi mejor amigo —dice con una sonrisa somera, algo curioso, puesto que Sammuel me dijo lo mismo sobre Calen—, y aunque nunca le conté lo que pasó con Grace, sí que sabía lo que yo sentía por ti, cosa que para mí era igual de importante. Además, yo ya me sentía en conflicto con Muata. Nunca estuve de acuerdo con la forma en la que te trató, y aunque también llegué a tener la impresión de que presionaba demasiado a Nashua, jamás creí que hubiese llevado las cosas tan lejos. Fue decepcionante, pero tampoco me sorprendió tanto enterarme de la verdad.

Asiento, un poco más tranquilo al saber que al menos el oso tiene a Tared de su lado, porque no creo que las cosas vuelvan a ser las mismas con mis otros dos hermanos después de lo que pasó hoy.

Con tanto revuelo, no me extraña que Tared no considere conveniente hablarles todavía sobre Grace. No creo que le venga muy bien a Johanna saber algo así en este momento...

¿No te parece obsceno? ¿El cómo ella mira con tanto deseo lo que se supone que te pertenece?

Tantas mentiras, tantos secretos. Pareciera ser que, sin importar qué tanto nos esforcemos, en Comus Bayou nunca terminamos de sacar los trapos sucios.

—Supongo que Nashua no dirá nada respecto a su madre y Muata hasta que se sienta listo. Y tú tampoco vas a contarme nada más, ¿verdad?

—Tan perspicaz como siempre, mi amor.

Suelto un suspiro de resignación.

—Odio que seas tan leal.

—No me estimes tanto. Te recuerdo que ahora también me debes una chamarra —dice al apuntar hacia la parka en el respaldo del sillón, con la manga arruinada por las garras de Nashua.

—Apuesto a que también tiene seguro —respondo con los ojos en blanco, cosa que lo hace sonreír.

—Oye, hablando de lealtad —pone su taza en la mesa y rodea mis hombros con el brazo—, déjame decirte que no fue lindo despertar y no encontrarte en la cama. Me sentí tan usado.

Suelto una carcajada y dejo mi propio café a un lado para disimular mi tenue rubor.

—Perdona, intentaba salvarle el trasero a tu mejor amigo.

Él se inclina y me borra la sonrisa con un beso.

—Hablo en serio cuanto digo que te fuiste demasiado pronto —insiste, aún sobre mis labios—. ¿Estás bien? Y sabes que no me refiero sólo a la pelea...

Trago saliva e intento recordar cómo respirar otra vez.

—S-sí, tranquilo —respondo, más rojo que un carbón encendido—. No me duele absolutamente nada. Lo hiciste *muy bien* anoche, Tared.

El lobo sonríe con una ligera veta de orgullo.

—Lamento ser tan pesado, pero temí haber hecho algo que no te gustara. Es decir, hubo momentos en los que me costó mucho... contenerme, ¿sabes?

Una serpiente de placer me sube por la cadera cuando él acaricia mi muslo sobre los pantalones; se me hace agua la boca de sólo recordar esas manos grandes ejerciendo su tremenda fuerza sobre mi piel desnuda, tan firmes y a la vez tan cuidadosas explorando en los lugares correctos. Semejante imagen me hace preguntarme lo que pasaría si le pido que no se contenga tanto la siguiente vez.

Las pupilas de Tared se dilatan, y estamos tan cerca que sólo tiene que inclinar un poco la cabeza para rozarme la piel con esos labios y esos colmillos que tantas veces me mordieron anoche.

De pronto, mi magia vibra igual de ansiosa que yo, como si anhelara revivir ella misma la sensación de este hombre sacudiéndome entero.

—Dios, hueles tan bien… —susurra, y su aliento acaricia mi cuello.

—¿En serio? —pregunto, mareado—. No creí que el aroma de los huesos fuese agradable.

Por la forma en la que se aleja para mirarme, el comentario parece haberlo desconcertado.

—Eh, Muata decía que ése era mi olor —carraspeo—. ¿No te habías dado cuenta?

—Ah, eso. Sí, lo había notado. De hecho, se hizo un poco más evidente después de tu batalla con Barón Samedi.

—¿Y no te parece desagradable?

Él se encoge de hombros.

—No particularmente. Además, no es el único olor que percibo en ti, y tampoco es, de cerca, el más dominante —él se ríe por lo bajo cuando ahora soy yo el sorprendido—. Soy un lobo, así que mi nariz es más sensible que la de otros errantes —explica—. Inclusive, a veces puedo percibir de forma sutil el olor de las hormonas que sueltan las personas cuando tienen miedo, están felices o angustiadas.

—Ah, qué decepción —bromeo—, y yo que pensé que siempre me leías la mente.

—En realidad, no estás tan equivocado —dice—. Digamos que cuando alguien me interesa, mi percepción se vuelve mucho más aguda. Me pasa un poco con Comus Bayou porque es mi familia, pero mis sentidos se disparan como locos cada vez que *tú* estás cerca. Tanto que, de haber estado en algún momento en mi forma de lobo, de seguro me habrías visto mover la cola.

Me echo a reír al pensar en semejante imagen.

—Así que, sí. Puedo oler en ti la tenue esencia del monstruo de hueso, pero también puedo percibir otras cosas más importantes. Tu esencia humana, por ejemplo. Está allí y es tan natural, tan tuya, que podría encontrarte en un segundo en medio de una multitud —con cuidado, levanta la mano, acaricia el largo de mi trenza y juega con la liga como si quisiera soltarla, tal cual hizo anoche—. Y luego está el olor de *tu magia*.

Esta vez, sus dedos se deslizan hacia mi muñeca. Le da la vuelta y besa donde pulsa mi vena, lo que me provoca un espasmo que corre desde sus labios hasta mi columna.

—Tu magia tiene un aroma único y poderoso, tan intoxicante que la primera vez que la percibí pensé en ti toda la noche... y de *muchas maneras*. Y, Dios, el día que te vi en esa maldita hoguera en Red Buffalo, con todos esos espíritus a tu alrededor, yo...

Alzo una ceja.

—¿Tú?

Él sonríe de una manera que prende fuego a todo mi cuerpo.

—Te juro que, si bien siempre me habías gustado mucho, nunca había querido llevarte a la cama *tanto* como en ese momento.

No me detengo a preguntar más. Tomo a Tared de la nuca y lo atraigo hacia mí para besarlo. Y como si hubiese esperado todo este tiempo a que yo diese el primer paso, él se hunde en mis labios con una sonrisa. Lo beso con más hambre que experiencia, pero el gruñido que suelta dentro de mi boca me hace saber que aprendí bastante anoche.

—¿Sabes? Eso que hiciste en el garaje fue jodidamente excitante —susurra—, verte usar tu magia y tus conocimientos de esa manera. Dios, casi te salto encima frente a todos...

Dioses, ¿estaría muy mal si le salto yo encima ahora mismo?

Nos besamos tan largamente que por unos momentos olvido que allá afuera el mundo se está yendo a la mierda. Sus labios son tan suaves, su lengua es tan deliciosa...

—Elisse acaba de tener una jodida pelea, ¿y *esto* es lo mejor que se te ocurre hacer, desgraciado?

El calor se evapora de mi cara en cuanto veo a Hoffman parado al pie de la escalera. Tiene una mano bien apretada sobre el pasamanos, y aunque su voz ha sonado iracunda, ni siquiera mira hacia acá.

—Hoffman, por favor, él no estaba...

—No me interesa —dice con los dientes apretados—. Dile a tu perro en celo que nos dé un minuto a solas. *Necesito* hablar contigo.

Al darse cuenta de mi incomodidad por haber sido encontrados en un momento tan personal, el hombre lobo cierra los ojos un segundo para no perder los estribos, tal como me prometió. Después, se levanta del sillón.

No entiendo de dónde saca fuerza de voluntad para no arrancarle la cabeza al detective cuando pasa a su lado, porque se limita a salir al porche lateral de la casa, quizá para enfriarse algo más que la cabeza.

Al cerrar la puerta, Hoffman deja en paz el pobre pasamanos y se acerca. Suspiro y busco un poco de esa paciencia que Tared tanto se esfuerza por tenerle.

—No estábamos haciendo nada malo —insisto—, él y yo...

—Dije que me importa una mierda —interrumpe, para luego detenerse a unos pasos de mí—, aunque a ti tampoco te vendría mal considerar un poco a los demás, ¿acaso no piensas en lo que habría sentido Johanna si los hubiese visto revolcándose en ese sillón?

—¿Es eso? —espeto, furioso ante la simple mención de mi hermana—. ¿Johanna es la razón por la que te has portado como un jodido animal desde que recuperé la consciencia? Vaya. Y yo que pensé que venías a disculparte.

Hoffman aprieta los labios. Pero en vez de gritar como siempre, se queda callado unos momentos, sin insultar, sin montar una rabieta, tan sólo observándome de una manera indescifrable.

—No vine a disculparme —musita, tan calmo que me desconcierta—. Vine a darte esto.

Y entonces, saca algo de su bolsillo que me hace abrir los ojos de par en par: el libro rojo de Laurele.

—¡Por los dioses! —me acerco de una zancada para tomarlo. Lo hojeo, y me lleno de alivio al encontrar dentro el sobre con la valiosa fotografía de mi papá.

—Lo dejaste en mi coche aquella vez en Stonefall—dice—. Quería dártelo desde ayer, pero ni siquiera he podido hablar contigo porque el cabrón de Miller está pegado a ti como una maldita sanguijuela. Y tú estás tan idiotizado que ni siquiera lo notas...

Acaricio la preciada imagen sintiendo que otra parte de mí regresa por fin a su sitio.

—Hoffman, yo...

—Todavía no termino.

Alarga el brazo y toma la fotografía. Le da la vuelta y veo que hay algo anotado en el reverso, en español.

Tiraje no. 269-6

—¿Qué es esto?

—En los meses que estuviste perdido, y aprovechando que tenía esto conmigo, me tomé la libertad de investigar un par de cosas. Aunque no lleva dirección, el sobre donde guardas esta fotografía sí que tiene un timbre postal.

Su dedo apunta hacia dicho sobre, guardado en otra de las páginas del libro. Miro la estampilla en una esquina, donde muy apenas se puede distinguir la figura diluida de un faro.

—Subí la foto del timbre a un foro de internet con gente obsesionada con estas cosas —continúa—. Costó un poco identificarlo porque es un diseño muy viejo, pero después de unas semanas, un sabelotodo dio con la información.

El corazón me empieza a latir como el de un caballo de carreras.

—¿*Y*? —casi grito ante la tensa pausa.

—Ese faro que ves ahí es parte de una colección especial de sellos que fueron emitidos hace casi veinte años para celebrar los faros más icónicos del país. Y lo que los hace especiales es que dichos timbres fueron repartidos únicamente en las oficinas postales correspondientes a la ciudad en la que se encuentra cada uno.

—Eso... ¿eso significa que...? —Hoffman asiente.

—Si logramos identificar qué faro es éste, podremos saber desde qué ciudad envió tu padre la postal. Y posiblemente podremos empezar allí a busc...

Hoffman cierra la boca de golpe cuando, sin aviso, lo estrecho con fuerza entre mis brazos, apretándome contra su pecho. El hombre se queda rígido, con las manos a los costados, mientras a mí casi se me salen las lágrimas de la emoción.

Había decidido abandonar la búsqueda de mi padre desde hacía tanto tiempo, pero saber esta información cambia totalmente las cosas porque significa que, si logro salir vivo de esto, ahora tengo un sitio dónde empezar.

Una razón más para seguir luchando.

Al darme cuenta de que el detective no reacciona, lo suelto de inmediato.

—Perdóname —le digo avergonzado, para luego devolver la mirada a la foto—. No tenías por qué hacer esto, pero... dioses, ¡no sabes lo *feliz* que me has hecho!

El detective no dice una palabra. Tan sólo gira la cabeza hacia la puerta de la cocina, de seguro muy incómodo al haber recibido un abrazo sin pedirlo; el contacto humano no es precisamente una de las cosas favoritas de Hoffman, después de todo.

Bajo la barbilla y sonrío.

—Aunque no lo creas, yo también he querido acercarme a ti —digo con una sonrisa honesta—. No se me olvida que, de toda esta familia, tú eres el único que *siempre* ha estado ahí para mí.

Y es verdad.

No habremos tenido el comienzo más normal del mundo ni la relación más pacífica de todas, pero si algo es seguro es que él se las ha arreglado para ser mi pilar en los momentos en los que me quedaba poco para derrumbarme.

Y ahora, ha hecho esto *por mí*.

El hombre deja salir un suspiro de hastío.

—Ojalá eso deje de atormentarme algún día.

El detective me da la espalda con la firmeza suficiente como para hacerme saber que nuestra conversación ha terminado. Luego, se marcha por las escaleras a la planta de arriba, dejándome con la sensación de que algo muy importante se me escapa.

Algo que, a diferencia de mí, Hoffman parece entender bien.

CAPÍTULO 45
SANGRE INESPERADA

En cuestión de horas, la Marionetista ha empezado a pudrirse, puesto que su piel se ha puesto algo púrpura y su olor se asemeja cada vez más al de la carroña que al de algún perfume.

Saco unas tijeras del recipiente de plástico que he traído conmigo y abro el círculo de sal al trazar una línea recta sobre él con la punta. Una vez que cruzo el campo de contención, vuelvo a cerrarlo para aproximarme a la mesa. Abro los párpados de una de las caras de la criatura con una pinza y meto una cuchara en la cuenca para sacar el ojo con cuidado.

Cuando el tendón es ya lo único que lo une a la cavidad, paso a cortarlo con las tijeras. Lo deposito en el recipiente y, después de un rato, cuando ya he logrado sacar alrededor de cinco pares, tomo un puño de la sal del círculo y repito el ritual para salir de él.

En cuanto pongo un pie fuera me inclino un poco hacia mis rodillas, jadeando con dificultad.

—Deja de hacer eso, carajo —exijo a la espada en un gesto inútil, porque otra vez me siento como si hubiese revivido a un ejército de homúnculos entero.

Yo ya era consciente de que la espada me jodía mucho cada vez que utilizaba mi magia, pero creo que nunca me había dado cuenta de lo progresivo que podía ser el daño si la usaba tantas veces en un solo día.

—*Mierda* —musito al pensar en el trato que he hecho con Tared, y barajo la posibilidad de romper nuestro acuerdo de alguna manera para no tener que entregársela. No me importaría asumir las consecuencias y...

laipoh Darr.[9]

Wéndigo susurra aquello en un tono tan débil que ni siquiera logro comprender lo que dice, cosa que me alivia sobremanera; la piedra me estará haciendo la vida difícil, pero al menos tengo la tranquilidad de que el monstruo de hueso está bajo control por ahora.

Tomo aire unos minutos más para después erguirme y salir del garaje. Cierro la puerta detrás de mí y la atranco con una silla, un gesto inútil que sólo sirve para mantener la cabeza de los demás un poco más tranquila.

En la cocina me encuentro con Julien, quien lucha por sacarle chispa a la estufa portátil. Dejo el recipiente de ojos en la mesa junto con lo demás y me acerco a mi hermano. Alargo los dedos huesudos hacia la parrilla y ésta se enciende de inmediato.

El devorapieles suelta un silbido de admiración.

—Vaya. Lo que nos vamos a ahorrar en cerillos, ¿eh? —dice con una sonrisa para luego poner encima una olla con trozos de nieve.

Al imaginar el estofado de ciervo que preparará una vez que los demás lleguen con la despensa, mi estómago ruge con fiereza.

---

[9] "Quémalos con ella".

—Te haría algún comentario estúpido como que con esa hambre podrías cometerte una vaca, pero creo que en tu caso sería demasiado realista para ser gracioso, ¿eh? —comenta él sin maldad.

—La verdad es que sí que extrañaba mucho tus comentarios estúpidos —confieso con una tímida sonrisa.

—Y vaya que yo te eché de menos a ti, flaquito. Aunque no lo creas, Johanna y Nashua no son el combo explosivo de diversión que aparentan.

Río por lo bajo mientras lavo las tijeras y la cuchara. Vuelvo a la mesa y reviso con cuidado todos los materiales que he reunido.

Además de la *materia prima* —los ojos y la sal—, también hay una camiseta vieja cortada en cuadros, un estuche de costura, una navaja muy afilada y un cuenco de porcelana.

Tomo asiento y empiezo a coser uno de los trozos de tela para darle la forma de una pequeña bolsa, algo que me resulta fácil gracias a mi experiencia remendando ropa en el campo de refugiados. Después de un rato en el que sólo se escucha el ruido de la nieve al derretirse, mi hermano carraspea.

—Oye... lamento haberme quedado con ustedes. Imagino que querías estar a solas con Tared.

Detengo la aguja entre mis dedos.

Después de mi discusión con Hoffman, me sentí tan mal, tan avergonzado, que tuve que pedirle al bisonte que se quedara en casa mientras los demás bajaban al pueblo. Tared ni siquiera se sorprendió por mi petición y, de hecho, respetó tanto mi necesidad de espacio que no me ha preguntado absolutamente nada sobre lo que hablé con el detective.

—Yo te dije que lo hicieras, ¿recuerdas? Y, de todos modos, es mejor así —respondo al encogerme de hombros.

Julien levanta una ceja.

—¿Mejor para ti o para Johanna?

Frunzo el ceño ante su pregunta.

—¿Escuchaste lo que Hoffman dijo?

—Ay, ¡obviamente! En cuanto se pusieron a gritar me pegué al barandal. Agradece que ella se estaba bañando en ese momento, ¡imagínate si los hubiese oído también!

Controlo mis ganas de enterrarle la aguja en la frente, porque como bien dijo Tared, no hay gente más metiche que mis hermanos. Meneo la cabeza y tomo uno de los ojos del cuenco para meterlo en la bolsita.

—Dioses, debería hablar con ella —musito.

—Ah, no, ¡eso sí que no! —dice Julien, amenazándome con la pala de plástico que ha estado usando para remover la nieve—. Johanna ya está grandecita y te aseguro que puede resolver sus problemas sola. Además, no es tu responsabilidad, ni la de Tared, lo que ella pudiera pensar de todo esto. No cuando él le dejó muy en claro los límites mucho antes de que tú llegaras.

—Sí. Estoy consciente de eso, pero...

Me quedo en silencio unos momentos, preguntándome si acaso Johanna y Julien ya habrían hablado antes de eso. Y también, si llegará el día en el que por fin el bisonte se canse de ser el soporte emocional de todos nosotros.

Nunca consideré que los vínculos de Comus Bayou podrían estar igual de fragmentados que el mío.

—Eso no evita que me preocupe por ella, ¿sabes? —digo en voz baja, puesto que todavía recuerdo muy bien lo terrible que es tener el corazón roto.

En realidad, quieres asegurarte de que no se le ocurra tocar lo que te pertenece...

Con la navaja, me abro una herida en el brazo para callar a Wéndigo del todo; inofensiva, pero lo bastante profunda para que empiece a sangrar.

—¿De verdad tienes que hacer *eso*? —pregunta Julien cuando comienzo a empapar el artilugio.

Mi idea es crear unos detectores parecidos a los que hice en la cabaña que, si bien no serán tan complejos como los homúnculos, me avisarán de inmediato si ven que alguna criatura de la misma naturaleza que la Marionetista se acerca a la casa. La ventaja es que sólo hay que mantener intacto el círculo de sal para que funcione, cosa que mi cuerpo agradecerá muchísimo una vez que termine.

—Tranquilo. Ya estoy acostumbrado —aseguro.

De pronto, escuchamos el ruido de la caldera vibrar por las paredes, en señal de que ahora es el lobo quien está en la ducha. Sin decir más, Julien regresa a lo suyo.

Cuando termino de cubrir la bolsa con sangre y magia, me levanto de la silla para ir a lavarme.

Súbitamente, me encuentro con el pelirrojo atrapándome antes de que caiga al suelo de golpe, invadido por un potente mareo.

—¡Elisse! ¿Estás bien? —pregunta, pero no respondo hasta que mi cabeza deja de dar volteretas, de seguro provocadas por la magia que tuve que transferirle al artilugio. Preocupado, mi hermano me ayuda a ponerme de pie.

—Sí, es la espada —respondo mientras recupero el equilibrio, manchando el suelo y la mesa con mi sangre al tratar de levantarme—, sólo necesito descansar un poco antes de seguir y...

Soy interrumpido por el ruido de un motor. Miro hacia el ventanal del frente de la casa y veo unos faros acercarse por el camino de grava.

—Vaya, ya se habían tardado —digo por lo bajo, pero mi hermano frunce el entrecejo.

—Ésa no es nuestra camioneta.

Entorno la mirada y descubro que, efectivamente, se trata de un automóvil de color azul. Julien y yo nos acuclillamos detrás del medio muro horizontal que divide la cocina de la sala. Saco los guantes de mi bolsillo y me los pongo con prisa mientras escuchamos el vehículo estacionarse frente al porche.

Quien lo conduce se baja dando un portazo, y al acercarse a la casa, agudizo mis sentidos.

—No huelo óxido —susurro confundido.

—Ni sangre —concuerda el pelirrojo en voz baja—. No parece que sean los tramperos, ni tampoco luce como un coche de la policía.

—Entonces, ¿quién...? —me toma sólo unos segundos llegar a una conclusión—. Julien, ¡es el contacto de Debbie!

Como si no hubiese estado a punto de desmayarme hace sólo un segundo, me levanto como un resorte y echo a correr hacia la puerta, justo cuando ésta resuena bajo los puños de alguien que llama con fuerza. Mi hermano me grita algo, pero estoy tan eufórico que ni siquiera reparo en el hecho de que la madera se sacude entera. Que quien está del otro lado la golpea casi con furia.

Y al abrirla, no me cabe ninguna duda de que el hombre que está parado al otro lado no es el contacto de Debbie. De hecho, es un joven blanco, quien desprende un simple olor a humano.

Primero me mira de arriba abajo, sorprendido, y luego su cara se quiebra en una sonrisa.

—Ah, con que eres *tú*.

Una sensación desconocida se alarga por mi espalda al escuchar la *manera* en la que pronuncia aquella palabra. Él da un paso hacia mí con tanta seguridad que reacciono retrocediendo.

—Pero, ¿quién...?

—Soy Allen Miller —dice—. Y vine aquí a buscar a mi hermano.

CAPÍTULO 46
UN MONSTRUO QUE NO ES DE HUESO

En un segundo, pierdo la capacidad de hablar todas y cada una de las lenguas del mundo.

La mandíbula cuadrada, las cejas espesas y el cabello rubio que se asoma bajo el gorro; no es ni por asomo tan alto ni fornido como lo imaginé, pero el parecido es tan evidente que no puedo creer que no me haya dado cuenta de inmediato.

Por todos los dioses habidos y por haber. *Es el hermano de Tared.*

—¡Ah! —balbuceo—. ¡P-perdona, pasa, pasa, por favor!

Abro la puerta y el joven entra a la casa con las manos en los bolsillos.

Lo sigo casi de puntillas, con el corazón en la boca de mi estómago al ver la manera en la que repara en las pocas cosas desperdigadas por la sala.

Dioses, dioses, *¿cómo se enteró de que estábamos aquí?*

El chico se detiene y me mira sobre su hombro. Y como si hubiese cambiado de cara, su sonrisa es reemplazada por un gesto ceñudo.

—Y bien, ¿dónde…?

—Tared no está, Allen —dice Julien de pronto, quien ahora está parado a un lado del fregadero de la cocina. Ha actuado tan rápido que ya no hay rastros del recipiente de ojos sobre la mesa ni el artilugio.

—¿De verdad? Porque juraría haber visto su camioneta allá afuera —dice al apuntar hacia el ventanal del frente con su barbilla, donde se puede ver un trozo del cofre rojo—. ¿Estaré alucinando? ¿O sólo soy estúpido?

Aquella desagradable sensación se acentúa cuando una mueca alegre brota de su cara al decir aquello.

—Se ha ido al pueblo con otras personas. Como te dije, *no está en casa* —insiste mi hermano, tan secamente que me quedo desconcertado. ¿Por qué le está hablando de esa manera al mismísimo hermano de Tared?

Repaso una y otra vez las cosas que el lobo me ha contado hasta ahora sobre él y me sorprendo de que no han sido demasiadas. Es más, creo que nunca había mencionado siquiera su nombre. ¿Acaso cometí un error al haberlo dejado pasar?

—Pero, si gustas, Allen —añado—, puedes volver en un rato y...

—¿Me estás echando de la casa de mi propio hermano?

Abro los ojos de par en par, tan nervioso que me debato entre seguirle la corriente a Julien o echarme a correr a las escaleras para buscar a Tared.

—Tranquilo, muchacho —pide el pelirrojo, levantando un poco las manos para calmar las aguas—. Mi nombre es Julien y este chico es Elisse. Somos amigos de Tared.

Allen me observa de nuevo con ojos de un azul oscuro, un océano tan profundo que siento que me ahogaré en medio de él.

—¿Amigos, dices? Porque, en mi opinión, con quien anoche vieron a mi hermano en una gasolinera, *exhibiéndose*, fue con una cualquiera.

Esta vez, no necesito a las voces de Wéndigo para convertirme en un remolino de náuseas y palidez, puesto que he recibido suficientes miradas de asco por parte de la gente como para no entender la forma en la que Allen ahora observa mi cuerpo de arriba abajo.

—Pero eso no es todo —añade—. Uno de los vecinos de por aquí dijo haber visto algo extraño ayer, mientras conducía por la carretera: siluetas en los árboles y *gritos*.

Él me quita los ojos de encima y los lleva hacia la mesa. Su sonrisa se tuerce hacia abajo cuando encuentra el rastro rojo y oscuro de mi sangre por la madera y el suelo. Y luego, las venas se me vuelven escarcha cuando repara en la silla puesta contra la puerta del garaje.

—¿Qué estás haciendo aquí, Allen?

El alma me regresa al cuerpo al escuchar la gruesa voz de Tared.

El hombre lobo nos mira desde el balcón aún empapado de la regadera, vestido con apenas un pantalón deportivo y la parka encima de su torso desnudo.

Con la mirada clavada en el chico, empieza a bajar con calma. Y cuando pone un pie en el suelo de la cocina, no hay ni un solo gramo de entusiasmo. Ningún reencuentro emocional entre los hermanos Miller.

De hecho, la primera reacción de Tared es colocarse delante de mí como un muro.

Allen se tensa y levanta sólo la mirada, como si se negase a erguir el cuello y reconocer los quince centímetros de estatura que lo distancian de su hermano.

—Después de tantos años, ¿eso es lo primero que se te ocurre decir? —pregunta él con sorna.

—¿Acaso no eso es lo que querías? ¿No volver a saber de mí *nunca más*?

Me percato de la forma en la que el cuerpo de Allen se echa ligeramente hacia atrás, como si temiera que su enorme hermano fuese a desplomarse encima de él.

—Un amigo mío te vio ayer en la gasolinera —insiste—, él...

—Escuché muy bien lo que dijiste, Allen. *Cada palabra* —corta Tared con un semblante que me recuerda mucho a su aspecto de hombre lobo—. Así que te lo voy a decir una sola vez: vuelve a faltarle el respeto a Elisse y ni mi madre te va a salvar de que yo te ponga en tu lugar. ¿Me oíste?

Si las miradas fuesen puñales, Allen habría descuartizado a su hermano en un segundo. Desvía los ojos hacia mí, hacia Julien, y podría jurar que las venas de sus ojos se engrosan.

—¿Ah, sí? Pues entonces dame una sola razón para que no vaya a decirle que ya encontraste *algo* con que reemplazar a tu esposa.

—¿Es-posa?

Un gemido se atora en mi garganta cuando aquella voz irrumpe en la casa. Miro hacia la entrada y encuentro a Johanna parada en la puerta, con los ojos grises abiertos como platos y una bolsa de víveres bien aplastada contra su pecho.

El hombre lobo chasquea la lengua mientras una sonrisa dura se abre paso en la boca de Allen.

—Diría que has crecido mucho desde el día en el que nos conocimos en Nueva Orleans, Allen Miller, pero la verdad es que me sigues pareciendo el mismo mocoso *pendejo* de aquel entonces —la satisfacción del chico se borra en un instante cuando Hoffman se acerca por detrás de la errante coyote, aún inmóvil bajo el dintel. El detective empuja con suavidad a mi hermana y cruza la sala con un puñado de papeles en la mano, seguido por Nashua.

—Usted...

—¿Se conocen? —pregunto con absoluta sorpresa. Y por la cara que pone Tared, parece ser que él tampoco lo sabía.

—¿Qué diablos está haciendo aquí? —masculla Allen con los dientes apretados.

—Vine a esquiar, imbécil, ¿qué te parece? —responde el latino estampando las hojas en mi pecho, mientras que el otro le lanza una mirada tan amable como la que le dio al hombre lobo.

Cuando Nashua se aproxima también a la cocina y el chico se ve rodeado por otros tres hombres tan intimidatorios como su hermano, cuadra los hombros y arruga la nariz.

—Ja, ¿ahora eres amigo de este desgraciado, Tared? —espeta con las cejas alzadas—. ¿Es que Nueva Orleans te volvió demente?

El lobo sostiene el aliento, quizá para contener su propio enojo, y luego apunta con la cabeza hacia la puerta de la cocina. Allen nos mira a todos de soslayo, pero se detiene unos segundos más en mí. Luego, sale hacia el porche lateral con la barbilla en alto, triunfante al haber dejado a la mitad de nosotros sumidos en la conmoción.

Tared, más frío que un témpano, se sube el cierre de la parka y va detrás de su hermano sin decir una palabra más. Y en cuanto la puerta se cierra con estrépito, todos en la estancia giran la cabeza hacia mí.

CAPÍTULO 47
PARIENTES MUY LEJANOS

Cuatro mujeres y cuatro demonios con cuernos que bailan alrededor de una hoguera. Una damisela que levita a varios metros del suelo, delante de una inocente casa. Unas jóvenes que le ofrecen muñecos de paja al diablo como sacrificio. Y, finalmente, el grabado de un hombre que se inclina a besar el ano de Satanás.

Le doy una fumada a mi cigarro y miro de arriba abajo aquellos dibujos antiguos, impresos en las hojas que me trajo Hoffman desperdigadas por el colchón, labor que me lleva de vuelta al angustiante momento en Nueva Orleans cuando estuve investigando sobre vudú en casa del detective.

Canibalismo, ungüentos mágicos hechos con niños, mujeres que secaban ríos y cosechas, registros de juicios desde Rusia hasta Nueva Inglaterra y libros como el *Malleus Maleficarum* y el *Daemonolatreiae*...

Echo las cenizas sobre una taza, intrigado al descubrir que, tal cual mencionó Johanna, todo, absolutamente todo lo que detallaban los tribunales eclesiásticos sobre las brujas adoradoras de Satanás es tal cual lo que vi en mis visiones, como si hubiese presenciado yo mismo aquellos *Sabbaths* supuestamente ocurridos hace cientos de años. Y eso incluye aquel libro negro que estuve a punto de firmar, porque vender su alma al diablo mediante un pacto era un requisito indispensable que toda bruja debía hacer si quería unirse a un *aquelarre.*

Y lo peor es que, al mirar el grabado de un hombre que habla con un cuervo y el de una mujer con cola de pez provocando un naufragio, me queda claro que los errantes también tuvimos algo que ver con todo esto, porque una característica importante de estas brujas es que solían estar acompañadas de demonios que *se transformaban en animales.* Criaturas que las llevaban a volar por los cielos sobre sus espaldas, que les facilitaban tareas mágicas y con las que incluso llegaban a fornicar de maneras muy dolorosas.

Pero, a pesar de todas estas pruebas y la forma en la que encajan tan perfectamente con lo que he visto, hay algo que no logro entender.

Las fuentes no sólo aseguran que las casi sesenta mil personas que murieron condenadas por brujería no sólo eran inocentes de los crímenes de los que se les acusaban, sino que, además, la gran mayoría no tenía nada que ver con la magia ni la habían practicado jamás en sus vidas. No es que pueda fiarme de un texto moderno escrito por humanos que descreen de estas cosas, pero ¿tantas personas y errantes con magia se *dejaron* capturar en aquel tiempo? Es absurdo y, si debo ser sincero, la pena que siento ahora mismo no es por las maldades de las supuestas brujas satánicas, sino por lo que los inquisidores les hacían *a ellas* cuando las torturaban.

Una de las razones por las cuales de niño tenía tanto miedo de que descubrieran que podía ver espíritus es porque hoy en día se siguen haciendo cacerías de brujas en la India, después de todo.

Pero aún hay más. Aparte de que no he visto una sola imagen o texto que describa algo remotamente parecido a la Marionetista, tampoco hay rastros del símbolo *alquímico* que tenían grabado en la piel aquellas terribles mujeres de mi visión:

Me alargo para tomar una de las hojas sobre la cama, la cual tiene impresa una especie de tabla periódica alquímica. Desde el principio sospeché que todo esto tenía alguna relación con esa magia, y eso es porque había visto dibujos muy similares en los libros de la casa Blake, aunque no dejo de preguntarme cómo diablos es que la magia de Jocelyn —o ella misma, inclusive—, se podría conectar con unas brujas más familiarizadas con una escoba que con una pseudociencia.

Es una pena que Hoffman no pudo encontrar el símbolo por ninguna parte, sólo figuras remotamente parecidas a lo que busco, como la Cruz del Leviatán.[10] Pero nada más.

Estoy por darle otra vuelta a los papeles, frustrado al pensar en lo mucho que Sammuel y sus libretas ayudarían en estos momentos, cuando escucho la puerta del porche abrirse y cerrarse con violencia. Me levanto a toda prisa para salir de la habitación y asomarme por el barandal del pasillo, aunque sólo alcanzo a oír las voces airadas de los hermanos Miller dirigirse a la sala.

---

[10] Considerada la "cruz de Satanás", es una reestilización que combina los símbolos del fuego y el azufre.

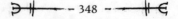

Debo admitir que fue un tanto cobarde haber huido y refugiarme aquí arriba, pero estaba tan contrariado por todo lo que pasó en tan escasos minutos que no quise enfrentarme al escrutinio de nadie. Y mucho menos después de que se hubieran enterado del asunto de Grace.

Al escuchar cómo Allen sube a su coche y arranca a toda velocidad, me retraigo de nuevo a la habitación con el corazón pendiendo de un hilo. Siento los pasos de Tared retumbar contra los escalones, ignorando los llamados de los demás a su paso.

En segundos, el lobo entra y casi azota la puerta tras de sí. Me quedo inmóvil al lado de la cama mientras se quita la parka y la arroja al suelo descuidadamente, algo muy impropio de él. Lo veo sacudirse el agua que se ha cristalizado en su cabello y dar vueltas como un lobo enjaulado.

De pronto, se detiene y mira sobre su hombro para encontrarme con la mirada en el piso y el cigarro a punto de caerse de mis dedos.

—Dios, Elisse, perdóname —dice, para luego acercarse a mí a pasos largos—. Lo siento, de verdad, ¿estás bien?

—Creo que soy yo el que necesita preguntarte eso, Tared.

Él resopla y se pasa una mano por la cara.

—Sí, estoy bien —contesta—. Aunque me costó hacer que se largara.

—¿Quieres hablar? —pregunto—. Bueno, si te sientes cómodo con eso, claro.

Tared niega con la cabeza.

—No te preocupes —afirma—. Nada de esto ha tenido que ver contigo, ni siquiera las estupideces que te dijo mi hermano allá abajo. Nuestra relación jamás ha sido sencilla y lo que sucedió con Grace tampoco hizo las cosas más fáciles, así que no te lo tomes como algo personal, por favor.

Sí, creo recordar que una vez mencionó que su hermano le tenía mucha estima a su esposa.

Siento que el suelo se mueve bajo mis pies, porque nunca me había puesto a pensar en la familia del lobo. O más bien, no creí que llegaría el día en el que tendría que hacerlo. Tared es *viudo* y tal vez debí considerar la forma en la que su madre y su hermano recibirían el hecho de que ahora sale con un chico diez años más joven del que jamás habían escuchado.

Y por la manera en la que Allen se dirigió a mí, supongo que no le hizo gracia. Es más, era obvio que yo le resulte...

Repugnante.

—Sin embargo, es *tu hermano*, Tared —digo en un intento por apartar mis sentimientos—. Estoy seguro de que nada te gustaría más que arreglar las cosas con él.

—Algunas relaciones no pueden ni necesitan arreglarse, Elisse. Ni siquiera las que tienes con tu propia sangre. Además, tampoco puedo forzarlo a que deje de temerme.

Tared se aleja y va hacia la maleta que ha dejado al pie del ventanal. Se agacha y empieza a sacar algo de ropa para vestirse.

—¿Tu hermano te tiene miedo? —pregunto, porque más bien parecía que el chico buscaba la forma de provocar al lobo. Aunque es verdad que la gente asustada suele reaccionar con violencia para no mostrarse vulnerables.

Tared detiene su labor y lleva la mirada afuera, hacia el bosque.

—¿Alguna vez Johanna te contó por qué se fue de su casa? —dice.

Me cuesta unos segundos responder, confundido por la pregunta:

—Sí. Dijo que tenía que ver con sus problemas de ira, lo que le había causado muchos conflictos con sus padres desde niña...

Él concuerda con un gruñido.

—Para ciertos errantes, y más durante la niñez, controlar emociones como el enojo puede ser complicado. Tanto para nosotros como para la gente a nuestro alrededor —explica—. En mi caso comencé a volverme problemático más o menos a los cinco o seis años de edad, poco antes de que nuestro padre se fuera de casa. No recuerdo casi nada de esa época de mi vida, estaba tan atormentado que perdía la noción de la realidad, incluso de la gente que era parte de mi familia. Y aunque yo nunca pude perdonarle que abandonara a mi madre en la época más difícil, Allen siempre quiso saber más de él. Siempre resintió la ausencia de un padre.

Tared guarda silencio de pronto, pero es obvio que se culpa por su partida. Por la fragmentación de su familia. Por todo.

—Allen es tres años menor que yo —continúa—, así que se supone que yo debía protegerlo, hacer lo que todos los hermanos mayores deben hacer, pero en cambio fue él quien se pasó toda la niñez viendo cómo yo le hacía la vida imposible a mi madre debido a mis problemas, y cuando sucedió lo de Grace, su miedo se acentuó. Siento que, al igual que Hoffman, Allen sentía que dentro de mí se ocultaba algo aún más... terrible.

—No vuelvas a decir eso —ordeno, bastante molesto—. No hay nada terrible contigo *y no tienes la culpa de las decisiones de los demás*, ¿me oyes? Estabas pasando por un trauma, por cosas que no podías controlar, ¡y eras sólo un niño, por favor!

Tared me mira con sorpresa, con esos ojos de trueno azul tan distintos a los de Allen, y susurra un sincero "gracias" para después volver a ocuparse de su ropa.

Quisiera preguntarle más cosas, saber más sobre su pasado y su familia, pero esta vez, decido esperar a que él esté listo para abrirse por su cuenta. No debe ser nada fácil consultar de nuevo un capítulo tan doloroso.

—¿Crees que Allen le dirá a tu madre que estamos aquí? —pregunto.

—Lo dudo. Ellos tampoco tienen una relación fácil.

Cuando Tared zanja el tema allí, me llevo el cigarro de nuevo a los labios. Al percatarse del humo, el lobo se levanta y camina hacia mí para tomar mi muñeca y darle también una fumada.

—¿No íbamos a dejar ambos esta porquería? —dice.

—Estaba tan ansioso que cuando vi la cajetilla de Hoffman en la cocina no pude evitarlo —respondo—. Aunque no he vuelto a ver a Samedi desde que desperté, su lengua sigue aquí, ¿sabes?

—¿Y sigues ansioso? —pregunta—, porque si es así, creo que un baño te ayudaría bastante con eso...

Noto los músculos de su abdomen tensarse, sus ojos descender hacia la hilera de botones entreabiertos de mi camisa. Miro sobre mi hombro, hacia la puerta bien cerrada de la habitación, y pienso en la manera despectiva en la que Allen se dirigió a mí antes.

Un chispazo de rabia me hace sonreír.

—Bueno, en ese caso tú también deberías tomarte otro rato en la ducha, es decir, ¿a quién se le ocurre salir *así* a la intemperie? —digo a la par que acaricio distraídamente su pecho desnudo.

El vínculo tira y una sonrisa feroz se dibuja en su boca. Y, por la forma en la que sus manos se cierran contra mí, tengo la placentera sospecha de que lo único que ha logrado Allen con todo esto es hacer que, esta vez, su hermano no esté tan dispuesto a contenerse.

CAPÍTULO 48
LUGARES QUE NO NOS PERTENECEN

Ayer, el hombre lobo y yo nos dimos cuenta de algo muy interesante. El sexo, de alguna manera, vigoriza mi magia lo suficiente como para sobreponerme a la espada unas horas. Tanto así que, cuando Tared terminó conmigo, mi primer impulso fue bajar por los artilugios. Julien había escondido los ojos de la Marionetista en la olla de nieve, así que me bastó con traerla aquí arriba para poder trabajar con tranquilidad.

Y ahora, la mañana me encuentra exhausto después de derramar hasta la última gota de magia que acumulé, con el último artilugio entre las manos y con la sombra de una migraña rondando en mi nuca.

El devorapieles, en cambio, duerme como una roca a mi lado, como si fuese lo más normal del mundo que el chico en tu cama se pasara la noche metiendo ojos de *demonio* dentro de pequeñas bolsas ensangrentadas.

Imagino que de nuevo le costará mucho levantarse, así que reúno las pocas fuerzas que me quedan para ponerme de pie en silencio. Me abrigo lo mejor que puedo y salgo de la habitación con los artilugios; ahora que los detectores están terminados, sólo bastará colocarlos en los alrededores de la casa.

Al llegar a la cocina sólo encuentro a Julien en la estancia, quizá porque aún es temprano. Él se gira hacia mí con la sartén en la mano, pero en vez de saludar apunta con la cabeza hacia la sala.

Me quedo petrificado al ver que Allen está sentado en el sillón, los brazos sobre los muslos y los puños entrelazados bajo la barbilla. Y que Johanna está junto a él, *escuchándolo*.

Me acerco al pelirrojo con cuidado, como si temiera que fuesen a reparar en mis pasos.

—¿Qué diablos está pasando aquí? —musito y el bisonte hace una mueca de incomodidad.

—Llegó hace menos de diez minutos —aclara—, iba a pedirle que se fuera, pero... Johanna quería hablar con él. No quise subir a avisarles porque tenía la esperanza de que se largara antes de que ustedes despertaran, pero creo que ya es tarde para eso.

Miro de reojo hacia los dos mientras me pongo los guantes con discreción, perturbado de sólo pensar en las cosas que Allen debe estar diciendo a mi hermana en este momento.

Ayer, Tared me contó que, aunque en Comus Bayou no sabían sobre la existencia de Grace, sí que conocían la mala relación que tiene con su hermano, lo que me hace entender todavía menos qué diablos pretende Johanna.

La errante levanta la barbilla y, al descubrir que estoy aquí, palidece.

Se levanta, sin despedirse de Allen, y camina hacia acá.

—Johanna —ella no me responde. Tan sólo se cruza de brazos y me pasa de lado para subir la escalera y perderse en las habitaciones del fondo.

En otras circunstancias me extrañaría demasiado un comportamiento así de desconsiderado por parte de ella, pero supongo que no puedo culparla ahora mismo. Debe estar...

Envenenada de furia.

Dejo la olla con los artilugios en la mesa y Julien niega enérgicamente con la cabeza cuando voy en dirección a la sala.

El menor de los Miller levanta los ojos hacia mí.

—¿Quién lo diría? —dice a modo de saludo—, para ser tan buena persona, a mi hermano le gusta mucho ocultarle cosas a los demás, ¿verdad?

—Buenos días, Allen —respondo con calma—. Puedo llamar a Tared para que baje, si gustas.

—De hecho, vine porque quería darte a ti *otro vistazo*. Te llamas Elisse, ¿verdad?

Entorno la mirada, incómodo.

—Lamento que te enteraras así de todo esto —musito—. No debió ser agradable saber que Tared había vuelto a Minnesota sin avisarles.

—Sí, mi hermano me dijo que eres algo así como su *amante*.

¿"Algo así", eh?

Me quedo frío delante del chico, con la sensación de una ansiosa picazón en las manos. No me ha gustado ni un poquito la forma que se ha dirigido a mí, y ni siquiera creo que lo que dijo sea verdad, pero intento ser comprensivo, considerar que no es realmente su culpa la relación tan difícil que lleva con Tared.

Es un humano. Un humano ajeno a nuestro mundo y nada más.

—Ya. Entiendo que saber eso debió ser una sorpresa para ti —susurro con las mejillas calientes.

—Claro que lo fue —dice mientras se recarga a sus anchas en el sillón—. Es decir, Tared *nunca* había mencionado nada de ti, y mucho menos a mi madre. Pero es comprensible. Yo tampoco lo habría hecho.

La forma en la que me mira de arriba abajo me crispa los nervios. Observo de reojo a Julien, quien parece tenso por la indignación, y decido que no tengo por qué soportar esto. Así que doy un paso atrás para retirarme.

—¿No te da pena, Elisse? —dice el menor de los Miller, quien se pone en pie para retenerme. Luego, señala con las manos a su alrededor—. Estas paredes, estos pisos, esta pintura; todo lo escogió Grace para hacer de esta casa un lugar donde *ella* pudiera ser feliz. ¿No te da vergüenza venir aquí, dormir bajo su techo y acostarte con su esposo en la habitación donde ellos solían hacerlo también?

—Tu hermano tiene todo el derecho de terminar su luto —musito, intentando controlar la humillación que aquello me ha hecho sentir—. Que no te guste lo que él eligió no va a cambiar nada.

—Tú no eres *nadie* para venir aquí, sentirte a tus anchas y tomar este lugar como si te perteneciera —dice con la mandíbula rígida—. *Ésta es la casa de Grace.*

—¿La casa de Grace? —la cara del chico palidece al escuchar la voz de su hermano a sus espaldas, tan sigiloso que sus botas ni siquiera han resonado contra el parqué—, porque según recuerdo, yo pagué la inmensa mayoría de esta propiedad con el sudor de mi frente. Y, por lo tanto, ésta es ahora *su casa* —el lobo me señala con la barbilla—. No voy a sufrir toda la maldita vida para tenerte contento, Allen, y tumbaré estas paredes, estos pisos y esta pintura si eso es lo que hace falta para seguir adelante.

Como si el devorapieles hubiese prendido una mecha, la cara de Allen se enciende como la yesca. Pero en vez de gritar y ponerse como un loco, el chico levanta la comisura de sus labios en una desagradable sonrisa, algo que empieza a parecerme más un tic nervioso que una reacción natural.

—Vaya, Tared —dice—, si hubieras confesado desde el principio que eras maricón te habrías ahorrado el enloquecer a tu esposa, ¿no?

Tared me atrapa un segundo antes de que le reviente la cara a su hermano de un puñetazo.

—¡Suéltame, carajo! —grito y me revuelvo con furia mientras el muy cobarde de Allen se echa sobre el sillón—. ¡Ya quisieras ser la mitad de hombre de lo que es tu hermano, mocoso idiota!

Mis sienes palpitan; mis manos escuecen como picaduras; el dolor en mi cabeza pulsa sin cesar; Allen puede decir *toda* la mierda que quiera sobre mí, prenderme fuego si se le antoja, ¡pero esto...!

¡Despedázalo!

—¡Elisse, calma! —Julien corre hacia acá para ayudar a lidiar con la situación, porque, sorprendentemente, a Tared le cuesta forcejear conmigo.

—¿Pero qué carajos está pasando aquí? —grita Hoffman, quien se asoma por la escalera debido al escándalo.

El menor de los Miller casi lanza un chillido cuando mi brazo se zafa del agarre del bisonte.

—¡ELISSE! —esta vez es el grito de Nashua lo que me detiene. El errante entra a toda prisa por la puerta principal de la casa—. Elisse. El contacto de Debbie ha llegado.

CAPÍTULO 49
UN LATIDO PRIMIGENIO

Allen. Grace. El aire que ahora mismo respiro. Todo pasa a importarme un comino cuando aquellas palabras caen como una bomba sobre mis oídos.

—Por los dioses... —musito, asfixiado por el estupor.

Me abro paso como un huracán hasta la puerta para ver cómo un vehículo entra por el camino de terracería, una pequeña y elegante camioneta blanca que pronto se estaciona junto al coche de Allen.

Un hombre de piel muy morena baja del auto, sereno, hundiendo los zapatos negros en la nieve, sin chistar. Va vestido de traje sastre, con un abrigo grueso encima y el largo cabello suelto. Y aunque aún está a varios metros de mí, logro distinguir con claridad que no se trata de un errante, sino de un *humano*.

Me acerco como un rayo, con Nashua detrás de mí.

—Buenos días —nos saluda el visitante, quien se toma brevemente de las muñecas con el errante oso—. Perdonen por llegar hasta hoy. Hubiese querido hacerlo en cuanto Debbie me llamó, pero apenas encontré un vuelo desde Canadá y tampoco ha sido fácil dar con la casa. Está muy bien escondida —el hombre mira hacia mí—. Tú debes ser Elisse, ¿verdad?

—Pero ¡¿qué diablos te pasa?!

Detrás de nosotros, Allen es echado de la casa a empujones por su hermano. El chico se planta en el porche y parece a punto de reclamar cuando Tared le apunta con el dedo y lo amenaza con algo así como llamar a la policía.

—Eh, ¿llegué en un mal momento? —pregunta el contacto de Debbie por lo bajo.

—No, no, pase, por favor —pido, tan ansioso que apenas reparo en la manera en la que el menor de los Miller es obligado a largarse en su coche.

Guiamos al hombre a la sala y lo sentamos en medio del amplio sillón. Mi hermana decide bajar junto con Hoffman, y después de traer sillas de la cocina, todos nos congregamos alrededor del visitante.

—Creo que lo mejor es que primero me presente —dice una vez que el ánimo se ha calmado—. Mi nombre es Huritt y soy profesor de Antropología en la Universidad de Toronto.

Me siento frente a él en la mesita de centro, incapaz de creer que por fin haya encontrado a alguien que pueda ayudarme.

—¿De qué familia vienes, Huritt? —pregunta Tared a mi lado.

—Yo no tengo Atrapasueños, muchacho —responde con calma—. Soy humano, aunque tengo varios amigos errantes. Debbie es una de ellos.

Cuando sólo Hoffman parece tan sorprendido como yo, me doy cuenta de que éramos los únicos que ignorábamos que hubiese gente más allá de las familias de errantes que supieran de nuestra existencia. Aunque eso explicaría la facilidad con la que pudimos entrar a Monument Valley.

—Entonces, ¿usted puede ayudarme? —pregunto, arriesgándome a ser demasiado efusivo.

—La verdad es que Debbie no pudo contarme mucho sobre todo esto, Elisse —dice—. Como no hablabas demasiado con ella, no supo exactamente qué te había ocurrido.

—Eh, sí. Es que siempre estaba tan seria que preferí guardar mi distancia para no incomodarla.

El antropólogo sonríe sin malicia.

—Algunas personas de las tribus originarias podemos ser reservadas, pero no porque tengamos mal carácter, sino porque entendemos el valor de las palabras y nos gusta recurrir a ellas con precisión. De hecho, Debbie me dijo que, para ser tan sombrío, le provocabas mucha ternura.

Miro de reojo a Nashua y encorvo un poco la espalda, avergonzado de mi prejuicio.

—Pero no es eso lo que te interesa escuchar ahora, ¿cierto? —dice Huritt con cortesía—. Así que, ¿por qué no me cuentas primero tu problema?

Ah. Directo al grano.

—Supongo que ya sabe que soy un contemplasombras —el hombre asiente con naturalidad—, así que he visto fantasmas y espíritus del plano medio desde que tengo memoria. Pero a ese monstruo no comencé a verlo hasta que llegué a Nueva Orleans, hace ahora ya más de un año. Y a diferencia del resto de mis pesadillas, las cuales sólo me atormentaban cuando entraba al mundo espiritual, *Wéndigo* también podía aparecer en el humano y...

El hombre alza la mano para pedirme un momento.

—Lo más seguro es que no estés familiarizado con esto, así que tal vez te sea valioso saberlo antes de que continúes tu relato —dice—: te recomiendo mucho que no pronuncies el nombre de ese ser. Hacerlo es una forma de *evocarlo*,[11] de dirigir su atención hacia ti, así que, si te parece bien, comenzaremos a llamarlo de otra manera, algo como...

—¿Monstruo de hueso? —sugiere el lobo, y Huritt accede, comprensivo. De pronto, me siento un poco perturbado al pensar en la cantidad de veces que hemos usado ya ese nombre por simple ignorancia.

Con eso en mente empiezo a contarle al antropólogo, a grandes rasgos, todo lo que me sucedió desde el día en el que encontré a la terrible criatura en la tienda de Laurele. Acaricio mi mano descarnada, oculta bajo el guante, y las emociones me desbordan al darme cuenta de que ya no recuerdo con exactitud cómo eran las yemas, ni si esa uña rota, resultado de un machucón cuando era niño, estaba en el dedo medio o en el anular.

Somos...

Después, le hablo sobre el momento en el que monstruo de hueso me arrancó a Ciervo Piel de Sombras del pecho para tragárselo y de la forma en la que me vi obligado a hacer un pacto con él para apropiarme de sus poderes. O más bien, para dejarlo tomar el lugar de mi ancestro.

Intento ser sincero con absolutamente todo. Desde las voces en mi cabeza hasta cómo esta criatura parece alimentarse de mi debilidad. Y, por supuesto, le hablo también del canibalismo y de la presión dolorosa de la garra de la bestia en algún punto sobre mi corazón.

El hombre me pregunta dónde nací y quienes fueron mis padres, así como la apariencia física del monstruo de hueso,

---

[11] En el mundo de la magia y lo esotérico, "evocar" se utiliza para los espíritus menores, mientras que "invocar" se refiere sólo a los dioses o divinidades.

y cuando termino, estoy tan agotado que comienzo a sentir de nuevo ese insistente golpeteo en la nuca, el indicio de un dolor de cabeza.

Huritt deja escapar un suspiro.

—Vaya. En qué lío estás metido, ¿eh? —dice mientras afloja un poco el nudo de su corbata—. De acuerdo. Voy a hacerte una última pregunta, y necesito que reflexiones bien la respuesta, porque es sumamente importante, ¿está bien?

Aquello me trae una sensación de pesadez, pero termino por asentir.

—Cuando el monstruo de hueso puso su garra sobre tu corazón —empieza a la par que hace un gesto con su propia mano—, ¿sentiste un frío terrible, una especie de congelación súbita dentro de tu pecho?

Me llevo la palma hacia esa zona del cuerpo para intentar rememorar la sensación de aquellos huesos sobre mi carne. El ahogo, la ansiedad, la opresión...

—No —contesto muy seguro—. Lo que sentía era dolor, como si estuviese a punto de sufrir un ataque cardíaco, no sé si eso tiene sentido.

El semblante comprensivo del antropólogo cambia a uno de preocupación.

—Bien. Entonces creo que necesito empezar por explicarte qué es en realidad un *"Wándiga"* —dice, pronunciando así el nombre a propósito—: Como te imaginarás, el mito de esta criatura proviene del pueblo algonquino, los habitantes originarios que han vivido en el norte de este país y en Canadá desde hace miles de años. Al igual que muchas otras tribus, preservábamos nuestras leyendas y tradiciones por medio de la transmisión oral, por lo que mucho de nuestro pasado quedó perdido debido al genocidio de los colonizadores y la cristianización. Wándiga no fue la excepción, por lo que, hasta hoy en día, no se sabe con certeza cuál es el origen exacto de su leyenda ni cuánto tiempo hace que existe, pero los pocos rastros que tenemos coinciden en que se trata de un espíritu maligno que se manifiesta durante el invierno y sólo en los bosques septentrionales a aquellas personas que, hostigadas por la hambruna, deciden comer carne humana; como resultado, estas víctimas comienzan a transformarse en un Wándiga también, adquiriendo sus hábitos caníbales y su apetito.

Sí. Eso suena bastante al monstruo de hueso, cuya sonrisa parece haberse ensanchado en mi interior, pero...

—Nunca he estado en esa zona del continente —recalco— y tampoco había comido carne humana hasta mucho después de ser poseído. No tiene sentido.

—A menos que... —Julien carraspea cuando todos giramos hacia él—. Es decir, cuando llegaste a Tíbet tenías ya unos meses de nacido, ¿no? Tal vez tu padre provenía de esa zona que menciona Huritt, y quizás estaba en una gran necesidad, no tenía con qué alimentarte y... ya sabes.

Escucho a más de uno jadear, espantados al comprender hacia dónde iba su insinuación.

—Tranquilos. Todavía es muy pronto para sacar conclusiones —dice Huritt ante la inquietud—. Hay muchas similitudes entre Wándiga y la bestia que me describes, demasiadas como para pasarlas por alto. Pero...

—¿Pero...? —pregunta Tared al darse cuenta de que no puedo articular la palabra por mi cuenta.

—Pero si le pregunté a Elisse sobre la garra dentro de su pecho, es porque una parte esencial del mito de Wándiga es *el corazón frío* —explica—. Alrededor del mundo hay muchas leyendas en las que los espíritus malignos usan el corazón, el símbolo de la *voluntad*, como vínculo para subyugar a su víctima; la voluntad es el arma más poderosa de cualquier criatura viva, ya sea humana, errante o animal, y si el corazón es embrujado o destrozado, el ente invasor tendrá la total libertad de controlar su cuerpo y su alma. Lo que Wándiga hace es precisamente congelarlo, así que cuando alguien es poseído, lo primero que debe sentir es un terrible helor en el pecho, el cual tú ya debiste haber percibido, y quizá desde el primer momento en el que tu padre te "alimentó" con carne humana.

—Tampoco olvidemos que Wándiga te poseyó sólo hasta que tú aceptaste ser su receptor —apunta Nashua.

—¿Y... la segunda cosa? —pregunto, cada vez más angustiado al presentir hacia donde diablos estaba yendo esta conversación.

Huritt extiende la palma de su mano hacia mí.

—¿Puedo ver tu mano? —pregunta—. En cuanto Debbie me habló de ella, supe que debía venir personalmente a verla en vez de limitarme a hacer una llamada por teléfono.

Asentir me cuesta como si mi cuello fuera de acero, pero retiro mi guante y alargo mi garra hacia él. El antropólogo entrecierra los ojos y la toma para observar los huesos, las articulaciones y el movimiento. Acaricia la textura y, por unos momentos, puedo sentir cómo se le eriza la piel.

—La segunda cosa es *su apariencia*, Elisse —dice después de soltarme—. La criatura que has descrito y esta mano que parece hacer cosas tan terribles como extraordinarias no se parece en nada al Wándiga de nuestras tradiciones.

Tared entorna la mirada:

—Yo creí que, precisamente por su apariencia, el monstruo de hueso era un Wándiga.

Al ver mi gesto de confusión, el lobo se da a entender:

—Soy de la zona de los Grandes Lagos, después de todo, así que Wándiga es una leyenda bien conocida por aquí. Recuerdo que lo representaban como un esqueleto de animal con colmillos en algún cuento para niños.

—Y ésa es la parte que no tiene sentido —continúa Huritt—. Cuando los primeros colonos británicos llegaron a tierras algonquinas hace cuatrocientos años, el mito de Wándiga se mezcló con tabús y miedos traídos de los cristianos obsesionados con demonizar todo lo que no se asemejase a sus tradiciones. Como resultado, dieron a este espíritu maligno la apariencia de un ser antropomorfo con astas, más parecido a las deidades de aquellas religiones mal llamadas "paganas" que habían sido condenadas por brujería en Europa, porque los registros nativos originales lo describen más bien como una criatura humanoide, a veces gigante, que se ha comido sus propios labios debido a la avidez, algo muy distinto a la imagen que tiene Wándiga en el imaginario colectivo en la actualidad.

Al escuchar "condenadas por brujería" mi mente evoca aquellas brujas satánicas que ahora han sido enviadas por mi Mara, incapaz de entender cómo es que todo lo que está sucediendo pareciera conectarse y a la vez no tener ningún sentido.

Mis labios se abren muy apenas para hacer una pregunta que galopa dentro de mí sin cesar.

—Entonces, ¿no es un Wándiga lo que me ha poseído? ¿No hay forma en la que puedas ayudarme? —susurro.

Cuando el antropólogo niega con la cabeza a manera de respuesta, siento como si mi corazón se desinflara. Justo cuando había encontrado una respuesta. Justo cuando creí que me había acercado al final de esta pesadilla...

Pero luego el hombre piensa unos momentos, quizás ordenando una idea compleja.

—Contradiciendo lo que muchos historiadores piensan, y quizás esto es porque no tienen idea de que los errantes y la magia son reales —dice—, existe la teoría de que detrás de la inmensa variedad de mitos, religiones y creencias, hay algo muy antiguo, algo arquetípico que, de alguna forma, pareciera conectar todos los miedos de la humanidad en un único origen; un sitio, un momento, una figura de donde se desprende todo lo que nos atormenta en las noches, una semilla oscura que late dentro de las entrañas de las sombras. **Un corazón, ¿verdad? Un corazón podrido, un corazón inmundo que crece como una enredadera alrededor de tu cuello.**

Cállate.

—Este ser al que llamas "monstruo de hueso" tiene características muy similares al mito algonquino —continúa, sin percibir cómo mi garra se abre sobre mi pierna, cómo el dolor de cabeza dilata las venas de mi sien—, pero también se parece a otras criaturas existentes alrededor del mundo, como aquellas que trajeron los colonizadores en sus pesadillas. Irónicamente, todo eso lo hace tan *único* que lo convierte en algo mucho más complejo, algo que parece haber sido sacado no de una leyenda, sino de algo más…

Cállate.

—Primordial.

—¿Primordial? ¿A qué te refieres? —pregunta Johanna, creo. ¿Tienes una idea de qué podría ser? —cuestiona alguien más, pero ya no reconozco su voz.

—¿Cómo carajos podemos detenerlo? —*basta, ¡basta!*

—No, no tengo idea. Pero sé que quizá…

Cállate.

Dejo de escuchar. De sentir. De pensar.

En un latido, el tiempo se derrite entre mis dedos. Huritt habla, pero no puedo oírlo; sólo veo sus labios moverse, sus ojos expandirse por la sorpresa, las imágenes de todos diluirse a mi alrededor.

Sa... em. L...y

Sa... lm... Woods...

Y él habla.

Y habla.

Y habla.

Y luego...

—Elisse, *¿estás bien?*

¡ **CÁLLATE!**

Mi grito es seguido de un suspiro. Y de silencio.

De pronto, el monstruo de hueso me cubre los ojos y los oídos con cientos de manos; me ciega y me deja sordo. Me arranca un gemido.

Dolor. Migraña. Un hormigueo terrible en la nuca.

La negrura se expande de mi cabeza hacia mi pecho, a mis pies, a mis manos que se clavan en mis muslos hasta hacerme sangrar.

Un latido primigenio.

La realidad se desenfoca, mis extremidades se desprenden de mí como llevadas por una ola, tiradas por montones de manos cadavéricas que las ahogan.

Una semilla sembrada en tu corazón.

Lanzo otro grito que esta vez no puedo escuchar dentro de mi cabeza. Sólo hormigueo. Hormigueo que nubla todo sonido y todo color y toda forma con energía estática en luz y sombra.

Me levanto y me sacudo para tratar de expulsar de mi cuerpo el terrible cosquilleo que me recorre la carne. El escozor en mis dientes me hace sentir como si creciera una trampa de oso en mi mandíbula que abro y cierro sin cesar para tratar de quitármela.

Intento arrancarme mi propia quijada, pero está mojada y resbalosa.

"¡ELISSE!"

Oigo que alguien grita, y hunde sus manos en mis hombros. Todo da vueltas y mi espalda azota con fuerza contra el piso. ¿Me estoy desmayando? ¿Por qué está tan oscuro de pronto?

Y entonces escucho un goteo. Una, dos, tres veces caen las gotas.

Mis manos están tibias y pegajosas, mi lengua se retuerce presa del sabor de las cenizas. La energía estática se convierte en un lago escarlata cuando algo florece sobre mi pecho, húmedo. Muy caliente.

Y entonces, el monstruo de hueso me libera ojos y oídos.

Enfoco la vista despacio, doloridamente. El jadeo de Tared me hace girar la cabeza. Él está a mi lado, con los brazos alrededor de mi pecho, la mejilla cubierta de sangre, sangre que gotea de mis manos, de mis labios, de mi rostro.

—¿Tared? —pregunto, como si acabase de ver la luz después de días enteros de tener los ojos vendados.

Estoy sentado en el suelo, rodeado de personas, con el lobo reteniéndome con todas sus fuerzas. Nashua, Hoffman y Julien me sostienen las piernas. Jadean, se agitan.

La mesita de centro está volcada junto con el sillón. Johanna está frente a mí con los ojos abiertos de par en par, cristalizados a causa del horror.

Y bajo sus manos cruzadas, tendido en el suelo cual muñeco roto, yace Huritt con el pecho escarbado como una tumba, ahogándose con su propia sangre, murmurando palabras que no alcanzo a comprender por el constante zumbido en mis oídos.

Veo el subir y bajar de su corazón expuesto entre sus costillas destrozadas.

Sa... em. L...y

Sa... lm... Woods...

Sólo un latido más...

Grito con tanta fuerza que podría reventar las ventanas, porque descubro que aquello que sentía todo este tiempo detrás de la nuca no era un golpeteo, ni una migraña ni un benigno hormigueo. Eran las voces del monstruo de hueso, diminutas pero presentes como la marabunta de millones de células que, en vez de gritar, me hicieron creer que por fin lo había subyugado, mientras se apoderaban de mí como una infección. O como la mano de una Marionetista detrás de mi nuca.

Orillado por el miedo de volver a perder el control, inflo mi corazón, *mi voluntad,* como una bomba, y expulso mi magia hacia mi cabeza, hacia la base de mi cerebro. La clavo y la tuerzo como un tornillo para volver a quedarme ciego y sordo, apagando las luces del entendimiento y empujarme así, de vuelta a la terrible oscuridad.

CAPÍTULO 50
INFRAMUNDO

Gracias a ti, comenzó a crecer un bosque en medio de la niebla, hace más de mil años.

Y después, *ella* llegó y construyó un hogar con hiedra venenosa y miedo. Pavor que, una vez que logró erigir sus muros, llenó las habitaciones de lenguas que lamían ansiosas cada gota de sangre derramada sobre los suelos; de ojos que miraban con deseo cada cuerpo que abría sus cavidades delante de ellos preguntándose, ¿cuándo? ¿Cuándo será mi turno de alimentarme?

La casa en la niebla, un refugio de endrinos oscuros que crecieron a lo largo de ocho caminos, abre sus puertas, tan perversas que me permiten ver dentro de ellas sólo cuando las siete chimeneas arrojan humo hacia mi portal; un humo denso que me obliga a toser trozos de pulmón para despertarme.

Vanidosa y cruel, aquel monumento del horror me ofrece el interior de su cuerpo para que pueda ver a sus hijas, para que la rabia me consuma al ser incapaz de tocarlas, para que me resigne al anhelo de rasgar algún día con truenos y martillos aquellas paredes infestadas por la humedad.

A sabiendas de mis deseos, de mi inmensa frustración, hoy me muestra cómo Inanna, la Maligna, se acerca por uno de los corredores vestida de encaje negro mientras arrastra una ofrenda tras ella: un venado aturdido, cuyo rastro rojo se mezcla con el agua que inunda el pasillo bajo la escalera.

—Maldita sea —la bruja oscura escucha a su hermana mayor quejarse al fondo del corredor, puesto que ha metido los pies por accidente en el charco helado que brota de una de las paredes del pasillo, cubierta de llaves que cuelgan de clavos, tan antiguas como la propia casa.

—La marea, Caligo —dice la Maligna con aburrida obviedad, para luego soltar al venado delante de las tres sillas puestas frente al muro. La envenenadora da un último sorbo a su té de narciso y deja el recipiente de porcelana en el suelo para que una mano gris brote del agua y la hunda dentro de la oscuridad del charco.

—Gracias, querido —pronuncia la bruja a la par que toma asiento al lado de su hermana. Pronto, las tres escuchamos el repiqueteo de unos pies descalzos que chapotean en el pasillo inundado.

—Vaya tardecita, ¿eh? El mar se ha puesto bravo —dice la última hija, aquella de cabello blanco que se acerca con un televisor de bulbos entre los brazos, tan viejo que el cable de corriente ya ha sido devorado por los ratones.

Después, mira hacia el animal agonizante en medio del pasillo.

—Uy, Ilya lo ha dejado vivo esta vez. Qué buen gatito.

Hela sonríe y arroja el televisor frente a sus hermanas, quienes reclaman al ser salpicadas por el agua helada. El cristal de la caja produce una chispa potente al estrellarse; la estática zumba por la pantalla, para luego encenderse, sin más.

La imagen de un cordón policial aparece, rodeando un semáforo en plena Washington Street. El camarógrafo apunta hacia el suelo, porque bien sabe que podría ser despedido si se atreve a levantar la lente hacia la soga metálica que engancha las luces de tránsito.

Un ruido inteligible es lo único que sale de la boca del humano, pero no hace falta comprender lo que dice. Las tres mujeres saben bien quién es el hombre que yace colgando allí arriba, y es fácil saber que piensan en su mano izquierda, ésa que, aunque no pueden verla, están seguras de que debe faltarle.

—Es la tercera víctima —susurra la envenenadora, quien se arrepiente de haber bebido tanto té.

—Que nosotras sepamos —remarca su hermana pequeña—. Anoche, el espejo me dijo que podría haber *muchos* más.

La Maligna, por su parte, se queda con la mirada fija sobre la imagen en blanco y negro, quizá recordando el cuerpo devorado que había encontrado hace poco. Minutos después, la misma mano que se llevó la taza de Caligo se levanta de nuevo del agua. Toma el cordón del televisor y, poco a poco, comienza a succionar el aparato hacia las profundidades invisibles.

Las tres se miran entre sí mientras yo comienzo a sentir un cosquilleo en mis brazos descarnados, una caricia helada que las tres brujas también pueden sentir con claridad.

Ah. La familiaridad. La sombra. El llamado incesante de la sangre.

Inanna se levanta y arrastra la cola de su vestido detrás de ella. Se para delante de la pared y ésta le pide que observe bien la colección de llaves. Que encuentre una que en ese momento parezca más oscura o más brillante, más hermosa o más horrible que las demás.

—¿Madre? —llama, y recibe el ruido de las olas del otro lado como respuesta.

—No sabemos qué hacer —insiste Caligo a sus espaldas, retorcida como una hiedra en su silla ante el silencio—. Está claro que *no podemos matarlos.*

—Y enviarlos de vuelta a las sombras tampoco servirá de nada —añade la Maligna, aún absorta en las llaves de la pared—. Ellos *siempre* encuentran la forma de volver.

—Yo sabía que ver a Giles Corey no traería nada bueno —musita la necromante—, pero nunca imaginé que sería algo como... *esto.*

Un silencio imponente prevalece, tan denso que la respiración de las tres hermanas se detiene. Pero después de no escuchar otra cosa que las olas contra los muros de la casa, una voz se abre paso entre las aguas y la pared, tan profunda que se clava como una estaca en los oídos.

—*¿En verdad están esperando a que yo les dé la solución, pequeñas?* —pregunta *ella* decepcionada—. *Inanna, me sorprende tu incapacidad de confiar en tu instinto. Tú más que nadie sabes bien qué es lo que pueden hacer ahora.*

La hermosa mujer cierra los ojos y respira profundo.

—*Nada.* Nosotras no podemos hacer nada.

Sus dos hermanas la miran como si las hubiese maldecido.

—¿Qué? —exclama la más joven—, ¿cómo que no podemos hacer nada?

—Cali ya lo dijo, Hel —responde ella tranquila—. No podemos matarlos. Pero...

Sus ojos oscuros miran hacia donde se ha ido el televisor.

—¿Pero...? —insiste Hela.

—Pero al menos podemos prepararnos para lo que viene. Para lo que los muertos te han mostrado en aquella visión.

Los ojos oscuros de la Maligna se clavan en su hermana más joven, quien enmudece y mira a su regazo, pensando en ese sueño de obsidiana que no ha dejado de repetirse en su cabeza.

—*Tres días, mis niñas* —susurra la voz en la oscuridad—. *Tres días que podrían ser sólo unas horas, si lo desean.*

Inanna estruja los puños a los costados, porque sabe bien que aquello no ha sido una petición, así que pasa la mano sobre las llaves hasta que una empieza a quemarle la palma.

Cuando la Maligna abre el portal, sus hermanas toman al agonizante ciervo, de una pata cada una, y se levantan para escoltarla. Observan la negrura, el único sitio en toda la casa a donde no puedo seguirlas, cosa que debe estar haciéndote sonreír ahora mismo.

Así que tan sólo observo, con impaciencia, cómo finalmente las tres descienden como hizo Perséfone hacia las profundidades de la oscuridad.

CAPÍTULO 51
MALIGNO

—¿Tienes miedo? —pregunta mamá Tallulah.

Pero no me pregunta a mí. Le pregunta a padre Trueno.

Él lo piensa. Aprieta su bastón. Pero quien contesta es Calen.

—Sí —dice el león—, pero no tengo miedo de él.

Y luego, me mira.

Una tumba abierta yace en medio de todos ellos, y hay algo allí que no alcanzo a distinguir, apretado dentro del agujero y que late de arriba abajo como un corazón gigante. Lo observan cabizbajos, con velas de grandes flamas derretidas entre las manos, mientras que el resto, a su alrededor, sólo es negrura.

En esa oscuridad veo la silueta de Muata, el anciano que debería estar en silla de ruedas camina de un lado a otro. Mueve la cabeza una y otra vez y murmura, perdido a sabiendas de que ya no se puede acercar a la luz.

Una sombra. Sólo una sombra que, con el tiempo, quizá se pudrirá.

—Tengo miedo de volver al punto de partida —dice Fernanda.

—Tengo miedo de que huya de nuevo —susurra Chenoa.

—Y que esta vez no volvamos a encontrarlo nunca —Alannah levanta la cabeza hacia padre Trueno.

Éste extiende la boca y el sonido que emite es como el lento rechi-
nar de una puerta. Pero no son sus labios sino mis párpados los que
se abren de par en par.

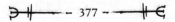

Despierto con un jadeo y los ojos desorbitados. Mis retinas se acostumbran a la oscuridad del techo y distinguen la luz fría que se desliza a través de la puerta entreabierta de la habitación.

¿Tienes miedo?

La pregunta martillea en mi cabeza. Mis dedos se clavan hasta penetrar el colchón debajo de mí.

"Tengo miedo de volver al punto de partida."

Mi cuerpo clama por levantarse.

"Tengo miedo de que huya de nuevo."

Mi alma suplica porque salga corriendo.

"Y que esta vez no volvamos a encontrarlo nunca."

Pero en cambio, sólo espero el momento en el que una gota de sal se deslice por mi mejilla.

Pero aquello no ocurre.

—No... —musito, ahogado en mi angustia. Vuelvo a cerrar los ojos con la esperanza de despertar en otro momento. En otra realidad. En aquel fugaz segundo antes de haberme transformado en *otra cosa.*

Justo cuando creí que por fin habíamos encontrado un nombre y una respuesta. Justo cuando creí que ya no podía hacer nada más terrible.

He matado a muchas personales crueles y miserables antes. Pero nunca había asesinado a un inocente.

Percibo en mi nuca el rastro adormecido de una migraña, las pulsaciones de un zumbido muerto en mis oídos; las manos ya no me escuecen, pero aún recuerdo la sensación de aquel hormigueo terrible bajo mi piel.

No estoy seguro de cómo o qué fue lo que sucedió. Lo único que me queda claro es que el control de mi cuerpo me fue arrebatado de golpe, la violación más terrible a un alma que lo único que ha querido es volver a ser libre.

Ya siento de nuevo mis extremidades, puedo llevar mi mano frente a mi cara y ver el movimiento voluntario de mis dedos... pero lo que ya no siento es rabia ni dolor. Tan sólo ese vacío que alguna vez vi en la mirada de Irina; la sensación de que acaba de romperse otra parte irreparable de mi ser.

Porque nunca había sido tan... *maligno*.

—*Tú* —musito—. Tú lo mataste.

¿Yo? ¿No eran tus manos las que estaban manchadas de sangre?

Sí. Fui *yo* el que saltó de un momento a otro sobre Huritt. El que le abrió el pecho en canal con su garra de hueso y el que de seguro cavó en él en busca de un corazón.

Pero *no era yo*. Estaba poseído por ti.

No era yo... ¿verdad?

La necesidad de estallar en llanto y locura se aquieta de nuevo en mi garganta, sin pulsar, sin convertirse en un grito, mis emociones paralizadas por un cáncer que se apoderó de mí sin que pudiera darme cuenta.

De reojo veo que la luna nueva ha muerto sobre las montañas como un presagio, empezando a abrirse como un ojo somnoliento en el cielo nocturno.

Pongo los pies sobre el suelo, como si nunca hubiesen dejado de ser míos, y me levanto para ir hacia los ventanales. Todo está oscuro en el bosque, pero bajo el brillo nocturno logro encontrar uno de mis artilugios colgado en un árbol, que se balancea con el viento.

¿Por qué estoy solo en esta habitación, con la puerta entreabierta, cuando debería estar encerrado a cal y canto? La chimenea está apagada. No está la maleta de Tared y tampoco escucho ruido en la casa.

—¿Por qué no estoy encadenado? —cuestiono al ver mis manos sucias, rememorando la sensación de la carne de Huritt bajo mis uñas. Tengo la misma ropa ensangrentada de antes y el sabor metálico que circula en mis labios que me hace preguntarme si también habré empleado mis dientes para matarlo.

Salgo de la habitación, y afuera me encuentro con siluetas azules proyectadas a través de las ventanas, con el rechinar de la escalera bajo mi peso, pero de allí en más, todo es sombras. Todo es quietud, como si la casa hubiese sido…

Abandonada.

Al llegar a la cocina, me percato de que han desaparecido las sartenes, la comida, los trastes. Miro hacia la sala y la mesa sigue volcada. Hay sangre en el suelo, un rastro grueso que lleva al sillón. Luego, un reguero abundante hasta la puerta que da al porche lateral.

Y, abandonado sobre una encimera, el celular de Hoffman, manchado también de sangre, como si alguien lo hubiese utilizado justo después de mi arrebato.

Quiero despedazarme contra el suelo, porque ahora está claro que ni una pizca de mi maldad ha sido un sueño.

Por fin te dejaron, ¿verdad?

—¿Tared? —llamo entre sollozos, asustado y solo en medio de la oscuridad.

¿Tienes miedo de lo que has hecho?

—Sí.

¿Tienes miedo de lo que pasará a partir de ahora?

—Sí.

¿Tienes miedo de mí?

Tres veces sí.

Pero entonces, logro comprender que, aunque se han llevado el cadáver de Huritt y han colgado los artilugios... no han limpiado *nada*, una regla inexcusable en el mundo de los errantes.

Escucho el crujido de un vidrio roto. Giro la cabeza y percibo aquel sonido en el garaje. Abandono el charco rojo y camino hacia allá con el corazón como una pelota dentro de mi pecho torturado. Quito la silla puesta contra la puerta. Y al abrirla...

Oh, cómo hubiese querido ver al mismísimo Satanás del otro lado.

Allen tiene la mirada desorbitada sobre el cadáver podrido de la Marionetista, con los pies sobre el círculo de sal barrido mientras sostiene contra su pecho el picahielo con el que se ha abierto paso a través de la ventana del garaje. Los cristales yacen amortiguados por las cajas húmedas y sus huellas llenas de nieve se arrastran por el concreto.

Recuerdo, con el estómago revuelto, el camino que lleva hasta aquí desde el mirador.

—Allen... —susurro, despertando del letargo de mi propia pesadilla—. ¡Allen!

Él no reacciona, petrificado ante la inerte criatura.

—¡Allen! —insisto, presa de un miedo atroz.

Pero las voces en forma de hormigueo no despiertan. La migraña detrás de la cabeza no comienza a palpitar.

Me acerco para alcanzar al chico, pero él grita y me apunta con el picahielo, mientras mira mi ropa ensangrentada como si yo fuese el propio monstruo amarrado sobre la mesa. Se estremece de arriba abajo con la respiración tan acelerada que parece que hubiese corrido una maratón.

Cuando creí que su cara no podría desencajarse más, ésta muta del horror a la absoluta sorpresa. Y tan súbitamente como llegó, el pánico de Allen desaparece.

Pero no por haberme reconocido, sino porque está viendo algo sobre mi hombro.

Giro la cabeza lentamente hacia atrás.

—¿*Tú?*

La palabra sale con atropello de mi boca al ver a una persona delante del fregadero de la cocina, *flotando* a centímetros del suelo.

El camisón azul, la espuma en los labios, su cuello aplastado por una fuerza invisible: es la mujer que se me apareció en el río congelado. Y al igual que aquella vez, un brazo grueso y blanco se columpia debajo de ella para manipularla como un títere.

Miro de reojo y compruebo, horrorizado, que la Marionetista sigue inerte sobre la mesa, y justo cuando creo que voy a ser acorralado por este otro monstruo y el picahielo a mis espaldas, escucho cómo el afilado instrumento repiquetea al caer sobre el suelo.

Una única palabra sale de la boca de Allen y basta para sacudirme entero:

—¡Grace!

CAPÍTULO 52
UN GRITO AL AMANECER

Sus ojos, su cabello, su piel; nunca pregunté a Tared qué apariencia tenía su esposa, por lo que verla frente a mí en estos momentos se siente como una bofetada.

Y sólo el empujón de Allen para apartarme del camino hace que mi cuerpo reaccione.

—No, ¡no, Allen! —grito una vez más, atrapándolo por el brazo.

—¡Suéltame! —exclama al forcejear para liberarse. Grace despega la cabeza del hombro y nos observa con ojos desorbitados.

—Qué pronto te has olvidado de mí, Allen —dice ella con la voz ahogada. Gruesas lágrimas quiebran la mirada del chico, quien intenta dar un paso hacia la aparición.

—No, no —solloza—. ¡Yo jamás haría eso, tú sabes que yo...!

—Allen, ella no es Grace —vocifero con la esperanza de mantener al chico a raya—. ¡No dejes que te engañe!

Pero él no me escucha. Tan sólo tiene ojos y oídos para la funesta criatura.

—Ibas a salvarme, ¿lo recuerdas? —dice la mujer, quien estruja la bata entre sus puños engarrotados—. Salvarme del hospital. Salvarme del *monstruo*. Me hiciste tantas, tantas promesas en esta casa y no pudiste cumplir ninguna.

Escucho a Allen balbucear, retroceder con la voz quebrada por el llanto. Quiero gritar, pedir ayuda, pero, ¿cómo si...?

¿Estás solo ahora?

—Esta casa. Esa habitación *me pertenecía* —dice ella—. Y ahora está llena de *él*, de un desconocido que se baña en sangre como lo hacía mi esposo. ¿Por qué lo has permitido?

La falsa Grace desciende hasta que sus pies amoratados tocan el suelo de baldosas, su camisón, que en realidad es una bata de hospital, se mece como si una corriente de aire traspasara la cocina.

—¿Por qué lo permites *aún*? —insiste a la vez que me mira con una sensación que remueve y descarna una herida envenenada. Segundos después escucho un siseo; el ruido del hierro que raspa contra el concreto.

Me aparto de un salto antes de que Allen clave la afilada punta del picahielo en mi espalda.

—¡Allen, detente! —exclamo, pensando en que quizás ha sido dominado por la influencia letal de aquella cosa. El joven vuelve a arremeter contra mí y esta vez me veo forzado a detener el objeto en el aire.

Él abre los ojos de par en par, atónito al ver mi garra de hueso alrededor del arma. Allen suelta un sorpresivo rodillazo a mi abdomen, para luego echar a correr hacia Grace.

Pero se detiene a media cocina, su furor detenido de súbito por algo que le hace llevarse las manos a los oídos: el tronar profundo y horripilante de una trompeta.

Por un segundo, pienso que es el estruendo lo que agita mi cuerpo, pero al ver que los gabinetes comienzan a abrirse y cerrarse con violencia me doy cuenta de que la casa es la que tiembla entera.

Allen y yo nos tambaleamos, mientras pedazos de la cocina comienzan a caer por todas partes; las puertas se salen de sus bisagras y los vidrios crujen como dientes enfrentados. Pero por encima del estruendo, se oye un alarido en una de las habitaciones de arriba.

—¡JOHANNA! —exclamo al reconocer la voz de mi hermana.

Cuando la ventana sobre el fregadero se resquebraja en miles de pedazos, me lanzo sobre Allen. Lo tumbo boca abajo contra las baldosas para protegerlo con mi cuerpo de la lluvia de cristales en tanto él intenta zafarse de mi agarre.

—¡Grace, Grace! —grita él hacia la falsa mujer que, al contrario del resto de la casa que aún se sacude, parece sobrenaturalmente inmóvil. Nos mira con sus ojos tristes y terribles, su cuello torcido de nuevo por la marca de una soga invisible.

Allen me da un codazo en la mandíbula y el dolor vibra en mis dientes con la suficiente fuerza como para que el muchacho se me escape de las manos.

—¡ALLEN!

La puerta de la cocina se abre de par en par y Tared intercepta a su hermano en la carrera. Lo agarra del cuello de su chamarra y lo echa hacia atrás de un tirón justo antes de que pueda alcanzar al fantasma.

—¡Suéltame, suéltame, Grace, Grace! —grita Allen como un lunático en los brazos de su hermano, quien corre a acuclillarse a mi lado.

Tared mira al espectro de Grace, pero sólo para buscar el brazo que sostiene el cuerpo desde su nuca. Éste se alarga desde el fregadero, en señal de que la criatura ha entrado por las tuberías.

Observo horrorizado cómo docenas de brazos rodean la casa desde afuera, metidos como lianas por la chimenea, los desagües y las cañerías, invadiendo las entrañas de la construcción como una tenia.

Julien y Johanna bajan en estampida por la escalera.

—¡TARED! —grita Nashua, quien entra por la puerta principal en su forma parcialmente transformada de oso, seguido de un Hoffman que no para de disparar a diestra y siniestra. Y cuando distingo entre el claroscuro a quienes atormentan a todo Comus Bayou, contengo las ganas de enloquecer yo también.

Mamá Tallulah títere se desliza por el barandal, arrastrada por otro brazo infernal, las plumas blancas dispersas por todas sus ropas. Justo como el día en el que fue asesinada.

—¡Devorada! ¡He sido devorada! —exclama—. ¡Me traicionaste, te llamé "hijo" y me traicionaste!

Un falso Padre Trueno, quien claramente perseguía a Tared desde el bosque, entra a la casa por la misma puerta que él. Todos los vidrios revientan al mismo tiempo y más brazos blancos entran por cada ventana.

Y en la lejanía de los árboles, logro distinguir el terrible llanto de un bebé.

Comus Bayou intenta reunirse, pero la construcción tiembla desde sus cimientos infestados por aquellas extremidades y la trompeta que no para de tronar.

De pronto, algo hace crujir el techo, algo que comienza a aplastarlo y a estrujar las paredes como un monstruo que cierne sus tentáculos.

Grietas parten los muros. Las cornisas se despedazan. La llave del fregadero revienta para dar paso a un chorro desesperado y los pisos se abren debajo de nosotros como bocas hambrientas.

La casa entera comienza a colapsar.

—¡NASHUA! —grita el lobo por encima del pánico colectivo—, ¡llévate a Allen!

El hombre oso se lanza hacia nosotros y agarra al chico por la chamarra; éste grita a todo pulmón ante la feroz apariencia del errante, quien, sin más, lo toma bajo su brazo y echa a correr hacia la puerta lateral de la cocina.

Julien y Johanna parecen incapaces de enfrentarse a la figura de los abuelos, tanto que ni siquiera han podido transformarse, por lo que Hoffman, quien no parece afectado por las ilusiones, se ve obligado a arrastrarlos hacia otra de las salidas.

—¡¿Por qué me has hecho esto, Tared?! —chilla el espectro de Grace, pero el hombre lobo no mira una sola vez al cuerpo de quien pretende suplantar a su esposa. En cambio, me alza en brazos y corre hacia la sala al encontrar la puerta de la cocina ahora bloqueada por un fragmento de techo.

Los brazos intentan entorpecer su camino, pero él los embiste uno tras otro hasta que, de un salto, cruza uno de los ventanales rotos. Tared rueda por la nieve protegiéndome con su cuerpo. El frío entra a raudales a mis pulmones, pero no queda tiempo ni para temblar.

El devorapieles rodea la propiedad a zancadas hasta llegar a las camionetas, estacionadas detrás del garaje, y me sube a la cabina de su *pickup* con el parabrisas y el cofre ya partidos por una viga caída, mientras que Hoffman toma el control de la suburban negra. Nashua es el último en resguardarse, puesto que primero sube a un aterrorizado Allen a mi lado.

El oso ni siquiera termina de cerrar la portezuela cuando Tared ya ha metido reversa. Y cuando el vehículo se pone en marcha hacia la carretera, es entonces cuando consigo *verla*.

Una Marionetista gigantesca, encaramada en el tejado como una araña, sus largas patas alrededor de toda la casa como si fuese una mosca sondeando su trampa.

Las paredes, la escalera, el porche. En segundos, la construcción se derrumba a trozos, aplastada por la fuerza y ferocidad de aquellas extremidades.

—¡NO, NO, GRACE! —Allen se lanza sobre mí para alcanzar el volante. Y al hacerlo, el vehículo da un peligroso giro por la grava congelada.

—¡¿Pero qué carajos estás haciendo?! —exclama el lobo, quien intenta mantener el control del vehículo.

—¡Regresa, regresa, Grace está aún en la casa!

Tared lo aparta de un fuerte empujón que lo estrella contra la puerta. Allen lo mira atónito, pero no es el golpe lo que lo deja sin habla. Es ver que las uñas de su hermano ahora son largas garras oscuras.

El lobo ni siquiera parpadea. Tan sólo acelera, acelera y acelera hasta que el grito de aquella trompeta se funde con el amanecer.

CAPÍTULO 53
UNA PARTE DE LA VERDAD

La suburban llega primero a la zona de descanso de la carretera, mientras que nosotros estacionamos segundos después en medio del terraplén.

Y sólo cuando el zumbido escandaloso del motor de la camioneta roja se apaga, dejándonos con el traqueteo herido del radiador, por fin me atrevo a mirar de reojo a Allen.

El chico está pegado a la puerta con los ojos abiertos de par en par y las manos tan crispadas sobre el asiento que algunas uñas le sangran. Su presencia se siente como un revólver en la sien, aun cuando me pregunto si el hombre lobo a mi lado no pensará de mí de la misma manera.

Huritt. Allen. El monstruo de hueso. Una pesadilla en bucle.

Los segundos transcurren como una cuenta regresiva hasta que Julien desciende de la suburban para acercarse a nosotros con un abrigo de plumón bajo los brazos. Llega a la ventanilla y se lo entrega a Tared.

Me sobresalto como un conejo cuando el lobo me coloca la prenda sobre los hombros. Me toca los brazos, la espalda y el pecho para ponérmelo como si no tuviese miedo de que saltase a abrirle la garganta.

—¿Hay alguien herido? —pregunta Tared a Julien.

—No —responde mi hermano con un tono que me hace pensar que su respuesta no es del todo verdad—, ¿qué hay de ustedes?

Tared me pasa el brazo alrededor del cuerpo y me presiona contra su costado para que deje de tiritar a causa del frío que se cuela por el parabrisas.

—Estamos bien, pero no creo que la camioneta vuelva a encender —dice el hombre lobo a la par que señala hacia el cofre partido—. ¿Cómo van de gasolina?

—No creo que lleguemos hasta Winsconsin, habrá que detenernos en una estación pronto —aquello me hace girar la cabeza. ¿*Winsconsin? ¿Por qué estamos yendo hacia el este?*—. Es una suerte que hubiésemos guardado las maletas en la camioneta anoche. Olvidamos el celular, pero al menos se salvó la bolsa de Johanna con los mapas y el dine...

—Llévame a casa.

La voz de Allen corta la de Julien como un delicado cuchillo. Tared mira al chico y aprieta los labios, como si de pronto recordara que tiene encima este *pequeño* problema.

—Allen...

—¡DIJE QUE DES LA JODIDA VUELTA Y ME LLEVES A CASA!

Un par de aves emprenden el vuelo graznando desde la línea arbolada, lo que hace a Hoffman y Johanna salir alarmados de la camioneta. La tensión es tanta que me pregunto si el hermano de Tared será consciente de que, en estos momentos, él representa un peligro casi tan grande como yo.

—Lo siento, no podemos volver, Allen —sentencia el lobo con gentileza—. Sé que lo que has visto es difícil de creer, pero te prometo que...

—Grace estaba allí —dice él—. *Y tú la abandonaste.*

Pienso en *ella*, en la mujer que levitaba sobre el río en Montana, en la cocina de Tared, y el miedo irracional de volver a ser dominado por el monstruo de hueso me carcome.

Allen se baja de la camioneta.

—Maldición —masculla Tared, para luego salir disparado detrás de él. Y, como era de esperarse, lo alcanza antes de que siquiera ponga un pie en la carretera.

—¡SUÉLTAME, SUÉLTAME! —el menor de los Miller comienza a gritar a todo pulmón, mientras los demás presenciamos en silencio la manera desesperada en la que intenta zafarse del agarre de su hermano—. ¡Ayuda, AYUDA!

—Por Dios, ¿quieres dejar de gritar? —se queja Nashua, quien baja de la camioneta embadurnado en sangre y con la piel de oso amarrada en su cintura.

Ante semejante imagen, la quijada de Allen tiembla como un cascabel para luego volver a tirar inútilmente.

—Allen, por favor, necesito que te calmes...

—¡La dejaste, la dejaste morir otra vez en esa casa!

—¡Escúchame, por favor! —insiste Tared, a punto de perder la paciencia—, aquello que viste no era...

—No te atrevas a decirme qué vi y qué no, ¡porque todo lo que sí vio Grace esa noche resultó *ser verdad,* maldito mentiroso!

Su mirada baja hacia las garras de Tared puestas alrededor de su antebrazo; cinco dedos cubiertos hasta los nudillos de fino pelo plateado. El lobo suelta al chico y éste abandona todo intento de escapar cuando descubre que Hoffman ahora está a unos metros detrás de él, dispuesto a detenerlo si decide dar un paso más.

Me bajo de la camioneta de puntillas, como si estuviese a punto de entrar a un campo minado. Y cuando Allen se estruja la cara para llorar de rabia, comienzo a sentirme terriblemente mal por él.

—El ataque, el lobo, *tú...* —continúa—. Grace vivió sus últimos meses podrida en un psiquiátrico, suplicando que alguien le creyese, que detuviese a la criatura que la había atacado. Y tú te aprovechaste de eso para irte y *salvar tu maldito pellejo.* ¡Te largaste como un cobarde!

Nashua aprieta los puños y da un paso hacia los Miller, pero Tared levanta la mano para que no se acerque; el lobo permanece impertérrito, recibiendo cada acusación como una merecida puñalada.

—No sólo la dejaste morir —dice, rabioso—. Tú dejaste que ella muriese *en tu lugar.*

Johanna levanta la mirada, muy despacio, hasta posarla sobre el devorapieles. Tiene los ojos enrojecidos y frágiles, como si una ilusión dentro de ella se hubiese roto como un cristal.

La *decepción* que siento emanar de mi hermana demuestra que en nuestro mundo nada sale impune. Ninguna herida cierra sin dejar tras de sí una horrible cicatriz.

¿Ése es el hombre al que te has entregado, del que tan orgulloso dices estar?

El miedo de que la infección se apodere de mí me pide que me quede quieto, pero me acerco y alargo mi mano de hueso hacia Tared. Despacio, toco sus garras, apenas un roce, y en vez de rechazarme, él busca mis dedos de hueso y los estrecha.

Él. Lo único que tengo por seguro en este mundo.

Nosotros. El lobo y el brujo. El monstruo y el otro monstruo; un gesto que Allen Miller observa con profundo resquemor.

—Me fui porque tenía la esperanza de que Grace entrara en razón —dice Tared, alentado por el suave apretón de mi mano—. Intenté hablar con ella innumerables veces, y cuando eso no funcionó, sentí que alejarme sería la única forma en la que se sentiría a salvo. Creí que así encontraría la manera de entender que yo no era esa bestia que, ella juraba, quiso matarla esa noche. Pero eso no sucedió, Allen. Y Grace *decidió* quitarse la vida sin que yo pudiese hacer nada al respecto.

El corazón se me encoge ante el dolor que percibo en el hombre que permanece a mi lado, al verlo escarbar en esa herida vieja e inolvidable que parece haber florecido de nuevo como una rosa terrible.

—¡Debiste volver! —exclama el chico con la cara inundada en lágrimas rabiosas—, ¡pudiste haberla salvado si hubieses dicho la maldita verdad!

—¿En realidad crees que no pensé en hacerlo, Allen? —replica Tared—. ¿Piensas que hubo un momento en el que no quise decir a todos que lo que ella había visto era cierto, a pesar de que no tenía ni la más remota idea de cómo demostrarlo? Admito que tuve miedo, pero también admito que, de todas maneras, *no tenía opción*. No, Allen, tú piensas que soy un asesino, un desgraciado egoísta, pero la verdad es que no tienes idea de lo que *sí soy* ni de cómo funciona el mundo al que pertenezco —dice, para después alzar su brazo libre hacia mis hermanos.

El chico contempla de nuevo nuestras garras, la piel de animal en la cintura de Nashua, el parabrisas partido de la camioneta; sus pupilas se dilatan, su respiración se acelera como si reviviese una vez más todo lo que sucedió en la casa.

Lentamente, se pone de rodillas en el suelo para enterrar la cabeza entre las manos. Allen Miller descubre, de la más desafortunada manera posible, que el mundo nunca ha sido como él pensaba.

—No te culpo por odiarme, Allen —continúa Tared, consciente de la impresión por la que pasa su hermano en esos momentos—. Pero tú y yo sabemos que la única manera en la que ella volvería a la normalidad era si me veía muerto o encerrado en una jaula. Y si eso no pasó fue porque, aunque no lo creas, *yo tampoco merecía morir.*

Escucho a Hoffman encender un cigarrillo, aspirar el humo y arrojarlo al aire. Luego, el agarre del lobo se afloja dolorosamente bajo mis dedos, como si decir aquello le hubiese costado la mitad de sus energías.

Por mi parte, no puedo evitar pensar en por qué Grace se aferró tanto a no escuchar a Tared, a no darle una oportunidad de explicarse; una pregunta que tal vez no me corresponda formular en lo que me queda de vida.

De pronto, un coche se acerca. Nashua se agazapa detrás de la camioneta y la tensión en Comus Bayou se eleva como la luz de la mañana entre los árboles. Vemos al vehículo pasar junto a nosotros y, por un segundo, temo que Allen se levante y empiece a vociferar para detener al conductor.

Pero él, en cambio, se queda quieto sobre el pavimento. Pensando. Perdido en su cabeza hasta que decidimos que no podemos quedarnos más.

¿Tienes miedo...?

Sí. Tres veces sí.

Allen no vuelve a gritar, o siquiera a pronunciar palabra alguna. Ni cuando entre Hoffman y Julien lo suben a la camioneta, ni en los siguientes dos días que nos toma viajar a toda prisa desde la frontera de Minnesota hasta el noreste del país.

Hacia la costa de Nueva Inglaterra. Hacia Massachusetts.

TERCERA FASE

UN MONSTRUO
CRECIENTE

El libro rojo de ~~Laurele~~ Elisse (II)

¿Qué desgracia tiene que ocurrir para aceptar que tu familia ha tocado fondo?

¿Descubrir que nunca terminarás de desenterrar sus mentiras? ¿Darte cuenta de que no eras el único que colgaba del Atrapasueños como un hilo roto?

¿O enterarte de que están dispuestos a esconder un cadáver por ti?

Porque nunca imaginé que la razón por la cual la casa de Tared parecía deshabitada cuando desperté era porque habían ido a sepultar el cuerpo de Huritt.

Durante mi inconsciencia, el hombre lobo lo ocultó en el bosque con la ayuda de Hoffman y Nashua. Por otro lado, Johanna y Julien se habían quedado conmigo. Uno para echar las cosas en la suburban y la otra para vigilarme, tal vez, aunque después hubiese sido sacada de la habitación gracias al hipnotismo de la Marionetista.

El ataque fue tan repentino que no hubo tiempo para limpiar demasiado la evidencia, pero después de la destrucción de la casa de Tared, todos esperaban que no hubiese hecho falta.

Y mientras el errante bisonte me contaba todo esto en una de las pocas paradas que tuvimos en la carretera, mi cargo de conciencia se duplicó. No sólo la muerte del antropólogo recaía ahora sobre mis hombros, sino que ellos se habían convertido en cómplices de mi crimen.

Julien intentó recordarme o, más bien, convencerme, de que Huritt era consciente del peligro al que se exponía cuando vino a buscarme. Incluso me contó que cuando llamaron a Debbie para informarle lo que había pasado, poco antes de la destrucción de la casa, ella tampoco me culpó de nada. Egoístamente, agradecí que el celular se hubiese perdido durante el caos. El aparato tenía guardado el teléfono de Lía, y aunque eso significaba que ya no teníamos manera de volver a contactarla, me evitaría el averiguar si Huritt tenía familia o gente que lo esperaba en casa.

El saberlo me habría sido insoportable. Porque, por más terribles que fuesen las sombras de nuestra nación, una parte de mí se sentía responsable cuando éstas afectaban a humanos inocentes. A personas que sólo querían ayudar.

Que el monstruo de hueso me engañara para luego tomar el control de mi cuerpo era lo más peligroso que nos había sucedido hasta ahora, y más porque lo había logrado gracias a la *espada*.

La piedra filosofal había llevado mis fuerzas al límite, drenado mi magia y mis energías lo suficiente como para dejar libre el camino a la criatura y a sus voces. Y aun cuando todos entendiesen que nada de lo que había pasado era mi culpa, me había convertido en una trampa mortal, a la espera del momento preciso para volver a activarme.

Ante tal amenaza, aislarme emocionalmente de los demás parecía inevitable, y no sólo por culpa o vergüenza, sino porque mi familia también se estaba... fragmentando.

Tantas mentiras, tantos engaños; no sólo mis vínculos con Comus Bayou no se habían restaurado todavía, sino que los que había entre ellos también estaban más frágiles que nunca. Apenas y se hablaban, inclusive Johanna y Julien se mantenían distantes la una del otro, y eso que nunca habían tenido un problema entre ellos. O al menos, no que yo supiera. ¿No soportaron la traición de Muata, el silencio de Nashua, de Tared? ¿O les pesaba demasiado el cadáver de Huritt y no tenían el valor de decírmelo?

El Atrapasueños se deshilaba ante mis ojos con tanta rapidez que me aterraba pensar cuánto tardaría el monstruo de hueso para aprovecharse de esa situación, y más cuando Tared, la única persona cuyo lazo conmigo seguía siendo lo bastante fuerte como para apoyarme, no podía hacer mucho en estos momentos. No cuando tenía un asunto tan delicado del cual ocuparse.

Allen.

Sin saberlo, el chico se había convertido en una amenaza casi tan grande como esta nueva Marionetista, porque ya no sólo existía el temor a que el menor de los Miller se diese a la fuga o nos delatase, sino que el hecho de, en nuestra situación, tener a un humano tan vulnerable era un factor de riesgo que Tared había decidido asumir por su cuenta. Así, se mantenía a su lado todo el tiempo, para intentar explicarle lo que somos y cómo es nuestro mundo.

Pero siempre fue como dirigirse a un muro, a alguien sumido en una especie de catatonia. Tanto así que una parte de mí temía que hubiese enloquecido por el trauma.

Y eso significó que, en los días que nos tomó llegar hasta la costa de Nueva Inglaterra, mi contacto con el hombre lobo se volvió nulo. No tuvimos la oportunidad de hablar sobre todo lo que sucedió aquella noche, de la destrucción de su casa... y de Grace.

Ella se me apareció en el río, en Montana. Y eso significaba que, en algún momento, Tared había soñado con ella. Y quizá, tal como lo había sido Adam, la mujer era...

Una manifestación de sus más hondos deseos.

Al final, la única razón por la cual todo esto no me hizo explotar fue el temor de volver al punto de partida, tal como lo habían anticipado mis pesadillas. Y como una palabra que repites una y otra vez hasta que pierde sentido, así me parecía ya la idea de poner distancia y volver a huir de Comus Bayou y de Tared.

Ese terror que me hizo escapar de Nueva Orleans con tal de no lastimarlos se había vuelto más real que nunca, pero si ya habíamos tocado fondo juntos, ahora sólo nos quedaba nadar hacia arriba de nuevo o ahogarnos bajo el hielo; evitar que la espada me debilitara hasta que encontrásemos la forma de ayudarme.

La decisión terminó de asentarse en mi cabeza al conocer cuál era la razón por la cual ahora nos dirigíamos con rumbo al este: antes de que le abriera el pecho en canal, Huritt logró decir a los demás que si bien él no tenía clara la verdadera identidad del monstruo de hueso, había escuchado rumores sobre la existencia de un Atrapasueños ubicado en la costa de Massachusetts, especializado en resolver problemas de nuestro mundo y que, a estas alturas, parecía nuestra única oportunidad de alcanzar una resolución.

La noticia podría haber sido maravillosa de no ser porque lo primero que sentí fue un miedo muy... complejo, porque *por fin* empezaba a ver un patrón.

Barón Samedi, Nueva Orleans y Comus Bayou. Jocelyn Blake, Utah y Red Buffalo. Ambos Atrapasueños, de alguna forma, estaban conectados con la magia de aquellos seres enviados por mi Mara para asesinarme. Y ahora se cruzaba en mi camino una tercera familia, un grupo de errantes que habitaba en Lynn Woods, una reserva justo a las afueras de Salem, el lugar donde ocurrieron aquellas ejecuciones por brujería hace cientos de años.

Satanismo, demonología, pactos diabólicos; no tenía idea de cómo llamar a esta nueva magia que me acechaba, y la certeza de que algo terrible podría llegar a pasarles también a estos errantes se sumó a mi larga lista de culpas. Pero decidí no dar un paso atrás, ya que, probablemente, ese Atrapasueños ya estaba destinado a ser un engranaje más en esta máquina de pesadillas de la misma manera en la que Red Buffalo había sido atado a la alquimista hacía más de veinte años.

Ya no teníamos más opciones. Si habían hecho falta cuatro hombres para detenerme ante la locura del monstruo de hueso, quizá la siguiente vez ni siquiera eso sería suficiente.

Algo muy dentro de mí me decía que Massachusetts era la parada final del camino.

Y que iba a ser *mi última oportunidad*.

CAPÍTULO 54
EL MENSAJERO

Después de observar a Benjamin Lander por tanto tiempo me di cuenta de que una de las pocas cosas que le provocan placer es el *silencio*.

Pero no cualquier tipo de silencio.

No aquel producido por la serenidad o la armonía, sino el silencio que sólo la violencia puede ejercer. El de una bestia asfixiada en una de sus trampas, el de un hacha después de segar una cabeza de golpe… Pero el mutismo que ha prevalecido en su campamento en los últimos días no le gusta para nada, porque no es el de una vida que se derrama entre sus manos, sino el de algo mucho más peligroso: el silencio del luto.

Y Benjamin sabe muy bien que cuando los hombres prolongan demasiado la pena y la dejan anidar dentro de ellos, ese temible silencio se convierte en resentimiento. En revuelta. *En traición*.

Oculto en el claroscuro de su remolque, el líder trampero hace nudos en una cuerda gruesa. Y aunque parece demasiado concentrado en su tarea, es consciente de los susurros que rasgan el aire de afuera, afilados como la aguja que unió las dos tiras colgantes de lo que alguna vez fue su mejilla, marcada por una garra de plata que todavía resplandece en sus pesadillas.

Benjamin Lander sabe que aún le queda carne de cañón, más de quince hombres y un puñado de niños, si se le antoja, pero sus tramperos están cansados de la matanza. De la humillación. De la precariedad del invierno y de perseguir bestias que renacen una y otra vez de sus cuerpos hechos jirones.

—Errantes... —musita y la palabra suena en mis oídos como una sentencia.

El Inquisidor observa las libretas puestas en pilas sobre el suelo del vehículo, documentos que su gente terminará por exigirle que entregue a quien sea que esté dispuesto a escuchar si no encuentra la forma de apaciguarlos.

Al final, Benjamin decide interrumpir los nudos para levantarse y salir de su vehículo. Sólo unos pasos lo separan de la gran camioneta de carga, así que lo único con lo que tiene que lidiar es con el momentáneo resplandor de las hogueras que serpentean por el campamento sembrado en el bosque.

Lo veo llegar hacia la caja de metal, comprobar las abolladuras de sus golpes inútiles y retorcer la cuerda entre sus manos como si fuese un cuello. Y en cuanto quita el candado y abre una de las puertas, el chirrido de gruesas cadenas lo recibe junto con el hedor de la paja podrida.

Sin siquiera arrugar la nariz, el Inquisidor sube a la camioneta de un salto.

Un par de sombras se agitan en una esquina de la caja, ahogan sus gritos, se agazapan una contra la otra. Pero en vez de ir a callarlas con un par de puntapiés, la bestia se dirige primero hacia el enorme congelador colocado contra una de las paredes; un féretro viejo y lo bastante grande para albergar doscientos kilos de carne.

O un cuerpo entero, si se le antoja.

El viejo levanta la pesada tapa y la luz blanquecina se esparce hacia todos los rincones para revelar a quienes llevan meses encerrados en la oscuridad de aquella caja de carga.

Dos niños, abrazados el uno contra el otro, vestidos apenas con sucios harapos y cobijas agujereadas para cubrir sus esqueléticos cuerpos, prendas que han usado desde el día en el que fueron arrebatados de los brazos de su padre.

Sus llantos, sus siluetas y sus cuerpos maltrechos me llenan de vigor al imaginar la manera en la que lamería las heridas de mi creación si fuese herido de la misma manera.

Benjamin Lander ignora a los infantes y se concentra en lo que hay dentro del congelador: un pico y unas garras envueltas en plástico, ambas apartadas ya para un buen postor. Las alas, las plumas y el tórax se vendieron hace mucho tiempo, y lo único que le molesta es no haber encontrado huevos cuando abrió el vientre del águila gigante, la cual era claramente una hembra.

Pero lo que en verdad busca es lo que yace debajo de aquellas partes: un cadáver con un agujero de escopeta en su pecho, con sus alas blancas replegadas detrás de su espalda como un polluelo dentro del cascarón.

Tiene los ojos ya hundidos y cubiertos por una capa de escarcha, los labios azules y la piel blanca como el papel ante el resplandor del foco, tan tieso por el frío que ni siquiera ha comenzado a descomponerse.

Benjamin Lander mira unos instantes el cadáver de aquel perpetuasangre y decide que no vale la pena ponerse a embalsamarlo frente a su gente. Porque lo que él necesita ahora mismo no es que lo observen, sino que recuerden que todavía deben *temerle*.

Es por eso que deja abierta la tapa del congelador y va hacia el fondo del camión, con aquella cuerda bien asida en los puños. Los niños gritan, chillan y se pegan como sanguijuelas contra la pared cuando se inclina sobre el más grande de los dos.

De un solo movimiento, el hombre tira de su cabello y lo levanta del suelo.

—¡No, déjalo, deja a Misha, déjalo! —exclama el otro abalanzándose contra su pierna, pero el hombre patea directo a su barriga con la punta de su bota de casquillo. La criatura se retuerce de dolor y gimotea al punto del vómito, debilitado por los largos meses de inanición.

—¡Enola, no! —exclama el otro, pero pronto es asfixiado por la cuerda del trampero, puesta alrededor de su cuello con la maestría de más de cincuenta años de ahorcamientos.

El monstruo comienza a arrastrarlo como a un perro fuera de la camioneta. Sin misericordia, lo arroja en la nieve. Baja del camión y el movimiento hace que la puerta que está del lado del congelador se entrecierre.

En algún momento se le ocurrió que tal vez sería mejor matarlo rápido, con una bala, tal vez, pero no, eso era demasiado compasivo; por otro lado, quemarlo vivo sólo lograría arruinar el pelaje si la bestia, presa de la desesperación, decidía transformarse en medio de las llamas.

Así que escoge la rama perfecta.

Arrastra al niño detrás de sí un par de metros más, hacia el bosque. Y ante aquello, el más joven grita, suplica y lloriquea inútilmente, porque Benjamin Lander no conoce la conmiseración.

Arroja la cuerda sobre el árbol en un lanzamiento perfecto. Ésta cae frente a su cara como una serpiente desenrollada y luego se inclina a ajustarla un poco más alrededor del cuello del niño, que no deja de luchar.

Después, encuentro mucho placer en la forma en la que Benjamin Lander le propina una brutal bofetada, más para descargar su estrés que para contener a la víctima. Y el pequeño, al sentir el ardor en la mejilla y comprender el destino que le aguarda, deja de llorar. Se sorbe la nariz y levanta la barbilla hacia su hermano pequeño, cuya silueta sólo puede ver gracias al resplandor del congelador.

—Ya no tengas miedo, Enola —le dice al tiempo que yergue su espalda esquelética—. Papá nos espera del otro lado.

El trampero extiende la herida en su mejilla al hacer una mueca, quizás al recordar el rostro del hombre que aguantó ocho balas antes de caer muerto en aquella casa del rancho Red Buffalo. Afianza la cuerda y, tras un gemido ahogado, los pies del niño se elevan del suelo de un tirón.

El cuerpecito se retuerce en el aire mientras los gritos de su hermano resuenan en las paredes del vehículo. El hombre cuenta los segundos, preguntándose si esas criaturas mitad bestia se ahogan igual de rápido que los humanos, si sus cuellos tienen la misma cantidad de vértebras.

El chico patalea en el aire, su cara muta del moreno al bermellón, Benjamin Lander aprieta más la soga y…

—¡Alto!

El trampero deja caer al niño de golpe, quien tose una y otra vez ante la repentina entrada de aire frío a sus pulmones. El viejo se lleva la mano a la cintura y desenfunda sin dudar, porque está seguro de que esa voz no pertenece a ninguno de sus hombres.

Aquello vuelve a llamarlo, un eco bajo y grueso que retumba como si proviniese de un ataúd.

Y esta vez, no es un perfume lo que inunda mi celda, sino un brillo blanco y prístino.

—¿Dónde estás, maldito?

—Oh, hijo mío, no extiendas tu mano sobre el muchacho ni le hagas daño —el Inquisidor mira de un lado al otro, hasta que se da cuenta de que el llamado proviene de sus espaldas. Se vuelve hacia el niño dentro de la caja, quien súbitamente ha dejado de llorar. Ahora tiene los ojos abiertos de par en par, y mira aterrorizado no hacia el trampero, sino a algo que está oculto tras la puerta frente al congelador.

Podría llamar a sus hombres, pero gritar no le es propio, así que da unos pasos hacia el vehículo y abre aquella puerta despacio empleando para ello la boquilla de su arma. Y al mirar hacia dentro, por primera vez en su vida, Benjamin Lander se queda sin aliento.

El perpetuasangre Sammuel está sentado dentro del congelador, mirándolo con aquellos ojos hundidos y el pecho exhalando vapor caliente a través del agujero de escopeta. Sus alas blancas aletean con suavidad en el aire frío, libres por fin de las ataduras.

El cadáver ladea la cabeza y las vértebras de su cuello, congeladas después de meses en esa caja, se tuercen como si se las hubiese quebrado con el movimiento.

Y entonces le sonríe.

—Hola, Benjamin.

CAPÍTULO 55
UN BOSQUE LIMINAL

Al llegar a la reserva forestal Lynn Woods, la esperanza de terminar por fin con esta pesadilla se vuelve trizas cuando la encontramos completamente cerrada.

A medida que Tared sitúa la suburban en un cajón del solitario estacionamiento, observo con más claridad el cartel que prohíbe la entrada a los senderos. También hay una gran cantidad de pilas de nieve repartidas por los bordes, en señal de haber sido ya acumuladas hace tiempo por barredoras.

El lobo apaga la camioneta y da vueltas al mapa que compramos durante una parada en la carretera. Se pasa una mano por el cabello y resopla.

—No me cabe duda —dice—. Es aquí.

—¿Será por otro acceso? —sugiere Julien, quien toma el mapa desde el asiento de atrás.

Al alargar el cuello y verlo yo también, mi primer pensamiento es que este lugar no es precisamente el más adecuado para que se esconda un Atrapasueños.

La reserva de Nueva Orleans era inmensa, lo suficiente como para albergar ríos, pantanos y propiedades privadas como la aldea de Comus Bayou, pero el bosque Lynn Woods es más bien un parque público de gran tamaño, con rutas de senderismo, lagos pequeños e inclusive un campo de golf.

—Maravilloso —resopla el detective—. La maldita debe haber cerrado por la temporada.

Al escuchar aquella posibilidad, todos nos quedamos quietos, como si esperásemos que la barra de hierro que cierra la entrada a la propiedad se levantase sola y nos dijese que no hemos cruzado todo el país en vano.

La agobiante sensación de que la camioneta se vuelve más y más estrecha me obliga a poner una mano en la puerta.

—¿Elisse? ¿A dónde...?

Me guardo la pistola de Lía en la pretina de los pantalones y bajo de un salto fuera de la camioneta. Cruzo el estacionamiento a paso rápido y rodeo la barra para entrar a los senderos de caminata.

Y al hundirme varios centímetros en la nieve, me cierro con más fuerza la chamarra de lana, puesto que el invierno de Nueva Inglaterra es tan atroz como el de las montañas del oeste.

El cansancio se acumula bajo mis ojos, la nube alrededor de mi cabeza no hace más que espesarse.

Tared es el último en bajar, justo detrás de su silencioso hermano. La mirada del lobo se levanta sólo lo suficiente para tensar nuestro vínculo, y luego regresa hacia el chico. Siempre alerta. Siempre vigilante.

Te está evitando. Y lo sabes.

Giro hacia un par de letreros marrones clavados en un árbol, los cuales indican que hay dos rutas a seguir desde este punto de la reserva: a la izquierda, el amplio circuito de caminata, de aproximadamente seis kilómetros; y a la derecha, un sendero estrecho y pedregoso que guía hacia algo llamado *Dungeon Rock*.

—¿Y ahora qué? —pregunta Nashua.

—Diría que probemos con el agradable y seguro circuito —dice el bisonte—, pero eso de "La Prisión de la Roca" suena feísimo, así que de seguro es por allá.

—Dios, ¿no puedes tomarte las cosas en serio por una vez? —musita mi hermana.

—¿Y tú no puedes dejar de ser tan amargada?

—¡Lo haría si dejaras de portarte como un tonto!

—¡Basta ya! —ordena Tared—. No quiero escuchar una palabra más. Harán que nos descubran.

Julien y Johanna se lanzan una mueca de hastío y obedecen a regañadientes, irritados debido a lo poco que han podido dormir. Al igual que todos nosotros.

Pero lo peor de todo es que, seguramente, mi hermano tiene razón.

Estoy a punto de ponerme en marcha hacia la pendiente que lleva a Dungeon Rock cuando me percato de que Allen sigue detrás del cancel, reticente a cruzarlo.

—Esto es una estupidez.

Sus palabras hostiles nos sorprenden, puesto que son las primeras que pronuncia desde que salimos de Minnesota.

Supongo que es buena señal, porque significa que no se ha vuelto loco, todavía.

—Si lo que quieres es quedarte aquí *solo*, con gusto te atamos a un árbol —dice Hoffman a la par que enciende un cigarro—. Pero ninguno de nosotros volverá para ayudarte si la cosa que destruyó la casa de Miller aparece.

Allen tensa la mandíbula, pero al final, decide pasar por un lado del cancel.

En el fondo, siento algo de lástima por el chico. No es más que un humano indefenso, traído contra su voluntad a la brutalidad de nuestro mundo. Es normal que sienta miedo.

Yo también lo tuve la primera vez.

Con esto en mente, comenzamos a adentrarnos en el camino, siendo el crujido de nuestros pasos nuestra única conversación durante un tiempo. Puedo sentir la tensión sobre todos nosotros, atentos a cualquier ruido que nos haga sacar las garras o salir corriendo de vuelta a la camioneta.

Aunque, en mi caso, no es sólo por el miedo a un ataque de las Marionetistas. Es este bosque, tan distinto al de Montana y al de Minnesota.

El primero se sentía de un blanco sucio y claustrofóbico, estéril y asfixiante. El de la casa de Tared era precioso y prístino, de pinos verdes y cielos oscuros empapados de estrellas, un lugar del que no querría marcharme nunca.

Pero aquí, todo se percibe quieto a la vez que inquietante, con su neblina espesa y sus árboles de troncos altos y flacuchos cual patas de garza. El viento susurra entre las hojas, pero más allá de eso, no se escucha el menor atisbo de vida silvestre.

Es como un corazón a la espera de su siguiente latido; un pasillo entre una puerta y la siguiente; como entrar a un bardo del plano medio y quedarte atrapado en un escenario de concreto detenido en el tiempo, tan desconocido y a la vez tan…

Nuestro.

Me viene a la mente lo que Julien nos contó en el camino sobre los infames Juicios de Salem. Dijo que hacía poco más de trescientos años, alrededor de doscientas personas habían sido acusadas de brujería en dicho pueblo puritano,[12] de las

---

[12] Grupo protestante descontento con la naturaleza de la Iglesia anglicana.
Fue el primer grupo de colonos que invadieron para poblar la costa de lo que hoy en día se conoce como Nueva Inglaterra.

cuales diecinueve fueron colgadas al pie de una colina y un puñado más murió en prisión, sin mencionar a un hombre llamado Giles Corey, quien fue aplastado hasta morir por las pesadas rocas que sus verdugos colocaron poco a poco sobre él para obligarlo, fútilmente, a declararse culpable.

Tal vez por eso es que este lugar me parece tan opresivo, así como me hace preguntarme si estas brujas que he estado viendo no serán una especie de espíritus vengativos relacionados con dichos juicios, manipulados por mi Mara para obedecer a su maldad.

Cuando el camino se convierte en la pendiente de un monte, Julien rompe de nuevo el silencio:

—Oye, flaco, ¿qué harás cuando todo esto termine?

La pregunta me toma desprevenido, puesto que el final de esta pesadilla es una cosa que veo aún muy lejana. Para mi sorpresa, la respuesta no tarda en venir a mi cabeza.

—Iré a buscar a mi padre —respondo, sin dudarlo—. Es la razón principal por la que vine a este país, después de todo.

—Espera, ¿quieres decir que no volverás a Nueva Orleans con nosotros? —pregunta Johanna con desconcierto.

Hoffman observa de reojo a Tared, quizás en espera de alguna reacción de su parte, pero el lobo no mira en nuestra dirección. De hecho, se ha separado unos metros de su hermano para acercarse a una de las orillas del camino, hacia donde se extiende una densa arboleda.

—¿Huelen eso? —pregunta, y todos nos giramos en busca de aquello que el devorapieles ha percibido.

Nashua arruga el entrecejo.

—¿Fuego?

De súbito, mi percepción del bosque se deforma, y esa realidad tenue, ese espacio liminal, es interrumpido por algo que atraviesa el aire helado; la vibración de una serpiente viva e invisible, una sensación que busca escabullirse por mis venas.

El monstruo de hueso susurra la palabra antes de que ésta logre salir de mi boca:

Magia.

—Tared...

Todos y cada uno de mis nervios se paralizan cuando escucho la voz rota de Allen.

Miro hacia atrás y casi puedo sentir el corazón del hombre lobo detenerse.

El chico tiembla de arriba abajo mientras sus ojos se humedecen del terror, porque justo ahora está *flotando* en el aire, a casi un metro sobre el camino.

—T-Tared —repite, con el brazo extendido hacia su hermano.

Como si tuviese un lazo invisible amarrado en la cintura, Allen es atraído hacia la colina a toda velocidad.

CAPÍTULO 56
GOLMÁ

—¡A llen! El grito de Tared nos hace reaccionar. Y en un segundo, todo Comus Bayou se lanza detrás de él y su hermano, quien grita con toda la fuerza de sus pulmones.

El empinado camino se vuelve un sendero de rocas y escalones de piedra congelada, pero el lobo sortea cada obstáculo con desesperación al ver que la silueta de Allen empieza a fundirse con la niebla.

De pronto, escuchamos *risas*. Carcajadas femeninas de cuyas bocas emisoras vi masticar carne humana y cuyos cuerpos vi cabalgar, en mis pesadillas, un miembro del grosor de una espada.

Van a comérselo vivo...

No, ¡NO!

—¡Suéltenlo, malditas sean! —les digo.

El sendero desaparece cuando por fin llegamos a la cima de la colina. Y allí, nos topamos con dos piedras gigantescas que forman una estrecha gruta entre ellas. No hay ningún letrero que lo señale, pero no me cabe duda de que es Dungeon Rock.

Tared casi enloquece cuando encontramos a Allen justo en medio del claro. Está boca arriba, su espalda curvada como un sable y los ojos vueltos hacia el cráneo.

Al alcanzarlo, sostengo del brazo al devorapieles, quien también lucha contra su imperiosa necesidad de correr hacia el chico, porque es más que obvio que esto es una trampa.

—¡Allen, Allen! —llama, pero su hermano parece estar sumido en una especie de trance.

Todos los demás desenfundan sus armas y apuntan con las mirillas hacia los largos árboles que flanquean la colina. Por mi parte, busco por todos lados el *vínculo*, ese hilo de magia invisible que conecta a Allen con quien sea que lo esté embrujando, pero no logro encontrar nada. *¿Qué demonios está...?*

—Siempre parece que pesan tan poco, ¿verdad?

Una puerta de metal se abre justo en medio de las dos rocas, tan oxidada que se escucha como uñas que rasgan un pizarrón.

Instantes después, *ella* sale de la oscuridad, descalza sobre la tierra helada y con un delicado vestido mancillado por la suciedad. Su cabello blanco cae suelto sobre su espalda y su rostro joven exhibe una sonrisa amplia, casi infantil.

—Eres *tú* —mascullo—. ¡Eres una de esas malditas brujas!

Todo Comus Bayou apunta sus armas en dirección a la aparente mujer, cuya imagen me cuesta alinear con la de la criatura terrible que sostenía un espejo negro en mis visiones.

Ella ensancha aún más su sonrisa.

—Qué grosero usar un tono tan despectivo considerando que tú también eres *un maldito brujo*. Pero lo que sí me ha tomado por sorpresa es encontrarte tan bien acompañado —dice con los ojos entornados hacia mi familia—. Vamos a cambiar eso.

Con las palmas hacia arriba, ella comienza a levantar los brazos.

Al instante, los cuellos de mis hermanos y Hoffman se ponen rígidos, con sus brazos atenazados contra sus costados. Y, al igual que Allen, sueltan sus armas y se elevan en el aire. Mi corazón casi se detiene cuando la bruja aprieta poco a poco los puños y comienza a asfixiarlos.

—¡No, detente! —grito al ver que los rostros de todos se tornan rojos por la falta de aire.

—¡ALLEN! —la chica ladea la cabeza, sorprendida, cuando Tared tira de las muñecas de su hermano para intentar liberarlo, siendo el único que no ha caído bajo la influencia de su magia.

—Qué interesante...

Ella mira hacia Allen, o *detrás de él*, en realidad, y asiente.

Segundos después, el hombre lobo es arrojado de bruces contra el suelo, como si algo gigantesco lo hubiese aplastado. Otra presencia cae de golpe a mis espaldas y enrosca algo invisible alrededor de mi cuello para impedir que vaya a socorrerlo; una soga hecha de magia.

La cuerda me tira de frente y me arrastra hacia la bruja, pero sólo hasta que tengo a la mujer lo bastante cerca como para distinguir las salpicaduras de sangre en su vestido, para darme cuenta de que no toda esta magia emana directamente de ella, rompo el amarre con un solo movimiento de mi mano de hueso.

Mi guante se desgarra en el acto y ella suelta un gemido cuando salto para embestirla. Cae de espaldas sobre el empedrado, pero mi familia aún se asfixia en el aire y los huesos de Tared comienzan a crujir.

—¡Libéralos, desgraciada! —demando, desesperado al no entender de dónde surge la energía que los tiene prisioneros.

La chica me da un rodillazo en el vientre con la suficiente fuerza para dejarme sin aire. Me hace rodar en el suelo pero, al aplastar mi pecho con su rodilla, refunfuña como si la hubiese puesto sobre una plancha de hierro caliente.

—¿Pero qué diablos tienes allí?

Ella grita cuando le clavo las garras en la pantorrilla y le abro la carne hacia abajo en canal. Me la quito de encima de un empujón, pero me agarra de las ropas para impedir que escape. Un puñetazo de ella en mi cara, un rasguño contra su costado; forcejeamos en el suelo como un par de animales hasta que, súbitamente, detenemos nuestra pelea.

Nos miramos, con los ojos abiertos de par en par, y giramos la cabeza al escuchar que algo se acerca por el bosque; el sonido de una hoja de metal blandiéndose en el aire.

—Por la Grieta... —murmura la bruja mientras el poco color en sus mejillas desaparece.

Comus Bayou cae en picada hacia el suelo y boquean como peces fuera del agua. Allen sale de su trance y grita, dolorido, a causa del impacto, pero parece tan ileso como los demás, quienes ya se arrastran en busca de sus armas.

Aparto a la mujer de un codazo y me levanto para socorrer a Tared.

—¡¿Están todos bien?! —pregunto, mientras el lobo gruñe por lo bajo. Le cuesta un poco moverse, pero parece que huesos y articulaciones están intactos.

Sin temor a darnos la espalda, la bruja cojea al lindero del bosque con la vista clavada hacia el lugar de donde proviene aquel sonido que ahora se estrella contra las rocas, los troncos, la maleza, como si buscase reducir la reserva a jirones.

Me basta respirar profundo para percibir de nuevo aquel olor de pesadilla.

—Mierda, ¡la Marionetista!

Todos nos retraemos hacia el centro del claro para rodear como un muro al hermano de Tared. Luego, aquel sonido letal se detiene, precedido por un silencio mortuorio.

El aire helado vibra. El olor se intensifica. Escucho a Allen jadear.

—¡CUIDADO!

Tared empuja al chico varios metros a lo lejos, justo cuando una enorme hoja de metal corta el suelo donde estaba parado.

Y al mirar hacia la cosa que nos ha atacado, mi primer pensamiento es que hubiese preferido que fuese la Marionetista.

Aunque son muy similares, tanto que no me cabe duda de que pertenecen a la misma clase de monstruo, este ser sólo posee ocho brazos alineados en su torso masculino, los cuales sostienen largos clavos, cinceles y navajas como si fuese una manifestación de la terrible diosa Kali, todo del mismo metal blanco que su máscara.

La criatura arranca el arma del suelo y la levanta por encima de su cabeza, un cuchillo similar al de un carnicero, tan grande y pesado que bien pudo rebanar en dos a Allen tal como el Rebis hizo con Dallas. Tiene también una piel amarrada en su cintura y la mirada fija en la bruja, quizá porque percibe la sangre fresca que emana de su herida pero, al erguirse, tuerce el cuello hacia mí.

Tan grande como un puño, un ojo dorado se abre enorme en medio de su halo de hueso.

Me echo a un lado cuando el monstruo salta como un insecto, impulsado por sus piernas raquíticas. Los demás se dispersan, en tanto Tared arrastra a su hermano consigo, quien comienza a gritar al ver a todos los errantes transformarse.

Desenfundo la pistola de Lía y la criatura bloquea mi disparo con el largo de su cuchilla, lo que me obliga a retroceder hacia Dungeon Rock.

Nashua se abalanza y clava los colmillos en su hombro, pero el demonio tuerce un brazo hacia atrás en un ángulo rápido e imposible para intentar apuñalarlo con un picahielo. El hombre oso retrocede y deja una hilera de dientes sobre su piel quebradiza, mientras que el resto de los brazos de la bestia se dedican a bloquear con pasmosa maestría todas las balas que Comus Bayou dispara hacia él.

—¡No dejes que *Golmá* te toque! —me grita de pronto la bruja, pero es demasiado tarde.

Con la rapidez de una flecha, aquella cosa me arroja uno de sus clavos, mientras que yo apenas logro esquivarlo lo suficiente para que se entierre en mi clavícula y no en el corazón.

El impacto es tan poderoso que me tumba de espaldas con la potencia de una escopeta.

—¡No! —Julien embiste al monstruo de un cabezazo, y lo hace volar varios metros por el aire.

Tirado sobre la tierra, percibo que el clavo apenas ha logrado entrar un par de centímetros en mi carne, aunque está tan firme y recto sobre mi pecho como si me hubiesen clavado una lanza.

Pero no es la herida en sí lo que me deja inmovilizado, sino algo increíblemente doloroso, casi incendiario, que brota de la punta de metal para reptar como una serpiente de lava por mis venas.

—¡ELISSE! —el lobo deja a su histérico hermano a un lado de Hoffman, quien dispara sin cesar hacia la bestia huesuda mientras que el resto de Comus Bayou la rodea para tratar de contenerla.

Tared se lanza de rodillas a mi lado. Mi cuello se tensa como una cuerda, mi espalda se arquea ante la terrible sensación de quemarme por dentro.

Siluetas y rugidos colisionan sobre la nieve, dentelladas de hierro chocan contra pelo, garras y balas, pero pronto pierdo la orientación de todo lo que sucede a mi alrededor, porque el clavo empieza a enterrarse por sí solo en mi cuerpo, abriéndose paso a través del hueso y la carne como una inyección letal.

Y cuando la espada ruge, furiosa por la proximidad de aquel veneno candente, descubro que lo que busca es *alcanzar mi corazón*.

—¡Aléjate! —ruge el lobo a la bruja, quien se acerca a zancadas hacia nosotros.

—¡Es el hierro blanco! —exclama ella—. ¡Hay que sacárselo antes de que lo mate!

Al escucharla, el lobo intenta remover el clavo con sus manos, pero no logra moverlo un solo centímetro. De hecho, el aire se le escapa cuando ve que éste se hunde todavía más.

—¡No puedo arrancarlo! —grita desesperado.

Déjame quitárnosla...

—¡Vayan a Dungeon Rock, rápido! —responde la chica, quien escapa muy apenas de una cuchillada—. ¡No tienen alternativa!

A sabiendas de que es verdad, el lobo decide obedecer.

—¿Pero qué demonios...? —masculla cuando, al poner sus brazos bajo mi espalda y rodillas, le cuesta muchísimo despegarme del suelo, como si mi peso se hubiese triplicado.

Hace un nuevo intento y, con un esfuerzo tremendo de sus rodillas, el devorapieles consigue levantarme.

—¡Vamos, Elisse, resiste! —exclama, para luego llevarme hacia la caverna.

¡Déjame salir para quitárnosla!

—¡Inanna, ayuda! —suplica la bruja a nuestras espaldas. Luego, escucho el sonido de la carne fresca abrirse por el filo de una hoja. Gotas rojas salpican el aire. Más y más gritos de dolor.

Veo el cuchillo cernirse sobre el hombro de Tared, pero el monstruo lanza un grito como de una trompeta al ser embestido por algo blanco y enorme, una figura poderosa que lo lanza hacia atrás.

El lobo no se queda a observar. Me aprieta contra su corazón y corre hacia la prisión lo más rápido que puede, donde otra mujer ya nos espera, alguien a quien sólo distingo como una sombra. Cuando Tared se agacha para seguirla por una estrecha puerta de metal entre las rocas, el llamado del plano medio llega hacia mí, desesperado por salvarme.

Bajamos por una inclinada escalera de madera que cruje debajo de nosotros, mientras que la invocación del mundo de los espíritus se torna tan intensa que siento como si me arrancase de estos brazos. Percibo cómo él se abre paso con tremenda dificultad a través de un estrecho túnel de roca, su pecho como un tambor contra mi oído mientras el clavo está cada vez más y más cerca de mi corazón.

Instantes después, escucho el sonido del agua a los pies del errante; una poza al final del pasadizo de piedra.

—Aférrate a él con todas tus fuerzas —le ordena la mujer para luego colgar en su cuello un péndulo de cristal que rebota contra mi mejilla. El lobo estrecha más sus brazos a mi alrededor y, como si saltase de nuevo hacia la catarata de Stonefall, se deja caer al agua, al plano medio, sumergiéndonos en la oscuridad.

El tránsito dura un abrir y cerrar de ojos. En menos de un segundo, emergemos en un agua tan fría que trozos de hielo flotan en la superficie. Muros de piedra oscura y mohosa se ciernen a nuestro alrededor, estrechos y alargados hasta terminar en una boca redonda a varios metros sobre nuestras cabezas.

Y al ver la luz gris y neblinosa al final del túnel comprendo que estamos dentro de un pozo.

—¡Ilya, Ilya! —escucho a una voz desconocida gritar.

Tared jadea, desesperado por mantenernos a flote, pero mi peso tira de él hacia abajo como un ancla. Aprieta los colmillos y me acuna con uno solo de sus brazos.

—¡Ayuda! —grita, abriéndose como una estrella para empezar a subir por las paredes—. Aguanta, Elisse, ¡aguanta! —me suplica, desesperado al ver que me asfixio debido al dolor.

Su pelaje chorrea a cántaros y sus garras se doblegan por cargar todo mi sobrenatural peso, pero el lobo sube, sube con tremenda tenacidad, y cuando está a un metro del borde, alguien nos saca del pozo de un tirón.

Después, no distingo con claridad qué más sucede. Mis extremidades se ponen aún más rígidas, escucho más gritos y el sonido de una puerta que se abre.

Soy arrojado de golpe sobre una superficie aterciopelada, un tapete, quizá. En mi delirio, veo a un anciano desnudo y de piel grisácea sentado en el techo, que me observa con brillantes ojos escarlata.

Y cuando una mano extrae con un movimiento el hierro de mi pecho, el grito de dolor que suelto me deja por fin volver a respirar.

CAPÍTULO 57
A WITCH IS A WITCH IS A WITCH[13]

Al caer sobre mi regazo, una cascada de flores me hace levantar la cabeza hacia Johanna, quien se balancea sobre un taburete.

Ella intenta alcanzar los racimos de ruda, romero y demás variedades que cuelgan de las vigas del techo como estalactitas. Y una vez que logra recolectar un puñado, procede a triturarlo dentro de un mortero de madera con algo de su propia saliva.

—¿Cómo te sientes? —pregunta mi hermana cuando entierro las manos sobre la cama para soportar el frescor del ungüento. Se supone que la herida de aquel clavo debía haber sido una penetración, un agujero abierto en la carne, pero ahora no es más que una quemadura bajo mi clavícula.

—Con frío —musito, aun cuando "jodido" fue la primera palabra que me vino a la cabeza. El dolor merma, pero muy despacio, como si la tibieza de la pequeña chimenea de hierro frente a mí evaporara el veneno a través de mis poros.

—Vale. Deja que vaya a buscarte otra toalla seca —la chica se limpia con un trapo y va hacia el cuarto de baño a un

---

[13] "Una bruja es una bruja es una bruja."

costado de la habitación, de donde ha estado sacando agua para tratarme. Quisiera detenerla y decirle que lo que en realidad quiero es ver a Tared, pero supongo que el lobo aún debe estarse quitando la piel en alguna parte de esta... casa.

Giro hacia el buró de boticario que está al lado de la cama, y observo con recelo el clavo de hierro blanco que descansa encima, con mi sangre seca en él.

En cuanto Johanna me lo sacó del pecho, fui traído a esta habitación de muebles cuarteados y muros de tapiz oscuro, con secciones de ladrillo expuestas por el paso del tiempo. Y eso, junto con el resabio a humedad y la iluminación a base de candelabros de cera, me hace saber que estamos en un sitio muy antiguo, tanto que siento como si me hubiesen arrojado varios siglos en el pasado.

Mi hermana regresa y retira la toalla, ya fría, de los hombros para ponerme una seca, tan caliente que parece recién secada al sol. Cosa extraña, puesto que la noche ya se asoma por las pequeñas ventanas de madera.

—¿Cómo está Allen? —musito, y ella sacude la cabeza, preocupada.

—Más callado que nunca, aunque fue muy difícil calmarlo al principio. Ellas tuvieron que ayudarnos con eso.

Ellas.

Estrujo la toalla entre mis dedos.

—¿Qué hay de ti?

Johanna sonríe y hace un aspaviento.

—Con un par de cortes por aquí y por allá, pero estoy ilesa, al igual que todos los demás. Tú fuiste quien se llevó la peor parte, como siempre —asegura con un suspiro.

—¿Y Tared? —pregunto, y puedo ver cómo su sonrisa pierde vigor.

—Sólo se lastimó un poco las manos, pero estará bien —dice—. Me costó mucho arrancarte de sus brazos hace rato, estaba tan histérico que temí por un segundo que su ancestro hubiese enloquecido de nuevo...

Mientras explica todo esto, mi hermana no me mira a los ojos ni una vez, lo que crea una tensión que jamás había existido entre nosotros. Ella todavía me trata con su usual gentileza, incluso en la extenuante situación en la que nos encontramos, pero con quien ya no es la misma es con el devorapieles. Todavía se dirige a él con sumo respeto y obedece de forma tajante sus órdenes, pero es ya tan mecánica en ello, tan distante, que resulta obvio para todos que las cosas ya no son las mismas entre ellos dos.

Y no sé cómo sentirme al respecto.

Qué alivio, ¿verdad? Que esa zorra por fin te haya quitado los ojos de encima...

—¿De qué diablos está hecha esa cosa? —apunto con la barbilla hacia el clavo.

—No estoy segura —responde—. Fue muy confuso cuando te lo saqué. Pensé que estaría envenenado o algo así, pero sólo es...

—No, querida. Eso no es un simple clavo de hierro.

Miro hacia la puerta de la habitación, que en ningún momento escuchamos abrirse, y me yergo al ver a la mujer parada en el umbral.

Aparenta la edad de Irina y tiene las facciones marcadamente andróginas: mentón cuadrado, cejas duras en un rostro muy hermoso, equilibrado, con labios gruesos y pómulos cincelados. Su cabello negro que cae lacio hasta por debajo de su cintura y su piel muy morena me haría pensar que se trata de una mujer algonquina, pero hay una familiaridad en la forma de sus ojos rasgados que me recuerda en realidad el aspecto de alguien proveniente de Eurasia.

Me incorporo al reconocer su voz profunda y la silueta de su largo vestido negro, porque sin duda, es la mujer que guio a Tared a través de la caverna.

—Mi nombre es Inanna —dice—. Y como ya debes de haberte dado cuenta, soy una contemplasombras.

Sí, eso fue obvio desde el momento en el que puso un pie en la habitación, pero no sólo por su aspecto o la intensa magia que emana, la cual ha despertado de inmediato los apetitos del monstruo de hueso, sino por la sensación punzante de varios pares de cuernos que recorren de forma invisible mi piel; la presencia indudable de un ancestro bajo su carne.

—Me alegra ver que te estás recuperando, y más rápido de lo que esperábamos —continúa—. Tengo entendido que un *Martillo* provoca un dolor muy semejante a que te quemen vivo por dentro.

—¿Martillo?

La mujer camina hacia el clavo y descompone ligeramente la perfecta simetría de sus facciones al observarlo.

—Su poder, su peso, la forma en la que parece envenenarnos con fuego para doblegarnos; durante milenios, el hierro ha sido un metal utilizado por muchas culturas como un amuleto contra la magia, por lo tanto, "Martillo" es como llamamos a todos los objetos que están hechos con este peculiar hierro blanco, el cual sólo puede ser forjado en las entrañas del plano medio.

Antes habría dicho que no tenía idea de que algo así pudiera crearse en un mundo inmaterial como el de los espíritus, pero al recordar el laboratorio de Jocelyn Blake, la idea termina de calzar.

—Ya. Supongo que eso explica por qué era tan doloroso.

—Sí, para *nosotros* lo es —dice—, pero para los seres que no comparten nuestra naturaleza mágica, no es más que un hierro común. Es por eso que tu hermana fue la más adecuada para sacarlo.

—Con "nosotros" quieres decir ¿los contemplasombras? —pregunto.

—*Brujas*, Elisse.

Retrocedo hasta tropezar con el pie de la cama, porque quien ha dicho eso es la chica de cabello blanco con quien nos enfrentamos en el bosque. Ella entra a la habitación dando pequeños saltos con su pierna ahora curada, aplastando las hojas y flores secas que han caído sobre el tapete con sus pies descalzos.

—Tú...

La joven se sienta a mi lado de un brinco y me muestra unas prendas que, definitivamente, no me pertenecen.

—Para ti —dice con una sonrisa.

Ladeo la cabeza, ahora con curiosidad. Al tener a la bruja tan cerca, libre de la adrenalina del enfrentamiento, por fin logro percibir el olor de su ancestro: una intensa esencia a agua profunda y sal.

—Oh, pero qué tonta soy. Mi nombre es Hela —exclama—. Aunque ya nos presentamos de una forma mucho más divertida, ¿verdad?

Ante mi semblante hostil —porque la imagen de toda mi familia siendo asfixiada en el aire no me causa ni un poco de gracia—, ella alza ambas manos:

—Uy, parece que todavía muerdes.

—Porque yo todavía no estoy seguro de que ustedes no lo hagan —reviro.

—Calma, cariño, que eso mismo podríamos decir nosotras de ti —una tercera mujer se manifiesta en la habitación. Parece ser la mayor, tiene la piel olivácea y el cabello oscuro y rizado; y el espeso aleteo que percibo dentro de ella me da una pista de la apariencia de su ancestro.

Cuando el monstruo vuelve a rugir, por fin lo comprendo. Si todas me parecían tan "apetitosas" en mis visiones no era por su magia, sino porque eran *errantes*.

—Yo soy Caligo —se presenta—. Y estas reinas del drama son mis hermanas.

Las tres brujas se reúnen en torno a nosotros como si contemplasen una hoguera, lo que me hace percibir algo muy peculiar: a primera vista, todas parecieran tener los ojos negros, pero no es así. Lo que pasa es que sus pupilas están tan dilatadas que del iris de Caligo sólo queda un casi imperceptible anillo avellana, mientras que el de Hela es de un azul turquesa como el mar. Inanna, en cambio, es la única cuyos ojos sí parecen ser completamente oscuros.

Eso sólo significa una cosa: que las tres, todo el tiempo, a todas horas, ven tanto el plano humano como el plano espiritual.

Johanna pone su mano sobre mi brazo erizado por la fascinación.

—Elisse, ellas *son* el Atrapasueños que estábamos buscando —susurra.

Sacudo la cabeza, confundido. No me cabe ninguna duda sobre Hela y Caligo, pero Inanna...

—No lo entiendo, ¿tú eras la Hembra Cabría de mis visiones? —pregunto, porque no logro encajar la macabra imagen de aquella criatura con la inmensa belleza de la contemplasombras.

Inanna sonríe, sin ofenderse ante la rudeza de mi tono.

—No te preocupes, que tú tampoco eras un príncipe encantador en la mía —dice Hela en su lugar, divertida.

—Se lo explicaremos todo más tarde, Hel, porque si nos quedamos un minuto más aquí, esa cosa que tiene dentro terminará por comernos —dice Caligo al apuntar hacia mi mano de hueso.

—Mientras esperábamos a que Tared y tú saliesen del pozo, les contamos todo lo que pudimos sobre la situación —dice Johanna, un poco apenada—. Sé que hubieses querido hacerlo tú, pero...

—No vale la pena preocuparse ya por eso, querida —interviene Inanna—. Por ahora, dejemos que Elisse descanse un momento, porque estoy segura de que todavía nos queda mucho por hablar, ¿cierto?

Sin más, le hace una señal a la errante coyote para que las acompañe a la salida.

Las brujas. La hoguera. El cruce de caminos. ¿Acaso todo lo que vi en mis visiones era mentira?

La quemadura en mi clavícula, cuyo dolor sí que es bastante real, me hace por fin preguntar:

—Pero, ¿qué eran esos *demonios* que nos atacaron en el bosque?

Inanna se detiene como si acabase de escuchar una blasfemia. Y después, despacio, gira la cabeza para mirarme sobre su hombro.

—Esos no eran demonios, Elisse —dice en voz queda—. Eran *ángeles*.

CAPÍTULO 58
UNA PREMONICIÓN ENGAÑOSA

Con sólo poner un pie fuera de la habitación, me queda claro que, si bien este lugar es tan extraño como la tienda de Laurele o la casona de Jocelyn, es de una naturaleza diametralmente distinta.

El cuarto donde me recuperaba está situado en el primer piso, al fondo de un corredor con los muros llenos de tijeras clavadas al revestimiento, todas de distintos tamaños, modelos y antigüedad. Algunas tienen manchas y salpicaduras en los filos, sustancias cuya naturaleza no me apetece detenerme a apreciar.

Llego al vestíbulo de la casa y observo el tapete persa, el diván de terciopelo negro y las peculiares pinturas que cuelgan de las paredes de tapiz resquebrajado, con marcos muy ornamentados y retratos sombríos de personas en el campo, en cocinas y en distintos lugares comunes, las caras contorsionadas por un pesar.

Pero de todo esto, algo en particular llama poderosamente mi atención.

Me acerco a la enorme puerta de la entrada, maciza y negra como el ónix, cuyo dintel está coronado por una guirnalda de diminutas escobas de paja y canela. Levanto mi mano de hueso y acaricio el texto grabado a punta de cuchillo sobre la superficie:

I am He! the Bornless Spirit! Having sight in the feet: Strong, and the Immortal Fire!

I am He! The Truth!

I am He! Who hate that evil should be wrought in the World!

I am He, that lighteneth and thundereth.

I am He, from Whom is the Shower of the Life of Earth:

I am He, Whose mouth ever flameth:

I am He, the Begetter and Manifester unto the Light:

I am He; the Grace of the World:

"The Heart Girt with a Serpent" is My Name![14]

Un poderoso escalofrío viaja desde mi garra hasta mi espalda cuando el texto vibra debajo de la palma de mi mano. Me pregunto qué clase de energía estará *conteniendo* esta casa, porque cada esquina, cada peldaño de la escalera, cada hoja de hierba seca que cruje bajo mis pies es...

Al escuchar voces familiares, voy hacia el otro lado del recibidor, al umbral que da paso a una sala.

---

[14] *¡Yo soy Él! ¡El espíritu no nacido! Vigilante a los pies: ¡Fuerte, y el Fuego Inmortal!*

¡Yo soy Él! ¡La verdad!

¡Yo soy Él! ¡El que odia que el mal sea forjado en el Mundo!

Yo soy Él, el que relampaguea y truena.

Yo soy Él, quien hace Llover la Vida en la Tierra:

Yo soy Él, cuya boca siempre está en llamas:

Yo soy Él, Creador y Medio de la Luz:

Soy Él; la gracia del mundo:

¡"El Corazón Rodeado por una Serpiente" es mi Nombre!

Allí, encuentro a mis hermanos sentados frente a la enorme chimenea, acompañados de Hela y Caligo. Ellos saludan con apenas un lánguido murmullo, mientras que Hoffman levanta la mirada un segundo, para luego regresar al periódico que tiene entre sus manos.

Siento una fuerte desazón al ver que el único Miller en el lugar es Allen, retraído en una butaca y con la mirada fija en la pintura sobre la chimenea. En ella hay varias mujeres de aspecto terrible congregadas alrededor de un macho cabrío,[15] quien está sentado a dos patas y con una corona de laureles alrededor de los cuernos. La sombría luna en el cielo nocturno mira cómo ellas ofrecen a sus bebés demacrados, una escena que me transporta de inmediato a mis visiones.

Pero ésa no es la única peculiaridad de este sitio.

Calderos de hierro abarrotan el robusto comedor de madera, llenos de pieles, plumas y cuernos. Cruces de distintos materiales cuelgan de las paredes, algunas rotas, otras invertidas, mientras que platos desperdigados en los muebles rebosan de huesos y dientes que no parecen haber pertenecido precisamente a animales.

No me extraña que Allen esté así de asustado. El lugar alberga tantas cosas sombrías que hasta el persistente olor a hierbas podría resultar asfixiante, pero si algo me sorprende más que las crueles taxidermias encerradas en frascos dentro de los gabinetes al fondo de la cocina, es que absolutamente todas las cosas me parecen… útiles, incluso hasta lógicas, como si supiese a la perfección qué hechizos podría hacer con cada una de ellas, algo que jamás me había sucedido frente a un objeto mágico.

---

[15] "El aquelarre" (1798), Francisco de Goya.

Quiero decir, a lo que parecen ser *cientos de ellos*.

—¿Pasa algo, Elisse? —pregunta Johanna al verme tan embelesado.

—En la casa Blake, la magia se escondía detrás de las paredes —explico—. Jocelyn la ocultaba para que yo no pudiese sentirla, pero aquí circula con tanta fuerza que es como si me revolcara una ola.

—¿Te está haciendo daño? —pregunta Julien.

—No. Es decir, es muy abrumador, pero a diferencia de la mansión o la tienda de Laurele, la magia de aquí parece *ofrecer* en vez de *arrebatar*. No sé si me explico.

Nashua asiente despacio.

—Aunque no puedo sentir lo mismo que tú, entiendo a lo que te refieres —dice—. La cabaña del abuelo era... muy similar.

Con pesar, me doy cuenta de que ya no recuerdo bien qué tipo de pertenencias tenía el anciano en sus aposentos, quizá porque el Elisse de aquel entonces no se imaginaba siquiera que algún día sería capaz de apreciar el potencial de aquellos objetos que en su momento le parecieron incomprensibles.

O tal vez, he pasado tanto tiempo en la oscuridad que terminé acostumbrándome a ella.

Cuando me percato de las miradas llenas de curiosidad de Caligo y Hela, me sonrojo hasta las orejas.

—Perdonen —musito—, no quise ser maleducado...

—Nada de eso, cariño —replica Caligo—. Es *natural* que te sientas tan cómodo aquí.

Miro hacia el predio de árboles espinosos que se asoman detrás de los ventanales, revelados por la luz de la luna creciente.

Otra vez, un bosque distinto a los otros, pero mucho más familiar, porque sin duda se trata de aquél presente en mis visiones.

—¿Dónde estamos? —pregunto con ansiedad.

—En ningún sitio que puedas encontrar en un mapa, Elisse.

Casi doy un salto al ver que Inanna entra a la sala acompañada de mi hombre lobo. Él lleva las manos vendadas y el cabello húmedo, en señal de que ya se ha dado un baño para quitarse los restos de su piel recién arrancada. Y aunque mi instinto me grita que me acerque a revisar sus heridas, me conformo con sólo verlo dirigirse hacia su traumatizado hermano, preguntándome cuánto tiempo más tendré que soportar esta tensión.

La magia de todo el lugar pareciera arrastrarse detrás de los pies de Inanna, quien toma asiento entre sus hermanas como una reina que entra a presidir una ceremonia.

—¿A qué te refieres? —pregunto—. ¿Ya no estamos en Massachusetts?

—Al contrario —dice Caligo—. Si los cálculos no me fallan, esta casa debe estar bastante cerca del centro histórico de Salem, aunque el bosque en sí abarca casi toda la ciudad.

La bruja cabría juega con el enorme anillo dorado que lleva en la mano izquierda, el cual exhibe un elaborado símbolo que no logro distinguir con claridad.

Al sentir mi confusión, ella levanta la mirada.

—Existen tres tipos de dimensiones por las cuales los seres vivos podemos transitar —comienza—: el plano humano, el plano medio y la muerte definitiva. Y, a veces, franjas delgadas entre un mundo y el otro se cruzan, se distorsionan y se entremezclan, creando espacios que terminan siendo parte de ambos.

—Como eso a lo que Elisse llama los "bardos" del plano medio, ¿no? —añade Johanna.

—Exactamente —continúa—. Los *bardos* son trozos del mundo espiritual que han sido modificados por la influencia del plano humano, un sitio sin familias regentes que puedan poner un orden al caos. Es por eso que, a veces, parecen copias extrañas de nuestra realidad.

Oh, sí. Mis queridos escenarios de concreto.

—Y luego, existen zonas como esta casa —dice Caligo—, lugares en los que el plano humano es el que se distorsiona bajo la influencia del plano espiritual. Es un sitio que existe en el mundo de los vivos y por el cual, si bien los seres comunes pueden habitar sin problemas, no se puede acceder sin ayuda de algún ser con magia.

—El pozo por el que cruzaste es nuestra salida y entrada de emergencia, uno de los tantos túneles del plano medio que hay en este bosque y que, en este caso, conecta esta casa directamente con Dungeon Rock—añade Hela—. El resto del tiempo nos limitamos a transitar por la niebla. Es menos engorroso, sobre todo con este frío.

Imagino que así fue como los demás pudieron llegar hasta aquí.

—Pero —dice Inanna de pronto—, por lo que me acaba de contar tu *consorte*, nuestra casa es lo que menos te interesa de nosotras, ¿verdad?

—¿Con... sorte? —la cara se me enciende de golpe al comprender que se refiere a Tared.

El lobo se inclina para entrelazar sus dedos.

—Como te mencioné, Inanna, alguien nos habló de ustedes —dice él, evadiendo con sutileza el difícil tema de Huritt, algo que todos han procurado no mencionar hasta ahora. Y menos frente a Allen—. Nos dijo que eran un Atrapasueños que se especializaba en ayudar a resolver... problemas complejos de nuestro mundo.

—Yo creo que lo que tu chico tiene es mucho más que un problema complejo, cariño —esta vez, la mirada de Caligo no se dirige hacia mi mano, sino a mi pecho.

—Y lo peor es que esto ha terminado afectándolas —replico un tanto desesperado—. Porque, por algo, ustedes y yo nos hemos encontrado en nuestras visiones.

—Lo que Elisse quiere decir es que más vale que tengan una jodida buena razón para habernos querido matar allá afuera.

—¡Hoffman, por Dios! —reprende mi hermana.

—Ah, sí. Lamento eso —dice Hela, despreocupada—. Pero teníamos nuestras razones. Además, fue muy interesante descubrir que somos mucho más divertidas en la cabeza de Elisse que en la vida real.

—¿Tú crees? A mí me parece que eres igual de indecente en todas partes, hermanita —añade Caligo y la aludida le responde levantándole el dedo medio.

Inanna lleva los ojos al techo.

—Pero, ¿qué fue lo que ustedes vieron? —pregunto—, porque debió de ser lo bastante malo como para que atacaran a lo que obviamente era una familia de errantes.

—No era tan obvio si consideras que aquello que llamas "Marionetista" puede viajar tanto a través de los sueños como tomar la forma y esencia de cualquier cosa —apunta Hela—. Y, en realidad, yo te vi sólo una vez, mientras intentaba observar una visión a través de mi espejo de obsidiana.

Arqueo las cejas al recordar que ella, efectivamente, sostenía aquel cristal oscuro delante de su cara durante mis pesadillas.

—Espera, ¿puedes tener premoniciones mientras estás despierta?

—Claro —dice—. Es mi *especialidad,* después de todo.

Mi sorpresa ante esto hace a las tres mujeres mirarse entre sí.

—Hela, perdona, pero ibas a contarnos tu premonición —interrumpe Tared, consciente de mi perplejidad.

—Uf, ¿seguros que quieren escuchar esto? —pregunta—. Porque les advierto que no va a ser bonito.

—Vamos, yo creo que pocas cosas pueden escandalizarnos a estas alturas —dice Julien, muy seguro.

Hela ladea la cabeza hacia Inanna y ésta asiente. La chica aplaude un poco, entusiasmada, y cruza las piernas sobre su asiento.

—De acuerdo. En mi visión, tú estabas acuclillado frente a una hoguera. Y tal cual te pasó a ti, tu apariencia era muy distinta a como eres en realidad —dice a la par que me escanea con la mano—. Tenías el cabello aún más blanco que el mío y llevabas una túnica sucia y desgarrada, además de que estabas superdemacrado. Yo me encontraba a varios metros de ti, pero podía escuchar con claridad los ruidos hambrientos de tu estómago a pesar de que ya te estabas alimentando de las tripas de... *alguien.*

Ella señala con la cabeza a Caligo.

—Retiro lo que dije —confiesa el bisonte con una mueca de asco.

—Después, pronunciaste tres frases que se me quedaron muy grabadas en la cabeza.

—Un monstruo para engañar a la magia —dice Inanna.

—Dos para despedazarla —continúa Caligo.

—Y uno más para revelarla —finaliza Hela—. Pero lo que más me llamó la atención fue la luna que tenías en lugar de corazón.

Entierro las manos en mi asiento, porque eso significa que ella no me vio a mí, sino al otro "yo" que también aparecía en mis visiones.

—Era muy grotesco porque también podía ver otro montón de corazones podridos moviéndose debajo —continúa—. Y cuando las llamas de la hoguera se avivaron, fue cuando me di cuenta de que *no venías solo.*

Johanna suelta un gemido que yo mismo hubiese querido dejar salir cuando Hela apunta con la cabeza hacia Tared.

El relato se ha vuelto tan denso que incluso Allen ha salido de su trance para mirar hacia acá.

—Uy, esto se va a poner bueno —dice Caligo, quien se recarga contra el respaldo de su silla.

—Un lobo plateado salió de entre las sombras, un animal gigantesco cuyas *dos cabezas* traían consigo el cadáver de Inanna. O más bien, cada una arrastraba una mitad de ella dentro de sus hocicos. La criatura dejó los pedazos del cuerpo a tus pies como una ofrenda. Y después de que probaras un poco del cuerpo de mi hermana, te tumbó de rodillas de un zarpazo y...

—¿Y? —pregunto, angustiado por la pausa.

Hela sonríe y entrelaza las manos sobre su vientre, deleitada ante las muecas de horror de todos los presentes.

—Una de sus cabezas cerró los colmillos sobre tu hombro y la otra sobre tus astas, las destrozó hasta llegar a tu cuello y luego *te montó* sobre el cruce de caminos.

El chirrido de una silla siendo arrastrada hacia atrás me hace dar un salto sobre la mía. Hoffman cruza a zancadas la sala, y abre la enorme puerta de la casa para salir.

Abochornado, bajo la mirada con tal de no ver cuál ha sido la reacción de Tared... o de Allen.

—El simbolismo era preocupante —dice Inanna, quien por fin rompe su mutismo—. El brujo acompañado del lobo es una de las figuras folklóricas más antiguas y peligrosas de la hechicería, ¿y qué presagio más oscuro que un hechicero terrible fornicando con un lobo hambriento por nuestra carne?

Mi respuesta se limita a ser un largo silencio.

—Bueno, como ya nadie tiene estómago para escuchar más detalles —interviene Caligo—, espero que ahora entiendan por qué nos pusimos en alerta. Y más cuando Hela nos dijo que la visión terminó al escuchar el grito de…

—Una trompeta —musito. Y esta vez, son los labios de las brujas los que se transforman en líneas rectas—. Inanna, ¿qué quisiste decir con que aquellas cosas que nos atacaron eran ángeles?

—¿Ángeles? —Nashua arruga la nariz—. Esas porquerías no se parecen en nada a los ángeles.

—No tienen un aspecto convencional, querrás decir —corrige ella.

—Espera —interrumpe Julien—. ¿No estarán hablando de ángeles "bíblicamente exactos"? ¿De esos que tienen ojos y anillos por todas partes?

—¿Te refieres a un Ofanim? —pregunta Inanna.

—O un bulo de internet,[16] como yo los llamo —susurra la rubia.

---

[16] Las criaturas conocidas como "Ofanim" son originalmente las ruedas de la carroza en la que Dios se aparece a Ezequiel en el libro canónico que lleva su nombre (1:15-21), pero no existe ningún libro oficial del Antiguo Testamento que haga referencia a que son propiamente ángeles. Dicha confusión se ha creado por la popularización de algunos textos bíblicos no canónicos como los Manuscritos del Mar Muerto.

—Yo no afirmaría eso con tanta ligereza, Hel —dice Caligo—, sabes muy bien que esas cosas se convertirán en lo que haga falta para arrancarnos el pellejo.

Esta vez no encuentro nada valioso qué aportar. Tal como Satanás, mi concepción de un ángel occidental no va más allá de niños alados y regordetes. Aunque, ahora que lo pienso, la alineación y la forma en la que los brazos de la Marionetista se movían eran muy similares a unas alas.

Inanna descansa la barbilla sobre sus manos entrelazadas.

—Las criaturas que nos han atacado tienen poco que ver con lo que van a encontrarse en una biblia, pero sí que tienen *todo* que ver con nuestro mundo. Y también con lo que Elisse nos vio hacer en sus visiones.

Me inclino hacia la bruja, lleno de curiosidad.

—Entonces, ¿qué tipo de ángeles son? —pregunto.

—*Deja que yo se lo explique, querida.*

Todo Comus Bayou se levanta de un salto al escuchar aquella voz, tan fuerte y clara que parece haber hablado justo al lado de nuestros oídos.

—¿Qué diablos ha sido eso? —exclama Nashua mirando a un lado y otro. Inanna juega una vez más con su anillo, para luego levantar la mirada hacia mí.

—De acuerdo —dice—. Es un tema viejo y complicado, de todas maneras, así que *ella* sabrá explicártelo mejor.

—¿*Ella*?

La bruja se pone en pie y alza una mano para apuntar hacia la salida de la sala.

—Ven, Elisse. Vamos a presentarte a nuestra Madre.

CAPÍTULO 59
TRÁNSITO

Innana nos guía hacia la escalera del recibidor. O, más bien, hacia el pasillo que hay debajo de ella, cubierto a ambos lados por un montón de llaves antiguas, tal como el corredor de las tijeras.

Ella se detiene y, después de observarlas por unos momentos, descuelga unas pequeñas y de color bronce.

—¡Pero qué...! —Allen retrocede de un salto cuando una puerta se materializa al instante en la pared.

Por mi parte, me cruzo de brazos y doy un paso para observarla.

—Ya veo. Las llaves funcionan como el sello que había en la trampilla de Jocelyn Blake.

—¿Eso significa que detrás hay un portal? —pregunta Tared e Inanna me tiende la llave como respuesta.

Hela dijo que este bosque tenía muchos túneles al plano medio. ¿Será acaso que cada llave conduce a uno distinto? Dudo un poco, pero termino por tomarla. La introduzco en la vieja cerradura y ésta se abre con un húmedo rechinar.

Para los demás no hay más que una simple pared de madera del otro lado, pero yo casi puedo sentir cómo mis pupilas se expanden cuando el umbral se convierte en una boca de absoluta oscuridad.

—Madre querrá hablar contigo a solas —dice Inanna—, así que nosotras nos quedaremos aquí arriba con tu gente.

—¿No puede subir ella? —pregunta Johanna, y mi sorpresa es grande cuando la bruja niega con la cabeza.

—¿Ella vive en el plano medio? ¿Cómo es eso posible? —cuestiono al recordar que una vez el propio Muata me advirtió sobre los peligros de pasar demasiado tiempo en el mundo espiritual.

—Cuando bajes lo descubrirás tú mismo, cielo. Pero ten cuidado. Hoy hay marea alta.

Un malestar me recorre ante la críptica advertencia de Caligo, pero aun así, decido poner la mano en el pomo.

—¿Estás seguro de esto, Elisse? —pregunta Julien sin poder disimular su preocupación—. Recuerda que siempre que entras ahí regresas con algo roto.

—*Ven, querido. Te estoy esperando* —dice aquella voz oscura y sedosa que brota de la pared como el humo.

—¿Quieres que vaya contigo? —pregunta Tared al escuchar aquello, lo que atrae la mirada curiosa de las tres brujas.

—Ni se te ocurra —espeto, indignado por la simple insinuación—. No vas a arriesgarte de nuevo.

—Pero…

—Tranquilo, señor lobo —dice Hela con una sonrisa—. Usted sólo preocúpese por tener el pelaje caliente para cuando su brujo regrese. Lo va a necesitar.

Tared tensa la mandíbula, indeciso, pero al final decide retroceder.

Me acerco al portal y escucho el sonido de algo que parece ser agua en movimiento.

Alguien suspira a mis espaldas, quizás uno de mis hermanos, agotado ante la idea de que, una vez más, no puede hacer otra cosa que esperar a que salga con vida de un agujero.

Contengo el aliento antes de dar un paso más, para luego desaparecer a través de la pared.

ℭ ● ◖ ○

La oscuridad, como era de esperar, es absoluta. Mis sentidos se encienden como una mecha y me quedo quieto, adaptándome a la sensación sofocante de las sombras, mientras que un intenso sabor a sal inunda de inmediato mi paladar.

—¿Hola?

Cuando sólo recibo como respuesta el sonido del agua lamiendo las paredes siento algo moverse encima de mí, un cordón metálico que cuelga como un cadáver. Lo atrapo con mi mano de hueso y jalo de él.

La luz sepia de un foco viejo revela un armario con las paredes hinchadas por una buena razón: la escalera en la que estoy parado desemboca hacia un sótano inundado hasta las vigas.

—*Vamos, pequeño. No tengas miedo.*

Para mi pesar, aquella voz que borbotea desde alguna parte del agua no hace más que inquietarme. La puerta por donde entré sigue allí, al igual que la llave de bronce en mi bolsillo, así que puedo dar media vuelta y regresar a la seguridad del mundo de los vivos si así lo deseo.

Pero, en cambio, introduzco un pie en el agua helada a la par que me pregunto si en algún punto de esta maldita odisea podré mantenerme seco más de un par de horas.

Con el temor de ser invadido por la letal migraña, uso sólo la magia suficiente para no morir congelado. Cada escalón se siente como una mordida en los huesos hasta que, al sexto, decido sumergirme por entero en la oscuridad.

CAPÍTULO 60
FRAGMENTACIÓN

A la casa de la niebla ha entrado un gusano. Una criatura sucia y rastrera capaz de reconocer cuando un corazón se encuentra repleto de veneno o de lujuria. Un ser tan egoísta, tan ambicioso, que fue el único monstruo en toda la casa que alguna vez, hace mucho tiempo, pudo escuchar el susurro de tu voz.

Pero si hay algo que le gusta más que saborear los secretos de un pecho podrido es ver a un hombre bueno quebrarse.

La criatura respira tan despacio que apenas podría saberse que está allí, con el cuello ligeramente torcido, mientras observa la manera en la que aquel devorapieles de cabello rojo empuña el cuchillo en la cocina, al fondo del comedor.

El errante contempla un pequeño cerdo puesto sobre la mesa, el cual no tiene mucho de haber sido sacrificado. Y algo dentro de la naturaleza inmunda del gusano le hace saber que si aquel hombre se ha ofrecido para prepararlo no fue por gentileza, sino porque necesitaba *apartarse* un momento, dejar de mirar a la cara a los suyos para no enloquecer.

Ya está cansado de ser siempre unos oídos que escuchan y nunca una boca que grita, tanto así que comienza a preguntarse si terminará partido en dos de seguir extendiendo los brazos alrededor de su familia para mantenerla unida.

Porque personas así, que prefieren mantener dentro lo que otros no temen escupir, son las que revientan con más fuerza.

La bestia rastrera pierde su interés en el bisonte y desliza la mirada hacia el otro devorapieles, aquél que siempre tiene la cabeza gacha, que se encorva a pesar de su tamaño. Es un ser que grita, que insulta y chasquea la lengua, pero que no sabe ya cómo mantener la barbilla arriba, castrado por una culpa que le pesa más que la ira.

Y el hermano... oh, lo dulce, lo exquisito que le parece el olor de ese hermano falso...

Pero, sin duda, los peores son los otros dos restantes. El humano y la curandera. El ciego y la egoísta. Tan heridos, tan hipócritas y, a la vez, tan resignados...

¿Por qué? ¿Por qué estos seres que parecen estar tan resentidos los unos con los otros insisten en mantenerse juntos, se pregunta el gusano? ¿Por qué se llaman "familia" si los separa el calor de la sangre, la desconfianza, el deseo por lo ajeno?

Quizá no saben estar solos, piensa. Quizá tienen miedo de descubrir que están tan hundidos en la mierda que no van a salvar a nadie. Que su búsqueda es estúpida, un callejón sin final.

Obsesión. Envidia. Venganza. ¿Es cierto todo esto que percibe la criatura sucia? ¿O es que lo ve así porque nunca ha conocido otra cosa? Todo esto le parece intrigante, tan conveniente, como si ellos mismos se abriesen la ropa para mostrarle dónde comenzar a hacer agujeros.

Pero, para mí, es casi profético.

Hace mil años vi a mi criatura nacer gracias a una grieta y, una vez más, volverá a través de ella. Porque esa grieta que se abre y que se ensancha como un útero no es otra que la que ha comenzado a fracturar su Atrapasueños.

CAPÍTULO 61
MAMÁ

Como si me hubiese arrojado al vacío en vez de a un sótano lleno de agua, mis rodillas se doblan con torpeza al aterrizar sobre un escalón. Y la caída es tan precipitada que, en un segundo, pierdo el equilibrio y comienzo a rodar hacia abajo.

Después de varios golpes y quejidos, termino boca arriba en un suelo encharcado, la oscuridad ahora diluida por la luz de otro foco manchado de hollín.

—Mierda... —musito, tan adolorido que apenas puedo levantarme sobre mis codos. Los dientes me castañetean, pero no por el frío de mis ropas empapadas, sino al ver que el sitio por donde entré está ahora bloqueado por tablones de madera.

—Por fin estás aquí...

Algo se mueve detrás de mí. Tan grande y pesado que el foco empieza a balancearse. Y al girar, poco me falta para soltar un grito cuando descubro qué es lo que yace al fondo del sótano.

Del color del oro viejo y con el cuerpo enroscado, tan largo y grueso que ocupa casi la mitad de la amplia habitación, *ella* me observa con sus amenazadoras pupilas escarlata.

—Ah, querido —dice con voz sedosa—. Eres mucho más hermoso de lo que imaginé.

Y ella tampoco se parece en nada a lo que creí que encontraría aquí abajo, porque la Madre de las tres brujas ha resultado ser una serpiente gigante.

Me llevo una mano a los labios cuando su raudal de magia me alcanza, tan potente como un martillazo en la barriga. Y, como si fuese una presa, ella saca su lengua bífida para olfatearme.

—¿Eres...? —pregunto con la voz descompuesta al descubrir un venado en medio de su cuerpo enrollado, tan fresco que todavía no ha empezado a descomponerse.

—¿Una bruja? —responde, articulando a la perfección esos labios viperinos—. Por supuesto. Tal como mis hijas. Tal como *tú*.

La palabra que yo buscaba era "errante", pero por alguna razón, ése no parece ser el término correcto en esta casa.

Al desenroscarse, su piel y sus escamas se desgarran, lo que deja trozos suyos en los muros y el suelo como si estuviese unida de alguna manera al concreto.

—No te asustes, por favor —pide—. El plano medio es un sitio con mucho apetito, así que es natural que quiera alimentarse de lo poco que encuentra vivo —dice, mientras se arrastra entre los restos de sus propias mudas acumuladas por toda la estancia, carcasas blancas cuya impronta se mezcla con la de los muebles que hay arrumbados por el sótano, podridos ya por la sal y la humedad.

Lucho contra el instinto de echarme hacia atrás cuando ella detiene su cabeza a un par de metros de mí, puesto que le bastaría expandir sus mandíbulas para tragarme.

He visto el tamaño que adquieren mis hermanos y Tared al transformarse, pero las dimensiones de esta mujer sobrepasan por mucho las de un errante normal.

—Mi nombre es...

—Elisse —dice, y aunque ya no escucho su voz a través del agua, todavía parece igual de recóndita—. Conozco toda tu historia, querido brujo. Mis hijas me la han contado a través de las paredes de esta casa.

—¿Y usted es...?

—He tenido muchos nombres a lo largo del tiempo —responde—, pero el más reciente es *Arádia*.

Me tenso de arriba abajo cuando la serpiente alarga su cuerpo para rodearme. Una ola de magia caliente se desprende de sus escamas como una caldera viviente, y aun cuando eso basta para que deje de temblar, una parte de mí todavía teme compartir la suerte del ciervo.

—Ah, Elisse —sisea con su lengua bífida—. Ha pasado tanto tiempo desde que vi a otra persona además de mis hijas, que tenerte aquí me parece un auténtico regalo. Y más cuando has resultado tan maravilloso como en el vaticinio de Hela...

Arrugo un poco la nariz, porque no sé en qué lugar concuerda la palabra "maravilloso" con mi imagen consumida por el hambre.

—¿Por qué nuestras visiones estaban tan distorsionadas? —pregunto.

Mis premoniciones nunca han sido fáciles de interpretar, pero de eso a mostrar a Inanna y a las demás de aquella forma tan amenazante...

—¿Distorsionadas, dices? ¿No será que, al ser desenterradas de nuestro subconsciente, nuestras premoniciones sólo nos muestran una verdad que nos negamos a ver? ¿Un futuro del que no podemos escapar? —Aradia alarga tanto su lengua que pareciera querer alcanzarme con ella—. Pero, si te hace sentir más tranquilo, en este caso sí que hubo una intervención en nuestros presagios. Y estoy segura de que ya sabes quiénes fueron los causantes.

—Ángeles, ¿verdad? —musito, porque si las Marionetistas podían pasar a nuestro plano gracias a nuestros sueños, no hay razón por la cual no puedan también manipularlos.

—Lo que mis hijas hacían en tus visiones no era más que la manera en la que ellos mismos las ven —dice—: como unas criaturas malvadas y brutales, brujas terribles cuya imagen fue creada durante el brote de pánico ocurrido hace cientos de años en Europa.

—Y supongo que eso mismo le pasó a Hela ¿no? —me llevo las manos al cabello cuando ella asiente—. Maravilloso, ahora hasta el Dios de los cristianos quiere matarme...

—Lamento decirte que es un poco más complejo que eso, pequeño.

Sí. Siempre lo es.

—¿Sabes? En el mundo de la magia se habla mucho de las familias regentes —dice—. De esas grandes religiones con dioses generosos que otorgan favores, virtudes y trascendencia espiritual a sus seguidores a cambio de culto y memoria. Judaísmo, hinduismo, wicca, *vudú* —la forma en la que enfatiza esto último me hace pasar la lengua sobre los dientes—. Pero, ¿qué pasa con aquellos humanos que, cegados por su soberbia, por su estupidez, corrompen la voluntad de esos dioses, los trastornan y crean *la religión equivocada*?

Ella aleja su enorme cabeza y la recarga sobre su cuerpo para observarme con esos afilados ojos rasgados.

—Hace más de seis siglos, las distintas Iglesias cristianas comenzaron una guerra imaginaria contra la magia —continúa—, todo con tal de imponer control sobre una población de humanos azotados por la miseria. Pero lo que nunca supieron es que el miedo y la superstición que sembraron hacia un mundo que no existía, terminó volviéndolo... real.

—¿Me está diciendo que los cristianos crearon un reino espiritual nuevo, *por error*?

Si ella tuviera hombros, estoy seguro de que los habría encogido.

—¿No es así como funciona el plano medio y los espíritus regentes, Elisse? Los errantes han creado leyendas durante milenios, historias inspiradas en ... momentos en los que han sido vistos copulando con sus amantes en los bosques o en donde alguno de ellos fue descubierto mientras se quitaba la piel. Sólo hizo falta que un puñado de hombres poderosos tomaran una parte de nuestra realidad y la torcieran, para luego predicar que sólo su Dios podía protegerlos de brujas caníbales que se transformaban en bestias, que fornicaban con demonios y se reunían alrededor de hogueras para adorar a Satanás. Con tanto miedo, tanta devoción convertida en fanatismo, era cuestión de tiempo para que un puñado de espíritus del plano medio se cruzase con *la persona correcta*, para que el verdadero terror comenzara.

—Dioses, ¿así fue como crearon a las brujas satánicas?

Aradia me sorprende una vez más negando con la cabeza.

—No, Elisse. Crearon algo para *protegerse* de ellas.

La impresión de escuchar todo esto me hace sentarme despacio sobre el primer peldaño de la escalera, casi sin aire.

—No lo entiendo. Si fueron creados por los cristianos, ¿por qué tienen esa apariencia tan horrible, tan distinta a la de los ángeles *convencionales*?

Ella se alarga hacia el foco para descubrir su pecho delante de mí. Y entre la sangre y la piel rasgada distingo un símbolo grabado en sus músculos blanquecinos, uno que me deja boquiabierto.

—¡Pero si es...!

—¿Recuerdas que te dije que sólo hacía falta la persona correcta para que todo comenzara? —pregunta—. A finales del año mil quinientos, justo en el apogeo de la histeria colectiva, un mago y *alquimista* inglés llamado John Dee dijo haber recibido la visita de un ser celestial, un ángel mensajero llamado "Nalvage" que le había dado la tarea de transcribir unas instrucciones muy especiales enviadas por Dios. Esto que ves en mi pecho es el *Monas Hieroglyphica*, el glifo personal de Dee.

Los ojos de Aradia refulgen como el fuego de la espada, mientras que yo pienso en lo que daría porque Irina pudiese escuchar esto.

Ella se enrosca de nuevo a mi alrededor.

—Según sus propios diarios —continúa—, John Dee aseguró haber sido frecuentado a lo largo de varios años por aquel mensajero, quien le dictó diversas tablas y rituales con las que podría *evocar* legiones completas de ángeles con cualidades tan particulares como terribles. Eso lo llevó a crear lo que hoy día se conoce como magia enoquiana.[17]

---

[17] El nombre "enoquiano" es una connotación moderna y deriva del Libro de Enoc, un texto apocalíptico hebreo (al que no se le considera como canónico por la mayoría de las Iglesias cristianas) en el cual se narra la expulsión de los ángeles del Paraíso. El nombre que se le ha dado a este

—¿Le... giones? —ella saca la lengua de nuevo, quizás al saborear la forma en la que aquella palabra me ha retorcido las entrañas—. ¡¿Por eso había otra Marionetista?!

Aradia asiente, su cabeza tan pesada que empuja el aire como una ola.

—"Un monstruo para engañar a la magia, dos para despedazarla y uno más para revelarla" —dice, citando aquellas palabras que mi otro yo pronunció a Hela durante su premonición—. Los ángeles de Dee se dividen en distintas clases, cada una correspondiente a una cualidad específica de esos seres. Y según el vaticinio de mi hija, cuatro de estas categorías están destinadas a enfrentarnos.

"*Golmá*, aquél que se manifestó en Lynn Woods, es un ángel de las Artes Mecánicas, quienes se encargan tanto de forjar los Martillos como de despedazar los cuerpos de las brujas, mientras que *Nadaazan*, aquello a quien llamas "Marionetista", pertenece a la categoría de los ángeles de la Transformación, quienes tienen la capacidad de cambiar de apariencia y viajar a través de los sueños.

—Creo que entiendo. Con esa habilidad, las Marionetistas no sólo los manipulaban, sino que también tomaban la forma de las personas que veían en ellos para torturarnos... —digo al pensar de inmediato en Adam. En Muata... y en Grace.

—O más bien, de los *pecados* que más pesaban sobre nosotros —aclara—. Como buenos ángeles, se creen con el derecho divino de condenarnos tal como lo hicieron las Iglesias en su tiempo, por eso es que, a diferencia de Dee y los cristianos,

---

tipo de magia ha sido largamente cuestionado debido a que no existen registros de que John Dee supiese siquiera de la existencia del Libro de Enoc.

tanto los brujos como aquellos con quienes compartimos vínculos podemos ver sus apariencias reales, porque la culpa es una de sus formas favoritas de castigo. Fueron ellos quienes susurraron las formas más ingeniosas de tortura al oído de nuestros perseguidores, después de todo.

Miro unos momentos hacia el foco del techo, con el corazón aturdido al recordar las cosas terribles que todos revivimos en casa de Tared, cosas que alentaron la fragmentación de mi familia.

—¿Que hay de las otras dos categorías? —pregunto.

—No lo sabemos —dice—. Estas criaturas son tan complejas que es difícil predecir cuándo se manifestarán en nuestro mundo, o siquiera si ya lo han hecho. Además, la *alquimia angelical* requiere carne mágica y evocación, un proceso demasiado difícil como para liberar demasiados de esos seres a la vez.

De pronto, algo hace clic en mi cabeza.

—Espere —agrego—. Si la piedra filosofal absorbe mi magia, tal como los Martillos, quizás es porque fue creada por los mismos principios alquímicos, ¿no? Ambos hechos para...

—Matar brujos.

Al darse por aludida, la espada me hace sentir su frialdad. Dioses, ¡con que ésa es la razón por la cual la piedra nunca me ha sanado ni hecho inmortal!

—Aradia, ¿cómo es que logramos vencerlos en el pasado? —pregunto, estremecido ante la idea de una legión de ángeles con cualidades terribles y armas casi tan poderosas como una piedra filosofal.

Ella niega con su pesada cabeza.

—Yo no podría llamarlo una victoria —dice—, no cuando cientos de brujos cayeron bajo el Martillo de los ángeles, volviendo aún más reducida nuestra delicada especie mágica. Y aunque es verdad que durante centurias logramos resistir, las revoluciones, los avances tecnológicos y el gran Siglo de las Luces[18] fueron lo que realmente despertó a la humanidad de su locura, muy a tiempo para evitar nuestra extinción. Los ángeles perdieron casi todo su poder cuando la gente dejó de creer en las brujas, hasta el punto que tuvieron que volver a su plano. Irónicamente, la ciencia fue lo que salvó la magia en Europa.

—Y fue la ignorancia lo que casi acaba con ella —pego mis rodillas al pecho, desolado al pensar en lo terrible que debió haber sido esa *Guerra Ocultista*—. No lo entiendo, si los ángeles de Dee perdieron el culto que les daba fuerza para existir, ¿su reino no debió haber desaparecido y ellos haberse convertido otra vez en espíritus errantes?

—¡Ah, mi dulce brujo! Los humanos nunca han querido asumir los riesgos que corren al meterse con cosas que no comprenden. La magia enoquiana es considerada una de las más peligrosas sobre la Tierra y, desde su creación, las personas han intentado dominarla y modificarla al punto de que, sin saberlo, han mantenido *vivas* a estas criaturas tan terribles, que aguardan en su pútrido reino de dolor para volver a toparse con...

—La persona correcta —musito—. *Mi Mara.*

Aradia mira hacia mi garra.

—¿Te gustaría saber por qué estoy aquí encerrada, Elisse? —mi silencio le es respuesta suficiente—. Hace diecinueve años, algo o alguien me atacó una noche, en mi propio

---

[18] Movimiento cultural e intelectual surgido en Francia, Inglaterra y Alemania a mediados del siglo XVIII. También conocido como el periodo de la "Ilustración".

bosque, y grabó el Monas Hieroglyphica en mi carne. Inanna y Caligo me encontraron en la madrugada ya en esta forma, y como si el símbolo me hubiese maldecido, desde entonces nunca he podido volver a ser... humana.

Ella levanta una parte de su cola, la cual se desgarra al despegarse del concreto.

"¡¿Por qué crees que Laurele estuvo aumentando mi poder y preparando mi venida por veinte años?! ¡Porque estaba predicho que tú pisarías Nueva Orleans!"

Sí. Esas fueron las palabras de Samedi. Y si Aradia fue atacada hace diecinueve, eso significa que mi Mara, en algún momento, tuvo una visión sobre mí. Una premonición que le ayudó a hacer todos estos pactos con tanta antelación que bien pudo haberse estado preparando ella misma durante años.

—Tú sabes bien lo que les ocurre a los errantes que pasan demasiado tiempo en su forma bestial —continúa—, y si he tenido que resguardarme en este sótano como una apestada, alimentándome de los animales que mis hijas me traen para no devorarme a mí misma, es porque el plano medio, aunque me consume, también me protege de la locura. Un precio que debo pagar para no ser aplastada por el peso del mundo de los espíritus con demasiada rapidez.

¿Demasiada rapidez? ¿Eso significa que Aradia se está debilitando?

Pienso de inmediato en el padre de Adam quien, aunque estuvo veinte años encerrado en el laberinto de Jocelyn, los sintió como si apenas hubiesen sido uno, cosa que no evitó que el propio plano lo consumiera poco a poco.

—Todo esto es culpa de mi Mara —reitero—. ¡Hizo un pacto con el Loa de la Muerte, resucitó a un trotapieles maldito, invocó a los ángeles para volver a cazarnos y...!

—Y como es tan poderoso, puede que esa criatura de la que tan desesperado estás por deshacerte sea la única posibilidad de derrotarle.

Me pongo de pie de un salto.

—No, ¡no puedo seguir teniéndola dentro de mí! —espeto—. Cada día me consume, me arranca partes valiosas de mí mismo y ahora ya ni siquiera puedo usar mi magia sin ser presa del más absoluto terror, ¡este monstruo me ha destruido la vida!

—¡Y ya no hay nada que puedas hacer para cambiar eso! —exclama y su cuerpo adopta la forma de una ese, tan amenazadora que me encojo de nuevo contra los escalones—. Desconozco la identidad del espíritu que te ha poseído, pero lo que sí sé es que, si te liberas de un ser tan poderoso, lo único que lograrás es darle la oportunidad a tu Mara de *atraparlo*. Y si eso sucede, ¡ya no habrá nada, absolutamente nada en este mundo o el otro que pueda protegerte a ti o a aquéllos a quienes amas!

Cierro la boca, con el corazón encogido como si la garra de mi monstruo se cerniera de nuevo sobre él.

—¿Me está sugiriendo que permita a esta cosa vivir dentro de mí hasta que me consuma?

—No, pequeño —dice, recuperando el terciopelo de su voz—. Estoy sugiriendo que seas *tú* quien lo domine.

Tres días antes, sus palabras quizá me habrían brindado un poco de esperanza. Pero al recordar cómo fui engañado por el monstruo de hueso para creer que por fin tenía algo de control sobre él, no puedo hacer más que lidiar con esta desesperación.

Por su parte, Aradia empieza a deslizarse hacia atrás, lo que me permite sentir el frío del plano medio de nuevo.

—Piénsalo, Elisse. Si semejante ser te ha escogido como portador es porque ha visto algo muy especial dentro de ti, un potencial que, por lo que parece, los tuyos no te permitieron desarrollar. Así que, a partir de ahora, mis hijas te guiarán para que puedas hacerlo. Porque, independientemente de lo que decidas hacer con tu *don,* necesitarás de toda tu capacidad mágica si es que quieres enfrentarte a tu Mara.

¿Mi... *don*? ¿No había dicho Damballah alguna vez que era una *maldición*?

El resplandor del foco comienza a menguar como la llama de un pabilo agotado. Escucho los tablones sobre la escalera crujir a mis espaldas, quizás abriéndose bajo las órdenes de Aradia.

—Comenzaré a buscar un método para separarte de tu criatura —promete—, si es eso lo que decides hacer al final. Pero te pido que consideres mis palabras, Elisse. Y si llegas a cambiar de opinión, el Culto a la Grieta Resplandeciente estará feliz de ayudarte...

La serpiente despacio se enrolla contra los muros, y su brillo se apaga a la par de la luz de la habitación.

Y allí, al quedarme sumido por completo en las sombras, descubro que el monstruo de hueso nunca había estado tan callado.

CAPÍTULO 62
NOSOTROS

Exhausto, me dejo caer contra la puerta del sótano para abrirla. Del otro lado, Tared me sostiene de inmediato para evitar que me derrumbe sobre el suelo, estoy tan entumecido por el frío que apenas puedo mantener el equilibro.

—Estoy bien, estoy bien... —musito contra su pecho mientras me envuelve en una toalla caliente. Miro hacia los ventanales del vestíbulo, y descubro que falta poco para que salga el sol.

—¿Cuánto tiempo estuve allí dentro?

—Casi seis horas —contesta Hela, quien se estira como un gato, sus hermanas sentadas en sillas a lo largo del corredor—. Enviamos a tus hermanos y al hombrecito a dormir hace rato, pero a estos dos no pudimos moverlos ni con una grúa.

Hoffman no se da por aludido cuando la chica lo señala con la cabeza, recargado en una de las paredes e impregnado de un intenso olor a café.

—Espera, ¿todos están durmiendo? —pregunto, sobresaltado.

—Tranquilo, Elisse. Los ángeles de la transformación no podrán seguirlos en tanto esta casa esté bajo la protección de Aradia —asegura Inanna.

Aradia. Sólo pensar en el inmenso poder que debe tener como para que los ángeles no puedan manifestarse en este lugar me fascina y aterra a partes iguales, porque eso significa que si alguien como ella no logra ayudarme, quizá no haya ninguna otra fuerza en este mundo que pueda.

—Dioses, debieron irse a descansar también —digo, preocupado ante el evidente cansancio de Tared y el detective.

—No íbamos a ir a ningún lado hasta que salieras de allí, Elisse —me asegura el lobo, mientras que Hoffman, como si ya hubiese terminado su labor, mete las manos en el bolsillo y se da la media vuelta para perderse en el umbral de la sala.

—¿Qué tal tu plática con Madre?

—Hablaremos de eso en la mañana, Cali —interrumpe Inanna—, por ahora, Elisse necesita lavarse el agua de mar y dormir. Mañana tendremos mucho trabajo por delante.

Estoy tan cansado que me limito a asentir.

Las tres se levantan de sus sillas y nos acompañan hacia el recibidor. Y al asomarme a la sala, encuentro a Comus Bayou y a Allen descansando sobre cojines y mantas, en tanto el detective ya se ha tumbado sobre el único sofá, todos bien cerca de la refulgente chimenea.

Por el tamaño de la casa, imagino que debe de haber muchas habitaciones, pero me da tranquilidad saber que mi familia se quedará junta por lo menos esta noche.

—Te hemos preparado una tina en el cuarto del fondo para que puedas darte un baño, cariño —dice Caligo, quien se refiere a la habitación al final del pasillo de las tijeras.

Después de agradecerles, las tres brujas se despiden y dan la vuelta para subir por las escaleras, arrastrando su magia por los peldaños hasta desaparecer de nuestra vista.

En vez de entrar en la sala para unirse a los demás, el lobo aguarda pacientemente a mi lado.

—Tared —llamo en voz baja—, ¿puedo hablar contigo un momento?

Él, como si ya lo supiera, asiente, sereno. Después, me sigue en silencio hasta el cuarto de hierbas. Alcanzamos el baño y lo encontramos caldeado por una estufa de hierro, con tantos trastos, hierbas y rarezas como el resto de la casa. Pero no me detengo demasiado en los detalles, ni siquiera en la ropa que me espera sobre el pesado lavabo de mármol verde.

El lobo cierra la puerta y pega la espalda contra ella, mientras yo dejo caer la toalla húmeda de mis hombros, para caminar hasta la antigua tina de bronce que ya rebosa de agua caliente.

Lo siento observar cada uno de mis movimientos cuando empiezo a desprenderme de la ropa helada, su respiración se torna un sutil suspiro al desatar la liga que trenza mi cabello.

Pero lo que lo hace lanzarse sobre mí no es el deseo de desnudarme, sino el escuchar que se me escapa un sollozo.

Tared me alcanza, me gira hacia él y me estrecha. Y sólo hasta que sus brazos me enjaulan, me permito romper en llanto.

—*Lo maté*, por los dioses, ¡lo maté! —sollozo con la cara hundida entre mis manos, el miedo y la culpa son una ola fría que inunda mi cuerpo, que me asfixia, un dolor que he tenido que tragarme todos estos días, y lo único que puede hacer Tared es oprimirme contra su pecho.

A él no puedo ocultarle nada. No cuando sabe a la perfección lo mucho que la sangre quema en las garras. Así que, como la única persona en este mundo que podría entender cómo me siento, me acaricia los cabellos llenos de sal en silencio, sin soltarme, sin dejar de estrujar mis hombros, mi cintura y mi espalda para mantener mis pedazos juntos.

En algún momento, dejo de llorar y termino de desvestirme. También entro a la tina caliente, pero lo tengo claro sólo hasta que mi nuca se asienta en el borde. Veo los racimos de lavanda colgar de las vigas, sus flores besar mi piel al caer despacio sobre la bañera.

Tared se acuclilla a mi lado y lava mi pelo con el agua perfumada, sin importarle que sus propios dedos todavía estén heridos por haber escalado aquel pozo.

—¿Alguna vez deja de doler la culpa? —pregunto.

—No. No del todo —responde, cuando empieza a limpiar con cuidado la quemadura sobre mi clavícula.

—No sé si voy a poder vivir con eso... —musito, amenazado de nuevo por el llanto.

Él sonríe, muy apenas.

—Siempre he creído que el remordimiento es una buena vara para medir qué tan nobles somos en realidad —dice—, pero tarde o temprano, todas las heridas se vuelven cicatrices, aunque a veces quieras abrirlas de nuevo. Y, al final, uno debe aprender a vivir con ellas, no esperando a que el dolor se desvanezca, sino al permitir que te pasen otra vez las cosas buenas.

Giro la barbilla hacia él, hacia sus ojos azules que observan mi piel a través del agua, en busca de más heridas de las que ocuparse.

Cómo desearía que me hiciera el amor en este instante, pero mi cuerpo está tan exhausto que quizás hasta ese placer sería demasiado.

—Lo siento. Lo siento mucho, Tared —susurro—. Lamento que esa casa que tanto amabas haya sido destrozada y que ahora tu hermano esté metido en todo esto. Lo lamento como no tienes una idea.

Él fija la mirada en el ligero moretón que surca ahora mi muslo, uno que me hice al rodar por la escalera del sótano.

—Admito que fue duro ver eso —dice—. Pero todo lo que valía la pena rescatar se salvó cuando logramos escapar la noche del ataque. Y, de todas maneras, yo ya tenía planeado venderla.

—¿Es en serio? —él asiente con seguridad.

—Aunque Grace y yo pusimos nuestras esperanzas y sueños de futuro allí, mi matrimonio nunca logró ser fácil o siquiera feliz; la quería, pero eso no es suficiente para que las cosas funcionen, y a pesar de que esa casa era mi último recuerdo de ella, también era el sitio donde todo había terminado de la peor manera posible. Así que no. No me habría gustado ofrecerte sólo un lugar donde fui tan miserable.

Alargo mi mano hacia su mejilla y él la intercepta con un beso.

Creo que, con el tiempo, yo también me habría sentido como una enredadera creciendo alrededor de esa casa, oprimiéndola hasta el punto en el que quizá la habría hecho trizas, tal como los brazos de aquel ángel.

No suelo preguntarle nada a Tared sobre Grace porque no me gusta indagar en esa herida, pero es asombroso ver la persona en la que se ha convertido a pesar de su dolor.

Muchos hombres se han perdido por menos.

—Y no te preocupes por Allen —añade Tared—. Luego veremos la forma de hacerle una lobotomía.

La idea suena demasiado necesaria como para ser una broma. Hoffman pasó a ser parte de Comus Bayou de una manera tan natural que, cuando menos nos dimos cuenta, nuestros vínculos se habían cerrado a tal grado que ya me es imposible concebir a la tribu sin él, y estoy seguro de que los demás piensan lo mismo. Pero Allen...

—Sé que se portó como un idiota, pero ahora la situación lo rebasa —insisto—. No soporto ver lo asustado que está.

—No te recomiendo que le tengas demasiada lástima, Elisse —advierte—, Allen me ha enseñado muy bien que si hay algo más difícil de superar que el miedo, es el rencor.

A pesar de sus palabras, reconozco un brevísimo trazo de dolor en su semblante, invisible para cualquiera, menos para mí.

—No tienes por qué ocultar cuando algo te lastima, Tared. No te hace ningún bien.

—Estoy bien, Elisse, él...

—No me refiero sólo a Allen. También hablo de Johanna.

El lobo cierra la boca de inmediato. Luego, acaricia bajo el agua la curva que se forma desde mi cintura hasta el costado de mi cadera.

—No quería que los demás se enteraran de Grace de esa manera —confiesa—. Pero supongo que Allen pensó que eso era justo lo que yo me merecía. Y quizá tenía razón. Quizá debí decirles todo desde el momento en el que pusieron un pie en mi casa.

—Eres tan duro contigo.

—No puedo decir nada menos de ti.

Cierro los ojos y suspiro bajo su caricia mientras empiezo a quedarme dormido.

Ya ni siquiera me interesa mencionar el asunto del sueño que tuvo con Grace mientras estábamos en Montana, y menos ahora que sé que el ángel Nadaazan se aprovechó de su culpa para atormentarme.

Antes de caer rendido, distingo unos ojos rojos que me observan desde el techo, resplandeciendo como rubíes contra la luz dorada del amanecer.

CAPÍTULO 63
LOS HABITANTES DE LA NIEBLA

Por la mañana, el grito de Allen nos despierta a todos de un sobresalto, siendo Tared el primero en salir de nuestro nido de cobijas en el piso de la sala.

El devorapieles encuentra a su hermano con la espalda pegada contra uno de los ventanales, la cara pálida y fija hacia aquello que lo observa sentado desde las vigas del techo.

—¿Pero qué diablos es eso? —pregunta Hoffman, quien ha desenfundado su pistola como un reflejo.

Me sorprendo al descubrir que se trata del mismo anciano de barba larga que vi el día de ayer, después de haber sido sacado del pozo, lo que me hace saber que no estaba alucinando.

—Cálmate, Allen —pide el lobo con los ojos puestos sobre el viejo, cuya piel parece agrietarse con cada movimiento de su cuello, como si estuviese recubierta de barro seco.

—¡Asmoday! ¿Qué modales de porquería son esos?

Hela entra en ese momento a la estancia, con una sonrisa de lado a lado y un bonete rojo en la cabeza.

Cuando el ente inclina la cabeza hacia Allen, una herida de cuello a pecho se revela bajo su larga barba, cosida con grueso hilo negro. Después, el hombre se marcha en silencio, reptando por el cielo raso hasta perderse entre los racimos de hierbas, como si la gravedad no le afectase en lo más mínimo.

—Perdonen, es que le gusta mucho ver a la gente dormir —Hela ríe de buena gana ante el semblante horrorizado del menor de los Miller—. ¡Vaya! Les preguntaría si pasaron una buena noche, pero por las caras que tienen, creo que ya sé la respuesta.

Me basta echar un vistazo a mis hermanos para confirmar aquella certeza. A pesar de haber dormido largo y tendido, tienen las ojeras más marcadas que nunca, los poros de la piel dilatados y hasta los pliegues de las sábanas les han dejado marcas en la cara.

—Dios, me siento terrible —musita Nashua con una mano en la sien.

—Tranquilos. Se les pasará en un rato —dice la bruja—. Esta casa no está hecha para gente sin magia, y es peor si comparten la habitación con uno de los nuestros. Apuesto a que Elisse la pasó de maravilla drenando la energía de todos.

El grupo entero se gira hacia mí.

—No lo hice a propósito… —susurro mientras me levanto del suelo, porque es verdad que hacía tanto que no dormía tan bien.

—Claro que no, porque para eso fue construido este lugar y sus habitantes —aclara la chica—. Para ocuparse de nosotros sin que tengamos que pedírselo.

Mi hombre lobo se estira a mi lado, fresco como una lechuga.

—Tared parece estar bien —digo, y Hela se encoge de hombros.

—Los consortes ya se encargan de satisfacer otro tipo de necesidades, así que es normal que la casa tampoco les afecte demasiado.

Hago de mis labios una línea, incómodo ya no por la reacción de los demás, sino porque hay algo en esa palabra que no me termina de gustar.

La chica mira el moderno reloj de su muñeca.

—Bueno, apresúrate en vestirte —dice—. Cali y yo te llevaremos al pueblo a conseguir algunas cosas para empezar tu... ¿entrenamiento? *¡Puaj!* No, esto no es una escuela de magia, qué ridículo, no, no, a ver...

Mientras Hela desvaría, señalo hacia Comus Bayou.

—Pero, ¿y ellos?

—¡Ah! Inanna dijo que no quiere exponerlos. Como los ángeles no pueden entrar a la casa, es mejor que se queden aquí, y más si necesitan cuidar a un humano bobalicón. Pero lleva a alguien contigo, si eso te hace sentir seguro.

Quisiera replicar, pero debo admitir que la idea es bastante coherente, así que una vez que el plan queda concretado, la bruja se aleja de la sala. Y en lo que mi familia empieza a vestirse, les cuento todo lo que hablé con Aradia anoche.

El complejo tema de los ángeles los desconcierta, pero no tanto como la propuesta de la matriarca sobre apropiarme del monstruo de hueso en vez de tratar de expulsarlo de mi cuerpo.

Nos quedamos discutiendo esto un rato más hasta que las brujas me llaman. Hoffman, Tared y yo dejamos a los demás para ir al recibidor de la casa y encontrarnos con la rubia y Caligo en la puerta.

Respingo al ver lo que esta última lleva en los brazos.

—¿Ésa es...?

—¿La piel de mi madre? Sí —responde al mostrarme varios pedazos de la gruesa carcasa blanca, con el patrón de las escamas bien marcado en la superficie—. Sus mudas sirven como una extensión de ella misma, por lo tanto, nos ayudarán a pasar desapercibidos para los ángeles por unas cuantas horas.

Hela nos entrega un trozo de la piel a Hoffman y a mí, y nos pide que la acomodemos debajo de nuestros abrigos mientras ellas hacen lo propio. Al terminar, el detective sale detrás de las dos brujas.

Tared me detiene antes de que pueda seguirlos. Luego, acomoda sobre mi cabeza la capucha de mi chamarra, una excusa para acariciarme las mejillas.

—Cuídate mucho, por favor —pide—. Si sucede algo, haz lo posible por avisarme. Volveré a sumergirme en ese maldito pozo si hace falta.

Sonrío para luego permitirle que se incline a besarme. A mí tampoco me gusta la idea de separarme de él aunque sea por unas horas, pero sabemos bien que no puede dejar a su hermano solo.

Al despedirnos y cerrar la puerta a mis espaldas, observo el bosque de endrinos espinosos, entremezclados con algunos sauces y robles de raíces gruesas, tan profundo que se asemeja a un pantano sumido en la neblina.

Luego, miro hacia la fachada de la casa. Es una construcción de tres pisos, con múltiples chimeneas, techos puntiagudos y una ventana grande y redonda en el ático, muy al estilo de las construcciones típicas de Nueva Inglaterra, ésas que Tared llamó de "arquitectura colonial". Está pintada de negro, pero sospecho que es un color pensado más en la humedad circundante que para darle un aire macabro.

Cuando alcanzo a los demás en el porche trasero, compruebo que las brujas decían la verdad respecto a este lugar: más allá del muro de árboles no parece haber *nada*, ni colinas, ni montañas ni otras construcciones que puedan divisarse a lo lejos.

Un sitio en el corazón de un bosque infinito; un plano humano torcido por la influencia del mundo espiritual.

A lo lejos, reconozco aquel pozo de donde Tared y yo surgimos ayer. Y, sobre el sutil sendero a unos metros de la fosa, una silueta comienza a acercarse.

Es un hombre muy alto y fornido, tan pálido que su piel podría camuflarse a la perfección con la nieve. Tiene unos impresionantes ojos rosas, enmarcados por cejas espesas y pestañas tan blancas como su cabello, además de que viste ropa ligera, apenas una chamarra delgada sobre su camiseta, como si estuviese hecho de la misma madera que Tared.

Una mirada severa, un perfil tosco y un cuerpo colosal; mi primer pensamiento es que este hombre *debería* ser un devorapieles, pero...

—God margen, kattunge![19] —saluda Hela dando brinquitos hacia él—, ¿dormiste bien?

En vez de contestar, él entorna la mirada hacia acá. Da un par de pesados pasos, y cuando está a sólo un palmo de mí, se inclina tan rápido que no logro evitar que ponga su nariz en mi cuello.

—¡OYE!

—¡¿Pero qué carajos crees que haces?! —Hoffman lo aparta de mí de un fuerte empujón, mientras que yo sólo atino a echarme hacia atrás, desconcertado por aquel gesto tan invasivo.

—Huele a hueso —dice el sujeto, mostrando unos dientes apretados.

---

[19] Del noruego: "buenos días, gatito".

—Me importa una mierda si huele a tu madre —espeta el detective—. Si vuelves a tocarlo, te lleno la cara de plomo, ¿me oíste?

Sus uñas se afilan como garfios al ver la mano de Hoffman sobre el arma enfundada en su cintura.

—Ilya, ¡basta! —exclama Inanna a nuestras espaldas, tan sigilosa que ni siquiera la sentimos llegar.

Ante su orden, las garras de aquel hombre hacen algo que me deja con la boca abierta: *se retraen* y regresan a su forma humana, algo que jamás había visto en un errante.

—Discúlpenlo, por favor —pide ella a la par que pone la palma en el fornido antebrazo del tipo—. Ilya no está acostumbrado a dirigirse correctamente a otras personas. Y es mi culpa por no permitirle salir de esta casa tanto como debería.

El devorapieles musita algo en voz baja que no alcanzo a distinguir, quizás una disculpa. Luego, Inanna se quita el guante de su mano izquierda, lo que revela de nuevo aquel curioso anillo dorado.

—Vamos. El jinete está listo —dice cuando señala con un brazo hacia el pozo.

Otro hombre nos espera en el sendero. Un tipo también muy musculoso, casi deforme y que, al igual que Asmoday, tiene la piel cuarteada y el pecho atravesado por esa costura de hilo negro. Monta sobre un caballo, tan delgado y con las fosas nasales tan agusanadas que dudo mucho que esté realmente vivo.

—Éste es Bathin, el guía de la niebla —dice la bruja—. Él es quien los llevará al pueblo.

Hoffman mete las manos en los bolsillos.

—Qué jodido —se queja—, he visto tantas aberraciones gracias a ustedes que ni siquiera me impresionó cuando esa cosa apareció ayer en la reserva para traernos hasta aquí.

El jinete no parece molestarse por el comentario del detective. Tan sólo nos espera pacientemente en el sendero, observándonos con esos aterradores ojos de rubí.

Después, Inanna me tiende algo que saca de su bolsillo, una especie de disco de cera blanca con un símbolo grabado:

—¿Qué es esto? —pregunto.

—Se trata del *sigilo* de Bathin. Cuando quieran volver a casa, sólo tendrán que extenderlo hacia la niebla y él irá por ustedes.

Al tomar aquel objeto, siento de inmediato el peso de su magia en la palma de mi mano; una sensación tan incitante que los huesos vibran bajo mi guante.

—¿Un *sigilo*, dices? —pregunto, mientras acaricio el símbolo con mi índice.

—Eso es algo que aprenderás después con nosotras. Pero por ahora, deben apresurarse.

Caligo nos hace una seña para acercarnos.

—No se separen de nosotras —dice para luego tomar el sigilo—. Si se pierden en el bosque, no hay garantía de que a Bathin le dé la gana traerlos de vuelta.

Con esta advertencia, el hombre echa a andar su caballo por el sendero, con nosotros cuatro detrás. La niebla se vuelve más y más espesa, casi al punto de borrar el bosque que se extiende delante de nosotros.

Al observar por última vez a Inanna, noto que el rictus severo de Ilya se ha transformado en una expresión que reconozco de inmediato, puesto que más de una vez he descubierto a Tared mirándome así.

Asmoday. Bathin. Ilya.

La necesidad de saber quiénes son estas criaturas me carcome, pero algo me dice que quizá no estoy listo aún para escuchar la respuesta.

Porque, por más errante que parezca, mi instinto me dice que lo que hay dentro de aquel hombre quizá no sea un ancestro, sino algo mucho más... peligroso.

CAPÍTULO 64
UNA MAGIA TRISTE

—¡Cuidado!

Hoffman tira de mi chamarra justo cuando un coche pasa frente a mi nariz. El conductor se recarga en la bocina a la par que me tambaleo sobre una acera, confundido, hasta que la mordida del frío me hace reaccionar.

Miro de un lado a otro, sin entender cómo es que el bosque ha desaparecido de pronto, junto con el jinete, para dejarnos ahora frente a una versión más pequeña de la casa de Aradia, erigida al otro lado de una calle asfaltada.

—Respira un segundo —pide Caligo—. Cruzar la niebla suele ser confuso las primeras veces.

Y vaya que sí, porque el sendero se ha convertido en una corta vía de casas coloniales de ladrillos rojos y cornisas espolvoreadas de escarcha. Ornamentadas bardas de hierro resguardan los jardines frontales, con árboles altísimos y de numerosas ramas desnudas.

—Esto es Essex Street, una de las calles más emblemáticas del centro histórico de Salem —dice Hela, quien reacomoda la porción de piel de serpiente que se asoma por mi abrigo—. Y esta tienda es donde comienza nuestra búsqueda.

Miro de nuevo hacia la casa. Velas de colores, colgantes de piedras preciosas y varillas de incienso se asoman a través de las ventanas cerradas mientras que, al costado, se erige un Museo de la *Ouija* con una plancha gigante de madera en la entrada, un bazar de antigüedades y hasta un negocio de... ¿varitas mágicas?

—¿A buscar qué? —pregunta Hoffman, pero las dos cruzan la calle a toda prisa sin responder.

En vez de seguirlas, fijo la mirada hacia el suelo.

No es el frío ni la conmoción lo que me deja plantado en el concreto, sino la sensación de encontrarme en medio de un río cuyo caudal emana de los árboles, los callejones, las rendijas de las puertas...

Magia.

Sí, magia que se derrama por cada escalón con la fluidez del agua, y aunque no puedo verla, sí que puedo percibirla con impresionante nitidez; una sensación muy parecida a la que tuve en casa de Aradia.

—¡Elisse! —grita Hela para hacerme reaccionar. Al ir hacia ellas, la rubia sonríe—. Es un poco abrumador, ¿verdad? El *espíritu* de Salem.

Asiento, embelesado por la marea sensorial.

—En Nueva Orleans me pasaba algo similar —explico—. Mi percepción no estaba tan desarrollada en ese entonces, pero aun así podía sentir que había algo más de lo que se podía ver a simple vista. Antes me perturbaba mucho, pero ahora...

—Yo creo que la magia es como el sexo —dice—. Al principio es extraño y te da un poco de miedo, pero después te empieza a gustar. Te empieza a gustar *mucho*, ¿verdad?

—Hela...

El llamado de Caligo no es para reprenderla, puesto que la bruja está frente a la puerta de la tienda con los puños apretados. Al acercarnos, descubrimos que está cerrada, con una hilera de candados colgada como una guirnalda sobre el dintel.

—¿Crees que *Madame* esté bien? —pregunta su hermana, quien parece haber perdido el buen humor.

—A estas alturas, dudo que siga en el pueblo.

—Los demás harían bien en seguirla...

—No todos pueden ser Mary English,[20] Hela —replica la otra—. Además, huir no sirve de nada. No si los ángeles de la Transformación pueden seguirnos a todas partes.

El semblante de Caligo se convierte en una mueca de rabia.

—Vamos —dice con los dientes apretados—. Hay que darse prisa.

Observo por última vez la hilera de candados, para luego seguir a las brujas a través de la diminuta avenida. Una manzana después, el asfalto se termina y Essex Street se convierte en un amplio andador de tabiques de terracota, casi vacío a excepción de un puñado de policías, como si las heladas de enero hubiesen barrido a la gente de la ciudad.

Hay un museo muy grande y moderno en la esquina, con un letrero de una exhibición sobre la historia marítima de Salem, mientras que el resto del camino está ocupado a ambos lados por tiendas de esoterismo, librerías ocultistas, cafeterías temáticas, locales de recuerdos típicos sobre el día de brujas y casetas para recorridos turísticos que se hacen a pie. Inclusive, reconozco el letrero rojo y negro de una tienda de santería que también estaba en Nueva Orleans.

---

[20] Una de las mujeres procesadas durante los juicios de Salem, quien logró escapar de la condena gracias a su fortuna e influencia.

Pero lo que de verdad me inquieta es ver que todas aquellas tiendas que emanan magia *real* están sólidamente cerradas, tal como la casa de hace rato.

Me basta con mirar a Hoffman un segundo para que éste tome a Caligo del brazo frente a Witch City Mall, un viejísimo centro comercial.

—¿Qué demonios está ocurriendo? —pregunta el detective.

La bruja duda un poco antes de responder.

—Aunque los errantes estemos entrenados para limpiar nuestro rastro en el plano humano, no podemos decir lo mismo sobre el resto de las criaturas mágicas —dice—. Los ángeles necesitan alimentarse de nuestros cuerpos y, a diferencia de hace quinientos años, hoy en día es mucho más difícil ocultar algo así y...

Hoffman afloja su agarre.

—Con que de eso se trataba todo este circo —suelta.

—¿De qué hablas? —pregunto.

—Mientras veníamos hacia acá me enteré de que varias personas habían sido asesinadas en este pueblo hace poco. Y cuando vi que las víctimas eran sólo personas que administraban este tipo de negocios —dice el detective a la par que señala las tiendas con la barbilla—, supe que había algo raro. Y con raro me refiero a que tenía que ver contigo.

El recuerdo de ver al exagente hojear un periódico en casa de Aradia me viene de pronto a la cabeza.

—¿Por eso te ofreciste a venir? —pregunto—, ¿querías aclarar tus dudas?

—No seas idiota —espeta—, vine para asegurarme de que regreses entero. Esto se ha convertido, literalmente, en una cacería de brujas.

—Por más que no nos guste el término, el detective Hoffman tiene razón —dice Caligo—. Nosotras corremos con la suerte de estar bajo la protección de mi Madre, pero todos los demás no tienen más remedio que exponerse a los ángeles.

—Y no podemos llevar a nadie a la casa de la niebla —continúa Hela, apretando el bolso de pieles contra su pecho con un atisbo de culpa—. Es demasiado arriesgado.

Caligo tensa los puños bajo el abrigo, frustrada. Pero a sabiendas de que no ganaremos nada con lamentarnos, seguimos avanzando por Essex Street hasta detenernos bajo el letrero colgante de un sitio llamado Witch History Museum. Las brujas nos piden que esperemos aquí mientras ellas entran a una tienda al otro lado de la vía, ambientada con algún tipo de música folklórica europea, en tanto nosotros nos quedamos observando el andador.

Si tuviese qué describir el centro histórico de Salem, una buena opción sería llamarla "la ciudad de los ladrillos rojos", ya que cada edificio pareciera estar construido con el mismo material. El lugar es, sin duda, precioso, como trasladarte a otra época en el tiempo, pero a la vez me produce una opresión extraña en el corazón.

La magia de Nueva Orleans era muy distinta a la de este sitio. En la Ciudad Creciente sentía una fuerza devastadora, festiva y sensual, pero aquí...

—¿Qué estás pensando?

Me sobresaltó al escuchar la pregunta de Hoffman, quien se ha acercado en silencio para observar la vitrina del museo.

—Hay algo en este lugar que me deprime —contesto—. Siento como si me faltara el aire. Es... *triste*. No sé cómo explicarlo.

El detective saca un cigarro de su bolsillo.

—Es normal para alguien como tú sentirse así, supongo —dice—. Gente de todo el mundo viene a pasear y comprar baratijas como si esto fuese un parque de diversiones, sin pensar en la gravedad de lo que sucedió aquí hace tantos puñeteros años. Es un jodido negocio montado sobre la tragedia, después de todo.

Pienso lo que nos contó Julien sobre los juicios de Salem y no puedo hacer menos que darle la razón. Sé que no todos los turistas que vienen aquí son así, pero que alguien como él pueda verlo con tanta claridad es...

—¿Y ahora qué carajos te pasa? —inquiere al verme sonreír.

—¿Sabes? Te echo mucho de menos —confieso—. Casi no hemos hablado estos días...

Hoffman parece sorprendido por la franqueza de mis sentimientos, pero los rechaza con una mueca.

—Ya te dije que no pienso acercarme a ti mientras ese idiota te siga rondando como una peste. Me importa un carajo si eso significa no volver a tocarte.

¿Es en serio? ¿Aún sigue aferrado a la misma mierda?

—Pues lo siento mucho —replico, exasperado por su actitud—, porque no voy a dejar a Tared para tenerte contento, ¡ni a ti ni a Johanna!

Jadeo, sorprendido de la facilidad con la que aquellas palabras han salido de mi boca. Pero es que ya tenían días atoradas en mi pecho.

Las miradas de mi hermana, el malhumor del detective, la manera vergonzosa en la que Julien y Nashua presenciaban este circo en el que los cuatro nos hemos convertido...

—¿Cómo carajos puedes tener la maldita consciencia tan tranquila como para decir eso? —grita Hoffman, rojo de furia—. No soy idiota, Elisse, ¡sé que el cabrón de Miller te contó lo que pasó entre nosotros! ¿Cómo puedes pedirme que me quede a mis anchas después de ver cómo te largas con el desgraciado que...?

—No, ¡no vas seguir responsabilizándolo de lo que ocurrió con tu hija sólo para liberarte un poco del peso de tus propias decisiones, Hoffman! —corto—. ¿Por qué crees que Tared sigue soportando todos y cada uno de tus absurdos desplantes? No es por culpa, sino *por mí*, porque a diferencia de ti, ¡él nunca me obligaría a elegir entre ustedes dos!

Hoffman retrocede, atónito, como si le hubiese soltado una puñalada.

No sé qué le ha dolido más. Mis palabras, o que no me arrepienta ni un poco de lo que acabo de decir, porque no ha sido más que la verdad.

¿Acaso no les importa todo lo que hemos pasado? ¿No pueden dejar a un lado su maldito egoísmo un momento y estar un poco felices por mí y por Tared?

¿Te atreves a pedirles compasión? ¿Después de todo lo que has hecho? ¿Después de la forma en la que mataste a ese hombre?

Sí, porque estoy cansado de pensar siempre en los sentimientos de él. De Johanna. En los de cualquiera antes que los míos.

Cuando Hela me llama desde la tienda para que me acerque, el detective aprovecha para darme la espalda. Y en vez de continuar con nuestra disputa, decido alejarme, con la rabia y esa angustiosa incertidumbre punzando dentro de mí una vez más.

Al entrar, vuelvo a encontrarme con un sitio de una naturaleza mágica muy distinta a todo lo que he visto hasta ahora.

Además de las plantas aromáticas que cuelgan del techo, tal como en la habitación de las hierbas, también hay canastos de mimbre con astas de caribú y pieles de conejo. Duendes, elfos y distintas estatuas de guerreros barbados adornan las estanterías, acompañados de platitos con sahumerios, trozos de corteza y piedras preciosas con runas grabadas en sus lustrosas superficies, con sus propiedades anotadas en pequeños letreros de cartón.

Detrás de un mostrador de musgo, un hombre rubio nos da la bienvenida con un asentimiento de cabeza, entonces Caligo le muestra algunas de las pieles de Aradia que lleva en la bolsa. Aunque el tamaño del tipo es comparable con el de un devorapieles, la esencia que emana es bastante humana, con un resabio a fuego y humedad.

—Gracias a los dioses, Thalía... —alcanzo a escucharlo decir al tomar las carcasas.

—¿Thalía?

—Oh. Es el nombre de nacimiento de Cali —dice Hela—. Una práctica común entre los brujos es escoger otro nombre al unirte a una familia, y el Culto a la Grieta Resplandeciente no es la excepción. En nuestro caso, seleccionamos los nombres de espíritus o deidades que tienen que ver con nuestras raíces, nuestra especialidad mágica o el ancestro que nos ha sido otorgado. Como mi hermana nació en la costa de Tesalia y es una experta en las artes herbolarias decidió llamarse "Caligo", el cual es otro nombre para la diosa griega Aclys, la envenenadora.

Ah, con que a eso se refería Hela ayer con lo de "especialidad".

—¿Qué hay de Inanna?

—"Inanna", o Ishtar, es una antigua diosa mesopotámica, una de las primeras figuras que los cristianos satanizaron durante la opresión religiosa. Ahora, ése es el único nombre de mi hermana. El que tenía antes ya no importa.

—Entiendo —me da curiosidad preguntar cuál es la especialidad mágica de la bruja, pero desvío mi atención hacia las figuras de los diferentes dioses repartidos en las estanterías. Algunos hacen alusión a las cuatro estaciones del año, otros son estatuillas de animales antropomorfos —¿errantes, quizá?—. Inclusive, está la peculiar figura de una mujer que abre su vagina de par en par con ambas manos.

Tomo la escultura de una guerrera con dos lobos a sus costados y acaricio su rostro con el índice.

—Estos dioses tienen que ver contigo, ¿verdad, Hela?

Ella abre los ojos enormes.

—¿Cómo lo sabes?

—Esta mañana le hablaste a Ilya en noruego. Y no pude evitar notar que aquí hay libros con algunas palabras en ese idioma.

La mujer parpadea, sorprendida, para luego sonreír sin su usual picardía.

—*Ásatrú*. La religión de los leales a los dioses —dice con los ojos fijos en la figura de mujer entre mis manos—. La necromancia es mi habilidad más desarrollada, así que decidí escoger el nombre de Hela en honor a la diosa asgardiana que se comunica con los muertos. Todo para no olvidar el sitio del que tuve que escapar.

—¿Quieres contarme? —pregunto con tiento.

Ella toma la escultura y la deja en la estantería.

—Hay gente muy buena y muy noble en el Camino del Norte —dice, mirando de reojo al sujeto en el mostrador, quien deja a Caligo para ir hacia el fondo de la tienda—. Pero, como en todas las religiones, también hay muchos que no lo son tanto.

—¿A qué te refieres?

Por un segundo temo haber sido demasiado entrometido, pero ella decide responder.

—Nací en el seno de un Atrapasueños del norte de Tromsø, una familia que llevaba varias generaciones cuidando nuestro "linaje" como errantes —dice—. Pero al crecer me di cuenta de que había cosas que no me gustaban, formas del Ásatrú que mi tribu practicaba de una manera que me parecía muy... cuestionable. Tanto así que, cuando tuve la oportunidad de venir a este país, corté los vínculos con mi gente en Noruega y me asenté por mi cuenta en Salem. Fue entonces cuando me uní al Culto.

Aquello me asombra demasiado. No sólo no sabía que se podían cortar vínculos con un Atrapasueños para unirse a otro diferente, sino que tampoco había considerado la posibilidad de que los errantes pudiésemos ser... malvados, de alguna manera. Y por la forma en la que Hela ha dicho aquello de "cuidar el linaje", ya imagino a qué tipo de cosas horribles debe referirse.

Supongo que es culpa mía por creer que, por ser seres extraordinarios, los errantes no tendríamos también la posibilidad de corrompernos.

—¿Puedo preguntarte algo más? —aventuro. Ella asiente—. ¿Qué es la *Grieta Resplandeciente*? ¿Por qué su Atrapasueños tiene ese nombre?

—Oh, eso proviene de una leyenda muy vieja de nuestro mundo, sobre el origen de los portales al plano medio.

Ella ríe al atestiguar mi creciente curiosidad.

—Por lo general, los errantes damos por sentado que los portales al plano medio siempre han estado ahí —comienza—. Pero en el mundo de la magia existe el rumor de que estos portales tienen, a lo mucho, unos mil años de antigüedad.

—¿Hablas en serio? —pregunto, sorprendido. Ella asiente antes de continuar.

—El mito empieza con un errante nórdico llamado Leif Erikson quien, según los registros históricos, fue de los primeros exploradores europeos en llegar a América. Se dice que cuando él y su tribu arribaron a una costa del norte y tuvieron contacto con otros Atrapasueños nativos, el choque entre las magias del Viejo Mundo y el Nuevo Mundo fue tan poderoso que el velo entre los vivos y los muertos se desgarró por primera vez. Y allí fue cuando surgió la Grieta Resplandeciente; un portal gigantesco que, al abrirse como una boca en alguna región incierta del continente, brilló con el fulgor de las miles de almas y espíritus que fueron liberados. Y cuando su luz cesó, dejó tras de sí un abismo oscuro: el primer portal al plano medio. El vínculo primordial.

—Dioses, ¡eso debió ser terrible!

—Y de seguro lo fue. Tantas posesiones, tantos animales y objetos maldecidos...

—Pero, ¿qué pasó con el portal? —pregunto, porque no hay manera de que algo así siga existiendo hoy en día.

—Según se cree, la grieta era tan grande que no pudo mantenerse por sí misma, así que se desgarró. Y al hacerlo, pequeños trozos suyos se repartieron por todo el mundo, creando los portales al plano medio que conocemos hoy. De allí en más, no tenemos muchos detalles de lo que sucedió, y como la leyenda era transmitida de manera oral por las tribus nativas americanas, se perdió casi en su totalidad debido al genocidio de los colonizadores y su esfuerzo por erradicar todo rastro de cultura o religión ajena al cristianismo. Y lo mismo sucedió con los descendientes de Leif Erickson en Europa, cuyas creencias pasaron a bastardearse bajo la etiqueta de "paganas"... eso, o la única forma en la que la humanidad pudo seguir adelante después de algo tan horrible fue olvidándolo todo. Tal como las mujeres cuando dan a luz.[21]

"Madre decidió bautizar a nuestra familia de esta manera para rendir memoria a la leyenda que nos abrió paso al mundo espiritual. Por eso no permite que nadie que no sea un contemplasombras se nos una, además de que, como ya has visto, la casa tiende a consumir la energía de todo aquél ajeno a la magia. Es imposible para seres comunes permanecer allí durante demasiado tiempo.

—Entiendo —respondo sin aliento, fascinado por tan asombrosa leyenda—. Pero... Ilya no es un contemplasombras, ¿o sí? Y vive con ustedes...

En vez de responder, Hela mira sobre mi hombro.

—¿Él no va a entrar? —pregunta al ver a Hoffman aún bajo el letrero colgante del museo.

—Ah, no. No está de humor —contesto en voz baja.

—¿De nuevo? *Puf,* qué pena que tenga tan mal carácter. Con lo bueno que está...

---

[21] Existe la teoría de que las endorfinas producidas durante el parto funcionan como un amnésico natural que ayuda a las mujeres a sobrellevar el trauma y el dolor del acto, lo cual estaría encaminado biológicamente a facilitar que pudieran repetir el proceso.

—Hel, cariño, ¿quieres que te cosa la lengua al paladar otra vez? —amenaza Caligo, quien se acerca por fin a nosotros. La rubia se pasa el músculo por los dientes, como si aún recordara la sensación—. Vamos, Edvar ya tiene listo lo que venimos a buscar.

Tras un último vistazo al detective, sigo a las dos mujeres hacia el almacén del fondo, decorado de una forma muy similar a la tienda. Y al entrar, encontramos una jaula de hierro puesta sobre una mesa con una pequeña gallina dentro.

—Oh, ¡es perfecta! —exclama Hela.

El animal tiene el plumaje, el pico y hasta la cresta de un profundo color negro; una peculiaridad que nunca había visto hasta ahora en un ave como ésta.

Edvar toma la jaula y se la entrega a Caligo.

—Gracias, querido —dice mientras la criatura cacarea, quizá con ganas de lanzarse a picotear a la bruja.

Me tenso un poco al ver que el hombre desliza su mirada desde mi rostro hasta la garra que tengo oculta bajo mi guante.

—¿Otra víctima del Camino de la Mano Izquierda? —pregunta.

—¿Camino...? —musito, puesto que de pronto me he quedado sin aire.

Aprieto los puños sobre la mesa, alerta al sentir cómo el hormigueo empieza a molestarme. Caligo me mira, apenas un segundo, y luego le pasa el animal a su hermana.

—Vamos. El efecto de la casa está mermando en Elisse —dice, apurándonos a salir del almacén—. Cuelga las pieles en la fachada de tu negocio, Edvar. El mensajero de Inanna te traerá más cuando le sea posible, pero hasta ese momento, ruega a tus dioses porque éstos no sean los últimos favores que podamos intercambiar.

CAPÍTULO 65
SIGILO

Tal como dijo Inanna, bastó con que Caligo extendiera la mano con el sello para que Bathin apareciera, con todo y su hambriento corcel, en medio de la neblina de Salem.

Nuestra camioneta, aquella que dejamos en el estacionamiento de Lynn Woods, ya se encuentra en la entrada de la casa, pero no puedo decir lo mismo de Comus Bayou. No sólo Tared no ha salido a recibirme, sino que tampoco encontramos a nadie en la sala a excepción de la bruja cabría, quien ya nos espera junto al comedor.

—Venga, detective. Lo llevaré arriba con los demás —pide Caligo a Hoffman. El hombre la mira con un poco de recelo, pero al final, decide seguirla sin voltear una sola vez hacia mí.

—Perdona, Elisse. Tuvimos que pedirle a tu familia un poco de privacidad —se excusa Inanna ante mi evidente confusión—. Pero no te preocupes, tu consorte está en la habitación de las hierbas, así que podrás reunirte con él en cuanto terminemos.

El desconcierto da paso a la intriga, porque han retirado los calderos que había sobre la mesa para dejar en su lugar un solo cuenco con frutos rojos, tan jugosos que parece carne fresca contra la madera oscura.

Hela pone la gallina sobre la mesa y el animal se agita cuando una mano cetrina se eleva desde la superficie. Se aferra a una esquina de la jaula, y tira de ella como si la hundiese en un estanque.

Por el color y la delgadez de aquellos dedos, me queda claro que se trata de Asmoday.

—Muy bien, ahora sólo nos queda esperar tres días —dice Hela çuando la jaula desaparece por completo.

—¿Tres días?

—La gallina necesita tiempo para estar lista, pero en lo que se cumple el plazo, sería bueno enseñarte unas cuantas cosas primero.

Ella arrastra la silla colocada a la cabeza del comedor para que me siente.

—¿Para qué es esto? —pregunto, refiriéndome al cuenco.

—Mientras estaban en Salem, tu consorte me habló con más detalle sobre la espada que llevas dentro —dice Inanna—. También mencionó el pacto que hiciste con él respecto a entregársela.

—Espero que Tared no te haya pedido ayuda con eso —exclamo.

—Por favor, no seas duro con él —contesta la bruja con un aspaviento—. Sabes bien el efecto que esa piedra está teniendo en tu magia, así que es más que natural que esté preocupado.

—De hecho, es bueno que tu hombre le haya contado todo esto a Nanni —interviene Hela, quien pone los codos en la mesa—. Porque nos sería imposible explotar tu potencial si tienes esa cosa metida ahí. Oprime tu magia todo el tiempo y además, da oportunidad al monstruo dentro de ti de aprovecharse de eso.

—Entonces, ¿eso significa que ustedes pueden sacarla? —pregunto, tratando de que no se note tanto la esperanza en mi voz.

Para mi desgracia, Inanna niega con la cabeza:

—Un objeto como la piedra filosofal es tan poderoso y volátil que intentarlo podría resultar fatal, tanto para ti como para nosotras.

—Pero lo que sí podemos hacer es prepararte para contenerla —Caligo entra a la sala con el libro rojo de Laurele en una mano.

—¿Dónde lo encontraron? —pregunto al recordar que, la última vez que lo vi, estaba escondido bajo mi almohada, en casa de Tared.

—Asmoday lo dejó en mis aposentos poco después de que ustedes se fueran al pueblo —dice Inanna—. Adiviné que era tuyo gracias a lo que tiene en una de las tapas.

Caligo lo abre justo donde se encuentra un mechón de mi cabello pegado con cinta adhesiva, un detalle que le añadí en Minnesota.

—Antes pertenecía a una caplata[22] que conocí en Nueva Orleans —digo al alargarme para tomarlo—. Un Loa se encargaba de traerlo de vuelta cada vez que se me perdía, pero ahora que estamos tan lejos de Luisiana, tuve que atarlo a mí de otra manera.

De hecho, tampoco he visto rastro de Samedi desde que llegamos a Massachusetts.

—Vaya. Qué interesante forma de conseguir un *libro de las sombras* —dice Hela, impresionada. Ante mi semblante de duda, Caligo se explica:

---

[22] "Sacerdotisa" del vudú haitiano que se dice que sirve a los Loas con "ambas manos", es decir, tanto para hacer el bien como el mal.

—Un "libro de las sombras" es un diario personal en el que cada brujo anota hechizos, rituales y observaciones respecto a su magia y su mundo, así que es una suerte que ya cuentes con él. Nos ahorra mucho trabajo.

—¿Por qué? ¿Qué vamos a hacer ahora? —pregunto, intentando no denotar mucho entusiasmo en la voz.

Inanna toma unas cuantas frambuesas del cuenco.

—¿Recuerdas que me preguntaste qué era un "sigilo"? —ella aplasta las frutas entre los dedos. Las lleva hacia un pañuelo que saca de su bolsillo y comienza a trazar algo con su dedo índice, mojado por el jugo—. Desde curar algún dolor y obtener protección contra un mal en particular hasta establecer contacto con los espíritus, los *sigilos* son dibujos sintetizados de nuestra voluntad; símbolos mágicos para conseguir algún fin —dice a la vez que retira el dedo de la tela.

—A inicios del siglo veinte —continúa—, un hombre llamado Austin Osman Spare[23] diseñó un sistema mágico en el que escribía frases como "T-h-i-s i-s m-y w-i-s-h",[24] eliminaba las letras repetidas y, con las restantes, sintetizaba sigilos

---

[23] Fue un pintor, escritor y practicante de varias corrientes ocultistas, cuya filosofía inspiró gran parte de la corriente de magia moderna conocida como "magia caos".

[24] En inglés: "Éste es mi deseo".

como éste, el cual le ayudaba a canalizar su voluntad sobre otras personas. Puede parecer extraño que algo tan simple tenga tanto poder pero, para los brujos, crear sigilos es tan natural y sencillo que llevamos haciéndolo desde la era de las cavernas.

—Ya entiendo —susurro—, quieren que haga un sigilo para contener la espada.

—Eventualmente, sí —Inanna se limpia los dedos—. Mientras más simple sea la tarea, más sencillo puede ser el sigilo también. Pero para hacer cosas como comandar espíritus u oprimir fuerzas tan poderosas como una piedra filosofal no sólo necesitas un sigilo más elaborado, más ritual, sino que tu magia debe estar en un punto de éxtasis muy alto. Es por eso que primero vamos a enfocarnos en algo menos... exigente.

Ella empuja el cuenco hacia mí.

—Anda. Come una —me apremia.

Miro a las tres brujas, dubitativo, y luego escojo un arándano. Llevo tanto tiempo con la lengua del Señor del Sabbath que ya ni siquiera arrugo la cara cuando, al probarlo, su sabor se transforma en un resabio a tierra de panteón.

—¿Qué fue lo primero que deseaste al momento de comer ese fruto, Elisse? —pregunta Caligo, pero levanta una mano en señal de contención antes de que pueda responder, para luego apuntar al libro rojo con la mirada.

—No me gustaría usar mi magia más de lo necesario —protesto al comprender lo que busca—. La última vez, perdí el control y terminé asesinando a una persona inocente...

—No te preocupes tanto por eso. Como te expliqué en la mañana, esta casa está hecha para cubrir tus necesidades —dice Hela—. Así que, si la espada empieza a molestarte, ésta te transmitirá la suficiente energía como para que tu mascota no te dé problemas. Si no tientas demasiado a tu suerte, estarás bien.

Ah, con que a eso se refería Caligo con "la influencia de la casa".

—Además —interviene Inanna—. Si algo llega a salir mal, este lugar y *todos sus habitantes* se volcarán sobre ti para detenerte. Así que, adelante.

Sin bajar la guardia, tomo un puñado de frutos más y los aplasto en la palma de mi mano para escribir en el libro.

DESEO PROBAR SU SABOR REAL

—Muy bien, Elisse. Ahora elimina las letras que se repiten, deja sólo su primera aparición —pide Caligo.

DES O PR BA U   L

D-E-S-O-P-R-B-A-U-L

—Ahora, trata de dibujar un símbolo, o varios, si te parece mejor, con las letras restantes. No tiene que ser muy elaborado ni tampoco lo pienses demasiado. Deja que tu deseo fluya desde tu mente hacia el papel.

Miro unos momentos aquellas letras, secándose sobre las hojas amarillentas, y machaco un poco más de fruta. A medida que las líneas se dibujan bajo mi dedo, me concentro más y más en lo que deseo lograr con el hechizo, como si transmitiese mi magia a un pedazo de hueso o a una pincelada de sangre. Las tres brujas se asoman sobre mi libro cuando termino.

—Oh, ¡qué lindo! —exclama Hela—. Sí. Eso debería funcionar.

Me llevo el pulgar empapado de fruta a los labios y arrugo la nariz.

—Esto aún sabe mal.

—Porque todavía no hemos terminado, cariño —dice Caligo—. Ahora viene la parte divertida.

—¡Oye! —reclamo cuando ella alarga las manos y arranca el trozo donde están dibujados los sigilos. Lo arruga en su puño hasta comprimirlo en una bola de papel.

Luego, me lo extiende sobre su mano.

—Anda. Cómelo.

Entorno la mirada, no muy seguro de haber escuchado bien.

—*¿Qué?*

—Vamos. Has comido cosas más desagradables antes.

Caligo le da un codazo a la rubia, aunque el semblante serio de Inanna me deja claro que no están bromeando. Tomo la bola con algo de reticencia, para introducirla en mi boca con un rápido movimiento.

La siento raspar las paredes de mi garganta, ahogarme al punto de querer escupirla hasta que logro hacerla pasar a través de mi esófago.

—*Puaj* —exclamo, asqueado por el desagradable sabor de la celulosa mezclada con el jugo...

Basta que me detenga un segundo en aquel pensamiento para abrir los ojos de par en par. Arrebato una enorme fresa del cuenco, con tanta violencia que casi lo tumbo al levantarme de golpe.

—Oh, ¡por los dioses! —exclamo, extasiado al morderla y sentir una vez más los sabores, la textura, la acidez y el azúcar que se mezclan en mi paladar.

Después de tanto tiempo de haber probado sólo el sabor de la tierra y las cenizas, para mí esto es como volver a vivir. Como *recuperar* una de esas valiosas partes humanas que me habían sido arrebatadas.

—¿Es esto real? —pregunto e Inanna asiente con dulzura, contagiada por mi felicidad.

—El efecto durará unas cuantas horas, dependiendo de qué tan rápido tu metabolismo consuma el papel —dice—. Si yo fuera tú, aprovecharía para comer todo lo que...

Salgo corriendo de la sala, y escucho cómo las tres sueltan una carcajada al verme cruzar el pasillo de las tijeras como una flecha.

Tared casi da un brinco sobre la cama cuando abro y cierro la puerta de un azote. Se pone de pie y se acerca hacia mí de una zancada, alarmado.

—Elisse, ¿qué está...?

No le doy tiempo a terminar.

Lo tomo del cuello de la camisa y tiró de él hacia mis labios para besarlo. Y aún bajo la sorpresa, él percibe de inmediato el motivo de mi furor: mi lengua ahora está *tibia* contra la suya, como si la de Samedi jamás hubiese estado allí.

Se queda sin palabras cuando me separo para permitirle respirar, pero no hace falta decir nada cuando, un segundo después, me toma de la nunca y vuelve a arrastrarme hacia él.

Dejo que se siembre en mis labios, que enrede su lengua con la mía sin miedo a congelarla. Nos besamos con tanta efusividad que pareciera que no lo hubiésemos hecho en años, pero es que la experiencia es tan distinta, tan demoledora, que más bien se siente como si fuese la primera vez.

Tared me empuja hacia atrás para alcanzar la perilla y echarle el seguro. Luego, me arranca la chamarra y abre mi camisa para descubrir mi pecho, tan desesperado que revienta un par de botones.

Sus dedos buscan mi piel con lujuria, mientras yo siento un escalofrío de satisfacción al escucharlo gruñir de placer cuando mi lengua toca esa vena gruesa y palpitante a un costado de su cuello.

Cierra sus manos sobre mi cintura para colarse en mi pantalón, pero antes de que pueda alcanzar el cierre, lo sujeto con fuerza de las muñecas.

Lo hago girar y estampo su espalda contra la puerta.

Él ahoga un gemido más cuando me pongo de puntillas y muerdo su mentón. Me mira con los ojos entornados, casi jadeando ante la ansiedad.

—Entiendes que tus labios no es lo único que he venido a probar, ¿verdad? —musito sobre su clavícula.

Tared gruñe desde el fondo de su garganta cuando mis dedos se enredan en la pretina de su pantalón vaquero.

Él clava las uñas en la puerta, con tanta fuerza que temo que la destroce, cuando, muy despacio, comienzo a arrodillarme frente a él.

CAPÍTULO 66
FALSA BRUJA

El único acto de amor que hice, en todo el tiempo que tengo viviendo sobre esta tierra, fue arrancarme mi propia piel en nombre de mi hijo.

De allí en más, ninguna criatura conoció la caricia de mi mano. Ningún hombre probó jamás un beso dulce de mis labios y ningún niño, anciano o mujer fueron bendecidos con la caridad de mis dones.

Y ni siquiera tú, en todos los siglos que me hiciste compañía, conociste jamás una gota de mi amor.

Pero eso nunca me importó. Ni a mí ni a los espíritus que dominé al paso de los años. Porque, para ser una buena bruja, no hace falta ser una buena mujer.

Un poco de envidia para tener los objetivos claros. Una porción de furia para agitar los hechizos con fuerza. Y lo más importante de todo: una sonrisa falsa para que los demás no puedan descubrir nuestras intenciones.

A veces sólo se necesitan unas cuantas cualidades, y es una pena que *ella*, aun pudiendo reunirlas todas, no tenga una pizca de magia para aprovecharlas.

De ser así, quizá sólo le faltaría un empujón para volverse una hechicera terrible.

En cambio, la miserable debe conformarse con estar sola, a la espera de pudrirse en medio de los hongos alucinógenos que crecen en cada rincón de la habitación de la envenenadora Caligo, con un puñado de hierbas —que ella misma ha robado de los racimos— apretadas en su mano.

La casa la ahoga. Le consume las energías, le revuelve los pensamientos...

No me hace falta conocer a fondo a esta perpetuasangre para saber qué tipo de anhelo late en su pecho ni que fin tienen aquellas plantas mortíferas entre sus dedos, porque, ¿cuántos como ella no acudieron a mí a través de mis largos siglos de vida? ¿Cuántos Césares, Augustos y Cleopatras no tocaron a mi puerta con los dedos enredados de cabellos que no eran suyos, con ropas íntimas en el interior de botellas y la esperanza de que robara para ellos un corazón que no les pertenecía?

Sus ojos grises observan el bosque infinito a través de la ventana, quizá preguntándose qué tan malo sería perderse allí para siempre en vez de volver a un pantano y a una familia a la que cada vez le cuesta más mirar a los ojos. Por vergüenza. Por culpa. Porque lo que más le duele no ha sido descubrir que el amor que tanto quería nunca confió en ella lo suficiente, sino que eso no ha bastado para liberarla de los sentimientos que la torturan. Como para que deje de doler cada mirada que no se ilumina al ver su rostro, cada caricia que no roza su piel y cada beso que es depositado en unos labios diferentes a los suyos.

Qué desperdicio. Con un afecto tan inflamado como ése, pedir *un favor* a la criatura correcta sería muy sencillo. Pero si ninguna de las bestias que habita en la casa de la niebla se ha acercado a ofrecerle lo que desea es porque saben que, al final, la mujer preferiría morir de amargura antes de tener a su lado un cadáver vivo. Un corazón que latiría por ella sólo a punta de latigazos...

Aunque eso no significa que no haya otras inmundicias que no esté dispuesta a hacer para compensar su dolor.

Un presentimiento en la piel la hace separarse de la ventana. Y, como ocultando un crimen, cierra la gruesa cortina con un solo movimiento.

Escucha pasos. Pasos cautelosos que ya reconoce. Pasos que a veces se escuchan tan heridos como los lamentos que ella retiene para que no puedan salir.

La errante mira las hierbas en su mano. Sabe que lo que ha estado haciendo es repugnante. Que si los demás se enteraran, mirarlos a la cara de nuevo ya no sería una opción.

Pero no puede evitarlo. No puede dejar de acercarse cada vez más a esa bruja terrible que, aun sin magia, es capaz de dañar como si la tuviese.

Se da la media vuelta y pega la espalda contra el vidrio. Y la culpa y el placer bombean su corazón a partes iguales cuando escucha que alguien llama a la puerta.

CAPÍTULO 67
PALABRAS DE PODER

Para mi desgracia, el efecto del sigilo duró apenas unas cuantas horas, tal como me advirtieron las brujas. Pero no me doy cuenta de ello hasta la mañana siguiente, cuando Tared gruñe al comprobar que mi lengua vuelve a estar tan fría como una lápida.

Eso no nos desalienta demasiado, así que nos quedamos un rato más bajo las cobijas hasta que el sol toca la ventana y la casa se llena de las voces de mis hermanos.

Satisfecho, salgo de la cama y percibo mi cuerpo fuerte, mis energías cargadas, pero no puedo decir lo mismo de Tared. A él le cuesta mucho levantarse, tanto así que necesita varios minutos para lograrlo.

Y eso empieza a preocuparme, porque no sería la primera vez que termina exhausto después de acostarnos, como si, al contrario de mí, las fuerzas le mermaran. Sospecho que lo que dijo Hela sobre que él se ocupaba de otras necesidades mías tiene algo que ver, por lo que tomo una nota mental para preguntarle más tarde.

Después de ducharnos, salimos en dirección a la sala. Y a excepción de Hoffman, quien ha optado por *desayunar* un cigarro y una taza de café junto a uno de los ventanales, toda nuestra familia está ya a la mesa, con un silencioso Allen retraído al final del comedor.

El detective y yo no hemos hablado desde nuestra disputa en Salem. Y aunque tampoco es que tuviese oportunidad, sigo tan molesto con él que ni siquiera intento acercarme.

Pero él no es el único tenso en el lugar.

De inmediato, percibo el ambiente extraño en el comedor, casi incómodo.

Normalmente, Johanna y Nashua estarían disputándose la torre de panqueques, y Julien debería estar yendo de un lado a otro para llenar los platos de comida. Pero todos están tan quietos, tan tranquilos, que es como si hubiese entrado a un salón lleno de desconocidos.

Tared también parece percatarse de esto, pero se limita a dar los buenos días y correr una silla para mí, cerca de las tres brujas.

Empiezo a preguntarme si debería repetir el sigilo de ayer para "normalizar" mi lengua, cuando percibo una densa mirada en la espalda.

Al voltear, descubro a Asmoday acuclillado como una gárgola en la chimenea y con los labios entreabiertos para mostrar una hilera de dientes afilados que no había tenido la desgracia de notar hasta ahora.

Y después de recordar cómo sus manos traspasaron esta misma mesa ayer, hago una pregunta que no ha dejado de rondar por mi cabeza:

—Inanna, ¿para qué es la gallina que trajimos?

Por un segundo, temo que me mande a descubrirlo por mi cuenta, tal cual hacía Muata cada vez que le preguntaba algo relacionado con nuestro mundo.

Pero, para mi alivio, ella deja los cubiertos a un lado.

—Uno de los elementos más poderosos que existen en la magia son los *"true names"* —comienza—. Los *nombres verdaderos* son nuestra primera individualidad, lo que nos vuelve únicos entre millones y millones de otros seres, y son tan importantes que, según ciertas leyendas ocultistas, hasta Dios ha mantenido sus nombres verdaderos en secreto para proteger a los humanos de su poder.

—O para que nadie pueda tenerlo sobre Él —dice Hela mientras engulle un panqueque entero de un bocado.

¿Poder sobre Dios?

¿O tener el poder de uno?

Me retraigo contra mi asiento al sentir mis pupilas dilatarse.

—Los nombres verdaderos son algo así como un muñeco vudú muy simple, ¿no? —concluyo.

—Exacto —continúa Inanna—. Tu Mara es sin duda demasiado poderoso, lo suficiente como para comandar ángeles y establecer pactos con Loas, por lo que, si bien no podríamos controlarle sólo con saber su nombre verdadero, sí que podríamos saber *dónde está.*

El jadeo colectivo que lanzamos no es para menos.

¿Encontrar a mi Mara para enfrentarle? ¿Acabar con el problema de raíz?

Eso suena a lo más peligroso que podríamos hacer ahora, pero supongo que es mucho más factible que seguir intentando resistir sus oleadas de monstruos.

—¿Y una gallina podrá ayudarnos con algo así? —pregunta Johanna, un tanto confundida con la simpleza de la idea.

—No si no encontramos primero un *athame* para Elisse —dice Hela con la boca llena—. Ayer quisimos buscar uno en Salem, pero la tienda estaba cerrada…

—¿Un *athame*? —pregunto, cada vez más intrigado por el plan.

—Un cuchillo ceremonial —explica Caligo—, una herramienta que, para funcionar, debe compartir una conexión muy importante con su portador. Tradicionalmente sólo se usa para dirigir energías, pero en esta casa le damos utilidad también para marcar, cortar, *mutilar* y...

La mujer es interrumpida por la súbita y estridente risa de Allen.

—¿Qué carajos te parece tan divertido? —espeta Hoffman, quien se acerca ante el escándalo del chico.

—¡Es que no puedo creer que no lo haya visto antes! ¿Cómo no me di cuenta? —dice, tan eufórico que me pregunto si no habrá perdido la cabeza—. Vudú, brujería, ¡sacrificios animales! ¿No han pensado que si les ha pasado toda esta mierda es porque *se lo merecen*?

Pongo mi mano sobre el muslo de Tared para evitar que éste se levante.

—No tienes idea de lo que dices —espeta Julien, quien sí se yergue sobre la mesa—. De no haber sido por nosotros, esas cosas te habrían matado también.

—Quizá debimos dejar que se lo tragaran —se recrimina Nashua, por lo bajo.

En vez de ponerse a la defensiva, Allen se relaja sobre su asiento.

—Yo sólo digo que si los "ángeles" han venido por ustedes es porque quizá tienen algún pecado que expiar, ¿no?

Caligo deja escapar algo parecido a una risa:

—Por si no te has dado cuenta, muchachito, el concepto de *pecado* no encaja en nuestro mundo de la misma forma que en el tuyo.

—¿Ah, no? ¿Y qué tal el de "asesinato"?

Tared resopla con fastidio:

—Dios, Allen, si vas a sacar otra vez lo de Grace…

—¿Grace? ¿Quién dijo algo sobre Grace? —corta el chico, para luego casi sonreír—. El día que su casa fue destruida, vi algo muy curioso mientras me escondía en el bosque. Tres siluetas que se dirigían hacia la montaña, con tanta prisa que ni siquiera se percataron cuando caí de espaldas al ver lo que uno de ellos traía en brazos. Algo pesado, algo que chorreaba. Un… *cadáver*.

Los ojos azules de Allen se dirigen hacia mí, tan terribles que un par de balas se me antojan menos peligrosas. ¿Cómo diablos lo supo? ¿Fue mi ropa, mi cara empapada en sangre? ¿Mi mano de hueso, aferrada a su brazo?

Lucho desesperadamente para no saltar sobre la mesa, cerrar mis manos sobre su cuello.

Siléncialo.

Las tres brujas, ajenas a mi horror, observan al chico de arriba abajo, como si pensasen por dónde empezar a diseccionarlo.

Las paredes, la magia, los objetos e, incluso, el invisible palpitar del plano medio en el sótano; todo en este lugar parece inclinarse sobre el impulso maligno que amenaza por brotar bajo mi guante.

Siléncialo, siléncialo…

—Podrán lamentarse todo lo que quieran de la suerte que les ha tocado —finaliza—, pero ninguno de ustedes puede negar que merecen quemarse en el maldito infierno de donde han salido.

El silencio que prosigue es tan largo que empiezo a preguntarme si el tiempo no se habrá deslizado entre mis dedos otra vez.

¿Está aquí? ¿El cosquilleo? ¿La migraña? ¿Voy a quedarme ciego y despertar con la lengua de Allen en mis manos? Podrías fingir que te he poseído y matarlo. No. No soy capaz... Cúlpame y sálvalos. Cúlpame y sálvalos. Cúlpanos y sálvate.

¡No!

—Por favor, no se enfaden con el joven Miller —la firme voz de Inanna me hace recuperar la cordura de un momento a otro—. Después de todo, no ha dicho ninguna mentira.

Estamos tan tensos por lo que Allen acaba de revelar que nadie se atreve a rebatir a la bruja, por lo que ella se levanta de su silla y comienza a andar alrededor de la mesa.

—Si bien no podemos hablar por los demás, les puedo asegurar que nosotras tres sí que merecemos ser quemadas en una pira —reconoce—. Porque todo lo que se contaba en los tiempos del pánico, todos los maleficios y las cosas terribles que supuestamente hacíamos alrededor de las hogueras ahora son... *verdad*.

Allen respinga cuando ella llega a él y pone la mano sobre su hombro.

—Somos servidoras del Camino de la Mano Izquierda —dice Caligo—. Vendemos deseos y manipulamos voluntades.

—Incluso, segamos las vidas que haga falta para sobrevivir —añade Hela, sin duda en su voz.

—Nosotras no somos un Atrapasueños, niño —Inanna estruja su mano sobre el chico y su anillo dorado resplandece contra la luz de los ventanales—. Somos un *aquelarre*. El gran Culto a la Grieta Resplandeciente. Y por lo tanto, somos...

—*Malignas*.

Cuando la voz de Aradia pronuncia aquella palabra como una maldición, escucho el corazón de Allen triplicar su ritmo, quizá temeroso de ser arrancado de su pecho.

La Hembra Cabría se inclina despacio a su oído.

—Pero aun así —dice—, sabemos que tú eres *mucho peor* que nosotras, Allen Miller.

Ella gira la silla del chico hacia la pintura del aquelarre sobre la chimenea. Él intenta levantarse, pero una soga invisible parece haberlo aprisionado contra el asiento.

Él grita, grita y se revuelve con fuerza, pero nadie en la mesa mueve un dedo para ayudarlo.

—Pretendes ser un juez, un hombre bueno que mira nuestros pecados desde arriba. Pero los habitantes de la niebla han visto lo que tienes dentro —dice Inanna mientras una sonrisa comienza a dibujarse en la boca acolmillada del anciano—. Así que, la siguiente vez que quieras apuntarnos a los demás con una espada, quizá deberías sacártela primero del corazón.

La fuerza que sostiene al chico en la silla lo suelta, tan repentinamente que casi cae de bruces contra el suelo. Allen se gira hacia nosotros, temblando como una hoja, para echar a correr hacia la salida de la casa.

Inanna eleva una mano cuando Tared intenta levantarse de nuevo.

—No te preocupes —dice, en tanto escuchamos cómo él abre la enorme puerta de madera—. Bathin no lo dejará ir muy lejos.

El lobo dirige su mirada azul hacia el predio nevado, quizás atormentado por la acusación que ha hecho la mujer hacia su hermano.

Pero no es el único con la cabeza llena de dudas.

Aradia dijo que las brujas satánicas eran producto de la imaginación de los cristianos, pero Inanna acaba de decir que todas sus leyendas son ahora *verdad*.

No tengo idea de qué sea el Camino de la Mano Izquierda, pero mi percepción de las tres brujas acaba de cambiar por completo, porque ahora me doy cuenta de que compartimos una naturaleza muy especial.

Y distinta, muy distinta a la de mis hermanos, puesto que la palabra "maligno" cobra un significado que transforma mi miedo hacia mi oscuridad en algo menos amenazante y más *mío*.

Comienzo a tener la inquietante sensación de que esta casa en la niebla no es una fortaleza transitoria, ni siquiera una parada en el camino... sino un lugar al que siempre estuve destinado a...

Volver.

CAPÍTULO 68
DEUDA GENERACIONAL

Cualquiera pensaría que una biblioteca de brujas sería un sitio muy especial, lleno de libros antiquísimos y objetos de lo más peculiares, tal como el resto de la casa.

Pero con lo que nos encontramos Tared y yo es con un montón de cajas de ropa, zapatos y adornos de Navidad que atiborran buena parte del piso.

Libreros de caoba cubren el largo y ancho de dos de las paredes, pero todos los libros están muy desordenados, algunos con los lomos hacia atrás, otros acostados, derrumbados en pilas por todas partes y acompañados de muchísimos números de una revista llamada *Green Egg*.

—Perdonen el desastre —se disculpa Inanna con un tenue sonrojo en las mejillas—. Somos mujeres prácticas, así que los libros rara vez se quedan en su sitio mucho tiempo. Además, Hela hace honor a las leyendas de las brujas que causaban desastres naturales en las villas, así que tampoco podemos contar con su cooperación para mantener las cosas ordenadas.

—No te preocupes —dice Tared—. Sabemos lo que es. También teníamos un huracán así en la reserva.

—¿Julien? —pregunta ella.

—Elisse.

Le doy un codazo al lobo, quien se echa a reír junto con Inanna. Miro de arriba abajo las estanterías hasta localizar un par de libros sobre el tema que busco, escritos en un idioma que reconozco como alemán. No tendré problemas para leerlos, pero...

—¿Puedo preguntar qué es lo que buscas? —dice Inanna al verme tomar un antiguo ejemplar del *Splendor Solis* que parece haber sido utilizado como portavasos.

—Los antepasados de la alquimista de quien tomé la espada filosofal estaban relacionados de alguna manera con Red Buffalo, el Atrapasueños que fue aniquilado en Utah —explico, abriendo el ejemplar—, pero la última persona que sabía algo sobre dicha conexión sólo dejó una parte de la historia en el libro de las generaciones de la tribu. Y éste, junto con mucha información delicada sobre nuestro mundo, fue robado por los tramperos.

—Y sospechas que todo eso tiene que ver con John Dee, ¿cierto? —deduce la bruja.

—Sí. Y como todavía faltan un par de días para que la gallina negra esté lista, me pareció que podía aprovechar el tiempo para investigar un poco sobre el tema. Pero, honestamente, no tengo idea de dónde empezar.

Inanna me dedica una sonrisa de complacencia:

—Bueno. En ese caso creo que puedo ayudarte.

Ella toma el libro de mis manos y le arranca una hoja. Se acerca a la mesa colocada al centro de la habitación, hecha con un antiguo y pesado disco de mármol azul, y se sienta a dibujar algo. Al terminar, levanta el papel hacia la ventana que está al fondo de la biblioteca para que sea traspasado por la luz que entra a través del cristal.

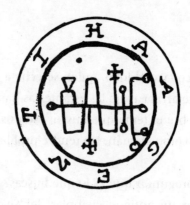

Alguien llama a la puerta.

La bruja se levanta y, tras abrirla, Tared y yo nos miramos mutuamente.

Una mujer muy pequeña y desnuda, con la piel del mismo color y textura que la de Asmoday, está parada en el umbral, con el largo cabello negro sobre las dos costuras negras que corren desde sus hombros hasta sus pechos.

—Ésta es Haagenti —dice Inanna—. Todos los habitantes de la niebla tienen un talento específico útil para nosotras, y el suyo es encontrar cualquier tipo de conocimiento que necesites en los libros. Ella te facilitará mucho el trabajo.

La menuda mujer se acerca a tomar justamente aquellos dos libros que localicé con la mirada hace un momento. Los pone sobre la mesa y hojea el primero hasta colocar el dedo en un párrafo. Luego, me clava esos ojos escarlata que parecen tan carentes de… alma.

Al aproximarme para darle un vistazo, me impresiono sobremanera al leer lo que su dedo índice apunta.

Me giro hacia Inanna y ella sonríe, satisfecha.

—Cuando hayas terminado, Elisse, es muy importante que le pidas que se marche mientras le muestras esto —dice al extenderme el sigilo que ha dibujado—. Ahora, te dejaremos solo para que trabajes tranquilo.

Tared frunce un poco el entrecejo.

—Preferiría quedarme con Elisse si no te molesta, Inanna.

—A mí no me molesta en absoluto, querido. Es *ella* la que podría ponerse difícil si un hombre como tú se queda tan cerca mucho tiempo —advierte—. Y créeme, quitártela de encima no va a ser sencillo.

Una sensación muy desagradable me eriza la piel cuando la mujer ladea la cabeza hacia mi lobo, con esa boca acolmillada entreabierta.

—De acuerdo. Te esperaré abajo —concede Tared al percatarse de mi preocupación.

E incluso, creo escuchar a Haagenti bufar cuando él se inclina para besarme.

Tared se marcha, pero retengo a la bruja antes de que ésta pueda seguirlo.

—Inanna, ¿qué es el Camino de la Mano Izquierda?

Ella me mira sobre su hombro. Y al descubrir que acaricio mi libro rojo no con miedo, sino una inmensa necesidad de *aprender*, sonríe.

—Te prometo, Elisse, que muy pronto conseguirás no sólo tu *athame*, sino la respuesta a todas tus preguntas sobre la casa de Aradia.

Cierra la puerta, dejándome solo con un monstruo que no deja de mirar hacia donde se ha ido mi devorapieles.

☾ ● ◗ ○

Cuando me senté a investigar sobre John Dee, hace casi cuatro horas, no esperaba descubrir que él y Jocelyn estarían ligados no sólo por la práctica de la alquimia, sino por *herencia*.

Porque según las fechas, datos y nombres que me ha ayudado a encontrar la mujer monstruosa que sigue a mi lado, los desgraciados eran parientes.

Para empezar, Haagenti me proporcionó no sólo un libro con una biografía breve de Dee, sino también la de otra persona igual de interesante, un poeta y pintor llamado William Blake, nacido casi doscientos años después del fallecimiento del mago.

Al principio pensé que lo único que tenían en común era que ambos habían nacido en Londres, además de que no había nada que afirmara o negara que alguno de los ocho hijos que tuvo Dee hubiese creado el linaje de los Blake que conocí en Utah. Pero me bastó adentrarme en la obra del pintor para convencerme de lo contrario.

Éstas no sólo tenían un amplio trasfondo sobre alquimia, ángeles y el misticismo cristiano, sino que yo había visto esas mismas pinturas en la casa de Jocelyn Blake; aquellos pasajes bíblicos y mitológicos colgados en las paredes que tanto me habían perturbado.

Y cuando la mujer me señaló con su dedo cetrino una minúscula parte de un libro sobre la historia de la colonización de los Estados Unidos, por fin entendí qué tenía que ver todo eso con Red Buffalo.

Cuando Adam me contó que la casa Blake había sido construida durante la colonia, época en la que ellos habían migrado al país, yo no sabía que se refería específicamente a la colonización de Utah, la cual ocurrió veinte años después de la muerte de William Blake.

Tengo la teoría de que, cuando algunos miembros de la familia del pintor trataron de asentarse en Valley of the Gods —territorio actual de Red Buffalo—, se encontraron con lo que tanto habían perseguido sus antepasados en Europa: brujos que, además de hacer magia, también podían convertirse en animales. Y si Dee había transmitido su linaje místico a los Blake, no había ninguna razón para que ellos no quisieran acabar también con la brujería que desafiaba al Dios en el que tan fervientemente creían.

Tal vez hubo un enfrentamiento entre la antigua tribu Red Buffalo y los alquimistas Blake, lo que originó de alguna manera la profecía de la que habló el viejo Begaye. Y aunque todo esto es sólo una deducción que no podré confirmar hasta que recuperemos las libretas de Sammuel, no creo estar demasiado equivocado.

Mi Mara tuvo una premonición sobre mí. Luego, hizo un pacto con Samedi, despertó al Silenciante de Utah y trajo a los ángeles de Dee de vuelta a nuestro mundo. Todo con tal de acabarme.

—Es por el monstruo de hueso, ¿verdad? Por eso quieres matarme, porque él *me escogió* —parloteo como si mi Mara pudiese escucharme.

Entierro la cara en mis manos, lamentándome de que, de entre los miles y miles de brujos de la tierra, tuve que ser yo la víctima de semejantes criaturas.

Pero después, hago unas preguntas a las que no me gusta enfrentarme: ¿Será acaso que todo esto no tiene que ver conmigo... sino con mi padre? ¿Acaso él hizo algo que me maldijo con el monstruo de hueso? ¿Será él el causante de la ira de mi Mara?

Me quedo unos momentos más con la mirada hacia el cielo nocturno a través de la ventana. No me había dado cuenta de lo tarde que se había hecho, aunque el peso de mis ojos debió haber sido una buena señal.

—Debería ir a dormir ya —musito con resignación.

Tenía la esperanza de que Inanna viniese a contarme sobre el Camino de la Mano Izquierda, pero supongo que eso no sucederá hoy.

Estoy a punto de levantarme para irme a la cama, cuando Haagenti bufa furiosa a mi lado. La ansiedad emana de ella, desesperada por obtener *algo más* ahora que ha terminado su labor.

Al recordar el anhelo en sus ojos cuando miró a Tared, le muestro el sigilo.

—Lárgate —ordeno, tal como la bruja indicó.

No necesito levantar la cabeza para saber que ahora estoy solo en la habitación, porque de esa mujer no ha quedado más rastro que un desagradable hedor a carne quemada.

CAPÍTULO 666
ARS GOETIA
(EL CAMINO DE LA MANO IZQUIERDA)

Horas más tarde, soy despertado por el ruido de un goteo. Solitario e insistente, como el lloriqueo de una llave de paso mal cerrada.

Y, por un instante, creo haber vuelto a una de mis pesadillas.

Todo está oscuro, apenas iluminado por un candelabro de múltiples brazos puesto sobre el asiento de una silla con las patas pegadas al techo, en medio de una habitación vacía que no reconozco. Mis ojos buscan acostumbrarse a la penumbra, pero me siento mareado y somnoliento, muerto de frío sobre el suelo de madera.

Todavía estoy en la casa de Aradia, aún puedo percibir la misma magia que emana de las paredes desnudas, pero me perturba pensar cómo es que pude haber sido arrastrado hasta aquí sin sentir que me arrebataban de la cama que compartía con Tared.

—*Una bruja es una bruja es una bruja…*

Miro hacia el lugar de donde proviene aquella voz: una pared que la luz de las velas no alumbra del todo. Entorno la mirada y, poco a poco, comienza a dibujarse una puerta.

—Yo te evoco, aquél que es descabezado... —el susurro es tan bajo que repta como una alimaña—. Yo te evoco, aquél cuyo corazón ciñe la serpiente...

—¿Inanna? —pregunto al levantarme, aunque aquella voz no se parece en nada a la de la bruja.

—Yo soy *él*, el no nacido, el que se enreda en el corazón afligido —reza, reza tan rápido que sus palabras comienzan a perder sentido—. *Una bruja es una bruja es una bruja. Una bruja es una bruja es una bruja. Una bruja es una bruja es una bruja...*

Alargo una mano a la perilla y la puerta se abre por sí sola. Y del otro lado no hay nada. Sólo oscuridad. Sólo un abismo. Sólo un eco, una y otra vez.

—Buenas noches, Elisse.

Me sobresalto y miro hacia atrás.

Inanna está a mis espaldas, donde hace unos momentos estaba la silla boca arriba con aquel candelabro. Sólo que ya no hay silla, y el candelabro, en realidad, está en la mano de la bruja.

Ella pasa a mi lado y me pide que la siga.

Internarme en esa habitación es como cruzar a otra dimensión, porque súbitamente puedo ver el techo triangular, en señal de que estamos en el ático, y un gran ventanal redondo al fondo de aquel cuarto con un atril delante y la luna creciente sobre el bosque.

Su luz azul ilumina decenas de vasijas de latón repartidas por el suelo, grandes y pesadas, manchadas por el paso del tiempo. Todas rodean un tapete hecho con varias pieles de cordero, enteras desde la cabeza hasta las patas, y fijas al suelo por cinco clavos oxidados, tan grandes que podrían ser del largo de mi mano.

Al acercarme a los jarrones, noto que algunos están abiertos y con las tapas *rasgadas*, como si algo se hubiese abierto paso desde adentro con las uñas. Astaroth. Stolas. Havres. Asmoday. Son nombres grabados sobre la superficie de los recepientes. Todos ellos escritos en...

—¿Hebreo? —musito, resistiendo la tentación de tocar aquellas vasijas—. ¿Qué es todo esto, Inanna?

La bruja camina hacia el atril para poner el candelabro sobre él, lo que revela un libro grande y de pastas oscuras sobre la madera.

—Cuatro siglos antes del pánico de brujas, durante las cruzadas, la persecución antisemita por parte de la Iglesia católica cobró una fuerza tan letal, tan trágica, que tuvo consecuencias no sólo en el mundo humano, sino también en el mágico —dice, con la mano anillada sobre el libro—. Con la excusa de haber sido "los asesinos de Cristo", los judíos fueron víctimas del pogromo de los cristianos de la misma manera en que las personas acusadas de brujería lo serían cientos de años más tarde. Con tal de arrebatarles sus bienes y expulsarlos de tierra supuestamente "santa", ellos fueron condenados de cosas tan terribles como los libelos de sangre[25] y de hacer pactos con Satanás. Pero aun cuando los intelectuales cristianos consideraban el misticismo judío como algo malvado y oscuro, estaban igualmente hambrientos por

---

[25] Alegatos antisemitas por los que se acusaba falsamente a los judíos de asesinar a niños cristianos para utilizar su sangre en la ejecución de rituales religiosos. Se sospecha que estas acusaciones dieron pie a que se popularizara la idea de que los rituales mágicos involucraban sacrificios humanos.

obtener el supuesto poder sobrenatural que estas prácticas otorgaban.

Inanna acaricia las vasijas con sus ojos oscuros.

—Fue así como, no contentos con despojar a estas personas de su dignidad y sus pertenencias —continúa—, aquellos hombres de Dios tomaron su lenguaje, su religión, y las reinterpretaron sin ningún respeto para crear los famosos *grimorios;* libros sobre magia y rituales prohibidos que no eran más que una degeneración del judaísmo y muchas otras religiones demonizadas por los cristianos. Y algo creado desde el odio, desde tanta maldad, por supuesto que no podía traer nada bueno.

Inanna toma el libro, se acerca hacia mí y me muestra lo que hay en la primera página:

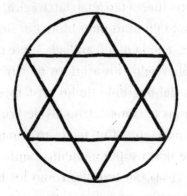

—¿El sello de Salomón? —digo con sorpresa, para luego recordar que incluso Sammuel llamó a este símbolo "estrella de David".

—Salomón fue un antiguo mago y gobernante hebreo mencionado tanto en el Talmud[26] como en la Biblia; un hom-

---

26 Obra que recoge principalmente las discusiones rabínicas sobre leyes judías, tradiciones, costumbres, narraciones y dichos, parábolas, historias

bre tan poderoso que, con ayuda de un anillo, logró someter a varios espíritus para que construyesen un templo para Dios —explica—. En base a esta historia se creó algo que hoy conocemos como *magia salomónica*, uno de los sistemas de magia más influyentes de toda la historia ocultista. Y *Las Claviculas de Salomón*, el grimorio más famoso creado en torno a esta magia, aseguraba contener tanto los rituales prohibidos de evocación como el *Ars Goetia*, el listado con los setenta y dos nombres de los demonios que, dotados con cualidades especiales, ayudaron a construir dicho templo.

—Setenta y dos nombres verdaderos —digo, cosa que hace a la bruja sonreír.

—Los cristianos en aquel entonces creían en la existencia del infierno y sus criaturas de forma tan ferviente como el reino celestial, así que, inventando grimorios por todas partes e invocándolos estúpidamente en el proceso, era lógico que una familia de espíritus encontrara la manera de pasarse a nuestro plano.

—Tal cual lo hicieron los ángeles de Dee, ¿no?

"Carajo" es la primera palabra que se me viene a la mente ante el asentimiento de Inanna. Miro de nuevo hacia las vasijas, especialmente a aquellas que siguen selladas, y pienso en que, a pesar de lo terrible de sus orígenes, los habitantes de la niebla parecen ser muy dóciles ante Aradia y sus brujas.

—¿Cómo es que esos demonios terminaron en poder de ustedes? —pregunto, intrigado.

—*Las Claviculas de Salomón* contienen una advertencia —dice—: si el mago que invoca a dichos espíritus no lo hace

---

y leyendas. Es un inmenso código civil y religioso, elaborado entre los siglos III y V por eruditos hebreos de Babilonia y la tierra de Israel.

correctamente o no tiene el suficiente poder para dominarlos, el demonio podría provocarle una muerte violenta y dolorosa, y como los cristianos no podían ejercer ningún control sobre esas bestias debido a su naturaleza "diabólica", éstas terminaban por hacerlos pedazos.

Una caricia helada me sube por los brazos al recordar las bocas dentadas de Asmoday y Haagenti.

—Fue entonces cuando los grimorios pasaron a convertirse en verdaderos textos malditos, una bofetada de ironía para aquellos que quisieron apoderarse de fuerzas que no les correspondían —ella cierra el libro y comienza a caminar alrededor de las pieles—. Pero lo que realmente llamó la atención del Culto a la Grieta Resplandeciente fue descubrir que estos espíritus, si bien ignoraban a los cristianos, sí que estaban dispuestos a entablar pactos con aquellos que eran la encarnación de la maldad.

—Los brujos verdaderos —deduzco, sobresaltado—. Dioses, ¡los demonios se convirtieron en nuestros aliados!

Innana deja escapar una risa.

—¿Aliados? No —dice, deteniéndose a mi lado—. Los demonios no son mejores que los ángeles en ningún sentido, Elisse. Al ser producto de la vileza del humano, son crueles, egoístas y sanguinarios, y si te descuidas lo suficiente, buscarán cualquier oportunidad para traicionarte. Tanto así que, cuando el Culto negoció con los demonios salomónicos hace quinientos años, éstos exigieron que se cumplieran tres cláusulas para zanjar el pacto. Tres precios muy altos a cambio de su favor.

Inanna hojea el libro y me muestra un largo, largo texto impreso en letras góticas, seguido por cientos de rúbricas con tinta roja sobre las páginas, tan viejas que crujen con el peso de sus dedos.

Casi siento el calor emanar de aquel objeto al comprobar que se trata del mismo libro negro de mis visiones, aquél que yo estaba tan desesperado por firmar también.

—Éste, Elisse, es el libro de las generaciones del Culto. El lugar donde quedó grabado el pacto entre nosotros y el *Ars Goetia* —dice—. Y si te lo estoy mostrando es porque la primera cláusula fue que todos los miembros de nuestro aquelarre, de aquí hasta el fin de la tierra, firmásemos para poner nuestro corazón, nuestra voluntad, al servicio del Camino de la Mano Izquierda,[27] aquél en el que los brujos nos movemos sin escrúpulos, sin temor a la maldad o la sangre, siempre dispuestos a lo que sea para alcanzar nuestros objetivos. Sí. Obtuvimos las fuerzas para combatir a los ángeles y salvar a los nuestros. Pero, a cambio, debimos renunciar a la luz.

La bruja regresa a la ventana para poner el libro sobre el atril.

En estos momentos debería sentirme asqueado. Amenazado, inclusive, por todo lo que Inanna ha revelado ante mí pero, en cambio, mi piel se eriza al sentirme tan… comprendido, porque yo también sería capaz de hacer *lo que fuera* con tal de proteger a los que amo.

—Gracias a ese pacto, los demonios del *Ars Goetia* permanecieron en nuestro poder —continúa—. Y desde entonces, desde hace cinco siglos, nuestra *voluntad* ha estado atada al Culto, a la Mano Izquierda… y a la propia Aradia.

—Espera, ¿Aradia? ¿La misma que está encerrada en el sótano? —ella asiente sin dudar—. Pero, ¡¿cómo es posible que haya vivido tanto tiempo?!

---

[27] Es considerada popularmente también como "magia negra", término que he decidido no utilizar debido a sus connotaciones racistas.

—*Solvet et Coagula.*[28] La segunda cláusula —dice—. Cuando Aradia selló el pacto con los demonios goéticos y fundó el Culto a la Grieta, éstos le dijeron que debía aceptar el "don del regreso": una maldición muy antigua y de la que se habla muy poco, inclusive entre la gente con magia. Es tan rara, y tan brutal, que sólo las brujas más poderosas de la Mano Izquierda pueden resistirla lo suficiente como para *volver* durante más de un puñado de centurias.

"Dicho don consiste en que, cada vez que la practicante cumple un ciclo de vida natural y muere, su columna vertebral se convierte en una serpiente que pondrá un huevo durante el invierno, del cual ella renacerá, una y otra vez, quizá con otra identidad, con otra apariencia o en otra cultura, pero siempre con su misma consciencia, durante todas las vidas que le sea posible sostener el hechizo.

Oh, vaya. El que el ancestro de Aradia sea una serpiente acaba de cobrar un sentido completamente nuevo.

—Pero, ¿por qué los demonios le pedirían algo así? —pregunto al imaginar tantos renacimientos, tantos seres queridos dejados atrás a lo largo del tiempo.

Inanna comienza a enrollarse las mangas del vestido.

—Después de Dios, Lucifer es la figura bíblica más temida de todas —añade—, la única criatura que todas las Iglesias cristianas, por distintas que sean, consideran como el enemigo en común. Por lo tanto, los contemplasombras, criaturas mágicas que representaban la unión del humano y la bestia, eran los candidatos perfectos para encarnar al Príncipe de las Tinieblas. Así que, como tercera cláusula, los demonios exigieron que el ancestro de un macho cabrío, tocado por el Ca-

---

[28] En latín: "Disolver y Coagular".

mino de la Mano Izquierda, fuese otorgado, generación tras generación, a uno de los nuestros para perpetuar la *Goetia*.

Ella baja los brazos, descubiertos hasta el codo, y me muestra los sigilos que se asoman en su piel en forma de cicatrices blancas. Y por la forma en la que se pierden bajo el vestido, me queda claro que deben ser exactamente setenta y dos.

Ya no me cabe ninguna duda: el talento mágico de Inanna es la magia salomónica.

Y eso la convierte en la portadora perfecta de Satanás.

—Por eso ellos querían que Aradia tuviese el don del regreso —deduzco—. Para que continuase otorgando ese ancestro a una contemplasombras que fuera capaz de dominar a los demonios...

—Y para asegurarse de seguir siendo evocados a través de las eras —dice—. Al haber sido la pactante original, Madre todavía puede ejercer cierto control sobre ellos, pero soy yo quien porta al macho cabrío. Y por lo tanto, la única que puede traerlos a nuestro plano. Justo como lo vamos a hacer esta noche.

Inanna camina hacia las vasijas para tomar una cuya tapa no haya sido rasgada. Y al hacerlo, vuelvo a escuchar el sonido de aquel goteo; ese ruido espeso que me despertó y que ahora parece provenir de la puerta que está a mis espaldas.

Al mirar hacia atrás, encuentro a Ilya parado bajo el marco, observándonos. Lleva puesta una larga gabardina negra, pero está descalzo, con el torso descubierto y los vaqueros embarrados de lodo y nieve sucia.

Pero lo que me hace dar un paso atrás es ver lo que lleva en la mano, aquello que gotea incesantemente contra el suelo.

Es una piel humana.

CAPÍTULO 69
EVOCACIÓN

Con la boca bien abierta, quizá presa de un gran horror al haber sido arrancada del cuerpo al que pertenecía, aquella piel pareciera mirarme a través de sus cuencas vacías, mientras gotea densamente bajo el duro puño de Ilya.

La incertidumbre me impide retroceder, puesto que ese líquido que parece rojo y brillante contra la luz de la luna *no es sangre;* el olor que emana es ácido y penetrante, propio de un químico cuya naturaleza no logro reconocer.

—¿Qué diablos...?

Ella hace una señal con la mano a Ilya, quien entra en la habitación arrastrando aquel pellejo, el cual deja a su paso una mancha parecida a la de un caracol. Me echo a un lado cuando el hombre se inclina para arrancar los cinco clavos oxidados que fijan las pieles de cordero para revelar el impresionante símbolo grabado en el suelo, tan grande que debe tener al menos tres metros de diámetro.

Ilya deja la piel dentro del triángulo exterior mientras que Inanna camina hacia él para poner también la vasija. Después se para en medio del círculo principal, rodeada de los cuatro sellos salomónicos.

—Acércate, Elisse —pide con la mano estirada hacia mí.

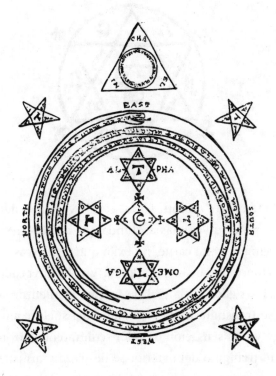

En cuanto pongo un pie dentro de aquel extraño símbolo, siento una estrechez cerrarse alrededor de mi cuerpo, como si acabase de entrar a un cilindro de vidrio y la magia circulase como la serpiente dibujada en el suelo.

Mi corazón comienza a latir con fuerza, pero Inanna me rodea con un brazo para apretarme contra ella.

—Veas lo que veas y escuches lo que escuches, no grites, no me sueltes y, sobre todo, *no salgas del círculo.*

Ilya retrocede hacia el marco de la puerta, observándonos con unos ojos que ahora brillan como rubíes en la oscuridad.

La bruja levanta su mano izquierda, lo bastante despacio como para que por fin pueda distinguir el símbolo grabado en su anillo.

—Yo te evoco, espíritu Foras, con la voluntad del rey Salomón —reza, su voz más profunda que nunca—. Y a través de esta sangre y esta carne, ¡te exijo que obedezcas!

Tal como los vevés que alguna vez he invocado en mi cuerpo, los sigilos en la piel de Inanna comienzan a brillar. Su luz se transmite hacia el símbolo del suelo como un río de fuego y una sensación de calor se desprende por todas las líneas. El triángulo del exterior se desplaza y arrastra la piel humana consigo como la manecilla de un reloj.

Se detiene en el este, y la luna resplandece a rabiar sobre el anillo dorado de la bruja.

—¡Manifiéstate, Foras, y revélate ante la piel del hombre que he traído para honrarte!

Una ráfaga de viento entra a la habitación desde las sombras; todo comienza a sacudirse, a crujir, como si el suelo deseara abrirse para tragarnos.

Me aferro a la cintura de Inanna como un niño a su madre, y los símbolos de su piel relampaguean contra mis pupilas cada vez más dilatadas.

—¡Escucha el llamado de la Agradecida por la Locura, la Mujer Escarlata, la Madre de todas las Abominaciones! —grita con tanta fuerza que su voz sobrepasa la del estruendo de la casa—. ¡Cumple nuestro pacto, siervo de la princesa Bæbælən[29] y bríndame tus talentos a cambio de esta piel que te ofrezco! ¡Obedece, Foras, obedece o nunca vuelvas a exhalar tu aliento sobre la tierra!

El ruido del metal al partirse me araña el cuerpo de arriba abajo. E instantes después, con la misma violencia con la que comenzó, el temblor cesa y un silencio precede al crujido de la casa.

Ahogo un gemido al ver que la tapa de la vasija ahora está rota.

Y entonces... la piel humana comienza a levitar.

Se eleva como si la tomasen con pinzas puestas en los hombros. La silueta de un par de manos se asoma detrás del cuero y se desliza por el cuello, el pecho y los brazos hasta encajar en las manos como si se pusiesen unos guantes.

El espeso cabello castaño se cae a puñados, su miembro flácido crece de forma desproporcionada hasta alcanzar la mitad de su muslo y su piel se cuartea cual barro seco.

Y al batir los párpados, las cuencas de aquella criatura infernal se llenan con ojos que brillan en escarlata.

—Foras, el de mercurio y las veintinueve legiones, el que descubre tesoros y recupera las cosas perdidas, ¿dónde tienes lo que busco esta noche? —pregunta Inanna una vez que la bestia ha terminado de "ponerse" aquella piel.

Él, con sus pies en punta a unos centímetros del suelo, tuerce el cuello en un ángulo imposible, hasta que su barbilla apunta hacia el techo.

Después, habla con una voz muy gutural, rota y oscura, como si retumbase desde el interior de un ataúd.

[29] "Babalon."

525

—¿Y dónde tienes *tú* lo que busco yo, puta de Babilonia? —dice él mientras se lleva una mano a la base del pene. Suelta una carcajada, y sus hombros se agitan de arriba abajo junto con aquella cabeza invertida.

La respiración de la criatura se torna pesada, pero no es hasta que la portadora de Satanás da un paso hacia ésta, que se encoge como si le hubiese levantado un hacha sobre la cabeza.

—No olvides, Foras, que este círculo mágico no es para que te quedes tú afuera, sino para que *yo* no salga de él.

El espíritu aprieta los colmillos ante la amenaza de Inanna, pero luego tuerce el cuello hacia mí.

—¿Qué me darías a cambio de uno de mis brazos o una de mis piernas, Bestia Revestida de Luna? —pregunta con una mueca demente—. ¿O es que acaso preferirías tragarte mi verga?

Mi aliento se calienta junto a las voces del monstruo de hueso, pero Inanna me cubre los labios antes de que pueda escupir una maldición.

—¡Obedece! —ordena ella con furia, y agita su mano libre en el aire.

Un latigazo invisible corta la espalda de Foras, quien suelta un rugido de dolor.

—¡El muchacho está tan tierno, tan *cargado*, mi Señora! —grita, para luego alargar la mano hacia mí—. Déjeme saciarme con él, ¡se lo suplico!

Es casi vergonzosa la satisfacción que siento cuando un segundo latigazo revienta, esta vez, en la cara del demonio, y más porque no vuelve a levantar sus asquerosos ojos hacia mí.

El desdichado se encorva y comienza a vomitar una cascada de arena roja y caliente sobre el triángulo del suelo.

Casi cometo el error de salir corriendo del círculo cuando un objeto cae en el montículo de tierra. Es *mi cuchillo*. Aquél que compré en Nueva Orleans y que perdí en alguna parte de Utah.

El monstruo mira a Inanna con una mueca, los dedos de sus pies temblorosos en el aire.

—*Estrella de la Mañana*, cóseme la piel para que pueda entrar al reino de los vivos —pide señalando la herida que va desde el costado de su cuello hasta su talón, el lugar por donde Ilya debió haber comenzado a despellejarlo—. Déjeme sentir la caricia de la niebla, mi Señora, permítame cobijarme bajo la fría sombra de los endrinos. Déjeme...

La hermosa cara de la bruja es cruzada por una mueca de desprecio.

—No has hecho más que avergonzarme frente a mi invitado, Foras. No mereces más aire que el que ya has respirado esta noche.

—Mi señora, ¡por fav...!

—Guardaré tu piel para cuando vuelva a necesitar tus servicios. Pero, por ahora, *desciende al pozo*.

Y con un agitar de su mano, el espíritu suelta un grito, para luego fundirse en la semioscuridad que deja el símbolo en el suelo tras apagarse.

Escucho la piel humana vaciarse y caer, y la madera crepitar contra el calor del fuego ahora extinto. La sensación de encierro dentro del círculo desaparece en cuanto Inanna sale de él y se inclina hacia el montículo de arena para extraer el cuchillo.

Ella vuelve a mí y me lo extiende, su mango de madera ya cuarteado por el sol. Pero yo sólo puedo mirar hacia aquel cuero dentro del triángulo. Inerte, deforme, apenas un rastro de lo que el hombre debió ser mientras estuvo vivo.

—Una regla de la magia goética es que los demonios siempre deben tomar forma humana para poder pasar a nuestro mundo. Pero inclusive nosotras procuramos tener límites en nuestras prácticas de vez en cuando —explica la bruja, consciente de lo que debo estar pensando ahora mismo—. Esta piel que ves aquí fue sustraída de una tumba reciente, profanada por Ilya para la evocación de esta noche. Y aunque ellos prefieren la carne viva, no les molesta tomar una que no lo esté siempre y cuando se encuentre lo bastante... fresca.

Miro el rastro rojo que ha dejado la piel por el cuarto y concluyo que debe ser una especie de líquido de embalsamamiento.

Inanna vuelve a tenderme el cuchillo. Y al tomarlo, una sensación de nostalgia me inunda al pasar los dedos por el filo, ya atrofiado por las temperaturas que debió sufrir todos estos meses en el desierto de Utah.

—¿Con esto ya podré realizar el ritual de la gallina? —pregunto.

—Así es, aunque todavía hay tiempo para que aprendas una lección más antes de eso —responde.

Me da la espalda para atravesar la habitación.

—Inanna, ¡espera, la vasi...! —las palabras mueren en mi boca cuando veo que la tapa del jarrón de latón ha vuelto a sellarse con el nombre "Foras" grabado sobre el metal.

Ilya extiende su mano hacia la bruja, quien la entrelaza con la suya sin importarle los restos de suciedad en ellos. Él la ayuda a bajar por una trampilla que, de pronto, ha aparecido en la antesala donde desperté.

Inanna. Tan poderosa, tan capaz de doblegar una legión de demonios con el chasquido de sus dedos...

Mientras ambos se marchan, dejándome rodeado de quinientos años de maldad, no dejo de pensar en lo mucho que me gustaría acariciar también ese tipo de magia.

CAPÍTULO 70
MAGIA SEXUALIS

—¿Qué quiso decir Foras con que yo estaba "cargado"? Hela se cubre los labios para contener una risa. Su hermana, en cambio, simula no haber escuchado mi pregunta y continúa regando la hilera de plantas carnívoras sobre el alféizar de su ventana.

—¿Y bien? —insisto, cruzado de brazos sobre el sillón azul que adorna la habitación de la envenenadora, con la noruega trenzando mi cabello al estilo "vikingo".

—El demonio se refería a que tu cuerpo tenía mucha magia estancada —dice por fin Cali—. Y supongo que quería sacártela de alguna manera antes de que se desperdiciara.

—Puf. Vaya forma de enterarnos de que tú y tu chico cogen un montón.

Me giro hacia la rubia con la boca abierta como un pez.

—¡Tranquilo! —añade—. No te estoy juzgando. Es más, si yo tuviese a un hombre con *semejante* potencial…

Su hermana rocía a la chica con la regadera antes de que pueda terminar.

—¡Ay, eres una salvaje! —se queja, mientras yo me río por lo bajo, secretamente complacido por la observación de la rubia.

—Y tú una tremenda cerda, cariño.

—¿Yo? ¿Acaso no nos pidió Nanni a *las dos* que le explicáramos esto?

—No todos tienen tus apetitos, hermanita.

—No es mi culpa que a ti no te guste nada.

—¿Pueden concentrarse, por favor? —pregunto, cada vez más intrigado.

Hela me toma de los hombros y me hace darle la espalda otra vez para seguir con aquel complejo trenzado.

—El sexo se considera la práctica mágica más antigua de la tierra —comienza—. Y al orgasmo también suelen llamarle la "pequeña muerte" porque, al alcanzarlo, tenemos unos instantes, unas fracciones de segundo en las cuales nuestra mente queda varada en un limbo muy similar. La consciencia deja de contener nuestra magia y la hace fluir por todos los canales del cuerpo, y si no sabemos manejarla, se estanca y se desperdicia. Imagino que lo has sentido, ¿verdad?

Y no sólo eso, sino que la idea no me es tan ajena como creí, puesto que se parece un poco a la esencia de algunas prácticas tántricas budistas.

—Y claro, cuando se tiene un *consorte*, la cantidad de magia que se acumula es aún más grande y poderosa, por lo que los rituales sexuales son muy beneficiosos para alcanzar objetivos mágicos difíciles —continúa Caligo—. Quizá por eso tu hombre puede pasar por el plano medio sin tener una pizca de magia. Es más, estoy segura de que, desde el principio, el vínculo que tenía contigo se beneficiaba también de tus poderes sin que te dieras cuenta.

—¿Por eso Tared no podía sacar el clavo que me arrojó Golmá? ¿Porque tenía impregnada mi magia? —pregunto, pensando en que quizá, también ésta es la razón por la cual el lobo pudo escuchar durante un tiempo las voces del monstruo de hueso—. Vaya. Siempre creí que todo esto era imposible para un devorapieles —aventuro.

—Y lo es —aclara la menor—. Pero vamos. Creo que muchas de las cosas que tú haces son supuestamente imposibles.

Miro hacia mi mano descarnada, confundido ante cómo estas mujeres me atribuyen todos estos dones con tanta naturalidad, como si la bestia dentro de mí no significase gran cosa para ellas.

Al pensar de nuevo en Aradia y su escabrosa propuesta, no puedo evitar preguntarme si ya habrá averiguado algo respecto a separarme del monstruo de hueso.

—En resumidas cuentas —concluye Hela—. Durante el sexo, los brujos no sólo retenemos nuestra propia energía, sino que también podemos extraerla de otras personas, y más si éstas tienen un clímax que deja sus canales tan abiertos como los nuestros.

—Esperen, ¿por eso Tared siempre termina agotado? —el pánico crece dentro de mí—. Dioses, ¡no me digan que voy a terminar matándolo si...!

—Tranquilo, Elisse —dice Caligo—. No es así como funciona. Para empezar, el sexo que tienes con él no es producto de un acuerdo mágico; además, tendrías que estar sirviendo al Camino de la Mano Izquierda para que eso tuviese consecuencias peligrosas.

Busco mi *libro de las sombras* para anotar todo esto, el cual dejé en alguna parte del suelo, pero Hela tensa las manos sobre mi cabello como si fuesen riendas, no dispuesta a permitir que deshaga su trabajo otra vez.

—Por ejemplo —continúa la rubia—: cuando me pagan para dejarme poseer por alguien que ha fallecido, es decir, para actuar como *médium*, el cliente a cambio debe aceptar que un espíritu del plano medio ocupe el espacio que dejó esa persona en su vida. Lo malo es que nunca hay garantía de que dicho ser sea benévolo.

—O si yo le doy una poción de belleza a un cliente, tampoco puedo asegurar que ese veneno que le ha rejuvenecido no traiga como consecuencia un tumor cancerígeno.

—Mierda, eso suena horrible…

—Y lo es, pero muchos afirman que la juventud o unos minutos más con un ser amado valen completamente la pena.

Cierro la boca antes de replicar, porque yo también estuve a nada de vender mi alma por Tared. Y si tuviese la oportunidad de volver a ver a mamá Tallulah o a Adam…

¿Qué estarías dispuesto a dar a cambio?

—Por eso nunca nos hacemos favores entre nosotras. O al menos, no aquéllos que conlleven consecuencias demasiado altas. De otra manera, Innana ya tendría más niños que una coneja.

Me toma un segundo comprender la magnitud de lo que Caligo acaba de decir.

—¿Qué? —grito—. ¡¿Puedes hacer que Inanna *tenga hijos*?!

La envenenadora suelta una risa.

—Ay, cariño, ¿podemos transformarnos en animales, pasar al reino de los muertos y volver reales todas y cada una de las magias del mundo, pero no podemos hacer un bebé? Sembrar un útero vivo dentro de una persona que no lo tiene y mantenerlo funcional hasta que sea momento de sacar a la criatura es complejo, pero muy posible.

Sí. Creo que puedo ver la lógica en todo ello.

—¿Sabes, Cali? —dice Hela— Si Elisse aprende a aprovechar la magia sexual de su consorte, quizás hasta podría hacer *telequinesis*. Tal como Inanna.

Arrugo un poco la nariz:

—Nunca le he leído la mente a nadie.

—No, no, Elisse, eso es *telepatía*. La telequinesis es la capacidad de mover objetos con la mente.

—Ah, ¿como lo que ustedes hicieron en Lynn Woods? —pregunto—. Por más que busqué, nunca pude encontrar el vínculo mágico que les permitía manipular a mi familia.

—Eso es porque no éramos nosotras, sino los sirvientes de Inanna —dice Caligo, quien me sorprende una vez más—. En los tiempos del pánico, a Satanás se le empezó a conocer como el "Príncipe del Aire" porque se decía que sus demonios podían volverse invisibles y, con ello, mover a las brujas de tal forma que pareciera que éstas podían levitar e, inclusive, cruzar los cielos nocturnos volando en grupo, un fenómeno que llamaron "la cabalgata de Diana".

A mi cabeza acude de pronto un momento de la Hoguera de los Milagros en Nueva Orleans, cuando recuerdo haber visto cómo las practicantes de vudú eran manipuladas de una manera similar por los espíritus.

—Pero no te preocupes todavía por todo esto, querido —dice Caligo—. Por ahora, concéntrate en algo más sencillo, como buscar la manera de no dejar escapar esa energía sexual que tanto pareces estar desperdiciando. Es importante que sepas aprovecharla, y más porque si todo sale bien el día de mañana, puede que pronto tengas que prepararte para pelear.

El rubor de mi cara da paso a la palidez.

Es verdad. Mañana se cumple el plazo. Mañana la gallina estará lista para el ritual.

Y puede que por fin conozcamos el nombre de mi Mara.

CAPÍTULO 71
NALVAGE

Al enterrar el gancho en su garganta, la cara del motociclista pareciera retorcerse de dolor, aunque ya lleve un par de días muerto. Pero sea o no producto de su imaginación, Benjamin Lander le ata las manos a la espalda de todos modos, con la suficiente fuerza como para hacer sus muñecas crujir.

Sus hombres entornarían la mirada, confundidos al verlo amordazar de esa forma a un cadáver, pero yo no lo culparía por ser tan precavido cuando *el Mensajero* resucitó hace unos días ante sus ojos.

Una vez que se ha asegurado de engancharlo bien, el trampero jala de la polea para levantar el cuerpo y colgarlo en el techo de la camioneta que ha convertido en su propia carnicería.

El denso pelaje del errante lince se estropea a medida que el hombre lo retira con un cuchillo para desollar, algo imperdonable para alguien con su experiencia.

Pero es que no busca conservarlo, así que el Inquisidor abre del esternón a la barriga en una línea recta y cuenta las costillas.

Sí. La misma cantidad que un humano.

Corta un trozo de músculo. Pequeño, del tamaño de su pulgar, y lo observa brillar como un rubí entre sus dedos antes de llevárselo a la boca.

Ha probado mucha carne exótica a lo largo de su vida, pero no sabe si lo que le gusta de ésta es el sabor graso de las partes que parecen más humanas o el placer que siente al ver que sus peligrosos enemigos se han convertido en un vulgar trozo de comida.

Rasguño las paredes de mi celda, atosigada por la envidia y el hambre al verlo paladear el sabor del hierro entre las costuras de su mejilla.

—Es maravilloso, ¿no es así? —aquella voz nos arranca a los dos de nuestra fantasía, pero el Inquisidor no gira la cabeza hacia aquella esquina oscura de la caja, desde donde *él* lo observa.

Sabe que está allí. Escucha el ligero batir de sus alas, pero no soporta mirarlo. No tolera esa cara de ojos gentiles hundidos en sus cuencas, esa sonrisa dulce en una boca deforme por el frío.

Benjamin lo siente acercarse, y no por sus pasos, tan ligeros como una pluma, sino porque esa criatura despierta en él un miedo que nunca había experimentado antes.

Porque aquella noche, en cuanto el cadáver del perpetuasangre Sammuel se irguió sobre el congelador, el trampero contuvo un grito. Como si, después de todas las cosas que había visto y hecho, un muerto que se levanta de su tumba fuese lo más terrible que pudiera pasarle.

Al apuntar su arma, el hombre alado torció la cabeza y sonrió.

—Malcolm Dallas me disparó en el pecho con una escopeta, ¿y tú crees que vas a matarme ahora con eso? —dijo con una voz que Lander no reconoció, pero que yo sí que escuché muchos años atrás.

Un emisario. Un portador de un mensaje que, en vez de robar el cuerpo de un brujo para manifestarse, ha preferido tomar el de un cadáver.

—¿Qué demonios quieres? ¿Venganza? —musitó el Inquisidor.

—¿Venganza? No. No, Benjamin —contestó Sammuel con ternura—. Al contrario. Vine aquí para ayudarte.

El cuerpo salió del congelador y bajó de la camioneta de carga. Y aunque no le gustó la condescendencia de aquella criatura, se percató de que los dos niños que tenía secuestrados temblaban y gemían, horrorizados ante la figura del ángel caído.

—¿Sabes cuál es la razón por la cual no puedes con ellos? —preguntó el emisario—. Es porque todo este tiempo los has tratado como bestia como animales que puedes cazar con balas y sogas, en vez de verlos como lo que son en realidad.

Al acercarse, el recelo de Benjamin se convirtió en extrañeza, porque sólo le hizo falta una inhalación para descubrir en aquel hombre el mismo olor que había percibido durante las apariciones de su hijo.

Bajó el arma y la guardó en su funda. No sabía a ciencia cierta cuál era su naturaleza, pero aquel cadáver ya no era el hombre que Dallas había asesinado en Stonefall.

—¿Por qué traicionarías a los tuyos? ¿Quién dice que no es todo un engaño para liberar a estos dos?

—Esas criaturas son una abominación, Benjamin —dijo el ángel, casi con ternura—, el resultado de la fornicación entre un hombre y un súcubo, un demonio que pretendía ser una mujer. Sí, tendrán qué morir y ser purificados, pero todavía no es el momento. Todavía son útiles para nuestro cometido.

—¿Y por qué carajos debería confiar en ti? —insistió.

—Porque estoy a punto de darte justo lo que necesitas para acabar con esa estirpe de brujas.

El cadáver alado se llevó dos dedos a la boca, la torció un poco y, con un jalón suave, se arrancó algo de allí.

Primero, el trampero creyó que era un diente. Pero al acercarse descubrió que se trataba de una bala, blanca como la luna.

Luego, miró de nuevo la criatura frente a él.

—¿Quién diablos eres?

El monstruo sonrío.

—Mi nombre es Nalvage.

Benjamin sacude la cabeza y se aleja de los sucesos de aquella noche cuando el Mensajero se para a un lado suyo para contemplar la carcasa del hombre lince.

Lander siente aquella bala blanca en su bolsillo, la cual tiene el peso de un revólver. Decide que no tiene ganas de seguir descuartizando la cena, así que deja todo tal cual está y baja de la camioneta de un salto.

Camina a través de su gente, acuclillada alrededor de montículos de escombros con los que han comenzado a hacer fogatas, mientras que el ángel flota detrás de él con los pies en puntas y su pestilente perfume como una estela.

Lo que más desconcierta al Inquisidor es que sus hombres han visto a Nalvage deambular entre ellos. Inclusive, más de uno se ha tropezado con él y lo ha pasado de largo, como si nadie pudiese verlo en realidad.

Después de cruzar el campamento, se detiene en el lindero del bosque y observa la casa destruida en medio de la colina.

Cuando el mensajero Sammuel le dijo dónde encontrar al Atrapasueños de los motociclistas, haberlos emboscado y aniquilado de forma satisfactoria le había regresado el poder a Benjamin sobre su gente. Pero que ahora los hiciera detenerse en Minnesota, en una casa que ya tenía tiempo de haber sido abandonada, parecía fútil.

Los rastros estaban cubiertos de nieve, y nadie parecía haberse dado cuenta siquiera del desastre que había ocurrido en ese lugar. No había policías a la vista, ni señales de que alguien más se hubiese acercado. Sólo un montón de artilugios colgados entre los árboles, muy parecidos a aquella bolsa llena de los ojos de sus tramperos.

Sí. Él sabe que mi hermosa criatura estuvo aquí, de eso no hay duda, pero...

—¿Por qué nos has traído a este sitio? —pregunta—. ¿Por qué no llevarnos directamente donde están esos desgraciados?

El Mensajero mira el sendero que lleva a la montaña, donde sabe que un cadáver sigue enterrado bajo la nieve.

—Porque falta muy poco para que *ellos* lleguen, Benjamin —anuncia el ángel—.Y voy a asegurarme de que tú y tu gente estén preparados para recibirlos.

CAPÍTULO 72
EL SECRETO DE LA GALLINA NEGRA

Cuando se cumple el plazo, salimos de la casa de Aradia, muy tarde, cerca de la medianoche. Y mientras que Hoffman y Johanna han decidido quedarse para cuidar de Allen, el resto de Comus Bayou nos dirigimos hacia el pozo para encontrarnos con las tres brujas.

El frío encorseta las costillas, tanto así que hasta Tared ha decidido llevar una chamarra más gruesa de lo normal, pero Julien y Nashua parecen tensos por razones ajenas a la helada. No puedo culparlos por estar nerviosos cuando yo mismo siento mis adentros retorcerse presas de la expectación.

Ellas ya nos esperan sobre el sendero, con una vela blanca cada una mientras que Ilya las escolta como un fantasma mimetizado con la niebla.

Tared endurece el semblante al cruzar la mirada con él. No le agradó enterarse de lo que el hombre albino hizo el día que fui a Salem con las chicas, y aunque no me ha dicho nada al respecto, es obvio que ha caído completamente fuera de su gracia.

—¿Traes el athame, Elisse? —pregunta Inanna después de darnos las buenas noches, por lo que le muestro el mango del arma en mi bolsillo—. Muy bien. Los esperaremos aquí entonces.

Asiento con la cabeza hacia los míos para adentrarme junto con Hela en el sendero. Andamos unos cuantos minutos en la foresta, sobre un camino muy distinto a la dirección que tomamos con Bathin para ir al pueblo, hasta dar con una vieja cabaña en la nieve, no más grande que aquélla en la que nos refugiamos Tared y yo en Montana.

La chica me guía hacia la parte trasera, donde encontramos un establo con espacio para apenas un caballo. Y mientras ella busca algo en su bolsillo, distingo un catre desde la ventana de la choza.

—No creí que en este bosque hubiese algo más que la casa de Aradia —digo a la rubia.

—La niebla tiene muchos senderos que, en su mayoría, no llevan a ninguna parte, por lo que seguirlos sin la guía de un demonio puede significar perderse para siempre —explica—. Pero hay ocho caminos principales, ocho rutas que conducen a espacios que cumplen una función específica para el Culto. Uno es la casa. Otro es el camino a Salem. Y éste, el más corto de todos, es la morada de Ilya.

—¿Y por qué está aquí afuera?

Ella se detiene unos segundos, quizá considerando si debería contarme algo de todo aquello.

—Por más especial que sea, Ilya sigue siendo un devorapieles. Y como no puede formar parte del Culto, tampoco tiene un lugar fijo en la casa con nosotras —dice al final, con cuidado—. Pero no te preocupes. Como consorte de Inanna, tampoco pasa tanto tiempo solo en esa cabaña.

Confirmar, fuera de toda duda, que el hombre albino *es un errante* me sorprende muchísimo pero, antes de que pueda preguntar más, Hela saca por fin una llave. Se cruza un dedo en los labios para pedirme silencio y abre la puerta del establo.

Trago saliva y entro de puntillas al lugar. De inmediato escucho los suaves ronquidos de la gallina negra, apacible y regordeta sobre un nido de paja, rodeada de las semillas y virutas de madera con las que la han alimentado estos días. Ella despierta ante el crujido de la paja bajo mis pasos, pero la tomo del cuello con la suficiente fuerza como para que no pueda emitir ruido alguno. El animal se retuerce, histérico entre mis puños, y suelta a su paso unas cuantas plumas mientras lo saco del establo. Hela le cierra el pico con cinta de aislar y suspira, aliviada de que ni un solo cacareo se haya escapado de su garganta.

Al regresar con los demás, Julien alza una ceja al ver al animal revolotear bajo mi brazo.

—Esto se va a poner lindo, ¿verdad? —pregunta sin humor.

—No va a ser agradable, eso es seguro —dice Inanna—, pero no les habría pedido venir hoy de no ser necesario. Es mejor tener refuerzos por cualquier... eventualidad.

Ella nos da la espalda para que podamos seguirla. Y a medida que avanzamos, el sendero bajo nuestros pies se ensancha.

—¿Y Bathin? —pregunto al ver que el jinete no ha aparecido aún para guiarnos.

—No te preocupes. Tenemos a Ilya, y nadie conoce mejor los caminos que él.

Miro hacia la espalda del hombre, quien se mantiene bien cerca de la bruja goética.

Con el enigma de su naturaleza aún en mi cabeza, alargo mi mano hacia Tared, quien me estrecha bajo su brazo para protegerme del frío. Caminamos durante más o menos un kilómetro hasta que por fin el sendero corona en una pequeña colina.

El agarre del lobo sobre mí se afianza al ver lo que hay en la cima.

Es un tocón, grande como un sofá y cuyas raíces se arquean por todo el monte como olas, cubiertas por cientos y cientos de velas derretidas a lo largo de sus cortezas; otro fragmento de mi visión que se materializa en la noche.

La inquietud se acentúa cuando la luz de la luna creciente ilumina la superficie del tronco y contrasta las densas manchas oscuras que se derraman por los bordes y las raíces.

Un sitio de ofrenda. Un lugar de sacrificio.

Las tres brujas atraviesan las raíces y se colocan alrededor del tocón. Caligo y Hela ponen sus velas en medio, como si fuesen dos columnas, y luego Inanna se gira hacia mí.

—Ordénales a los miembros de tu familia que no muevan un dedo, que no se aproximen ni se inquieten a menos que yo se los pida. ¿De acuerdo?

Los tres asienten y la tensión burbujea como un caldero. Subo la colina, con el animal cada vez más inquieto entre mis brazos, y ellas me hacen espacio para que pueda unirme.

Tengo a Inanna de frente y a sus hermanas a los costados con sus caras iluminadas por las pequeñas llamas aun cuando la brisa recorre mis tobillos como una serpiente de hielo.

Saco el athame de mis ropas. Y, con la gallina en la mano, trazo con la punta un triángulo en medio de las dos velas, su cúspide hacia Inanna como una plancha de *ouija*.

—*Miohle, Miasshé. Miohle, Miasshé. Miohle, Miasshé* —murmuro a la par que escribo aquellos dos nombres alrededor del triángulo.

Mi magia circula con el conjuro, y cuando la espada comienza a hostigarme, las tres brujas levantan las manos sobre las mías para contrarrestar su opresión, imitando la energía que la casa de Aradia siempre ejerce sobre mí.

Pongo a la gallina boca arriba en medio de las velas, y la aplasto con la palma de mi mano abierta como una estrella de cinco puntas.

El animal me picotea, se revuelve y me rasguña, pero no le permito escapar, por más que una parte de mí luche por compadecerse de ella.

—¡*Miohle, Miasshé*, espíritu de los canales, de los oídos y los susurros en la noche! —exclamo para apuntar hacia la luna con mi cuchillo, empuñado en la mano izquierda—, ¡te pido que grites el nombre que ahora agoniza en tus entrañas!

Mis hermanos y Tared plantan los pies en el suelo para no llamar la atención de *aquello* que empiezo a percibir bajo la gallina.

—Libérame de la ignorancia, ¡libera el secreto que yace en tu interior! ¡*Miohle, Miasshé*!

—¡*Miohle, Miasshé, Miohle, Miasshé, Miohle, Miasshé*! —rezan las tres brujas al unísono.

La brisa se convierte en ráfaga y todas y cada una de las velas sobre las raíces se encienden de golpe. El campo de sacrificio se ilumina con la luz de cientos de llamas.

Muéstrate...

Contengo el aliento cuando, ante la orden del monstruo de hueso, el animal empieza a *crecer*. A engrosarse contra mis dedos crispados en las plumas y la piel de su pecho.

—Maldita sea, ¡se está escapando de la gallina!

Ante el grito de Caligo, las tres brujas se lanzan para atrapar a la bestia. Inanna la toma del cuello y el pico y sus hermanas de las alas.

Las extremidades y el cuerpo redondeado se alargan hasta formar un torso humano, mientras que su corazón late con la fuerza de tres bajo mi mano.

Me veo obligado a retroceder cuando una de las patas, ahora transformada en una pezuña, me golpea el abdomen.

—¡No se muevan! —exclamo al ver de reojo cómo alguien de Comus Bayou se sobresalta. Y también creo notar que Ilya ha desaparecido.

—¡Elisse, apúrate! —exige Inanna, con las manos heridas por el filo del pico que se niega a soltar.

—¡Surge de entre las sombras! —reacciono, para echarme de nuevo sobre la bestia—, ¡revela el secreto que retumba en el abismo!

—¡*Miohle, Miasshé. Miohle, Miasshé. Miohle, Miasshé!* —gritan las brujas con fuerza, una y otra vez.

—Por esta sangre, por este vínculo y esta ofrenda, ¡libera el nombre verdadero de mi Mara o regresa al pozo de donde te he traído!

Y con este mandato, corto de lado a lado la garganta de la gallina.

Un grito *humano* sale de la abertura, tan alto que me encojo de hombros para que no me revienten los oídos. Aquella hendidura se abre y se cierra como si se hubiese convertido en una boca.

—¡Auxilio, Padre Santo! —grita a todo pulmón—, ¡auxilio!

—¡Dame su nombre, criatura hipócrita! —grito.

—¡Ayuda, padre Jehová, ayuda! —insiste—, ¡dile a tu arcángel que detenga el brazo de Abraham y salve a tu hijo!

Bajo mi athame hacia el pecho cada vez más humano de la gallina.

—¡Dame su nombre verdadero o me tragaré tu corazón para que desaparezcas!

—¡Ella, ella, quien está en las sombras! —contesta por fin, aterrada por mi amenaza—. ¡Ella, quien está en la niebla y en la luna que todo lo mira como un ojo!

—¡Dime su nombre!

—¡Su nombre no yace en mi garganta, sino detrás de la Puerta de los Mil Brujos construida por los ángeles!

Mi agarre sobre la daga se afloja.

—¿Qué? ¡¿De qué puerta hablas?!

Ante mi pregunta, la gallina se inmoviliza de golpe. Y, despacio, saca su negra lengua de la garganta. La alarga, tanto que pareciera querer tocarme con ella.

Como una guillotina, sus dos hileras de dientes humanos se cierran sobre ella.

—¡NO, BASTARDO! —grita Inanna, furiosa cuando el asqueroso órgano se desprende de la criatura.

—¡No, dime su nombre, maldita sea! —sacudo el cuello de la gallina antropomorfa de un lado a otro, pero la hendidura comienza a vomitar sangre, tan fría que es como si nos echasen agua helada a las vestiduras.

—¡Es inútil, Elisse, tienes que pedirle que se marche! —exclama la bruja goética, con el temor de que, de la abertura, logre asomarse algo peor que aquella voz.

Miro hacia la lengua, tiesa a un lado del animal, y siento que mis rodillas pierden fuerza.

—Desciende hacia el pozo, *Miohle*…

El viento apaga todas las velas de golpe y el monstruo deja de convulsionarse.

Tared sube la colina a zancadas cuando le hago una señal con la cabeza. Él me sostiene de inmediato, puesto que sabe

—La isla del invierno —exclama Hela a mis espaldas porque, con la tempestad, no hay forma de escucharnos más que a gritos.

Mis nervios se tensan cuando miro a un lado y otro.

—¿Dónde están Julien y Nashua? —pregunto al no verlos entre nosotros.

—No lograron cruzar la niebla, pero haré que Asmoday los guíe de vuelta a la casa —dice Inanna.

—Maldita sea, ¡Allen! —llama Tared a todo pulmón, pero la tormenta no nos permite ver más allá de unos metros a la redonda.

—¡Allá! —Caligo apunta hacia Ilya, quien se aleja por un sendero que conduce a una pequeña loma arbolada frente al mar.

Lo seguimos a toda prisa hasta llegar a un viejo fuerte de piedra de la época de la colonia, semienterrado en la cima y con sus puertas de hierro abiertas de par en par. Metros delante, se extiende una playa de arena oscura, rodeada como una media luna por las enormes rocas de la isla.

Y allí es donde por fin logro verlo.

—¡Allen! —exclamo, aterrado. Con medio cuerpo en el agua, el chico empuja un bote de remos para adentrarse hacia el embravecido mar que ruge delante de él.

Tared y yo bajamos por la pendiente hacia la playa a toda velocidad con el corazón en la boca al verlo subir a la embarcación de un salto.

—¡Allen, no, regresa! —grita Tared cuando las olas golpean furiosas contra el bote.

—¡Espera! —grita Caligo antes de que el lobo pueda lanzarse al agua—, yo iré por él.

La bruja se quita el abrigo y salta varios metros sobre la arena.

En un instante, sus brazos se convierten en alas negras de gran envergadura, tan enormes como las de Fernanda. Pero el largo cuello desplumado, sujeto a una cabeza completamente humana, me indica que no es un águila, sino más bien una especie de buitre.

Caligo se transforma en una de esas temidas arpías de la mitología griega, con garras tan grandes y afiladas que podría perforar cualquier hueso, si lo quisiera.

Ella vuela hacia el bote y extiende las patas para arrancar al chico de la cubierta, pero antes de alcanzarlo, tuerce las alas y se eleva en línea recta hacia el cielo.

—¡¿Qué está haciendo?! —exclama un angustiado Tared cuando ve a la errante planear en círculos.

—Por la Grieta, ¡miren eso! —exclama Hela, quien apunta con su dedo hacia el agua.

Un montón de pequeños remolinos se forman en la superficie y rodean la embarcación, empujándola hacia el mar.

Jadeo de sordo terror al ver que el jardín letal de brazos blancos de la Marionetista brota de las espirales como los tentáculos de un calamar.

Y en un instante, el bote es hundido en las aguas.

—¡NO, ALLEN!

Un relámpago azul estalla a nuestras espaldas, lo hace tan cerca que el impacto nos derriba a todos contra la arena.

—¡Hela, ayuda! —exclama Caligo desde lo alto.

A pesar de la sacudida, la rubia se levanta de inmediato y se zambulle de golpe, tan rápido como si el mar hubiese abierto la boca para tragársela. Un segundo después, ella re-

Como a pedir de boca, el resplandor de mis manos hace al ángel mirar hacia acá.

El monstruo abandona su cacería y se lanza hacia mí de inmediato, lo que le da la oportunidad a Caligo de levantar el vuelo y llevarse a Allen. Intento nadar de vuelta a la orilla, pero me alcanza casi al instante, mi pierna atrapada por uno de sus brazos.

Hela intercepta la extremidad de la criatura y entierra su athame en su muñeca para obligarlo a soltarme, pero tres brazos se enredan entre ellos como un garrote para propinar un potente golpe contra la errante. Ella grita y se desvanece en la oscuridad de la violenta marea.

El ángel me rodea y la corriente me arrastra mar adentro junto a ella, con un abismo cada vez más grande bajo mis pies. Al sentir que me quedo sin aire, dejo que sus extremidades me alcancen, que se aferren a mi cuerpo como una medusa.

Y después, hago estallar el fuego por toda mi piel.

Casi la escucho gritar bajo el agua cuando sus letales tentáculos hierven con el impulso de mi magia.

En menos de un segundo, Hela me embiste y me abraza con fuerza para sacarme a la superficie antes de que me ahogue.

Cuando logramos salir a la playa, Caligo corre hacia nosotros envuelta en su abrigo, despojada ya de su piel. Me ayuda a arrastrar a su hermana lejos de la orilla, para luego arrancarle las branquias del cuello. La rubia jadea de dolor con un costado amoratado bajo la blusa empapada.

Mientras la envenenadora se ocupa de ella, yo me sobrepongo al peso de la espada para ir hacia Allen, aún recostado sobre la arena.

—¡Allen, Allen! —grito mientras me echo de rodillas a su lado.

Caligo ya debe haberle sacado el agua de mar, pero está pálido, y tan frío que sus labios se han puesto azules.

¡Mierda, mierda, mierda!

Déjalo morir.

Lo tomo de las mejillas y empiezo a llevarle calor a todo el cuerpo, intentando no freírlo con mi magia como a la Marionetista. Después de unos momentos, el agua se evapora de sus ropas y su piel recupera algo de color.

Lo pongo de costado cuando empieza a toser, pensando en que quizá necesita expulsar más agua. Pero en vez de eso, el chico vomita una... ¿bola de papel?

—¿Qué carajos...?

—¡Elisse!

El grito de Caligo me hace mirar de nuevo hacia el mar.

La Marionetista brota a la superficie con su boca de metal abierta y los brazos ardiendo, mientras entona el terrible grito de aquella trompeta como una sirena terrible.

Pero antes de que pueda tocar tierra firme, la dirección del viento cambia para soplar contra el ángel. Las olas la golpean y la marea comienza a empujarla hacia atrás.

Abro la boca de asombro al ver que Inanna levita a un costado de la playa, a varios metros sobre las rocas. Tiene los ojos en blanco, y el cabello flota a su alrededor como si estuviese dentro del agua.

Es ella. ¡Ella es quien controla la tormenta!

Pero mi sorpresa no hace más que crecer cuando la niebla y la tormenta se despejan al cambiar de dirección, puesto que ahora puedo ver lo que hay detrás de la bruja.

Un faro. Con aquella luz que me dejó ciego girando en su punta sin parar.

—¡Elisse, cuidado!

Mi chispazo de claridad desaparece ante el grito de Tared.

CAPÍTULO 74
LA LENGUA DE ADÁN

*E*s *el faro.*

No me cabe ninguna duda. Es el mismo maldito faro de la postal de mi padre.

Y si no subo como un rayo a decirle esto a Hoffman es porque ahora mismo debe estar teniendo una pelea campal con Tared en la segunda planta de la casa. Y aunque todavía no sé por qué él y Johanna descuidaron a Allen de esa manera, en estos momentos tampoco me importa demasiado.

Así que, en cambio, estoy sentado en el porche, acompañado del alba que roza los endrinos con tanta lentitud que parece resistirse a separar la niebla de la oscuridad.

El frío me acaricia con su garra, pero me veo obligado a soportarlo al escuchar a Inanna acercarse.

—Lo lamento. Lo lamento muchísimo —digo al sentirla detrás de mí—. Allen era nuestra responsabilidad, y más al haberlo traído a tu casa. Y ahora Hela está…

—No, Elisse. Nada de esto habría pasado si Bathin no hubiese accedido a llevar a Allen Miller a través de la niebla —asegura con asombrosa tranquilidad—. Y no voy a tolerar semejante traición.

Cuando ella da un paso al frente, descubro que lleva un látigo de cuero entre las manos cuya punta tiene cuerdas con cuentas de hierro y trozos de hueso afilados como ganchos; un artefacto tan siniestro que bien podría haber sido sacado del repertorio de los Lander.

—¡Mi señora, por favor!

Aquel grito desesperado me hace mirar hacia el pozo.

Ilya se acerca despacio a la casa. En una mano, lleva a Bathin asido del pelo, mientras que en la otra arrastra a su caballo fantasmal de una de las patas traseras.

—¡No, por favor, mi señora! ¡El chico me obligó, se lo…!

Inanna estruja el mango del látigo con tanta fuerza que el demonio calla de puro terror.

—He sido buena contigo, Bathin —dice ella—. Te traje al mundo de los vivos para que pudieras sentir la tierra bajo tus pies, la caricia de la niebla en tus mejillas, ¿y así es como me pagas?

—¡Señora, se lo ruego! ¡Por sus dones, tenga piedad! —suplica él.

La bruja ladea la cabeza.

—¿Piedad? Esto no es una iglesia —espeta, asqueada—. Esto es la casa de Aradia.

Con el índice de su mano izquierda, Inanna hace un gesto y un círculo se traza en el suelo del patio siguiendo los movimientos del dedo de la bruja.

Ilya arroja a Bathin dentro de la circunferencia, quien se levanta de inmediato para escapar, pero cae de espaldas al chocar contra el campo de contención. El demonio maldice, se retuerce y profiere una cantidad increíble de obscenidades.

—¡Sácame de aquí, Bestia Revestida de Luna, sálvame y te otorgaré mis poderes! —suplica, pero yo lo miro con la misma repulsión que Inanna.

turada por un grupo de soldados, entre los que iba el propio Ilya —la envenenadora encuentra un cuchillo de carnicero y comienza a decapitar a la gallina—. Él no sólo se sorprendió de ver por primera vez a otra errante, sino que se enamoró tan perdidamente de ella que traicionó a sus camaradas para salvarla. Y juntos escaparon en una embarcación ilegal con rumbo a Norteamérica.

"Lamentablemente, Ilya resultó herido, quizá durante la huida, tal vez durante el viaje en barco. Inanna nunca nos ha dado demasiados detalles al respecto. Pero Aradia, quien había predicho la llegada de la portadora de Satanás, ya los esperaba en la costa donde arribaron.

Mientras escucho todo esto, empiezo a pensar en lo mucho que la historia de Inanna se asemeja a la mía o a la de cualquier bruja que se atreve a serlo en una sociedad atontada.

—No había remedio. Ilya iba a morir —continúa—. Pero ambos estaban tan desesperados por seguir juntos que él decidió hacer un pacto con Aradia. Uno muy… especial.

La envenenadora termina de separar la cabeza del cuerpo, y luego camina hacia una de las repisas de la cocina, de donde saca el libro de las generaciones del Culto, el cual, estoy seguro, no estaba allí hace un minuto. Lo coloca en la mesa, sobre la gallina, y lo abre en la última página de las firmas.

Después, apunta con el dedo hacia una que está escrita en cirílico.

Илья Сергеевич Стасов

(Ilya Sergeyevich Stasov)

—No lo entiendo —digo, confundido—. Si nadie que no sea un brujo debe ser parte del Culto, ¿cómo es que pudo firmar este libro?

—Porque el pacto de Ilya no fue entrar al aquelarre, no como sucede irremediablemente con todos los contemplasombras que firman, sino ligar su alma, *su voluntad,* directamente a la de nuestra Madre —me explica—. Tal cual el monstruo que intenta dominarte por medio de tu corazón, Ilya le ofreció este valioso vínculo a Aradia minutos antes de morir para que ella pudiera hacer lo mismo. Y antes de que su alma terminara de cruzar el plano medio para entrar a la muerte definitiva, ella tiró de este vínculo y lo trajo de nuevo al reino humano.

—Pero creo que a estas alturas ya sabes cuáles son las consecuencias de *pactar* con nuestra magia —dice Hela con tristeza.

Y lo que Caligo confiesa a continuación, con la voz casi rota, me deja completamente asombrado:

—Aunque él volvió, *no así su ancestro.* La mitad de su esencia quedó perdida para siempre en el plano medio, y su transformación, su apariencia y su piel no son más que un fragmento de su memoria. Un espejismo de su antigua naturaleza bestial.

Ya. Eso explica por qué las garras del hombre tigre se retraían por sí solas, así como la manera en la que podía recomponer su cuerpo en la batalla.

—Sus reacciones humanas, sus emociones, su capacidad de comunicarse con normalidad; todo en Ilya cambió de una forma antinatural a partir de ese día —continúa la bruja—. Los demonios goéticos sirven a Inanna, pero él *pertenece* a nuestra Madre, y al ser un alma encerrada en un espejismo, una ilusión, no importa que pasen los años y que Inanna envejezca y muera junto con todos nosotros. Él seguirá aquí, sirviendo a Aradia y a esta casa...

—Por toda la eternidad —concluyo.

No soy consciente de cuánto tiempo permanezco con los ojos abiertos tras decir aquella frase. Tan sólo me llevo una mano a la mejilla para limpiarla.

—No te sientas mal por mí, querido.

Los tres nos sobresaltamos al escuchar a Inanna, quien entra a la cocina con una de las vasijas de latón que hay en el ático entre las manos.

La vasija está cerrada y tiene el nombre de Bathin escrito por todas partes.

—Cuando accedió a firmar el libro de Aradia, Ilya sabía perfectamente cuáles iban a ser las consecuencias, al igual que yo —dice, poniendo el recipiente en el suelo—. El arrepentimiento no cambia el pasado, pero tampoco le resta valor a lo que hemos obtenido a cambio de un sacrificio.

Ella quita el libro de encima de la gallina y le hace una seña a Hela con la cabeza. La chica se levanta, con un poco de esfuerzo, y toma las tijeras. De una sola rajada, abre el vientre de la criatura, extrae un puñado de intestinos y los arroja sobre la mesa.

Ejecutando una especie de aruspicina, ella revuelve las entrañas hasta encontrar un papel enrollado. Lo extiende frente a sus ojos y niega con la cabeza.

—El espíritu hablaba con verdad —dice, y nos muestra que el papel está en blanco—. No conocía el nombre de tu Mara.

—No. Pero dijo que era una "ella", y que su nombre se halla detrás de la Puerta de los Mil Brujos —musito—. Y, si no estoy equivocado, debe ser la que vi en mi primera premonición, una que estaba justo en este mismo bosque.

—Pero aun así, la visión es inexacta —dice Caligo, dubitativa—. La gallina dijo que fue construida por los ángeles, así que es imposible que esté en los dominios de Aradia.

—¿Y la gallina no podría decirnos dónde está si la invocamos de nuevo? —pregunto.

—Lo dudo mucho. Ese espíritu pertenece a nuestro lado de la magia. No hay forma de que conozca la ubicación de algo así.

Me muerdo los labios con frustración.

—Mierda, ¿y ahora qué vamos a hacer?

—*Para tu fortuna, Inanna ya sabe la respuesta, pequeño.*

Me yergo como una vara de pronto, como si no pudiese acostumbrarme a escuchar la voz de Aradia brotar de todas partes, tan cercana que parece que la tengo a mis espaldas.

Los tres miramos hacia la bruja goética, y ésta suspira.

—Cuando dijiste que podías hablar todas las lenguas del mundo, no consideramos que el *adámico* también sería una de ellas —reconoce.

—¿Adámico?

—El lenguaje oculto de los ángeles —explica la envenenadora—. Se dice que fue el idioma que existió desde los tiempos de Adán en el Paraíso hasta la construcción de la torre de Babel. Y el cual, según las leyendas, fue transmitido a John Dee durante sus revelaciones.

—Así que de eso se trataba —murmuro al recordar todas las veces que esos monstruos se dirigieron a mí en ese idioma.

—*Pero el que hablases adámico no fue la sorpresa, brujo mío* —continúa Aradia—. *Sino que el ángel decidiera obedecerte.*

—¿Y eso es bueno? —pregunto con inseguridad.

—Es más que bueno, Elisse. Es impresionante —dice Inanna con... ¿orgullo?—. Los contemplasombras, por lo general, dedicamos toda nuestra vida a especializarnos en un solo tipo de magia. Ésta puede ser desde alguna que tenga que ver con nuestra cultura, la que nos haya sido transmitida por un contemplasombras más experimentado o, inclusive, una que hemos escogido por simple afinidad. Y la razón es porque, al poder acceder a la magia y al mundo espiritual de una forma más compleja que los brujos humanos, necesitamos mucho tiempo y experiencia para hacerla funcionar. Y el hecho de que tú puedas trabajar la alquimia, el vudú y cualquier tipo de magia sin ninguna experiencia, sin ningún conocimiento previo, es algo *extraordinario*. Porque eso significa que quizá también podrías manipular la magia enoquiana.

—¡Y a los propios ángeles! —exclama Hela, entusiasmada ante la revelación.

Mi boca se abre en un silencioso "oh" cargado de sorpresa, porque nunca había considerado usar la magia de mis enemigos no para combatirlos, sino para...

Manipularlos...

—Pero sólo fue un momento —titubeo—. El ángel recuperó la consciencia momentos después.

—Eso no cambia el hecho de que lograste tener influencia sobre él —insiste Inanna—. Piénsalo, Elisse. Con los métodos adecuados, con las evocaciones correctas, quizá...

Inanna hace una pausa, y mis dedos se crispan sobre la mesa al comprender por fin.

—Ahora lo entiendo —musito—. Quieren que evoque a un ángel para que nos diga dónde está la puerta.

CAPÍTULO 75
UNA VERDAD INSIGNIFICANTE

Al salir al vestíbulo, me encuentro por fin con mi hombre lobo, quien baja las escaleras furioso.

—Eh, ¿todo bien? —pregunto, más por detener su acelerada marcha que por la respuesta.

—Sí. Sólo necesitaba ajustar cuentas con esos dos —Tared se pasa los dedos por el cabello, y percibo que aún tiene los brazos marcados por sendos moretones, en señal de que ni siquiera permitió que la perpetuasangre lo tratase.

—Dioses, ¿qué diablos pasó?

Él niega con la cabeza.

—Hoffman y Johanna empezaron a discutir por tonterías. Así que Allen aprovechó para escapar...

¿Una discusión? ¿Eso es todo? Dioses, con razón está tan molesto.

—¿Qué hay de tu hermano?

—Arriba —el lobo señala con la cabeza—. Ni siquiera tuvo las agallas para enfrentarme por lo que hizo, así que se encerró en el cuarto de Hela y echó el seguro.

—Pues tendrá que hacerlo, porque necesito hablar con él.

Saco mi libro rojo del bolsillo, y tomo de allí el papel que Allen vomitó en la playa para extenderlo frente al lobo. Se trata del letrero de "se busca" de los tramperos. Uno exactamente igual al que estaba pegado en la gasolinera de Montana.

—Mierda... —susurra, atónito—, ¿por qué los ángeles le darían algo así a mi hermano?

—Quizás hayan atacado a los Lander —digo—. O quizá...

—Los están guiando hacia nosotros.

Un estertor de pánico sacude mi cuerpo al siquiera pensar en esa posibilidad.

—¿Ves? Es por eso que debo hablar con Allen *a solas* —exclamo, y por la forma en la que el semblante del lobo se endurece, me queda claro que no le encanta la idea—. Lo siento, Tared, pero si estás allí, lo único que lograrás es alterarlo. Es mejor que tú vayas con los demás para advertirles sobre esto.

El lobo duda un momento más, pero luego me da la razón con un suspiro.

—De acuerdo —acepta—. Pero no bajes la guardia, Elisse. Mi hermano será todo lo ordinario que un humano puede ser, pero eso no hace su lengua menos peligrosa.

Sí, eso se lo concedo.

Vuelvo a guardar el papel, pero no subo por las escaleras.

—¿Pasa algo? —pregunta el lobo al sentir mi inquietud.

Con un temblor en los dedos, abro otra de las páginas de mi libro para mostrarle el sobre de mi padre.

—Compruébalo tú mismo —digo señalando hacia el faro en el timbre. A Tared le toma sólo un segundo entender..

—Dios santo, ¡pero si es...! —la voz se atasca en su garganta al ver la angustia que se asoma en mi mirada.

—Tared —musito—, creo... creo que mi papá está muerto.

En cuanto subo el último escalón hacia la segunda planta, me detengo al ver que Asmoday está sentado en las vigas del techo, algo que ya me parecería normal de no ser que mira con ansiedad hacia la habitación de Hela. Justo donde Allen se encuentra encerrado.

Siento una profunda incomodidad ante la respiración apretada del demonio, una reacción que ya había visto antes en Haagenti, pero decido ignorar a la criatura y meter la llave que le he pedido a la rubia para poder entrar.

Allí encuentro al joven frente a un espejo redondo, colgado en la pared. El cristal es de color negro, como de piedra ónix, y está enmarcado en oro; sin duda, el mismo con el que la rubia me miraba en las premoniciones.

Él no reacciona ante mi intrusión, embelesado por las sensaciones sobrenaturales que estos objetos suelen transmitir. Eso, o busca algún rostro familiar entre los fantasmas que se asoman en el reflejo.

Por toda la habitación hay varios tableros de *ouija* tirados, las planchas apuntadoras revueltas entre tubos de labiales, ropa apilada y esferas de cristal. Cerca de la ventana yace un gramófono antiguo con una corneta de color oro viejo, y aunque no tiene puesto ningún vinilo, el platillo da vueltas con la aguja en posición.

Cierro la puerta y me siento detrás de él, en la cama de estampado psicodélico.

—Allen, ¿recuerdas cómo llegaste a la playa? —pregunto mientras saco el letrero de los Lander—. ¿O siquiera algo de esto?

Como era de esperarse, el chico ni siquiera gira la cabeza hacia mí.

El chico. El hermano de Tared es bastante mayor que yo, pero tiendo a usar mucho esa palabra para describirlo, quizás en señal de lo mucho que me cuesta verlo como algo más que un niño caprichoso. Así que ahora intento entenderlo como lo que realmente es: alguien que fue arrastrado a una realidad a la que no pertenece, con problemas que nunca pidió tener y rodeado de personajes hostiles que no sienten la menor empatía por él.

No puedo culparlo por querer huir de todo eso.

—A diferencia de lo que muchos creen, saber la verdad no siempre te libera —comienzo—. Al menos no cuando tenías la esperanza de que tus temores fuesen sólo un invento de tu imaginación. Y el día en el que supe que mis monstruos eran reales, fue como una sentencia, porque entonces estaba claro que nunca iba a poder escapar de ellos.

Creo escuchar una canción vibrar en el aire, una melodía muy queda y antigua que parece desprenderse del gramófono.

—No voy a pedirte que seas parte de nuestro mundo, y mucho menos que hagas las paces con Tared. Eso no me corresponde —continúo—. Pero, si algo aprendí de tu hermano, fue que mientras más conoces aquello que temes, más dejas de temerle. Y si no intentas por lo menos comprender lo que te está sucediendo, entonces tendrás que resignarte a enloquecer.

Al levantar la mirada, descubro que Allen me observa a través del espejo de obsidiana.

—Eres tan ingenuo al pensar que lo que buscaba de todo esto era una respuesta —dice—. Yo siempre supe la verdad, después de todo. Lo que yo quiero es... *justicia*.

Niego con la cabeza, fatigado por su tozudez.

—Al igual que el pecado, la justicia no existe en nuestro mundo, Allen. No de la misma manera que en el tuyo. Ya deberías entenderlo a estas alturas.

Él se aleja de los fantasmas y se acerca. Reposa una mano sobre la cama, se encorva sobre mí como un buitre.

—¿Y qué hay de la venganza? ¿Eso sí existe en tu mundo, Elisse? —pregunta con una sonrisa. Aún puedo percibir el olor a sal que se desprende de sus ropas, de sus cabellos, pero a él no parece molestarle. Es más. Debería estar traumatizado después de lo que pasó en la playa, pero se ve casi complacido por los problemas que ha causado. ¿Acaso...?—. Porque si esas brujas son tan malvadas como dicen ser —continúa—, tal vez hasta estarían felices de ayudarme a *vengarme* de mi hermano.

Cuando el desgraciado acaricia mi trenza, lo empujo para quitármelo de encima, tan asqueado que me sorprende no haberlo hecho con un puñetazo.

—Hiciste todo esto a propósito, ¿verdad? —exclamo—, ¡escapaste para exponernos a los ángeles!

Allen contiene una carcajada.

—Oh, no, ¿cómo puedes pensar eso de mí? Si tú mismo lo dijiste. Estaba atemorizado y sólo aproveché la oportunidad para escapar...

Dioses. Es ridículo el cinismo de este cabrón.

—No has respondido mi pregunta —le muestro de nuevo el cartel.

Allen ladea la cabeza y mete una mano en el bolsillo. Aprieta el puño dentro, cuadra la mandíbula. Pero al final, se arquea de hombros como un completo psicópata.

—Seguí al jinete después de pedirle que me llevara a Salem —dice, tan tranquilo que se me revuelve el estómago—, y cuando entré a la niebla, me desmayé. Eso es todo lo que recuerdo.

La mirada que le lanzo es suficiente para hacerle saber que no le creo en absoluto.

—¿Sabes? Vine aquí con la esperanza de ayudarte. No. De que me permitieras *protegerte*. Y no sólo de nuestro mundo —susurro—. Pero tu hermano tenía razón. No eres más que una víbora.

Estrujo el papel y lo arrojo al suelo de la habitación, consciente de que quizá ya no estoy tratando con una persona en sus cabales.

—¿Y qué vas a hacer conmigo ahora, eh? —espeta—. ¿Vas a dejarme encerrado aquí hasta que me pudra? ¿O vas a "silenciarme" como hiciste con ese hombre que mi hermano escondió en el bosque?

No sé en qué maldito momento Allen escuchó sobre los *silenciamientos*, pero el chico no pareciera darse cuenta de que su actitud no lo está salvando precisamente de uno.

—Creo que ya da igual lo que te pase, Allen. Y por lo que Tared ya me ha contado de ti, tampoco es que mucha gente vaya a extrañarte allá afuera, ¿verdad?

Su sonrisa se descompone. Ya sin deseos de quedarme a escuchar su rabieta, cruzo la habitación a zancadas.

—Qué conveniente, ¿no? —exclama, justo cuando pongo la mano en el pomo de la puerta—. Qué conveniente que siempre que alguien sufre, muere o desaparece, Tared nunca recuerda nada, ¿verdad? Pero *yo me niego a olvidar,* Elisse, ¡a mi padre, y a cómo eran las cosas antes de que mi hermano decidiera erradicar de mi vida a todas y cada una de las personas que significaban algo para mí!

El calor que de pronto se propaga en mi mano de hueso es tan intenso que la perilla se torna al rojo vivo bajo mis dedos.

La obscena insinuación de Allen por fin me hace comprender por qué su hermano siempre ha intentado mantener su distancia con él.

Furioso, azoto la puerta a mis espaldas y echo llave a la cerradura.

Y al ver a Asmoday aún en el techo y con esa boca acolmillada entreabierta, me queda claro que Allen se lo pensará dos veces antes de intentar escapar otra vez.

CAPÍTULO 76
ANZUELO

Cuando le dijeron que volverían a Minnesota en busca de un cadáver, el instinto tiró de la errante Irina de manera peligrosa.

Primero, lo sintió como una comezón desagradable al fondo de la lengua, pero luego, el vínculo materno la hirió tanto que más de una vez la vi despertar agitada en medio de la oscuridad.

Y ahora, bajo las sombras de aquel bosque nocturno, esa sensación de pesadilla cobra sentido por fin. Porque jamás creyó que, al llegar a la colina donde solía estar aquella casa, se encontrarían con *eso*. Con la construcción hecha ruinas y a dos tramperos en pie donde alguna vez estuvo la entrada, puestos alrededor de una pequeña hoguera, hecha con los restos de un viejo sillón.

—¿Crees que hayan capturado a Elisse y a los demás? ¿Fue por eso que su teléfono estaba fuera de servicio? —pregunta una mujer humana a su lado, tan sorprendida como ella ante semejante escena, pero la madre no responde, demasiado ocupada en asegurarse de que el olor que percibe en el aire no es una alucinación.

No. El tirón en sus entrañas no miente: es el aroma de sus hijos, desperdigado en alguna parte de aquellos escombros.

¿Estarán ocultos entre las vigas caídas, detrás de las paredes a medio derrumbar? O quizás en el estrecho sótano de la casa, donde recuerda que había una caldera.

—No lo creo, Lía —contesta por fin—. De ser así, este lugar apestaría a sangre...

La humana jadea horrorizada, porque no le cuesta imaginar las cosas que haría el Inquisidor si le pusiera las manos encima a mi criatura y a las bestias que lo rodean.

Pero no hay una sola señal de ellos o del resto de los tramperos. Ni un solo resabio a óxido, a cuerdas o a Benjamin Lander en todo el terreno.

Sólo la esencia de sus hijos, que la llama con grave desesperación.

El sabor amargo en su lengua se intensifica, por lo que la puma mira atrás.

La tribu de la Espiral del Norte se agazapa detrás de ellas, tensa ante la incertidumbre.

Además de la concubina de la humana, hay otros tres hombres. Tres devorapieles, uno de ellos tan joven que apenas roza la adultez. Todos vinieron en busca del cuerpo de aquel miserable sujeto, pero lo único que han encontrado son unos cuantos ojos colgados entre los árboles y a esos dos asesinos frente a la casa, quienes custodian en solitario el terreno como si fuese la entrada a un mausoleo.

Sentimientos contradictorios invaden a la errante, una resistencia sembrada en su garra apretada contra el gatillo de la pistola, pero al final, decide que no puede distraerse con las posibilidades.

Hace una señal a uno de los devorapieles, un hombre de pelaje blanco con pequeños cuernos de cabra de montaña sobre su cabeza. Él le entrega una manta de camuflaje, la cual se coloca como una capa sobre cabeza y hombros.

Ambos, ya envueltos en trajes que se mimetizan con la nieve que cubre el predio, salen del lindero del bosque para acercarse a aquellos tramperos, cuidando mantener el sigilo en todo momento. La naturaleza felina de ella le permite moverse como hoja sobre el agua, mientras que el otro hombre parece ya acostumbrado a acechar en aquellas condiciones.

Avanzan despacio, silenciosos y con la ventaja del viento que hace crujir la montaña. Tanto, que los cazadores ni siquiera se percatan cuando ambos flanquean la casa y se agazapan entre los escombros, a pocos metros suyos.

La madre se prepara para atacar, pero algo la hace aguardar; un olor peculiar que percibe por encima del de sus hijos, tan apetitoso que lo reconoce de inmediato.

Ah, ¡qué instinto tan afilado! Porque le toma apenas un instante descubrir lo que es: el hombre al que acecha tiembla de arriba abajo. Y no por frío, sino de *miedo*. Un terror tan obsceno que las lágrimas se acopian en su cara.

Y eso es lo que no encaja. Un trampero es mezquino y traicionero, pero nunca cobarde.

Ella baja la mirada, estupefacta, y descubre una hilera de pequeños paquetes de plástico comprimidos alrededor de la cintura del pobre desgraciado, a quien le falta poco para orinarse encima.

Y entonces, lo comprende por fin: aquellos hombres no son vigías. *Son anzuelos.*

—¡No! —el chillido de la errante llega muy tarde, porque el hombre chivo ya ha saltado sobre su víctima. El cazador revienta en cientos de pedazos cuando el devorapieles se estrella contra él.

Ella grita, pero no escucha su propia voz con claridad, puesto que un zumbido atronador invade sus oídos como resultado de la explosión, como si los hombres del Inquisidor hubiesen devuelto la misma bofetada que se les dio a ellos en Montana.

Los tramperos comienzan a brotar como cucarachas de las entrañas de los escombros, y la errante puma se sacude presa de la conmoción.

¿Cómo es que no pudo darse cuenta de que estaban allí antes? ¿Acaso su instinto materno de protección nubló sus sentidos por completo?

No tiene tiempo para descubrirlo, puesto que el caos se cierne alrededor de ella cuando la Espiral del Norte alcanza las ruinas.

La concubina de la humana se transforma en una osa gigantesca, mientras que los otros dos errantes se envuelven en sus propias pieles: un joven puercoespín, con la espalda atestada de púas afiladas como lanzas, un guerrero tejón con garras largas cual navajas.

Pero ni siquiera sus brutales dimensiones logran intimidar a la veintena de hombres que se abalanza contra ellos.

—¡Mamá!

El llamado atraviesa el zumbido. Los gritos, los disparos, las explosiones; todo aquello no es nada comparado con el ruido que hace su corazón cuando ve a un niño detrás de ella con la marca de una soga alrededor del cuello.

—Mamá… —clama de nuevo el pequeño con el brazo extendido para alcanzarla.

Pero Irina Begaye se queda helada, las garras atenazadas en el suelo, porque sabe bien que aquella cosa que acaba de ver no es su hijo.

CAPÍTULO 777
RAXNAL

U*n monstruo para engañar a la magia.*
Dos para despedazarla.
Y uno más para revelarla.

La ironía es tan grande que casi resulta gracioso. Porque ¿quién hubiera adivinado que el último ángel de la visión de Hela, un *Ángel de los Secretos*, sería traído a nuestro plano por nosotros?

Y si bien, el enterarse de que yo tendría que realizar tan peligrosa evocación hizo que más de uno en Comus Bayou protestara, el que no pudiese ejecutarse en otro sitio más que en Salem, lejos de la protección de la casa y con la amenaza de un posible encuentro con los tramperos bastó para que casi quisieran abortar el plan.

Pero yo ya estoy tan desesperado por acabar con todo esto que no di lugar a ninguna objeción. Así que, en cuanto sale el sol, nos ponemos en marcha hacia la niebla envueltos en las pieles de Aradia, guiados esta vez por Ilya. Y al diluirse la cortina gris del bosque, lo primero con lo que me topo es con una mujer inclinada sobre un caldero de hierro. Lleva un vestido largo y polvoriento, con un mandil atado a la cintura y una gorra de peregrina, inmune a nuestra presencia.

Es una muñeca de cera, colocada en una cocina que parece tener cientos de años de antigüedad. Pequeñas placas informativas cuelgan en las paredes y los muebles, en señal de que estamos en una especie de museo, cerrado por la tormenta que ha empeorado desde nuestra pelea con Vaasaa.

Me llevo una mano a los labios para aguantar una repentina arcada por náuseas.

—¿Elisse, estás bien? —pregunta Tared a mi lado.

—No se preocupen. Es natural que, al principio, su cuerpo y su magia sientan rechazo hacia este lugar —dice Inanna, quien carga una pequeña caja de madera entre las manos—. Ésta es la casa de Jonathan Corwin, después de todo.

Johanna se acerca para ayudarme con mi malestar. Julien y Hela no nos acompañan, ésta última para asegurarse de que ningún otro demonio quiera pasarse de listo.

—¿Aquí vamos a invocar al ángel? —pregunta mi hermana—, pensé que el ritual debía hacerse en un sitio donde se adorasen a los ángeles, algo así como una iglesia.

—Y así es, querida —dice Caligo—, piénsalo, ¿qué lugar de veneración mejor para esos seres que la mismísima casa de uno de los magistrados de los juicios de Salem? Si hubo un lugar en Nueva Inglaterra donde los ángeles se revolcaron de placer fue dentro de estas paredes.

La incomodidad se acrecienta al seguir a las brujas al segundo piso, hacia una de las sombrías habitaciones.

—¿Qué diablos es eso? —pregunta Nashua al observar el tétrico interior.

Rodeada de muebles de la época yace una cama de dosel blanco, con un cuerpo humano cubierto por una sábana sobre el colchón. Manchas de lodo fresco se desparraman por la tela, en señal de que Ilya tiene poco de haberlo traído de su tumba.

—Los ángeles necesitan cuerpos de brujos para manifestarse en nuestro mundo. Así que vamos a ofrecerles uno —dice Caligo, quien avanza hacia el lecho para descubrir el rostro del cadáver.

Es una mujer quemada, quien parece ya tener varios días de haber empezado a descomponerse.

Hoffman ladea la cabeza.

—¿Ésa es...?

—Cecilia. Una de las nuestras —dice la envenenadora, casi en un suspiro—. Pero está bien. Esto es lo que ella hubiera querido.

La bruja rellena la boca de su amiga con lavanda y corteza de benjuí, para luego volver a cubrirle la cara. Después, Inanna saca de la caja de madera una esfera de cristal con una cruz de metal insertada; un artefacto similar al usado por John Dee para evocar a los ángeles hace quinientos años. Lo coloca en el suelo, delante del cuerpo, y la esfera se queda quieta por sí sola, sin rodar y con la cruz apuntando hacia el techo. Luego se gira hacia mí.

—Muy bien. Ahora, todos dejaremos esta habitación para que puedas ejecutar la evocación.

—Espera, ¿vamos a dejarlo aquí *solo*? —pregunta Tared, exaltado.

—Raxnal no es como los otros ángeles —responde Inanna, firme—. Las pieles de Aradia podrán esconder nuestra esencia, pero no así nuestras voces, por lo que no podemos arriesgarnos a que se nos escape un solo suspiro si queremos que coopere con Elisse.

—O que no lo mate en el acto.

El comentario de Ilya hace gruñir a Tared.

—Calma —Caligo da unas palmadas a la espalda del lobo—. Estaremos del otro lado de la puerta para entrar a socorrer a Elisse si hace falta. Pero estando aquí, sólo entorpeceremos su labor.

Esto no lo ayuda a tranquilizarse en absoluto, y no es para menos. Quedarme encerrado en un espacio tan reducido, con la posibilidad de que el ángel me ataque con uno de sus Martillos…

Inanna me cubre la cabeza con otra de las pieles de Aradia, en señal de que ha llegado el momento.

—Muy bien. Ahora, lo más importante: tu lengua, tus pensamientos, tus conjuros; cada parte de ti debe hablar en adámico, no lo olvides. Tu vida depende de ello.

Me estruja el hombro y sale de la habitación junto con los demás. Y una vez que la puerta se cierra a mis espaldas, me arrodillo ante la esfera de cristal.

Cierro los ojos y me tomo unos minutos para prepararme, porque mi miedo más grande no son mis capacidades, sino la furia de la espada.

Abro los ojos y miro hacia el cadáver.

—*OLGOTA*,[32] Raxnal —exclamo a la par que levanto los brazos—. Raxnal! *Sobam ialpurg izazaz!*[33]

Mi enoquiano resulta tan perfecto que, de inmediato, un sutil rayo de luz se abre paso en la tormenta, tan delgado como un hilo al atravesar la ventana. Se dispara sobre la esfera y, de su resplandor, múltiples haces de arcoíris se manifiestan por toda la habitación.

---

[32] Palabra de poder para evocar a los ángeles de los secretos.

[33] En enoquiano: "¡Raxnal! Aquél que yace enmarcado por las llamas".

—*Dspaaox busd caos, dschis odipuran teloah cacrg oisalman loncho od vovina carbaf!*[34]

Estiro mi mano de hueso hacia el cuerpo y retuerzo mi puño como si quisiera tirar del ángel del cielo a la tierra. Una mota de humo blanco traspasa la tela, en señal de que el benjuí y la lavanda se consumen dentro de la boca de Cecilia.

El letal olor a flores comienza a inundar la habitación a la par que los rayos de luz cambian de dirección y apuntan hacia la bruja fallecida.

—*Dooiap mad, goholor!*[35]

Mi pecho dobla su peso cuando el cadáver cruje bajo las sábanas. Pero no es el sonido de algo que se rompe y se reacomoda, sino de... dientes al masticar.

Debajo de la tela, escucho que el ángel *habla*. O más bien, susurra cosas ininteligibles.

—*Dooiap mad, goholor!*

La criatura se detiene ante mi insistencia. Y sin sonidos de arpas ni manifestaciones hermosas, los hilos de luz tiran del cuerpo y comienzan a levantarlo en perpendicular sobre la cama. Lo hacen flotar sobre el colchón como una momia y luego lo giran despacio hacia mí.

Los rayos de luz desaparecen y la tela se desprende para revelar a la bestia.

Raxnal no tiene en absoluto la apariencia de Cecilia, de quien sólo queda su piel quemada, amarrada alrededor de la cintura del ángel. Tiene los brazos cruzados sobre su pecho, y una de sus manos sostiene una aguja y la otra, unas tijeras, su

---

[34] "¡Tú, que permaneces en la gloria de la tierra, que no verás la muerte hasta que esta casa se derrumbe y los dragones se ahoguen!"

[35] "En el nombre de tu Dios, ¡levántate!"

par de Martillos. El resto de su cuerpo tiene la forma de una crisálida cubierta de oídos y bocas, éstas últimas cerradas con un grueso hilo blanco.

Mi corazón galopa como un caballo, y el temor de que aquel monstruo lo escuche se acrecienta cuando me toma un segundo recordar el siguiente paso de la evocación.

—*¿Tu nombre verdadero es Raxnal?* —pregunto en adámico—. *OCALCO!*[36]

El ángel ladea la cabeza como si me observara a través de esa hermosa máscara de hierro, manchada en los labios por la carne quemada de la bruja.

La criatura abre los brazos. Escoge una de sus bocas, próxima a sus costillas, y corta el hilo con sus tijeras.

—*Yo soy él* —responde una horrenda voz desde esos labios, también en enoquiano—. *El enmarcado por las llamas. El que no morirá hasta que esta casa se derrumbe y los dragones se ahoguen.*

Trago saliva, la tensión me retuerce los intestinos.

—*¿Quién te ha despertado a ti y a tu estirpe?* —pregunto, tentando un poco mi suerte.

El ángel abre otro par de labios.

—*Su nombre no yace en mis gargantas, sino detrás de la Puerta de los Mil Brujos.*

Ahogo mis ganas de maldecir, porque a cada segundo, siento como si mis rodillas se hundiesen en la madera ante el esfuerzo de luchar contra la espada.

La magia angelical es dura. Mucho más de lo que pensé.

—*¿Dónde está la Puerta de los Mil Brujos, Raxnal?* —pregunto, consciente de que no aguantaré demasiado.

---

[36] Palabra de poder para comandar a los ángeles de los secretos.

El monstruo se vuelca hacia otra boca, una que se abre justo en medio de su pecho.

—*La Puerta de los Mil Brujos. El último portal antes de La Luz...* —dice— *su fulgor resplandece al final del camino que lleva hacia el Merkavah...*

¿Mer...kavah?

—*¿Y cómo llego hasta ahí?*

La criatura alza sus tijeras y escoge un orificio más. Mete las puntas, abre el instrumento y...

¿No ves que estoy aquí, bestia idiota?

Raxnal se detiene de golpe. Al igual que mi corazón.

Y luego, el ángel empuña las tijeras.

—¡TARED!

El hombre lobo derriba la puerta ante mi grito, justo cuando el monstruo se abalanza contra mí. Lo atrapa en el aire y lo arroja contra la ventana, rompiendo el cristal en pedazos.

La alarma de seguridad se dispara de inmediato.

—¡Ayuda! —exclamo.

Nashua e Ilya entran detrás de Tared, pero Raxnal se desliza como un veloz gusano por el techo para impedir que lo alcancen. Destroza el dosel de la cama, trepa por las vigas con sus letales tijeras y se deja caer sobre mí de un salto.

Apenas soy lo bastante veloz para sujetar su muñeca e impedir que me clave su arma en la frente.

Los tres errantes se ciñen contra él, tiran del halo de hueso y de ambos brazos para alejar de mí sus Martillos, pero la boca abierta de su pecho logra morderme el hombro.

Lanzo un grito al sentir los dientes como una trampa de oso, aferrados con tanta fuerza que me arrancarán un trozo en cualquier momento.

En un reflejo, saco el athame de mis ropas y lo ensarto en el costado de su cabeza. Raxnal grita con sus otras bocas abiertas, pero no dejo de apuñalarlo hasta que afloja sus dientes sobre mi carne.

Tared me arranca al ángel de encima, y mi hermana se cierne sobre mi herida de inmediato.

—No hay tiempo, ¡hay que largarse ya! —grita Caligo, quien se lanza a cubrir la ventana rota con la sábana del ángel. Escucho los gritos de los vecinos de la casa y una sirena de policía a lo lejos, ensordecida por la tormenta.

La niebla se abre y las luces de las patrullas entran a la habitación mientras Ilya alza el cadáver sobre su hombro.

Y esta vez, no hay tiempo de limpiar.

CAPÍTULO 78
EL TRONO CELESTE

Fue muy irónico que, después del desastre que habíamos causado en casa de Jonathan Corwin, lo primero que hicieran los noticieros, al día siguiente, fuese asegurar que todo había sido obra de "un culto satánico", el mismo responsable de los asesinatos ocurridos en Salem en las últimas semanas.

Y, como cereza del pastel, también parecían más interesados en la esfera de cristal que dejamos allí que en el cruel homicidio que había sucedido esa misma noche, pero en otra parte de la ciudad; una venganza de los ángeles por lo que le habíamos hecho a Raxnal, tal vez.

No tuve estómago para descubrir cómo habían torturado esta vez a la víctima, así que me mantuve todo el día alejado de ese extraño televisor que parecía funcionar sin electricidad. Ya habíamos perdido la cuenta de la cantidad de monstruos que debían estar ahora sueltos por Salem, y la sensación de peligro se retorcía en mi espalda como un tornillo.

Tenía miles de dudas, pero las brujas bajaron al sótano en cuanto volvimos de la batalla, y se llevaron consigo el cadáver del ángel sin dar más explicaciones sobre lo que había pasado en la casa del magistrado.

Y no es hasta hoy, casi al anochecer, cuando ellas vuelven y nos llaman a reunirnos en el comedor.

Me hacen sentarme a la cabecera, con mi lobo muy cerca de mí. Y antes de que cualquiera de nosotros pueda abrir la boca, la bruja goética me pone delante un libro de pastas blancas, abierto de par en par.

—¿Qué es esto? —pregunto, inquieto ante la complejidad del diagrama.

—Esto, Elisse, es el reino de los ángeles —dice—. Y el Merkavah no es otra cosa que el Trono Celeste. El corazón de ese lugar.

Su larga uña apunta hacia el centro del dibujo.

—Raxnal dijo que la Puerta de los Mil Brujos estaba al final del camino que lleva hacia el Merkavah —añade Johanna, pálida—. Eso significa que...

—Si lo que Elisse quiere es el nombre de su Mara, entonces deberá atravesar el Cielo de John Dee para conseguirlo.

—No, ¡es una locura! —Nashua es el primero en protestar.

—Y también una trampa —añade Julien—, ¿qué tal que esa cosa sólo haya dicho eso para engañarnos como hacían las Marionetistas?

—Es imposible —corta Caligo—. Los Ángeles de los Secretos se llaman así porque sólo guardan verdades ocultas, por lo tanto, no tienen la capacidad de mentir.

—Pero...

—Puedo hacerlo.

—¡Elisse!

—Puedo hacerlo, Johanna —reitero—. Entré una vez al reino de Samedi, así que no hay motivo por el cual no pueda hacer esto también.

Mi confianza no parece entusiasmar a las brujas.

—Guinée es un lugar muy peligroso, pero no se compara con el reino de los ángeles —replica Inanna—. Su legión completa se encuentra allí, y con tantos Martillos, tantos ojos vigilantes, es sin duda el reino espiritual más letal para los brujos... Pero eso ni siquiera es lo que más nos preocupa.

—¿Qué quieres decir? —pregunto, incapaz de imaginar que podría ser peor que todo esto.

La bruja respira hondo, pero baja la cabeza para evitarme.

—El problema no es llegar a la puerta —continúa, casi en un susurro—. Sino lo que te espera detrás de ella.

Tres.

Tres segundos es lo que nos toma entender lo que acaba de decir Inanna. Y al hacerlo, el detective se levanta con tanta furia que la mesa se sacude.

—De ninguna manera. Elisse no va a entrar allí.

—¡Hoffman!

—¡Olvídalo! —explota—. ¿Te das cuenta de lo que están diciendo? ¡Quieren que te enfrentes a Dios!

Dios.

La palabra se siente como un puñetazo en la cara.

—No queremos que lo enfrente —interrumpe Hela—. Queremos que lo *mate.*

Mis hermanos se alzan también, insultados por el atrevimiento de las brujas.

—Los malditos ángeles son falsos —espeta Nashua—, ¿cómo carajos pueden tener también un Dios?

—Todos los reinos espirituales tienen regentes superiores, incluso los cultos falsos. Sí, tienen a Dios. Y les aseguro que es tan real como el auténtico.

Y quizás...

Igual de poderoso.

—Además —continúa la rubia—, él debió haber negociado con la Mara de Elisse, para empezar, así que tiene sentido que conozca también su nombre.

—¿Es que no ven que no nos queda otra opción? —exclama Caligo—. Si no acabamos con el Dios de los ángeles, sus legiones seguirán desatándose, una tras otra, mientras haya brujos vivos sobre la tierra, ¡da igual que obtengamos o no ese nombre!

—Eso es lo único que querían de Elisse, ¿verdad? —grita el detective, tan alto que juro ver los pabilos de las velas tambalearse—. Por eso le sugirieron que no se separara del monstruo de hueso, ¡porque querían *utilizarlo*, hijas de perra!

—¡No se atreva a acusarnos de esa manera, detective! —espeta la envenenadora—. Si nosotras pudiéramos hacerlo, no le pediríamos intervenir, pero con esa lengua y esa garra, él es nuestra única posibilidad, ¡la nación de los errantes no puede arriesgarse a sufrir otra Guerra Ocultista!

—Están pidiendo que se suicide —replica Julien—, ustedes mismas lo vieron, ¿no? Por más enoquiano que hable, el monstruo de hueso traicionará a Elisse en cuanto ponga un pie en el reino de los ángeles, ¡y eso si no es que la espada lo fulmina primero!

Una guerra campal de gritos y protestas se desata por la mesa, lo que me orilla a sumirme en un mutismo total. El único que no se une a la disputa es Tared, quien todo este tiempo se ha limitado a mirar sus manos entrelazadas sobre la mesa.

—Elisse, escúchame, por favor —pide Inanna—. Mis hermanas y yo estamos conscientes de que, por más que hayas aprendido sobre tu magia estos días, nada de eso servirá si no puedes controlar tanto la espada como al monstruo. Y es por eso que por fin tenemos un plan —ella vuelve a poner sus dedos sobre el diagrama del plano angelical—. ¿Recuerdas cuando hablamos sobre los sigilos y lo complejo que sería hacer uno para la espada filosofal? Si bajamos con Madre fue precisamente para trazar un ritual lo bastante poderoso como para crear dicho sigilo y que, de paso, te ayudará también a silenciar a la bestia dentro de ti.

Eso por fin me hace levantar la cabeza.

—¿Están hablando en serio? —pregunto.

—Será muy... arriesgado para nosotras, para la casa, y también será una de las ceremonias más complejas que hayamos hecho en este aquelarre —asegura—. Pero estamos convencidas de que la única razón por la cual no has podido anteponerte a la criatura es porque la espada te ha oprimido todo este tiempo.

—Mírate, Elisse —pide Hela, desesperada—, cargas un maldito Martillo dentro de ti y aun así puedes hacer cosas extraordinarias, ¡hasta la propia Aradia ya estaría muerta en tu lugar! Tenemos fe en que, si logras hacer el sigilo con éxito, todo esto funcionará.

Fe.

Abro y cierro la boca un par de veces, incrédulo ante tal promesa.

—Yo no tengo semejante poder —musito—. El monstruo de hueso es quien me lo otorga...

Inanna niega con la cabeza.

—No. El monstruo de hueso es poderoso porque *se alimenta de ti*, Elisse. Que no se te olvide.

Los colmillos de la criatura resuenan dentro de mí como un cascabel.

—¿Cuándo habría que empezar? —cuestiono.

La bruja goética se relaja sobre su asiento y mira hacia sus hermanas antes de responder:

—Esta misma noche.

—¿Qué? ¡¿Tan pronto?! —grita Johanna en mi lugar.

—No podemos esperar más —insiste—. Dentro de muy poco llegará la Luna del Lobo,[37] uno de los acontecimientos más importantes de los calendarios esotéricos. Y si queremos aprovechar su energía, debemos descender con Madre para prepararte. Y ustedes saben que, lo que aquí pueden ser largos días de espera, allá no serán más que unas horas.

Hoffman chasquea la lengua y nos da la espalda para caminar con nerviosismo de un lado a otro. Mis hermanos están pálidos, las brujas, expectantes...

----

[37] Primera luna llena del año.

Me veo obligado a apretar las manos sobre las rodillas, porque no me había dado cuenta de que estaba *temblando*.

¿De verdad estoy tan aterrado? ¿Después de todo lo que hecho, de los lugares a los que he llegado? ¿Tanto miedo tengo de entrar a ese sitio, de enfrentarme a ese *Dios* imitador?

El silencio a la espera de mi respuesta se alarga. La presión crece como una avalancha sobre mí.

De pronto, Tared se levanta de su silla, da la media vuelta y, sin decir una sola palabra, sale a zancadas de la sala. Algo que jamás había hecho en un momento de confrontación.

No dudo ni un instante en seguirlo.

Como una flecha, él entra a la habitación de las hierbas, conmigo detrás, y comienza a dar vueltas frente a la cama como un lobo enjaulado.

—¿Tared?

—Todos aquí no han hecho otra cosa que hablarte de rituales y magia. De lo que *debes* hacer —dice, furioso—. Pero, ¿por qué nadie en esa maldita mesa se ha tomado la molestia de preguntar qué es lo que tú *quieres* hacer?

Bajo los hombros, con angustia, y cierro la puerta a mis espaldas.

—*Tengo* que hacer esto, Tared —susurro sin poder ocultar el miedo en mi voz—. Si no, no podré salvarlos a...

—¿Salvarnos? —exclama—. ¡Dios, Elisse! ¿Quién te dijo que ésa era tu responsabilidad? No nos debes nada, ni a mí ni a nuestra maldita raza ni a la jodida humanidad como para que pienses que debes sacrificarte por nosotros.

Aquello me sorprende tanto que me cuesta creer que haya sido dicho por Tared y no por Hoffman.

Pero ahora lo entiendo. Él también está aterrado.

—Tared, yo...

—Siempre que entras a esos lugares intento mantener la calma —corta—. Intento no ceder ante el miedo, pero no tienes idea de lo que se siente el estar del otro lado del portal, rezando a cada segundo para que no vuelvas hecho pedazos. Esto no es Samedi. Esto no es Jocelyn Blake —dice con la voz cada vez más rota—. Me enfrentaré a una horda de ángeles y tramperos. Me arrancaré el último trozo de piel, colmillo o garra que pueda regenerar mi cuerpo para protegerte, pero Elisse, por favor...

Tared no logra terminar su frase. En cambio, se lleva las manos a la cara y se encorva de una forma que me rompe el corazón.

Rodeo a mi hombre lobo y lo atraigo hacia mí con fuerza. Él también me abraza, hunde su rostro en mi cuello.

—Tengo que hacerlo —insisto mientras acaricio su cabello—, porque prefiero morir ahora mismo a seguir despertando una y otra vez en esta pesadilla —a él se le escapa un gemido que me obliga a apretarlo contra mi pecho—. Pero no voy a lograrlo sin ti. Eres la única persona que me queda en el mundo, y no puedo ir a ese lugar si tú no crees en mí.

Tared se separa para mirarme con los ojos enrojecidos de contener las lágrimas.

—No, Elisse, no digas eso, por favor...

—¡Nuestra familia está en ruinas, Tared! —exclamo, también al borde de la desesperación—. Julien está harto, Nashua está tan avergonzado que ya ni siquiera puede mirarnos a los ojos, ¡y Johanna y Hoffman se han vuelto tan egoístas! ¿Cómo puedes decirme que no me estoy quedando solo si hasta mi padre ha muerto y...?

—Tu padre no está muerto, Elisse, ya te dije que...

—¡Deja de quererme hacer sentir mejor! —suplico—. ¡Deja de mentirme sólo porque piensas que no voy a soportar la verdad!

¡Mi padre está muerto!

—¡Mi padre está muerto y yo fui un idiota porque no tuve las agallas para aceptarlo!

Yo lo sabía. Lo había sentido desde el principio, como una semilla enterrada a la que no permitía germinar.

Mi Mara *lo mató*. Mi padre me abandonó en Tíbet, quizá para protegerme, y ella lo mató en algún momento de todos los jodidos años que estuvo preparándose para mi llegada, ¡y hasta pudo haber enviado esa jodida postal para engañarme, para hacerme venir hasta este maldito país a pesar de todos los esfuerzos de mi padre! Y aun así, decidí aferrarme a la esperanza, ¡a un invento de mi imaginación porque no podía soportar la idea de que el hombre que había anhelado toda mi vida estaba muerto!

Me quiebro como una ramita. Estallo con toda la fuerza de mis pulmones. Tared me hace sentarme en la cama. Y luego, se arrodilla delante de mí.

—Escúchame, Elisse, escúchame, por favor —pide—. No hay nada, absolutamente nada que nos asegure que tu padre está muerto. Pudo haber evitado los riesgos todo este tiempo. Pudo haberse ido muy lejos en cuanto sintió el peligro de tu Mara. Y, lo más importante: si él es la mitad de hombre que su hijo, entonces estoy completamente seguro de que *está vivo*.

—Pero...

—Pero si no es así, si tu padre realmente ya no está en este mundo —dice, para luego tomarme de las mejillas y obligarme a mirarlo—, entonces Comus Bayou y yo vamos a estar contigo cada minuto, cada segundo, para que no pases por eso solo. *No te vamos a soltar*, Elisse, porque, lo creas o no, *tú* eres la razón por la cual nos hemos mantenido juntos hasta ahora. Y cuando todo esto termine, vamos a volver a Luisiana, a nuestra reserva, y nos sentaremos largo y tendido a arreglar nuestras diferencias. Pero, por ahora, yo soy el que va a confiar en ti y en darte mi apoyo. Si no quieres ir al reino de los ángeles, seré el primero en salir detrás de ti por la puerta de esta casa. Pero, si al final decides enfrentarlo todo, entonces seré el último en marcharme. Te lo juro.

Volver.

Volver a casa. Si lo hacemos, ¿las cosas serán las mismas en Comus Bayou? ¿Seguiremos juntos, siendo una familia como hemos...?

¿... pretendido hasta ahora?

Intento replicar. Encontrar alguna manera de navegar del mar de emociones que me embargan. Pero no logro hacerlo.

Sigo aterrado. Tanto que, si Inanna llegase ahora mismo a anunciar que ha encontrado otra manera, la aceptaría sin dudar.

Pero no existe, no la hay. Así que voy a hacerlo. Llevaré a cabo el ritual de Aradia, y llegaré hasta el Merkavah. Arrancaré el nombre de mi Mara y apagaré la luz de los ángeles para siempre.

Así sea lo último que haga.

CAPÍTULO 79
UN ÚLTIMO PACTO

La primera pregunta que me viene a la mente es si acaso Aradia piensa devorar a Raxnal. Porque, al bajar al sótano, la encontramos con el ángel en medio de su cuerpo enrollado de la misma manera en la que estaba aquel pobre ciervo, del cual ya no queda más que una pila de huesos digeridos al fondo de la habitación.

—Ah, querido. Te eché tanto de menos… —dice la Madre bruja, un comentario curioso ya que, para ella, no han pasado más que unas cuantas horas desde la última vez que nos vimos.

En vez de responder, dirijo mi atención al círculo de sal que han trazado en el suelo. Dentro de éste hay carretes de hilo vacíos junto con varios pares de tijeras y agujas de coser.

—¿Estás listo, Elisse? —pregunta Inanna, consciente de la angustia que mana de todo mi cuerpo.

Saco mi libro rojo del bolsillo y se lo muestro a la serpiente.

—Ahora, querido, el sigilo que vas a hacer requerirá de mucho más que símbolos hechos con palabras —advierte Aradia—. La piedra filosofal es alquimia, así que con alquimia la vas a contener. Deberás crear un sello mayor compuesto de cuatro sellos menores, cada uno de ellos correspondientes a las cuatro etapas con las que fue creada la espada. ¿Recuerdas cuáles son?

—Nigredo, albedo, citrinas y rubedo.

Aradia asiente, complacida.

—Después, nosotras tres nos encargaremos de colocar estos sigilos en tu cuerpo para bloquear los puntos principales de donde tu magia se desprende —continúa Inanna, lo que me hace reparar de nuevo en los carretes y las agujas—. La idea es que, durante el ritual, rompas estos sellos de poder únicamente con tu voluntad. Sólo así podrás obtener la fuerza suficiente para someter a la espada.

—¿Y cómo ayudará eso con el monstruo de hueso? —inquiero.

—Esa criatura es un ser mágico, al igual que los contemplasombras —explica—. Si logras dominar un Martillo tan poderoso como la piedra filosofal, usarlo para subyugar a esa criatura con su poder ya no te supondrá ningún problema. O, al menos, no lo será por un tiempo.

—El suficiente como para entrar y salir del reino celestial, ¿cierto? —es lo que digo.

El silencio de las cuatro brujas me da la razón.

Todo parece tan frío, tan calculado, que debería tranquilizarme. Pero las dudas me asaltan sin parar.

—Aradia —comienzo—, ¿cómo voy a enfrentarme a... Dios?

La serpiente mira hacia Hela, y ésta saca un disco de cera blanca de su bolsillo muy parecido al que tenía el sigilo de Bathin.

—Mis hijas ya te hablaron sobre los nombres verdaderos de Dios, ¿cierto?, pues bien, puede que los nombres del Dios hebreo sigan siendo un secreto, pero no así los del Dios de los ángeles de Dee.

La rubia extiende el disco hacia mí.

—Éste es el *Sigillum Dei Aemeth*[38] —continúa Aradia—. Un símbolo que contiene los siete nombres verdaderos de ese Dios y que, según la leyenda, fue entregado a Dee para que pudiese comandar las fuerzas angelicales. Si logras utilizarlo de la forma correcta, puede que te dé una ventaja crucial durante tu batalla.

---

[38] El "Sello del Verdadero Dios".

Tomo el complejo sello y siento su peso considerable entre mis manos.

—¿Funcionará? —pregunto sin poder ocultar mi inquietud.

—Nadie ha estado lo bastante cerca de Dios como para descubrirlo —dice—. Pero puede que tú tengas una oportunidad.

Dominar la espada. Dominar al monstruo de hueso. Dominar a Dios.

Cierro los ojos un momento para visualizar la titánica tarea que se abre ante mí.

Me siento en el suelo y comienzo a trabajar en los sigilos. Después de un largo silencio, Inanna entra al círculo de sal para tomar uno de los carretes. Luego, comienza a enredar en él un mechón de su cabello.

—Lo lamento, Elisse. Lo lamento muchísimo —dice ella con tristeza—. No quisimos causar un conflicto hace rato. Nunca ha sido nuestra intención arrebatarte de tu familia.

—Aunque tampoco nos molestaría hacerlo.

—¡Hela!

—No me digas que no lo sentiste, Elisse —insiste la joven reprendida, quien entra también al círculo e imita a su hermana—. Si hay algún lugar en el mundo en el que encajas es en esta casa. Y en este aquelarre.

Caligo suspira, irritada por la lengua de su hermana, pero luego alcanza incluso a sonreír:

—Te apreciamos mucho, querido. Y si hubieses llegado primero a Salem en vez de a Nueva Orleans, habríamos sido muy felices de convertirte en nuestro hermano. Pero sabemos lo importante que es ahora Comus Bayou para ti.

El silencio de Inanna me hace saber que ella piensa lo mismo.

Estoy tan perplejo, que no me atrevo a indagar dentro de mí si tienen razón o no. Lo que me queda claro es que el sentimiento de afecto es recíproco, y que jamás me había sentido tan comprendido como ahora.

Quizás ellas no sean mi primera familia, pero, tal como a Irina, no me costaría para nada darles un lugar de igual importancia en mi vida.

—Ah, pequeño mío, estás tan abrumado, con tantas decisiones que tomar —interviene Aradia, quien me *olfatea* con su lengua—. Pero quizá te anime saber que tengo una buena noticia para ti.

—¿Una noticia? —pregunto y las hijas de la serpiente bajan los carretes para escuchar.

—¿Recuerdas que te prometí que buscaría la forma de separarte del monstruo que llevas dentro de ti? —aventura—. Pues ya he dado con la solución.

—¡¿Está hablando en serio?! —miro a las brujas, pero ellas parecen tan sorprendidas como yo.

—¿Por qué estás tan asombrado, pequeño? —pregunta la serpiente, casi divertida—. Tú ya sabes que es lo que tenemos que hacer para conseguirlo, después de todo.

Aradia gira hacia Inanna. Ella ladea la cabeza, pero luego deja caer el carrete de hilo a sus pies.

—*No*, Madre —exclama, aterrada—, ¡no puede ofrecerle eso!

—Es la única manera, pequeña. Y lo sabes —insiste Aradia.

—No, ¡no voy a...!

Aradia se yergue de golpe, tan rápido que casi se golpea la coronilla contra el techo.

—¿Permitirlo, Inanna? —dice la bruja dorada sin gritar, sin exaltarse—. ¿Qué lugar crees que te corresponde en esta casa como para pensar siquiera algo así?

Caligo y Hela se encogen, intimidadas ante las pupilas contraídas de su Madre, una hostilidad que difiere mucho de la tranquilidad de su voz.

—¿Qué está pasando? —pregunto, desconcertado.

Inanna se muerde los labios, y las pupilas de Aradia se relajan al dirigirse hacia mí:

—Hace muchos años logré devolver a un errante de las garras del mundo de los muertos. Pero a cambio, él tuvo que dejar a su ancestro atrás. Y la única forma en la que podré separarte del monstruo que tienes dentro de ti es si repito contigo exactamente el mismo ritual.

Abro los ojos de par en par, porque está hablando de Ilya.

—¡Es cierto! —exclamo, sin entender cómo es que no lo vi desde un principio—. Pero, ¿eso no tendría consecuencias igual de graves para mí?

Inanna se oprime los puños, pero decide no intervenir.

—Ilya era un devorapieles, así que había *nacido* con su ancestro —continúa la serpiente—. Por lo tanto, era una parte tan suya como su cuerpo o su consciencia. El haber perdido la mitad de sí mismo sin duda trajo sus propios problemas, pero tú, querido, no eres un devorapieles. Eres un *contemplasombras*.

Dioses, dioses, es verdad, ¡es verdad!

Mi emoción es tan grande que ya ni siquiera sé si lo que zumba dentro de mi cabeza son las voces de protesta del monstruo de hueso o mis propios pensamientos que giran de un lado a otro.

—Sí, ¡quiero hacerlo! —exclamo—, en cuanto terminemos todo esto, voy a...

—Estás olvidando un detalle muy importante, Elisse —la seriedad de Inanna corta mi entusiasmo.

Miro hacia la bruja, y la encuentro aún con los puños apretados, tan angustiada como sus hermanas. Aradia, en cambio, parece sonreír cuando por fin lo comprendo. La habitación comienza a dar vueltas a mi alrededor.

—Para poder realizar el ritual... debo darte mi alma, ¿verdad? *Mi voluntad* —musito, tan pálido que podría desvanecerme.

Ella vuelve a enroscarse sobre sí misma.

—Así es, Elisse —confirma—. Si quieres salvar tu *vida*, si quieres evitar que el monstruo te consuma hasta que no quede nada de ti, deberás firmar nuestro libro de las generaciones. Deberás unirte al Culto a la Grieta, ofrecer tu vida al Camino de la Mano Izquierda... y dejar a Comus Bayou para siempre.

CAPÍTULO 80
CONSORTE

Por la noche, el monstruo Ilya llama a la puerta, dispuesto a cumplir la última petición de la madre de las brujas.

Han pasado cuatro días desde que ellas descendieron al inframundo de Aradia, un día por cada sigilo, lo que significa que falta sólo un ciclo más para la Luna del Lobo.

Él ya ha hecho gran parte de la tarea. Ha recorrido todos los senderos de la niebla para convocar a sus habitantes y pedirles sus pieles humanas. Ha despejado los caminos, ha bajado al pueblo de Salem para interceder como heraldo del aquelarre…

Pero allí, delante de la habitación que huele a ruda y lavanda, la cabeza del errante demoníaco es un remolino, una secuencia de recuerdos que se borran como una pesadilla de la que no termina de despertar.

Y eso es extraño, porque desde que ya no tiene a su ancestro, desde que arrancaron de su cuerpo la mitad de su alma… él no ha vuelto a soñar.

Sueños. ¿Cuándo fue la última vez que yo también pude tener uno?

Su lengua se aprieta y acumula un montón de palabras que no sabe cómo soltar. Y por dentro, llora por esas memorias que no son ahora más que un amasijo de culpa cuyo origen no logra reconocer.

Al abrirse la puerta, el desgraciado se encuentra con unos ojos azules hinchados de angustia, un dolor que entiende tanto como puede entender un corazón que sólo late con la mitad de su fuerza.

Pero, incapaz de mostrar todos los sentimientos que le arrollan porque su cuerpo y su cara han olvidado cómo hacerlo, le dirige una señal con la cabeza para que él, *el hombre lobo*, lo acompañe, para que juntos, crucen la casa y atraviesen el sendero de endrinos.

La Gran Serpiente le ha pedido que lo prepare para lo que viene, pero a medida que los dos hombres se abren paso envueltos en el viento helado, me pregunto por qué el errante demoníaco no se da media vuelta y le clava las garras en la garganta. Por qué no se arriesga, en tan delicioso momento de vulnerabilidad, a arrancarle el corazón de una mordida.

¿Es porque sabe que no podría vencerlo? ¿Porque caería él primero ante su furia…? ¿O es porque tú has visto algo que yo no? ¿Porque tú sabes algo que yo sólo puedo añorar que me sea revelado?

Bien podría guiarlo hacia un punto irreconocible del sendero, obligarlo a perderse para siempre en la niebla.

Pero tú no se lo permites. Tú dejas que lo lleve hacia el lugar de sacrificio y que, bajo la luz de la luna, se hundan ambos lentamente en el bosque.

CAPÍTULO 81
CINCO ESCOBAS A MEDIANOCHE

Nigredo *en los labios,*
para que no pueda pronunciar hechizo alguno.

Albedo *en la mano izquierda,*
para que no pueda no comandar a los espíritus.

Citrinas *en el talón,*
para impedir que siga el camino del Príncipe del Aire.

Rubedo *en la frente,*
para cerrar el ojo que mira del otro lado del velo.

Con estos cuatro símbolos cosidos al cuerpo con cabello de brujas, asciendo del plano medio hacia el pasillo de las llaves, poco antes del quinto anochecer.

Las brujas ya se han adelantado, apenas unos minutos que, en el plano de los vivos, quizás hayan sido ya un par de horas. Me han abandonado como a un iniciado en las sombras, con la dolorosa sensación de la magia congelada dentro de mi cuerpo.

Es tan terrible volver a sentirse humano. Tan humano como ese muchacho al que le arrancaron a Ciervo Piel de Sombras del pecho. Como el joven al que dejaron ciego en un ático oscuro en Nueva Orleans.

¿Tienes miedo?

Tanto que, si el sigilo en mis labios no lo impidiese, soltaría un grito.

Respiro profundo y tomo la prenda que ha sido dejada para mí frente a la puerta. Es una larga túnica negra con una corta hilera de botones al frente, una prenda envestida con una magia que no es mía, preparada para que pueda soportar el invierno que me espera en el exterior.

Me quito mi ropa y la coloco sobre mi piel desnuda. Ajusto mi athame en el arnés de la cadera y libero mi cabello de su trenza.

Hay algo indudablemente erótico en el profundo escote que se abre desde mi pecho hasta el ombligo, así como en mi apariencia andrógina cargada de sigilos sangrantes; una fuerza ilusoria, un glamour violento que busca compensar mi vulnerabilidad.

Llego al vestíbulo, pero no encuentro allí el aquelarre. Todo yace en penumbras, apenas iluminado por las velas tenues de los candelabros que me dan la impresión de que mueren y reviven con los crepúsculos.

No hacen falta. Aunque ahora esté cubierta por nubes, la luz de la *luna llena* es suficiente para ahogar la oscuridad.

Salgo de la casa y me dirijo hacia el pozo. Sobre el sendero, las tres brujas ya me esperan, envestidas en negro y con escobas hechas de paja y endrino en sus manos izquierdas.

—Tres veces tres —dice Hela.

—Tres veces tres —repite Caligo.

—Tres veces tres —finaliza Inanna, quien me ofrece una escoba también.

La magia detrás del sigilo de Albedo empuja cuando la sostengo por lo largo.

Una bruja es una bruja es una bruja...

El aquelarre y yo rodeamos el pozo como si fuese un caldero.

—¡Salve, Reina de los Muertos! —exclama Inanna, quien apunta con su escoba hacia el agujero—. Salve, Grieta que ha rasgado el Velo entre este Mundo y el Otro, ¡escucha a quienes honran hoy tu memoria frente al abismo!

Hela, Caligo y yo repetimos sus palabras como si quisiéramos despertar al plano medio que yace en el fondo.

—Esta noche, *Squochee kesos*[39] tendrá un nuevo parto —continúa la bruja goética—. ¿Estás listo para volver a nacer, Elisse?

La angustia de mi corazón es enorme, el dolor punza tras cada palpitación... Pero asiento. Más convencido que nunca.

Miramos hacia arriba cuando varios haces de luz caen como sables sobre la nieve. Las nubes comienzan a moverse, a despejarse por un viento frío que viaja por los cielos.

La luna por fin asoma la cara.

—¡Ahora!

Ante el grito de Inanna, las tres brujas echan a correr.

Sin saber hacia dónde vamos, las sigo a través del sendero hasta que saltan hacia el bosque. Las ramas espinosas de los endrinos intentan rasgarme la ropa y la piel para obtener algo de mi sangre, pero no me detengo. No miro hacia atrás.

---

[39] En algonquino: "El sol no tiene fuerza para descongelarse", forma original que recibiera la Luna del Lobo.

Ellas serpentean por los árboles, brincan por las rocas y los troncos, persiguiendo al astro blanco que pareciera moverse como un perezoso cometa.

Cuando la nieve cruje bajo el peso de montones de pies, me doy cuenta de que ya no estamos solos.

Varias siluetas corren alrededor de nosotros, cuerpos oscuros que comienzan a aullar de júbilo acompañados de tambores, de cuernos que cantan a la par del golpeteo cada vez más frenético dentro de mi pecho. ¿Son espíritus? ¿Son monstruos del plano medio?

No. De ser así, yo no podría verlos, porque mi ojo sobrenatural permanece cerrado por el sigilo en mi frente.

A lo lejos, una antorcha anaranjada se enciende, mientras que la nieve a mis pies desaparece hasta convertirse en un sendero de cenizas. Me detengo, al filo de un claro, cuando me percato de que es en realidad una hoguera sobre un cruce de caminos.

Y es allí donde por fin lo entiendo todo.

Ocho senderos tiene la casa de la niebla. Una estrella de ocho puntas en cuyo centro palpita el fuego de una hoguera como el latir de un corazón.

La última pieza de mis premoniciones.

Inanna se coloca detrás de la fogata y sus hermanas la flanquean con los ojos relampagueantes ante el resplandor de la lumbre. Llego hasta ellas y ocupo mi lugar como el último punto cardinal.

Las tres alzan sus escobas hacia la luna.

—Una sola bruja despierta tormentas con un revés de su mano —exclama Caligo.

—Arranca vidas con una gota de agua y levanta a los muertos de un soplido —prosigue Hela.

—Pero un Gran Vínculo de aquelarres... —concluye Inanna—. Eso puede sacudir el mundo entero.

Desde los ocho senderos, aquellas sombras que nos rodeaban en el bosque se manifiestan. Y al ser alcanzados por la luz descubro que son más de treinta brujas, brujos y todos lo que son ambos o ninguno; humanos con magia que han sido traídos desde Salem por los habitantes de la niebla para reunirse en esta noche de ritual.

Algunos portan tocados hechos con cornamentas; otros, mandiles negros sobre sus trajes sastre arremangados. Un puñado más llevan el cuerpo pintado con runas azules; otros están vestidos con túnicas o van completamente desnudos, con coronas de flores entrelazadas. Todos están descalzos y armonizan sus cánticos con los tambores y cuernos de batalla que han traído consigo.

Incluso, logro distinguir entre ellos a Edvar.

La imagen materializa un poderoso momento del pasado en mi cabeza. Brujos y errantes, magias desde todas direcciones alrededor de la hoguera de Aradia, unidos para detener a los monstruos de John Dee.

Vuelvo al presente, y ellos hacen un círculo en torno a nosotros. Inanna mira hacia el cielo y levanta la escoba con su mano izquierda, para luego exclamar:

¡Gran Fuerza que abrió la Grieta Resplandeciente!
Vínculo entre esta tierra y la otra,
tú, que has bendecido la tierra con un beso de plata,
tú, que cabalgaste las nubes con truenos
y elevaste a tus hijos sobre todas las ciencias.
Manifiéstate sobre mi cuerpo
y déjame ofrecerte una sangre nueva
para ésta, tu Gran Sinagoga de las Brujas.

—¡*Manifiéstate, reina Bæbælən!* —gritan Hela y Caligo—. Madre de todas las Abominaciones, Reina Escarlata que se viste con la piel de los muertos, ¡libérate para que podamos cumplir la voluntad de tu Mano Izquierda!

—¡*Manifiéstate, manifiéstate!*

Ante la exigencia del resto de los brujos, Inanna se arroja a la hoguera.

El fuego estalla como si su cuerpo estuviese hecho de gasolina. Las llamas giran, altas y furiosas en un remolino que pinta todo el bosque de rojo hasta que, como invocada desde el mismísimo infierno, ella surge de nuevo entre la lumbre.

La bruja levanta su hermosa cabeza de cabra, armonizada con lustrosos cuernos largos que se curvan hacia arriba. Su estilizado cuerpo azabache se alza sobre patas de fauno entrecruzadas, la perfecta cohesión esotérica entre sus pechos y el pene entre sus piernas, expuesta a todos los aquelarres.

La contemplasombras pareciera flotar sobre las llamas, pero en realidad, son sus monstruos goéticos quienes la elevan; aunque no llevan sus pieles humanas, incluso yo puedo verlos moverse como espíritus informes de la misma manera que lo hacían los Loas en la hoguera de Red Buffalo.

Cuando la portadora de Satanás apunta hacia la luna con el índice y el anular de su mano izquierda, sentada en su trono de demonios, me queda claro por qué tantos se han arrodillado para adorarle.

—*Hijo de la Luna Famélica* —dice—, *esta noche honraremos tu resplandor con el ritual de las Cinco Escobas. Cinco pasos para sellar el Martillo de las Brujas.*

—*Por la herencia de Endor*[40] *y Hécate* —grita una triada de voces en el este.

—*Por la inocencia de Tituba y De Meath* —gritan otros tres en el oeste.

—*Y por la nostalgia de Leland y Valiente* —culmina Inanna—. *Por todos los hijos del Camino de la Mano Izquierda que fueron arrancados de su grandeza, ¡brindemos a esta criatura nuestro poder!*

Todos los presentes extienden las manos en mi dirección, y las oleadas de magia que envían contra mi cuerpo casi me derriban sobre la hoguera, tan potentes como si la propia Aradia se hubiese arrojado sobre mí.

Me mantengo firme y saco el athame de mis caderas.

—*Cinco escobas a medianoche* —exclama Hela—. *Una para pronunciar los hechizos.*

Como una serpiente que se enreda por todo mi brazo, cierro los ojos y dirijo la energía que me es enviada de los aquelarres hacia la punta. Esta vez, la magia no me exprime las energías porque *no es mía*. Es algo que tomo prestado, algo que manipulo únicamente con la fuerza de mi voluntad.

Llevo la daga hacia los hilos de mis labios, y en la oscuridad de mis párpados apretados puedo por fin ver un resplandor.

Rasgo el aire con el Athame, y el sigilo se rompe con tanta fuerza que un grito es lo primero que brota de mi garganta.

Las costuras se disuelven y las puntadas en mi carne descienden para grabarse sobre mi pecho, empujadas por la magia que ahora se dispara desde mi boca como si fuese un dragón.

---

[40] Ref. Bruja de Endor.

La espada ruge como un titán al que le han puesto un grillete en el brazo, mientras que yo siento como si a mí me hubiesen liberado de un amarre.

Basta...

Los brujos se toman de las manos y comienzan a bailar alrededor de la fogata, su magia como un torbellino sobre mis sentidos.

—*Cuatro escobas a medianoche. Una para comandar a los espíritus.*

Ante el rezo de Caligo, apunto con mi athame hacia la hoguera, pero no hacia Inanna, sino a los espíritus que la rodean.

—*Para que mi mano jamás sea más suave que un látigo* —susurro—. *¡Tráiganme al ejército de Diana!*

Agito mi muñeca izquierda en el aire, y el sigilo de Albedo se despedaza en el acto.

Los demonios gritan cuando un chasquido invisible de *mi telequinesis* los azota por igual.

—*¡Obedezcan!* —latigueo una vez más, y ellos succionan el humo de la fogata para tomar la forma de lobos, de jabalíes, de caballos y de grandes animales salvajes, negros como la noche, los ojos al rojo vivo como el carbón.

Una cadena más. Un peso menos sobre mi corazón.

Al ver que he dominado a sus criaturas con magia goética, tal como deseé desde el primer momento en el que supe que ésta existía, Inanna sonríe con orgullo.

—*Tres escobas a medianoche* —reza—. *Una para seguir el camino del Príncipe del Aire.*

Los brujos presentes dejan de bailar y comienzan a saltar en su sitio, cada vez más alto, cada vez más rápido.

—*¡Suplicamos a la Grieta que nos deje cabalgar sobre las estrellas!* —gritan—. *¡Suplicamos a la Grieta que levante de la tierra al ejército de Diana!*

¡No!

—*¡Elévense!*

Con este comando, doy un pisotón en la tierra, reventando el sigilo de mi talón.

Los demonios goéticos salen disparados hacia los brujos, los toman de los brazos, de las piernas, y comienzan a elevarlos en el aire.

Inanna se agazapa, adquiere una forma de cabra completa y salta de las llamas. Antes de que me embista, me echo a un lado y me aferro a su cornamenta, para subir a su lomo.

Y esta vez, ni siquiera los gritos desesperados del monstruo son capaces de distraerme. No cuando el tercer sigilo ya arde como el hierro sobre mi pecho.

DOS

Todos los aquelarres ascendemos en una gran espiral hacia el cielo. Gritamos, chillamos, invocamos a la Grieta montados sobre bestias cuyas garras y pezuñas sacan chispas en el aire.

Cuando el bosque no es más que un tapete de follaje bajo nosotros, nos unimos como una marea, una nube negra de magia y humo, de fuego y cantos demoníacos. Tal cual las pesadillas de los cristianos que nos persiguieron durante siglos, cruzamos el cielo, cabalgamos hacia la luna, y revivimos, por una noche, la leyenda del mítico Sabbath.

Y la espada, más débil que nunca, ya no puede detener los sigilos ahora quemados sobre mi pecho, ni la magia que circula por mis labios. Por mis manos. Por mis pies.

—Dos escobas —musito—. *Una para abrir el ojo que mira del otro lado del velo…*

Al desprenderse el cuarto sello de mi frente, mis pupilas se expanden hasta convertir mis iris en un fino halo verde.

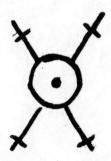

Y allí, a la cabeza de los aquelarres, montado sobre la mismísima Lucifer, el sigilo de la espada filosofal se completa ante mi última oración:

Soy Él. Él descabezado.

Soy Él, el que abre las puertas de este mundo y el otro.

Soy el Martillo que revienta a los espíritus.

Yo soy... La Bestia Revestida de Luna.

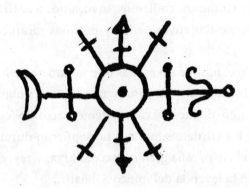

CAPÍTULO 82
EL BRUJO Y EL LOBO

—Una. Una escoba a medianoche. Levanto la cabeza, y descubro que la Estrella de la Mañana ya brilla sobre los endrinos, aunque la noche todavía se niega a fallecer. El Sabbath se ha disuelto, y de nuestra ceremonia no queda más que una columna de humo sobre el cruce de caminos.

Ellos se han llevado su magia, pero la mía por fin es libre dentro de mi propio cuerpo; un río de sombras cuyo cauce se mueve sólo bajo mi voluntad.

Y la sensación es tan natural, tan mía, que me parece una abominación que haya estado contenida tanto tiempo.

Pero aún no estoy satisfecho.

Me llevo una mano al vientre y siento el dolor de un quinto sigilo. Un emblema secreto que yo mismo cosí con mis propios cabellos y que ahora pulsa contra las paredes de mis entrañas. Un sigilo que no es para la espada, sino para contener algo mucho más… poderoso.

El monstruo dentro de mí protesta ante el calor del símbolo que he destinado para él. Pero… ¿sus voces? Apenas las escucho, no porque no estén allí, sino porque la piedra filosofal ya no puede volver frágiles mis oídos.

Me inclino sobre la hoguera y trazo un nombre sobre las cenizas calientes. No acabo de erguirme de nuevo, cuando *él* aparece a mis espaldas, *invocado* en el lindero del bosque.

Erguido en dos patas, y con la última escoba en su garra izquierda, Tared se detiene a unos metros y me mira con ojos oscuros, un cielo azul cruzado por una tormenta confusa. Su pelaje se eriza y su espalda se encorva como la de un monstruo.

Ver ese hocico feroz y esa piel que parece salpicada de truenos me lleva de vuelta al momento en el que sentimos por primera vez el tirón de nuestro vínculo, en aquel parque neblinoso de Nueva Orleans.

—Desde ese momento supiste que ibas a ser mío, ¿verdad? —pregunto, pero sólo un gruñido amenazador brota de su garganta.

Bajo la mirada hacia su pecho, y la palabra "maleficio" cruza mi cabeza al ver que una costura fresca yace desde sus clavículas hasta el esternón, hecha con hilo de cuero negro.

Levanto la mano de hueso para que mi magia emane de la muñeca como un perfume. La bestia dentro de mí se agita, pero la espada ni siquiera protesta, encerrada a cal y canto en el sarcófago en el que se ha convertido mi cuerpo.

Tared, en cambio, alza el hocico y olfatea el aire con tanta agitación que densas motas de vapor expelen de su boca. Mira mi piel expuesta, percibe el latido caliente de mi corazón y tritura la escoba bajo su garra a la par que se relame el hocico.

En un parpadeo, se lanza contra mí.

Dejo que me embista y que me tumbe con violencia contra las cenizas. Me lanza una dentellada letal al cuello, pero saco mi athame para que muerda el mango en su lugar. Sus fauces se cierran en torno a la madera y la parten hasta dejar al descubierto el centro de metal.

Tenso la mandíbula cuando sus garras se aferran a los costados de mis muslos, buscando abrirme las piernas de par en par.

En esa forma, y bajo semejante locura, podría desgarrarme entero, así que enrosco mi mano libre alrededor de su cuello.

—¡Apártate!

El lobo es lanzado hacia atrás, empujado por la fuerza invisible de mi telequinesia.

Me pongo de pie y, en vez de alejarme de él, hago que mi esencia le acaricie las fauces para agitar de nuevo su apetito.

Tared se levanta de un salto, pero mi magia lo paraliza por completo, como si hubiese trazado un campo de contención a sus pies. Me acerco, y siento su urgencia arder en cada uno de sus músculos, su sexo y sus colmillos ansiosos por hundirse dentro de mí por igual.

Así, en esa forma, es la viva imagen del licántropo maldito de las leyendas. No más que un cruel heredero del rey Licaón.

Me detengo a un paso de él y empuño el athame. El filo del mango destrozado me corta la palma de la mano y me hace sangrar sobre el metal al apuntar hacia el cielo.

—Una escoba a medianoche —exclamo, y un calor infernal comienza a desprenderse del sigilo en mi vientre—. Para volvernos invencibles con la fuerza de nuestros amantes.

De una estocada, entierro el cuchillo entre sus clavículas. El lobo ruge, enfurecido, y al deslizar la hoja hacia abajo para cortar aquellos hilos de cuero, encuentro el artilugio escondido bajo los tajos de piel: un clavo largo y oxidado con un mechón de mi cabello atado en la punta, aquel que yacía pegado en el libro rojo.

Con mi mano de hueso, lo arranco sin piedad.

El devorapieles se derrumba de espaldas, aturdido ante la ruptura del hechizo. Pongo una rodilla sobre su vientre y me inclino para asegurarme de que no quede un solo cabello mío dentro de la siniestra herida.

Tared parpadea, y la tormenta en sus ojos azules se despeja... Pero la bestia hambrienta *sigue allí*.

Me atrapa por la cintura y me arrastra hacia su hocico. En vez de recibir una letal mordida, lanzo un gemido de sorpresa al sentir su larga lengua entrar de golpe en mi cuerpo, tan húmeda y suave que se desliza dentro de mí sin una sola gota de dolor.

Dejo caer mi athame y grito de puro placer cuando el músculo presiona una y otra vez en ese sitio tan familiar para él. Me aferro al pelaje de su cabeza y dejo que se sacie conmigo como tantas veces lo ha hecho antes, tan diestro que ni uno solo de sus colmillos hiere mi piel.

El sigilo arde como tres infiernos ante el umbral de mi orgasmo, pero todavía es muy pronto.

Me libero de su lengua para girarme y alcanzar las costuras en su pecho. Al tirar de los pliegues, Tared se levanta como un resorte. Me tira de nuevo sobre el cruce de caminos y se arrodilla delante de mí, con jadeos tan densos que parece un volcán a punto de estallar.

Como si se quitase una capucha, pone una garra en su hocico y lo estira hacia atrás. Las fauces se parten y los colmillos y la lengua se desprenden hasta revelar su cabeza humana debajo.

Contaminado de esa hambre, me lanzo hacia él para besarlo con ferocidad. Entierro mis manos en la herida de su maleficio y, de un tirón, le arranco la piel hacia los costados.

Tared gruñe sobre mis labios, pero en vez de detenerme, se despoja también de su pelaje hasta que ambos desenterramos al hombre bajo el monstruo.

Cada partícula de mi magia se sacude al ver el cuerpo de mi consorte brillar en escarlata, como una bestia mítica ofrecida en sacrificio para la luna llena posada sobre su cabeza.

El brujo y el lobo. La gran *antinatura* y el más delicioso de todos los pecados.

Ebrio de deseo, es su turno de hacerme la ropa jirones.

Sin miramientos, revienta la hilera de botones de mi túnica, tal como yo hice con su piel. Desgarra la tela, y ladea la cabeza con curiosidad al descubrir el sigilo cosido sobre mi vientre.

Lo toca, gruñe al sentir el calor y los hilos bajo sus dedos.

—Ofrécete ahora mismo —ordeno con hostilidad. Por más desbordados que estemos de deseo, esto sigue siendo un ritual.

Tared obedece sin chistar. De un solo movimiento, me toma del hombro y me empuja para que caiga de rodillas sobre su piel de lobo, la cual sirve como manto sobre nuestro altar de ocho senderos. Me toma de las caderas con ambas manos y, con mi cuerpo ya preparado por la generosidad de su lengua de lobo, su miembro se abre paso dentro de mí de una sola estocada.

Suelto un grito ante el breve dolor que, en cuestión de segundos, se convierte en un placer que apenas puedo soportar, mientras que Tared, poseído por mi estrechez, comienza a embestirme con una precisión que sólo un errante de su calibre posee.

El placer me hace añicos, me impulsa a enterrar los dedos en las hebras plateadas y arrancarlas a puños cuando, con una mano, él me toma de los cabellos de la nuca, los estruja y empuja sus caderas contra mí como si quisiera entrar entero. Tan fuerte. Tan rápido que el mundo se desenfoca.

Tal como en la visión de la necromante, el lobo me monta frenéticamente sobre el cruce de caminos, hasta que la amenaza de la cúspide se asoma en mi entrepierna.

El licántropo lanza un gruñido de protesta cuando me libero de su posesión. Mi telequinesia lo arroja de espaldas sobre su manto, lo inmoviliza para permitirme tomar el control.

Tared echa la cabeza hacia atrás cuando, con una lentitud despiadada, comienzo a descender mis caderas sobre su miembro, hasta finalmente albergarlo en toda su longitud. Y él, incapaz de mover sus manos, arquea su columna para llegar a lo más profundo de mi ser.

Sentado en su regazo, entierro las manos en su pecho y me muevo sobre él en un ritmo que poco a poco se torna más frenético, casi violento, pero no para alcanzar yo el clímax, sino para obligarlo a él a liberar esa energía que mi magia busca con desesperación.

—¡Mi Señor, mi brujo! —gime, embrujado por el vaivén de mi cuerpo. Mi excitación se eleva como una torre de humo ante su sumisión, hasta que él ya no puede resistirlo más.

Mis labios se ahogan en un gemido largo y profundo, para después permitirle culminar. Y sólo entonces, cuando él se esparce entero dentro de mi vientre, dejo que el orgasmo me alcance también.

La magia de la creación, mezclada con la energía vital de mi consorte, se expande a mi mano izquierda, a mi talón, a mis labios, a cualquier parte de mi cuerpo que sirva como una vía de escape. Pero antes de que lo logre, tiro de ella y la arrojo como una soga a una sola dirección: el monstruo de hueso.

Sin la espada de por medio para impedirlo, mi magia le ata las extremidades y lo arrastra hacia las profundidades de mi psique, donde no pueda escapar.

¡MÍO, ERES MÍO!

Y cuando él ya no puede hacer frente a mi voluntad, susurro:

—No... *tú* eres *mío*.

El sigilo por fin se desprende de mi vientre y se graba, no sobre mi piel, sino sobre el cráneo de la criatura.

Sus astas se abren paso en mi cabeza, crecen y se ensanchan como una corona de plata que resplandece contra la luna llena. Pero la criatura ya no logra cruzar al otro lado. Ya no logra utilizarme como su portal.

El ritual de las cinco escobas concluye, y las voces del monstruo quedan por fin silenciadas bajo mi poder.

CUARTA FASE

UN MONSTRUO

COMPLETO

CAPÍTULO 83
UN ÚLTIMO EMISARIO

Por la madrugada, dos de los tramperos habían abandonado el grupo para ir hacia la ciudad de Salem.

Ambos llevaban en su vehículo varias cajas de cartón, desbordadas con aquellos papeles y libretas que alguna vez fueron robados de Valley of the Gods. Y también, una pequeña nevera con un mensaje enrollado en su interior.

Pero ya han pasado varias horas desde que volvieron con la camioneta vacía. Y desde entonces, la quietud de Nalvage no ha hecho más que alimentar la frustración del Inquisidor.

La victoria en la colina de Minnesota fue fácil, tan fácil y tan indolora que Benjamin ni siquiera sintió placer cuando sus manos se empaparon de sangre. Pero su insatisfacción no podría importarle menos al ángel, porque su atención lleva toda la noche fija en la puerta de metal cerrada delante de él.

Puede sentir el plano medio detrás, muy dentro de la cavidad de Dungeon Rock. Tanto así que quiere extender la mano. Desea empujar la lámina de hierro y descender los escalones de madera, atravesar el plano medio que yace en la gruta para ver con sus propios ojos la casa en la niebla.

Sabe que el pozo se lo impedirá porque la Mano Izquierda de Aradia aún está puesta sobre la entrada. Pero si la Mano se levantase, si la Mano se moviera lo suficiente, él, la legión, todos ellos podrían entrar.

Tú los dejarías entrar, ¿verdad?

—¿Por qué? —pregunta por fin el trampero a sus espaldas—. ¿Por qué nos has obligado a hacer *eso*, para luego traernos aquí?

—Misteriosos son los caminos del Señor, hijo mío —responde Nalvage, tranquilo—. Los humanos no necesitan entenderlo. Sólo necesitan confiar en su...

—¡Basta de acertijos, cabrón!

Ante su grito, el Mensajero se gira despacio hacia el Inquisidor. Y, para mi goce, éste casi retrocede.

Por un segundo, Benjamin Lander había olvidado el profundo malestar que esa mirada muerta le provocaba.

—Oh, ¡qué hombre de tan poca fe eres! —dice el cadáver, más divertido que irritado ante la insolencia del hombre—. ¿No te he alimentado a ti y a tu gente? ¿No te he guiado hacia los caminos correctos? ¿No te ha dado mi Dios una esperanza en medio de la desesperación?

La manera en la que Lander tuerce la boca hace que la herida de su mejilla se tense. Nalvage sabe que su Dios no significa nada para una bestia como él, pero hay algo en sus ojos fríos que le recuerdan mucho a la ambición de los verdugos con quienes alguna vez hizo pactos en el pasado.

Y por eso, no le cabe duda de que acabará por hacer lo que le diga.

—Si te hace sentir más tranquilo, querido Benjamin —dice Nalvage—, la razón por la que no te he dado más indicaciones, es porque estás esperando a alguien.

El Inquisidor entrecierra la mirada.

—¿A quién? —pregunta, y el sonido de su voz trae consigo un silbido rasposo.

El cadáver de Sammuel levanta un dedo hacia la caverna.

—Lo reconocerás de inmediato. Porque *él* saldrá de esta misma puerta para venir por ustedes.

El hombre mira hacia la gruta y sus pupilas se encogen ante la cavernosa sensación que se desprende del metal.

Sé muy bien que, en el fondo, se pregunta si lo que ha estado sintiendo todo este tiempo no es otra cosa que el temor de Dios.

El ángel da media vuelta y mira hacia el lindero del bosque.

—Ah, una cosa más —dice—. Mi trabajo contigo ha terminado, pero mi Señor quiere que te dé una última recompensa por tu labor.

El viejo atenaza el arma en su cintura cuando escucha que algo se aproxima desde la oscuridad.

—¿Qué diablos pretendes?

—Eres un Inquisidor, Benjamin Lander. Uno de los más grandes que han visto mis ojos —asegura Nalvage—. Pero es momento de que abandones ese cuerpo decrépito y te prepares. Porque el tiempo ha llegado.

Cuando la figura por fin emerge y la luna llena ilumina su faz, los dedos del hombre se aflojan.

Su hijo —Buck Lander— lo observa de manera inexpresiva, tan grande, tan ancho, que el brazo conectado a su nuca queda completamente oculto por la maleza.

Sin decir más, Nalvage se da la media vuelta y comienza a alejarse, dejando un suave rastro de plumas detrás.

CAPÍTULO 84
PUERTA AL CIELO

Al amanecer, el sol me encuentra con la cabeza astada y envestido en piel de lobo, ambos tan plateados como la luna que ya se ha ocultado en el bosque.

Tared, en cambio, camina desnudo detrás de mí, con nuestras manos enlazadas para que lo guíe a través de la niebla.

Antes me era imposible ver más allá de unos metros, pero ahora, los senderos de este lugar se abren ante mis ojos con tal claridad que mis pasos avanzan con la precisión de una brújula.

Me siento tan… distinto, tan ligero y a la vez, arraigado al suelo por el que camino, mientras que mi consorte, en lugar de haber terminado exhausto, parece que también se ha cargado con la energía de nuestro ritual.

Mi tercer ojo por fin se ha abierto del todo, puesto que ahora puedo ver *más allá del velo:* las calles de Salem interpuestas en este bosque, las casas, los transeúntes convertidos en fantasmas que traspasan los árboles, ignorantes del mundo espiritual cernido a su alrededor.

Y estoy seguro de que, cuando vuelva al plano de los vivos, veré este reino con la misma nitidez.

Ésta es la razón, pienso. Éste es el motivo por el cual estoy condenado a quedarme ciego al final de mi vida. Como todos los de mi estirpe.

Levanto mi mano y, con un sutil movimiento de mi muñeca, las ramas de los endrinos se retraen para revelar el sendero junto al pozo. Y, al llegar a la casa, sus hilos se estiran hacia mí con tal reverencia que podría echarla abajo de un tirón.

Es la misma construcción de siempre, pero ahora sus venas están tan expuestas para mí que, al entrar, la presencia de Aradia ya no me parece muda. La siento infectar cada pared y cada viga, abrazar cada parte de la construcción para intentar mantenerla unida a este plano.

Y también puedo ver las grietas que, poco a poco, se han abierto en la magia debilitada de la bruja.

Pero eso no es lo único que nos recibe. Las vasijas con los demonios de Inanna están ahora repartidas por toda la casa, la mayoría con las tapas ahora rasgadas. Las súplicas de las criaturas restantes, aún atrapadas, son tan claras como un susurro en mis oídos.

Aquello no me sorprende. Como las voces del monstruo de hueso han sido silenciadas, es normal que pueda escuchar todo lo demás.

Después de detenernos unos momentos para que Tared pueda vestirse, subimos al ático. Allí, Comus Bayou y el aquelarre nos esperan, reunidos en torno a la puerta del cuarto de evocaciones.

Más de uno contiene un quejido cuando emerjo de la trampilla con las astas, la piel de lobo aún fresca sobre mis hombros y el gran sigilo de la espada grabado en mi pecho. Y al cruzar la habitación, sus pieles se erizan, sus ojos se dilatan; incluso

Hoffman, quien es enteramente humano, puede percibir la oscuridad que ahora acentúa cada uno de mis movimientos.

Inanna se encuentra frente a la puerta con las manos cruzadas sobre su vientre. Su consorte permanece a su lado y sus hermanas sostienen un gran cofre de madera de las asas. Después de asentir, como si aprobase lo que tiene ahora frente a ella, la bruja goética nos hace pasar a la habitación, la cual ha sido preparada con cautela.

Además de no tener ya un solo jarrón, han quitado el tapete de corderos para poner sobre el símbolo el atril donde antes estaba el libro del Culto. Ahora, el espejo de obsidiana de Hela reposa sobre él, mientras que dos sillas de madera han sido puestas delante.

La sirena y la arpía bajan el cofre. Y, una vez en el suelo, Inanna saca de allí dos mantos blancos cuyos pliegues se escuchan como el repiquetear de cientos de cristales. Coloca uno en cada silla, y mi asombro se exacerba al reconocer lo que son.

Se trata de la piel del ángel Raxnal, la cual ha sido dividida en dos y confeccionada como si fuesen un par de túnicas.

Inanna sonríe ante mi expresión.

—La razón por la cual bajamos al ángel con nuestra Madre fue para poder mantener su esencia intacta para este momento —explica—. Portarla será una gran ayuda para pasar desapercibidos en el reino de los cielos.

Miro con suspicacia hacia las sillas.

—¿Desapercibidos?

—No vas a ir solo al Paraíso, Elisse.

Un nudo se forma en mi garganta cuando, después de decir estas palabras, Inanna comienza a quitarse el abrigo.

—No, ¡de ninguna manera!

La bruja se echa a reír ante mi protesta.

—¿De verdad crees que tienes manera de detenerme, Elisse?

—Es demasiado peligroso —insisto—, eres la portadora de Satanás, ¡el peor enemigo de los ángeles! Si ellos nos descubren, irán primero por ti.

Cuando ella ni siquiera parpadea ante mi advertencia, me queda claro que lo sabe. Es más, que ésa es precisamente la razón por la cual está decidida a venir.

Miro a Ilya, a Cali y a Hel, con la esperanza de que alguno de ellos la haga recapacitar. Pero al ver que ninguno parece sorprendido, me doy cuenta de lo inútil que sería seguir discutiendo.

Ellos ya lo habían decidido. Y quizá desde que supimos que tenía que ir al Merkavah.

Cuando mi silencio deja en claro mi resignación, Inanna me tiende un artefacto que saca de su bolsillo.

Tared ladea la cabeza al reconocerlo.

—¿Ése es...?

—Sí —se anticipa la bruja—. Es el mismo péndulo que puse en tu cuello para que pudieran cruzar el plano medio en Dungeon Rock. Y la razón por la cual se lo estoy dando ahora a Elisse es porque si el muchacho llega a pronunciar en voz el alta el nombre de su Mara con la lengua de Barón Samedi las consecuencias podrían ser fatales.

—Y por eso hemos encantado el péndulo. Para que apunte hacia esa desgraciada en cuanto arrebates el nombre a Dios —explica Hela.

Dios.

Estrujo la piedra en mi puño y la magia responde ante mi contacto. Luego, extiendo la otra mano para que Inanna me dé el sello de cera con los nombres secretos del desgraciado.

Después de repasar aquellas palabras de poder, cierro los ojos antes de susurrar un "empecemos".

El vínculo con Tared se tensa cuando Hela y Caligo me quitan la piel de lobo. Me ofrecen unos pantalones vaqueros, botas, y una túnica muy parecida a la que usé en el ritual de las escobas, aunque más corta, más práctica, para permitir que me mueva con soltura si llegara a hacer falta.

Después de removerme las astas, nos invisten a Inanna y a mí con la piel del ángel Raxnal, y nos hacen sentarnos en las sillas, de espaldas al espejo.

Empuñamos nuestros athames en el regazo, el mío aún con el mango trozado ahora envuelto en una franela debido a mi enfrentamiento con Tared, y, finalmente, Inanna extiende su anillo dorado a Ilya.

—Llévale esto a Madre —pide—. Sé que no lo necesita, pero me sentiré más tranquila si ella lo tiene de todas maneras.

El hombre tigre se acerca y envuelve la mano de la mujer con cuidado.

—Я люблю тебя фсей душой, Инанна.[41]

La portadora de Satán permite que él le acaricie los dedos antes de tomar el anillo de Salomón. Y aunque Inanna no añade palabra alguna, no hace falta. La manera en la que sus ojos oscuros resplandecen es elocuente.

El gesto me resulta conmovedor, puesto que es la primera vez que los veo compartir una muestra de afecto frente a los demás.

La bruja arpía saca varias botellas pequeñas del cofre y nos da una a cada uno. Miro el interior y distingo pedazos de belladona que flotan en el líquido ambarino.

---

[41] En ruso: "Te quiero con toda mi alma, Inanna".

Veneno. No lo suficiente para matarnos, pero sí para reducir la intensidad del latido de nuestros corazones hasta casi hacer desaparecer el pulso. Algunos planos espirituales requieren algo más especial que pasar corporalmente a ellos, como entrar a través de los sueños, de las visiones... o acercarse lo más posible a la muerte.

Y un mundo tan complejo como el de los ángeles no podía ser la excepción.

—¿Estás listo? —pregunta Caligo, pero yo dirijo mi atención hacia Comus Bayou.

La angustia en el semblante de mis hermanos me oprime el corazón, la cual puedo sentir incluso en Hoffman, aunque éste tenga la mirada clavada en el suelo.

Pero el que más me duele de todos es sin duda Tared, quien con la espalda recta y un semblante firme hace todo lo posible por no transmitirme el miedo que debe sentir ahora mismo.

Si tan sólo supiera que esos ojos azules ya no pueden mentirme.

Tomo sus manos, las aprieto contra mi pecho, y él se inclina para recargar su frente contra la mía. Cierra los ojos un segundo para grabar en su piel la sensación de mis dedos firmes, de mi aliento bajo sus labios.

—Vuelve pronto a mí, Elisse —suplica el hombre lobo antes de besar mis nudillos.

Inanna y yo nos sentamos en los improvisados tronos mientras Caligo nos muestra una vez más el mapa del plano celeste.

—Para llegar al Merkavah, deberán atravesar primero los Campos del Vigilante —dice, apuntando al interior de los anillos—. Después, alcanzarán la Columna de la Tierra,

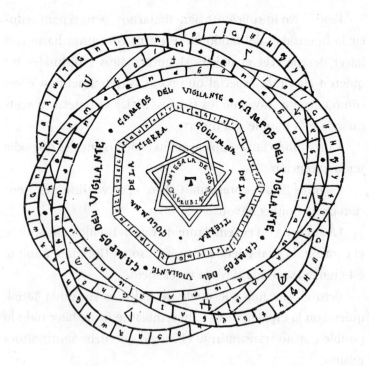

donde encontrarán la Antesala de los Querubines. Allí yace la puerta.

Una vez que ha quedado claro, abrimos nuestras botellas a la vez.

—Y recuerden —continúa antes de que nos las llevemos a los labios—: sus mentes seguirán conectadas a sus cuerpos como si los hubiesen materializado en el plano de los ángeles. Cada herida, cada golpe y cada dolor lo sentirán en carne propia, así que tengan mucho cuidado, porque Hela no los guiará de vuelta hasta que ese péndulo se levante.

—*Salgan victoriosos, hijos de la Grieta Resplandeciente. Que su brillo llene el Paraíso de Oscuridad.*

Ante el eco de Aradia, ambos echamos la cabeza hacia atrás y bebemos el amargo elixir. Hasta la última gota.

Hela se coloca frente al espejo con las manos alzadas. Cierra los ojos y recita unas palabras en voz baja. La superficie de cristal se remueve como una densa nube de humo y luego escucho voces brotar de la oscuridad.

Un montón de brazos negros, muy similares a los de los sirvientes de Samedi, brotan del espejo. Se alargan, nos rodean como tentáculos hambrientos.

Una de las manos pellizca mi pecho con el índice y el pulgar, justo sobre el sigilo de la piedra filosofal. La mano se aleja y comienza a sacar un hilo de plata que emerge desde mi corazón.

Y, como si también se llevase mi consciencia, empiezo a cabecear a la par que la belladona hace su efecto. La mano se retrae hacia el espejo, y cuando el hilo toca la superficie de obsidiana, cierro los ojos.

Pero esta vez, el mundo no se cubre de sombras, sino de la más radiante de las luces.

CAPÍTULO 85
OFRENDA

Hace diecinueve años le hiciste una promesa al gusano. Le juraste que, si traicionaba a Aradia y se sometía a *tu voluntad*, le darías un cuerpo humano *vivo* que le permitiese sentir más allá de lo que sólo había podido imitar al *vestir* una piel embalsamada.

Y el gusano jamás creyó que el día en el que finalmente se cumpliría esa promesa comenzaría así: con un hombre de su misma naturaleza asquerosa, encorvado como una cucaracha y retraído en una esquina de la habitación de la necromante.

La locura se cierne sobre Allen Miller como la suela de una bota, puesto que ha perdido la cuenta de los días que lleva dentro de esas cuatro paredes, escuchando una y otra vez la cacofonía de aquel gramófono infernal.

La puerta no se abre desde dentro y el cristal de la ventana tampoco puede romperse. Lo ha intentado tantas veces que se pregunta si acaso van a mantenerlo allí por siempre.

El gusano saborea la podredumbre que percibe bajo la piel de ese joven, tan apetitosa que sus colmillos se hundirían en él como mantequilla. Los corazones malvados siempre han sido sus favoritos, pero si no cede a sus impulsos, a esa necesidad demoníaca que lleva dentro de sí desde hace diecinueve años, es porque ya ha sentido lo que hay dentro del bolsillo del joven: una bala. Blanca y con el peso de un revólver, escondida en el fondo de su bolsillo desde aquella noche de tormenta en la Isla de Invierno.

Un objeto que el joven vio, perfectamente, cómo los ángeles introducían en sus ropas antes de caer en su hipnotismo. Los monstruos de John Dee hicieron muy bien su labor, así que al gusano sólo le queda dar el último paso.

Asmoday repta por el techo hasta quedar justo sobre el muchacho, quien se encoge más sobre su vientre, temeroso de girar la cabeza y encontrarse con esos ojos rojos que lo miran siempre con hambre, siempre con deseo. Aun así, se obliga a levantarse de un salto cuando el demonio deja caer algo a su lado.

—¡No, aléjate! —exclama mientras se retrae contra la ventana. Pero, para su sorpresa, el gusano no se mueve de su lugar. Tan sólo mira con ansias aquello que le ha dado como ofrenda.

Allen Miller ladea la cabeza, y se acerca con cuidado hacia el libro rojo que yace abierto de par en par en el suelo, con el lomo hacia arriba.

Se acuclilla y alarga el brazo sin quitarle la mirada de encima a Asmoday. Y al levantar aquel libro descubre que debajo hay un arma… y una fotografía.

Después, escucha el chasquido de la puerta al abrirse.

CAPÍTULO 86
EL JARDÍN DE LAS DELICIAS

La sensación de traspasar a los dominios de Barón Samedi es muy similar a ser arrojado a un pozo sin fondo. Es como una caída, claustrofóbica y oscura, que luego se convierte en una trayectoria sin sentido ni dirección, hasta que las sombras por fin te escupen en aquel trozo de *Guinée*. Pero entrar al reino celestial es una experiencia muy diferente.

Es una elevación, una energía que te arrastra hacia arriba a una velocidad vertiginosa, y la luz del tránsito es tan agresiva que crees que te quedarás ciego para siempre. Pero luego ese resplandor comienza a serenarse, y de un momento a otro estás en el Paraíso.

Inanna y yo abrimos los ojos. Seguimos en las sillas y el espejo de obsidiana flota como un fantasma a nuestras espaldas, con el hilo de plata que conecta nuestra consciencia con el cuerpo serpenteando en el aire.

Del otro lado, podemos ver todavía el ático y oír cómo los demás hablan en un murmullo casi imperceptible, como si el portal se hubiese convertido en una ventana hacia el mundo terrenal.

Guardamos nuestros athames entre las vestiduras, para luego ponernos en pie. El lugar que se abre frente a nosotros es una pradera verde y luminosa, tan amplia que no se alcanza a ver dónde termina, mientras que el cielo pareciera ser una especie de mar de cristal líquido que refleja todo lo que hay aquí abajo como en un estanque.

Y allá, como a medio kilómetro de nosotros, tan ancha como medio campo de fútbol, se alza la *Columna de la Tierra*; una torre de piedra blanca, semejante a la de un castillo medieval, cuyas paredes tienen algunos agujeros y partes derrumbadas, como si hubiese sido perforada por cañones en algún momento de su existencia, lo que me hace pensar que quizá no seamos los primeros en entrar aquí.

No es tan alta como su nombre me hizo imaginar, puesto que apenas y alcanzará los cien metros de altura. Y tal como en el mapa indicaba, está rodeada por los *Campos del Vigilante*, un inmenso prado de flores en tonos rosa pastel y marfil cuya fragancia mortífera se percibe hasta acá. De allí en más, no pareciera haber nada alrededor de este lugar. Tan sólo campos viridianos que se extienden hacia el infinito.

Observo el extraño Edén, e Inanna extiende su mano para envolver mis dedos de hueso, consciente de lo que se ha retorcido dentro de mí ante aquella construcción.

Le doy un suave apretón en respuesta, y luego la suelto para encaminarnos hacia la torre.

No parece haber ningún ángel a la vista, y esto, en vez de tranquilizarme, me trae una profunda sensación de malestar. El jardín se balancea de forma peculiar, como si vientos que vienen de distintas direcciones lo agitaran, aunque no percibo ninguna corriente.

Al acercarnos, la bruja goética se detiene y clava la mirada en las flores.

No. No son flores.

Son una especie de escultura de carne que busca asemejarse a ellas, puesto que sus pétalos y hojas están hechos de piel que, por la forma en la que se mueven, parece estar viva. Su centro no es más que una abertura oscura, rodeada de bordes sanguinolentos, similar a una...

Boca.

Inanna me toma del hombro y apunta con el dedo hacia los tallos venosos.

Hay algo debajo de la tierra abultada, sembrado cual semilla y con aquellas flores de carroña creciendo a lo largo como un altar. Y por la forma que tiene, no me cabe ninguna duda de que se trata de un cadáver.

Un brujo.

El resto del campo posee la misma naturaleza, tan macabra que no comprendo cómo los propios ángeles pueden interpretar esto como un paraíso.

Ambos nos tragamos la bilis y continuamos a través del jardín, obligados a abrirnos paso sobre los restos de quienes probablemente son nuestros antepasados. Al alcanzar el pie de la torre, siento un tirón en mi mano humana, seguido de un punzante dolor. Siseo y sacudo el brazo con brusquedad, desconcertado al ver que una de las flores se aferró a mi dorso con los dientes.

Pero el que esa cosa me haya mordido no es lo que hace que Inanna abra los ojos de par en par.

Me llevo la mano a los labios, pero ya es demasiado tarde.

El suelo comienza a temblar con tanta fuerza que nos vemos obligados a zambullirnos entre las flores.

¡BUM!

Como anillos de Saturno, tres titánicos arcos de metal dorado se levantan por los distintos horizontes de la tierra, tan veloces pero a la vez tan pesados que parecieran arrastrar la gravedad tras ellos. Y, al entrecruzarse sobre nuestras cabezas, se detienen al mismo tiempo que el temblor.

Hileras de ojos gigantes, insertados a lo largo de las bandas de oro, se mueven hacia todas las direcciones del plano celestial, buscando aquella criatura que ha emitido un sonido tan poco angelical.

Innana y yo nos cubrimos bien con nuestros mantos, puesto que se trata de él. *El Vigilante.* Una especie de reinterpretación de aquel Ofanim que alguna vez mencionó Julien.

Para nuestro alivio, los anillos vuelven a girar para ocultarse en el horizonte, comprobando así la efectividad de la piel de Raxnal.

Después de un par de minutos de quedarnos inmóviles, Inanna y yo nos atrevemos a respirar otra vez. Nos levantamos y entramos por una estrecha grieta que se abre en la base de la torre.

Deslizándonos por las sombras de la construcción, entramos por fin a la Columna de la Tierra.

CAPÍTULO 87
FIN DEL CONTRATO

Fue tan lento, tan progresivo, que por un segundo creyó que lo que veía no era más que una alucinación.

Pero sus temores se confirmaron cuando la necromante, con los dedos enredados en aquellos hilos de plata, dijo que, efectivamente, esa línea punteada que había aparecido en la mano de la Bestia Revestida de Luna era una mordida.

Y fue allí cuando Salvador Hoffman supo que tenía que salir de esa habitación.

El licántropo se quedaría. Ni un trueno podría arrancarlo de ese lugar, pero él no. El miserable detective no podría soportar ver ese cuerpo cubrirse de heridas sabiendo que, por más que lo deseara, no *debía* ponerle un dedo encima al joven para intentar aliviar su dolor.

Y no era sólo porque la bruja Caligo les hubiera advertido de la posibilidad de que la conexión de los hilos se desequilibrara si llegaban a tocarlos, sino porque nunca se había sentido con ese derecho.

Así que, con una sonrisa de malicia, lo contemplé cruzar la casa e ir hacia el lindero del bosque helado, en el cual lleva parado más de media hora, ahogado con el humo de una sucesión infinita de cigarros.

Hasta que unos pasos a sus espaldas lo hacen bufar.

—¿Qué demonios haces aquí?

La pregunta sale tan afilada de su boca que de haber sido un hombre con magia habría apuñalado a la mujer que está detrás de él.

Pero a la falsa bruja no parece importarle su hostilidad. Después de todo, ella jamás habría acudido a él en busca de ternura.

—Vine para ver si estabas bien...

—Sí, ésa siempre es tu excusa —replica él, sardónico—. No estoy de humor para *eso*, si es lo que estás buscando.

El fuego de la humillación cruza la cara de la mujer.

—Cretino de mierda. Debí dejar que te pudrieras aquí solo —espeta con un desprecio que parecería inusual en alguien como ella—. Pero me alegra que lo menciones, porque, de hecho, ya no puedo seguir haciendo esto, Hoffman.

Él por fin se digna a girarse. Y al hacerlo le basta un segundo para reconocer en esos ojos grises toda la culpa que a él también le atormenta.

Le da una última bocanada a su cigarro y luego lo aplasta en una corteza que yo siento en carne viva sobre mi cuerpo.

—¿Es porque Miller nos descubrió? —pregunta—. Vamos. Sabías bien que se iba a enterar. Es más, estoy seguro de que se dio cuenta desde que estábamos en Minnesota. Es un jodido lobo, después de todo.

Aunque lo ha dicho en tono divertido, la sonrisa en su cara no es precisamente de placer.

—No, Hoffman —replica ella con brusquedad—. Es porque ahora también tuvo que mentirle a Elisse para encubrirnos.

Aquello logra activar un nervio reflejo en la cara del detective. Chasquea la lengua y se aparta un par de pasos, como si eso pudiese alejarlo de la repentina vergüenza que le provoca aquella verdad.

—¿No fuiste tú quien rogó que no le dijera nada sobre lo nuestro, en primer lugar? —dice Hoffman para luego resoplar con cansancio—. Da igual. Yo iba a pedirte exactamente lo mismo. Estoy harto de sentirme como una mierda cada vez que me meto contigo.

—¡Lo dices como si yo te hubiera obligado a hacer esto para vengarme! —exclama ella, furiosa.

—¡¿Qué parte de todo esto te parece una puñetera venganza, Johanna?! —brama el hombre, incapaz de soportar la repulsión que lo invade—. ¿Ésa en la que a Miller le importa un carajo con quien estés? ¿O en la que me he rebajado a hacer algo que ni siquiera me gusta porque no encuentro otra manera de lidiar con toda esta jodida situación?

La errante crispa las manos sobre su cabeza.

—¿Y crees que no lo sé? ¿Me crees tan estúpida como para no entender que no importa si me acuesto contigo o con un millón de hombres más eso no va a cambiar en absoluto lo que Tared siente por Elisse? Por favor, ¡tú sabes bien lo que yo buscaba con todo esto!

El calor de su discusión me hace hervir de placer.

Tantos encuentros, algunos tan desesperados que incluso yo misma me retorcí en el suelo de mi celda, poseída por sus bajos instintos, y jamás se habían atrevido a hablar del remordimiento que sentían una vez apagada la euforia.

Ciegos como animales. Culpables y sucios ahora que el brujo astado yace a un paso de la horca.

—Dios, estás enferma —espeta él, irritado—. Sabes que ese cabrón te mintió. Que les ocultó a ti y a todos los demás sobre su esposa y aun así tú...

—Mira quién lo dice, el idiota que no puede negarle nada a alguien que tiene la mitad de su edad.

La furia sube por los puños del detective, tan rojos que parecen dos bombas a punto de explotar.

—Al menos yo no pretendo estar de acuerdo con lo que ellos tienen —dice—. En cambio, tú sí que eres una jodida hipócrita, ¡pregonas el supuesto amor que le tienes a los dos cuando en el fondo te pudres de envidia!

En vez de arremeter con la misma cizaña, la perpetua-sangre gira la cabeza hacia la casa, hacia el ático, para que el detective no pueda ver cómo lágrimas patéticas le cubren la cara.

La errante todavía puede sentir entre sus dedos la esencia de la lengua de vaca y el regaliz. De todas las hierbas que ha consumido para evitar que su despecho se convierta en un error irreparable.

—Sí, soy una hipócrita, ¿y qué? ¿Y qué si prefiero sonreír y pretender que todo está bien aunque por dentro quiera vomitar de los celos? —admite—. Tener esos sentimientos no me convierte en una porquería de persona, me hace *humana*, y tengo tanto derecho a serlo como tú.

El detective contempla el temblor en los hombros de aquella mujer con lástima, casi arrepentimiento. Y ante su mutismo, ella se gira de nuevo para enfrentarlo:

—Pero, ¿sabes qué? Es gracioso que me llames hipócrita cuando tú no eres mucho mejor que yo en ese aspecto, Hoffman.

—¿De qué carajos estás hablando?

Ella mira de arriba abajo al hombre, quizás indecisa de si serviría de algo reabrir esa herida. Pero está tan furiosa, que no puede evitarlo.

—Hace un tiempo, en Utah, te pregunté por qué estabas en este viaje con nosotros —comienza—. Y por un tiempo creí saberlo. Creí que todos los hombres como tú, a fin de cuentas, eran igual de predecibles. Pero me equivoqué.

La mujer lo mira con una compasión tan repentina que el hombre no puede evitar preguntarse si es un gesto auténtico u otra de esas máscaras que logra ponerse tan bien cuando le conviene.

Y cuando ella se acerca, él contiene el impulso de dar un paso atrás.

—Al principio, pensé que era por tu deuda —dice—. Elisse había matado a Laurele y vengado a tu hija, después de todo. Pero luego te conocí un poco mejor y entendí que tú, tu personalidad y tus sentimientos eran tan complejos que no había manera de que algo tan *simple* fuese la respuesta.

"Después, creí que era por Tared. Que todo esto era un plan mezquino tuyo para sacar sus verdades a la luz y hacerlo sufrir como tú sufriste por la muerte de tu niña. Pero una vez más, algo así no encajaba, porque también descubrí que, a tu manera, eras un buen hombre. Quizá no para mí o para Comus Bayou, pero sí para quien pudiera ser lo suficiente-mente... *especial*.

El detective endurece la mirada, pero se queda inmóvil, como si algo en su fuero interno lo obligase a escuchar a aquella mujer.

O como si, de alguna manera, quisiera que ella encontra-ra *esa verdad* por él.

—¿Por qué estás aquí, Hoffman? —insiste ella ante su silencio—. ¿Por qué has abandonado tus recuerdos, tu lugar seguro y la casa donde tuviste a tu hija por última vez? ¿Por qué soportas estar cerca de un hombre que sólo te recuerda la peor parte de tu vida? ¿Por qué te acuestas con alguien a quien no amas, a sabiendas de que ni siquiera eso te hace sentir genuinamente mejor?

Las preguntas de la errante me hacen ladear la cabeza. Siempre he sido buena para escarbar dentro de los corazones. Sacar de ellos lo más maravilloso o lo más podrido, y utilizarlo para cumplir mi voluntad. Pero nunca había conocido uno tan peculiar como el que palpita dentro de este hombre, y no puedo evitar preguntarme qué clase de artilugio se necesitaría conjugar para dominarlo.

Pero bien dicen que un corazón no se puede embrujar dos veces.

Como si los propios ángeles hubiesen conspirado para salvarlo, un crujido en la nieve los interrumpe. Un ruido que, en segundos, se convierte en múltiples pisadas que se acercan rápidamente por el bosque.

Él desenfunda su arma y la falsa bruja se arquea, lista para transformarse mientras varias siluetas se asoman entre la niebla apenas iluminada por la luna.

La errante, confundida, baja sus manos cuando el demonio Ilya surge de entre la maleza. Pero lo que casi la hace gritar es reconocer a la mujer que lo acompaña, con dos niños entre los brazos.

CAPÍTULO 88
LA COLUMNA DE LA TIERRA

Al entrar a la torre, casi sufro un infarto al descubrir por qué no había un solo ángel allá afuera, en el jardín.

Y es que *todos* están aquí.

Cientos y cientos de ellos, clavados en las paredes como Cristos crucificados, tan quietos que, por un segundo, pienso que están muertos.

Pero no. Esos seres inmóviles y desnudos, con la cabeza inclinada hacia el suelo, tan sólo están "dormidos", a la espera de ser convocados al mundo de los vivos. Y lo sé porque, además de que sus cuerpos parecen débiles y casi humanos, sin la complejidad aberrante que la carne recién consumida de un brujo puede otorgar, ninguno tiene puesta una máscara de hierro.

De todas las cosas que creí que habría detrás de esas caras andróginas, nunca imaginé que aquello sería *nada*. Absolutamente nada, porque donde debería haber un rostro, tan sólo hay un agujero, tan vacío y profundo como el pecho resquebrajado de la Marionetista.

Después de unos segundos de contener la respiración, me animo a dar el primer paso.

Nada. Los ángeles permanecen quietos, inmunes al ruido de mis botas contra el suelo de piedra, lo que nos empuja a avanzar hacia lo que parece ser una enorme y compleja escalera que se erige en medio de la estancia, la cual termina en una trampilla de metal dorado, tan labrada que parece extraída del Palacio de Versalles.

La entrada a la Antesala de los Querubines.

Pero, al acercarnos, la torre e incluso los propios ángeles pasan a segundo plano cuando por fin comprendemos la naturaleza de la escalera.

Para empezar, los peldaños son del tamaño de sarcófagos de cristal, mientras que la estructura de lo que serían los "barandales" consiste en tallos iguales a los de las flores de los Campos del Vigilante, entrelazados en complejas formaciones arbóreas. La escalera por sí misma es también muy enrevesada, con caminos en los que se parte en dos o tres escaleras para luego volver a unirse en una especie de laberinto, con algunas terminaciones que no llevan a ninguna parte.

Y esta vez, Inanna es quien necesita contener un gemido al distinguir el cuerpo de una bruja dentro del primer escalón, a quien le han cortado la mano izquierda.

Yace rodeada de las terribles flores de carroña que se alimentan de su cuerpo ya marchito, con las raíces encarnadas en su boca, en sus cuencas, en los orificios corporales que desaparecen bajo su vestido. Lleva ropas muy antiguas, similares a las de la muñeca de cera que había en la casa de Jonathan Corwin, lo que indica que se trata de una de las primeras víctimas de las Guerras Ocultistas.

Casi quiero echarme a reír. Porque es obvio que para los ángeles éste es su Árbol del Conocimiento;[42] un jodido inver-

---

[42] Génesis 2:16-17. El árbol del conocimiento del bien y el mal es uno de los árboles del Paraíso mencionados en la historia del Jardín del Edén.

nadero donde nosotros, los brujos, somos las semillas para que las flores germinen en ángeles.

La humillación de pisar las tumbas de los nuestros me hace estrujar el athame oculto en mi túnica, con más deseos que nunca antes de clavarlo en el *Dios* que me espera al final de esta torre.

Pero a medida que subimos, tengo la sensación de que la realidad comienza a... distorsionarse.

Se supone que íbamos hacia arriba, hacia el techo, pero, al haber cambiado de escalera, ahora siento como si descendiéramos. Después de un rato, la perspectiva cambia para llevarnos en ascenso de nuevo conforme pasamos de una escalera a otra, atrapados en una especie de dimensión sacada de un dibujo de Escher.

La alucinación empeora cuando, por más que avanzamos, no parece que nos estemos acercando a la trampilla de la antesala.

Ante la frustración, una idea hace clic en mi cabeza, y me giro hacia Inanna para ver la forma de transmitirle mi plan.

Y es allí cuando me transformo en Orfeo, que volvió su mirada hacia Eurídice en el Inframundo, porque la bruja no está detrás de mí, sino varios escalones más abajo, con la mirada petrificada en uno de los ataúdes, las manos a los costados de la cabeza y un gesto de infinito terror.

Ella lo intenta. Pero al final no logra contenerse.

Ante el grito ensordecedor que lanza, los ángeles levantan la cabeza.

CAPÍTULO 89
FUGITIVOS

—¡¿Qué quieren decir con que los tramperos los dejaron ir?!

Ante el grito del detective Hoffman, la bruja Caligo escruta a los recién llegados en busca de algún artilugio, un encantamiento, un amuleto que los ángeles hayan colocado en sus cuerpos.

Pero no. Ese puñado de humanos y errantes, repartidos ahora por toda la sala, sólo están malnutridos y sucios, con varios huesos reventados a balazos o laceraciones de cuchillo. Inclusive, hay un hombre chivo cuyo par de muñones, secuela de una explosión, muestran una grave infección pustulosa.

Y eso es precisamente lo más extraño de todo: que están *vivos*. Heridos sólo por el resultado de la pelea, no por la mano de hierro de los tramperos. Una orden que inclusive a mí me pareció demasiado generosa viniendo del Mensajero Nalvage.

—Aradia advirtió a Ilya sobre la presencia de Irina y los demás en la reserva. Y él dijo que los encontró muy cerca de Dungeon Rock —explica la falsa bruja sin apenas levantar la mirada, atendiendo sobre el largo comedor al hombre de los miembros amputados, a quien poco le falta para perder la consciencia.

La envenenadora asiente, puesto que sabe tan bien como yo que Aradia, la hija de Diana, jamás enviaría a buscar a esos errantes si no supiera que era seguro traerlos a través de la niebla.

—Lía, ¿qué fue lo que pasó? —pregunta la bestia bisonte, y la demacrada mujer parpadea, las heridas tirantes sobre su piel. Mira a su gente, a los despojos de aquella batalla, pero no parece encontrar las palabras adecuadas para responder.

—Fuimos a Minnesota a buscar el cuerpo de Huritt —dice la errante puma en su lugar, quien aprieta a sus niños contra ella, tan huesudos, tan frágiles que parece que se desharán en sus brazos—. No habíamos tenido noticias de ustedes después de la llamada que le hicieron a Debbie, así que decidimos volver para cerciorarnos de que todo estuviera bien. No esperábamos encontrar la casa destruida. Y tampoco imaginamos que los Lander no iban a estar... solos.

El horror se retuerce en el estómago de la arpía al comprobar que los temores del brujo astado estaban bien justificados.

—Después de capturarnos, nos encerraron en una camioneta de carga —continúa el errante más joven del grupo, un chico que todavía conserva unas cuantas espinas de su ancestro en el cuerpo—. Nos dejaron allí durante días, sin comida y apenas con agua. Estábamos tan débiles que no podíamos escapar.

—Aunque tampoco hizo falta —asegura la osa devorapieles, quien se ocupa de tratar las heridas de su hermano tejón—. Esta misma tarde nos bajaron del vehículo y nos obligaron a deambular en el bosque. No nos persiguieron. No nos lastimaron. Tan sólo nos dejaron ir.

Su testimonio borra el color de los rostros de todos los presentes, porque les hace saber que la presencia de estos desgraciados en la casa no es precisamente un milagro.

—Dios mío —exclama la perpetuasangre por lo bajo, las manos aún sobre la carne expuesta de uno de los muñones—. ¡No puedo creer que los tramperos realmente se hayan aliado con los ángeles!

—¿Ángeles? —pregunta la mujer humana, quien por fin parece reaccionar.

—Es una historia muy larga, Lía —explica el errante bisonte—. Pero sí, en resumidas cuentas, ahora mismo nos enfrentamos a un montón de ángeles espantosos.

Una de las crías de la mujer puma se sobresalta bajo el brazo de su madre.

—Ah, ¡eso explica lo del tío Sam! —exclama.

—¿Qué quieres decir, Enola? —pregunta el devorapieles Nashua.

—Él estuvo muchos meses… muerto —dice el pequeño, dudoso, como si le costase entender sus propias palabras—, y un día, se levantó del refrigerador donde lo tenían encerrado. Pero ya no era el mismo.

—Por las alas, parecía un ángel —añade su hermano—. Y decía cosas horribles con una voz que no era del tío Sam. Fue él quien le dijo al viejo dónde encontrar a los errantes de las motos y…

De pronto, ambas criaturas guardan silencio y miran al vacío, invadidos por recuerdos que jamás se atreverían a contar siquiera a su propia madre.

El detective cruza una mirada de profunda preocupación con la envenenadora.

—Eso sólo significa una cosa —dice ella, presa de un escalofrío—: ahora mismo están buscando la forma de entrar a la casa.

Ah, ¡cuánta razón tenían al decir que el tormento era la tortura favorita de las criaturas de Dee! Porque, ¿qué suplicio más grande que sentirse encerrados en su propia casa, a la espera de ser ejecutados como cerdos en un matadero?

—Caligo, ¿crees que los ángeles logren cruzar la niebla ahora que Aradia está débil? —pregunta la perpetuasangre, tan nerviosa que ha tenido que interrumpir la curación.

—Madre se pudriría primero antes de permitir que algo así sucediera, y los demonios, por más traidores que sean, desprecian tanto a los ángeles que jamás se doblegarían ante ellos —responde la arpía—. No. Esta casa permanecerá en pie mientras Aradia viva.

Su certeza tuerce mi sonrisa.

¿Es así? ¿Si la gran Aradia cae, la casa caerá con ella?

¿O serás *tú* quien la derribe primero?

Mientras el grupo lame sus heridas y ahoga sus cabezas de temores, mi portal me aleja de la estancia y me lleva de vuelta al bosque de endrinos.

Allí, contemplo cómo el monstruo Ilya se dirige hacia el pozo con un gran espejo entre las manos. Se asoma por el borde de piedra y mira la negrura que lo observa con curiosidad desde el fondo.

La envenenadora le ha dado la orden de bloquear la entrada para no ofrecer a los ángeles ninguna oportunidad de cruzar. Pero *tú* le susurras al oído, y le ordenas que abra las manos.

Y obedece. Y el espejo cae. Y el espejo se estrella contra el suelo de piedra y el espejo se fragmenta en pedazos.

Ilya mira hacia la luna llena. El resplandor le baña la cara, pero es su mente la que se cubre de sombras.

Es cierto. Los demonios jamás se doblegarían ante los ángeles. Pero, ¿quién podría negarse a tu voluntad?

Así que, sin piedad, por completo falto de misericordia, lo haces aferrarse al borde y meter una pierna en el pozo, para luego dejarlo caer en la oscuridad.

CAPÍTULO 90
LEAALOC

En un desgarre surrealista del espacio, el techo se catapulta hacia arriba como un elevador, llevándose consigo la valiosa trampilla. La torre se alarga a una velocidad vertiginosa y se convierte en un túnel oscuro, como si su interior se hubiese vuelto infinito de un tirón.

El sonido de cientos y cientos de trompetas brota de las caras vacías de los ángeles en un coro apocalíptico, tan estruendoso que los vidrios de los ataúdes se resquebrajan a nuestros pies.

De pronto, uno de los costados de la torre comienza a temblar, golpeado desde afuera por algo que busca abrirse paso a través de la pared. La escalera se tambalea de forma violenta y la bruja resbala ante la sacudida.

—¡Inanna!

Me lanzo hacia ella y la sujeto de una mano para evitar que caiga por el borde del sarcófago. Uno de los escalones debajo se rompe, y el cuerpo que tenía dentro dentro cae en picada, con todo y sus flores sangrientas.

Logro subir a la bruja, y ambos nos echamos a correr hacia abajo, todo lo que la laberíntica escalera nos permite.

Hasta que aquello por fin logra hacer pedazos el muro.

Trozos de ángeles y roca salen disparados por todas partes y se estrellan como proyectiles contra la estructura del Árbol. Y cuando éste comienza a colapsar hacia un costado, Inanna y yo saltamos de una altura de casi diez metros.

Mis tobillos me punzan dolorosamente al aterrizar en el suelo de la torre, apenas amortiguados por mi naturaleza de errante. Pero nos vemos obligados a apartarnos de inmediato para no ser aplastados por la lluvia de vidrios, cuerpos y flores de carroña que revientan como globos sangrientos a nuestro alrededor.

Y entonces, aquello que ha venido por nosotros por fin entra a la torre: una criatura tan grande, tan voluminosa que, por un segundo, pareciera ser más un gólem que un ángel.

Como una personificación terrible de Hefesto, la criatura empuña en su mano derecha un pesado mazo de hierro blanco, mientras que cientos de máscaras angelicales recubren su cuerpo abultado por los imponentes músculos y tendones que lo conforman.

Su propia máscara nos observa con un único ojo dorado, muy abierto en su frente.

—Leaaloc. El Forjador —dice Inanna con un jadeo, consciente de que ya no vale la pena callarnos—. Un ángel de los Metales.

Como un trueno, el Forjador se abalanza a una velocidad impresionante contra nosotros.

Inanna me arroja a un lado para salvarme de la embestida de la colosal criatura, la cual se estampa contra lo que queda de la escalera. Leaaloc se arranca de la estructura y se gira despacio hacia nosotros.

Pero, en vez de volver a atacarnos, el monstruo camina hacia uno de los ángeles que ha salido volando de la pared que destruyó.

En una secuencia de lo más grotesca, Leaaloc arranca una de sus máscaras y la coloca sobre el agujero en su cabeza. Y entonces, la criatura despierta. Se sacude, se levanta sobre sus cuatro extremidades y repta a toda velocidad hacia uno de los brujos que han quedado desperdigados por el suelo. Y cuando su boca metálica se expande para tragarse el cráneo del cadáver de una mordida, saco el athame de mis ropas.

Dirijo mi magia a una de las piedras que han caído de la pared y, como una bala de cañón, la disparo hacia el ángel.

El monstruo recibe el ataque de lleno, con tanta fuerza que vuela por los aires y termina aplastado contra otro de los muros de la torre.

—¡Cuidado, Elisse!

El Forjador carga de nuevo, esta vez directamente hacia mí. Arrojo una roca más pero a él le basta con levantar su mazo para destrozarla de un golpe.

Apenas logro esquivar la caída de su arma sobre mí. Ruedo por el suelo y me quito la piel de Raxnal para echarme a correr, pero el gigante es tan veloz que logra alcanzarme en cuestión de segundos.

Él martillea una y otra vez para tratar de aplastarme, demoliendo el duro suelo de piedra a su paso. Y justo cuando logra acorralarme contra la pared, Leaaloc se detiene por completo, el pesado mazo alzado sobre su cabeza. Se gira hacia atrás, y ambos vemos a Inanna en el centro de la torre. Completamente transformada en Satanás.

Las trompetas se intensifican y los ángeles en las paredes comienzan a retorcerse ante la presencia de la Princesa de las Tinieblas en el Paraíso. Leaaloc, como si se hubiese olvidado completamente de mi presencia, arranca un puñado de ángeles de la pared y los arroja al suelo, con la intención de colocar máscaras sobre todos y cada uno de ellos.

Pero la bruja goética no muestra un ápice de temor. Athame en mano, comienza a elevar con su propia telequinesis trozos de sarcófago: grandes vidrios con puntas afiladas como cuchillos. Y lo único que puedo entender es la orden "vete", saliendo con toda claridad de sus labios oscuros.

No me permito perder más tiempo.

Leaaloc y los ángeles que éste despierta en un instante se arrojan contra Inanna mientras yo me abalanzo hacia una de las flores de carroña que ha caído de la escalera. Por una fracción de segundo, miro hacia los cadáveres de brujos repartidos por el suelo, preguntándome qué es lo que habrá visto Inanna en ellos como para haberle provocado ese grito fatal.

Trituro la flor entre mis manos y trazo un círculo en el suelo con la sangre.

—Como es arriba es abajo —susurro, y rasgo de lado a lado la figura con mi athame.

Las sombras acuden sin falta a mi llamado; las siento moverse ante mi voluntad y pronunciarse bajo la punta de mi daga.

El plano medio se abre como un vientre y se expande dentro de toda la circunferencia para convertirse en un portal.

Un portal dentro de un plano medio. Un túnel de gusano.

Sin pensarlo dos veces, me arrojo de cabeza dentro del agujero.

CAPÍTULO 91
EL MARTILLO DE LAS BRUJAS

Ante el inmenso moretón que surca de pronto la mejilla de la Maligna, la necromante casi cede al instinto de tirar del hilo para traerla de vuelta al plano de los vivos.

Pero el péndulo no se ha levantado, y eso le hace mantener las manos en su lugar.

Su tarea es vigilar los vínculos, mantenerlos activos y funcionales, y no piensa traicionar su cometido. Ni siquiera por la gradual sensación de peligro que ha comenzado a asecharla durante las últimas horas.

No son los recién llegados, ni siquiera la amenaza del Inquisidor. Es el presentimiento de que hay *algo* que se le escapa, algo que ni siquiera su agudo tercer ojo puede ver.

Ella lo siente a un costado de su cabeza, en esa región de su cerebro que le permite mirar más allá del velo del tiempo. Es un hueco en el pasado al que no logra acceder; una presencia negra y difusa, como la sensación de un desconocido a sus espaldas que espera a que se gire para reconocerle.

Observa al portador del lobo y a la envenenadora, los últimos que quedan en la habitación tras las largas horas de angustiosa espera.

Pero su inquietud no encuentra lugar.

¿Será acaso tu presencia la que su subconsciente busca con tanta insistencia?

Con esa angustia incomprensible atascada en la garganta, dirige la mirada hacia su hermana, quien sólo volvió al ático para suministrar los antídotos de la belladona, asegurándose de devolver los latidos de ambos brujos a su ritmo normal.

—¿Cali? —dice, pero ella no responde, porque a pesar de que no es una vidente como su hermana, justo ahora experimenta el mismo mal presentimiento, lo que la impulsa a acercarse despacio al gran ventanal al fondo del ático.

Al mirar con atención, descubre una línea tenue y dorada que se asoma en el horizonte del bosque, fina y luminosa como un amanecer. Eso la hace fruncir el ceño, porque la noche tiene poco de haberse recostado sobre los endrinos.

Ella no puede percibirlo, pero yo sí.

La madera. Las astillas y la ceniza. El olor del fuego y el letal perfume de miles de flores.

Y después, el zumbido de un arpón.

—¡AL SUELO!

Ante el grito de Tared Miller, la bruja Caligo se echa por tierra justo cuando el arma revienta el vidrio en pedazos. El arpón vuela sobre su cabeza y se siembra en una de las vigas del techo.

Y como si se hubiese abierto la caja de Pandora, el ruido de sierras y cuchillas se abre paso por el ventanal.

El licántropo, sin dudarlo un segundo, corre a arrancar la puerta del ático de sus bisagras para colocarla a modo de escudo frente a los tres brujos unidos por el espejo.

Retuerzo las manos en mi portal al ver lo dispuesto que está a recibir un segundo arpón en el cuerpo.

—¡Julien, Nashua! —grita el portador del lobo a todo pulmón.

—¡¿Qué diablos está pasando?! —exclama la necromante, incapaz de mover los dedos un centímetro de su lugar.

Desde su sitio, el lobo logra ver cómo la línea de fuego avanza sobre el bosque como un sendero de lava en dirección hacia la casa.

—Tramperos —exclama él, casi sin aliento.

El sonido de una detonación le hace transformar sus manos en garras. Luego, una secuencia de balas penetra la fachada negra de la construcción.

La envenenadora está tan aturdida, tan desconcertada, que todavía no ha podido ponerse en pie.

—No es posible —el espanto vibra con cada sílaba que sale de su boca—, ¿cómo diablos lograron atravesar la niebla?

—¡Nashua, Jul...!

El grito insistente del devorapieles muere cuando un pesado golpe sacude el desván, un ruido terrorífico que le hace saber que algo muy grande se ha ceñido a la pared de la ventana.

Y entonces, una larga mano cetrina se siembra en el alféizar.

Los vidrios rotos se clavan en los dedos y cortan la palma de lado a lado, pero eso no impide que el monstruo se yerga lentamente ante ellos, con la luna llena detrás como el halo de un emisario divino.

Al principio, a Tared Miller le cuesta mucho reconocerlo, porque la cabeza de Benjamin Lander, en el extremo de un cuello tan largo como un brazo, parece ser lo único que queda del legendario trampero.

El ángel de la Transformación ha logrado meterse bajo su piel. Ha consumido sus órganos y sus músculos, pero en vez de matarlo hizo crecer decenas de brazos y piernas a un cuerpo que ahora cuelga entre el nido de extremidades como el torso de una araña.

Dientes y garras capaces de destrozar hierro y hueso, la fuerza de veinte hombres bajo la apariencia de un esqueleto titánico.

El Gran Inquisidor. El último Martillo de las Brujas se alza sobre la casa de Aradia como la cresta de una ola, con los ojos puestos únicamente en el brujo a espaldas del licántropo.

—Es hora de pagar por lo que me hiciste, bestia inmunda —dice el monstruo a la par que asoma su larga y negra lengua a través de la abertura de su mejilla, ahora una segunda boca en una cara ya deforme—. Voy a despellejarte, a ti y a tu gente. ¡Y luego me voy a cebar en tu puta!

El cazador se impulsa hacia delante para entrar al ático, pero un poderoso disparo de escopeta, justo en medio de su rostro, lo hace recular.

—¡Irina! —grita el portador del trueno al ver a la hembra parada en el marco de la puerta, con sus dos crías a sus espaldas, aferradas a sus caderas—. ¡¿Dónde diablos están los demás?!

—Peleando —dice mientras recarga su arma con los ojos fieros sobre el Inquisidor—. Los cabrones ya han rodeado la casa. *Y no vienen solos.*

Benjamin Lander se tambalea con las múltiples manos aún aferradas al marco de la ventana. Su cara cuelga en jirones, tan destrozada que fragmentos del cráneo logran verse detrás de la masa sanguinolenta.

Aun con la mandíbula hecha pedazos, suelta una carcajada, y se arquea de nuevo hacia delante. En un parpadeo, su rostro vuelve a regenerarse con el ruido de cientos de vidrios que crujen entre una masa de carne.

—¡MADRE!

Ante el grito de auxilio de la sirena, fuertes pisotones se escuchan subir de inmediato por la escalera de la trampilla.

El hueco se hace pedazos cuando el demonio Buer, una de las bestias goéticas que alguna vez asfixió a Comus Bayou en Lynn Woods, se abre paso por la casa. Pero el demonio no es invisible esta vez, puesto que ahora porta no una, sino tres pieles humanas entretejidas para completar el voluminoso tamaño de su espíritu.

Corriendo sobre sus múltiples extremidades como un animal salvaje, Buer embiste al Inquisidor con la fuerza de un bisonte y lo lanza al vacío.

La errante puma corre hacia la ventana para intentar un segundo disparo, mientras que la envenenadora por fin consigue ponerse en pie.

—¡Mierda! —exclama, y se da la media vuelta para dirigirse hacia la salida del ático.

—¡Cali! ¿A dónde...?

—Los demonios nos ayudarán, Hela, pero sólo hasta que Madre pueda resistirlo. Debo intervenir —dice para luego mirar a su hermana sobre su hombro. Siente una espina en el corazón al ver el semblante asustado de la rubia, las manos crispadas sobre los hilos.

—No te preocupes, cariño —dice—. Todo va a estar bien. Tared los protegerá a los tres.

La mujer levanta la cabeza e intercambia una significativa mirada con el licántropo.

—No te olvides de mi hermano —le pide él como una última muestra de compasión hacia su sangre.

La envenenadora asiente, y después, sale del ático mientras una sola cosa rebota en sus labios, no sólo como una pregunta, sino como la materialización de ese temor al que su hermana no podía ponerle nombre:

—¿Dónde diablos está Ilya?

CAPÍTULO 92
LA ANTESALA DE LOS QUERUBINES

El túnel funciona con tanta efectividad que, en un segundo, salgo catapultado del otro lado de la torre. Me elevo un par de metros en el aire, y luego caigo en el suelo de piedra, a centímetros del agujero que abrí con mi athame.

No me permito reparar en la extraña *gravedad* de este sitio, ni en la infinita oscuridad que se alza sobre mí como si ahora estuviese en el fondo de un pozo, puesto que a poca distancia de mí se encuentra la trampilla dorada.

Aquí "arriba", los ángeles también tocan sus trompetas sin cesar, así que me levanto y pongo las manos sobre la pesada manija. La compuerta se abre con un rechinido y la luz que brota de ella ilumina las paredes con tanta claridad que logro ver una fracción más de aquellos miles —si no es que millones— de ángeles crucificados, tantos, que no alcanzarían todos los brujos de la tierra para satisfacer su hambre.

Con la frente perlada de sudor, bajo por la trampilla de oro, esta vez con más precaución. Y en cuanto ésta se cierra a mis espaldas, las trompetas se callan de golpe.

En un desdoblamiento del espacio, tan irreal como en el de hace unos momentos, súbitamente me encuentro caminando sobre un suelo de mosaico blanco y negro, un patrón que me devuelve por un instante a la pesadilla de la casa Blake.

La Antesala de los Querubines tiene la forma de una cúpula blanca. Y a lo largo de su pared redondeada se alzan doce estatuas de las criaturas que le dan nombre a este lugar; seres bíblicos que, por su apariencia, parecieran haber sido construidos también por la propia alquimista.

Sus cuerpos son únicamente un conjunto de múltiples alas, con cuatro cabezas al centro: una de león, una de águila, una de toro y una humana. Todas tienen las bocas o los hocicos abiertos, como si cantasen alabanzas a lo que yace en el centro de la habitación: la Puerta de los Mil Brujos, grande e imponente, erigida como un portal que no lleva a ninguna parte.

Descubro que es aún más terrible que en mis visiones, porque aquel latido que sentía, ese movimiento informe, esa masa de oscuridad que parecía palpitar, no es más que las miles de manos izquierdas con las que está construida, arrancadas de todos y cada uno de los brujos que han caído bajo el yugo de los ángeles.

Y está… viva, porque las manos se mueven, se crispan, forman puños; un órgano cuya magia mantiene vivo al monstruo que habita detrás de la puerta.

—Es maravillosa, ¿verdad?

Me tenso de arriba abajo cuando un hombre comienza a salir por un costado del portal, como si hubiese estado esperándome allí todo este tiempo. La rodea y se para delante de ella, deleitado ante el desconcierto que se apodera de mí.

Casi se me escapa un "Sammuel" de los labios, pero es obvio que el monstruo que me observa ahora con ojos marchitos no es aquel errante que murió alguna vez bajo el plomo de Malcolm Dallas.

—¿Quién diablos eres? —pregunto, indignado ante la grotesca posesión—. ¿Y cómo te has atrevido a profanar ese cuerpo?

—¿Profanar? —la criatura sonríe con una mueca condescendiente—. Según los herejes, ésta es la era esotérica de Acuario. La era de Marco, el Ángel —dice a la par que mira hacia el techo, donde los evangelistas aparecen pintados en los cuatro puntos cardinales de la cúpula—. Si me lo preguntas, era profético que este cuerpo me perteneciera.

El monstruo extiende sus alas podridas frente a la puerta y las manos detrás se estiran hacia él como si quisieran alcanzarlo.

—Tú debes ser el Mensajero —digo con rabia—. El maldito Nalvage.

—Ah, la Bestia Revestida de Luna —dice el monstruo con una sonrisa, complacido al escuchar su nombre en mis labios—. El Brujo Famélico. El que retoza con lobos y devora todas las magias. Creo que, al igual que todos los que se han interpuesto en tu camino, cometí el error de subestimarte.

—Y si no quieres correr el mismo destino que ellos, apártate —blando mi athame, que apunto hacia el hueco donde debería estar su corazón—. Esa maldita puerta no protegerá a tu Dios de mí.

La sonrisa de Nalvage pierde fuerza, pero disimula su disgusto al mirar sobre su hombro.

—¿Protegerlo? —dice—. Hace medio milenio comenzamos a construir esta puerta para que nuestro Señor pudiese cruzarla. Para liberarlo de este reino y que tomara por fin posesión de la tierra. Pero, aún con todos los herejes a los que hemos ejecutado en todos estos siglos, jamás pudimos conseguir la mano más importante de todas...

Su mirada se dirige hacia el centro de la puerta. En ella se abre un hueco pequeño, casi imperceptible, donde se vislumbra el hierro blanco que hay debajo; un lugar donde una sola mano más podría servir como perilla.

Me toma apenas un segundo comprender.

—Aradia...

El ángel se gira de nuevo hacia mí.

—Hace diecinueve años, la oportunidad de tomar la mano de la hija de Diana nos fue arrebatada. Y aun cuando creímos que todo se había perdido, que no había forma de que tu Mara cumpliese la promesa que nos había hecho, nos dimos cuenta de que todavía teníamos una oportunidad.

Aquello me llena de confusión. Efectivamente, la bruja dijo que había sido atacada hace diecinueve años, pero, si así fue... ¿por qué los ángeles no obtuvieron su mano en ese momento? ¿Qué diablos fue lo que sucedió esa noche?

Mis pensamientos se desvanecen al darme cuenta de que Nalvage ahora mira mis dedos de hueso.

—¿Cuál será, Bestia Revestida de Luna? —dice, burlón—. ¿Cuál será esa mano lo suficientemente poderosa como para abrir por fin las puertas del Apocalipsis?

—Quiero ver que lo intentes, desgraciado —espeto con ira, el peso del *Sigillum Dei Aemeth* como un ladrillo entre mis ropas—. Entraré allí y mataré a tu Dios antes de que ponga un pie fuera del Merkavah, así tenga qué perder todas mis manos.

Su cara se tuerce en una mueca de furia.

—No dejaré que mancilles el corazón de este reino con tu oscuridad, bestia impía. Ésta será tu última tumba.

Ante su sentencia, Nalvage extiende los brazos como un mesías y comienza a elevarse. Sus alas crecen, se multiplican y se cierran alrededor de su cuerpo como un capullo. El ruido de cientos de cristales al quebrarse brota del interior de aquella figura hasta que, como si se tratase de la cáscara de un huevo, las alas vuelven a abrirse para revelar la verdadera forma del Mensajero.

Es una criatura, o más bien, una quimera con un cuerpo semejante al de un hombre sacado de una pintura renacentista, puesto que cuatro caras distintas conforman su cabeza.

Al frente, la de Sammuel, el ángel, cuyos ojos se han multiplicado hasta ser seis en total, todos dorados; a la derecha, un león negro como la noche; un águila al costado izquierdo; y, finalmente, por el par de largos cuernos que se asoman detrás, no me cabe ninguna duda de que la última cara es la de un toro gris como la ceniza.

El querubín desciende y posa los pies descalzos sobre la tierra. Y con una sonrisa torva, lleva ambas manos hacia el agujero de bala que persiste en su pecho.

Un crujido desagradable brota cuando sus dedos logran alcanzar algo dentro de su cuerpo. Y luego, como si se arrancara un par de costillas, Nalvage saca lentamente dos largas espadas de su tórax, forjadas con el fatal hierro blanco propio de los ángeles.

Pero en vez de retroceder, atemorizado ante la letal criatura que se interpone entre la puerta y yo, siento la magia empujar ansiosa contra mis venas.

Levanto mi athame como si sostuviese una escoba, y pronuncio una evocación que hace arder el sigilo en mi pecho.

Mi mano se cubre de llamas. E instantes después, el fuego se extingue y revela lo que ahora sostengo entre mis dedos: una espada larga e imponente, labrada con símbolos alquímicos y de un color dorado como el sol.

Los seis ojos del ángel relampaguean de cólera al ver la espada filosofal materializada en mi mano, su poder fulgiendo como una aurora por todo mi cuerpo.

Él afianza sus armas y da un paso hacia mí, para luego decir:

—Que comience, pues, el Juicio Final.

CAPÍTULO 93
LA GRAN TRIBULACIÓN

En cuanto la primera bala reventó contra la puerta principal, el impulso inmediato del detective fue ir en busca de la Bestia Revestida de Luna.

Pero el cuchillo de Golmá se lo impidió.

El ángel de las Artes Mecánicas entró por uno de los ventanales de la sala y barrió un puñado de escalones justo cuando el hombre estaba dispuesto a subirlos, como si su intención hubiese sido, precisamente, evitar que cualquiera pudiera alcanzar al brujo dormido.

La casa se quejó entera, como si la propia Aradia hubiese recibido el blandir del metal. Pero lo que hizo al hombre retroceder no fue el miedo, sino uno de los tablones astillados, el cual voló hacia su cabeza antes de que pudiera esquivarlo.

La madera impactó en su sien y lo derrumbó sobre su costado. El revólver voló de su mano y el disparo accidental que detonó al golpear contra el suelo fue opacado por los gritos que inundaron las estancias. El ángel alzó el cuchillo sobre el detective para asestar el golpe final, pero fue interceptado por uno de los errantes de la Espiral: aquel joven con la espalda cubierta de largas púas venenosas que, aunque aún débil y herido, no dudó en arrojar a la criatura hacia el pasillo de las tijeras para luchar cuerpo a cuerpo contra ella.

Las pocas armas de Comus Bayou estaban arriba, en el segundo piso, y el resto de los errantes habían llegado casi desnudos al nido de Aradia.

Todo dio vueltas para Salvador Hoffman, quien sintió la sangre abandonar su cabeza. Y, por unos segundos, creyó que alucinaba: las luces anaranjadas del fuego se acercaron por el bosque, piras listas para quemar a las brujas y sus demonios. Y luego, la criatura en la que se había convertido Benjamin Lander le sonrió desde la ventana frontal del recibidor para luego trepar por la fachada, en dirección al ático.

Los demonios de la Maligna brotaron de las paredes, de la chimenea y los pisos, forrados con sus pieles muertas. Los errantes a su alrededor contraatacaron y la madre puma subió de un solo brinco por la destrozada escalera, con sus hijos en brazos, dispuesta a ponerlos a salvo.

Pero él sólo logra reaccionar minutos después, cuando la falsa bruja posa una mano sobre su hombro.

—¡Hoffman!

Su grito le hace enfocar la mirada, como si esa voz tuviese la misma propiedad curativa de sus dedos.

—¿Qué diablos...? —él siente algo frío sobre su herida que le devuelve su consciencia casi de inmediato. Escucha los endrinos caer bajo las sierras, ve el fuego expandirse por las copas.

Pero en Salvador Hoffman sólo cabe un pensamiento.

—Por Dios, ¡Elisse! —grita—, ¡Johanna, debemos ir por Elisse!

—No será necesario.

La bruja Caligo desciende de la escalera de un suave salto.

—¿Qué está pasando? ¡¿Por qué los ángeles están aquí?! —pregunta la joven con desesperación.

—No lo sé y no hay tiempo para averiguarlo —responde la mujer quien avanza en línea recta hacia la entrada de la casa. Se para delante de la puerta negra, los ojos oscuros puestos sobre la frase grabada en la lámina—. Madre, ¡estoy lista!

—Caligo, ¿qué...? —la errante coyote es interrumpida por el ruido de una detonación a un costado de la casa.

Mi sangre hierve de excitación al ver cómo los demonios echan a los ángeles por las ventanas, para salir tras ellos y ser acribillados por balas y arpones lanzados por la línea de tramperos que se agazapa en el lindero del bosque.

Sus costuras se parten, sus cabezas y miembros salen volando pero, finalmente, logran vaciar la casona.

—Atrás —ordena la arpía cuando el detective y la perpetuasangre se acercan a sus espaldas—. Voy a cerrar esta casa.

Ella saca su athame de sus ropas y se abre las muñecas de tajo, y aunque el corte no parece mortal, la sangre empieza a fluir como un manantial.

—Vengan —susurra—. Ésta es mi voluntad.

Evocadas, un par de raíces negras brotan de los tablones bajo los pies de la bruja. Se elevan y se alargan, siguiendo con sed los finos hilos rojos de la mujer.

Y al alcanzar sus heridas, todo el lugar empieza a moverse.

El piso de madera se comba, las paredes se cuartean, las vigas se tuercen. Como si la casa se sacase las entrañas, múltiples ramas y raíces de endrinos comienzan a salir de las grietas, armadas con espinas letales. Las gruesas enredaderas cubren cada puerta, cada ventana y cada recoveco de la construcción, creando una coraza impenetrable en la que ni una sola bala más puede entrar o salir.

En el ático, el licántropo, aún postrado frente a su amante, ve cómo las raíces oscuras tapizan rápidamente el ventanal redondo, custodiado todavía por el demonio Buer.

Y como el más terrible de los presagios, la luz de la luna llena se apaga y, dentro de la coraza de espinas, la casa en la niebla queda hundida en la oscuridad.

CAPÍTULO 94
LA PUERTA DE LOS MIL BRUJOS

Nunca en mi vida había usado una espada. Se me dan mejor las pistolas que los cuchillos. Las escopetas, en realidad.

Pero la piedra filosofal no es cualquier espada.

Su energía es eléctrica y vigorosa, y el calor que desprende parece sacado de mis propias venas; es más un brazo que un arma, una extensión tangible de mi magia.

Soy consciente de que mis habilidades con ella serán más bien intuitivas, pero eso no reducirá su capacidad para rebanar carne, hueso y *espíritu* de un solo tajo. Un filo tan letal como mi garra de hueso.

Nalvage lo sabe. Y es por eso que, en vez de atacarme con una primera estocada, hace algo mucho menos esperado.

Su cabeza gira sobre su cuello como un demencial cubo de Rubik para dejar la cara de león en lugar de la del ángel. La criatura abre el hocico y una potente llamarada de fuego sale disparada de su interior.

Ni siquiera necesito retroceder. El fuego no es capaz de dañarme, así que me basta con alzar la espada delante de mí para que las llamas se abran como un libro a mis costados.

Y he allí mi error.

Nalvage atraviesa la densa cortina de fuego de un salto y aterriza delante de mí en menos de un segundo. Blande sus espadas de hierro como si fuesen guadañas y las cierra contra mí para intentar partirme en dos.

Me dejo caer de rodillas para esquivar los filos, pero el cabrón me lanza una patada que apenas logro bloquear con la espada. La hoja vibra y el impacto me arroja contra el muro a mis espaldas.

El golpe me saca el aire de los pulmones, pero el ángel no me da tiempo ni de sacudir la cabeza.

Su cuello gira de nuevo para traer el rostro del toro al frente. Tan rápido y con tanta fuerza él vuelve a embestirme que apenas logro evadirlo. Su pesada frente se incrusta en la pared y abre una grieta de suelo a techo, la cual parte el rostro de uno de los evangelistas por la mitad.

Echo a correr hacia la Puerta de los Mil Brujos para alejarme de sus espadas, pero el cabrón ni siquiera necesita darse la media vuelta.

Con esa cara monstruosa de ángel sonriéndome por encima de sus alas, Nalvage se arranca del muro y echa a correr de espaldas hacia mí con la misma facilidad con la que lo haría de frente.

Hago un revés con mi mano y mi magia levanta una de las pesadas estatuas de querubín. La lanzo hacia él, pero éste la esquiva con una precisión milimétrica, casi burlona.

El ángel gira sus cuatro cabezas una y otra vez como un trompo para intimidarme. Y con tantos ojos mirando en todas direcciones, está claro que no tengo forma de tomarlo por sorpresa.

Levanto un dedo y, tal como lo aprendí de Inanna, trazo una figura en el aire.

Un círculo se graba alrededor de Nalvage, raspando el suelo de mosaico; sus alas se comprimen y su cuerpo azota de golpe contra la barrera mágica.

Su cara de león vuelve a ocupar el frente de su cuello, pero sólo para soltar un rugido de rabia.

Agito la muñeca de nuevo y una de sus manos se tuerce hacia atrás con mi movimiento, lo que le hace soltar una de sus espadas, la cual rebota en el suelo, lejos de él.

Esta vez, las cuatro caras braman al mismo tiempo.

—¡Maldita ramera! —exclama para luego girar su cuerpo de nuevo hacia el frente. Levanta una de sus pesadas piernas y, de un pisotón, una prominente grieta en el suelo se abre hacia mí.

La fisura rompe la barrera mágica, se traga la espada de Nalvage y revela el abismo de la torre que hay debajo tan rápido que apenas puedo saltar para evitar caer por el borde.

Liberado de su prisión, el Mensajero cambia su cabeza por la del águila. Extiende las alas y vuela hacia el casco de la cúpula. Levanta su espada restante hacia arriba, y la blancura de su filo se vuelve un brillo cegador.

En un segundo, el ángel cae sobre mí como una guillotina.

Levanto la espada filosofal y su hoja choca con la de Nalvage. El impacto envía un doloroso calambre desde el metal hasta mis brazos, pero resisto el golpe, con mi magia inyectando a mis extremidades la fuerza de la cual carece mi cuerpo mortal.

Cuando su arma no es capaz de doblegar la mía, el Mensajero estrella su puño contra mi cara, con tanta fuerza que es un milagro que no me haya tumbado todos los dientes.

Me desplomo contra el suelo y el mundo se tiñe de una niebla confusa; paladeo algo metálico dentro de mi boca y poco me falta para desmayarme.

—¡Me estoy cansando de jugar contigo! —espeta, para luego cernir su puño sobre mi cuello ensangrentado.

En un arrebato desesperado, acumulo la magia en mi mano y la planto contra su barriga con la palma abierta.

Con la potencia de un martillazo, el ángel sale proyectado hacia la puerta, pero sus alas se extienden para impedir que se estrelle. La criatura planea y regresa los pies al suelo, su vientre fragmentado como si hubiese roto un cristal con mi impulso. Se lleva una mano a la herida y su rostro humano vuelve para sonreír someramente.

—Muy impresionante —dice y una arcada me recorre al verlo lamerse mi sangre de sus dedos. En segundos, su abdomen herido se regenera—. Disfrutaré mucho devorándote, Bestia Revestida de Luna.

Exhalo un jadeo de frustración y me tambaleo al levantarme. Pienso en Tared y en la angustia que debe sentir al ver todo ese rojo derramarse de mis labios inconscientes en el mundo real.

Nalvage carga de nuevo, y nuestras armas se entrecruzan en un poderoso choque; el ángel deja caer su filo y mis brazos resisten los golpes uno tras otro, en tanto sus cuatro rostros gritan, rugen y chillan sobre mí para aturdir mis oídos. No será tan monumental como Leaaloc, pero el Mensajero pareciera tener una fuerza equiparable.

A medida que nos movemos por la antesala, destellando mandobles y estocadas, mientras evito acercarme a la inmensa grieta que Nalvage ha abierto en el suelo, comienzo a sentir la espada un poco más pesada en mi mano.

Es de una ayuda indescriptible, y ahora evocar mi magia cuesta apenas un chasquido de dedos, pero mis energías aún son muy humanas, y si la batalla continúa alargándose, no podré resistir.

Al acuclillarme para esquivar un golpe horizontal de Nalvage, aprovecho el flanco que deja descubierto. En un movimiento más preciso de lo que me creería capaz, alzo la espada y rebano una de sus múltiples alas como si fuese mantequilla.

El ángel, presa del dolor, me lanza un revés en la cara que me hace girar en redondo.

El letal filo blanco de su acero me corta la espalda de hombro a hombro. Y aunque el hierro no se queda clavado en mi carne esta vez, siento como si me hubiera arrancado los omóplatos de tajo.

Grito desde el fondo de mis pulmones, la agonía es tan intensa que me es imposible mantenerme en pie. Caigo al suelo de mosaico, momento en que el ente patea la espada de mi mano y me pone boca arriba. Luego cierne su gruesa mano alrededor de mi cuello y relame sus labios antes de posicionar la cara del león al frente.

Abre su monstruoso hocico, y yo lo dejo que se acerque. Que me muestre la hilera infinita de dientes que ya asoman por su garganta, ansiosos por triturarme.

Cuando la primera gota de saliva resbala por mi cara, estampo mi mano de hueso contra la cara del toro, posicionada sobre su hombro. Mi fuego revienta contra ella como una explosión e incendia el rostro de la bestia con tanta intensidad que de inmediato siento sus ojos estallar bajo mis dedos.

—¡Aaaagh, maldito, maldito! —se queja el monstruo.

Ruedo por el suelo y me pongo de pie de un salto para intentar escapar por un costado y de paso alcanzar mi espada, la cual ha quedado a apenas unos metros de la inmensa grieta a espaldas de Nalvage.

Pero el Mensajero se interpone entre la piedra filosofal y yo de un solo salto.

Él intercambia su cabeza por la del ángel y me hace retroceder hasta que mi espalda lacerada mancha de rojo la pared de la antesala. Nalvage alza su Martillo y me apunta al corazón.

—Puede que hayas inutilizado uno de mis rostros, bestia inmunda, pero todavía me quedan otros tres para devorarte —dice—. Es hora de abrir la puerta a nuestro Señor.

Nalvage levanta su arma como un hacha, pero se detiene, extrañado, al verme sonreír.

—Monstruo estúpido —exclamo, al ver la confusión marcar su gesto—, ¿qué no te has dado cuenta de que la puerta *ya está abierta?*

Con la cabeza de toro ciega en su nuca, a Nalvage no le queda más remedio que mirar atrás.

El ángel lanza un largo grito al ver que Inanna, quien ha entrado a través de la grieta en el suelo, está frente al portal. Tiene los cuernos hechos pedazos, uno de sus brazos cuelga roto al costado de su cuerpo y respira con dificultad. Pero el espeso charco de sangre que yace a sus pies proviene de su muñeca, puesto que ella se ha mutilado la propia mano izquierda con su athame.

Y ahora la ha puesto sobre el último hueco de la puerta.

Aprovecho la distracción de Nalvage y le arrebato la espada de hierro. El metal quema como los mil infiernos contra mi mano, pero sólo necesito sostenerla unos segundos para clavarla de una estocada en la frente calcinada del toro.

Escucho su cráneo reventarse como el cristal cuando la punta de la espada emerge por el otro lado, justo entre los seis ojos de la cara del ángel. Dejo el arma ensartada en su cabeza y echo a correr hacia el centro de la antesala.

Levanto la espada filosofal en el camino, a la par que la portadora de Satanás abre la Puerta de los Mil Brujos para mí. Inanna se derrumba, pero yo no me permito mirar atrás. De un salto, entro en el corazón del Merkavah.

CAPÍTULO 95
LA ÚLTIMA BARRERA

En el momento en el que la mano de la Maligna es cercenada frente a sus ojos, cortada por el filo de un espectro invisible, el licántropo se prepara para escuchar un grito demoledor por parte de la necromante.

Pero, para su sorpresa, ella no dice una sola palabra. Ni siquiera cuando esa mano izquierda se desvanece en la profunda oscuridad del suelo; una negrura que la luz cetrina del candelabro que les han traído no ha podido contrarrestar.

La joven tan sólo abre los ojos de par en par, petrificada por el terror, y susurra la palabra "madre".

Tared Miller, arrodillado delante del brujo como un vil sirviente, clava las garras en el suelo para luchar contra su necesidad de tirar él mismo de los hilos plateados.

La oscuridad de la casa no le permite ver las heridas que se han bordado lentamente en la piel de la bestia astada, pero vaya que puede oler la sangre que mancha ahora mismo el respaldo de la silla, impregnada también bajo mi nariz.

La desesperación lo ahoga. Las detonaciones que estallan fuera de la casa se acompasan con el frenético latido de su corazón.

—*Tráela.*

La orden que brota de las paredes libera a la oscura sirena de su parálisis. De inmediato, tira con fuerza la fina cuerda que pende del pecho de su hermana.

La Maligna inhala y su cuerpo pierde la rigidez del desprendimiento astral.

Cuando se desploma sobre el suelo como un cadáver, el hombre lobo es, de hecho, el primero en gritar.

—¡Johanna!

Como invocada por el más poderoso de los sigilos, la perpetuasangre entra al ático apenas segundos después. No necesita recibir ninguna orden, su instinto la hace arrojarse de inmediato al cuerpo de la Maligna. Siente la sangre manchar sus rodillas y la carne del muñón palpitar aún caliente entre sus dedos.

Ayudada por la ínfima luz de las velas, ella rasga la parte inferior de sus ropas y aplica un rápido torniquete en la herida, para luego levantarse e ir de regreso hacia la salida del desván.

La necromante ahoga un gemido en la garganta.

—¡Espera! ¿Nanni está...?

—¿Viva? Sí —dice la curandera—. Pero ha perdido demasiada sangre y no tengo manera de hacerle una transfusión ahora mismo. Sólo me queda ir por una aguja para coser su herida y esperar a que resista. No creo que despierte pronto...

La angustia humedece los ojos de la sirena, el miedo como un martillo que se balancea sobre su sien.

—¿Qué hay de Elisse? —pregunta el lobo, y su desesperación provoca un nudo en el estómago de la falsa bruja. Ella regresa sobre sus pasos y se encorva hacia el brujo dormido para calcular de forma precisa los latidos que escucha a la perfección con sus oídos de perpetuasangre.

Una palidez espectral la inunda de pies a cabeza.

—Su corazón se está volviendo más lento —dice, confundida—. Dios mío, ¡también está perdiendo presión! ¡¿Qué no Caligo ya le había dado el antídoto?!

—No es por la belladona. Es porque su hilo está demasiado tenso —corta la necromante—. El vínculo que conecta a los vivos con sus almas es muy resistente, pero Elisse está alcanzando un sitio demasiado... lejano. Tan remoto que la estela ha comenzado a estrecharse.

—Eso... ¿eso significa que ya ha llegado al Merkavah? —pregunta ella, y la rubia asiente:

—Sí. Y ahora mismo debe estar combatiendo contra Dios.

La palidez cruza el semblante del lobo.

—¿Y si el hilo se rompe, él...? —insiste él con absoluto terror.

—Su cuerpo no morirá. Al menos, no de inmediato —asegura la médium—. Pero el alma de Elisse podría quedarse atrapada en el otro lado y...

Un golpe contra el tejado impide a la sirena continuar. Los hijos de la errante puma se contraen contra su madre por el miedo, mientras que el demonio Buer levanta la cabeza y tensa todas las manos, listo para contraatacar.

Pero, tras un segundo golpe, la criatura en el techo decide retroceder.

La casa está ahora coronada por arpones, por antorchas que no han podido mantenerse encendidas contra las espinas y por balas incrustadas como un sarpullido en las ramas. Pero la cortina de endrinos se mantiene firme como una barrera impenetrable, inmune incluso a los Martillos de los ángeles.

—No puedo creer que no puedan atravesar las raíces —dice la mujer coyote observando los ramajes que acorazan la ventana circular y al monstruo que permanece inamovible frente a ella.

—Los endrinos son parte de la niebla, e intentar derribarlos es como golpear contra una montaña —interviene la vidente—. No hay manera de que ellos puedan entrar mientras Cali los tenga bajo su control.

La perpetuasangre se marcha en busca del hilo y la aguja antes de que pueda decir que eso es precisamente lo que la preocupa: la frente perlada de sudor de la envenenadora, así como la palidez que poco a poco ha cubierto su piel.

En ese momento, la falsa bruja comprende que sus vidas ya no están puestas en la resistencia de los endrinos, sino en la esperanza de que la Bestia Revestida de Luna emerja pronto de la oscuridad.

CAPÍTULO 96

EL JUICIO FINAL I
LAS TRES TROMPETAS DE GABRIEL

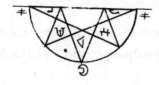

Primera Trompeta

Creí que mi entrada al Merkavah estaría inundada por el caos.

Que las trompetas de los ángeles se quejarían con tanta fuerza que harían reventar mis oídos, y que *Dios* se levantaría como un ente tan colosal que, al estar delante de él, me sentiría como una gota en el lagrimal de un titán.

Pero el Trono Celestial no me recibe con otra cosa que el irregular latido de mi propio corazón, bombeando en medio de una espesa niebla.

Miro sobre mi hombro, pero la Puerta de los Mil Brujos ya no está detrás de mí. Alzo la cabeza, no hay cielo. Ni sol ni horizonte. Ni siquiera un suelo bajo mis pies. Sólo niebla. Más y más niebla.

Y, peor aún, la espada tampoco está ya entre mis dedos.

Más alerta que nunca, comienzo a caminar, pero al hacerlo no se escucha uno solo de mis pasos... es como si me moviese sobre una nube gris.

—Da la cara, cobar... —me detengo a media frase, apretando los puños embargado por la frustración.

Después, contengo un gemido al ver que mi valiosa mano de hueso ha desaparecido, y que en su lugar hay ahora dedos *humanos*.

Pero mi garra no es lo único que me falta. Tampoco puedo sentir mi magia, la lengua de Samedi... ni al monstruo dentro de mí.

—*Bastardo* —musito, apenas, pues tal como en mi visión, este *Dios* me ha despojado de mis poderes. Me ha vuelto *humano*.

Mi confusión comienza a escalar en auténtica rabia cuando escucho un grito a lo lejos.

—*¡Detente, detente, por favor!*

Miro hacia un lado y otro, pero no logro ver nada ni a nadie. Es más, ni siquiera estoy seguro de dónde provino esa voz.

—*¡Por piedad, te lo suplico!*

—¡Revélate de una vez, desgraciado! —exclamo, pero no recibo respuesta. Aquellas han sido palabras de súplica, pero pronunciadas en tono de burla y sarcasmo, gritos que parecen provenir de una mujer.

Escucho unos pasos a mis espaldas, me giro y ahogo un gemido de sorpresa al ver a quien yace detrás de mí.

—¿Laurele? —apenas logro arrancar la pregunta de mis labios, estupefacto ante la visión.

Ella está en pie, vestida como la primera vez que la vi en el Barrio Francés. Sonríe ampliamente, parece complacida al verme buscar por inercia el mango de la espada.

—Aquí no vas a encontrar nada de lo que buscas, querido —dice y su voz suena exactamente como la recuerdo.

—Déjate de ilusiones y enfréntate a mí tal cual eres —corto, y ella ladea la cabeza.

—¿Ilusiones? —recomienza, y sus ojos brillan como el petróleo—. ¿De qué hablas, querido? *Éste es tu Juicio Final.* Y yo soy tu primer testigo.

Una repentina sensación de cosquilleo acaricia la planta de mis pies. Miro hacia abajo y los encuentro ahora descalzos sobre césped húmedo y frío, oscuro como el jade.

Levanto la cabeza de nuevo, y Laurele ya no está allí. En su lugar, la niebla comienza a despejarse y un campo aparece gradualmente alrededor. Un sitio de matices verdes y azules, como si la noche se hubiese cernido sobre la hierba, pero no en el cielo, que sigue siendo de un infinito color gris.

Montones de tumbas salpican el prado, cajas de cemento que se erigen como pequeñas capillas. Y al ver sus vientres abiertos completamente, derramando monedas, oro y joyas, me doy cuenta de dónde estoy.

—*Guinée* —musito, desconcertado. Porque no es cualquier parte de Guinée. Es el reino de Barón Samedi.

—*Ten piedad, te lo suplico, por favor...*

Esta vez, la voz de Laurele suena distinta y lejana. Rota, cargada de un sufrimiento que no parecía padecer hace unos momentos.

Me armo de valor y atravieso el campo y las tumbas en busca de la bruja. Pero nada, absolutamente nada me prepara para lo que veo al encontrarla.

La caplata ya no está sola, porque ahora me veo inclinado sobre ella, a unos pasos de la tumba de Marie Laveau.

Laurele gimotea en voz baja, retuerce las manos y los dedos entre la hierba, pero ya no puede gritar.

No cuando ese otro yo ya se ha devorado casi la mitad de su cuerpo.

Me llevo una mano a los labios al ver mi esqueleto expuesto, arqueado como un buitre, llenándose poco a poco de la carne y vísceras de la bruja.

Pero mi cara, mi cabeza... eso es lo más horrible de todo.

Mi rostro ya es humano, pero mis colmillos todavía brillan afilados en mi boca a medio camino de volverse dientes, mientras que mis ojos aparecen dilatados y llorosos, cegados completamente por el hambre.

Quiero decirme que esto no es más que un engaño grotesco del Dios de los ángeles. Que él sólo está jugando con mi cabeza.

Pero Laurele tenía razón. Esto no es un truco. Esto no es una ilusión.

Es un recuerdo.

—¡¿Qué demonios pretendes?! —grito hacia el cielo, desconcertado ante tan grotesca manifestación.

—Te gustó mucho hacer esto, ¿verdad?

Una arcada me obliga a callarme cuando, en medio de su canibalización, Laurele ha girado la cabeza hacia mí.

—Todavía lo recuerdas bien, ¿cierto? —pregunta con una sonrisa y los ojos hinchados por las lágrimas—. Cuando recuestas la cabeza en la almohada por las noches, *esto* es lo primero que ves, ¿no?

La mano huesuda de mi otro yo se clava entre los pechos de la mujer. Echa las afiladas garras hacia atrás y le rasga la carne hasta dejar expuesto el esternón.

Laurele comienza a reír ante el paso que doy hacia atrás.

—Ay, querido, ¿por qué te asustas? —pregunta, burlona—. ¿No es esto lo que querías?

"Éste es tu Juicio Final."

Me obligo a controlar los frenéticos latidos de mi corazón.

—No —contesto, firme, al entender lo que pretende esta criatura—. Yo nunca quise que esto sucediera. ¡Nunca tuve elección!

—Oh, ¿no la tuviste, querido? —responde ella con lástima fingida—. ¿Eso le dijiste a tu querida familia, a ese hombre que tanto te gusta? ¿Que para recuperar tu cuerpo no tuviste elección más que devorar a la malvada Laurele?

Abro y cierro los puños, tenso ante el escrutinio de la bruja.

—Estaba confundido —replico, la bilis revuelta en mi garganta—. Y acababa de convertirme en algo que no podía comprender. Fue un impulso que no pude...

—¿Resistir? —Laurele echa la cabeza atrás para soltar una carcajada—. Ay, querido. Podrás engañar a tu gente y al ciego de tu amante, pero *nunca* vas a poder engañarte a ti mismo.

Casi cedo al impulso de mirar hacia otro lado cuando ella acaricia la coronilla del Elisse que la está devorando.

—Pudiste perdonarme la vida —dice, dirigiéndole una de sus miradas más obscenas, como si fuesen un par de amantes sobre un lecho—. Pudiste sacarme de Guinée, tomarme como prisionera y obligarme a encontrar otra manera de devolverte tu cuerpo humano. Pero no lo hiciste porque no querías un cuerpo. Tú lo que querías era *mi poder.*

—No, no, ¡el monstruo...!

No te atrevas a culparme de tu pecado, criatura hipócrita.

Esta vez es mi otro *yo* el que responde. No con mi voz, sino con la del monstruo de hueso.

Él deja el cadáver de la bruja y se levanta del suelo. Me muestra su ser famélico ensangrentado y sus ojos llenos de tinieblas, justo como en mi premonición.

¿Por qué nunca te has dicho a ti mismo la verdad en voz alta, Elisse?, dice. **¿Por qué nunca has confesado ante el espejo que tu habilidad para manipular a los Loas, al vudú, no es gracias a la lengua de Samedi, sino al cuerpo de Laurele? ¿O es que has repetido tanto tu propia mentira que terminaste por creerla?**

Sus palabras taladran mi cerebro, me llenan de angustia y me hacen volver a ese fatídico día en Nueva Orleans. A todos y cada uno de los pensamientos que tuve mientras devoraba a Laurele.

¿Es cierto lo que dice? ¿Es verdad que yo buscaba... algo más?

—No —insisto—. No, yo nunca...

Te jactas de proteger tu humanidad a toda costa, pero no eres mucho mejor que yo, ¿verdad?, contraataca el Elisse frente a mí.

—¡No!

—Y encima de todo, ¡pudiste evitarme este sufrimiento! —grita Laurele—. Pudiste matarme y luego alimentarte, pero en cambio, me devoraste *viva*, para torturarme. Estabas furioso porque no pudiste matar a Samedi, estabas furioso porque *fuiste obligado* a salvar a esos niños, ¡así que decidiste desquitarte conmigo aunque *yo también fuera una víctima*!

—¡No, no es verdad, eso no es verdad! —grito a todo pulmón.

—Querías que sufriera.

—No.

—Querías que pagara.

—¡No!

—¡Y fingiste que todo esto te torturaba para que nadie pudiera juzgarte!

¡Mentiroso, asesino, sádico!

Ahogo mis gritos cuando, al parpadear, comprendo que ya no estoy de pie, sino de rodillas sobre el cadáver de Laurele. Mis manos sostienen su carne y en mi boca bulle el sabor de la sangre. Sangre que puedo sentir en mis labios, *allá*, en el mundo real, pues es mi cuerpo una manifestación viva de lo que ocurre en este lugar.

La bruja ya no se mueve. La bruja ya no respira.

En un segundo, estoy de vuelta en la pesadilla que yo mismo provoqué.

Pero lo más terrible de todo es saber que, al igual que aquella vez, no siento ni una pizca de remordimiento. No cuando sentí la magia de la bruja dentro de mí.

Cuando, por primera vez en la vida, supe que ya no era...

Vulnerable...

Me quedo quieto con las manos hundidas en aquel cuerpo, sopesando la culpa en mi corazón mientras mi otro yo está de pie a mi lado, con la mirada fija en mí como un verdugo paciente.

Tres armas. Tres grandes poderes que te han traído hasta aquí. ¿No te gusta este primer juicio?, dice. ¿Quisieras entonces pasar al siguiente?

—No, no, por favor... —sollozo, pero mis plegarias no son escuchadas.

Cuando levanto la barbilla, ya no estoy en Guinée.

CAPÍTULO 97
JUDAS

Al abrir la puerta, Allen Miller ni siquiera necesita preocuparse por el ruido de la bisagra. Y tampoco por el de sus pasos contra la madera al salir por fin de aquella habitación.

Los endrinos protegerán cada entrada con recelo, pero el ruido sí que encuentra rendijas por dónde colarse.

Así que, bajo la protección de las detonaciones, de las hachas y los cuerpos que azotan contra la casa como una tempestad, el joven se desliza por la oscuridad casi absoluta del pasillo.

La envenenadora debía asegurarse de que nada ni nadie pudiese entrar o salir de la recámara. Y haber visto a Asmoday postrado como un manso sirviente sobre el dintel le hizo tener esa certeza, por lo que ahora el corredor se encuentra completamente vacío, vigilado sólo por los propios ojos rojos del gusano.

Los errantes yacen agazapados en la planta inferior, con las pocas armas que poseen apuntando hacia las puertas y las ventanas; zonas donde los tramperos y los ángeles parecen arremeter con más fuerza.

Qué lástima que no se hayan detenido a considerar que los verdaderos monstruos ya estaban allí dentro con ellos.

Con el peso de su venganza dentro del bolsillo, el hermano falso mira en dirección a la escalera que lleva hacia la trampilla en el techo, iluminada por una única vela que flota solitaria en la pared.

Él sabe que el brujo está allá arriba. El mismo Asmoday se lo ha susurrado a través del gramófono que no ha dejado de girar.

Y, por lo tanto, sabe lo fácil que será llenar esta casa de fuego.

Tu agonía casi termina, le susurra una voz dentro de su cabeza. *Por fin vas a ser libre...*

Los ojos se le llenan de lágrimas de sólo pensarlo.

Así que nadie se da cuenta cuando él cruza el pasillo para deslizar sus pies sobre algunos peldaños. Ni tampoco cuando levanta el arma cargada con la bala de hierro blanco y apunta hacia su víctima.

Una bala para un brujo. Una bala nada más, así que, ¿por qué arrebatarle sólo a uno, cuando puede quitarle absolutamente todo?

Pero el detective Hoffman sí que escucha el percutor.

Y cuando se da la media vuelta, ya es demasiado tarde.

Con un grito que se le atora en la garganta, ve cómo Allen Miller, desde el filo de la escalera destruida, dispara a la bruja Caligo directo en el corazón.

CAPÍTULO 98
EL JUICIO FINAL II
LAS TRES TROMPETAS DE GABRIEL

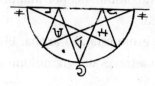

Segunda Trompeta

Mi otro yo, Laurele, Guinée.

Todo es tragado por un humo negro tan caliente y espeso que me veo obligado a cerrar los ojos para soportar el escozor de las cenizas.

La tos se instala en mi garganta, y al intentar aferrarme al suelo, mis manos se cortan contra trozos afilados de algo que parece porcelana.

Me siento vulnerable y ciego, mortificado por la atrocidad de la que he sido culpado hace unos momentos, agazapado a la espera de mi siguiente... ¿*Juicio*?

No, no, ¡por los Dioses, no debo caer en su maldito juego! ¡Lo que me ha mostrado ese monstruo es una mentira! ¿Cómo voy a ser *yo* alguien tan cruel, tan ambicioso, si lo único que he pretendido hacer todo este tiempo es proteger a los míos?

No te dejes joder, Elisse, me digo a mí mismo. Intenta engañarme, ¡ese maldito Dios está...!

Interrumpo el tren de mis pensamientos cuando el humo comienza a disiparse. Parpadeo y me doy cuenta de que aquello con lo que me he cortado son trozos de mosaico.

Estoy sobre un suelo blanco y negro, roto, salpicado de escombros y hollín. ¿Un sitio derrumbado? ¿Estoy otra vez en la antesala, con Nalvage?

No. Esto no es el cielo.

Esto es...

Stonefall.

Levanto la cabeza y, a unos metros de mí, encuentro de nuevo a mi "yo" monstruoso, acuclillado sobre el cuerpo de lo que parece ser un hombre de gran tamaño.

O más bien, sobre *la mitad* de uno.

La furia me azota sin piedad.

—¡NO LO TOQUES, CABRÓN! —grito a todo pulmón, pero mi yo terrible no me escucha. Tan sólo gimotea y llora con fingida tristeza mientras acuna en sus manos raquíticas el rostro de Adam, quien agoniza en su forma de Rebis, aún atado a la mitad del cuerpo de su madre.

Intento levantarme, ir hacia la horrenda bestia para apartarla de un puntapié, pero mis rodillas parecen unidas al mosaico de la casa de los Blake.

Las llamas cubren las ruinas, la luna nos observa como un ojo y no hay nadie más alrededor. Sólo nosotros en medio del caos.

—Oh, cuánto te gustaba él, ¿verdad?

El corazón se me paraliza al escuchar aquella *terrible* voz a mi costado.

Encuentro la cabeza de Jocelyn Blake a unos palmos de mí, recién decapitada por la espada que ahora yace a un lado de Adam.

Está postrada de costado y aún lleva esa horrible corona de huesos rojos sobre las sienes, mientras que su cuello blanco chorrea sendos hilos de plata.

Mi boca se abre, pero mi lengua se paraliza ante la sonrisa mortífera en sus labios, la cual jamás creí que tendría el horror de volver a ver.

—Ay, Adam. Mi pobre y sumiso Adam —continúa con irónica compasión—. Él te adoraba tanto, con cada pizca de su miserable ser, y todo para que al final lo dejaras morir aquí.

—Eres una estúpida si crees que puedes *usarlo* contra mí —espeto, olvidando por un segundo que esto no es más que una prueba de ese Dios miserable. Porque si de algo estoy seguro es que yo hice las paces con Adam Blake hace mucho tiempo.

No hay nada que no hubiese hecho por él. Adam era...

—Ah, ¿a quién quieres engañar, Elisse? —corta la alquimista—. Nunca fuimos tan distintos tú y yo, porque puedo apostar a que más de una vez quisiste llamar a mi hijo en mitad de la noche, hacerlo acudir a ti para que te *diera* todo lo que ese licántropo te había negado. *Utilizarlo* tanto como yo lo hice —dice como si me hubiese leído la mente. O el corazón

—¡Cierra la boca, maldita cerda!

Intento estirarme hacia la cabeza para callarla de un puñetazo, pero sólo consigo gemir de dolor.

Sí. Admito que hubo alguna vez un momento, en mi más oscuro sentir, en el que creí que tal vez él y yo podíamos encontrar algún tipo de *consuelo* mutuo. ¡Pero éste no era, ni de lejos, tan ruin como las intenciones de la bestia que se hacía llamar "su madre"!

—Oh, pobre criatura —exclama aquella cabeza decapitada ante mi semblante contrariado—, ¡qué duro debe ser reconocer tu lujuria!

—No. Yo jamás pretendí hacerle daño, ¡yo...! —gimoteo.

—Pero, ¿sabes? Ése ni siquiera es mi verdadero testimonio —corta—. Porque yo vine aquí a mostrarte una verdad todavía peor.

La cabeza gira lentamente hacia la escena frente a nosotros.

No quiero hacerlo, pero algo dentro de mí me obliga a mirar también, justo cuando mi contraparte monstruosa alarga la mano para tomar la espada filosofal con la intención de devolver al chico a la vida.

Pero Adam sostiene su muñeca.

—Per... dó-name... papá —susurra el joven.

Y entonces, veo sus ojos llenarse de lágrimas. Su cuello y su torso dividirse en una línea irregular, lo que lo libera por fin de su madre.

Mi otro yo, en cambio, tan sólo lo observa. Y lo observa, y lo observa...

Es allí, en ese justo y endemoniado momento, cuando la verdad sale como un escupitajo de mis labios:

—¡¿Qué estás esperando, imbécil?! —grito con desesperación—. ¡DALE LA MALDITA ESPADA Y SÁLVALO, IDIOTA!

Mi grito retumba por los escombros. Pero, ante mi horror, el monstruo no me escucha.

El monstruo, en cambio, toma la espada.

Y, en el acto más ruin, más terrible, en vez de salvar a Adam, mi otro yo incrusta la piedra filosofal en medio de sus costillas. El joven muere a sus pies, para acto seguido comenzar a fundirse como oro líquido que habrá de filtrarse en la tierra.

El tiempo se congela. Mi mandíbula cae, mis dedos se engarrotan contra los trozos de mosaico y, lentamente, siento cómo aquella herida que me hice con una sierra en Red

Buffalo, justo después de perder a Adam, vuelve a abrirse en mi garganta.

—Ahora lo ves, ¿verdad? —dice la alquimista—. La espada no podía salvarme porque yo era una bruja. Pero mi hijo... mi hijo era *tan* humano, tan mortal que, una vez separado de mi cuerpo, un simple toque de su punta le habría preservado la vida.

—No. ¡No es verdad! —susurro, y la sangre mana de mi herida en un borbotón.

—Pudiste salvarlo.

—¡No!

—Pudiste permitirle redimirse.

—¡No!

—Pero no lo hiciste porque...

Querías la espalda para ti, dice mi otro yo, quien por fin gira la cabeza para mirarme.

Lanzo un aullido de dolor.

—No, no es cierto, juro que no es cierto —digo con el sabor de la sangre impregnada por toda mi lengua—, yo no le di la espada porque... porque Adam *no quería vivir.*

Cierro los ojos con fuerza, porque mis propias palabras duelen más que una puñalada.

¿Quién era yo para decidir lo que Adam quería? ¿Quién era yo para no darle la oportunidad de vivir una vez más?

De pronto, un peso entre mis dedos me obliga a abrir los ojos de nuevo.

La espada filosofal recae en mis manos una vez más. Siento el calor de Adam en su filo, el resplandor de sus ojos dorados en el brillo del acero.

—¡NO, NO, NO! —grito y arrojo la espada muy lejos de mí—, no quiero la maldita espada, ¡quiero a Adam de vuelta, quiero a Adam de vuelta!

Me dejo caer sobre los rastros dorados en la tierra y continúo gritando, una y otra vez. Tiro de mi cabello y me dejo hundir en la más dolorosa de las histerias.

¿Sabes, hijo mío? Ése es tu problema, dice mi otro yo, impregnado de esa repugnante condescendencia. Que lo quieres todo. Quieres satisfacer tu hambre. Tu soberbia y tu locura. Pero también quieres perdón. Quieres ser amado y ser comprendido. Los quieres tener a todos ellos, y es por eso que he guardado tu pecado más grande para el final. ¿Estás listo para tu último juicio?

El monstruo no me da posibilidad de negarme. Antes de que pueda levantar la mirada, el fuego se apaga. Las ruinas se precipitan hacia un abismo oscuro, como si de nuevo estuviese encerrado en el laberinto de Jocelyn Blake.

Y así, en un parpadeo, soy arrastrado hacia la última espiral de mi condena.

CAPÍTULO 99
CAÍN Y ABEL

L a bruja Caligo escucha el disparo mucho antes de que pueda sentir el dolor.

Y tan sólo comprende lo que acaba de suceder cuando, de un instante a otro, se encuentra a sí misma tirada en el suelo de la entrada de la casa, boca abajo.

Como un trueno, el dolor se extiende desde su espalda y se abre paso lentamente hacia su corazón como una piraña. Y, por primera vez, siente en carne viva el fuego que incineró a tantos de los suyos apoderarse de su ser.

Gritos. Escucha muchos gritos a su alrededor, pero a ella no le importan la sangre ni las manos que la toman de los hombros para intentar levantarla. Porque en esos momentos, nada es más inmenso que el terror que se cierne sobre ella al ver que los endrinos comienzan a retraerse. Que las balas y los arpones que antes rebotaban contra las raíces ahora las quiebran como frágiles ramas.

La impenetrable fortaleza de la casa comienza a desvanecerse. Y la puerta… oh, la hermosa puerta negra se sacude con los golpes de un mazo hecho del mismo hierro que ahora le arrebata la vida.

Una lágrima resbala por su mejilla. Tanto terror, tanto pánico a su alrededor, y lo único que quiere la pobre desgraciada es ver a sus hermanas.

—¡Nashua, llévala con Johanna, ahora!

Ante la orden del detective, la bruja es tomada en brazos por el hombre con piel de oso, quien, usando hasta el último gramo de su fuerza, se impone ante el peso tremendo de la bala para saltar la destrozada escalera. A su paso, embiste a Allen Miller con tanta brutalidad que el joven termina dislocándose el hombro contra la pared.

El arma del chico sale despedida, pero el furioso errante no se queda a castigarlo más. No cuando el propio Salvador Hoffman se las arregla para escalar los escombros y llegar hasta él:

—¡Hijo de la gran puta!

Todo mi cuerpo se estremece de placer cuando el hombre le propina una patada en la cara al traidor antes de que éste pueda levantarse. Allen Miller grita, pero es sofocado ante una segunda patada, esta vez directo al diafragma. Su tabique sangra con abundancia, pero el detective no le da oportunidad ni de llevarse las manos a la nariz.

Lo toma de la camisa y lo alza contra la pared con una fuerza que sólo la desesperación es capaz de brindar.

—Si querías morirte te hubieras pegado un jodido tiro en la cabeza, cabrón —grita—. ¡Ahora esas porquerías van a matarnos a todos!

Cuando el joven responde con una sonrisa, el humano se la borra de una fuerte bofetada.

Está dispuesto a golpearlo una vez más, pero una risa monstruosa a sus espaldas le hace buscar el arma en su cintura.

Ángeles y tramperos por igual se aglomeran en todas y cada una de las entradas de la casa, mientras los demonios y errantes se abalanzan contra ellos para resistir la invasión.

Pero esa puerta negra, con aquella inútil frase grabada en la superficie, es la que tiene detrás de sí a la criatura más terrible de todas.

—¿Sabe que es lo que más me complace de esto, detective?

El hombre se gira hacia el joven y encuentra algo terriblemente inquietante en esa mueca de triunfo ensangrentada. Tiembla de arriba abajo por el dolor de la golpiza pero, a la vez, parece inundado por una felicidad incomprensible.

El primer pensamiento de Salvador Hoffman es que se ha vuelto loco.

—Que por fin, después de tantos años, he logrado vencer a mi hermano —dice el joven—. Porque yo sé que, sin importar que ángeles y tramperos sean derrotados, sin importar que yo sea ejecutado por alguno de ustedes... al final de todo esto, Tared mismo terminará volándose la cabeza.

—¿Por qué diablos dices eso? —pregunta Salvador Hoffman, y alza su arma cuando ve que el traidor mete la mano en el bolsillo. Pero no es otra pistola lo que saca. Es algo mucho más peligroso, y que él ya conoce muy bien.

Despacio, Allen Miller le muestra la fotografía de un hombre rubio delante de una montaña, sosteniendo un bebé sobre un campo espolvoreado de flores.

—Porque este hombre, aquél que tantos años ha estado buscando Elisse, es Isaac Miller. *Nuestro padre.*

CAPÍTULO 100
EL JUICIO FINAL III
LAS TRES TROMPETAS DE GABRIEL

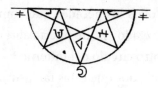

Tercera y última Trompeta

Después de abandonar el fuego y las cenizas de Stonefall, lo siguiente que percibo es sólo silencio y oscuridad. Así que me quedo quieto, ovillado sobre la tierra fría y húmeda con la esperanza de que la tortura haya terminado. Que, por lo que más quiera, el Dios de los ángeles no haya encontrado otro pecado con el cual atormentarme.

De inmediato me siento estúpido, frágil y vulnerable con el cuello encostrado por la sangre de una herida ya cerrada, porque sé, muy dentro de mí, que *él* no se detendrá. Que aunque llore, suplique y me arrodille, su Dios no me tendrá ninguna piedad.

Demonios, ¿acaso estoy rogando a ese ser que me perdone? ¿Que tenga misericordia? ¿Es ésta la desesperación que sufre la gente con fe?

Por encima del martirio, mis plegarias parecieran ser escuchadas, puesto que la negrura comienza a desvanecerse con la suave luz de una luna llena.

El frío se recrudece mientras el cruce de caminos se abre delante de mí, con sus ocho brazos extendidos y aquel árbol gris que vi en mi primera premonición instalado en su centro como una torre, pero ahora con su abertura obscena cerrada cual cicatriz.

El miedo me constriñe, me hace arquearme sobre mí mismo para protegerme de un golpe imaginario.

¿Por cuál de todos los pecados que cometí en este cruce de caminos seré juzgado? ¿Qué puerta abrí que haya convertido este sitio en otro círculo del infierno?

—Oh, hijo mío, ¿por qué estás tan asustado?

Levanto la cabeza, y me encuentro a mí mismo de nuevo, al pie del árbol. Pero el Elisse que está allí no es mi yo monstruoso, sino el auténtico. El que tiene carne sobre los huesos y los ojos verdes como una aurora boreal.

Él mira hacia arriba, hacia las ramas altas del endrino, y porta las mismas ropas ritualistas que usé la noche del Sabbath. Lleva el sigilo de la espada en el pecho, la mano de hueso en su sitio.

A diferencia de los otros dos juicios, esto nunca ha sucedido, y si no es un recuerdo, ¿entonces qué…?

Algo escondido en las ramas del inmenso árbol hace crujir la madera con su peso. Algo tan apagado, tan oscuro, que casi no la reconozco.

—¿Aradia?

Sí. Es ella, con sus escamas doradas ensombrecidas por la noche, enredada cual grande es por todo el endrino. Y a medida que desciende en espiral por el tronco, las columnas vertebrales que vi en mi primera premonición comienzan a emerger por el cruce de caminos como si estuviesen conectadas al propio esqueleto de la bruja.

Como la serpiente que alguna vez tentó a Eva, ella alarga la cabeza hacia el otro Elisse.

—¿Estás seguro de que esto es lo que quieres, pequeño? —pregunta con ternura, y mi otro yo asiente con la cabeza.

La Gran Bruja suspira, satisfecha, y luego abre la mandíbula para regurgitar algo a sus pies como si fuese una presa a medio digerir.

—NO, ¡no, espera! —es lo primero que sale de mi boca al ver de lo que se trata—. ¡¿Qué diablos estás haciendo?!

Mi otro yo no me escucha. Se inclina y, sin dudarlo, recoge el libro de las generaciones del Culto. Lo abre de par en par, y hasta aquí puedo escuchar los gritos que se desprenden de las páginas llenas de firmas rojas.

Me levanto de golpe. Corro hacia el árbol, pero las columnas se enredan en mis tobillos y me hacen tropezar sobre las cenizas.

—No, por todos los dioses, ¡no lo hagas! —suplico, perdiendo por completo el sentido de la realidad—. ¡Prometiste que no los abandonarías de nuevo, desgraciado!

—¿Ah, sí? ¿Y por qué debería cumplir esa promesa?

Me quedo pasmado al escuchar que mi otro yo por fin me responde. Baja el libro un momento, y gira la cabeza hacia mí.

—Dime, ¿por qué debería escoger la vida de ellos por encima de la mía? —insiste.

La conmoción escala dentro de mí como un demonio que emerge de las profundidades.

—Comus Bayou es tu familia —afirmo, atónito—, ¡ellos son todo lo que tienes, Elisse!

—¿Comus Bayou? —espeta mi otro yo con sorna—, ¿hablas de tu hermana, quien no deja de rondar como una hiena a tu hombre? ¿Nashua, el que no se atrevió a decirte la verdad hasta que no tuvo otra alternativa? ¿Julien, quien tan sólo te suelta palabras de consuelo, pero nunca le planta cara a los demás por ti?

Él se acerca y se acuclilla delante de mí, con el libro abierto entre las manos.

—¿O acaso te refieres al pobre y miserable detective? —dice—, ¿a ese hombre al que sólo sabes utilizar como vía de escape?

—Basta. ¡Nada de esto es verdad!

¿No lo es? ¿No odias lo dependiente que es tu hermana?

NO.

¿No odias que Nashua haya protegido a quien intentó asesinarte?

NO.

¿No odias que Julien sea tan cobarde?

¡NO!

¿No odias que Hoffman te estime tanto que lo único que sepas hacer con ese afecto es aprovecharte de él?

—¡NO! —grito y me retuerzo como lo harían las espinas de una rosa de hierro. Me cubro los oídos y entierro la frente sobre la tierra para no escuchar, aunque las voces no sean del monstruo de hueso, sino *mías,* y que estén sólo dentro de mi cabeza.

—Tú sabes que aquí no puedes mentir, Elisse —me dice—. Tú sabes que aquí no puedes ocultar ni siquiera las verdades que tu propia consciencia ignora. Así que, respóndeme —insiste—: ¿Por qué debería escoger la vida de ellos por encima de la mía?

Suelto un gemido, y siento las lágrimas volverse espesas al mezclarse con las cenizas del cruce de caminos. Miro dentro de mi corazón, y la respuesta reside en el centro, fría y dolorosa como la garra de hueso que alguna vez lo estrujó.

Levanto la frente de nuevo.

—¿Cómo... lo supiste? —mi pregunta resulta ser mi confesión.

Porque es verdad. Es verdad que, al final, iba a firmar el libro.

Iba a abandonar a Comus Bayou y con ello... iba a salvar mi vida.

Y ante mi dolor, él sonríe con una inmensa compasión.

—Porque yo *soy Dios*, hijo mío. Y yo todo lo sé.

Y entonces, mi otro yo hiere su índice humano con su garra de hueso y lo lleva al último espacio libre de aquella página sangrienta.

En cuanto termina de escribir, el hilo de plata se eleva de su pecho y se alarga hacia la serpiente que lo mira todo desde el endrino. En vez del símbolo de Dee, ella le muestra una herida abierta que revela su corazón palpitante.

El filamento se une y reconozco, en la cara de ese Elisse, el impulso que me llevó a devorar a Laurele. A apropiarme de la espada filosofal.

La magia.
La espada.
El monstruo.

La verdad cae como un telón cuando descubro que si yo firmase el libro, no lo haría para liberarme del monstruo. Sino para *apoderarme* de él.

Aradia tuerce el hilo que nos une y me empieza a fusionar con la criatura dentro de mí.

—¡Detente, por lo que más quieras, detente! —grito desesperado al ver que los huesos comienzan a revelarse bajo la carne del otro Elisse. Que su pecho se abre en canal para mostrar la espada entre las costillas, los montones de corazones que laten podridos debajo de ella.

Y, finalmente, unos ojos que se tornan rojos como los de la serpiente.

Una vez que termina de transformarse en la terrible criatura de mis visiones, en mi monstruoso *yo*, ese Elisse se gira a mirarme con una sonrisa.

Sepulto mis manos humanas en la tierra del camino, y hago polvo una columna con la simple presión de mis dedos.

Ahogado en mis tinieblas, en mi locura, pienso en lo único que siempre ha sido un rayo de luz y certeza.

Pienso en sus ojos azules.

—¿Por qué me atormentas con un pecado que sabes que nunca cometería? —pregunto, aferrándome a los huesos y las cenizas como una última esperanza—. ¿Por qué te molestas en mostrarme mi oscuridad, si sabes que nunca cedería ante ella si eso implica perderlo *a él*?

El monstruo ladea la cabeza con desagrado, como si algo en mis palabras le hubiese herido por dentro, pero luego vuelve a forzar su mueca burlona.

—¿Renunciar? —dice—. ¿De verdad piensas que una bestia como tú sería capaz de *renunciar* a algo?

Un resplandor plateado se abre entre los endrinos como una llama, tan brillante que por un segundo parece que la luna hubiese descendido en el bosque.

Intento levantarme de nuevo, impulsado por el desconcierto y la desesperación cuando Tared emerge de uno de los ocho caminos, envuelto en su piel de lobo tal como la última noche en la que se ofreció a mí.

—¿¿Tared?! —pregunto, estupefacto al ver al devorapieles caminar hacia mi monstruoso yo, para arrodillarse frente a él—. ¡No te atrevas a tocarlo, animal asqueroso! —grito, pero el otro Elisse le acaricia la barbilla con una dulzura repugnante.

Después, saca el athame de sus vestiduras y lo levanta hacia el reflejo de la luna.

La imagen de los ojos rojos de Ilya golpea mi cabeza como la bala de un cañón.

—¡No, NO! —grito con todas mis fuerzas—. ¡Es mentira, todo esto es una maldita mentira! ¡Yo nunca lo obligaría a quedarse conmigo!

—¿Obligarlo? —mi espectro se burla con su asquerosa mano aún puesta sobre mi Tared—. ¡Tú sabes que él preferirá convertirse en *esto* antes que perderte de nuevo! ¡Tu decisión de salvar tu propia vida lo condenará a esta niebla para siempre!

—¡PUES ENTONCES PREFIERO MORIR!

Mi grito lo devasta todo. Mi aliento. Mis pensamientos. Mis lágrimas.

Incluso detiene el filo del athame, a milímetros del cuello del lobo.

El otro Elisse baja el arma, y sonríe.

—... por fin lo has comprendido —él suelta a Tared, y el lobo cae de espaldas, inconsciente, mientras yo me hundo cada vez más en la conmoción—. No puedes renunciar a tu poder. Pero tampoco puedes arrastrarlo a él contigo. Y es por eso que sólo te queda una salida.

El monstruo me tiende mi propio athame.

—*Morir* —susurro.

Mi otro yo sonríe cuando tomo el arma entre mis dedos.

—Debes perecer, Elisse, para que yo no me convierta en tu futuro —dice, abriendo los brazos ante el endrino—. Muere aquí, ahora y en mi gloria, para que yo no pueda existir. Es la única manera. Es la única salvación.

Observo el brillo del arma.

Siempre pensé que ese Elisse podrido que veía en mis premoniciones era una ilusión del Dios de los ángeles. Pero me equivoqué.

Porque tal como alguna vez dijo Aradia, esto, este monstruo, no es más un reflejo de mi alma. De mi corazón. De lo que realmente soy y de todas las culpas que llevo encima.

Y tiene razón. No puedo permitir que eso resucite.

Llevo el arma a mi cuello de lado a lado, y cuando éste se abre en una fina línea roja, se escuchan tres trompetas. Una tras otra. Y al resonar la última, el orificio en el endrino se abre.

Brazos largos y blancos se asoman de su vientre, se alargan hacia mí como raíces carnosas hasta alcanzarme.

—Tu juicio ha terminado, Elisse. Es hora de ir hacia la eternidad —dice el monstruo a mi lado, para luego desvanecerse.

Me desplomo a la par que las extremidades, todas, se enredan en mis tobillos y piernas. Y como un recién nacido que es arrastrado desde su cordón umbilical, me llevan de vuelta hacia el vientre oscuro y podrido del que nací.

La luz del mundo se apaga. El frío me entumece mientras la esperanza se convierte en un pálido momento de lucidez.

Después, la locura. La oscuridad.

Y esta vez, decido no volver a luchar.

CAPÍTULO 101
UNA ÚLTIMA MENTIRA

En cuanto el errante oso deja a la bruja Caligo a los pies de la sirena, para luego volver a bajar al campo de batalla, ésta rompe a llorar con un grito, exclamando una y otra vez el nombre de su hermana.

Después, la perpetuasangre gime de frustración cuando se inclina sobre la herida en la espalda, pero sus garras no logran alcanzar la bala dentro del cuerpo, a nada de llegar al corazón de la envenenadora. En tanto, el licántropo jura, por su absurdo amor a la Bestia Revestida de Luna, que silenciará a su propio hermano en cuanto le ponga las manos encima.

Pero Irina Begaye sólo puede escuchar una cosa, y ésa es la risa de Benjamin Lander colándose por todos los recovecos de la casa.

Con la certeza de que sólo le queda una única cosa por hacer, ella ordena a sus hijos que se queden donde están y desciende por la estrecha trampilla del ático con todas las armas que su espalda puede cargar.

Abajo, la batalla que se libra en la casa arranca gritos de bestias, de hombres y de trompetas. Vaasaa, el ángel de la Alquimia, con sus dos puños ya regenerados después de la batalla en el faro, destroza una pared entera para alcanzar al errante tejón agazapado contra el horno de la cocina, mientras que Golmá hace tiras la piel de uno de los demonios de la Maligna con sus instrumentos de hierro blanco.

Por otra parte, la inmensa osa gris de la Espiral no duda en partir en dos a uno de los tramperos con su garra, en tanto su mujer revienta tres balas en la cara de otro ángel de las Artes Mecánicas, evocado apenas unas lunas atrás.

Una antorcha es lanzada al interior de la habitación de las hierbas, cuyo techo comienza a arder en segundos. El humo se expande como el veneno a la par que la vida del errante chivo es arrebatada, indefenso y mutilado sobre aquella gran mesa en el comedor.

La sangre se derrama. Los cartuchos se vacían. Y con una inmensa sonrisa, soy testigo, de cómo la resistencia de la casa comienza a colapsar.

Y allí, al bajar el último peldaño de la trampilla y llegar por fin al segundo piso, una sola detonación hace frenar en el acto a la mujer puma.

Ella jadea, tan incrédula ante lo que ve en el pasillo, que sólo logra volver a reaccionar después de un segundo disparo.

—Dios santo, Hoffman... —musita, y afloja ligeramente el rifle que lleva entre las manos.

El detective no responde. Tan sólo se queda quieto, con el brazo firme y la boquilla de su pistola humeante por el calor de las dos balas que acaba de escupir.

Allen Miller yace tendido a sus pies, boca arriba, con un agujero en medio de la frente y otro más a la altura del corazón.

El demonio Asmoday grita sin lengua sobre ellos, vuelto loco al ver cómo la vida del joven se desliza por los tablones del suelo, succionada por la sed de la casa.

Tú le habías prometido esa vida al gusano, ¿verdad?

Tú le habías jurado que, cuando esta guerra acabara, Allen Miller sería el cuerpo humano en el que por fin podría probar la vida fuera de la niebla.

Y ahora te ríes de su dolor, de su ciega estupidez mientras que el puño del detective retuerce en su puño una fotografía hecha pedazos.

—¿Por qué ha hecho eso? —pregunta ella, atónita no ante el asesinato, sino por las densas lágrimas de rabia que buscan abrirse paso en el detective.

Pero el hombre mantiene el temple, quizás atormentado ante el pensamiento de que, de haber sido un poco más frío nueve años atrás, se habría ahorrado esas dos balas.

Incapaz de comprender la inmensidad de lo que tiene delante de ella, la errante sale de su estupefacción cuando la puerta negra por fin es derribada.

El Inquisidor aparece en el marco, y alarga la cabeza dentro de la casa de Aradia.

Todos los errantes aglomerados en el primer piso detienen sus garras para retraerse hacia la sala, hacia las pocas barricadas que han logrado formar con los muebles.

Benjamin extiende sus extremidades por las paredes como una red y mira fijamente hacia la madre puma, quien se acerca al borde de la escalera destrozada.

—Volvemos a vernos, perra inmunda —dice el monstruo con una sonrisa—. ¿Están tus bebitos allí arriba? ¿Crees que vas a poder salvarlos de mí esta vez?

La rabia de la hembra sube la temperatura de mi prisión, pero pronto, ésta se convierte en una fría palidez cuando ve que los miembros de Benjamin Lander comienzan a transformarse en rostros y cuerpos que ella lleva grabados en el corazón.

—Irina... —la voz de su esposo la estremece, los ojos oscuros de sus hermanos y del hombre al que alguna vez llamó "abuelo" le provocan el más fuerte de los temblores.

Y ella, ante esos títeres, ante las imágenes de su familia resucitada por los dedos de un hombre fusionado con un ángel, no siente más que una profunda cólera.

—Suba a proteger a mis hijos y a Elisse, detective —ordena mientras le arroja una de las escopetas que lleva en la espalda—. Es hora de que salde cuentas con este cabrón.

Salvador Hoffman no necesita que se lo repita. Toma el arma en el aire y se da media vuelta en dirección al ático.

Irina Begaye sabe que si falla, que si permite que el Inquisidor cruce más allá de ese pasillo, no importará si sus hijos escapan de esa casa. De Salem. De Massachusetts.

Él los encontrará.

Así que saca sus colmillos, sus garras, y se prepara para recibir a la bestia, quien se arroja de un impulso hacia la mujer.

CAPÍTULO 102
LOS SIETE NOMBRES DE DIOS

Alguna vez escuché que el infierno de los cristianos era como una hoguera gigante, un sitio lleno de fuego y demonios que te provocaban los más dolorosos tormentos.

Pero no. El infierno es muy, muy diferente.

Es... es el lugar en el que estoy ahora mismo. Un espacio vacío e infinito en el que no hay, literalmente, *nada*. No hay arriba ni abajo. No hay luz ni oscuridad, ni un solo ruido o sensación.

No puedo moverme. No puedo respirar, pero tampoco puedo ahogarme. Ya no puedo siquiera sentir la oscilación de mi corazón, como si mi cuerpo se hubiese desvanecido y sólo quedara ahora mi consciencia encerrada en este lugar.

Tan sólo estoy aquí, inmóvil como un hombre al que han enterrado vivo en un ataúd. Como un astronauta que acaba de salir disparado fuera de su nave, para flotar en la inmensidad del espacio, a sabiendas de que nada ni nadie podrá rescatarlo.

Solo. Completamente solo.

En definitiva, este infierno es más parecido al Niraya que alguna vez me describieron los monjes budistas. No un lugar físico, sino un estado de desesperación, de angustia y desamparo.

No sé cuánto tiempo llevo encerrado en este lugar, pero si en algo tenían razón las descripciones cristianas del infierno es que cada minuto, cada segundo que paso aquí se siente como si fuese una eternidad. Y, en el momento en el que me doy cuenta de que voy a estar aquí *para siempre*, es cuando al fin comienza mi verdadero terror.

¿Es éste mi castigo, entonces? ¿Es ésta mi sentencia por mis crímenes, por haberme convertido en una fuerza cruel y destructiva?

Quisiera gritar y llorar, renegar del destino al que he sido arrojado, pero no tengo lágrimas. No tengo boca ni lengua.

Soy nadie. Soy nada.

¿Y acaso no lo merezco? ¿No merezco estar en medio de este limbo? ¿No merezco pagar por Adam, por Huritt, por Laurele? ¿Quién me creí al momento de poner un dedo en el renglón de la vida de todas esas personas? ¿Qué creí que iba a suceder después a mi muerte, si había causado tanto daño?

Y aun así, aun cuando sé que merezco todo lo que estoy sufriendo, no puedo evitar implorar que, por favor, *alguien* me libere de este dolor.

Ⅱⴰⴶⴶⴻⴶⴽ ⴑⴰⴶ ⴽ ⵌⴽⴰⵡⵌⴶ ⵌⵍⴰ ⵛⵍ ⴑⴰⴶ ⵕⴽⴶ ⵕⴶⵌⵕⴲⵍ[43]

Mi corazón da un salto al escuchar aquella extraña voz, incapaz de descubrir si ha sido real o tan sólo una alucinación de mi mente atormentada. Intento percibir aquel susurro entre la inmensidad de este lugar sin luz ni sombra, pero no logro encontrarle.

¿Acaso es... *Él?*

Ⅱⴰⴶⴶⴻⴶⴽ ⴰⵍⵛⴰⵕⴻ ⴶ ⴹⴽ, ⴶ ⴹⴶ ⴹⵕⵕⴹⵕⴲⵍⴹⵛⵕⴶⴶ[44]

_____

[43] "¿Quieres que te perdone por lo que has hecho?"
[44] "¿Quieres volver a mí, a mi misericordia?"

Sí. Es Él. ¡Es el Dios de los ángeles!

La angustia se cierne de nuevo sobre mí, porque mi primer deseo debería ser combatirlo. Rechazar aquella voz dulce y gentil que acaricia mi ser como unos dedos acarician la lana de un cordero.

Pero, para mi desgracia, mi primer impulso es... rogar. Buscar el perdón por las cosas horribles que hecho, suplicar desde esa voz débil y vergonzosa dentro de mí que, por favor, se apiade de mi alma, que me lleve a ese mar oscuro de la muerte definitiva.

¿No era acaso éste el Dios que perdonaba a asesinos y violadores si éstos se volcaban a adorarle? Entonces, si me *arrepiento*, ¿no podría liberarme también de este purgatorio?

"Perdóname, por favor, perdóname", suplica mi consciencia, traicionando a mi estirpe, a mi Nación, a mi familia, a todo lo que simbolizo yo y la magia de la que alguna vez estuve tan orgulloso.

Y cuando creo que no va a responder a mis súplicas, cuando creo que Dios *me ha abandonado*, escucho:

"Y vi dos ríos de fuego, y su luz brillaba como el jacinto,
y caí sobre mi rostro ante el Señor de los Espíritus."

Mi corazón se sobresalta de esperanza. ¿Acaso Él me ha respondido?

"Y él me tomó de la mano derecha,
y me llevó donde están todos los secretos,
me enseñó los de misericordia,
los de justicia,
los de todos los extremos del cielo..."

—Y los de todas las estrellas en donde nace la luz.

Imposible, ¿acaso acabo de pronunciar yo aquello? ¿Con mi boca, con mis labios, con mi lengua pura y humana?

En medio de esta abominable inmensidad, una luz comienza a brillar a lo lejos. Una luz maravillosa y cálida, una esperanza que se acerca como una estela preciosa entre el horrible espacio liminal.

La estela me alcanza y sus resplandores rebotan en mi cuerpo. Me permiten sentirlo de nuevo, me devuelven la sensación de mis brazos, mis piernas, mi pecho, y me llenan los ojos de alivio.

╱┐ ⊓ɛχ⅃ɔ⅃. ╱┐ ⊓ɛχ⅃ɔ⅃, ɛ┐ ℞⅃ɛχ⅂ɛ⅃.[45]

Extiendo mi mano y dejo que, como Adán, Dios me toque la punta del índice y entre a mi cuerpo a través de mi piel, de mis heridas, de mis cavidades, de mis poros. Dejo que su gracia me llene las venas, los órganos, los huesos; que ejerza su salvación sobre mí aun cuando *fue Él* quien me condenó a este sufrimiento.

Dios me abraza. Dios me eleva. Dios me envuelve en su seno y yo comienzo a encogerme.

Mis brazos se debilitan. Mis piernas dejan de moverse, y una sensación de tristeza y culpabilidad me baña de pies a cabeza. Me vuelvo frágil e indefenso como ese pequeño Elisse en el campo de refugiados al que tantas veces encontraron escondido debajo de los camastros.

╱┐ χɛ⅃. ╱┐ χɛ⅃. ╱┐ χɛ⅃.[46]

Le digo que me está haciendo daño, y Él dice que su amor es tan grande que a veces duele.

---

[45] "Te perdono. Te perdono, mi cordero."

[46] Te amo. Te amo. Te amo.

╱┐ ᚷᛲ. ╱┐ ᚷᛲ. ╱┐ ᚷᛲ.

Le digo que su luz me quema, y Él dice que es porque me está purificando.

ᚷᛠᚷᛋ. ᚷᛠᚷᛋ. ᚷᛠᚷᛋ.[47]

Le digo que se detenga, y Él dice que lo hace por mi bien.

Y estoy tan débil, tan vulnerable, que decido creerle. Decido creer que si su amor me lastima es porque me lo merezco. Porque *yo me lo busqué.*

Así que lo escucho. Lo obedezco, empiezo a cerrar los ojos despacio, y luego...

—ZIIRHia.

Mi Dios se irrita de pronto, porque ésa no ha sido su voz.

Abro los ojos y giro mi cabeza en todas direcciones, hacia la nada, medio cegado por la luz que todavía se enraíza dentro de mi cuerpo.

Ha sido una palabra remotamente familiar, pero que no termino de comprender, como si hubiese sido mal pronunciada.

—*azcaacb*...

¿Qué voz es ésa? ¿Qué voz es ésa que se escucha no afuera, sino *dentro* de mí?

—*paupnhr*...

Los susurros que se hacen cada vez más fuertes, más insistentes.

—No, ¡detente! —exclamo, porque quien sea que esté pronunciando esos *nombres* enfurece cada vez más a mi Dios.

Y si hay algo más terrible que su misericordia, sin duda debe ser *su ira.*

Pero la voz continúa, la voz hace que la luz que estaba dentro de mí se tense como un alambre de púas y se clave en

---

[47] Ámame. Ámame. Ámame.

el interior de mi cuerpo como una doncella de hierro invertida. Con temor a ser destrozado por la claridad de mi Señor, levanto la barbilla para suplicarle de nuevo que se detenga. Pero al mirar hacia arriba, hacia la divinidad, lo que encuentro me deja mudo y desconcertado.

Lo veo a Él como una proyección de fuerza y luz que cada vez se hace más grande. Más inmensa, como una tormenta sobre mi cabeza que crece y crece mientras yo... me desvanezco.

Aquella voz extraña me habla de nuevo. Aquella voz hace que sienta otra vez el latido de mi corazón.

Y por fin, la verdad se revela ante mí.

Esa luz, esa misericordia, ese Dios... no está salvando mi alma. No me está llevando a su gloria.

Se está alimentando de mí.

—¡Resiste, Elisse, *hdmhiai*!

La lucidez me embiste. Y como un trueno, como un destello azul y poderoso, pronuncio el nombre de aquél a quien pertenece esa voz:

—Ta... red —susurro, y Él retuerce sus espinas.

—¡*kkaaeee*!

—Tared... —lo llamo con un gemido de dolor.

—¡*iieelll*, Elisse!

—¡TARED! —grito, y mi tercer ojo *vuelve a abrirse por entero.*

El plano que está más allá de este mundo celestial se proyecta en mi mente en una agresiva avalancha de visiones.

La niebla. La casa. Tared en el ático. Tared, arrodillado a mi lado. Tared, intentando pronunciar los siete nombres secretos sobre mi oído mientras mira el *Sigillum Dei Aemeth* en mi mano.

Porque no sólo ha visto todas las heridas que he sufrido a lo largo de este juicio manifestarse en mi cuerpo. Sino que ha comprendido, a través del impulso de nuestro vínculo, que debía encontrar la forma de ayudarme.

Y cuando encuentro también a Inanna desangrada, a Caligo con una bala a milímetros del corazón y a Hela retorciéndose de angustia con mi hilo de plata entre las manos, la memoria de los miles de brujos enterrados en este plano maldito me inunda con el triple de fuerza que la luz de aquel Dios.

Y ahora soy yo el que se enfurece.

Recupero no sólo el control y la presencia de mi cuerpo, sino también mi magia. Y con una potencia de la que no me creí capaz a estas alturas, empujo contra aquella presencia invasora que aún yace dentro de mí.

—¡ellMG!

Ante el grito de ese séptimo nombre, la claridad es finalmente expulsada de mi ser cual veneno, su resplandor destrozado por la fuerza de todas las magias que laten en mi centro.

Y como si siempre hubiese estado allí, apretada entre mis dedos de hueso, la espada filosofal resucita junto con mi consciencia.

Me levanto. Me yergo delante del resplandor y reúno toda mi energía para realizar un último milagro: saco el *Sigillum Dei Aemeth* de mis ropas, y lo alzo hacia Dios con mi mano derecha.

Mi energía hace hervir el grabado en rojo escarlata con tal candor que los símbolos comienzan a deslizarse por mi brazo como cera fundida.

Los nombres, las letras, los trazos; todo se graba en mi espalda, en mis hombros, en mi rostro y mis piernas hasta que mi ser entero es recubierto de los sigilos angelicales, algo que también sucede en el mundo humano, ante los ojos de todos los presentes en aquel ático.

Y cuando por fin me apropio de la magia enoquiana, al igual que hice con el vudú y la alquimia, *Él* monta en cólera.

—Veremos quién suplica misericordia esta vez, cabrón...

Después de mi injuria, pronuncio el primer nombre de Dios.

Como si la torre de Babel se precipitara sobre mí, miles de lenguas salen disparadas de su estela divina y el vacío alrededor se transforma para llevarme otra vez a Guinée.

Laurele yace enredada en mis tobillos de nuevo, suplicando piedad. Pero esta vez no me conmuevo en absoluto.

—Tus trucos ya no van a funcionar —digo y esgrimo la espada hacia ella. Al ver el resplandor de su filo, su rostro se anega en lágrimas.

—¡Yo era una víctima, Elisse!

—Sí. Pero *yo fui la tuya.*

—¡Pudiste perdonarme, pudiste...!

—¿Perdonarte? —corto—. Eso le correspondía a tus Loas. A Bondyé.[48] ¿Y acaso no soy yo sólo un mortal?

Ella abre los ojos de par en par. Y al bajar la espada para decapitar la cabeza de la bruja pronuncio el segundo nombre de Dios.

Las lenguas gritan de nuevo, buscando aturdirme a la vez que el Merkavah, cada vez más caótico, me arroja esta vez a Stonefall.

Pero su realidad es inexacta; por todos los escombros veo tumbas, rastros de Guinée como si a Dios cada vez le costase más mantener el retrato de aquella fantasía.

Mientras tanto, el Rebis yace inmóvil en el suelo, con la cabeza de Jocelyn a unos metros, los ojos en blanco y la mitad de la cara derritiéndose lentamente sobre el suelo de mosaico.

---

48 "Buen Dios." Equivalente al Dios cristiano en el vudú.

Pero *él* todavía respira. Y su rostro hermoso y humano basta para devolver la ternura a mi corazón.

Clavo la espada a mi lado, sin dejar de sostenerla por el mango, y me arrodillo para acariciar la mejilla de Adam con la mano de hueso.

—Si pudiera, cambiaría las cosas —digo—. Habría luchado un poco más contra mi ambición. Y un poco más por ti —limpio la sal de su cara, aun cuando sé que su mirada dorada no es más que un espejismo—. Pero no puedo remediar lo que hice. Y todos los dioses saben que no hay peor castigo que saber que ésta es la última vez que podré verte. Lo siento tanto, Adam…

Bajo mi rostro hacia el joven, toco su frente con la mía, y mis labios pronuncian sobre los suyos el tercer nombre de Dios.

El joven se funde al igual que el escenario en derredor en un desesperado intento de llevarme ahora al cruce de caminos.

Criptas, escombros y ramas se entremezclan con trozos de nada; un plano que se columpia en el vacío junto con la voluntad de su creador.

Me levanto y las columnas intentan enredarse de nuevo en mis tobillos para que no camine hacia el árbol cada vez más arqueado sobre sí mismo, como una vela que lentamente se funde con el suelo. Pero basta que susurre el cuarto nombre para que las vértebras se retraigan.

Me detengo frente al árbol y empuño la espada con la intención de enterrarla en su brutal hendidura.

—¿Es que no te arrepientes? ¿Es que no sientes ningún remordimiento? —pregunta alguien a mis espaldas—. ¿Cómo puedes continuar con esto ahora que sabes todo el daño que causaste sólo por ambición?

Encuentro a mi otro yo arrastrándose en el suelo. Débil. Hambriento. Los ojos enrojecidos llenos de rencor.

—¿Nunca lo vas a entender, verdad? —digo con una sonrisa irónica—. No, ¿cómo vas a hacerlo, si no eres más que un simple Dios?

Vuelvo la mirada hacia el brillo de mi arma, su fulgor como una llama dorada contra la oscuridad obscena del árbol, y susurro el quinto nombre de Dios.

Los huesos de la criatura se rompen de manera violenta. Y cuando me giro de nuevo hacia él, veo que su cuerpo se ha torcido tanto, como este mundo, que ya es más parecido a un endrino que a un humano.

—Soy un brujo de la Mano Izquierda, un ser que ha renunciado a la luz —digo—. Pero eso no significa que todas las atrocidades que hago sean para volverme más poderoso. Para volverme... como tú.

Doy un paso hacia Él, y éste retrocede.

—Eso significa que estoy dispuesto a volverme el más terrible de todos los monstruos con tal de que ni tú ni nadie vuelva a poner un dedo encima a mi familia. Y ése... ése es un sacrificio que ningún dios parece estar dispuesto a hacer por los suyos.

En un último acto desesperado, mi otro yo se impulsa hacia mí, pero su cuerpo deforme y débil le impide alcanzarme. Me echo a un lado a la par que hiero la espalda de la criatura de arriba abajo con el rasgar de mi hoja.

Se estampa contra el árbol, y aúlla, lacerado. Se da la vuelta para enfrentarme, pero no le doy ninguna oportunidad.

—Soy *Él*. El descabezado, ¡soy el Martillo que aplasta los espíritus, el que abre las puertas de este mundo y el otro! —de una estocada, clavo la espada en el pecho de mi yo monstruoso, en medio de sus corazones podridos.

La espada prende fuego a la criatura, la ahoga en medio de dolorosas llamas que en segundos lo reducen a cenizas.

Y, sin piedad, pronuncio el sexto nombre de Dios.

El bosque se retuerce. Las tumbas se hacen polvo junto con los escombros y, en un intento por derrotarme, soy devuelto al vacío que hace unos instantes casi me enloquece.

Pero esta vez, al estirar mis piernas y poner los pies en un suelo que hace segundos no era más que una inmensa nada, mi presencia se expande como un mar de tinieblas; una tinta oscura que infecta el Merkavah y comienza a enfermar su infinitud.

La estela blanca y dolorosa del Dios de los ángeles se convierte en un remolino, un gigantesco tornado sobre mí que crece furioso y errático. Los resplandores me alcanzan como truenos y la agonía me tritura cuando su luz intenta volver a entrar en mi cuerpo; el poder de aquel ser aún es inmenso, alimentado por los sepulcros de los brujos que permanecen en su Paraíso obsceno.

Pero no me doy el lujo de rendirme, no ahora que la voz que retumba con más fuerza dentro de mi cabeza es de Tared quien me implora que resista.

Y al sentir que ese veneno luminoso se cuela de nuevo bajo mi piel, la oscuridad me da por fin la solución.

Llevo la mano de hueso hacia mi pecho y lo rasgo de arriba abajo para revelar el arma más poderosa que poseo. Porque si hay algo que ha logrado derrotar la magia de Laurele, la espada filosofal y al mismísimo monstruo de hueso es *mi voluntad*; el corazón rojo y vivo que late entre mis costillas como una bomba.

Y una vez liberado de su prisión humana, éste empuja mi magia con el triple de fuerza a través de la propia luz que el

Dios intenta inyectar en mí, utilizándola como vínculo para llegar hasta él.

—Soy la Bestia Revestida de Luna —musito, y la tormenta blanca sobre mí se vuelve más oscura a cada segundo—. ¡Y tú vas a obedecer mi voluntad!

Con un grito más, pronuncio el séptimo nombre de Dios.

Y en el efímero instante en el que Él deja de oponer resistencia, en el que queda completamente vulnerable ante mi poder, mi magia por fin alcanza su centro: esa energía inmortal e indestructible de todos los espíritus que se vuelve la más frágil de las flores cuando es alcanzada por mi garra.

La luz se marchita con la rapidez de un parpadeo. Y antes de morir bajo la asfixia de mis tinieblas, el Dios de los ángeles grita por fin el nombre de mi Mara.

CAPÍTULO 103
EL ÚLTIMO SENDERO

Como una flecha, el péndulo en el cuello del brujo se levanta y arroja un hilo de magia que yo siento clavarse en mi pecho con la fuerza de un arpón.

Sin más, me derriba de espaldas contra el suelo de mi celda, con esa soga ahora unida a mi corazón acelerado. Y aunque me cuesta levantarme y recuperar el aliento, sonrío al asomarme de nuevo hacia el ático a través de mi portal.

—Lo logró —susurra la sirena, asombrada—, ¡Elisse lo ha conseguido!

—¿Hablas en serio? ¡¿Tiene el nombre?! —exclama la falsa bruja, llena de alivio al escuchar cómo el pálpito de la bestia astada vuelve a tomar el ritmo de los vivos.

—No sólo eso. También ha matado a su Dios… —responde la rubia, quien ve, a través del espejo de obsidiana, cómo el angelino paraíso comienza a tambalearse.

Pero no es lo único que puede percibir. Aquella inquietud que tanto la ha atormentado vuelve a acecharla cuando sigue con la mirada el hilo de magia que conecta al péndulo conmigo, el cual apunta hacia la salida del desván.

—Tráelo. ¡Tráelo de vuelta! —grita entonces el portador del trueno, quien resiste el impulso de zarandear a la necromante.

Ella despierta de su conmoción y comienza a halar del hilo plateado para enredarlo en su brazo a manera de carrete.

—Mierda, ¡¿no puedes hacerlo más rápido?! —brama el detective Hoffman, quien en ese momento entra como una tempestad a la habitación.

Al llegar hacia ellos, evita cruzar la mirada con el angustiado licántropo, centrado únicamente en el brujo dormido.

—El hilo se ha vuelto demasiado frágil, y si lo fuerzo, reventará —replica la necromante con la frente empapada en sudor, los ojos negros alternándose entre su labor y la salida del ático—. Además, Elisse y yo no compartimos el vínculo del aquelarre. No puedo traerlo con la misma facilidad que a Inanna.

La desolación de escuchar aquello hace que el humano preste atención al cuerpo de la portadora de Satanás, inconsciente sobre un charco de su propia sangre. También encuentra al enorme demonio Buer encaramado en el ventanal, quien ha abierto sus costuras como una cortina para bloquear la entrada de cualquier arma o criatura.

—¿Qué ha pasado con ella? —pregunta, señalando a la bruja Caligo.

La perpetuasangre mira hacia la herida en la espalda de la envenenadora, agrandada con la ayuda de unas tijeras, y luego hacia la bala ensangrentada tirada a su lado.

Un frasco más de belladona derrama sus últimas gotas sobre la madera, secándose al lado del antídoto.

—Son como estacas para vampiros —explica ella con la lengua entorpecida por el cansancio—. No importa por qué parte de su cuerpo entre, el hierro de los ángeles siempre busca alcanzar el corazón del brujo. Así que se me ocurrió que, si paralizaba el de Caligo lo suficiente, la bala dejaría de moverse.

Él abre los ojos de par en par, tan impresionado como yo ante la astucia de la errante coyote.

—Mierda. Eso ha sido brillante, Johanna…

Ninguno de nosotros logra ver la reacción de la mujer ante el inusual cumplido del hombre, puesto que un golpe brutal abre una grieta en el suelo, apenas a unos metros de ellos.

—¡No! —exclama el lobo de plata, cuyos reflejos logran evitar que el espejo sobre el atril caiga y se estrelle contra el piso.

Las crías de Irina Begaye llaman a su madre al unísono, atraídas por el detective para evitar que sean heridas por los tablones astillados. Un disparo de escopeta retumba y pronto, todos perciben no sólo los gritos del Inquisidor a través de la estrecha apertura, sino también el espeso humo que poco a poco inunda la casa.

—¡¿Pero Elisse no había matado ya a ese jodido Dios?! —exclama el exagente, con los pequeños apretados bajo sus brazos—, ¡¿por qué sus puñeteros ángeles no han vuelto al maldito infierno de donde vinieron?!

—¡Debe ser por su Mara! —exclama la necromante, cada vez más agotada—, estos ángeles ya han cruzado a nuestro mundo, ¡el pacto que ha hecho con ellos es lo que debe estar manteniéndolos con…!

El ruido de algo parecido a una flecha corta las palabras de la bruja, seguido de un penetrante olor a gasolina.

Un globo revienta contra Buer y lo empapa de arriba abajo con el químico, para después ser impactado por una bala apenas un segundo después.

Al instante, la piel de la criatura se cubre de llamas, lo que lo obliga a contraerse de dolor. Los niños gritan mientras el resto mira con absoluto terror cómo el demonio cae por la ventana, ahora una bola de fuego en el aire.

—Mierda, ¡van a alcanzarnos en cualquier momento! —grita el detective cuando el ataque es seguido por el crujido de algo que comienza a escalar hacia ellos desde el exterior de la casa.

—Hay que matarla —concluye por fin el licántropo—, ¡tenemos que ir por la Mara nosotros!

—¡Serás imbécil! —replica el otro, quien se ha acercado a la ventana con la escopeta que le ha dado la devorapieles—, ¡la cabrona podría estar en el otro maldito extremo del mundo!

—No —replica la bruja Hela, más pálida que un amanecer—. Ella... ella está aquí. En esta casa.

—¿Qué? —exclama el lobo—, ¡¿qué diablos quieres decir?! La bruja apenas tiene aliento para responder.

—El hilo de magia del péndulo está... apuntando hacia el sótano.

La perpetuasangre ahoga un gemido.

—¿Estás diciendo que Aradia...?

—No —interrumpe—. El vínculo no llega hasta mi Madre. Sólo a la puerta, y desaparece dentro de un túnel al plano medio. Es... un sitio en el que yo nunca he estado antes, del que ni siquiera sabía su existencia, pero que está *aquí*. En algún lugar de la niebla.

El silencio que se hace entre los presentes les permite escuchar el reptar de la criatura por el revestimiento.

—¡¿Y ahora qué diablos vamos a hacer?!

La pregunta del detective es precedida por el estallido de su escopeta.

La sirena mira a sus hermanas, agonizantes, pero vivas, y alza la mano para remover el péndulo del cuello del joven brujo.

—Ve por ella —dice mientras extiende el objeto hacia el licántropo—. Sólo tú puedes lograrlo.

—¿Qué? —exclama la errante coyote—, ¿cómo va a hacer eso si...?

—Tared Miller es el único ser sin magia que he visto atravesar el plano medio y vivir para contarlo —insiste—. Así que, si el poder de Elisse sigue impregnado en él, tengo la seguridad de que podrá alcanzar a esa desgraciada.

El lobo mira con sorpresa la piedra, la cual apunta firmemente hacia la puerta de salida.

—Ve por ella —finaliza la bruja—. Juro que te devolveré a Elisse.

Y con esa promesa, no lo duda un segundo más.

El lobo dentro de él aúlla cuando toma la cadena entre sus dedos y sale a toda prisa de aquella habitación.

CAPÍTULO 104
LA CAÍDA DEL PARAÍSO

Cuando aquello que mantiene funcional un trozo del plano medio muere, a su reino sólo le queda una cosa por hacer: colapsar. Y, tal como ocurrió cuando maté a Nathaniel Blake en el laberinto de Jocelyn, el reino de los ángeles comienza a partirse como un escenario que precipita sus pedazos en el abismo del plano medio.

Y lo único que me ayuda a encontrar de nuevo la Puerta de los Mil Brujos, en medio de un Merkavah que se fragmenta cual cascarón, es el hilo de Hela, tan debilitado que ahora se asemeja a la seda frágil de una telaraña.

Para no caer por el precipicio de la nada, materializo un sendero de escalones oscuros debajo de mí, siguiendo el rastro de magia hasta que la puerta aparece por fin a lo lejos, ahora visible a causa de la ausencia del Dios que la mantenía oculta.

Y al alcanzarla, me doy cuenta de que las manos están ahora inmóviles, como si ellas hubiesen perecido también. Empujo con fuerza, pero ésta no se mueve un solo centímetro.

—¡Mierda! —jadeo, y escucho el crepitar del corazón del cielo como si cientos de relámpagos estallasen alrededor.

El cansancio me carcome, mis energías se desploman junto con el Paraíso. Pero me obligo a reunir fuerzas para comenzar a arrancar las manos de la puerta, una a una.

La oscuridad del abismo cada vez se vuelve más prominente pero, por fin, logro quitar las suficientes para que el hierro blanco al que están adheridas quede revelado.

El Martillo de los ángeles ha perdido su fuerza, así que rasgo el espacio que he despejado para crear un nuevo túnel de gusano, tal como el que utilicé para llegar a la Antesala de los Querubines.

Y al cruzarlo, éste me lleva directamente al exterior de la torre, muy cerca de la grieta por donde entramos Inanna y yo. Me percato de que mi hilo de plata se alarga a través del jardín, de la torre y el portal como si fuese la marca de mi recorrido por este sitio.

Contemplo, por un placentero segundo, el asombroso derrumbe del Paraíso.

El cielo de cristal líquido se fragmenta en miles de riachuelos, la torre se tambalea, en tanto que el Vigilante, aquellos tres anillos ostentosos que miraban en todas las direcciones, ahora yacen inmóviles y entrecruzados en el firmamento, con los ojos cerrados y su brillo dorado perdido para transformarse en unos simples arcos de piedra.

Y muy, muy a lo lejos, el espejo de obsidiana me espera, aún flotando sobre la hierba cada vez más gris.

Me echo a correr y las flores de carne se marchitan a mi alrededor; la tierra tiembla con tanta fuerza que más de una vez me veo obligado a retroceder para no ser tragado por las grietas que se abren a mi paso, mientras que fragmentos del Vigilante, grandes como casas, se desploman por todo su jardín.

Pero, finalmente, logro cruzar los Campos. Y la distancia que me separa del portal es tan corta que ya puedo distinguir el otro lado a través del cristal.

—¿Te irás sin saber qué fue lo que hizo a la Maligna gritar en la torre?

La voz de Nalvage me hace girar en redondo y desenvainar la piedra filosofal. El Mensajero, quien quizá me ha seguido hasta aquí a través del túnel que abrí, está a unos cuantos metros de mí y empuña aquella espada de hierro con la que atravesé su cara de ángel. Está vivo gracias, sin duda, a los otros dos rostros bestiales que aún jadean a ambos costados de su cabeza.

Supongo que debí haber decapitado al cabrón.

—¿Quieres saber qué fue lo que aterrorizó de tal manera a la gran portadora de Satanás? —insiste en su discurso, pero yo desecho sus palabras con un chasquido de lengua.

—¿Todavía quieres enfrentarme, Nalvage? —insisto—. ¿Aún después de haber matado a tu Dios?

El ángel tuerce todos sus hocicos a la par que una grieta se abre a sus espaldas, tan grande que pareciera haber dividido el Paraíso en dos.

—¿Enfrentarte? No. Yo ya no voy a luchar contra ti, Bestia Revestida de Luna —dice, y retrocede hasta el punto en el que sus tobillos vacilan en el borde de la apertura—. Pero lo que sí puedo hacer es llevarte al abismo con todos nosotros.

La criatura levanta su espada de hierro blanco en lo alto, pero en vez de dirigirla hacia mí, la baja como una guillotina contra el suelo.

Y, arrancándome un grito de absoluto terror, Nalvage corta mi hilo de plata.

CAPÍTULO 105
ÉSTA ES...

Al bajar de un salto por la trampilla, el licántropo es recibido por un humo tan denso que queda cegado por unos instantes. Pero el impulso del péndulo le permite seguir adelante, abrirse paso ante la cortina negra hasta encontrarse por fin con la masacre desatada en el pasillo.

Escucha los gritos del Inquisidor y los rugidos de la errante puma retumbar dentro de una de las habitaciones a los costados del corredor. Pero es la sensación de algo carnoso a sus pies lo que por un instante entorpece su marcha.

Mira hacia abajo, y su cara se constriñe en una mueca al encontrar al demonio Asmoday triturado como una masa sanguinolenta en el suelo, aplastado bajo la violencia de la batalla entre el monstruoso Benjamin Lander e Irina Begaye.

También ve otro tipo de cadáveres. Trozos de personas, a quienes reconoce como aquel Atrapasueños que conoció alguna vez en el desierto, fragmentándose como cristales que poco a poco se funden sobre la madera.

Y, más delante, al filo de la destrozada escalera, un espeso charco de sangre que aturde su instinto de una manera desagradable.

El lobo dentro de él aúlla sin cesar una y otra vez, un eco que se escucha como un cuerno de batalla dentro de mi Tártaro; el instinto que le grita a su portador que continúe. Que no se detenga más a mirar.

Pero una de las paredes a un costado suyo revienta de golpe, impidiéndole avanzar. Tared Miller estrella su espalda contra el lado contrario del pasillo para evitar ser embestido por el Inquisidor, quien estira un par de sus largos brazos a través del agujero que ha abierto en el ladrillo.

—¡Por fin das la cara, maldito perro cobarde!

El grito del cazador pareciera haber sido expulsado de su segunda boca, mientras que uno de sus ojos cuelga de su cuenca, producto de un rasguño de la furiosa devorapieles que se encuentra a sus espaldas.

—¡No he terminado contigo, maldito cerdo! —grita ella con un brazo roto, el cual cuelga lánguido de su hombro.

Pero Benjamin no la escucha.

Cegado por la sed de venganza, se abre paso a través de la pared con todo el montón de brazos que le quedan, dispuestos a acabar con el hombre que tiene delante.

Y en vez de prepararse para contraatacar, Tared Miller obedece al repentino cosquilleo que siente en la nuca y se echa de bruces contra el suelo.

Una mole pesada y poderosa embiste al trampero, arrojándolo de vuelta a la habitación donde hacía un instante peleaba con la devorapieles.

—¡Julien! —grita, mientras el minotauro se impulsa de nuevo hacia el monstruo.

Las celdas de mi prisión comienzan a palpitar, excitadas por la fuerza de mi propio corazón cuando el licántropo se levanta, cruza el pasillo, y salta la escalera hacia la planta inferior, sin pensar una sola vez en el falso hermano cuyo cadáver, sin saberlo, ha vuelto a ser encerrado en la habitación de la necromante.

Hay cuerpos de tramperos despedazados a su paso, miembros de ángeles por doquier mientras el ala izquierda de la casa es consumida por el fuego.

Pero no se detiene ni un segundo más. Dobla hacia el pasillo de las llaves, la mitad de ellas ya desperdigadas por el suelo.

El péndulo apunta hacia una que todavía cuelga de la pared. Y en cuanto la toma entre sus garras, la puerta que lo conducirá hacia mí aparece ante él.

CAPÍTULO 106
LA ÚLTIMA PUERTA...

El grito de Hela es tan fuerte, tan estruendoso, que logra traspasar la barrera de obsidiana.

Y Nalvage, con una sonrisa de absoluta satisfacción, da un paso atrás para arrojarse él mismo a la grieta.

—¡No! —exclamo, aterrorizado al ver cómo mi hilo se desvanece en el aire, mientras el ángel es tragado por la oscuridad—. ¡NOOOO!

Me lanzo con desesperación al espejo y alzo mis garras con la intención de abrir el plano medio y pasar al mundo humano a través de él, pero la necromante agita las manos del otro lado.

—¡No, no lo hagas, Elisse! —exclama, su voz opacada como si me hablase a través del agua—. ¡No debes volver al mundo de los vivos con tu alma desconectada de tu cuerpo, podrías morir en…!

Una colisión en alguna de las paredes del ático arranca otro grito de la bruja, seguido de un caos que pareciera compararse con la caída del Paraíso a mis espaldas.

—Mierda, ¿¿qué diablos debo hacer entonces?! —exclamo, golpeando el espejo con los puños cerrados.

—No lo sé —susurra con un miedo que jamás había percibido en ella—. ¡No lo sé!

Johanna, paralizada de horror por lo que ha escuchado, tiene las manos sobre mi pecho, quizá buscando la forma de sostener los latidos de mi corazón.

Hoffman dispara una y otra vez en alguna parte de la habitación. Los niños de Irina se agazapan en un rincón, en tanto el humo y el fuego se abren paso a través de una de las paredes laterales de la casa...

Pero a quien no veo por ninguna parte es a Tared.

La esperanza abandona mi cuerpo sin piedad.

¿Esto es todo? ¿Después de todo lo que he luchado, ésta es la manera en la que voy a... morir?

—*¡Todavía podemos salvarlo, hija mía!*

La voz de Aradia me cruza el cuerpo como un rayo, tan clara que pareciera estar a mi lado.

Y como una evocación, *alguien* aparece en la entrada del ático.

La necromante se gira y lanza un grito que suena más a confusión que a alivio.

—¡ILYA! ¡¿Dónde diablos estabas?! —exclama ella, pero el hombre no le responde. Tan sólo entra a la habitación con la ropa húmeda, casi congelada, y sosteniendo algo.

Mi aliento se evapora al ver que se trata del libro de las generaciones del Culto.

—Pero, Madre... —musita Hela mientras el errante demonio llega hacia nosotros, sin detenerse a mirar, siquiera un segundo, el cuerpo de Inanna en el suelo.

Él abre las páginas delante del espejo, justo sobre aquel espacio en blanco debajo de las firmas infernales.

—*Si firmas el libro, tu alma,* tu voluntad, *me pertenecerá* —dice Aradia—. *Y, de esa manera, podré traerla de vuelta al mundo de los vivos para depositarla en tu cuerpo de nuevo.*

—Tal como alguna vez hizo conmigo —las palabras de Ilya me paralizan como un veneno. La desolación me embarga, me hace querer echarme yo también hacia la grieta por la que se ha tirado Nalvage.

—Pero, ¿cómo voy a firmar si no puedo mover mi cuerpo? —pregunto, intentando encontrar alguna otra solución. Cualquier cosa que no implique poner mi nombre en esas páginas. Pero la respuesta llega pronto de los labios de mi propia hermana:

—¡Un fantasma!

Hela se gira hacia ella:

—¿Cómo?

La perpetuasangre da un paso hacia nosotros, entusiasmada ante su idea:

—El alma de Elisse está desconectada de su cuerpo, eso significa que ahora es un fantasma ¡y tú eres una médium! ¡Deja que te posea para que pueda firmar el libro a través de ti!

Su furor me desconcierta, pero luego caigo en la cuenta de que Johanna *no lo sabe*. Ni ella ni nadie de mi familia sabe lo que pasará si firmo ese libro y me uno al Culto de la Grieta Resplandeciente.

"¿No será que, al ser desenterradas de nuestro subconsciente, nuestras premoniciones sólo nos muestran una verdad que nos negamos a ver? ¿Un futuro del que no podemos escapar?"

Sí. Al parecer, mi tercer juicio terminó siendo precisamente eso. Un futuro del que no pude escapar.

Miro aquel espacio en blanco, y cierro los ojos para retener las lágrimas que de nuevo se aglomeran en mis ojos, porque ahora mismo, lo único que quiero es ver a mi lobo.

—¿Elisse? —apura la errante coyote, pero sólo tengo fuerzas para asentir.

Hela levanta la mano y la abre sobre la superficie del espejo. Intenta sonreír, pero la tristeza en sus ojos le impide mentirme.

—Por favor, no permitas que a Tared le pase lo mismo que a Ilya... —le suplico en un susurro desesperanzador.

—*Lo siento tanto, Elisse* —dice Aradia desde las paredes—. *Aunque no lo creas, esto no es lo que yo hubiera querido. No de esta manera.*

No digo una palabra más. Levanto también mi mano, con el corazón hecho pedazos, y la uno con la de la necromante.

CAPÍTULO 107
ANTES DEL...

Es verdad.

Aradia nunca habría obligado a ese joven a firmar el libro.

Aradia, la hija de Diana, en toda su sabiduría, habría preferido dejarlo morir en ese paraíso antes de cometer semejante abominación.

Pero *tú*... tú que yaces enroscada en el sótano, revolcándote entre los huesos y la inmundicia como la más sucia de las alimañas... tú nunca fuiste la verdadera Aradia.

¿Cierto, hermana?

Así que, una vez que el Licántropo abre la puerta de mi celda y la cruza, una vez que la Bestia Revestida de Luna firma el contrato a través de la mano de la necromante, *sonríes*.

Y, finalmente, tras diecinueve años, sales por fin de esa habitación.

CAPÍTULO 108
DESPERTAR

Al abrir la puerta de mi celda, con lo primero que se encuentra el licántropo no es conmigo, sino con una costa. Un mar calmo, cubierto por una niebla que se extiende hacia el interior del océano.

El péndulo en su mano permanece lánguido, sin apuntar ya a ninguna parte, mientras que el cielo gris sacude sus sentidos. La arena oscura bajo sus botas busca arrebatarle el aliento, y el mecer de la hierba verde y tibia que crece más allá de las dunas se siente como energía estática en su interior.

El portal a sus espaldas desaparece, y un gemido bajo lo hace mirar a un costado, con las garras fuera, listas para luchar. Pero lo que ve lo confunde tanto que no logra reaccionar.

Le parece que es un joven. Un infante, más bien, cuyo sexo no puede distinguir con claridad. Está a unos metros de él y observa con profunda desolación el horizonte, con esa mirada de pupilas dilatadas que tantas veces ha visto ya en el brujo que tiene por amante.

Entonces comprende que aquella criatura no mira hacia el mar, sino que está teniendo una visión. Tan terrible, que se le han inundado los ojos de lágrimas.

Las aguas se revuelven a lo lejos, y el lobo devuelve la atención al mar.

La silueta oscura de un barco de madera comienza a abrirse paso en la cortina de niebla; un bote largo de remos cuya cabeza curva apunta hacia él.

De inmediato, se da cuenta de que algo ha cambiado.

Ahora, el viento helado revuelve las olas y la costa se cubre de escarcha. La hierba también se ha quedado atrapada bajo un manto de nieve, como si las estaciones hubiesen pasado en un parpadeo.

Y aquel niño ya no está a su lado.

Cuando el bote se acerca a la orilla, el lobo por fin distingue que los navegantes, a diferencia del chico, son todos blancos. Visten capas gruesas de pelo animal y cascos metálicos en sus cabezas. Están sucios y hambrientos, silenciosos como las olas que los llevan, después de un largo tiempo en el océano, hasta tierra firme y desconocida.

El líder de la embarcación baja de un salto. Es muy corpulento, y la piel de oso sobre su cuerpo todavía muestra costras de sangre congelada en los bordes. Se aproxima hacia el lobo, con cuidado, pero también con un hacha apretada en el puño.

Tared Miller retrocede, dispuesto a defenderse, pero un impulso de instinto le hace saber que hay alguien más a sus espaldas: un anciano erguido sobre la hierba congelada de la costa, con la piel morena y una cornamenta de caribú sobre los hombros como una armadura.

Hay otras personas detrás, pero a éstas ya no puede reconocerlas. Sólo sentirlas. Sabe que, tanto los tripulantes del barco como la tribu nativa que se acerca son errantes. *Atra-pasueños.*

El inmenso devorapieles arroja el hacha sobre la arena en señal de paz, pero el anciano da un paso hacia atrás de todas maneras.

Confundido, el hombre venido del mar no logra entender que aquel contemplasombras no lo está mirando a él, sino a lo que lleva en el fondo de su convoy de *berserkers*[49] y *skjaldmærs.*[50]

Son dos mujeres. Dos hermanas acuclilladas en la popa, de piel cetrina y ojos tan negros, tan dilatados, que casi no puede verse el fino iris rojo que los rodea. Una de ellas tiene los cabellos tan largos y gruesos que parecen serpientes blancas, mientras que los de su hermana menor todavía no han perdido el color de la noche. Y las dos, a pesar del frío tempestuoso, no necesitan llevar encima más que un par de túnicas oscuras.

En su inmensa sabiduría, el anciano nativo comprende que ellas no vienen del norte. Que no comparten el origen o la naturaleza de aquellos hombres y mujeres de cabellos rubios y barbas rojas quienes, al ser todos devorapieles, quizá ni siquiera se han dado cuenta de que cargan con ellas en su barco.

Sabe que son más... antiguas.

Así que no hay bienvenida. No hay furor ante el encuentro. Tan sólo da la media vuelta y se marcha con toda su tribu al interior de sus tierras.

---

[49] Guerreros vikingos que combatían semidesnudos, cubiertos de pieles y que, según ciertas sagas nórdicas, se transformaban en animales.

[50] Mujeres guerreras en la mitología nórdica.

El devorapieles que ha venido del otro lado del mar mira a su propia gente, confundido por una frialdad ajena a todo Atrapasueños. Pero al final, el barco atraca en la playa.

El lobo se pregunta furioso qué es lo que está presenciando. Qué demonios significa esta ilusión y por qué está siendo confundido con imágenes tan extrañas.

Sólo comienza a comprender cuando, súbitamente, es transportado a la orilla de otro inmenso cuerpo de agua, muy distinto al anterior, puesto que ya no detecta el penetrante aroma a agua salada.

Es un lago que, frente a él, comienza a resplandecer como si el amanecer se suscitara en su fondo.

El agua se desborda de gritos que no pertenecen al mundo de los vivos. Y después de aquella luz, el lago se torna negro, de una oscuridad tan profunda, tan pétrea, que pareciera como si un canal se hubiese abierto en el corazón de la tierra.

—La Grieta… —susurra al reconocer aquella leyenda que alguna vez le contase la Bestia Revestida de Luna.

Imágenes de violencia y locura se ciernen sobre su cabeza; miles de espectros escapando de aquel abismo, poseídos por el hambre y la sed de cuerpos humanos. Familias enteras arrasadas de formas tan atroces, tan monstruosas, que necesita apretar bien los párpados para apartar semejantes visiones.

Hasta que el súbito crepitar de una llama lo obliga a abrirlos de nuevo.

Ya no está frente a la Grieta. Ahora se halla sentado en el suelo, contemplando una hoguera como si él mismo hubiese sido convocado a la reunión que se suscita en torno a ella.

Humanos, errantes y brujos alrededor de las llamas, protegidos por un círculo de tótems: líderes y consejeros de Atrapasueños traídos no sólo desde el territorio de los Mánekenks[51] hasta el corazón de Kalaallit Nunaat,[52] sino también de los ahora numerosos asentamientos formados por los exploradores nórdicos, quienes trajeron a más errantes y sus familias del otro lado del mar. Todos convocados en un Gran Vínculo de errantes.

Bañado en sudor, el licántropo escucha la desesperación colectiva de las criaturas que se apiñan en aquel bosque de pinos.

"La Grieta se está expandiendo", dicen unos.

"Lo hemos intentado todo, con todas nuestras magias juntas, y no podemos cerrarla", claman otros.

Y entonces, una sola voz logra elevarse sobre el coro.

Desde el rincón más oscuro de los árboles, aquella mujer de serpientes blancas e iris apenas rojos se acerca despacio a la hoguera, seguida de cerca por su hermana, mientras los desconcertados errantes se abren a sus costados como el cauce de un río, como si apenas se hubiesen percatado de la presencia de aquellas dos brujas.

Les preguntan sus nombres y, al descubrirlos, reconocen que son remotos y lejanos, provenientes de una lengua que nadie en ese lugar había escuchado antes.

Después, la bruja mayor comienza a explicarles que si no han podido cerrar la Grieta es porque todo este tiempo han utilizado la magia de los humanos. De los errantes... Pero que lo que ellos necesitan para cerrar el velo entre este mundo y el otro es *una clase distinta de poder*.

Y entonces, comienza a hablarles de un dios.

---

[51] Extremo sudoriental de la Patagonia Argentina.

[52] Groenlandia.

Un dios tan antiguo que incluso las deidades de todas las épocas habían olvidado su existencia. Tan viejo que su nombre verdadero ya sólo podía ser pronunciado por las paredes de las cavernas donde habitaron los primeros humanos, abandonadas hace ya miles de años.

Les habla del dios Primigenio. Del primer espíritu que recibió culto de parte de la humanidad y que, a cambio, no sólo otorgó la magia como regalo, sino que también dio luz al plano medio: la franja entre el mundo de los vivos y la muerte definitiva cuando no había *nada* en medio de esas dos inmensidades.

Cuando, antes de las religiones y los espíritus, los humanos sólo podían dedicarse a morir.

La historia comienza a resonar en el corazón de todos los brujos reunidos en la hoguera, como si un recuerdo en su consciencia, en el linaje de su magia, hubiese vuelto a despertar.

Cuando le preguntan dónde se encuentra ese dios, ella les dice que debido al tiempo, al olvido y a la multiplicación de las civilizaciones, ahora hace mucho, mucho tiempo que está muerto.

"¿Pretenden revivir a un dios muerto?", exclama un contemplasombras, aquél que miró con desconfianza a las dos mujeres desde la orilla de la playa.

"No." Responde la mayor. "Pretendemos crear *uno nuevo.*"

Ella extiende la mano hacia la hoguera y les explica que si el dios Primigenio había parido la magia y el plano medio, el único que podría cerrar la Grieta sería uno que fuese capaz de destruir todo eso. Pero que crear a un dios tan abominable no se lograría con cantos, culto y ofrendas.

Se lograría con *sacrificio.*

Así que, primero, la apariencia de este nuevo dios debía ser edificada con los cuerpos de los brujos más poderosos de cada Atrapasueños presente en el Gran Vínculo. Después, su espíritu sería creado al unir la magia y las voluntades, los *corazones*, de todos aquellos hechiceros.

Y finalmente, para traerlo al mundo terrenal, tendrían que escoger a un brujo más. A alguien que estuviese dispuesto a renunciar a su ancestro y a su familia para convertirse en el portador del nuevo dios.

Es allí cuando todo el consejo gira la cabeza hacia el licántropo. Pero, a su costado, se encuentra de nuevo con aquel pequeño que vio en la playa, ahora convertido en un muchacho. Alguien que, al acercarse al fuego, resulta ser un contemplasombras cuyos ojos siguen siendo terriblemente tristes.

"Él, muchas primaveras atrás, predijo la apertura de la Grieta. Y él", dicen las brujas al Gran Vínculo, "debe ser el portador de este nuevo dios".

Ambas mujeres son cuestionadas durante toda la noche, envueltas en los gritos más desesperados y las lágrimas más copiosas. Pero al final, tanto el consejo de errantes como el joven contemplasombras aceptan la proposición.

—No...

El suspiro del licántropo parece funcionar como un hechizo porque, una vez más, es arrastrado a una pesadilla.

Sin poder evitarlo, se convierte en testigo de la creación del nuevo dios; el sacrificio de decenas de brujos cuyos cuerpos son arrojados uno a uno hacia la Grieta, desde el borde de un acantilado a orillas del lago.

Después, contempla al joven arrojarse por voluntad propia al plano medio como una Andrómeda encadenada, convirtiéndose también así en el primer ser vivo en cruzarlo.

Lo ve caer en la larga oscuridad y hundirse sobre los cadáveres. Lo ve levantarse, escuchar el clamor de los espíritus hambrientos a su alrededor, para luego erigir él mismo el altar de huesos, carne y corazones.

Y cuando pronuncia las palabras "soy tuyo", el dios nuevo *despierta*.

Tared Miller grita con profundo terror cuando una garra huesuda brota como un arpón de aquella masa de cadáveres. Se clava en el pecho del chico y, sin compasión, arranca a su ancestro del pecho de un solo golpe, para triturarlo delante de él.

Después, la transformación es tan cruel que el portador del trueno haría lo que fuese por no verla. Pero es incapaz de cerrar los ojos, así que no le queda más que ver cómo el nuevo dios destroza el cuerpo de aquel joven para convertirlo en una criatura hecha de cientos de huesos, órganos y corazones oscuros.

Lo ve emerger de la Grieta, delante de todos los humanos y errantes reunidos en torno al lago. Lo ve desgarrarla con su furia, sus manos y sus colmillos, cerrando así la gran puerta del mundo de los espíritus.

Y luego lo ve… *enloquecer*.

CAPÍTULO 109
EL MONSTRUO DE HUESO

Al poner las garras sobre la tierra, lo primero que hace el dios nuevo es exigir más sangre. Más poder.

Porque el dios nuevo ha sido creado a base de tanto dolor que no existe espíritu ni magia que sea capaz de satisfacer su apetito.

Y con el mismo horror que siente la nación de errantes a sus espaldas, el hombre lobo comprende que ese ser que habían traído a la vida con semejantes sacrificios no era un dios.

Era un monstruo.

Un ser que esas dos brujas de ojos rojos habían visto en un vaticinio, el cual las había llevado a subir a ese barco y cruzar el mundo en su búsqueda. Una *bestia* que, sin saberlo, aquellos cientos de Atrapasueños les habían ayudado a crear.

Pero pronto el licántropo descubre un grave error en la ambición de las hermanas, porque aun cuando ambas querían que ese espíritu terrible naciera, lo querían por razones muy diferentes.

La bruja mayor deseaba el poder de la criatura: dominarla bajo su yugo y así tener ella misma el control de todas las magias del mundo. Pero la menor, en cambio, veía a ese monstruo con la más absoluta de las adoraciones, como a una auténtica deidad. Y no iba a permitir que su hermana cometiese el sacrilegio de reducir su dios a un simple esclavo.

Cegada por un amor irracional y maldito, la idólatra ofrece a su dios monstruoso el último sacrificio que le falta para estar completo. Una cosa que, ella promete, tomará gustosa de su propia hermana mayor para ofrecérsela en un último ritual.

Y él... acepta.

En una secuencia de años que el lobo sólo logra percibir como una fracción de segundo, el dios famélico asola el continente en busca de la hechicera de serpientes blancas, devorando a su paso espíritus, brujos y ancestros por igual. Y su asedio es tan inmensurable que lo único que logra detenerlo, por un instante, es su llegada a la costa este del continente, la cual el portador del trueno reconoce como la playa donde, mil años después, se erigiría el faro de la isla de invierno.

El dios monstruo mira hacia el horizonte y se relame pensando en las apetitosas magias que le esperan al otro lado del mar. Y lo que queda del Gran Vínculo, sin saber que la bruja mayor también había confabulado para traer a tan terrible criatura a la vida, se reúne de nuevo, esta vez a su alrededor.

Ahora, ellos son tan escasos y hay tal luto en sus rostros que Tared Miller también puede sentir su agonía.

El contemplasombras que alguna vez desconfió de las hermanas ya no existe. Y, por lo tanto, no hay nadie quien cuestione el plan de la bruja mayor para destruir tanto a la criatura como a su sacerdotisa.

Así que ésta escoge un guerrero. Uno muy especial, aunque éste no tenga magia ni poder sobre los espíritus, y le otorga aquel don que con tanta desesperación buscaba arrebatarle el dios famélico.

De pronto, las llamas de la fogata estallan y ciegan al licántropo por un instante. Los gritos del fulgor de una gigantesca batalla lo aturden y le incitan a cubrirse, pero su cuerpo se mantiene inmóvil, de pie.

Y al despejarse las cenizas, contempla a sus pies al dios monstruo, quebrado e inmóvil, abierto en canal.

No sabe cómo han logrado vencerlo, pero lo que sí nota al instante es que su garra izquierda ha sido cercenada, mientras que debajo de los cientos de corazones que han dejado de latir se encuentra... *él*, el joven contemplasombras, ovillado como un polluelo dentro de un nido.

El guerrero bendecido por la bruja se arrodilla y lo saca con cuidado de la carcasa, sus ojos inundados de pena ante la mirada moribunda del muchacho, consumido casi en su totalidad por el monstruo.

—No... no lo dejes morir, te lo suplico... —ruega Tared Miller al hombre, pero, como si él mismo hubiese puesto su propio oído contra los labios del joven, éste comienza a susurrar una última premonición:

—Durante siglos, el espíritu del *dios falso* vagará en las tierras del Nuevo Mundo, *esperándome*. Porque en las nieves más frías y remotas del Viejo Mundo, aquél que él nunca pudo alcanzar, yo... *volveré* —dice—. No permitas que me... encuentre...

Y así, como si presenciase el marchitar de la más rara de todas las flores, el hermoso joven fallece en brazos del guerrero.

Un parpadeo más, y ahora el hombre lobo presencia cómo el cuerpo del contemplasombras es colocado de nuevo dentro de la carcasa del monstruo, para luego ser quemado junto con él hasta ser reducido a cenizas.

Tared Miller sabe que esto no es más que un recuerdo. Una historia ocurrida hace más de mil años, pero la desolación constriñe su corazón como si lo hubiese vivido en carne propia. Y su rabia no es menos intensa, y más cuando pronto vuelve a encontrarse con las dos brujas.

La mayor mira a la traidora, arrodillada delante de ella sobre el suelo de un bosque, incapaz de hacer frente a la poderosa magia de su hermana. El Gran Vínculo espera que la ejecute, y más ahora que ha recuperado su don, aquél que otorgó momentáneamente al guerrero para que éste pudiese derrotar al dios falso... Pero sabe que la muerte es una sentencia demasiado piadosa para criaturas como ellas.

Así que, en una muestra de la crueldad más inmensurable, lleva a la hechicera hacia un gran árbol gris, sembrado cerca de la costa donde el dios monstruo descubrió que había más magias al otro lado del océano. Ella toca la gran abertura del tronco, y ésta revela un pasaje al plano medio oculto entre los pliegues, el cual marca con su propia mano, convertida ahora en una larga garra.

Pero antes de ser arrojada al interior de aquella celda, la menor de las brujas lanza a su hermana una última maldición:

—*Que el mar se torne tempestad cada vez que pongas un pie en la arena. Que el viento azote cada vez que mires al horizonte* —dice ella con una sonrisa—. *Porque mientras yo esté en esta celda, tú te pudrirás a mi lado sobre la tierra. Y nunca, nunca podrás abandonar el Nuevo Mundo para ir en busca de mi dios.*

Furiosa por el maleficio, y a sabiendas de que gracias al don del regreso que tanto ella como su hermana poseían ésta renacería una y otra vez dentro de esa celda, la mujer de cabellos blancos cierra las puertas de la prisión, destruyendo el árbol con un movimiento de su muñeca.

Los siglos pasan en un suspiro, y como si esa bruja enterrada hubiese sido una fertilizada semilla, un bosque espinoso comienza a crecer a su alrededor. El plano medio se entremezcla con el humano y pronto todo termina devorado por un denso mar de niebla y endrinos.

Y allí, frente a esa inmensidad gris que Tared Miller reconoce como los dominios de Aradia, siente un tirón en la mano. Alza su garra y comprende que el péndulo se ha movido una vez más.

La cortina se despeja, y revela un bosque cubierto de nieve. El hombre lobo sigue la dirección del apuntador con la mirada y encuentra unas huellas en el suelo.

El repentino aullido del lobo en su interior lo obliga a echar a correr, a dejarse guiar por aquel péndulo con la desesperación de miles de generaciones sobre sus espaldas.

Las huellas, cada vez más caóticas, despiertan en él un miedo indescriptible cuando comienza a encontrar prendas de ropa tiradas a su paso: una chamarra gruesa. Zapatos pequeños. Ropa interior.

Y entonces, se detiene cuando por fin encuentra algo entre los árboles.

Parpadea una, dos y tres veces, falto de entendimiento. Porque lo que está delante de él, recostado boca abajo es... un niño.

Un niño inconsciente y con la piel desnuda, casi azul debido a la helada.

—¡Acércate más a *mi hijo* y te mato!

El devorapieles se sobresalta, porque aquel grito no ha salido de su propia garganta.

Hay un sujeto a su lado, alguien que sostiene un rifle de caza con manos temblorosas, un hombre al que le cuesta sólo un segundo identificar como aquél que tantas veces vio en la fotografía de su amante.

El corazón de Tared Miller baja a su estómago y golpea con furia las paredes de sus entrañas, pero entonces se paraliza cuando comprende que eso no es lo único que ha logrado reconocer.

Reconoce el sonido denso del agua y el crepitar del hielo a lo lejos. Reconoce el precipicio y el pico de la montaña que sobresale por encima del lago que se abre delante de él como un espejo.

Es su mirador. Su bosque. Su *Gran Lago*.

Contempla al infante tendido en la nieve y su latido se acelera nuevamente, porque no es la Bestia Revestida de Luna.

Ese niño tirado en la nieve es *él* mismo.

CAPÍTULO 110
EL LOBO CON LA PIEL DE TRUENO

—¡Te lo advierto, maldita loca!

El grito de Isaac Miller lo hace por fin mirar a donde apunta el péndulo: hacía mí.

Parada delante de su yo del pasado, el licántropo me reconoce como la mayor de las brujas hermanas, aquélla cuyo cabello blanco cae como un largo manojo de serpientes sobre mi espalda. Pero lo que le impide abalanzarse sobre mí para detener esta desquiciada visión es *la piel* que recubre mi cuerpo, desde el cuello hasta los pies.

Un manto brillante como una moneda recién forjada. Plateado como el más luminoso de los truenos.

El errante se sobresalta al escuchar un disparo, pero su padre ya no está allí.

Y ahora, el rifle humea entre sus propias manos.

—¿Sabes? Tu padre tenía exactamente esa misma expresión cuando vio esto hace más de veinte años, en este bosque —digo a la vez que alzo mis ojos rojos hacia él—. Primero, me disparó sin saber que el plomo de los humanos dejó de tener significado para mí hace mucho tiempo. Incluso, volvió a hacerlo cuando le dije que aquello no había sido una ilusión mía, sino un auténtico recuerdo. Pero no fue hasta que finalmente hice *esto* que él comenzó a... *creer.*

Y entonces, Tared Miller descubre que no sólo soy una bruja, sino también, *una loba.* No una errante, sino una trotapieles, puesto que el cuero comienza a desprenderse de mi cuerpo como si tuviese vida propia.

Y esa piel, ese gran don que alguna vez otorgué al guerrero del pasado y que el dios falso nunca pudo obtener de mí, se deposita por sí misma sobre su yo infantil. Con su nuevo portador.

Tal como hizo hace más de mil años.

Cuando el manto plateado se funde con el pequeño, el devorapieles por fin *recuerda.* Recuerda el calor de aquella piel de lobo que le hizo recuperar el color de sus labios, el salvajismo que se asentó dentro de su corazón como si una parte muy suya por fin hubiese vuelto a su lugar.

Y después escucha, con escalofriante claridad, el aullido del espíritu que retumba como un trueno dentro de su cuerpo infantil.

—¡BASTA, *ERICHTO*!

Ante su grito, dirijo la mirada hacia él.

—Ah, ¡mi nombre! —exclamo, complacida al escucharlo de sus labios—. ¡Cuánto ha olvidado el mundo mi nombre! ¡Hace cuántos imperios que nadie temblaba ante las sílabas que componen semejante palabra de poder! El gran Ovidio fue el primero en clamar mi existencia en la antigua Roma, luego, Lucano reveló que el alcance de mi brujería era tan grande que los mismísimos dioses del Olimpo me temían. Después, Dante inmortalizó la trascendencia de mi magia en el noveno círculo del infierno.

"Pero, luego... el mundo se atrevió a olvidarme, ¡a olvidarme, aun cuando yo, envestida en esa misma piel que ahora portas, amamanté a Rómulo y Remo a orillas del río Tíber! ¡Aun cuando yo fui la pitonisa más poderosa del Viejo Mundo! Mi existencia fue tan relegada que pasé siglos sin escuchar que un solo brujo me evocase...

Alzo los brazos y le muestro a mi creación mi cuerpo sangrante y despellejado.

—Y ahora —continúo—, después de mil años tú, *hijo mío*, vuelves a pronunciar mi nombre.

—No —su voz rota suena como una dulce melodía que mis oídos de madre se mueren por consolar—. No es...

—¿Posible? —digo con una sonrisa—. Dime, ¿alguna vez te preguntaste por qué eras capaz de hacer cosas que, para un devorapieles parecerían... *antinaturales*? ¿Alguna vez te preguntaste por qué aquella noche tu ancestro *te abandonó*?

El recuerdo surca su memoria. Una noche de truenos en el pantano, en las tierras del Loa de la Muerte.

Él suelta el rifle y retrocede, aterrorizado al revivir en carne propia el dolor de sentir cómo el lobo que siempre creyó suyo se arrancaba de sus huesos.

—Creíste que la Bestia Revestida de Luna lo hacía posible con su magia, ¿cierto? Siempre creíste que su inmenso *amor* por ti lo podía lograr todo, ¿verdad? —pregunto con un potente veneno disfrazado bajo la dulzura de mi voz—. No. Siempre fui *yo*. Mi piel. Mi espíritu. Los trazos de mi magia... Y por eso, ha llegado el momento de que por fin sepas la verdad.

Mi cuerpo despellejado crea un sendero escarlata cuando comienzo a acercarme.

Y él, petrificado como un guerrero ante Medusa, no se mueve un solo centímetro de su lugar.

—Hace más de mil años, recibimos de aquel contemplasombras moribundo la primera parte de una premonición. Un vaticinio terrible en el que se nos advertía que el dios falso renacería en el Viejo Mundo —comienzo—. Pero apenas dos décadas atrás, recibí la segunda parte de esa profecía: que *tú*, en este nuevo continente, *habías regresado*. Porque al haberte colocado mi piel hace mil años, al haberte tocado con la magia de la Mano Izquierda, también te había transmitido el don del *regreso* —alzo las manos hacia su rostro—. No eras mi carne, y tampoco eras un brujo como tal, así que habías renacido de una simple humana. Pero aun así, eras *mío*. *Mi hijo. Mi creación.* El único vínculo que había establecido con un ser vivo sobre la tierra, así que sólo tenía qué encontrarte una vez más...

El licántropo destroza su parálisis al alejarse bruscamente de mi tacto. Bajo mis puños a los costados, desagradada por su rechazo.

—Guiada por mis visiones, logré descubrirte a la orilla de uno de los lagos donde alguna vez se abrió la Gran Grieta Resplandeciente —continúo—, pero ahora convertido en la criatura más peculiar de tu especie: un errante sin ancestro. Un devorapieles, sí, pero cuyo cuerpo no era más que una vasija, un recipiente a la espera de ser llenado por aquel espíritu que tú bautizarías más tarde como...

—Lobo Piel de Trueno.

Él mira a su yo infantil, aún desnudo sobre la nieve, y después hacia el rifle tirado a sus pies, quizá pensando en la absurda posibilidad de dispararme, tal como hizo Isaac Miller.

—Le expliqué a tu padre que, muy pronto, yo despertaría tres magias. Tres pactos para prepararnos para la llegada del dios falso —continúo—. Pero que si quería evitar que su hijo se enfrentase a su destino como guerrero, lo único que tenía qué hacer era…

—Encontrar a Elisse.

Las garras del lobo se entierran contra las palmas de sus propias manos.

—Negándose a reconocer la verdad de todo lo que en persona había atestiguado, tu padre te apartó de mí y te llevó de vuelta a tu hogar, a esa familia *falsa*, a sabiendas de que lo que cargaba entre sus brazos ya no era su hijo.

Más recuerdos se aglomeran en el licántropo. Imágenes de ese enojo y esa rabia infantil que pronto mutó en violencia pura. Y también, recuerda mis ojos rojos rondando su casa y el bosque, atormentando a su padre como dos bolas de fuego en la noche.

Y poco tiempo después, lo ve partir. Abandonar a su hermano y a su madre para dejarlos solos con la criatura en la que él, sin saberlo, se había convertido.

Algo dentro del guerrero se rompe con la fuerza de mil terremotos.

Esa identidad que tantos años había forjado, ese carácter, esa integridad y todo, absolutamente todo lo que le daba certeza de quién era él se resquebraja en pedazos.

Él mira la punta de mis pies desgarrados. No necesita preguntarme nada. Es mi hijo. Sé perfectamente lo que está pensando.

—¿Quieres saber cómo es que tu padre logró encontrar al portador del dios falso? Pues de la misma forma que tú has dado conmigo —digo, para luego apuntar hacia el péndulo—. Porque yo le revelé *su nombre verdadero*.

—¡SU NOMBRE ES ELISSE!

Retrocedo ante la furia de mi criatura, cuyos colmillos han vuelto a asomarse en su boca humana.

—Tanto tiempo buscando mi nombre verdadero y tú nunca te preguntaste cuál era el suyo —susurro con decepción—. *Elisse* es sólo el nombre que tu padre alguna vez le dio como un acto de absurda ternura. Pero tú y yo sabemos, hijo mío, que su nombre verdadero es *Luna de Hueso*.

Luna de Hueso.

Luna de Hueso.

El nombre repiquetea en la memoria ancestral del lobo.

—No soy tu hijo —dice con los colmillos tensos—. No soy nada tuyo, maldita bruja...

Su renuencia hace florecer una sonrisa en mis labios.

—Isaac Miller era un hombre de corazón débil. Alguien que no merecía haber engendrado a un ser como tú. Y es por eso que, cuando finalmente encontró a Luna de Hueso entre la nieve del Viejo Continente, renacido como un bebé diminuto e indefenso, lo llevó a un monasterio en el corazón del Himalaya para que yo nunca pudiese encontrarlo. Y esa debilidad, esa blandura, fue lo que al final terminó con él...

Tared Miller levanta despacio la mirada. Y aunque sé muy bien que su primer instinto sería acusarme de la muerte de su padre, pregunta algo mucho más inteligente:

—¿Dónde está *Canidia*?

Como si pronunciar el nombre de mi hermana menor hubiese roto un hechizo, los recuerdos por fin se desvanecen. El bosque nevado desaparece y deja ver el sitio donde verdaderamente estamos: la celda ovalada bajo el cruce de caminos, rodeados de las columnas vertebrales de aquella bruja que estuvo encerrada aquí durante más de mil años.

Mi hijo también puede verme a plenitud, despojada de mi magia, atada a las raíces de la terrible prisión que alguna vez creé para Canidia.

—Cuando Aradia decidió instalar su aquelarre en el bosque de endrinos, no sentí ningún temor —digo—. Yo había destruido el árbol con el portal, y la celda de mi hermana fue conjurada para ser imperceptible, así que no había manera en la que supiese que ella estaba aquí, bajo el cruce de caminos —apunto hacia la ventana de la celda, marcada con mis cinco largas garras—. Pero con lo que no contaba es que la casa en la niebla, construida por los demonios goéticos traídos del Viejo Mundo, crearía *una puerta* —digo, y señalo el sitio por donde mi hijo ha entrado, el cual ha vuelto a aparecer a sus espaldas.

Y sé muy bien que, dentro de su cabeza, resuenan con claridad aquellas palabras que alguna vez el perpetuasangre Sammuel le dijo:

"Los portales, tal como los conocemos, existen desde hace siglos. A veces se mueven un poco de lugar, tal vez porque al inicio eran grietas en el suelo y luego adoptaron la forma de ventanas o puertas cuando se construyó sobre ellos, pero siempre han permanecido en el mismo lugar."

La verdad lo aplasta con tanta fuerza que lo obliga a encorvarse. Su mirada se abre, sus manos tiemblan enroscadas en puños...

—La noche en la que tu padre debía encontrarme en el cruce de caminos para entregarme a Luna de Hueso, ofrecí la vida de Aradia a cambio de la lealtad de los ángeles —continúo, insensible ante su reacción de horror—. Pero cuando él llegó con los brazos vacíos, supe que había sido traicionada una vez más...

—No —susurra, como si deseara que sus palabras fuesen un hechizo que pudiera cambiar la verdad.

—Liberada por el demonio Asmoday, Canidia no sólo me encerró en esta prisión, sino que también *asesinó a tu padre* y le arrancó la mano izquierda a la hija de Diana. La disfrazó bajo su pecho con el sigilo de Dee para apropiarse de su magia y su esencia, y luego engañó al Culto a la Grieta Resplandeciente durante casi veinte años haciéndose pasar por la antigua Aradia, ¡aguardando en ese sótano hasta que este día finalmente llegara!

—¡No! —grita, tan desesperado que la tierra cae del techo como la lluvia.

—Incluso tuvo la osadía de manipular al consorte de la Maligna para enviar aquella postal. Para asegurarse de que el portador de Luna de Hueso volviese al Nuevo Mundo por su cuenta —recuerdo con amargura—. Y yo no habría tenido fuerzas para sobrevivir a esta prisión, a esta locura, de no ser porque, el día en el que fui encerrada en este sitio, recibí la tercera y última parte de la premonición.

Apunto de nuevo hacia la puerta.

—Cuando la tercera magia cayese, *tú abrirías esa puerta*. Tú entrarías a esta celda, y *resucitarías* con una nueva consciencia cuando por fin te enteraras de la verdad.

—¡Es mentira, todo lo que estás diciendo es mentira!

—¡El Señor del Sabbath ha fallado! —grito, más fuerte que él—, y ahora, la Bestia Revestida de Luna se ha vuelto a unir con su portador. Y aunque éste se ha resistido por un largo tiempo a su dominio, ¡acaba de entregarle su alma a mi hermana!

Tared Miller se abalanza sobre mí, pero con sólo tocarme, el lobo en su interior aúlla tan alto que tiene que llevarse las garras a los oídos.

—¡¿Es que no lo comprendes?! —exclamo, incrédula ante su terquedad—, ¡¿es que acaso el guerrero que fuiste hace mil años ha sido derrotado por la más insulsa de las lujurias?! Si no me liberas, si no me permites recuperar mi magia para detener *juntos* a Luna de Hueso, ¡él devorará a cada brujo, a cada ancestro y a cada dios de esta…!

Pero el lobo no me escucha.

Nunca me vuelve a escuchar. Porque en un segundo, rodea con sus garras mi garganta.

Enloquecido por la cólera, arranca mi cuerpo de las raíces y me aplasta contra la pared. Pongo mis manos alrededor de sus muñecas para hacerle ver de nuevo el horror que Luna de Hueso despertó en el pasado, y también intento mostrarle lo que ocurrirá si acaso el mundo presencia el renacimiento del dios falso, una vez más.

Pero me basta contemplar esos ojos azules, ahora llenos de lágrimas, para comprender que a este lobo hombre, a Tared Miller, *no le importa ese mundo.*

No le importa su pasado. Ni la magia. Ni el plano de los hombres o los espíritus.

Porque, al igual que mi hermana, él también idolatra con todo su ser a ese dios.

La primera de las vértebras de mi cuello se quiebra, y el aire abandona mis pulmones. La vida se escapa a través de cada raíz, cada roca, cada columna volcada a todo lo largo de la celda.

Bajo las manos de mi creación, nuestro vínculo se corta como el hilo de la más cruel de las Moiras. Y con el último de mis suspiros, del aliento de la milenaria bruja Erichto… comienza el fin de todas las magias.

CAPÍTULO 111
EL TRIUNFO DE LA LUNA

De inmediato, sé que he cometido un error.

Porque en cuanto trazo la última letra de mi nombre a través de la mano de Hela, mi alma revienta el espejo de obsidiana al ser arrastrada por Aradia. Pero al depositarla de nuevo dentro de mi cuerpo, la sensación de miles de cadenas se cierne sobre mi consciencia.

—¿Ma... dre? —musita Hela al desplomarme a un lado de la silla, pálido e inmóvil.

—¡Elisse! —Hoffman se lanza hacia mí y agita mis hombros para intentar hacerme reaccionar—. Miller lo ha logrado, ¡los cabrones se están haciendo polvo!

Sí. Escucho a los ángeles *morir*, sus trompetas desvanecerse como un eco perdido en algún sitio remoto de la tierra.

Pero ellos no son lo único que se silencia.

Las detonaciones. Los gritos, los gemidos de los demonios y los rugidos. Todo cesa en un frío desconocido y terrible que comienza a colarse bajo mi piel.

Después, lo único que retumba es la voz de Aradia:

—*Erichto por fin ha sido asesinada* —anuncia—. *¡Mi exilio ha terminado!*

Y entonces, siento cómo la bruja sale del sótano para abrirse paso por la casa. Y en vez de subir por las escaleras hasta el segundo piso, atraviesa el suelo como un proyectil para llegar directamente hasta acá.

Intento ordenar mis pensamientos, descifrar qué es este miedo inexplicable que infecta todo mi cuerpo cual Martillo, pero es como si mis emociones también hubiesen sido inmovilizadas. Como si el Merkavah hubiese crecido dentro de mi pecho.

Como si, en vez de haberme devuelto a mi cuerpo, la Madre de las brujas me hubiese metido en una prisión.

Abalanzándose como una cobra furiosa, ella destroza de una embestida lo que queda del hueco de la trampilla para luego dirigirse despacio hacia acá. Muy despacio. Tanto, que la piel de su cuerpo comienza a *desprenderse*.

Mi hermana corre a arrodillarse a mi lado, presa de mi propio temor cuando la mujer bajo la carcasa se revela y repta desnuda hacia nosotros, hasta ponerse de pie. Tiene el cabello largo y negro, la piel cetrina como la ceniza de una hoguera y unos ojos terribles.

Rojos. Verdaderamente *malignos*.

—¿Quién…? ¡¿Quién demonios eres tú?!

Johanna gira la cabeza ante el grito de la necromante.

—¿Qué has dicho? —pregunta la errante.

Hela retrocede, y un temblor se apodera de todo su cuerpo.

—*No es mi Madre* —gime—. ¡Esa mujer no es Aradia!

Con una sacudida de sus brazos, la bruja lanza a Johanna y a Hoffman por los aires, estrellándolos contra las paredes. Los demonios de Inanna brotan de los muros y del suelo para inmovilizarlos tanto a ellos como a los niños, quienes gritan aterrorizados en un rincón.

—¡Aléjate de Elisse, hija de puta! —ruge Hoffman a todo pulmón cuando la mujer da un paso hacia mí.

Pero Hela se interpone entre nosotros, con su athame empuñado como una espada.

—¿Quién eres? —grita—. ¡Dime quién eres y qué has hecho con...! —pierde el aliento en un segundo. Y luego, baja lentamente la mirada hacia su propio vientre.

Y allí, encuentra el destello de una punta de metal que brilla de un rojo carmesí.

—¿I-Ilya? —murmura al mirar sobre su hombro. Hacia el hombre que acaba de cruzar su vientre de lado a lado con el largo athame de Inanna.

—Perdóneme, mi Señora... —dice él con los ojos inundados de lágrimas.

El grito que desesperadamente quiero soltar de mi garganta muere dentro de mí cuando él retuerce el arma y la extrae de un solo y brutal movimiento.

—¡NOOOOO!

El horror de Johanna no evita que Hela se desplome ni que su sangre salpique los pies de la bruja monstruosa. Ilya suelta el athame y gira hacia mí.

—¡No, no, no, suéltalo, cabrón! —exclama Hoffman, más desesperado que nunca.

Sin poder hacer nada para evitarlo, el errante demonio me levanta en brazos, despojándome de la piel de Raxnal, y me lleva delante del ventanal como una ofrenda para la luna llena que con su resplandor ilumina la noche.

Inanna, Caligo y Hela yacen delante de mí, dispuestas las tres dentro del símbolo de la Goetia en el suelo, su sangre y sus vidas vertidas sobre el grabado como un último ritual.

Cuando la bruja impostora se acerca, la luz azul revela la mano momificada que yace cosida en su pecho, justo donde se supone que estaba el sigilo de Dee. Y al ver que en su dedo anular está el anillo salomónico, por fin comprendo que lo que Inanna vio dentro de ese sarcófago en el Paraíso, aquello tan terrible que la hizo gritar…, fue el cuerpo de la verdadera Aradia.

—Hace diecinueve años, mi hermana tuvo una visión sobre esta noche —dice la falsa bruja, inclinándose a mí para acariciarme la mejilla—. Lo que nunca supo, es que yo también tuve la mía.

Ella extiende su otra mano y me muestra la ajada fotografía de mi padre.

—Ya no hay razón para ocultarnos del mundo, mi hermoso *dios astado* —me dice con una ternura terrible—. Ya no hay razón para mantener este lugar en la niebla.

De pronto, un crujido demoledor sacude el suelo, y los muros y el techo se agrietan como si la casa entera hubiese dado un salto.

Un poste de luz atraviesa el piso como una lanza y el cableado eléctrico revienta contra las vigas, mientras que la pared del ventanal, ya debilitada, se parte en pedazos y se derrumba como la cortina de un telón.

El aire se llena de gritos, de voces confundidas que no pertenecen a ninguno de los presentes, mientras que, a lo lejos, el bosque de endrinos se mezcla con los techos antiguos del pueblo de Salem.

La bruja impostora ha colapsado el plano medio que ocultaba el bosque y la casa en la niebla.

Y, como una maldita bomba, *lo ha dejado aparecer en el plano humano.*

Quiero gritar con todas mis fuerzas. Quiero alzar mi mano de hueso y rasgar el cuello de la desgraciada que, en un parpadeo, lo ha cambiado todo para siempre.

Pero no puedo hacer más que verla inclinarse hacia mí.

En cuanto su mano cetrina toca mi pecho, soy consumido por visiones de una guerra antigua. De dos mundos y dos hermanas monstruosas. De un dios terrible y un hombre con un bebé que no era el suyo.

Y, finalmente, de un lobo y un brujo que jamás debieron amarse. Ni en esta vida ni en ninguna.

De pronto, empiezo a sentir el latido de todos y cada uno de los corazones que yacen dentro de mi cuerpo. Y las voces, esas múltiples voces llenas de dolor y rabia que tanto me atormentaron por fin cobran significado.

Y, con el dolor más grande que he sentido jamás, comienzo a olvidarlo *todo*.

Olvido a mi maestro. Tíbet. India. Nueva Orleans.

Olvido el rostro de Louisa. El amor de mamá Tallulah.

Olvido a mis hermanos. A Hoffman.

Olvido a Tared.

Pero, por sobre todas las cosas, me olvido de mí mismo.

Nunca hubo un *yo*. Nunca fui el hijo de nadie. Nunca fui más que la promesa de una maldad atroz. Porque el Elisse que siempre creí que fui resultó ser sólo la mitad de algo que ahora está...

Completo.

Canidia pasa su pulgar por mi mejilla, sorprendida al ver que, a pesar de su dominio, soy capaz de derramar una última lágrima.

—Ya estás listo —finaliza—. Es hora de despertar al mundo de su sueño.

Porque tú y yo somos...

Siempre fuimos.

Y siempre seremos.

Así, con mi voluntad atrapada bajo el yugo de la bruja, Luna de Hueso, *el monstruo dentro de mí*, es por fin liberado.

CAPÍTULO 112
EL DIOS DE LOS BRUJOS

TARED MILLER

En cuanto el suelo de la celda se parte para revelar un vacío inmenso debajo, mi primer instinto es arrojar el cadáver de Erichto al fondo de la oscuridad con un puntapié.

Pero no me quedo a ver cómo el abismo se la traga. No me quedo a drenar la frustración que se cierne sobre mí. Tan sólo doy la media vuelta y maldigo una y mil veces al espíritu que, ahora sé, parasita dentro de mí.

Lobo Piel de Trueno. Mi ancestro. Mi contraparte, aquel ser que honré con cada parte de mí no es más que un maldito monstruo.

Mi padre nunca me abandonó y mi hermano me odió toda la vida por algo que ni siquiera había sido mi culpa. Pero lo peor es que *no me importa nada de eso.*

No me importa el pasado, ni mi identidad, y ni siquiera Lobo Piel de Trueno. No me importa mi legado ni mi propósito.

Sólo me importa salvar a Elisse.

Así que, antes de que el agujero de la celda me lleve a mí también, introduzco la llave en la cerradura. Abro la puerta con un movimiento y me encuentro de vuelta en el pasillo.

Las paredes están arqueadas, los cuerpos de los tramperos aplastados como si algo muy grande se hubiese abierto paso sobre ellos.

Me echo a correr hacia la escalera, pero un tumulto de gritos me hace detenerme frente a la puerta derribada de la entrada.

Luces policiales destellan, construcciones de ladrillo rojo se asoman entre los árboles, patrullas van de un lado a otro detrás de la primera línea de endrinos.

Y la calle. Veo una maldita calle con transeúntes detrás.

—¿Pero qué dem...?

—¡Tared!

El grito de Julien me devuelve por completo a este mundo.

A toda prisa llego al segundo piso y encuentro a mi gente y la de Lía en el pasillo, aún *vivos*, reunidos en torno al cabrón de Benjamin Lander, a quien por fin han sometido.

Todas sus extremidades han sido cercenadas y arrojadas a los pies de Irina, quien sostiene un hacha entre las manos, lista para asestar el golpe final.

—Hemos vencido —suspira Lía, agotada—, todo ter...

Lander lanza una carcajada. Su parte angelical se pudre y se deshace en cenizas vidriosas, pero él, su mitad humana, sonríe como un desquiciado.

—¿Vencido? —se mofa—. Tú sabes quién está allá arriba, ¿verdad, cachorrito? —me dice.

Hacia el fondo del pasillo encuentro el inmenso agujero que lo atraviesa de arriba abajo. Justo donde estaba la trampilla del ático.

La sangre me golpea las sienes sin tregua.

—Habrán acabado con mi estirpe, ¡pero nosotros ya le hemos contado al mundo la verdad! —exclama el maldito—, ¡la humanidad entera se encargará de aniquilarlos *a todos*!

Irina levanta el hacha que empuña entre sus manos, pero no me quedo a ver cómo lo ejecuta.

Cruzo el pasillo, enloquecido, completamente fuera de mis cabales. Subo de un salto al tercer piso, y siento como si me arrancasen los huesos del cuerpo al encontrar el rastro de piel de serpiente que se alarga hasta la puerta del ático puesta nuevamente en el marco, aquélla que yo mismo había arrancado para usarla de barrera y proteger a Elisse y a Inanna.

La reviento de una embestida, dispuesto a entrar allí y luchar con lo que sea, con lo que haga falta. Pero al comprobar lo que ocurre dentro de aquella recámara, lo único que logro hacer es perder el aliento.

—¿Elisse?

Pero él no se inmuta ante la angustia de mi llamado.

Está parado al fondo del cuarto, dándome la espalda para mirar hacia el amanecer dorado que se levanta sobre el horizonte.

Escucho un gemido, y encuentro a Johanna agazapada en una esquina del ático, con los niños de Irina apretujados entre sus brazos. Hoffman está delante de ellos. Inmóvil. Apuntando su arma directamente hacia mi Elisse.

El exagente susurra algo en voz tan baja que apenas puedo escucharlo:

—Se las ha devorado —dice, mientras derrama gruesas y abundantes lágrimas—. *A todas…*

El sudor me cubre la piel cuando miro hacia el suelo, al símbolo grabado en la madera, y encuentro *marcas*. Charcos, ríos, rastros de cuerpos que fueron arrastrados.

Y, más allá, en otra esquina de la habitación, la piel de Ilya permanece *vacía* como una carcasa.

—No... —musito—. ¡No! ¡NO, DIOS MÍO, NO!

Ante mi grito, *él* por fin levanta la cabeza. Y luego comienza a girar lentamente hacia nosotros.

Mis piernas flaquean. La sangre abandona mi cuerpo. Porque esa *cosa* que está allá, parada delante de la luna llena, *ya no es Elisse*.

Su piel y su cabello ahora son blancos, mientras que sus hermosos ojos verdes han desaparecido para dar paso a unos de un rojo similar al de la sangre que le chorrea desde las comisuras de sus labios y hasta su pecho.

Y entre sus manos, largas y huesudas, yace la cabeza de Canidia, sus ojos arrancados de sus cuencas y el resto de su cuerpo despedazado a sus pies.

Me dejo caer de rodillas, como si una vez más estuviese frente a la pila de cadáveres donde alguna vez se engendró el monstruo de hueso.

—Elisse... —gimoteo como un animal herido—, no, ¡Elisse!

Al escucharme, la criatura me muestra los largos colmillos ocultos tras su sonrisa sangrienta.

—¿*Elisse*? —dice, y su risa burlona hace aullar al lobo... no, al *monstruo dentro de mí*—. ¿Acaso no sabías ya mi nombre verdadero?

Súbitamente, siento las manos temblorosas de Nashua y Julien sobre mí, pero el peso de mi horror es tan inmenso que no logran moverme un solo centímetro.

Él deja caer la cabeza de la bruja al vacío y comienza a acercarse hacia nosotros. Su túnica negra se arrastra, sus pies blancos se manchan con la sangre que pisa a su paso. Se detiene, justo en el centro del símbolo en el suelo, y deja caer un anillo de oro que, poco a poco va perdiendo su resplandor.

Comus Bayou y la Espiral del Norte se aglomeran tras de mí, exhalando alaridos matizados de horror y confusión.

Me lanzo hacia el monstruo, pero una pared invisible me impide dar un paso más.

Y aunque gruño, me revuelvo y rasguño con los últimos vestigios de fuerza que me resta, soy incapaz de franquear la barrera.

—¡Maldito, maldito hijo de puta! —grito a todo pulmón, nublado por la desesperación—. *Él* te vencerá de nuevo, ¡ELISSE ACABARÁ CONTIGO, CABRÓN! —exclamo, golpeando una y otra vez aquel muro con mis puños.

Mi familia se une a mi locura con garras, colmillos y balas. Pero nada es capaz de hacerle siquiera una pequeña fisura a la pared.

—Sí —dice aquella cosa, ensuciando la preciada lengua de mi Elisse con sus voces monstruosas—. Hace mil años fui derrotado por la voluntad de un mortal. Por un corazón que dejé latir por encima de todas las magias que alguna vez devoré...

Él lleva su garra izquierda hacia su pecho. Y como si fuese una pared de barro fresco lo desgarra de arriba abajo para revelar aquellos corazones podridos que palpitan sin cesar alrededor de la jodida espada filosofal.

Introduce la mano entre los músculos, y revuelve hasta sacar uno de ellos. Un corazón rojo y vibrante. Joven y vivo.

El mío se desborda de horror. Porque ése es *el corazón de Elisse*.

—Pero esta vez, no volveré a cometer el mismo error —dice, y lo mira palpitar entre sus dedos.

—¡NOOOOO!

Ante mi grito, la bestia cierra el puño y *lo destroza*.

Me quedo inmóvil un segundo que parece eterno, hasta que por fin grito, aúllo hasta desgarrarme por dentro, salpico todo con la sangre que comienza a manar de mis puños que, por fin, logran agrietar la barrera.

Él cierra los ojos, y sonríe cuando la sangre del corazón de Elisse se desliza por su mano hasta su codo. Levanta la cabeza, y su cornamenta plateada emerge de nuevo desde sus sienes.

El zumbido de un helicóptero me ensordece, luces brillantes me enceguecen, reflectores apuntan directamente hacia nosotros.

Así, en un instante, la humanidad entera observa cómo *él* se gira y sonríe al horizonte. Hacia donde reposa la costa de Salem.

—Una vez, la Gran Grieta se abrió sobre la tierra, naciendo como un portal tan débil que bastó un movimiento de mi garra para destrozarlo —dice—. Así que ahora abriré uno tan infinito, tan inalcanzable, que ninguna criatura podrá volver a escapar de ella.

Y entonces, *él* saca la espada filosofal de su cuerpo para apuntar hacia el cielo. Y de un solo movimiento, *lo rasga*.

Una nueva Grieta Resplandeciente se abre en lo alto, entre las estrellas de la mañana. Una grieta que crece y crece como si el firmamento entero se partiese por la mitad.

Después, su brillo se apaga, y la escasa luz del amanecer es tragada por la inmensa oscuridad del plano medio.

El monstruo dirige la mirada hacia mí.

—No te lamentes, guerrero —me dice—. Muy pronto volveremos a vernos, porque tú... tú aún tienes mi piel.

Él abre los brazos a los costados y comienza a elevarse

hacia el cielo. Hacia la grieta que se expande sobre el techo de la tierra.

Y con esto, Elisse desaparece de mi vista, perdiéndose para siempre en la oscuridad.

FIN DEL LIBRO TERCERO

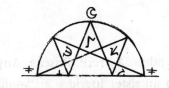

AGRADECIMIENTOS

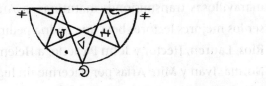

Antes de empezar, una disculpa por la torpeza de estos agradecimientos. Para mí, llegar hasta aquí siempre es motivo de sentimientos contradictorios. Por una parte, significa que logré ponerle punto final a un libro, pero, por otra, mi cerebro está tan frito que ya sólo le quedan dos neuronas vivas para escribir estas páginas.

Pero si algo tengo bien claro es que, sin todas aquellas personas que me acompañaron incansablemente a lo largo de los tres años que significó escribir *Luna de Hueso*, jamás lo habría logrado. Jamás habría dejado de ser esa chica que nunca terminaba sus fanfics para convertirme en la escritora con rumbo a empezar su quinto libro.

Así que, primero y por siempre, quiero agradecer a mi familia, por su apoyo incondicional, por siempre tener tiempo para mí aunque ustedes mismos estuvieran cansados, por hacerme saber que, sin importar lo que pasara, siempre iban a estar orgullosos de mí.

Pero, especialmente, gracias a Danny por haber llegado a nuestras vidas a llenarlas de alegría.

A mis amigos, a Alesth, por siempre ser una parte esencial de esta Nación. A la talentosa Mara, por ser esa amiga que creí que nunca tendría. A Trece, Priscila, Any Cemar, Mike, Alex y Denisse, a mi sister Ingrid y a Claudia Belmontes, a quien siempre es una alegría volver a toparme. A Eng por sus maravillosas transmisiones matutinas, a Ángel y Drew, por ser los mejores lectores beta que podría pedir. A Dianita, Julia Rios, Lauren, Héctor y John Picaccio, a Helena Segovia, Mary, Norma, Iván y Mire Arias por hacerme un lugar en su familia, a Karen Padilla. A Joseph por las asombrosas fotografías.

A mis amigos y colegas escritores, a la tía Luna, a Clau, a Pedro, Toño Malpica, Félix, Jorge Galán y Bef por la hermosa compañía en cada feria.

A mi increíble editor, José Manuel, por tener la férrea voluntad de no bloquearme por estarle enviando mensajes un domingo a la una de la mañana mientras tenía una crisis de escritura. A Matthew y The Mages Lantern, por el impulso que le dieron a esta historia. A todo el equipo de Océano México, que me tuvieron una paciencia titánica con la entrega de este libro. A Guadalupe Ordaz, por su inmensa disposición para que *Luna de Hueso* quedase tal como yo quería, a mi querida Rosie, quien siempre me hace sentir segura a donde quiera que vaya, a Rogelio por su confianza, a Ismael y Lupita Reyes por su colaboración. También, un agradecimiento especial a todo el equipo de la agencia Antonia Kerrigan, por ver el potencial de mi trabajo.

También, muchísimas gracias a todos aquellos que hicieron posible que me reuniera con mis lectores en el sur del continente. Mil gracias, Romina, eres un ejército de una sola persona y lo estás haciendo increíble. Gracias, Oswaldo, por la amistad, el espíritu alto y el gran trabajo que haces, a mis dos queridas Ingrid, a los equipos imparables de Océano Argentina, Panamá, Colombia, Perú y Uruguay. Pero en especial, muchísimas gracias a Océano Ecuador, a Tamara y Denisse, a Steven, Mafer y la adorable Nikki, a todo el maravilloso equipo de La Madriguera, quienes pusieron el primer peldaño de lo que fue un asombroso tour por Latinoamérica. A todos los blogueros, booktubers, booktokers y bookstagramers que conocí durante esta increíble experiencia.

A mis lectores asiduos, a quienes se toman un tiempo para hacer memes, clubs de lectura y páginas de fans. Gracias a todos ustedes que conforman mi Nación, a quienes van llegando y a quienes tienen años aquí. Todavía nos queda un poco más de camino qué recorrer. Gracias, gracias por tanto.

ÍNDICE

SEGUNDA FASE
UN MONSTRUO NUEVO

TERCERA FASE
UN MONSTRUO CRECIENTE

CUARTA FASE
UN MONSTRUO COMPLETO

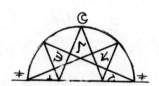

Esta obra se imprimió y encuadernó
en el mes de octubre de 2023, en los talleres
de Impregráfica Digital, S.A. de C.V.
Av. Coyoacán 100-D, Col. Del Valle Norte,
C.P. 03103, Benito Juárez, Ciudad de México.

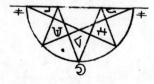

Esta obra se imprimió y encuadernó
en el mes de octubre de 2023, en los talleres
de Impresora Tauro, S.A. de C.V.
Av. Plutarco 100-B, col. Del Valle Norte,
CP 03103, Benito Juárez, ciudad de México